THE DISSOLUTION OF
THE HABSBURG MONARCHY

. . . . Speaking generally, there is something peculiar in national hatred. We always find it strongest and most vehement on the lowest stage of culture. But there is a stage where it totally disappears and where one stands, so to say, *above* the nations and feels the good fortune or distress of his neighbor people as if it had happened to his own. . . . .

GOETHE

THE DISSOLUTION OF THE HABSBURG MONARCHY

OSCAR JÁSZI

THE UNIVERSITY OF CHICAGO PRESS

CHICAGO AND LONDON

TO THE MEMORY OF MY FATHER

DR. FRANCIS JÁSZI

A PHYSICIAN ON THE MAGYAR-RUMANIAN BORDER, WHO
CONVINCED ME IN MY EARLY CHILDHOOD THAT ANY
PUBLIC POLICY NOT DIRECTED BY MORAL
PRINCIPLES IS ONLY A FORM
OF EXPLOITATION

International Standard Book Number: 0-226-39568-5

Library of Congress Catalog Card Number: 29-22812

THE UNIVERSITY OF CHICAGO PRESS, CHICAGO 60637

The University of Chicago Press, Ltd., London

PREFACE

When the task of describing the mass-psychological process of the disintegration of the Habsburg Monarchy and of the failure of the conscious elaboration of a common will was tendered me, I was hesitant for a long time in accepting it. Before all a motive of a rather sentimental character was in my way, expressed by the words of Aeneas: *Infandum, Regina, jubes renovare dolorem.* Besides I clearly felt that such an undertaking would mean the work of many years and the energies of a man equally qualified as a historian, a sociologist, and an economist. How could one dare to do such a work in a comparatively short time without being an expert in all these fields? My doubts, however, were counterbalanced by the consideration of a single advantage which I possess over many of the writers who might be appointed to the task: I lived through, in a conscious and active way, the last quarter of a century of the Dual Monarchy and foresaw its dangers and difficulties, and amidst an apathetic or hostile world, tried to convince my compatriots that without deep organic reforms (reforms in the agrarian constitution, in public administration and education, in the national organization of the various peoples) the whole edifice would collapse. And, finding that my feeble voice was constantly drowned by the beneficiaries of the old system, two years before the War, in a last effort, I tried, in a rather comprehensive book,[1] to describe the diagnosis and cure of the national pathology. The present volume is in a sense the continuation of my former book: it shows how the experiences of the last decade of the Monarchy were the logical consequences of deep social and economic causes previously analyzed. Therefore, that of which I treat in the following pages is not books but men; the processes which I elucidate are not theories but social realities.

There was also another consideration which encouraged me to accept the challenge. During my lifetime I have witnessed a twofold tragedy. Not only will men not understand social realities which are for them disagreeable or disadvantageous when they face them, but also, a posteriori, they try to get rid of the painful past experiences. There is a tendency to falsify history in order to absolve the crimes of the past and to obtain transitory gains among the difficulties of an adverse situation. Both the victorious and the vanquished nations show this marked tendency. The so-called "War Guilt" literature is an evidence of the whitewashing of facts in order to alleviate the responsibilities of the past and to obtain momentary diplomatic advantages.

[1] *The Evolution of the Nation States and the Nationality Problem* (in Hungarian; Budapest, 1912).

It is an almost intolerable spectacle to see how the four or five great
lessons of the terrible catastrophe are obscured and distorted by the
leaders of a world which continues along the vicious road of the past.
And a falsified history always means envenomed actions and new opportunities for armed conflicts. I feel it my duty to put into a correct
light that part of the tragedy through which I lived.

Perhaps the reader will say that such a pragmatic position is dangerous in itself for the task which I am undertaking. I think it is not,
provided it is combined with a sufficient amount of impartiality and
universal sympathy. Even before the war, but after it still more completely, I had grown away from the old local patriotisms of Europe.
At present there does not exist for me an isolated Hungarian problem; and, though with an unbroken loyalty to my own, I have the same
sympathy for all the suffering peoples of the Danube Basin.

But here a more serious objection may arise, on the part of those
who would discredit the reliability of my attitude. They will say a man
living in exile for a decade after having lost his cause will inevitably
have the tendency to extol his own point of view and misrepresent that
of his adversaries. However, there are two considerations which will
absolve me of this charge. The one is that the principles and conclusions which I advocate in the present book are not the results of a belated wisdom, for I can demonstrate that I maintained the same principles and conclusions for the last two decades before the collapse.
The other is that there is nothing eccentric or startling in my conclusions. As I emphasize in my bibliography and explain in my book, my
chief conclusions and principles are in entire harmony with those of
the best thinkers of the Monarchy, who for the last three generations
have been occupied with the same problem. What I did is scarcely
more than to make an organic synthesis and a many-sided elucidation
of the efforts and opinions of those whom I regard as the deepest observers of the Habsburg drama. There are only two points concerning which I claim a stricter originality in my researches. The one is
the analysis of the dissolving economic forces of the Monarchy. The
other is the elucidation of the mass-psychological situation in Hungary.

There is a further argument which I would adduce to demonstrate
the impartiality of my book. Fate ordered that I should be, if not *au
dessus de la mêlée*, at least outside of it. I was compelled to live outside
of my country for the last decade because I had a small share in the
endeavor to democratize Hungary and to remold the old feudal state
into a confederation of free nations. This effort failed completely,
and, as far as sociological prognostications can be indulged in, I regard my present position as final and unchangeable for the remainder
of my life. I have no longer any personal interest, except that of my
ideals, in the Danube region, having become a humble worker in the
great American Republic in one of its historical colleges which has al-

ways been associated with the idea of personal liberty and international solidarity. This book is therefore neither an apology nor a program, but a sincere effort to elucidate a problem which still deeply
influences the future of Europe and of mankind. It may also become
useful in a coming age, when the present nationalistic dementia will
ebb, as a kind of political testament.

Some minor remarks may be added. One of the greatest shortcomings of the present volume is the fact that among the many languages
of the former Monarchy I read only German, Hungarian, Italian and
Rumanian whereas the Slavic literature I know only through transla-
tions and excerpts made by my friends. However, this serious draw-
back is somewhat compensated by the fact that in consequence of my
policy of national conciliation I lived always in good and close personal contact with many leaders of the Slavic nations, who honored
my peaceful endeavors with their confidence.

The other point which I beg to mention is an apology for the great
number of quotations which I use throughout the book. Though I feel
the distastefulness of too many quotations, in the present book I was
compelled to resort to them. As my task was the interpretation of certain mass-psychological currents, I found the necessity of demonstrating that I do not express in the analysis of the social realities personal
opinions but widely spread mass conceptions. However, in order to
avoid a superabundance of footnotes, I included only such references
as seemed to me very important or of a controversial character.

I would also mention that the manuscript of the present book was
finished by contractual engagement in the fall of 1927, but difficulties
outside of my control delayed its publication. Therefore, to the literature published after this date I could only refer in notes and with occasional remarks so as not to destroy the unity of the composition.

Finally, I would like to express my personal thanks to those who
helped me in my task. Professor Charles E. Merriam, of the University of Chicago, Professor Karl F. Geiser, of Oberlin College, and
Professor Robert J. Kerner, of the University of California, gave me
some important suggestions and expurgated many Hungarianisms in
my style. My good friend Madame Anna Lesznai (Vienna) offered me
some excellent hints concerning the social psychology of the last generation. Two other Viennese friends, Arnold Dániel and Dr. Joseph
Rédei, sent me valuable excerpts from the libraries. Besides, the former assisted me with keen and original observations in the economic
field. I am sorry that I cannot express publicly my acknowledgments
to some of my Budapest friends, for reasons which are perfectly clear.
More than anyone else I wish to thank my wife, whose co-operation
and care I felt on many pages of this book.

OSCAR JÁSZI

OBERLIN COLLEGE

REMARKS ON THE LITERATURE OF THE SUBJECT

The author of the present volume has somewhat heretical opinions concerning the values of bibliographies. It seems to him that the power of our intellectual assimilation is as limited as that of our biological; that creative thoughts must have their natural growth, which too many references choke rather than promote; that literary footnotes are like a pedigree: they are more decorative than essential. As a matter of fact a detailed bibliography of the subject would be a book in itself. Concerning the Austrian part of the Monarchy, a careful bibliography was compiled by Richard Charmatz, the distinguished Austrian historian: *Wegweiser durch die Literatur der österreichischen Geschichte* (Stuttgart und Berlin, 1912). Concerning Hungary, a similar work was undertaken in the Appendix to Count Paul Teleki's book, *The Evolution of Hungary and Its Place in European History* (New York, 1923), mostly from the pen of the noted Hungarian bibliographer, Mr. Charles Feleky.

Therefore, I offer only at the end of this volume a restricted list of books which either impressed me or will show the reader an opposite outlook on the situation. Generally I omitted, with few exceptions, those books in the foreign languages most inaccessible to English readers, namely those in the Hungarian, Rumanian, and the Slavic tongues. (Some few of these I inserted in translation.) Similarly, I omitted the so-called "war literature," which has only an indirect connection with this book. An almost complete list of this will be found in R. W. Seton-Watson's book *Sarajevo* (London, 1925) and in S. B. Fay's comprehensive work on *The Origins of the World War* (New York, 1928).

However, in order to make the position of the present volume clearer, I would like to emphasize those authors and books of the following bibliography whose conception helped or influenced me mostly. Among the men of a previous generation, the remarkable statesman and diplomat, BARON VICTOR ANDRIAN-WERBURG analyzed in a masterly way the structure and the main tendencies of the Habsburg Monarchy. Later the keen and courageous historian, ANTON SPRINGER, realized the forces which would lead to the deadlock of the Empire. Among the responsible statesmen, the great economist and sociologist, A. E. F. SCHÄFFLE, has shown more insight into the problem than any of the leading ministers of Austria. DR. ADOLF FISCHHOF, the brilliant representative of the great liberal generation of 1848, developed an acumen and discrimination in the deepest foundations of the Monarchy which was never surpassed. Among the Hungarian statesmen and publicists of the same period, the state philosophy of BARON

Joseph Eötvös is unique from the point of view both of breadth and penetration, whereas the prophetic vision of Louis Kossuth concerning the formation of a Danube federation inspired my speculations very much concerning the future. Within the narrow circle of the few faithful followers of the great tribune, it was Louis Mocsáry who, with an exceptional moral courage and independence, pointed out the right road for a half-blind generation.

Among my own contemporaries, on the Austrian side nobody has so much aroused my admiration as Professor Joseph Redlich, who, with an unrivaled mass of information and deepness of judgment, has unveiled the most intricate aspects of the Habsburg problem. Though I feel the point of view of Professor Victor Bibl too pro-German, I think his *Der Zerfall Österreichs* is the most complete and sincere historical description of the catastrophe. He was especially successful in the gathering of what was called *unique facts* concerning the historical forces of the past, and I often used his rich repertory of significant data. Another Austrian, a man of the higher bureaucracy, Friedrich F. G. Kleinwaechter, wrote the best book concerning the psychology of the imperial administration and showed an unusual grasp of the problem of the irredentas. The artistic and moral side of the problem found a brilliant and sensitive exponent in the writings of the Viennese art critic and novelist Hermann Bahr. I am also very appreciative for the remarkable works of two Austrian socialist leaders, Dr. Karl Renner and Dr. Otto Bauer, who with the one-sided strength of a revolutionary ideology of a new class have introduced fresh points of view into the stagnant waters of Austrian public life.

Among my Hungarian contemporaries, I wish to mention the original and independent work of Baron J. Szillassy, one of those rare diplomats who clearly visualized the relation between the inner and outer policy.

Among the foreigners who were in more intimate touch with the problems of the Monarchy, none saw the situation more penetratingly than Henry Wickham Steed, R. W. Seton-Watson, and Louis Eisenmann (all three, until the World War, convinced supporters of the Habsburg Monarchy and hoping for her rejuvenation).

Finally, I wish only to mention two authors who, though disconnected with my special problem, influenced the general trend of my argument. Though I disagree with certain conclusions and constructions of Professor Carlton J. H. Hayes, I regard his studies on nationalism as an important contribution to the general problem. On the other hand, the fundamental inquiries of Professor Francis Oppenheimer concerning the social consequences of the feudal system supported very much my own diagnosis of the downfall of the Monarchy.

TABLE OF CONTENTS
PART I
SOME PRELIMINARY CONSIDERATIONS

PART II
THE HISTORICAL ATMOSPHERE

PART III

THE CENTRIPETAL FORCES: THE EIGHT PILLARS OF INTERNATIONALISM

PART IV

THE CENTRIFUGAL FORCES: THE DRAMA OF THE GROWING NATIONAL DISINTEGRATION

CONTENTS

PART V

THE DYNAMICS OF CENTRIFUGAL FORCES

PART VI

THE DANGER OF IRREDENTA

CONTENTS

PART VII
CONSCIOUS EFFORTS IN CIVIC EDUCATION

PART I
SOME PRELIMINARY CONSIDERATIONS

CHAPTER I

THE PROBLEM

Among those studies in which the University of Chicago has undertaken to investigate the evolution and the present state of civic education in the various countries of the world, the writer of this book has been given the charge of elucidating in detail that big, historical experiment which was carried on in the field of civic education within the limits of the former Austro-Hungarian monarchy. In this vast empire, which concentrated more than fifty-one million inhabitants in an area of two hundred and sixty thousand square miles, were almost ten nations and twenty more or less divergent nationalities in political or moral bonds. These constituted two distinct states (Austria and Hungary), seventeen provinces or crownlands in Austria, an "associated country" with Hungary (Croatia-Slavonia), a "separate body" (city and harbor of Fiume) annexed to Hungary, and a province of colonial nature (Bosnia-Herzegovina)—all of them with distinct historical consciousness and more or less extended territorial autonomy. In this vast empire there was going on, during more than four hundred years, an effort to keep together this variegated mosaic of nations and people and to build up a kind of universal state, a "supranational" monarchy, and to fill it with the feeling of a common solidarity.

This experiment, which the greatest state of the European continent (leaving out of account Russia and the powers with colonies outside Europe) undertook with colossal military, economic, and moral forces through almost sixteen generations, was one of the greatest and most interesting attempts in world-history. Had this experiment been successful, it would have meant more from a certain point of view than all other efforts of state-building ever recorded. For, if the Habsburgs had been able really to unite those ten nations through a supranational consciousness into an entirely free and spontaneous co-operation, the empire of the Habsburgs would have surpassed the narrow limits of the nation state and would have proved to the world that it is possible to replace the consciousness of national unity by a consciousness of a state community. It would have proved that the same problem which Switzerland and Belgium have solved on a smaller scale among highly civilized nations under particular historical conditions should not be regarded as a historical accident, but that the same problem is perfectly solvable even on a large scale and among very heterogeneous cultural and national standards.

We can go even farther and say that this experiment of the Habsburgs would have signified a higher and more promising principle of evolution, not only compared with the old national states but also with the English and American kind of confederative state. For the British Empire and the United States are in reality a continuation of the old national type. In the United States the unity of the Anglo-Saxon culture and hegemony is uncontested, whereas the greatest part of the commonwealth of British nations is still under Anglo-Saxon leadership and the non-European stock of this commonwealth is scarcely beginning to participate in the political life of the whole organism. Neither the United States nor the British commonwealth can be regarded as a supranational type of state life.

And again, if the Austro-Hungarian state experiment had been really successful, the Habsburg monarchy would have solved on its territory the most fundamental problem of present Europe, which is also the problem of the League of Nations. How is it possible to unite national individualities of very divergent ideals and traditions in such a way that each of them can continue its own particular life, while at the same time limiting its national sovereignty enough to make a peaceful and effective international co-operation possible?

This historical experiment in the society of nations under the patronage of the Habsburgs has proved unsuccessful. The centripetal forces of a supranational consciousness were more and more disintegrated by the centrifugal forces of national particularisms. In the unnational and patrimonial body of the Habsburg empire there arose always more distinctly several differentiated national embryo states which, under the formidable birth-pangs of the World War, split the once unified framework of the monarchy into six distinct states.

In spite of the tragic collapse of the Habsburg experiment, this problem of state organization has still a great theoretical and practical importance. For the question is, whether the Danubian experiment was due to fail because it was in its essence an organic, almost a natural impossibility, or because it was only a consequence of factors depending on will and insight which could have been avoided by a more advanced statesmanship, a more clear-sighted policy, and a better-organized civic education. The answer to this question will determine almost *sub specie aeternitatis* the fate of all future experiments intending to unite various and antagonistic national wills into a harmonious international order, protecting and supplementing the interest of each nation. This problem is not only a problem of the remote future but the vital problem of those states which were established on the ruins of the Habsburg monarchy, for these new states are not unified nation states but states resulting from the co-operation of different national elements. At the same time our problem is closely connected with the general problem of Europe. The saving of that Continent, destroyed by the unbridled forces of nationalism, depends on whether or not we are compelled to accept national antagonisms as final necessities or whether we can eliminate these national rivalries or at least replace them by other methods.

We can even affirm that the unsuccessful experiment of the old Habsburg monarchy affects not only the European future but also those problems by which the Far East is menacing the European powers and the United States, because all these problems are intimately connected with a national conflict aggravated by racial and religious antagonisms.

CHAPTER II

THE DISSOLUTION OF THE HABSBURG MONARCHY WAS NOT A MECHANICAL BUT AN ORGANIC PROCESS

Before proceeding to examine the causes which made the attempt at consolidation of the Habsburg empire a failure, a word may be said in anticipation of objections that may be taken to my viewpoint. There will be those who will resolve this whole problem into a sham by asserting that the dissolution of the monarchy was not the result of inner forces, but that it was due exclusively to external factors which had nothing to do with the psychic and political structure of the empire. This point of view, which in a former book I termed the "Habsburg legend" and which is disseminated by the propaganda of very influential dynastic and feudal groups, represents the Habsburg monarchy as an innocent lamb, a victim of the antagonism of German and English imperialism which, arousing the World War, buried under its ruins the free and happy Danubian League of Nations.

This historical materialism *à la Habsburg* has been recently advanced by a naïve and superficial historical and sociological literature which, investigating the responsibility for the World War, looks only on the diplomatic side of the problem, its chief interest consisting in the inquiry whether the world-catastrophe was actuated by the diplomatic maneuvers of Berchtold, Poincaré, Izvolsky, or Grey, or whether the Serb government did or did not have a previous knowledge of the murderous attack at Sarajevo. Such a point of view, which sees in the world-catastrophe exclusive personal intrigues and responsibilities, makes the real problem appear both shallow and obscure. For however great may be the crime of the individual politicians and statesmen in setting the date of the world-catastrophe, it is sufficiently clear that these men did not do more than detonate that mass of dynamite which the social and national unrest of Central Europe had piled up during the last hundred years.

Therefore, if we wish to understand history more clearly both from the point of view of the present and the future, and if we really try to follow a constructive policy of peace, we must have an end of that sentimental pacifism which considers all wars simply as the private affairs of criminal kings and diplomats or of capitalistic interests, and does not understand that the real causes of modern conflicts lie far deeper in the impeded evolutionary processes of the masses checked by stupid or criminal internal policies. I have no place here to amplify this point of view; I wish only to say that the warlike liquidation of the former Habsburg monarchy is no sane argument for the assertion that its collapse was purely a mechanical process and not the end of an organic development of almost two hundred years. We know not a single national or social crisis on a large scale in world-history which could have created a radical new equilibrium without awakening a series of international and warlike complications. This concatenation of the inner evolution and of outer warlike complications is also clearly demonstrated by the genesis of the other national states; and it is not a sane argument against the organic nature of English and French national unity to say that the movement toward unity of the moral and economic forces was very often protected in both countries by the militaristic and political centralization of the respective dynasties.

The dissolution of the Habsburg monarchy and the establishment of new national states on its ruins was, in its essence, the same process which in many other states of Europe led to the state integration of those peoples having a common language and culture. The same fundamental causes working for unity in the nationally homogeneous states worked toward dissolution in the ethnographical mosaic of the Habsburg empire. Even the World War can only be fully understood from this historical perspective. The detonator of the European explosion was perhaps a capitalistic one, but its violence would have been unimaginable without the powder magazine formed by the unsolved and accumulating national and social problems of Central and Eastern Europe.

In whatever manner we may regard the Habsburg problem—whether we analyze its historical atmosphere, the mass psychology of its people, or the international complications arising from its national and economic conditions—from all these points of view we must come to the same conclusion, namely, that this vast historical drama was not the result of diplomatic quarrels, but grew out of the inevitable logic of a long series of social causes.

This conception is not merely an *a posteriori* assertion, but it was already alive many years, even decades before in the consciousness of all those who were capable of regarding the problems of the Danubian monarchy with sufficient intellectual force. Many of the best statesmen, poets, scholars, and publicists were unanimous in the understanding that the empire of the Habsburgs had become an anachronistic impossibility, that it was doomed to death or at least could have been saved only by a major operation. Such and similar declarations, even well-founded sociological analyses, are so abundant that I must limit myself to the most characteristic and conspicuous ones.

Mickiewicz, the great Polish poet, almost a hundred years ago wrote the following startlingly clear-sighted description of the Habsburg empire:

This Empire counts thirty-four million inhabitants, but in reality it has no more than six million people; namely six million Germans keeping twenty-eight millions of other stocks in bondage. If one subtracts from these six millions the numbers of peasants, artisans, merchants, etc., who have no share at all in the government, there remain at most two million Austrians who rule all these masses. These two millions or rather their interests and opinions are represented approximately by a hundred families which are German, Hungarian, Polish, or Italian but which commonly speak French and have their capital largely outside the country. Using in their service two million bureaucrats and soldiers they rule through them the other thirty-two millions. That is a society modelled on the pattern of the English East Indian Company. . . . . Ordinarily, people have a false idea of this Austrian Empire which never was a German, Hungarian or Slavish empire, but a kinship of all those who aim at drawing out the marrow of so many extensive countries rich in population.

Even more striking than this were the diagnoses and prognostications several times expressed by the great apostle and theoretical founder of the national idea, Giuseppe Mazzini. He clearly described the irresistible movement both of the Northern Slavs and the Southern Slavs toward unification. He prophesied that this movement, combined with the struggles for emancipation of the Greeks and the Rumanians, would inevitably destroy both the Austrian and the Turkish empires, "these two serpents which paralyze the heart of Europe." Already in 1843 he wrote that "in the Austrian Empire a movement of the Slav population is progressing" (he even foresaw the unification of Bohemia and Moravia with the Slovak tribes of Hungary) "for which nobody cares and which one day, united with our own efforts, will cancel Austria from the map of Europe. . . . ."[1]

In another direction, but scarcely less pessimistically, the situation of the monarchy was elucidated in 1822 by Charles Sealsfield, a brilliant German-American who fled before Austrian absolutism into the New World where he later wrote his powerful denunciation of the system of Metternich, an arraignment which is one of the most direct and penetrating documents of the empire of Emperor Francis. Sealsfield characterizes Austria as a "big agglomeration of provinces," and describes with vivid colors the exasperated public mind of the Slav majority against the German absolutist rule. He writes:

One can even hear the Bohemians gnash their teeth if one begins to praise English liberty. They are filled with unspeakable sorrow if their own country is mentioned, the battles which they were obliged to fight for a strange cause, the armies for which they furnish the soldiers and bear the costs and which in reality serve for their oppression. They feel depressed that they exist for a dynasty which remained foreign to them and

[1] These and many similar statements of Mazzini belong to the most miraculous products of political foresight. A luminous analysis of his theory and prognostication will be found in the book of Alessandro Levi, *La filosofia politica di Giuseppe Mazzini*, Bologna, 1917.

their wishes in spite of a rule of several hundred years, and which in its incapacity cares only how to subdue Bohemia and how to kill its national aims.[2]

This system, according to the opinion of Sealsfield, is untenable. The country as a unified whole is very near a crisis. Though it will not come to a general upheaval since the provinces are too sharply watched and the inner antagonisms are too great (the Bohemians would march against Hungary, the Poles against the Italians, and the Germans against both), the inner immorality of the system and its disregard for all loyal principles will ultimately destroy itself.

About ten years later the same *facies hippocratica* of the monarchy was seen by a Russian observer, by the Pan-Slav historian, Pogodin, who made several trips of investigation in Central Europe and gave an account of them to his government. He wrote:

The Slavs seem to be on the eve of a renaissance, the empire of the Danube must tremble even more than the Turkish empire in the face of twenty millions of a hostile race in its interior. Austria is a white sepulchre, an old tree which is rotten within, though it still bears leaves on the outside, but which the first blast of wind will uproot.

Again, ten years later, quite similar was the diagnosis of Charles Montalembert, the eminent French conservative statesman who spoke the following words (1846) on the tribune of the French Parliament: "The Austrian monarchy is a bizarre composition of twenty nations which justice could have maintained but which injustice will push into dissolution."

The same mood is reflected in the opinions of many other foreign observers. Napoleon III called Austria a corpse with which nobody can make a contract. At the other pole of social life Karl Marx fixed the death-sentence of the Habsburg empire: "The only circumstance," he wrote in 1860, "which legitimates the existence of Austria since the middle of the eighteenth century is its resistance to the advances of Russia in eastern Europe . . . . a resistance helpless, inconsequent, cowardly, but tough." And, following the trend of thought of his master, Frederick Engels in 1888 made the assertion that the destruction of Austria would have been a misfortune for European civilization before the approaching triumph of the Russian Revolution; after which its annihilation becomes unnecessary, for Austria, becoming superfluous, will go asunder by itself.

Similar considerations were expressed from a quite different angle by the noted French historian, Louis Leger, who on a pamphlet published in 1866 and treating the problem of Austria, alluding to the oppressed nationalities, put the following significant motto: *Ave*

___

[2] This quotation and those which follow are a translation from the German edition (*Österreich wie es ist,* Wien, 1919), because the original English was not available.

Caesar resurrecturi te salutant! And in a more comprehensive work, in 1879, he wrote this judgment: "Abandoned to the blind egotism of the Germans and the Magyars the Habsburg Monarchy could not solve the problem of the East. She will witness its solution against its own interests."

It may be objected that the assertions quoted above emanate from strangers and from the enemies of the monarchy, but we shall soon see that the friends of the empire did not think otherwise than its enemies. Let us continue our survey with the opinion of two Hungarian statesmen of whom the first cannot be counted among the enemies of the dynasty. Count Stephen Széchenyi, the conservative promoter of the Hungarian renaissance, whom his noted political antagonist, Louis Kossuth, called the greatest Hungarian, prophesied as early as 1813 the dissolution of the monarchy. When, after the battle of Dresden, he was convalescing in a Prague hospital, he exposed before his officer colleagues the probable future of the monarchy. Of this conversation, a court spy (these men of Metternich filled even the hospitals) reported to Vienna that the count before an audience consisting chiefly of Prussian officers made the declaration that in spite of its victories, Austria would go asunder "within a century because its parts are unequal and they separate more and more from each other."

Louis Kossuth, in 1881, was naturally more capable of describing accurately the pathology of the monarchy. The Viennese secret police sent an able *agent provocateur* to Turin in order to extract from the great man in exile his point of view concerning the international situation. The maneuver succeeded, and Kossuth, knowing not to whom he was speaking, gave his unveiled opinion concerning the future of Austria, which was later reported to the Viennese commissioner by the spy. According to this report, Kossuth predicted the approach of the Russian Revolution which he thought would be a deathknell for Austria. As Augustulus was the last Roman emperor, so Rudolphulus would be the last Habsburg. That was an allusion to Crown Prince Rudolph who died in 1889. It can scarcely be doubted that if the catastrophe of Meierling of which Rudolph became a victim had not happened and Rudolph had remained alive, the prophecy of Kossuth would have been literally realized.

But even the guiding spirits of Austria were not more optimistic over the situation of the monarchy. One may say, in terms of recent psychology, that the whole policy of Metternich stood under a "dissolution complex," and this attitude fomented his almost monomanical struggle against democracy and liberalism. His wife, the princess Melanie, called him often the "Cassandra of the monarchy," for he was saturated with alarming news about the collapse of the empire. It is quite natural that in such a milieu the judgment of the more liberal and freer spirits was even more emphatically unfavorable to the reigning system and its consequences. So in 1830, after the revolution of July, Grillparzer, the greatest poet of Austria, wrote the following really visionary lines:

The whole world will be strengthened by the unexpected change, only Austria will go to pieces by it. The shameless Machiavellism of the leaders who, in order that the reigning dynasty should remain the only connecting tie of the state, have fomented and nourished the reciprocal national antipathies of the separate provinces, is responsible for it. The Hungarian hates the Bohemian, the Bohemian hates the German, and the Italian hates them all, and as horses absurdly harnessed together, they will scatter in all directions as soon as the advancing spirit of the times will weaken and break the bonds.

This conviction of the grave danger facing the monarchy gained a deep statesman-like elucidation ten years later in a book anonymously published at Hamburg in 1842, which, under the title *Austria and Its Future*, gave a pitiless analysis of the formidable inner antagonisms of the monarchy. The author of this book was Baron Victor Andrian von Werburg, a chamberlain and a high official in the court administration, and later vice-president of the National Assembly. As one of the most cultivated aristocrats of his time, his opinion may be regarded as representative. Andrian was of the opinion that "Austria is a purely imaginary name which does not signify any compact people, any country, any nation . . . . a conventional term of several nationalities sharply distinct each from the other." There are Italians, Germans, Slavs, Magyars, but there is no Austrian national consciousness. The idea of the state is annihilated by the principle of nationality. There arose a Slav, a Hungarian, and an Italian national feeling which consolidated itself more from day to day, rejected all foreign elements, and expanded with a prophetic vehemence. The system of these particularistic consciousnesses menaces the very existence of Austria. Only inertia succeeds in holding the monarchy together. "This state of mind is like the buried corpses in Pompeii which, preserved during many centuries, fall into dust and ashes as soon as a beam of God's free sun or a blast of wind touches them." How could such a state resist the growing consciousness of unity of the Slavs which begins to form a compact phalanx from Troppau to Cattaro?

Thoughtful men of later generations judged the future of the monarchy with the same pessimism. Ferdinand Kürnberger, the greatest Austrian publicist of the second half of the nineteenth century, agreed with these opinions, and he always regarded Austria as an anachronistic country and contrary to the spirit of Europe. He repeatedly emphasized the essentially Asiatic nature of Austria.

And lest these remarks be regarded as the impressionist utterances of exacerbated poets and publicists, I would call attention to the diagnosis of Ottokar Lorenz, the distinguished historian who, though a native Austrian, did not hide his deeply pessimistic opinions.

He too talked of the second "sick man of Europe," and he never took the so-called new constitutional era of Francis Joseph seriously. On the contrary, he considered the various constitutional experiments to be like the experiments of England to remold the Turkish empire, because he was of the opinion that the old Austria had died as a consequence of the Revolution of 1848.

This pessimistic attitude also gradually took possession of the leaders of practical politics, and Count Taaffe, prime minister of Austria during two decades, called his own policy, with crude honesty, the policy of *Fortwursteln* ("to go on in the old groove"). That this policy would earlier or later demoralize the national forces was clearly understood by the enlightened elements of the state. Professor Masaryk, now president of Czecho-Slovakia, disgusted by the petty compromises without principle, called the Austrian parliament a *Tandelmarkt* (a "junk market"). And Ernest Körber, one of the last premiers of the monarchy "saw the situation of the monarchy as darkly as Metternich did after 1848."

This pessimistic public opinion penetrated even the circles of the Viennese court itself. General von Margutti, one of the leaders of the chief military bureau, narrates in his memoirs that beginning with his earliest youth he heard that the monarchy was not an up-to-date state, that it had no right to existence, and that it was only upheld by the personality of the old Emperor after whose death it would fall asunder "like an old barrel robbed of its hoops." This conviction exasperated and perhaps drove to death Crown Prince Rudolph himself. "I am only anxious to know as a silent observer," he once wrote to a friend, "how much time such an old and tough edifice as this Austria takes before it cracks in all its joints and falls asunder." The successor of Rudolph, Archduke Francis Ferdinand, heir apparent, was even more impressed by the approaching catastrophe, and endeavored in vain to avoid the fate which menaced not only the state but his own life. This feeling of an approaching disaster dominated the more clear-sighted elements of the army also. Conrad von Hötzendorf, later the chief of general staff during the war, emphasized for many years in his memoranda to the Emperor that the Italian and Jugo-Slav *irredenta* threatened the monarchy with collapse. Similarly, General Auffenberg as minister of war judged the situation in 1912. At the time of the Balkan crisis he uttered the following prophetic words to the German ambassador:

We need at least a half century of peace in the Monarchy to put the southern Slavs in order and this quietness can be maintained only by eliminating all the hopes of the southern Slavs for Russian protection, otherwise the Monarchy goes to pieces.[3]

[3] *Die grosse Politik der europäischen Kabinette: 1871–1914* (Berlin, 1926), XXXIII, 372–73.

This insecurity of the future oppressed even the old Emperor in spite of the fact that those around him tried carefully to keep all alarming news from him. A documentary witness of this pessimistic mood is a testamentary provision of the Emperor of 1901 in which Francis Joseph established a family property in trust of sixty-million gold crowns the purpose of which was determined by the following words:

If in the course of events and in the historical evolution, the form of government of the Austro-Hungarian Monarchy should suffer a change and, what God may prevent, the crown should not remain in our house, the order of succession for the family property in trust established by me should be determined by those principles of common right which are in existence in the ordinary code of law from June first, 1811.

The chief ally of the Dual Monarchy, the German government itself, was also haunted by the ghost of the approaching dissolution of the Danube empire. The German chancellor, Prince Bülow, in order to avoid possible dangerous conflicts in the case of the disaster of Austria, suggested in 1905 through his ambassador in St. Petersburg, a plan of a "Treaty of Disinterestedness" according to which both Germany and Russia would declare not to make an annexation in the case of collapse of the Danube monarchy.[4]

These many and various declarations and utterances, which all denounce the extreme uncertainty of the existence of the monarchy, cannot be a pure accident, but are a symptom and almost a symbol of a deeply rooted organic crisis. There can be no doubt that many of the better intellects clearly saw or felt that the monarchy was being pushed toward disaster by irresistible historical forces.

[4] Quoted verbatim in *Der Krieg*, May, 1928.

CHAPTER III

THE DOUBLE WAR OF THE HABSBURG MONARCHY

Not only does the foresight of isolated men demonstrate that the dissolution of the monarchy was not a mechanical accident, but the final crisis, the final collapse itself, proved this truth even to the satisfaction of those who are distrustful of the more subtle, causal connections in social things.

There is, before all, the striking fact that the World War and the Sarajevo plot, which was its immediate cause, were in the closest connection with the outer policy of the Habsburg monarchy which again was determined by the social and national structure of the monarchy. At this place I cannot enter now upon the detailed analysis of this connection as this can only be done after the reader understands the statics and dynamics of the empire.

At this juncture I wish only to say that the monarchy's collapse was due not only to its struggles with foreign enemies, but in a no less degree to another war which the monarchy was constrained to carry on with its own so-called inner enemies, that is to say, with a very important mass of its own peoples. There is no fact, as far as I see, which could prove the inner organic dissolution of the Habsburg monarchy with such an almost symbolical force as this double war of the monarchy amid the frightful embarrassments of the world-crisis.

The history of this inner war of the monarchy has not yet been written as the most influential personalities of the old régime, who knew the warlike events the most intimately, do not like to lift the veil from the inner disintegration of the empire which would put in an unfavorable light the problem of war responsibility. On the other hand those elements who face this problem objectively or even with sympathy have naturally only a fragmentary knowledge concerning the facts since the official archives relating to this period are still closed.[1]

In spite of these difficulties sufficient facts about the inner war of the monarchy became manifest to convince any objective observer of the inner motivation of the crisis. In this connection nobody can deny

---

[1] Recently an important book was published connected with this matter by Edmund von Glaise-Horstenau, the director of the Viennese War Archives, under the title *Die Katastrophe* (Wien, 1929). Though the author has a natural tendency to show the loyalty of the peoples of the former monarchy, he is far too conscientious a historian to shut his eyes to the symptoms of inner dissolution. Even the facts mentioned by him would suffice to show the seriousness of what I call the inner warfare of the monarchy. At the same time Glaise-Horstenau describes very vividly the growing economic misery and technical inefficiency of the Austro-Hungarian army which was due to a large extent to maladministration and corruptive influences.

that the warlike absolutism nowhere took such rigid and uncouth forms as in the Habsburg empire where not only all military operations were strictly withdrawn from the control of the parliamentary corporations, but the economic life, the administration, the judiciary itself was put under a rude military control.[2] The only official organ to supervise the foreign and military policy, the so-called "Delegations," were not even convened during the first three years of the war because the leading circles were aware that the critics from the Slavs and the Socialists would destroy the prestige of the monarchy. For the same reason the Austrian Parliament ceased to function during three years and when the young emperor, terrified by the many signs of dissolution, gave general amnesty to the so-called "traitors of the country" and called the Parliament together, declarations were heard which made the blood chill in the veins of the old Austrian patriots. Victor Bibl, the excellent Austrian historian with a very outspoken German tendency, writes:

The secession movement in Bohemia encouraged by this sign of feebleness lifted its head of Medusa now more and more audaciously and recklessly. The Czech representatives did not hesitate to praise openly in parliament those soldiers who deserted; they did not abstain from the menace that the destiny of Bohemia would be decided on the conference table of the Allied Powers and not in Austria. The culminating point of the national frenzy and of an open high treason was reached by a declaration of the Czechs on the Day of Epiphany in 1918 in which they manifested their conviction that the independence of their state could not be reached in a constitutional way and they claimed a participation in the peace parleys in order that they might fight in full liberty for their rights.

The patriotic exasperation of the German historian can be understood, but on the other side the young Emperor possessed sufficiently reliable information concerning the probable developments of the war to know that the inner crisis of the monarchy could not be solved any more by the violence of a victorious war, therefore he saw the only means of saving his throne in a compromise with the dissatisfied nations of his empire. On this point he was really right because the whole repertory of terror and violence was consistently and excessively applied in the first years of the war; the disloyal regiments were mixed with loyal German and Magyar soldiers; the greatest part Czech, Serb, and Rumanian middle classes was declared a treacherous *maffia* and was supervised by the military authorities;[3] an interminable series of prosecutions for high treason were made (in Moravia

[2] As early as the spring of 1916 Baron Bolfras, the Adjutant-General of the Emperor, could make the characteristic remark: "The chief command of the army is now the exclusive government in our country."

[3] An excellent analysis of the war situation in this respect is given by Joseph Redlich in chapter iv of his *Österreichische Regierung und Verwaltung im Weltkriege* (Wien, 1925).

alone there were five hundred such prosecutions, and in the Rumanian and Jugo-Slav countries, especially in Herzegovina, a great number of the so-called "doubtful element" were brought into court on the same charge) ; without any serious judicial investigation many hundreds of persons were shot by the court-martial of nervous officers; the naïve religious Pan-Slavism of the unhappy Ukraine people which sometimes led to real treasons but more often only to a sentimental outburst of solidarity with the Russians drove great masses of the peasantry to the slaughter-house of the Austrian army in Galicia and in the Carpathians; entire villages were encircled and burned by the Austro-Hungarian regiments because they found the attitude of the population to be dangerous.

Generally speaking, the situation of the hinterland near the front cannot be imagined in sufficiently dark and terrifying colors. For instance, the descriptions of Dr. Vladimir Čorović, of the University of Belgrade, concerning the persecution of the population in Bosnia and Herzegovina cannot be read without horror, and Dr. Tresić Pavičić (later ambassador of Jugo-Slavia to the United States) made a vehement accusation in the Austrian Parliament of the brutal procedure by which he and many hundred of Dalmatians were treated by the Austrian authorities. Dr. Čorović gives a long list of cases in which men, women, and children were shot without any judicial inquiry. Also the custom of the taking of hostages in the civic population of the hinterland was carried on in an unheard-of measure and many hundred people became the victims of this crude kind of justice.[4] Very reliable witnesses from the Hungarian side corroborate the description given above of the mass psychology during the war. Ladislas Fényes, the brilliant Hungarian publicist who during the war went with the army into Serbia in order to study the social and military situation and who was in intimate touch with the peasant population, narrates that in the hinterland near the front he always had the distinct impression of being in the territory of enemies. Execution without any trial was the rule; especially in the villages near Zemun the attitude of the population became so alarming that the commander of the army proposed to the government the urgent evacuation of the whole civic population.

Hermann Wendel, the noted German historian of the Jugo-Slav unity, described in a very pathetic way the calvary of the Southern Slav hinterland during the war and remarks sarcastically that finally the long-desired Jugo-Slav unity was created by the Habsburg "by the unity of the gallows, of the court-martial, of the internment-camps, and of the jail-cells."[5]

[4] Dr. Vladimir Čorović, *Black Book* (Beograd-Sarajevo, 1920). In Serb.

[5] *Der Kampf der Südslaven um Freiheit und Einheit* (Frankfurt am Main, 1925), pp. 707–17.

But all these bloody activities of the military absolutism were incapable of maintaining the inner cohesion of the monarchy. On the contrary, among the Slav and Rumanian population there was an intense hatred which no thinking observer could behold without being terrified. What from a moral point of view made the war of the monarchy more horrible and unbearable than in any other country was the fact that this war was carried on by the broadest masses of population without any inner motives, nay very often against their real national feelings, and only under the stress of physical constraint. These feelings were dramatically expressed by a leader of the Czechs in the following memorable words: "We must fight for our liberation from the yoke of the Hapsburgs in order to avoid in the future those terrible moral tortures which signify for us the necessity of fighting side by side with our enemies."[6] At the beginning of the war several Czech regiments proved to be unreliable, indeed, they were very often in open treason. Especially the laying down of arms *en masse* became a common practice of the Czech soldiers. Out of these deserters was formed a Czech army of about 130,000 soldiers a part of which after the Russian Revolution became the only reliable armed force in the hands of the Allies in Russian territory. Not only on the Russian fronts but in the French and Italian trenches too one very often met Czech military formations. The Czech nation indeed accepted the admonition of its political leader, Mr. Kramář: "Not to undertake anything which could have the semblance of an approval of the war!" No, the Czechs themselves boasted that approximately one-half of their citizens who were in active military service, about three hundred thousand soldiers seceded to the enemies of the monarchy and a keen correspondent of the *Frankfurter Zeitung* wrote during the war that the souls of nine-tenths of the Czech people were in the camp of the Allies. And, when observing the growing symptoms of disloyalty, the supreme military authorities tried to check it by a severe example and, at the beginning of 1916, a court-martial sentenced Kramář to death, all of the more serious politicians and the Emperor himself clearly realized that this sentence could not be executed because by carrying it out all moral ties between the Habsburgs and the Czech people would have been definitely broken.

Under such circumstances it was tacitly accepted that the Czechs could not be regarded as reliable combatant forces. But not only from a military point of view did the monarchy become undermined by the Czechs, they also did a greater harm by their vehement anti-Austrian propaganda in foreign countries. The London lectures of Professor

[6] Even such a staunch pro-Austrian writer as Mr. Glaise-Horstenau, describing the new elements of the army after the terrible initial losses in trained soldiers, says: " . . . . These workers and peasants recently provided with the grey field-uniforms were far more cannon fodder than self-conscious fighters."

Masaryk, the flaming book, *Détruisez Autriche-Hongrie*, of Professor Beneš (now foreign minister of Czecho-Slovakia), and the activity of the other members of the Czech emigration made a great impression on the whole world and became one of the chief causes, according to a tradition, of the intervention of President Wilson. The other dissatisfied national groups of the monarchy too did their utmost for the moral discredit of the Habsburg empire. As a matter of fact, all these dissolving tendencies were skilfully utilized through an enormous ruthless scientifically managed propaganda by the press agencies of the Entente and the reflecting waves of this campaign reenforced again the growing revolutionary dissatisfaction both in the trenches and the hinterland of the Habsburgs.

The resistance of the other peoples of the monarchy was not so well organized nor so vigorous as these peoples were far more feeble and stood on a lower degree of national consciousness. The majority of the Slovaks remained loyal and great masses of the Croats fought heroically, especially on those fronts where they defended the Croatian littoral against the Italian aggressors. On the contrary, the mood of the Rumanians in Transylvania became more and more inimical. Already, at the beginning of the war, many intellectuals escaped to Rumania (among them the whole editorial staff of the *Tribuna* of Arad) and under the leadership of Octavian Goga, later minister of interior in Rumania, they developed an exacerbated propaganda in books and pamphlets and open meetings against Hungary. As early as 1915, Rumanian sources estimated ten thousand Transylvanians who seceded, championed Rumania, and took up arms against the old country. This revolutionary activity naturally had a very widely spread repercussion in Transylvania, and the military authorities continued with double energy the persecution of the Rumanian *maffia;* and a Rumanian writer, Jon Clopotel, gives us statistics according to which during the first four years of the war, twenty-six thousand Rumanians of Transylvania made a more or less intimate acquaintance with the military prisons. Meanwhile, following the Czech example, Rumanian battalions were formed among the captives and it was asserted that to the end of the campaign about two thousand officers and nearly twenty-three thousand soldiers fought side by side with the Allies.[7]

And the more oppressive the war situation became, the more the great masses of population sank into a state of slow starvation, and the more the militaristic terrorism aggravated the hinterland: the more the war of the monarchy became a war of the two privileged nations, the Germans and the Magyars. Even the Poles, who at the beginning were friends of the monarchy, later abandoned entirely this attitude. The so-called *bread peace* with Ukraine in which substantial interests of the Poles were betrayed in the hope of getting foodstuffs

[7] *Revolution of 1918* (Cluj, 1926). In Rumanian.

from there made the Pole a bitter enemy of the monarchy, both in the Parliament and on the battlefields, though at the beginning of the warfare Pilsudski energetically protected the cause of the Central Powers and made a raid against Russia. Now, in consequence of the hostile foreign policy of the monarchy, the rest of Pilsudski's legions went over into rebellion and one part of them was successful in leaving the country and joining the Allies on the Western Front to fight the Germans.

The Ukraine policy, too, had no better result. After the Bolsheviks were evicted in the newly formed Ukraine state, the Central Powers protected the old reactionary elements against the Ukraine people and the intelligentsia, the old Czarist generals and officers. There came a period of cruel requisitions and foreign rule which made the great majority of the Ukraine people an enemy of the monarchy. Under these circumstances it is no exaggeration when Otto Bauer, the brilliant socialist historian of the period of the collapse, exclaims:

In this manner the circle was drawn. The Habsburgs began the war against the Jugo-Slavs, passed through it in the most vehement conflict with the Czechs, lost the Poles during the War and were incapable of winning the Ukrainians. All the Slav peoples now stood against the Habsburgs. All hoped for the victory of the Allies. Austria-Hungary led the war not only against external enemies but against almost two-thirds of its own citizens. The destiny of the Habsburg monarchy was sealed.[8]

As the war situation became worse and worse the leading circles were of the opinion that their awkward position was caused by the treachery of the unreliable elements. Bertrand Auerbach, the French historian of the collapse, quotes a hidden decree of the minister of war which ordered a severe supervision of all the soldiers not belonging to the German and Hungarian nationality with the charge of special control over the baggage and correspondence of the Slav soldiers. This vexatious procedure evoked vehement interpellations in the Austrian parliament.[9] A state which puts under police supervision and under the control of its spies the majority of its fighting people! Could there be a more symbolical expression of the inner crisis of the monarchy? Perhaps this crisis would still have been bearable if at least the alliance of the two privileged nations of the monarchy had been a substantial one. But just the opposite was true. There arose in the Hungarian Parliament passionate and exasperated declarations that the leading military circles spared the other nationalities at the cost of Hungarian blood. At the same time in Austrian public opinion and in the Austrian Parliament, one heard excited complaints that agricultural Hungary lived in plenty while she let the other half of the monarchy cruelly starve!

[8] *Die Österreichische Revolution* (Wien, 1923), p. 48.

[9] *L'Autriche et la Hongrie pendant la Guerre* (Paris, 1925), p. 259.

At the end of the war when slow starvation became open hunger and the news of the abuses of the administration at home against the members of the soldiers' families embittered the fighting army, there began the dissolution of the fronts and the formation of so-called *Green Cadres*. These formations alarmed the military commanders because they were constituted from two highly undesirable elements: deserters who in compact groups, armed and often even provided with machine guns, tramped about and robbed, and a great number of soldiers on leave who with falsified documents avoided a return to their regiments. In the spring of 1918 even open mutinies occurred very often which the military authorities were incapable of checking by armed force. Serbs, Bosnians, Magyars, Slovenians, and Czechs refused, in many cities of the monarchy, to continue the military service.

This disorganization of the army was followed by the growing rebellion of the working population. Whereas at the beginning of the war the working mass had a kind of sympathy for it because the official ideology, accepted also by the socialist leaders, was that the Central Powers were fighting against Russian Czarism and the liberation of its oppressed peoples, later this hypothesis became untenable when military absolutism destroyed all the constitutional guaranties of the Dual Monarchy. An almost symbolical outbreak of this changed public opinion was the attempt of Frederick Adler, the socialist leader, against the life of the Austrian premier, Count Stürgkh who was killed by his bullet (October, 1916). The assassin, a man of high culture and moral ideas, took this desperate step in order to revolutionize the masses against the system of military absolutism and the war. The example of Adler was really a turning-point in the war history of the monarchy. From this date an open resistance of the working-classes had begun which found its culmination during the Russian revolutionary events. After the fall of Czarism the prophecy of Frederick Engels verified itself: Austria became superfluous in the opinion of the working-classes. Now a new political theory arose represented by the left wing of the party entirely in sympathy with Frederick Adler which with sufficient clearness declared even during the war that the right of self-determination for every people must be accepted even at the cost of the destruction of Austria. The disclosures of the socialist daily *Arbeiterzeitung*, about the bloody crimes of the war-absolutism, envenomed the whole situation still more; and, when Frederick Adler appeared before his judges, the socialist leader instead of being accused became the accuser and with a sincere moral pathos which exercised an enthusiastic influence far beyond the socialist camp, unveiled the moral bankruptcy of the whole Austrian system.

The moral indignation of a very great number of the middle classes found a passionate expression in one of the most interesting products of the war literature, in the tragedy of the Viennese poet and critic, Karl Kraus, entitled *Die letzten Tage der Menschheit* (written in the fateful years from 1915 to 1917 but published, naturally, only in 1919). It is worth while to compare this terrible document of the anti-war literature, with *Le Feu* of Henry Barbusse. Though both works are animated by the same hatred of war, their attitude is entirely different and demonstrates the radically antagonistic nature of the French and the Austrian anti-war feeling. Barbusse described the war as a catastrophe, an anachronism, a result of bad human institutions, a hideous nonsense from both an intellectual and moral point of view, but his solidarity with the French cause is not questioned. Just the opposite was the attitude of the Austrian poet. He depicted the war simply as a criminal plot of military adventurers and of greedy business men, a conscious conspiracy of scoundrels and idiots against the people. There is no place for higher motives.

Not only the working-classes and the oppressed nationalities abandoned the old state but even among the German and Magyar military organizations grave signs of disintegration were witnessed in the last months of the war. Both the Magyar and the German regiments felt more and more distinctly that they were fighting for a foreign cause. Many Magyar regiments declared that they were not willing to continue the fight for the monarchy but they desired to defend the endangered frontiers of Transylvania, of their real fatherland. This attitude of a national disintegration became victorious over all the nations of the monarchy. At last even some German military formations collapsed under this ideology. Not bolshevized masses, not even Socialists, but military formation of the most loyal Crownland of Tyrol would not continue to fight, but returned to southern Tyrol because the poor soldiers realized that their homes, houses, wives, and children were endangered by the aggression of the enemy. Tyrol remained the real fatherland, whereas the Habsburg monarchy became a concept void of any sense.

Under such circumstances and such a military situation, it was too late when, in October, 1918, the government of Mr. Hussarek made an official declaration that the aim of the Emperor and his cabinet was to rebuild the monarchy on a confederative basis. If this idea had been announced clearly and openly about two years earlier, it would perhaps have saved the monarchy. But at that time it signified nothing: all the peoples of the monarchy refused the program of the government. The spokesmen of the Czechs, of the Poles, and of the Jugo-Slavs did not hide their real intentions any longer. The famous manifesto of the Emperor of October 18, which can be regarded as a real liquidation of the monarchy, did not alter the situation. The sovereign declared in it that Austria should be transformed into a confederative state *(Bundesstaat)* in which every nation should form an independent community on its national territory. At the same time the manifesto promised the unification of the Polish territories and a particular status for the harbor of Trieste. The monarch made an appeal to all his nations that they should co-operate in this vast work by electing their national councils. "In this way our fatherland should be reconstructed as a confederation of free peoples out of the tempests of the World War."

From the German side this imperial manifesto was denounced as a "pitiful surrender," as "a digging of the grave of the monarchy," as "a suicide of the dynasty." But these statements are manifestly untrue. The manifesto was not a cause of the dissolution but only the fixing of the date of this dissolution, the acknowledgment of the fact that the old monarchy had lost all its entire cohesion. Its effect, however, was rather a beneficial one as the inevitable process of disintegration became legalized by the authority of the throne which made it possible for the entire bureaucratic staff of Austria to co-operate without violating their oath of loyalty in the creation of the new national states. And at this juncture one who can grasp the real meaning of the whole historical process will see more in the imperial manifesto than the tragi-comical vacillations of the Habsburg Romulus Augustulus. On the contrary he will see in this manifesto the last point of a logical series, a kind of *List der Idee* (the "trickery of the Idea") in the sense of Hegel. The half-conscious, half-unwilling incarnation of this historical process, the Habsburg dynasty has incubated, if I may say so, the eggs of the national states and even gave the first help in the science of flying to these fledglings of national liberty by giving them the opportunity to utilize the old administration and bureaucracy of the dynasty in building up their national states. In this manner the imperial manifesto made the way free by avoiding unnecessary revolutionary convulsions.

Otherwise, as a more critical observer could have forseen, the manifesto was entirely unfit to obtain the intended *Bundesstaat*. The nations disgusted by the war-absolutism, under the sway of their leaders in the emigration, had no interest at all in the maintenance of the Habsburg monarchy, the less because the insincerity and lack of seriousness of the whole document was manifest. The Slav nations rejected it in a rather contemptuous way. The national council in Prague and in Zagreb asked for complete independence.

Not only the Slavs, but even the privileged Germans manifested no better feeling toward the Habsburg state. When the German deputies proclaimed the Austrian German state at the end of October 1918, the president of the German parties opened the meeting with these memorable words:

History made us Germans the founders of the old state of Austria, and we have given to this state through centuries in unbroken fidelity and in unselfish sacrifice our best in culture and in economy. We take leave of this state without thanks in order to put our national strength on itself and to build up hopefully out of its inexhaustible well a new commonwealth serving our people alone.

This same feeling also took hold of the other privileged nation of the monarchy, the Magyar. The Hungarian national council in its first proclamation of October 26, 1918, announced as its chief aim the saving of the Hungarian state, but greeted at the same time the newly formed Polish, Ukraine, Czech, Jugo-Slav, and Austrian states, and emphasized the necessity of co-operating with them very closely both economically and politically.

Aside from the imperial manifesto there is another symbolic document of the spontaneous disintegration of the Habsburg monarchy. When it became obvious that the newly formed national councils rejected not only the old Austria but also the Habsburg rule, the young Emperor in order to save his throne made an appeal to the soldiers on the fronts and asked them to give a plebiscite whether they wished a republic or a monarchy, because the official circles cherished the hope that the fighting army was more propitious for the Emperor than the disenchanted population at home. This curious plebiscite—unique in history!—also came too late, for in the majority of the disintegrating fronts it could not be carried on. But many regiments gave a vote, mostly in favor of the republic.

Before closing this necessarily very cursory chapter demonstrating that the World War was not the *cause*, but only the final liquidation of the deep inner crisis of the monarchy, I beg to quote the conclusions of two eminent Austrian historians, both loyal to the former Austria and representing the best of its tradition. (By this I hope to avoid the suspicion that my presentation of the facts was one-sided or artificial.) Victor Bibl wrote this:

The death struggle of the Danube Monarchy has come to its end. She was—we have seen it—gravely sick for a long time, sentenced to collapse. "We were compelled to die," said Ottokar Czernin, "we could choose only the manner of death and we have chosen the most terrible." One can dispute whether we could really have chosen and whether the end could have been even more terrible. But this is absolutely correct: *the Habsburg Empire was no longer capable of life, it had become an anachronism.*[10]

And Alfred Francis Pribram expressed the following weighty opinion:

I trust that you gathered from my statements that Austria-Hungary broke down in consequence of the disastrous war. She might, but for the War, have existed as a great power, for many years longer. The World War was therefore the immediate occasion for the downfall of the Monarchy. But the deeper causes of its collapse lay in the irreconcilable antagonism of the different nationalities which aimed at an independence incompatible with the idea of imperial unity and of the ascendancy which the German had enjoyed for hundreds of years.[11]

[10] *Der Zerfall Österreichs* (Wien, 1922), II, 558. Italics mine.
[11] *Austrian Foreign Policy, 1908–18* (London, 1923), p. 128.

CHAPTER IV

ESSENCE AND POSSIBILITIES OF CIVIC EDUCATION

Though the description of the facts which I have arranged above concerning the process of dissolution of the Habsburg monarchy may be fragmentary, they are, as I hope, sufficient to prove that the dissolution of the empire was not a mechanical accident but only the end of a long organic process.

In this negative experiment the problem of civic education manifestly plays an important rôle since, for centuries, there were not lacking conscious endeavors to fill the citizens of the monarchy with such ideas and sentiments as should promote the harmonious co-operation of the ten nations and the many nationalities of the empire and which should develop and foster loyalty toward the common state.

We must seek the means and methods of such a civic education not only in the system of public teaching (from the elementary classes to the universities), but also in other more efficacious factors. For instance in the collaboration of religious forces; in the intellectual and moral training of the army; in the ideology of press, literature, and science, influenced by the state; in the historical traditions maintained by the state; and in that social directive which the imperial court and the upper classes connected with it gave to the bourgeois society so appreciative of their favors.

But an inquiry exclusively devoted to these factors would not be sufficient to solve the problem in which we are interested. Though a conscious civic education can do a great deal, still it cannot accomplish more than to direct and enforce certain forces which result from the statics and dynamics of the state at a given moment under the law of sociological determination. The division of wealth, the sphere of activity of the individual citizens delineated by the constitution, the co-operation and struggle between the classes, the problems of international relations, the degree and extension of public culture, the religious-ethical surroundings, and the continuity of the historical traditions are the factors of primary importance which determine in a given epoch and society the quality and efficaciousness of the civic consciousness. This consciousness can without doubt be directed, influenced, and modified to a certain degree by a careful educational activity of the state, exactly as the gardener can modify and influence the right development of his trees by improving the soil, by pruning the branches, and by altering to some extent the climatic relations. But in spite of this still the general conditions of the soil and climate will be decisive for the development of the trees in all cases where there is no possibility of creating a purely artificial kind of environment, transferring the plant from the normally natural conditions into a hot-house atmosphere.

This analogy illustrates sufficiently the possibilities of civic education. Against those mass psychological tendencies which emanate from the real economic, moral, and political structure of society even the most careful and detailed civic education will lead to failure. A spontaneous loyalty cannot be created where the real interests of the people are constantly sacrificed to this so-called loyalty. National solidarity cannot be fostered where the progress of one nation is sacrificed to the interests of the other. Harmonious co-operation among classes cannot be established where the exploitation of the laboring-classes keeps the masses in constant dissatisfaction. No democratic civic education is possible where the real type of life is a dictatorship or the rule of caste.

Therefore, if we wish to measure the real force and results of civic education, we must study before all else those forces which have determined the social and political life of the Habsburg monarchy. We must know precisely the flood and speed of a river before we are entitled to judge those technical equipments by which we wish to modify its flood in the interest of certain aims. We must know exactly the centripetal and centrifugal forces which emanated from the inner structure of the monarchy before we can have a right conception of how a conscious statesmanship endeavored to strengthen the centripetal forces and to check the centrifugal ones by utilizing the possibilities of a civic education.

Many of us are inclined at the present day—especially under the sway of an extremely formulated theory of historical materialism—to contemplate this problem exclusively from the point of view of present-day interests and of a purely materialistic reasoning. But to put the problem in such a manner would be too restricted and short-sighted. The scale of values and world-view, which was constituted in a given historical co-operation in the continuity of many generations in the consciousness of the leading factors, influences the historical events sometimes deeper than the purely materialistic and rational interests of the recent past.

Therefore, before we investigate the most important centripetal and centrifugal forces which determined the fate of the monarchy in order to understand the real rôle of the bulwarks of civic education amid their irresistible flood, we must try to bring the reader in touch with those traditional forces, judgments of values and mass impulses, which we might say constituted the river-bed of the currents just mentioned. A mechanical recapitulation of the history of the monarchy would not be of much use even if we would have sufficient space (which is not the case) for it in the frame of this inquiry. Dates and facts alone give us no close touch with the reality if we do not understand the psychological structure by which those dates and facts were determined and qualified. This psychological structure depended in the Habsburg monarchy more on the will and aims of the dynasty than perhaps in any other modern state because this empire remained, in its essence from the very minute of its birth until the hour of its death, an absolutistic system. Therefore, if we try to understand the political aims of the most outstanding and powerful Habsburg emperors and investigate the ways and means which they employed, we shall come nearer to the reconstruction of the social and moral atmosphere of the whole historical complex. This we shall try to do in the next part of the book.

But before undertaking this task I must face a probable objection. In our historical reconstruction the accent will very often be put on Hungary, and some of my readers will perhaps see in this attitude a kind of national bias and will be of the opinion that I ascribe a disproportionate importance to the Hungarian evolution compared with the rôle given to the other nine nations of the monarchy. I think, however, that this criticism would not be to the point, for, in the problem of the unity of the Habsburg monarchy, Hungary took an exceptional position from the beginning, being the only country of the empire over which the Habsburg absolutism did not become triumphant, which never lost completely its state independence, which was a continuous source of international complications for the Habsburgs, which created later the dualistic constitution of the monarchy, the exceptional power of which made a confederative rearrangement of the nations impossible. On the one side the centralized mechanical unity of countries and provinces which lost their historical independence (Austria in the proper sense) : on the other side the more or less independent Hungarian state which never abdicated from its national sovereignty. On the one side a conglomerate of nations and countries in a bureaucratic militaristic and capitalistic frame; on the other side a united territory where the rule of the feudal classes continued. On the one side a continuous though sometimes impeded progression toward the realization of a state of various nationalities[1] on a confederative

[1] The terms *nation* and *nationality* are very ambiguous in the sociological and political literature. Very often they are used in the same sense denoting a multitude of people of the same history, tradition, language, literature, and custom. Sometimes, however, we find a slightly different meaning for each term: "nation" means a fully mature nationality which has reached its complete independence as a state building organism; "nationality," on the contrary, means a struggling national entity which under the sway of a dominant nation has not yet reached its complete independence. In this sense some writers in the former Austro-Hungarian monarchy spoke of the two dominant nations whereas the other nations were regarded only as nationalities. That was especially the attitude of the Magyar nationalists who regarded only the Magyars as a real nation. All the other peoples constituting Hungary were called nationalities, a kind of second-rank nations. That is the reason why I shall speak of "Magyars" and not "Hungarians" (this distinction does not exist in the Hungarian language in which there is no adequate expression for the term

basis; on the other side the fiction of a united nation-state which tried to unify and assimilate all its various nations. Reduced to a few sentences this was the fundamental antagonism which determined in the last analysis the fate of the monarchy. The chief actors of the great drama were, on the one side, the dynastic forces and on the other, the Magyar ruling classes. All the other nations, even the other privileged nation of the monarchy, the Germans, played only a second or a third rôle in the big historical experiment. That is the reason why I am compelled to emphasize in the next part the psychological situation of the Hungarian nation in a seemingly disproportionate manner.

"Hungarian," a Latin derivative) whenever I speak of the ruling nation in Hungary as opposed to the other nations which lived in the former Hungary. Though the racial unity of the ruling nation is more than doubtful (Professor A. Vámbéry, the great student of the early ethnical origins of the country called the Magyars "the most mixed people of Europe") the denomination "Magyar" assumed more and more a racial and linguistic significance and became the expression of a common political front against the non-Magyar nations, the so-called "nationalities." By this the former situation changed radically since, before the Constitutional era, the idea of the *Hungarian Nation* ("Natio Hungarica") covered all the noblemen though they belonged to the non-Magyar nations. Even the Nationality-Law of 1868 interpreted the political nation as embodying all the nations of the country.

PART II
THE HISTORICAL ATMOSPHERE

CHAPTER I

DIFFERENCES BETWEEN THE WESTERN NATIONAL STATES AND THE HABSBURG EMPIRE

In the formation of all the great European powers, the rôle of some dynasty was predominant for its armed force was the power which swept out the system of feudal particularisms and, in the majority of cases in alliance with the cities, it made an economic and administrative unity out of the loose medley of petty local rules. What Ernest Renan said from the point of view of his own fatherland: "The king of France, if I dare say it, was the ideal type of a state crystallizer, the king of France who created the most complete national unity," is more or less true concerning all the other modern national states. Whereas in these great national states the centralizing royal power became more and more the chief executive of the national will or at least the representative of an overwhelming national majority, the Habsburg dynasty carried on this work almost as a private enterprise of the imperial family.

Why did Habsburg not succeed in a work which in the western states was completed, why was it unable to put the political unity on the basis of a compact linguistic, and national unity? Some readers will not see any problem in this question and they will simply allege that the western states were from the beginning national unities. But the situation is not so simple. The truth is that England and France in the earlier Middle Ages were also states of an extreme racial and national complication and there, too, an assimilating and unifying process of several hundred years was necessary in order to create a national solidarity. It would be one of the most attractive sociological tasks to compare the unifying function of the Habsburg dynasty with that of the English and French crown and to seek for the causes which made the Habsburg dynasty unsuccessful—in spite of the protection of the German empire and the economic and cultural supremacy of the Germans—in creating an efficacious national majority opinion. There is no place for the more detailed analysis of this problem; I can mention only as a kind of hypothesis the following points: (1) The ethnographical basis was in Austria far more mixed. (2) The geographical divisions and the cultural antagonisms among various races, nations, and religions were far deeper, especially the struggle of the Byzantine culture with the western established here an antithesis which the western states did not know. (3) The territory of the state became a closed structure far later. In consequence of the continuous occupations and expansions the work of unification always confronted more new and difficult problems. The Italian territories, Galicia, Bukovina, and Bosnia-Herzegovina were such morsels which Habsburg was incapable of digesting. (4) The Turkish occupation of more than two hundred years kept an important part of the monarchy under the sway of a foreign racial and cultural structure which made not only the work of unification impossible on vast territories, but also became the source of constant political and diplomatic struggles. After the expulsion of the Turks, on the other hand, a gigantic reimmigration and colonization took place which produced a thoroughly new psychological atmosphere. (5) The causes above mentioned retarded the evolution of the monarchy about two hundred years. (6) Whereas the unifying function of the royal power in the west was carried on at a time when the racial, linguistic, and national consciousness of the great masses were yet rudimentary: in the Habsburg monarchy the process of political and administrative unification went on in a period in which nationalism became a conscious force. (7) The Habsburg dynasty could not give a home to all the peoples living in its territory in their integrity but one part of those peoples, often the greater part, remained outside the frontiers of the monarchy and constituted there the germs of a national state (Serbia, Rumania, Polish, and Ukraine territories).

Whatever may be the opinion of some people concerning this hypothesis, there can be little doubt that the essence of the Habsburg rule was without a national character and it was far more of a private nature than that of the other unifying dynasties. This truth is very succinctly and clearly stated by Arnold von Luschin, the eminent Austrian law historian, in these words:

Our empire did not grow on a homogeneous national ground but it is the result of a conscious activity of many hundred years of its dynasty which succeeded in combining its German territories with non-Germans at a time when these latter in their isolation were incapable of fulfilling their mission as a state. Therefore the history of Austria is not so much the history of a people or a country as a history of a state.[1]

[1] *Grundriss der Österreichischen Reichsgeschichte* (Bamberg, 1914).

CHAPTER II

THE HABSBURG EMPIRE AS A FAMILY ESTATE
(FIDEI COMMISSUM)

The Habsburg monarchy remained until its end a species of medieval entail held together by the same imperial will, and by the same insatiable desire for consolidation and expansion. Metternich, the mighty chancellor, said the following words to the ambassador of the German Bundestag after the death of Emperor Francis I (while Roman emperor, Francis II), in order to emphasize the continuity and unchangeableness of the Habsburg state:

Where the basis is not deranged, there is no serious danger; the old house stands solidly. The successors of the entail, of the *fidei commissum* is another but this other wishes nothing else than his predecessor has wished. In the same direction with the same force and endurance.

This sentence can be regarded as a most characteristic feature of the Habsburg rule, of the fundamental ideology which remained always the categorical imperative of *my house, my army,* a kind of a dynastic religion. The real founder of the dynasty, Rudolph Habsburg, who at the end of the thirteenth century had defeated the Czech King Ottokar and laid down the basis of the so-called Habsburg *Hausmacht,* the patrimonial nucleus of the later empire, was one of the most successful and daring state *accapareurs.* His family of *Alleman* blood already possessed in the eleventh century widely extended estates in Alsace and in Switzerland and had family connections with some of the most important dynasties of the age.

This desire for expansion, this trend of *l'art pour l'art* imperialism remained a chief motive force also in the successors of Rudolph in the interests of which the family practiced such a successful and extended activity in marriages and contracts for succession which was strange even in a period when there was a widely spread habit of gaining sovereignties by marriages, donations, and exchanges. On this field Maximilian I (1493–1519), called the "Last Knight," was particularly skilful, and obtained by his marriage the Netherlands and Burgundy; by the marriage of his son Phillip, Spain and the Indies; while he gained by marriage contracts a right for his grandson Ferdinand both to the Hungarian and the Czech crowns. As a consequence of these feverish and fortunate marriage activities, with the purpose of uniting the most heterogeneous and remote countries under the scepter of his family, Charles V (1519–56) became really the proprietor of a world-empire so big that the "sun never sets on its frontiers." This marriage expansion made such a great impression on the contemporaries that it gave rise to the often-quoted locution: *Bella gerant alii, tu felix Austria nube!* ("Let others make wars, thou happy Austria, marry!")

This continuous imperialistic expansion of the Habsburg house found an almost symbolical expression in the title of the dynasty which until the end, not without a certain comic aspect, was the record of the innumerable marriages, hucksterings, and captures of the Habsburgs in many parts of the world and in various periods. I will fully quote this title because it seems to me that it will introduce the reader to the psychic structure of the monarchy more than many abstract considerations. This so-called *grand imperial title* was the following:

We, ... by God's grace, Emperor of Austria; King of Hungary, of Bohemia, of Dalmatia, Croatia, Slavonia, Galicia, Lodomeria, and Illyria; King of Jerusalem, etc.; Archduke of Austria; Grand Duke of Tuscany and Cracow; Duke of Lothringia, of Salzburg, Styria, Carinthia, Carniola and Bukovina; Grand Duke of Transylvania, Margrave of Moravia; Duke of Upper and Lower Silesia, of Modena, Parma, Piacenza and Guastella, of Ausschwitz and Sator, of Teschen, Friaul, Ragusa and Zara; Princely Count of Habsburg and Tyrol, of Kyburg, Görz and Gradiska; Duke of Trient and Brixen; Margrave of Upper and Lower Lausitz and in Istria; Count of Hohenembs, Feldkirch, Bregenz, Sonnenberg, etc.; Lord of Trieste, of Cattaro and above the Windisch Mark; Great Voyvod of the Voyvodina, Servia, etc., etc.

CHAPTER III

THE FATA MORGANA OF THE HOLY ROMAN EMPIRE

This expansion over countries far and near, well known and exotic, of which some are at present only known by the specialists of historical investigation, this incoherent and chaotic imperialism had three consequences of very great importance from the point of view of our problem: the first is of a biological nature, the second of an international, and the third of an inner political.

Under biological I mean the marriage contracted by Philip the son of Maximilian I, with the heiress of the Spanish throne, Johanna the Crazy. By this marriage the Habsburg and Burgundian blood, "already showing symptoms of degeneration, received a positively pathological synthesis" which in some successors to the throne manifested itself now as a childish playfulness, now as a tyranny inclining to melancholy.

Not less dangerous was the international consequence of Habsburg imperialism concerning the future of the monarchy. The Austrian dominions of the *fidei commissum* gave sufficient strength to the Habsburgs so that they were capable of securing the German imperial crown for the dynasty since the first half of the fifteenth century. This *Holy Roman Empire of the German nation* like a *fata morgana* was always before the Habsburgs and threw them into a series of warlike and diplomatic complications which meant very often the sacrifice both of the Austrian and Hungarian interests which often impeded the inner consolidation of the monarchy. Mr. Henry Wickham Steed, the keen English observer of the Habsburg drama, says correctly:

For centuries the Habsburgs had sacrificed the strength of Austria to the Roman German imperial dream. From Ferdinand I to Charles VI their aim had been to exercise universal sway. Maria Theresa, Joseph II, and Leopold recognized the chimerical nature of the dream but still struggled for undisputed hegemony in Germany. Not until the defeat of Sadowa in 1866, nor in reality until the foundation of the new German Empire at Versailles in 1871 did the Habsburgs give up their German ambitions and turn their eyes resolutely to their own realms.[1]

This situation through centuries gave to the Habsburg policy the character of an *activity without a center*. The great Western dynasties realized more keenly the proper force of their powers and the real forces of which they disposed. But the Habsburg dynasty always vacillated between its two centers: they tried to base their rule now on

[1] *The Hapsburg Monarchy* (London, 1913), p. 12.

35

36   DISSOLUTION OF THE HABSBURG MONARCHY

the family possession on the Danube, now on their loose imperial connection. If the Emperor had concentrated himself on the Austro-
Hungarian possessions and had avoided the awful complications of
the Spanish War of Succession after the extinction of the Spanish
branch, he could have attacked the Turks with quite another energy
and could have assumed the work of unification in his restricted realm
with a far greater efficaciousness. Especially after the Thirty Years
War, which was a victory of German feudalism, the German imperial
connection became more and more a source of political complications
and intrigues for the Habsburgs. There were, even in the eighteenth
century, some three hundred little sovereignties on the territory of
this chaotic empire, which did not have even fixed frontiers. Many of
the princes were ruling inside and outside of the Empire. This confusion was so great that the greatest political thinker of the epoch of
Emperor Leopold I, Philipp Wilhelm von Hörnigk, who in 1684, wrote
a treatise which was considered for many years as an oracle under the
title *Österreich über Alles, wann es nur will* (Austria above all, if only
it wants to) was incapable of forming a clear idea of the relation of
Austria to Germany.

"Nobody could exactly determine at this time," says the historian of
the Austrian state idea, Professor Bidermann, "how far the German territory extended into the Austrian and what part of Austria belonged to
the Roman-German Empire."[2]

It is clear that this German imperial phantom and the chaotic
system of petty sovereignties of this anarchical *Kleinstaaterei* had
very disastrous results from the point of view of Austrian unity, the
more as the rival powers, in the first line of which stood France, utilized often and successfully this centerless state of the Habsburg dynasty. Ernest Lavisse writes ingeneously:

The French policy pays the great electors and sometimes boasts of
having bought the German crown. It buys the Protestant princes, the enemies of Catholic Austria, it buys the Catholic princes who in their capacity
as princes are enemies of the imperial power. In France the price of a
prince of such and such rank was accurately known, as was the cost of a
minister or a court mistress: Versailles was familiar with the price list of
the German consciences.[3]

This international situation naturally had a further consequence;
the third mentioned above which I called an inner political. The continuous hucksterings and conquests of the Habsburg foreign policy—
as I have already mentioned in another connection—made the formation of a united public opinion impossible in countries so different in

[2] H. T. Bidermann: Geschichte der Österreichischen Gesamt-Staats-Idee (Innsbruck, 1867), Vol. I, p. 50.
[3] *Vue générale de l'histoire politique de l'Europe* (Paris, 1904), p. 128.

economy, culture, and traditions. Especially the annexation of Belgium and Lombardy, as the result of the Spanish War of Succession and later the participation in the Polish booty, proved fatal to the monarchy which was incapable of giving an organic unity to all these territories so remote from its center and being more developed in culture and national consciousness. The eagle with the double head, the symbol of the Habsburg weapon, looked with its one head toward the Slavs, with the other toward the Germans, according to the changing sinuosities of the foreign policy which aimed now at a Western hegemony, now at an Eastern supremacy.

CHAPTER IV

THE UNIFYING FORCE OF GERMAN COLONIZATION

However great may have been the indistinctness of the structure of the Habsburg empire, and however preponderant may have been the rôle of dynastic absolutism in this conglomerate of countries, it would be an error to consider the whole, as many did, simply as an accidental formation held together only by armed force, by marriage intrigues, and by contracts obtained by violence. Though this empire as a whole did not have a unified national and geographical basis,[1] still important popular forces were at work to form a vague feeling of solidarity in the nucleus of the empire among Austria, Bohemia, Hungary, and Croatia. This situation was manifested by the fact that even before the definite integration of the monarchy, the work of unification was tried by several princes: now by an Austrian, now by a Czech, now by a Hungarian. But when Ferdinand I (1521–1564), elected on the basis of contracts of his grandfather, Maximilian I, succeeded in combining his Austrian possessions with Bohemia and with a part of Hungary, he already had in this effort a solid background in some important social forces. Among these forces the first in time and also the most important objectively, was the German colonization, the state-building character of which was duly and often emphasized. The Austrian state is indeed a result of this powerful migratory wave which pushed the peasant youth of Germany out of the old country already saturated by the narrow limits of the feudal structure and drove them toward the northeast and southeast. The Austrian state became a fruit of this southeast expansion, as the Prussian state, a result of the northeast. This colonization signified that the more developed German agriculture and superior town life introduced the germs of Western civilization into the backward and primitive social structure of Central and Eastern Europe. Everywhere indeed in Bohemia, Moravia, Hungary, Transylvania, in the southern Slav countries, renewed swarms of German colonizers flooded the farthest regions. Sometimes they accompanied the feudal conquerors, but very often too, they came as invited guests of the respective governments which pampered these foreigners with all kinds

[1] Already in the tempest of the World War a noted Austrian professor, Dr. R. Sieger, undertook the task of demonstrating the geographical unity of the Habsburg empire, in his book, *Die geographischen Grundlagen der österreichisch-ungarischen Monarchie und ihrer Aussenpolitik* (Leipzig und Berlin, 1915). His argument is ingenious but seems to me not sufficiently solid. On the contrary, with the liberties he takes it would not be difficult to prove the geographical unity of France and Germany or of almost any two European countries.

of privileges in order to secure for their kingly powers the financial, cultural, and political protection of a higher type of civilization. The kingly powers in their continuous fight against the feudal lords and other local territorial resistances needed foreign warriors, priests, financiers, artisans, and agriculturists. This endeavor is expressed with striking lucidity and plasticity in the famous admonitions of the first Hungarian king, Saint Stephen (1001–38), which can be regarded not only as a Hungarian governmental doctrine in those times, but also as a general public opinion among the sovereigns of Central and Eastern Europe. The admonitions of the great king advised his successor as follows:

The utility of foreigners and guests is so great that they can be given a place of sixth importance among the royal ornaments. The Roman Empire, too, became powerful and its rulers glorious and august by the fact that from everywhere the wise and noble men were flocking into that country. For, as the guests come from various regions and provinces, they bring with them various languages and customs, various knowledges and arms. All these adorn the royal court, heighten its splendor, and terrify the haughtiness of foreign powers. For a country unified in language and in customs is fragile and weak. Therefore I order thee, my son, to receive them with good will and to nourish them honestly in order that they abide with thee more joyfully than elsewhere. [*Proptereo iubeo te, fili mi! ut bona voluntate illos nutrias et honeste teneas, ut tecum libentius degant quam alibi habitent.*]

This policy remained in later centuries, too, the spirit of the royal policy in all those countries where its work of centralization against the native feudalism had to be protected with foreign forces. The Saxons of Transylvania, for instance, were invited *ad retinendam Coronam* according to a document which gave them extended privileges in that country. It is only natural that the Habsburg dynasty found allies in these German colonists based not on a conscious national conception which in those times was scarcely dawning, but according to the necessities of the developing state power which consciously utilized the greater economic and financial force of the German civilization.

CHAPTER V

COHESION CREATED BY THE TURKISH PRESSURE

Another great force which protected the unifying work of the Habsburg rule was the need of the masses for protection against the Turkish danger. The real date of the formation of the Habsburg empire was the Battle of Mohács in 1526 when the Turks destroyed the completely demoralized and impotent Hungarian feudalism. The defeat at Mohács and the sudden death of the Hungarian king, Louis II, made the marriage contract of Maximilian valid and Ferdinand became king of the western parts of Hungary whereas the central parts, the most fertile third of the country, went under Turkish rule and Transylvania took the rank of a semi-independent principality under national rulers, but under Turkish suzerainty. From this time the nucleus of the Habsburg empire, the Austrian, the Czech, and the Hungarian center was from a military point of view united under Habsburg rule, which began a fight of two hundred years for the acquisition of the two other parts of Hungary by eliminating step by step the Turkish invasion.

The Hungarian dominions of Ferdinand formed for a long period a species of military bulwark of the West against the Turkish danger and the Austrian Archduke alone, in his quality as German emperor, disposed at this time of the financial means and military organizations on the basis of which the defense of the West became possible and the gradual expulsion of the Turks could be undertaken with the hope of success. And the more completely we understand the economic and social history of this epoch, the feudal disorganization and anarchy of the Hungarian and Czech state, the more we must acknowledge that the Habsburg dynasty was during those centuries the only sufficiently centralized and militarily organized power which could resist the growing trend of Turkish imperialism and begin later with its expulsion. The unrivaled heroism of some Hungarian and Croatian captains in their isolated fortifications (of a Zrinyi, a Dobó, a Losonczi) aroused the enthusiasm of the suffering nation but was utterly incapable of checking the terrible force of the highly efficient Turkish army.

We really witness that in the same measure as the danger of the Turk occupation grew more prominent since the fall of Constantinople, as the despair of the Christian people was augmented by the fall of Athens, of the Balkan states, of Belgrade, and of Buda, the more grew the conviction among the nations of the Danube basin that the old isolated state frames were no longer sufficient for the obstruction of the formidable Asian danger. Already as early as the first half of the fifteenth century, King Sigmund of Hungary, of the Luxemburg dynasty, urged at his deathbed the unification of the Hungarian, Czech, and German crown in order to form a bulwark against Turkish aggression. The same need was felt even by the eternal antagonists of the dynastical power, by the upper classes and, from the beginning of the sixteenth century we often meet plans and aspirations which try to combine the nobility of various countries in order to support the Habsburgs in their struggle against the Turkish invasion.[1] This international co-operation of the noble classes, however, evoked the suspicion of the dynasty which in its continual fight against the feudal forces regarded this alliance of its natural opponents as a menace against its absolutistic system and impeded systematically these unifying tendencies from below, from which a kind of moral cohesion could have been evolved between the various countries of the monarchy. Therefore the struggle against the Turks became more and more a private enterprise of the Habsburgs for the consolidation and strengthening of their own power. That is the reason for this unheard-of indifference with which the liberation of Buda, of the heart of the country by the imperial troops in 1686 was accepted by Hungarian public opinion at a time when this exploit was greeted by the West with an outburst of enthusiasm. Those who know the deeper history of the epoch will, however, find this attitude not surprising, for there was no real feeling of national cohesion: the largest strata of the nobility hated the dynasty as the destroyer of the ancient privileges; the masses of bondsmen deprived of all rights regarded with a perfect indifference whether the imperial, the Turk, or the national armies would squeeze out of them the expenses and the blood-tribute of the war, whereas the lower middle classes, a very uninfluential factor, were exasperated by the religious persecutions of the dynasty to such an extent that Protestant priests began to consider the Turks as a bulwark against the intolerance of the Habsburgs. Whereas the fight of the French king for the unification of France against English foreign rule laid the cement for the first foundation of French patriotism, the struggle against the Turks was not accompanied in the consciousness of the contemporaries by any kind of international cohesion among those peoples the sons of which were the real instruments of this work of liberation. In spite of this, the great masses themselves felt more and more clearly the growing power of the dynasty in the face of which the chances of the feudal forces became weaker and weaker. Needless to say that in this growing military bureaucratic and financial force of the dynasty there were certain elements of a moral cohesion: in the leading German element a kind of a dynastical

[1] Bidermann, *op. cit.*, I, 6–7.

state consciousness began to evolve and in the imperial army, created by the genius of Eugene of Savoy, the prestige of victories evoked a feeling of military solidarity among the soldiers which gained the force of a popular movement. Those songs which glorified the hero, the great French *condottiere*, were, even during the World War, a powerful instrument for creating enthusiasm in the imperial army and remained real pillars of the military consciousness of the monarchy. In these songs which were taught in the Austrian schools until the collapse of the monarchy, we would seek in vain for the expression of a national or state solidarity: the great war lord had no real connection with any country or people. His genius served exclusively the interests and glory of the Habsburgs of whom he became the ardent supporter after the offenses which he suffered in the French court. How characteristic, for instance, are the following lines of one of the more representative songs:

> Prinz Eugenius, der edle Ritter
> Wollt dem Kaiser wieder kriegen
> Stadt und Festung Belgerad.
> (Prince Eugene, the noble knight,
> Would try to capture for the Kaiser
> The city and fortress of Belgrade.)

The song is exclusively militaristic and dynastic and has no bearing on fatherland and state.

CHAPTER VI

ALLIANCE BETWEEN THE DYNASTY AND THE OPPRESSED CLASSES OF THE PEOPLE

But in spite of this dynastical, patrimonial, and imperialistic nature of the Habsburg rule, we very early witness in it a character and tendency which became a further sustaining force in its work of centralization and unification. As the great Western national dynasties, the Habsburgs too, realized more or less clearly that, against the particularist forces of the feudal ages, against the petty kings, the robber knights, and the privileges of the estates, they needed the sympathy and protection of broader popular forces in order to get a more effective money and military support from the bondsmen and to strengthen the economic and financial power of the cities against the chronic rebellions of the feudal lords. There are many facts which demonstrate the growing tendency of the dynasty to protect the broader masses of population not only in the German provinces but also in other parts of the empire, even in rebellious Hungary. This character of the royal power was already clearly delineated under Ferdinand I. His constant fight against the misgivings of the feudal anarchy gained for him the sympathy even of a part of the lower nobility. Since 1545, he urged energetically the Hungarian Diet to abolish the *glebae adstrictus* ("tied to the soil") condition of the serfs and to give them back the right of the free migration because "their lamentations rise to the heavens continuously."

In a later period Basta, the cruel and bloody imperial general, of Italian origin (1550–1607), enjoyed the support of the Hungarian peasantry in Transylvania against the national nobility and he got a certain popularity among the poor masses. "Even a beggar could call on him," says one of the documents. The old policy of the former dynasties of the Árpáds and of the Anjous and of the great popular king Matthias Corvinus, the Just, defending the peoples against the extortions and robberies of the feudal classes became also a constant trait of the Habsburgs at least of their better type of representatives. Unfortunately this tendency could not have the same effects as in the West because the dynasty was foreign to most of its peoples and operated with a foreign army and bureaucracy. It awaked with its absolutistic despotic and bigoted Catholic tendencies the antipathy even of those masses which would have been its natural allies: of the German citizens of the cities. In spite of this the anti-oligarchical attitude of the Habsburgs was sometimes very prominent and found in the policy of Maria Theresa and Joseph II, as we soon shall see, a real sys-

tem of social policy of a very advanced kind. Even the rigidly absolutistic system of Bach, after the suppression of the Revolution of
1848 which we shall analyze more in detail, carried on a long series of
almost revolutionary measures against the petrified rule of the feudal
classes. Francis Joseph himself, though a typical absolutist in thought
and feeling, pressed universal suffrage on the old régime in Austria
and coquetted with it even in Hungary where he got into conflict with
the Magyar feudal classes. This tendency was even more accentuated
in the political conception of the two heirs apparent: Rudolph regarded feudalism as the chief enemy of his empire and Francis Ferdinand
was determined to break the rule of Magyar nobility in order to obtain
legal equality for the oppressed Slav and Rumanian nationalities.
The last off-shoot of the family, Emperor Charles I (called King
Charles IV in Hungary), made a final and almost desperate effort to
save his throne by democratic reforms and tried to enforce universal
suffrage on the recalcitrant upper classes of Hungary headed by
Count Stephen Tisza.

Under the sway of this continuously renewed effort there undoubtedly arose in many parts of the monarchy a kind of moral cohesion among the Habsburgs and the oppressed classes, especially the
peasantry of the nationalities which was very often protected by the
Habsburgs against German and Magyar rule. Many years after the
death of Crown Prince Rudolph, Daszynski, the Polish socialist leader, narrated in the Austrian Parliament that, according to the belief
of large masses of the peasant population in Galacia, Rudolph was
not dead but that he traveled in disguise over the countryside in order
to make preparations for the liberation of the suffering people. The
writer of these lines also observed very often during his trips in
Transylvania that the idea of the Emperor (the Rumanian peasant
always called him emperor and not king which was the official Hungarian denomination) enjoyed almost a kind of religious sacredness
among the backward Rumanian peasants. The ardent loyalty of the
Jugo-Slavs toward the emperor and against the Hungarian nobility
in the period of the Revolution of 1848 constituted one of the most
outstanding forces which saved the throne of the Habsburgs. But all
these important tendencies on which a really constructive state policy
could have been built were never consequently and systematically utilized by the Habsburgs and the ruling classes allied to them. Here, as
on all other grounds, the characteristic of the Habsburg policy given
by Grillparzer remained true: this policy was always a policy of
"half-deeds and half-ways."

CHAPTER VII

THE FIGHT OF THE ABSOLUTISM
AGAINST THE ESTATES

The unity created in the realm of Ferdinand I remained a very loose unity during all his long rule in the first half of the sixteenth century. His power was in conflict, in all his provinces, especially in the Hungarian and Czech kingdoms, with the ruling classes, the powerful nobility of those times. There were indeed in this epoch two powers in the empire: the power of the dynasty based on its own finances, army, and bureaucracy reinforced later by the prestige of the imperial title; and that of feudalism in the various countries and crownlands which continued its medieval life almost unaltered.[1] There was no real connection between the Emperor and the great masses of the peoples of his empire. The people, the millions of serfs devoid of any rights, stood under the exclusive rule of their landlords, the greatest of whom regarded the Emperor almost as a *primus inter pares*, as the most powerful and the richest landlord who had the largest estates, most money, and the biggest army. The barter economy in the distribution of wealth, the undeveloped system of communication, and the insecurity of daily life made it possible for the more powerful landlords to play the rôle almost of a state with the real rights of a sovereign. The alliance of these petty kings, capable sometimes of moving the impoverished nobility and the abused peasantry in complots against the Emperor and their eternal intrigues with foreign rulers, was a continuous danger for the dynastic power.

The Habsburgs understood this situation very well because, in their Spanish territories and in the other western states, they clearly saw that without the elimination of the feudal authorities there was no place for unification and a centralized type of administration in a country. Therefore, the state idea of the Habsburgs in those times could not be other than to overthrow the second state of the nobles and to put in its place their own administration, jurisdiction, and army. This process dominated the history of the Habsburgs during more than two centuries.

When Ferdinand I, who was born in Spain and had grown up at the imperial court, ascended the Austrian throne, he not only utilized his Spanish experiences but he constantly surrounded himself with those military leaders and diplomats who were, so to say, masters of the struggle against the feudal world. In this manner the Habsburg

[1] This dualistic character of the Habsburg state was vigorously demonstrated by Arnold Luschin, *op. cit.*, I, 196–228.

rule became a foreign rule not only in the eyes of the Hungarian and the Czech nobility but also in the view of the German estates. The young archduke came first of all in conflict with these latter elements. He had scarcely come into the country when his new system was opposed by the nobility of lower Austria whose resistance was strengthened by the cities. Ferdinand, accustomed to Spanish absolutism regarded this formal, rather than actual resistance as high treason and in the so-called Blood Tribunal of Wiener Neustadt in 1522 condemned to death and executed six prominent men of this movement, among them the mayor of Vienna. With this there began the bloody weeding out and breaking down of the feudal world which under the successors of Ferdinand not infrequently resulted in spreading fire and anarchy to many parts of the empire.

But later as emperor he found the noble classes allied with another power which impeded his work of unification. The feudal world was converted to Protestantism in order to sustain its local particularism by a freer and more rational religion against the papal and imperial universalism. Though Ferdinand did not yet dare to begin his struggle against this other front with full vigor, he keenly realized the danger which the alliance of the estates and Protestantism would mean for the royal power. In his testament he emphatically admonished his sons to abstain from Protestantism. "I would rather see you dead than to be affiliated with the new sects." Indeed already under his rule there began the process of counter reformation and of the expansion of the Jesuits.

At the same time Ferdinand undertook the work of unification with great energy and he is regarded not without reason as the founder of the German bureaucracy. He built up the organs of administrative unity, the privy council, the army council, and the court treasury. At the same time he endeavored to establish the organs of a local administration which would control the feudal bureaucracy. In this manner a new type of administration was created which in France under the name of the *artistocratie de robe* had such a prominent rôle in the foundation of royal unity, a staff of eminent lawyers and administrators which, amid the primitive feudal administration, introduced a higher conception of law and state and a more effective protection of city life and productive work in general.

After the death of Ferdinand this unifying policy was continued by Emperor Rudolph II (1576–1612), but his mental derangement threw the whole system into such a vacillating and reckless condition that it made it hateful to the whole empire. In Hungary, for instance, with the help of some wicked lords and under the most flimsy pretenses, a long series of high-treason processes was started against all those feudal persons who were regarded as opposed to the dynasty or whose estates were coveted by some of the Emperor's favorites. All those accused were sentenced to death and their property confiscated by a corrupt judiciary.

The cruel war of Rudolph against the Protestants became the beginning of a policy which fatally influenced the later destinies of the monarchy. In the whole empire both in the Austrian provinces, in the proper sense, and in Moravia and Bohemia and in Hungary, there went on a ferocious extermination of Protestants who were mostly allied with the nobility and with large masses of the peasantry. This struggle was carried on by armed force and ideologically with the co-operation of the Jesuits. So-called "armed commissions of religion" were installed which captured the Protestant churches one after the other. This movement in the Czech countries, especially in Moravia, the country of the "iron barons," took on a strictly national character in the form of a specific Czech Puritanism. Especially the so-called "Bohemian-Moravian brothers," successors of the great Czech reformer, John Huss, who was an inspired disciple of Wycliff and who suffered a martyr's death in 1415, became the chief supporters of the anti-Habsburg movement. They combined their Protestant traditions with a strong national feeling against the Viennese Roman Catholic court and its German-speaking bureaucracy. A Czech nobleman for instance told his son, speaking German, "I would rather bark like a dog than speak the language of the foreigners."

The religious persecutions of the imperial policy led also in the German countries to a long series of popular outbursts in which religious feeling was sometimes mingled with social discontent against those feudal lords who oppressed the peasantry. In Hungary, too, a vehement national and racial antipathy arose against the Habsburg. In his fight against Protestantism the method of the Emperor consisted in playing the feudal elements against the citizens of the towns and vice versa. This was an imitation of the proceedings which were applied previously in Styria against the Protestant nobility. The work of counter-reformation was initiated in the royal cities as the court knew very well of the great hatred which existed among the cities which were mostly German and among the feudal classes. The Hungarian higher clergy always urged the king to combat the churches by armed forces in the cities. Only later the same process turned on the Protestant nobility.[2]

In such a manner the ill-famed Habsburg principle of the *divide et impera* (divide and rule) was introduced for the first time in its Machiavellian self-consciousness on religious grounds. It later became, in the national field, the chief factor in the creation of a political and moral atmosphere entirely unfit for the formation of an organic solidarity in the Habsburg empire. Under the sway of this

[2] Acsády, *History of the Hungarian Empire* (Budapest, 1903), II, 240–43. In Hungarian.

ferocious policy of religious persecution and in consequence of the fight of the imperial power against the liberties of the noble estates, there arose a kind of an alliance between the nobility, ousted from their landed properties by arbitrary processes, and the large strata of citizens and peasants molested in their religious life and overburdened with taxation and military service against the absolutism of the Habsburgs, against the German bureaucracy, and the Catholic high clergy allied with them.

This movement, partly social, partly religious, and partly national aroused a long series of semi-national rebellions against the Habsburgs which sometimes in the hands of a mighty and ambitious personality shook the very foundations of the Habsburg empire as the national and social discontent was strengthened and financed very often by the foreign enemies of the Habsburgs. The first national hero of this type was the remarkable personage, Stephen Bocskay, who as an almost legendary leader of the dispossessed smaller nobility and of the peasant masses persecuted in their religious faith and overstrained by a system of arbitrary taxation, organized such a widely spread rebellion against the Habsburg with the help of the Turks that their throne became endangered and Rudolph was compelled to guarantee the religious liberty of the Hungarian Protestants in the Peace of Vienna (1606). At the same time the semi-independent principality of Transylvania became more and more the center of the old feudal world which created a special type of Magyar nationalism directed against the Habsburgs and combined with the protection of the persecuted Protestantism. Transylvania became a bulwark of religious freedom against the clericalism of the Habsburgs and the Diet of Torda, by the codification of religious liberty, was an early protest against the methods of the counter reformation (1557).

CHAPTER VIII

THE INTRODUCTION OF THE SPANISH TERROR

The cruel and unbalanced policy of Rudolph overstrained the chord. The feudal world became more and more conscious of the danger which menaced it by Habsburg absolutism. Under the milder régime of his successor, we witness a greater activity of the noble classes. We see the beginnings of a conscious foreign policy of the estates which the growing pressure of Turkish aggression made even more prominent. Already, under the rule of Rudolph, the Austrian feudal classes made a close alliance with the Czech, Moravian, and Silesian nobility as well as with the Hungarian, Transylvanian, and Croatian estates. We can even observe a conscious endeavor to establish a central council of the noble classes for the administration of all those affairs in the internal and foreign policy in which the nobility of the various countries were equally interested. This feudal coalition took a more and more menacing attitude against the centralizing policy of the Habsburgs. When Ferdinand II (1619–1637), an entirely bigoted, passionate personality of a purely Spanish type succeeded to the throne, the conflict between Protestant particularism and Habsburg Catholic universalism, a struggle of life and death, became inevitable which under the tempests of the Thirty Years War led to an atomization of Germany and to a consolidation of the Habsburg dynasty.

The personality of Ferdinand II was a real incarnation of the Jesuit ideal which did not know any moderation or regard. "A desert is better than a country with heretics," he used to say, and he remained loyal to this slogan. The extermination of Protestantism and by it the annihilation of the resistance of the nobility to the final establishment of the absolutistic rule upon the whole territory of his empire, that was his ideal of a state. The aristocratic Spanish priests who were always with him took care that the Emperor should not know hesitation and milder compromises. He heard every day two masses and he visited constantly the monasteries and often personally rang the bell in the hermitage of Neustadt for the vespers. He initiated the historical custom according to which the Kaiser at Vienna assisted publicly the procession on Corpus Christi Day and, beginning with 1622, the Emperor walked among the crowd with a candle. (This practice remained unaltered until the end of the monarchy.) Ferdinand regarded his political enemies simply as the enemies of God and he was devoured by a burning desire to annihilate the hated sect of Protestantism.

Such was the individual who, at an important turning-point of history, found himself opposed by a big coalition of the feudal classes, especially by the proud and inflexible Czech and Transylvanian estates, which, under the leadership of Count Mathias of Thurn and of the powerful and clear-sighted Prince of Transylvania, Gabriel Bethlen, laid siege to Vienna and endangered his throne. Ferdinand made his first offensive against his Czech enemies and won a decisive victory over them in the Battle of the White Mountain in 1620. This signified a new epoch in the history of Austria. Ferdinand, with the cruelty of the religious fanatic and of the despot of God's grace, now undertook systematically the work of the extermination of the reformation and of the Czech national nobility. Perhaps there is no second example in history of such a total annihilation and extirpation of a whole political system. More than a score of noblemen were executed in Prague with cruel brutality. Before the execution even the Emperor seemed to vacillate but the mighty Jesuit, Lamormain, put an end to his meditations by declaring that he would take the whole matter on his conscience. The Emperor yielded but previously he did something in the interests of his victims. He prayed when they were executed for the salvation of their souls. For this purpose he went to the famous madonna picture of Maria Zell in Styria, where he knelt before the picture and implored the Virgin that the Czechs should obtain at least in their last moments an illumination and that they should be conducted before their death within the pale of the church.

It became his dogma to make the people blessed by terror. He boasted of torturing and executing his subjects out of love in order to save their successors from the damnation of heresy. But beside his transcendental aims the Spanish humanitarian did not forget his worldly purposes. He made colossal confiscations in Bohemia and Moravia, the value of which is estimated at fifty million golden florins, in those times an immense fortune, which he applied as a fund *to create a loyal aristocracy for his throne*. From all parts of the world hungry adventurers eager for booty poured into the unfortunate country as the representatives of Catholicism and of the Habsburg state idea, as bureaucrats and war lords of the Emperor. The pressure of executions, imprisonments, and confiscations upon the nation was so formidable that, beginning with 1623, a long wave of emigration began from Bohemia and Moravia. In the year 1628 alone thirty-six thousand emigrants left the country, among them one hundred and eighty-five noble families.[1]

With this reign of terror Ferdinand reached his aim: he extirpated almost entirely the recalcitrant Protestant nobility in the Czech countries which signified in those times the complete extermination of the whole national life, because the real supporters of it belonged then to the noble classes. The whole Czech people sank into a long

[1] For other interesting details see Dr. Eduard Vehse, *Geschichte des österreichischen Hofes und Adels und der öst. Diplomatie,* Dritter Teil (Hamburg, 1851).

torpor of peasant unconsciousness. The new nobility, the so-called *Brief- und Hofadel* (nobility of letter and court) which Ferdinand put in the place of the feudal one, became an obedient instrument of the imperial will. In this way the mechanical unity of the empire was secured in the countries of the Czech crown, and the monarch, had no ulterior purposes or aims. The old struggle between the dynasty and nobility ceased and the servile court nobility seemed to be a sufficient basis for the unification of the empire. No new kind of administration was introduced into the country purged from feudalism, but the old administration of feudal nobility continued under the direction of the new nobility.

Thus the system of Ferdinand became a prototype of absolutist and Catholic concentration which remained a salient trait of the Habsburg rule. The idea that the state can be held together by purely military forces with the help of a court nobility entirely dependent upon the throne and with the protection of the Roman Catholic church, this conception of a *Machtstaat,* became as we shall see later in detail the chief obstacle to real co-operation and psychic penetration between the various peoples and classes of the monarchy. And the system had also another quality which slowly but surely ground up the moral forces of the monarchy. To press anything and anybody into the bed of Procrustes of the dynastic and patrimonial ideal, to persecute all originality and independence which sought for new ways and means and for a freer kind of co-operation, to reward the servile routine, and a formal loyalty revelling in words: these elements of the Spanish system infiltrated deeply into the Habsburg *fidei commissum* and envenomed its blood circulation.

But what still more undermined the system was its entire political immorality. Ferdinand II and Leopold I (1657–1705) applied literally the principles of Machiavelli though they probably were not familiar with them. Let us illustrate this spirit by a document produced by the official historian of the Habsburgs, Hormayr, who became the most severe critic of the system after he abandoned the country of Metternich. This document is almost symbolical of the methods of the *divide et impera* of Austrian absolutism. The document in question is a protocol of the state council which under the chairmanship of Ferdinand II was held relative to the matter of the pacification of Hungary. The council was assisted by the Papal Nuncio, by the family ambassador of Madrid and Florence, the governor of Bohemia, Cardinal Franz Dietrichstein, and by the chief military leader Wallenstein and other outstanding personalities of the epoch. The Spanish ambassador made a proposal according to which his lord and king would be inclined to supply for forty years forty thousand soldiers to the Emperor, in order to crush rebellion in Hungary. "In this manner this whole nation, so disloyal to the imperial majesty, could be exterminated root and branch and the capital and its neighborhood could be made safe from the aggressions of these monsters." And when some members of the council expressed doubts concerning this plan because of the well-known bravery of the Hungarians, the Spanish ambassador continued his argumentation as follows:

The best wisdom would be to buy the Turks at any price and separate them from the Hungarians. . . . . The Hungarians should be constantly irritated, the Turks should be made distrustful towards them and if possible an eternal peace should be settled with the latter. . . . . The best method would be that already experienced in Spain: foreign governors should be set over these Hungarian barbarians to give them new, entirely arbitrary, laws without the possibility of any legal redress. . . . . If the Hungarians complain at Vienna, the answer ought to be: His Majesty does not know anything about these procedures which are very disagreeable to his most high person. In this manner these beasts who do not see beyond their noses could not make any accusations against the emperor and would turn all their hatred against the governors. . . . . In this way the Hungarian nation unaccustomed to such a yoke would attempt a rebellion against its severe governors. This rebellion would give a desired opportunity to punish the traitors with inhuman penalties and tortures.

This awful and almost incredible declaration given here in practically the same words as Hormayr reports it, was undersigned by the whole state council and the Emperor. On the basis of this document Wallenstein and the other military chiefs were charged with the control of all popular movements in Hungary.[2]

[2] *Anemonen aus dem Tagebuche eines alten Pilgermannes* (Jena, 1845), I, 116–19.

I know that the authenticity of this document will be questioned by a certain group. Baron Joseph Hormayr (1781–1848), a historian of immense knowledge and brilliancy became in 1816 the official historiographer of the Habsburgs, but in 1828 he abandoned the country and accepted a position in Bavaria in order to avoid the vexations of the Metternich system. From this time the historiographer became an acute critic of the Habsburg system and I will not question that he was biased against it. Nevertheless, I believe in the authenticity of the document (although it was not found in certain parts of the Viennese Archives) for the following reasons: (1) Some of the best Hungarian historians believed firmly in the trustworthiness of Hormayr. (2) Also competent Austrians told me that though he sometimes colors his statements they regard him incapable of a conscious falsification. (3) The disappearance of documents disagreeable to the Habsburgs was not exceptional. (4) The later spirit of the Habsburg policy in Hungary corroborates the principles of the document. (5) Some passages of it were already quoted in a sensational book of the noted Viennese critic and publicist, Hermann Bahr, in 1907. The book was mutilated by the censors and later seized by the police. Professor Joseph Redlich and his friends brought the matter before Parliament where the authenticity of the document was not questioned as far as I know.

My guess is, therefore, that Hormayr told the truth though he colored and vivified certain expressions. And another point: why should we be surprised by the infamous cruelty of this document from the beginning of the seventeenth century, when we have another analogous from August 30, 1905, a letter in which William II, so much admired by certain American radical pacifists, tells Prince Bülow that an alliance should be made with the Sultan in order "to put the Mohammedan forces under Prussian leadership," but, "before all the Socialists must be shot down, beheaded, and made harmless, if necessary, by a blood-bath and the foreign war later!" (Published by the *Berliner Tageblatt,* October 14, 1928.)

If we even take into consideration all the mitigating causes, the brutal atmosphere of the period, the cruel methods and eternal intrigues of feudalism, its predatory spirit against the working-classes and the poor, its continuous plots and treasons in the pay of foreign interests, the document quoted still remains a horrible reminiscence of the governing spirit under Ferdinand which remained the real spirit of the imperial policy under his successor Leopold I. The influence of a small group of prelates, Jesuits, rapacious aristocrats, the so-called *Viennese camarilla,* became even more preponderant and the Emperor continued the policy of the counter-reformation and of an absolutistic centralization in the whole monarchy, especially in Hungary, with a renewed vigor. The terrible "Blood Tribunal" in the city of Eperjes under Count Caraffa, the war lord of Leopold, crushed all constitutional and religious resistance. "From March to September, 1687, the butchery lasted," says an independent Hungarian historian, "and already in October the Diet was opened which surrounded by foreign military forces, voted all which was expected from it."[3] The re-Catholization of the whole aristocracy in Hungary formerly belonging almost entirely to Protestantism was accomplished. In 1655 there were only three Protestant families and the work was continued with the forceful conversions of the cities and of the counties. A systematic warfare was carried on against the Protestant churches and many hundred processes of high treason were inaugurated. The fate of the Protestant-Hungarian galley slaves was so pathetic in Buccari and Naples that their condition repeatedly moved European public opinion. The system of confiscating landed property of the disloyal nobility continued and the new aristocracy loyal to the throne was reinforced. Especially the complot of some feudal aristocrats under the leadership of Nádasdy (all Catholics!) in which the motives of national exasperation were curiously intermingled with the purely private business interests of the rebel magnates was an excellent instrument for the court absolutism to complete the final blow against the deeply wounded feudalism. The rebellion was cruelly revenged, its leading men were executed. In 1670 about two thousand men, nobles, and distinguished citizens were imprisoned. Immense treasures in land and jewelry were confiscated. A terrible despair took hold of the whole country and the hatred against the court and the absolute system and the procedures of counter-reformation developed in the naïve consciousness of the great masses into a form of hatred against the Germans, and in those times were born those popular slogans which remained veritable symbols in the soul of the Hungarian people: the hatred against the *German* Vienna which sucks out the Hungarian blood and treasure. "The faith of a German

[3] Professor Aladár Ballagi in his commemoration of the 250th birthday of Francis Rákóczi, II.

is a faith of a dog . . . . he promises all when he is in anguish but later he grants nothing . . . . rather under any devil than under the German. . . . ." Such and similar outbursts were deeply rooted in the subconscious strata of the popular public opinion and made it always an easy manoeuver for the feudal classes to direct and canalize against Vienna all social or political discontent which could become dangerous for them. After the suppression of the feudal rebellion many thousands of fugitives fled to Turkish or Transylvanian territory and became the nucleus of a series of insurrections called *kurucz insurrections*, the ideology of which was a curious mixture of the feudal interests with the social and religious unrest of the disinherited classes.

In connection with the counter-reformation there was another movement in favor of Habsburg Catholicism which was directed against the Graeco-Oriental church and embittered the life of vast masses of Rumanian serfs. The effort of the Roman Catholic church to push back toward Rome the masses of people living in Graeco-Oriental communities was protected by the Habsburgs with armed force. The history of the Greek-Catholic union constitutes one of the most horrible pages of the work of conversion made in the Habsburg monarchy, and contributed much to the exasperation of the bondsmen population.[4]

Besides the counter-reformation and the extirpation of the disloyal feudal elements, a third great fact completed the final consolidation of the Habsburg rule in this epoch. That was the continuation and the victorious accomplishment of the war against the Turks under the brilliant leadership of Prince Eugene of Savoy. The Peace of Karlovicz, in 1699, put all of Hungary under Habsburg rule with the exception of the Banat of Temesvár. This event changed the whole situation of the monarchy. From this time on there was no further organized power against the Habsburgs. The resistance of the feudal classes was entirely broken before the prestige of the imperial dynasty and the new army organized by Prince Eugene on a modern Western pattern. This ascendancy of the Habsburgs was so elementary that immediately after the reconquest of Buda, the heart of the country, in 1687, the Diet accepted not only the legal succession of the male line of the Habsburgs but it extended this privilege also to the Spanish branch of the dynasty and renounced the old right of armed resistance against unlawful imperial acts. The same diet gave citizenship to 167 foreigners to the new aristocracy of the Habsburgs which became a reliable bodyguard of the now hereditary Habsburg monarchy.

But a more solid foundation than the constitutional guaranties

[4] Benedek Jancsó, *History and Present State of the Rumanian National Aspirations* (Budapest, 1899), I, 733–97. In Hungarian.

above mentioned was bestowed upon the Habsburgs by a complete reorganization of the system of land ownership in the country. Following the advice of the Archbishop Kollonics, a leader of the counter-reformation and Germanization in Hungary, the Emperor constituted a special commission, the so-called *neoacquistica commissio* with the purpose of controlling the legal title of all those landed properties which were previously under Turkish rule. This whole territory was considered as conquered by the army of the Emperor and the committee claimed a heavy ransom from all those proprietors who now became imperial subjects. And as eight-tenths of the country was originally under Turkish domination the commission was able to extort large sums from the landed interests for decades and put above them the sword of Damocles of expropriation. All undesirable elements could easily be eliminated under the legal disguise. At the same time the Catholic and loyal elements were strengthened by opulent donations and the power of the high clergy with growing Germanizing tendencies became more and more preponderant. Many foreign ecclesiastic bodies and priests flooded the country with the purpose of paralyzing the native clergy of national tendency. Under such conditions the trend of the counter-reformation became almost irresistible. The Hungarian tradition attributes to Kollonics the ill-famed dictum, "I will make Hungary first a prisoner, then a beggar, and finally a Catholic." This maxim may be apocryphal but it expresses without doubt the state of mind, the hatred, and profound exasperation with which the great masses of the Hungarian population regarded the triumphant predominance of the Habsburgs.

CHAPTER IX

MERCANTILISM AND PRAGMATICA SANCTIO

The forces outlined above made the power of the Habsburg monarchy irresistible at the beginning of the eighteenth century in its whole empire. Against this daily growing power all resistances and rebellions of the feudal classes became futile. The last leader of all the dissatisfied elements of Hungary, a man of a remarkable and tragic personality, Francis Rákóczi II (1675–1735), of the famous stock of the Transylvanian princes, the hero of the last *Kurucz* insurrection against the hated world of the *Labancz* forces (the nickname of the Austrian crowd) tried in vain to oust the Habsburg rule. The whole movement was a curious mixture of narrow feudal local interests and of the aspirations for religious freedom and social emancipation. On the one hand stands Rákóczi the leader, a man with almost kingly powers who possessed in Hungary and Transylvania 445 villages on an area of 1,400,000 yokes.[1] On the other hand were all the impoverished masses of the country: noblemen whose estates were confiscated; poor priests; teachers driven by the counter-reformation from their offices; small peasants ruined by the eternal *kurucz-labancz* conflicts; soldiers dismissed from the imperial, Turkish, or national armies; and other uprooted parts of the population without bread and without any chance for the future. This fundamental contradiction, like a red thread running through the whole plot, of a feudal leader like Rákóczi with his immense landed estates and loyal Catholic feelings joining forces with the Protestant masses and with the disinherited peasantry, gave to the whole movement a kind of psychological danger and a lack of balance which the prince could scarcely appease by very vague and uncertain promises. In spite of this dilemma his standards *Pro Deo et libertate* and his famous proclamation issued in 1703, *Recrudescunt inclytae gentis Hungarae vulnera* ("the old wounds of the glorious Hungarian nation reappear"), and the kind, humanitarian spirit of the leader in sympathy with the sufferings of all the peoples oppressed by the Viennese absolutism evoked such a mass of popular enthusiasm that he succeeded for seven years in fomenting the spirit of rebellion against the Habsburgs whom he dethroned at the memorable Diet of Ónod in 1707. Large parts of the country were again covered with blood and the rebellion menaced not only the Austrian elements but at the same time the noble and wealthy circles of Hungary. Rebellions of famine and anarchical plunderings

[1] A Hungarian yoke *(hold)*=1.066 acre.

disturbed very often the campaign of Rákóczi who got into an entirely helpless position in face of the highly disciplined and efficient Austrian army and his destiny was sealed when his foreign allies and in-
spirers, especially the shrewd diplomacy of the French, abandoned
him. Though noble and enthusiastic in his intentions the prince remained always a semi-conscious instrument in the hands of foreign
diplomatic intrigues. The lack of any serious financial and administrative background made the whole insurrection die from hunger.[2]

Rákóczi was compelled to flee and in his exile he made a last unsuccessful attempt to reconcile himself with the Habsburgs. The
Viennese court became completely triumphant. The sequestration of
the Rákóczi estates and the unheard of servility of the nobles who dis-
honored in a special law the memory of their former chief made the
Habsburg rule in the country firmer than in any previous time. The
possibilities of personal feudal wars were over. The lords abandoned
their eagle nests, and their fortifications were demolished. At the
same time a colonizing activity on an immense scale had begun in order
to repopulate colossal territories devastated by the Turks and the
civil wars. Many hundred thousands of foreigners, especially Germans, Rumanians, Ruthenians, and Serbs, came into the liberated
areas of Hungary. One of the best experts of this movement thinks
that the gigantic proportions of this new immigration can be compared only to that directed toward the United States in the nineteenth
century. Very often the aims of colonization were connected with
those of Germanization. These new immigrants having had no moral
connection with the old traditions of the country became as a matter
of fact ardent supporters of the Habsburgs both from an economic
and a political point of view. Especially on the *military confines*,
bulwarks erected on the frontiers of the liberated territories which
remained under a strict military administration, there arose a proverbial Habsburg patriotism perhaps the only real one which the Habsburgs were capable of fomenting in their realm. The name of *graničar*, the soldier and citizen of these military confines, became a mock
name for politicians who showed an exaggerated loyalty toward the
Habsburgs.[3]

The great international events of this epoch only accentuated the
predominance of the monarchy. As a result of the Spanish War of

[2] The romantic uprising of Prince Charles-Edward in 1745 for the reconquest of
the throne of Scotland presents startling analogies with the upheaval of Rákóczi
demonstrating the common traits of feudalism under different racial and political
conditions. (See for particulars: R. Pauli, "Entstehung des Einheitstaates in Gross-
britannien," *Preussiche Jahrbücher* [Berlin, 1872].)

[3] An old song expressed this loyalty in the following way:
  "If the Glorious Emperor desires,
  The graničar jumps into death."

Succession, Charles VI acquired the Italian possessions of the Bourbons in the Peace of Utrecht (1713). On the other hand, in the continued war against the Turks, Prince Eugene conquered Belgrade and in the Peace of Passarowicz (1718) he restored the whole Banat of Temesvár to the empire and placed the Habsburg sovereign in control of Serb and Rumanian territories. The unifying work of Ferdinand I was finished and made an overwhelming impression on all the countries, especially on Hungary where the Emperor, as Hungarian king, came into the possession of a power which no other Hungarian king since Matthias Corvinus (1458–90) could rival.

Under these advantageous inner and outer conditions for the monarchy, we witness a more and more conscious effort in the imperial court and among the leading elements to replace the mechanic and military unity of the empire with one that is economic and political. During the reign of Charles VI, as Hungarian King Charles III (1711–40), there was beginning a conscious and consequent mercantilistic policy. Until then every kingdom, province, or crownland constituted an economic unity but now the so-called *transito* was introduced, that is, measures were taken to make it possible for goods introduced in any of the Habsburg countries to pass from one into the other without paying custom duties over again. This policy was energetically continued by later kings and in 1775 it was successful in uniting the Bohemian countries and the Alpine countries (with the exception of Tyrol) in a single custom union. By and by all the countries grew into a vast united market. The local merchants of the former periods who supplied only a closely limited area with their goods were replaced by big industrial and agricultural producers who possessed privileges for the whole economic territory. A kind of division of labor between the various provinces made its first appearance. Wool and glass were manufactured in Bohemia, clothes in Moravia, iron in Styria, and fancy goods in Vienna, for the whole economy of the empire. Only Hungary remained until the middle of the nineteenth century a strictly separated economic unit resisting the unified circulation of the monarchy. This situation was not a result of a Hungarian chauvinism (on the contrary, it was an old grievance of the Hungarian diets that the custom barrier between Hungary and Austria was very detrimental to Hungarian economic progress) but a consequence of the narrow-minded fiscal policy of the Hungarian nobility who refused on the basis of their ancient feudal privileges to pay taxes and, therefore, the only means of getting a financial contribution from them was the indirect way of custom duties on Hungarian corn and cattle.

This quickly growing military economic, and administrative unity of the monarchy aroused in the best minds of the empire the effort to unify and centralize the vast territory—following the examples of

Louis XIV and Peter the Great—in a homogeneous system of law and constitution. The book already quoted, of von Hörnigk, emphasized the fact that the countries of the Emperor formed a *natural body* and by the exchange of their raw materials they *constituted a small world* which could exist by itself. A similar thought was expressed by the great philosopher Leibniz who encouraged Emperor Leopold to become a second Justinian by elaborating a new system of civil law for the whole territory of his empire. The same effort was renewed and continued by the victorious military leader, Prince Eugene of Savoy in 1726 when he advised Emperor Charles VI: "It would be necessary to make as far as possible a *totum* from the extended and glorious monarchy of your majesty. . . . ."

But perhaps nobody saw more clearly the position of the monarchy at the beginning of the eighteenth century than the ingenious secretary of the court treasury, Christian Julius von Schierendorff, who, under the influence of the union between England and Scotland completed at this time, expressed the opinion in a scholarly memoir that the empire would be seriously endangered (and here the author was surely influenced by the experiences of the Hungarian rebellions) if it did not succeed in combining its various parts into a common constitution and a common order of succession for the throne. But this plan could only be achieved if a real popular representation were bestowed upon the whole in which all the classes of the monarchy, even the lower, would participate. This thinker, so much advanced for his age, at the same time emphasized the fact that the unjust and wretched state of the peasant masses especially of the Hungarian and Czech serfs, was the chief impediment of the consolidation of the monarchy. Therefore, the bondsmen of the noble rebels should be liberated. The *arcanum dominationis* (the secret of domination) would be a just policy of taxation.[4]

But these revolutionary ideas of a liberal centralization did not have a wide echo. Both the Habsburg absolutism and the particularism of the estates abhorred equally these measures. But his ideas concerning the legal succession to the throne had probably an effect on the carrying on of the *Pragmatica Sanctio* by which Charles VI, deprived of a male successor, proclaimed the hereditary right of the female line in case the male line should die out. This fundamental decision which was in Austria a purely personal decree of the Emperor emanating from the old patrimonial principles for the maintaining of his *fidei commissum* gained on the Hungarian Diet such a constitutional form and motivation that it was rightly called the "first declaration of a unitary state idea" in the empire. The Hungarian law of 1722–23, indeed, proclaimed not only the hereditary right of the fe-

---

[4] See for the particulars of Schierendorff's reform-plans, A. Fischel, *Studien zur österreichischen Rechtsgeschichte* (Wien, 1906), Abschnitt II.

male line in Hungary but at the same time declared that all the king-doms and countries of the Emperor outside of Germany should come *indivisibiliter ac inseparabiliter* ("indivisible and inseparable") in contact with Hungary and its annexed countries and territories under the scepter of the Emperor entitled to the throne. This document, though it emphasizes solemnly the liberties and privileges of the Hungarian estates, nevertheless acknowledges the permanent connection of the countries of the Hungarian crown with the other countries of the dynasty and explains this connection as a defensive alliance established by the struggles against Islam. And though we know very well that the law was not a spontaneous act of the Hungarian upper classes but that it was the result of much previous softening, pressure and of a long series of grafts: still one cannot deny that the Habsburg empire which was a purely military dynastic and patrimonial unity until this moment, got in the *Pragmatica Sanctio* its first jural formulation and by it a certain moral cohesion.

CHAPTER X

THE SYSTEM OF DOUCE VIOLENCE

It was said that every Habsburg felt himself to be an instrument of Providence and interpreted this mission *à sa façon*. This statement is particularly true in the case of Maria Theresa (1740–80) who continued with new and personal means the realization of the traditional aims of the dynasty: the work of unification, Germanization, and Catholization. She worked with an unbending energy for these ideals but she partly replaced the former methods of military violence by means of a feminine captivation, of patient compromises, of sugared violence, and even, if necessary, with the tears of the persecuted woman in all the cases in which she faced a more serious resistance. Indeed the only feudal opposition which remained dangerous for her in her empire, the opposition of the Hungarian nobility, she was able to disarm, at least transitorily, by these methods of feminine refinement; nay, she was successful in inducing Hungarian feudalism to make great efforts for the defense of her throne when it was threatened by a formidable coalition of her enemies. "The beautiful, brave young lady with the Hungarian face" as she was called in the circles of Hungarian nobility drew the estates into a veritable enthusiasm which among the luxuries of her Viennese court and in the refined social life of the baroque culture forgot more and more their former offenses and complaints.

The first lady of the empire lured the Hungarian aristocrats to Vienna and encouraged them for a permanent stay and for marriages with Austrian ladies. She adorned them with her decorations (even establishing a new Hungarian order for this purpose, the Order of St. Stephen) and founded for their sons a special institute and college, the so-called *Theresianum* where the noble Hungarian offsprings were educated together with the Austrians in the honor of the dynasty and in the cult of the empire. (More than a century ago in the same spirit another institution, the so-called *Pazmaneum*, was established by the brilliant leader of the Hungarian counter-reformation, Peter Pázmány, where the Hungarian theological pupils grew up in the spirit of the court and centralization.) Later she surrounded herself with the "Hungarian noble bodyguard," a corporation into which every county was entitled to send two youths. By this policy she laid a moral foundation for the Austrian court nobility. The successors of all those adventurers who poured into Vienna from all parts of the empire were melted for the first time into a conscious class regarding the service to the throne as their real life profession. The supreme measure for all values became the imperial grace and the imperial will.

Though through her husband, Francis of Lorraine, Grand Duke of Tuscany, to whom she presented sixteen children, new blood and a more liberal spirit was introduced into the reigning house now called Habsburg-Lorraine, the Empress adhered stiffly to her Catholic and anti-Protestant religious traditions, perhaps not only from fanaticism but because she hated the reformed religion as the fomenter of the national resistance in Hungary and as the state religion of her rival, Frederick the Great, the Prussian king, to whom she was compelled to abandon her province Silesia. We may say that her religious policy was scarcely more humane than that of her predecessors. The Empress, on the other hand, regarded the business of conversions as one of her chief royal functions. When she sent one of her sons abroad to study the world she wrote the following severe instruction for him: "You must blindly follow your confessor in all that pertains to your conscience, religion and morality. Without his permission you must not read a single book, not even the smallest pamphlet." She enforced these rigid principles not only in her family life but also in the policy of the empire and, in the middle of the eighteenth century, a new cruel wave of persecution of the Protestants fell on Hungary.

However, the Empress not only continued the old absolute and clerical traditions of her dynasty but, at the same time, she introduced two new elements of the greatest importance into the Austrian state ideal. The one was her work by which she formed from the former loose conglomerate countries a more and more united and strongly centralized bureaucratic state. That great organizing task which was carried on in France by Louis XIII and Louis XIV and in Prussia by her powerful contemporary, Frederick the Great, was achieved by her genius in Austria. She swept out definitely the organs of feudal particularism and built up the whole vast machine of the modern state in all spheres of public administration, in the center, in the middle instances, and in the field of local affairs. Vienna was now able to carry out its will over the whole territory of the empire, even in the newly acquired Galicia and Bukovina (with the partial exception of Hungary where they still did not dare to apply in full rigor a complete centralization) by means of its own organs, and by its own bureaucracy in the spirit of a unified system of law and administration. The unification of Bohemia, for instance, with the other countries of the empire, was no longer a mechanical but an administrative and organic process. The old *Ständestaat*, the ancient feudal state, the state beyond the state, (with the exception of Hungary) was now completely annihilated. Therefore, not without reason is Maria Theresa regarded as the *founder of the unified Austrian state* which is no longer a sheer military and power-organization for the taming of the estates and the continuation of a warlike imperialistic policy but a *Beamtenstaat*, a state of civil officials, which is intended first of all as an administrative system.[1]

And with this great change a second and not less fundamental one comes into Austrian state life. Now for the first time the imperial power appears to be in a constant, direct, and vital contact with its real subjects, with those millions of bondsmen who, by the old feudal state, were hermetically separated from the throne. In consequence of imperial finance, administration, and justice, Maria Theresa made the great discovery of enlightened absolutism: an Austrian sovereign got a clear consciousness of the fact that the force of her army, the stability of her throne, depended in the first place on the economic and cultural conditions of the great masses of population. And a really grandiose state activity began in this direction. The government of Maria Theresa carried on in the territory of the whole empire, even in Hungary, a long series of fundamental social reforms which infused fresh blood in the torpid veins of the former feudal state. Useful agricultural arts were encouraged by means of public administration and education, by a rational regulation of forest exploitation, by the promotion of horse and sheep breeding, by the diffusion of potato culture, and by the betterment of communication. But the greatest achievement of the social policy of the Empress was the reconstruction of the relations of the bondsmen by the preparation of the so-called "urbarium," which by fixing a minimum acreage for the use of each serf and the maximum for their burdens, tried to make the situation of the poor peasants tolerable. In these efforts the Empress exercised great energy: "I must do justice both to the rich and the poor, I must satisfy my conscience and I won't lose my soul for the interest of some magnates and noble persons." In vain was she threatened by the Hungarian lords with the specter of serf rebellions. The Empress strenuously continued her work. She received the delegations of the peasantry personally and under her government and that of her wonderful son, the later Joseph II, was established that almost mystical authority of the imperial power before the oppressed peoples which could not be annihilated thoroughly even by impotent and reactionary successors to the throne.

In the field of popular education, too, from the elementary schools up to the universities, the work of rebuilding and reorganization continued, of course in a strongly Catholicizing and Germanizing spirit. But this Germanization was not directed against the mother-tongue of the people but it aimed rather to establish in the place of the dead Latin language which remained the language of the nobility, particu-

[1] The meaning and significance of the whole system was masterly analyzed by Joseph Redlich: *Das österreichische Staats- und Rechtsproblem* (Leipzig, 1920), I, 25–37.

larly in Hungary, a modern language for the use of international communication and the state administration. Indeed, her famous decree, the *Ratio educationis*, delivered a deadly stroke in Hungary and in her annexed parts against the exclusive rule of the Latin language. Beside the Latin language she declared the German literature as the "only source of civilization" and she intended to make German in a short time the general language of the whole empire.

On the other hand the great and comprehensive cultural work of the Empress continued the same spirit of a rigid absolutism under the exclusive influence of the court and the Jesuits. She wished sincerely the welfare of the common people but entirely in the old Habsburg spirit and its narrow limits. She sought even to conserve the rule of the nobility in the social sphere. A progressing peasantry, *but under their old rulers:* this was her aim. "Those who are born in boots should not desire to wear shoes," she said on one occasion. Similarly in the realm of the spirit she abhorred modern notions. Her censors made a veritable war on condemned books. Pascal, Voltaire, Montesquieu, Locke, Milton, even the great historical work of Gibbon, and the *Werther* of Goethe were tabooed, according to notes of contemporaries. The bishop of Eger alone burned four thousand books. The list of prohibited books was officially printed by the government, but later this list too was forbidden that the public should not be informed about books of which they did not previously know.[2]

From the Austrian side it was often asserted that Maria Theresa had actually solved the very problem of the monarchy which she grasped not only from a jural and military point of view but with a woman-like warmth and intuition (she was often called the *Landesmutter*, the mother of the country), and if her successors, especially her son, had not abandoned the *douce violence* system of the grand lady by which she softened step by step the Hungarian feudalism and incorporated it in an almost unconscious way into her unified realm, then many crises of subsequent periods could have been avoided and the *Gesamtstaat*, the unitary state, could have been achieved without revolutionary convulsions. This point of view seems to me very shortsighted because it tries to explain great historical changes exclusively from the point of view of a single ruling coterie. It will suffice to allude to the fact that even in Bohemia they did not succeed in the extirpation of national separatism in spite of the total elimination of the old patriotic feudalism and cessation of the old constitution. It is almost certain that the national idea would have arisen even with an entirely tamed nobility. We can go even farther and assert that the very methods of the Empress led inevitably toward the creation of the national feeling and idea by laying down the fundamentals for the material

[2] Acsády, *op. cit.*, II, 522–23.

and spiritual culture of the great masses. However Austrian, even Germanizing, the tendencies of the Empress may have been, her work must have become revolutionary from a national point of view, too, in the sense that by it the great masses of the peasantry were lifted up from their somnolent existence of many centuries and the first dawning of a civic consciousness was infiltrated in these skulls thickened by feudal absolutism. From here until the vague presentiment of national consciousness is only a step. Her work was also revolutionary concerning the better elements of the noble classes themselves. The German and French cultural influences, with which they came into daily contact in the splendid international court of the Empress, aroused in them *a contrario* the consciousness of their own vegetating and backward national language and literature. This process really occurred in the noble bodyguard of Maria Theresa where some enthusiastic young Magyars, critical or poetic souls, lifted the standard of the languishing Hungarian literature and elaborated a program for its reconstruction. "We became very cramped in things Magyar," they said, and began courageously to fish out "the precious gems" of their mother tongue "from the thick, dirty dust" of the feudal Latinity. The Germanizing Empress became against her will the regalvanizer of the national consciousness and this propaganda *malgré elle* was continued in exactly the same unintentioned manner by her son, and successor to the throne, who began again new methods of dealing with the Habsburg state idea.

CHAPTER XI

THE SYSTEM OF THE REVOLUTIONARY ABSOLUTISM

Joseph II (1780–90), who had already functioned during a part of his mother's reign as a co-regent saw distinctly the shortcomings of this system, that it remained on the surface, that it was based too much on feudalism and clericalism, and that it was incapable of solving the greatest problem of the monarchy, the problem of the serfs. Traveling extensively in Europe, and sometimes entirely incognito in his own countries, and studying intimately the historical and philosophical literature of his epoch, (he admired Voltaire and once he called personally on Rousseau) this conviction of his matured into a real political passion the more because he was in heart and in mind a real child of the great rationalist century who had not the least doubt that a sovereign could transmit directly the abstract philosophical truths into life provided he possessed sufficient energy and consequence.

And indeed, history has seldom witnessed such an idealism, such a humanitarianism, and such a sense of duty on the throne as that by which this revolutionary despot was characterized. For Joseph II remained just as stiff a type of autocratic ruler as his predecessor. He hated the estates and in his times there was not a sufficiently developed bourgeois public opinion which could have participated in political power. And in the question of militarism his policy was very rigid. The slightest neglects of duty in the army were punished with the cudgel.[1] Especially the example of his famous rival, Frederick the Great, enforced on him this absolutist and militarist conception. In any case, the fact that after the loss of Silesia within the German empire a new German great power arose beside Austria, the more and more menacing Prussian state became a decisive motive in the hearts of the Habsburgs.

However, the new state ideal of Emperor Joseph differed radically from the conception of his mother. He no longer wanted to be a gorgeous sovereign with a prestige lent from the church and surrounded by the greedy luxury of the court nobility. In his nineteenth year he said:

The inner force, good laws, an honest judiciary, an orderly finance, an imposing military force, a progressing industry, a ruler held in esteem are more worthy of a great European court than festivals, parades, expen-

[1] Further interesting details will be found in Beidtel, *Geschichte der österreichischen Staatsverwaltung, 1740–1848*, I, 59–66.

sive clothes, diamonds, golden halls, precious vessels and brilliant sleigh-
ing parties. . . . . I would never demand from my subjects any gorgeous
display.

When he became sovereign he remained true to this early conception
and he wished to be in the first place the first official and soldier of the
country who with an admirable tenacity worked for the realization of
his ideal, the essence of which remained the traditional Habsburg conception: unity, centralization, German state language, powerful imperial administration, and the elimination of feudal particularisms.
But the state ideal of Joseph had two other very important aims. The
one was that he regarded his state more and more as the state of the
citizens and of the peasants. The second, that he tried to make the
state independent of the church. "The state is not a monastery," he
said, and he undertook with an iron energy the fight against the spirit
of intolerance. A lay state which determines for itself the kind of religious life which it will employ and a governing activity according to
the principles of his philosophy for the welfare of the great masses
with the purpose that the Emperor should have the greatest weight
and authority both inside and outside: that was the essence of his system called after his name *Josephinism*. And he displayed so much perseverance and so great an élan in the propagation of his principles,
that though the greatest part of his positive achievements collapsed,
his spirit did not die and remained almost to the end of the monarchy
a real source of all liberal initiatives.

Joseph clearly perceived the revolutionary character of his state
conception and he also knew that he could not realize it by the narco-
tizing half-measures of his mother. In particular he keenly visualized
that he was compelled to fight a death struggle with Hungarian feudalism which made the realization of his great reforms impossible.
"The Sarmatian spirit of the estates," this eternal rumination of dead
paragraphs for the maintenance of their class rule, their never-ceas-
ing policy of *gravamina*, their complaints for their offended privileges, their persistent sabotage against all measures tending to promote the interests of the peasant masses, their corrupt and impotent
Latin administration, their endless judiciary procedures, the unchecked rule of the latifundist system, emaciating the popular energies, and constantly fomenting national dissentions and animosities,
the eternal flickering of the fire of peasant revolts, "the servile and
slavish humiliation of the working masses," which he witnessed in
Transylvania with his own eyes, this whole backward feudal atmosphere exasperated so much the great humanitarian reformer, that he
decided not to care for the void formulas of this antiquated constitution (he saw only its nature of class domination but he did not realize
that it was at the same time a certain bulwark against the autocratic

Austrian militarism and counter-reformation), but to carry on his
lofty plans with entire disregard for it. He refused to be crowned lest
his constitutional oath should impede him in the destruction of that
feudal constitution which he felt as the chief impediment to the consolidation of his empire. Therefore, as an uncrowned, as a "hatted king"
as the popular language called him, he began the realization of his
great work and the holy crown of St. Stephen imbued with a mysterious force, according to the Hungarian traditions, a symbol of national independence, he ordered transferred to the Viennese treasury
as an anachronistic symbol. The Viennese treasury already contained
many other useless symbols of a past glory, such as the crown of
Wenceslaus and the ducal hat of Lower Austria. Now the proud symbol of Hungary was relegated to the same limbo.

Disregarding all national susceptibilities he began a long series of
social reforms all serving his philosophical conception. With a single
stroke he put an end to serfdom and introduced the duty of general
taxation. He wished to wipe out forever the hated name of bondsman.
He announced the unlimited right of free migration for the serfs, He
permitted them to marry, to learn a profession, to go to school, and to
enter a learned profession without the permission of the landlord. All
these measures quite alarmed the Hungarian feudal society, the more
so since serfdom without any culture misunderstood completely the
plans of the humanitarian Emperor and in some places they went into
open revolt, for instance in Transylvania, where the consequence was
a terrible peasant revolt under the leadership of Hora and Kloska
which led to the extermination of more than a hundred villages and
4,000 people. The exacerbation of the nobility was heightened by the
order for general taxation. In vain the Emperor announced, to sooth
the nobility, that in recompense for the new reform he would be inclined to comply with the old request of the country by eliminating the
custom barriers between Hungary and Austria and by suppressing
all intermediary duties. The feudal classes affirmed, however, that
without the Diet, which the Emperor refused to convoke, they were incapable of expressing their wishes. On the other hand the Emperor
wished to have nothing to do with the Diet because he held that the
Diet of the nobility was a sheer anachronism, the country having 40,-
000 nobles and 5,000,000 peasants: the former were the legislators,
the latter the slaves. It was quite unthinkable—this was the argument
of the Emperor according to a contemporary—that the nobility would
spontaneously abdicate its privileges and therefore permit the constitution to be remolded by a single man. The 40,000 noble families were
represented by 500 on the Diet but from these 500 only the ten most
influential had a real rôle in the legislation. Therefore the constitutional proceedings would have been senseless.[2]

    [2] Acsády, *op. cit.*, II, 545–46.

In the field of local government with disregard for the old territorial divisions, he placed the state administration in the hands of imperial officials. He separated the judiciary from the administration and tried everywhere to eliminate the old feudal authorities. He tried to atomize and standardize the Old World. He saw in every historical structure only an anachronism and tried to overthrow every traditional institution instead of transforming it and filling it with a new spirit. Into the non-German parts of the empire, more and more foreign German-speaking officials were sent in order to promote the unification of the realm and to counterbalance the local influences. Besides, to keep the old nobility in check the Emperor endeavored to create a new small nobility by extended distribution of letters of nobility. "Innkeepers, retailers, tanners, printers, lackeys of the counts, court officials, Armenians, and other such despicable peoples arose to the rank of nobility in our country" complains a popular writer of the Magyar nobility. At the same time the Emperor had pleasure in the cultivation of a literature directed against the historical nobility which lashed with sharp irony the privileges, the customs of the nobles, and their cruelties against the peasants.

With the same energy and relentlessness he tried to reform the church which he considered merely as a part of the state administration. In his memorable edict of 1781 in the so-called *Patent for Tolerance* he wished to put an end to the terrible sufferings of the Protestants and though he did not abolish the privileged position of the Roman Catholic church, he extended religious freedom to the Protestants and the Greek Orientals. The Emperor was fully aware of the historical importance of his decree. "Nobody should suffer any more tribulations in consequence of his faith, nobody should be constrained any longer to accept the evangelism of the state if it is against his conviction," he wrote in one of his letters. A murmur of alleviation swept over the whole monarchy especially over Hungary where a large Protestant minority was living. The humanitarian spirit of the Emperor did not stop here, but he expanded the privileges of tolerance to a certain extent even to the Jews who until his epoch lived without any civil rights on the properties of the nobility and on the imperial estates.

At the same time he tried to curb the haughtiness of the Roman Catholic church. He put in force the *Ius placenti* according to which no papal bull could be made public without the previous consent of the monarch. Even his reformatory zeal and revolutionary rationalism developed into the grotesque when he regulated by imperial decrees ecclesiastical ceremonies, processions, Lent, burials, and even purely individual and family relations. His plans for religious reforms aroused such an excitement that Pope Pius VI hastened to Vienna in 1782 in order to check the Emperor in his dangerous career, admonishing him that his reforms might cause serious revolts in his Italian provinces. But the Emperor went farther on his way and ordered the conscription of the incomes of the rich prelates in order to eliminate the terrible antagonism between their princely luxury and the misery of the lower clergy. He did away with 700 monasteries and nunneries with nearly 40,000 conventuals. The remaining ecclesiastical orders were put under severe supervision of the state. As a logical consequence of his policy, he took away the sacramental character of marriage and made it a simple civil contract.

These revolutionary decrees of the great rationalist naturally remained mostly on paper. Disregarding the really existing historical forces he came more and more into conflict with them and they proved to be mightier than the will of the enlightened autocrat. The feudal and clerical elements of the empire indulged in initiating an astute sabotage against his humanitarian proscriptions. He was therefore often constrained to take off the edges of his decrees and to soften them to the extent that the faith of the persecuted masses became doubtful of his intentions. In spite of these shortcomings the monarchy never was inspired with so much ardor for the public good from any of its regents as from this perhaps unconscious Benthamite.

The same work of centralization, unification, and modernization was continued by a vast codifying activity; both the civil code and the penal code were based on advanced principles and introduced in the whole empire. At the same time he undertook an almost feverish activity of colonization in order to introduce skilled artisans from every part of Europe. The peasant colonization of his predecessors was continued with an outspoken Germanizing tendency. The German language was introduced as the state language over the whole territory of the monarchy and at the same time the whole educational system was reorganized in order to give instruction in this tongue to the youth. This audacious but hasty policy which misunderstood completely the whole psychology of national evolution became the beginning of a new epoch not only in Hungary but also in Bohemia and in Croatia. Joseph II became, against his will, the real promoter of the national renaissance. Feudal public opinion, till then almost entirely indifferent to national matters, under the sway of the medieval Latinity, regarded the linguistic reforms of the Emperor as humiliating and as whip cuts under which their dreamy national consciousness began to prance. This resistance could not be reduced to genuine national motives; it was rather a growing fear of the nobles that their jobs in public administrations would be taken by the German imperial bureaucrats. Béla Grünwald, the best historian of this epoch says:

The vindication of the use of the Magyar language could not be a sincere one. The same counties which (arguing against the decree of the Emperor) emphasized the possibility of an administration in the Magyar tongue, declared it in 1811—that is, twenty-seven years later—an impossibility. . . . .

And about two decades later in a very nationalistic county, famous for its *kurucz* traditions, it was said that "the introduction of the Magyar language would endanger our constitution and all our interests . . . . and religion would be ruined if the Latin language would be eliminated."[3]

Regarding such and similar facts one must really doubt the sincerity of the resistance of the nobility against the reforms of the Emperor. The resistance, indeed, was not a serious one. In a few years German was introduced in all the Hungarian counties and the old Magyar bureaucracy remained in service complying with the new policy of Vienna. A similar opposition arose in Bohemia even among the already tamed aristocracy of this country. The Bohemian nobility suddenly remembered the time when their predecessors were masters of the country and they attributed their diminished might to the expansion of the German language. A historian of this period narrates that those opposed to the Emperor immediately discovered their own Czech mother-tongue which they formerly despised as the language of the peasants and servants. Nay, it became fashionable to promote and to foster the old forgotten language.[4] A similar exasperation overwhelmed the Croatian nobility which made common cause with the Hungarian against the Germanizing despot though they were almost entirely Latinized and without any contact with the real popular movement.

In this world, without a genuine national feeling the Emperor himself was not led by any nationalistic tendency in a modern sense when he undertook his policy of Germanization. He did not fight for instance against the Magyar language but he fought against the Latin. Following the example of the great national states he thought that, on the basis of the medieval Latin administration of the nobility, no effective work in the interest of the masses could have been carried on. The necessity of a unifying language connecting all the parts of his empire seemed to him a peremptory claim. Under this necessity he could not choose any other language but German, the only one which had a vast culture and literature under its sway and which had a considerable minority in all his provinces. His so-called policy of Germanization was therefore not a result of the national feeling but rather of the entire misunderstanding of this force. He was not aware that the colossal economic and cultural activity which he inaugurated in the interest of the material and spiritual elevation of the great masses must inevitably have led toward a national renaissance of all

---

[3] The whole political and social structure of feudal Hungary was brilliantly analyzed by Béla Grünwald in his wonderful study, *The Old Hungary* (Budapest, 1910). It is deplorable that the book was not translated into any foreign language.

[4] Some other interesting details concerning the development of the Czech nationalism were collected by Alfred von Skene in his *Entstehen und Entwickelung der slavisch-nationalen Bewegung in Böhmen und Mähren im XIX Jahrhundert* (Wien, 1893).

the nations. It is an interesting fact which explains the whole process
that the most nationally apathetic elements of the Hungarian society
were the most ardent enemies of the Emperor and even the German-
speaking population of Transylvania, the Saxons, were fiercely opposed to his policy which disregarded their ancient privileges. On the
other hand the great promoters of the Hungarian renaissance, the
champions of Magyar language and literature, had a vivid sympathy
with the monarch. Why? Because these refined spirits who were longing for Western civilization had the same conception that the Emperor had: they saw in the German culture the best vehicle for linking
the backward country with Western civilization. Francis Kazinczy,
the noble leader of the Hungarian renaissance, later wrote:

> It was superb to see in the pharmacy of Joseph, how the better souls
> of the society became interwoven in spite of their divergencies in color
> because they were united by the same love of the commonweal. Great and
> small, patriot and foreigner, official and private, civilian and soldier, were
> for solidarity if they found merit in each other.

But whatever may have been the real motives of the resistance of
the nobility, there can be no doubt at all that the Germanizing policy
of the Emperor aroused to a new life the paralyzed national consciousness in very large stratas of the population. And when the first
news of the great French Revolution arrived, there came an outburst
of the hatred of foreigners and of the antipathy against the German
language. A patriotic contemporary observer wrote:

> In many places the German hat was thrown away and they put the
> Hungarian fur cap and shako on their heads. The German dress found on
> a Hungarian was pulled off. . . . . Nay, everybody spoke Magyar and
> those who did not know it learned the language, though some few months
> previous, especially in elegant society, you could not find anyone speaking
> this language.

And this anti-German tendency broke out with equal vehemence in
other parts of the monarchy, too, when the Turkish war seemed to
take an unfavorable turn. Belgium was in open revolt and the Hungarian feudals conspired with the Prussian king. Even the loyal German
Tyrol, defending its ancient privileges, started rebellion. The resistance of the Emperor, gravely sick, collapsed. He decided to return to
the way of the old constitution and withdraw all his decrees and pat-
ents with the exception of those relating to tolerance and the liberation of serfdom. To demonstrate the sincerity of his purpose and to
indicate the change in the system he sent back the Holy Crown into
Hungary. The Austrian historian, surely not biased against the dynasty, says:

> A delirium of enthusiasm swept over Hungary when the crown of St.
> Stephen was transported to the country. Old and young danced on the

streets, even the lame, according to a report of a contemporary, jumped for joy and everybody clamored: "hurrah for Hungarian freedom!" And even the Viennese expressed a common joy with the Hungarians. When the Hungarian crown jewels were fetched from the treasury the people pressed together before the imperial castle and their joyous cheering penetrated into the room of the dying Emperor. . . . .[5]

A symbolical fact: the unselfish work of a whole life in the interest of the commonweal, the disinterested struggle of a great man against the dark powers of the past, a long series of brilliant reforms for the people, all were suddenly forgotten but the returning of the mystical medieval symbol threw them into raptures of enthusiasm. The poor Emperor, indeed, could not have received a more illustrative object lesson from the historical method against purely rationalistic deductions.

[5] Viktor Bibl, *Der Zerfall Österreichs* (Wien, 1922), I, 25.

CHAPTER XII

BULWARK AGAINST THE FRENCH REVOLUTION

The convulsions of the French Revolution which had already shaken the foundations of the system of Emperor Joseph had even greater and more general consequences for the future of the entire Habsburg monarchy. For all those complex questions which made the fate of the Danube monarchy problematical, which opened a process of long disintegration driving the monarchy from crisis to crisis, were a direct consequence of the French Revolution. The resistance of the old feudal society was no longer a serious menace to the Habsburg rule which was growing more and more powerful. But, at the end of the eighteenth century, two new currents met and became the source of a pernicious synthesis for the Habsburgs. One of these currents was formed by the popular forces aroused by the social policy of Maria Theresa and Joseph II. The peasantry and the bourgeoisie ceased to be passive objects of the patrimonial state and they assumed a more and more critical attitude against it. At the same time the waves of the French Revolution stirred these masses, alarmed by new purposes and aspirations infiltrated from the West, and which were in strict contradiction to the old traditional absolutist and patrimonial order of the Habsburg state.

The Habsburgs and their leading statesmen themselves realized the seriousness of this situation. They understood that if these ideas of national and political democracy should get a hold on the Danube monarchy, the system of imperial absolutism which they identified with the monarchy itself could be maintained no longer. Fearing dangerous consequences, similiar to those which resulted in the execution of one of the mightiest rulers of Europe and of his wife, the daughter of Maria Theresa, and which created a panicky atmosphere, the most influential political leaders perceived that the only possibility of salvation would be to check by police and military force the ideas codified by the great revolution and propagated by the imperialistic policy of Napoleon. Under the sway of this terrified attitude Emperor Francis II (1792–1835) took the lead in the coalition against Napoleon and drove his empire into a war which lasted twenty-three years, which in its early stages, caused the humiliation of the Habsburg dynasty but later its political hegemony in Europe. As the leading state of the Holy Alliance, it elaborated the most complete internal program of international reaction. This program in the hands of the almighty chancellor of the Emperor, who during thirty-eight years conducted the whole inner and outer policy of the realm, became

74

almost a state religion of the *ancien régime*. This system, called the "system of Metternich," which dominated Austria during the whole first half of the nineteenth century, represents one of the most consequent and audacious attempts in history to conserve an antiquated order. This system in conscious opposition to its predecessor, to the "Josephinist system," was also called, not without reason, by the name of the Emperor, the "Francisist" system, for recent historical investigations have demonstrated sufficiently that this system of *stability* —not without a certain grandeur—this system of *Ruhe und Ordnung* ("Calmness and Order"), of the absolutism *sans phrase*, of a modern despotism of God's grace was not an invention of Metternich (if we are entitled at all to reduce great historical currents to the name of a single man) but it emanated from the very personality of the Emperor, from "his conviction, heart, and conscience."

We must consider somewhat more closely this system of Metternich and Emperor Francis both in its theoretical foundations and in its practice, because it has become almost a *communis opinio* of recent historians that we must seek the deepest causes of the dissolution of the monarchy in the very dialectics of this system. It is highly characteristic of the psychic structure of the former empire that this correct historical conception was only accepted after the collapse of the monarchy and the dethronement of the Habsburgs. Today it is difficult to doubt the truth of the opinion, elaborated in the most trenchant manner by Joseph Redlich, that this system of Francis and Metternich made the whole structure of the monarchy so rigid during its rule of half a century, not counterbalanced by any other influence, that it developed, with such a terrible consequence, the militaristic *Machtstaat* centralizing and bureaucratizing to death all institutions; that it so totally suppressed every germ of a free thought and political criticism with the help of a devouring police and clerical mechanism that the empire became absolutely unfit to assimilate the real postulates of the epoch, to introduce those reforms without which no state could exist in the freer and more democratic atmosphere of Europe. It is impossible not to observe that the *facies hippocratica* of the dissolution of the monarchy can be clearly diagnosed in this period of so-called splendor of the empire when Metternich was the "coachman of Europe" and when as the leading power of the Holy Alliance it seemed to swim in the luxury of its world power.

Naturally it is impossible to give here in this sketchy outline a whole picture or even all the fundamental traits of this famous system. All that we can do is to continue the analysis of the previous chapters and try to give to the reader a moral insight into the mass psychology of the system. For this purpose we shall be obliged to separate things which in reality belonged together and had the character of a unitary governmental program.

As has already been emphasized the *real front of the system was directed against the great French Revolution*. In the ideas of the French Revolution Francis-Metternich saw only a *French fancy good* which could be stopped at the frontier by appropriate customhouse chicancrics. The best expert and defender of the system, Heinrich Ritter von Srbik, so reconstructs the opinion of Metternich and his collaborators:

The revolution, the greatest misfortune which can afflict a country and which according to its nature destroys all, has a Proteus nature. The remembrance of the greatest manifestation of this evil, still producing its after effects, justifies the name of Jacobinism. It appears now as religious and spiritual, then as political, again as mysticism, philanthropism, liberal fanaticism, or as Italian Carbonarism or the *Giovine Italia*.

The real supporter of these confused, wicked, and cracked ideologists is the newly established bourgeois middle class which the system considers as its chief enemy. Against this theory of professors *(Professorentheorie)* against this swindle of the universities *(Universitäts-schwindel)* is directed the whole hatred of the system. The middle class of the cities is the real source of the Jacobinism. This enlightened demagogy *(aufgeklärte Demagogie)* corrupts the whole life of the state and begins to envenom also the lower classes of society which remained safe from the moral cancer of presumption *(moralischer Krebs der Praesumption)*. "People are like children and nervous women; they believe in ghosts and the injudicious attitude of the masses is characterized by Metternich with the words: the simpletons called the public."[1]

Based on these axioms the problem for the system was sufficiently simple. These products of decomposition of crazy or wicked spirits must be kept isolated from the naïve and good soul of the people. It became necessary to introduce a sort of spiritual custom duties, more complete and ramified than perhaps the world had ever seen, the chief administrator of which became a police and spy organization. Metternich, one could say without exaggeration, created a *Spy International* and his paid agents and denouncers swarmed in all the capitals of Europe. But naturally the real center of gravity of the system was in the monarchy itself and its insidious, polypus arms entangled not only the suspected *litterati* and politicians but often even the leading elements of Viennese society. Step by step even the more prominent archdukes came under police control; and Metternich seized the correspondence of the Empress Maria Ludovica (the third wife of Francis) with her brother-in-law Archduke Joseph, the Hungarian Palatinus (governor), and presented it to the Emperor in order to arouse his matrimonial jealousy (wholly without foundation in this case), to put

[1] *Metternich, der Staatsmann und der Mensch* (München, 1925), I, 381–86.

an end to a somewhat liberal political current which he felt disagreeable to him. One can imagine how this system could chicane the life of simple citizens; and there can be no doubt that the following description by Charles Sealsfield of the police system of his time can be accepted without qualification:

Since the year 1811 ten thousand *Naderer* or secret policemen are at work. They are recruited from the lower classes of the merchants, of domestic servants, of workers, nay even of prostitutes, and they form a coalition which traverses the entire Viennese society as the red silk thread runs through the rope of the English navy. You can scarcely pronounce a word at Vienna which would escape them. You have no defense against them and if you take with you your own servants, they become within fourteen days, even against their own will, your traitors. . . . .

The persecutions of the so-called demagogues and Jacobins and other dangerous elements continued. Very often many men were sent up for execution and into prisons for harmless political discussions and for a mostly naïve and romantic play with the humanitarian and cosmopolitan ideas of the French Revolution. This cheap defense of the state served only to give a new field of activity to the growing crowd of police spies and helped to make the Viennese people amiable, careless enjoyers of life without backbone and without political judgment, to create that *Capua of the spirit* the marks of which remained deeply engraved in the mass psychology of the Viennese population. The descriptions of Mme de Staël of the Viennese society in its joyous hedonics without a semblance of serious discussion or an intelligent interest in the real problems of the epoch, its cult of mediocrities, and its distrust of all original talents prevailed until the end of the monarchy as an artificial flower of the system of Metternich.

This system menacing with the gallows and with imprisonment the serious patriots interested in the benefit of the country, and rewarding generously every spy and mixer in intrigues, was a diametrical antithesis of what could be called a reasonable civic education. Indeed, even the more thoughtful conservative contemporaries clearly understood the dangers of this situation relative to the corruption of civic consciousness and some ponderous voices arose against it. Thus, for instance, the far-sighted aristocrat already quoted, Baron Andrian, wrote the following embittered lines:

Men should be merry, should become drunk, should tell obscene jokes, or at best should establish a cotton factory, or read the theater paper of Adolf Bäuerle, but all interests concerning their community, their province, their state, the most important question of the epoch, however much they affect their purse and their whole existence, they should politely leave alone in order not to incommode the governing gentlemen.

This situation bore down the more heavily upon society because the police activity of the system was not only concerned with politics in a proper sense, and with the investigation of imaginary plots, treasons, and so-called "ramifications" (secret political connections on a large scale) but it choked the whole scientific and literary life, too, by the control of its political and ecclesiastical spies. One of the victims of the system, Hormayr, the brilliant writer already mentioned, characterized in the following manner the hopeless attitude of the Austrian intellectuals of his day:

In all the higher branches of knowledge with the exception of the *sciences exactes* there is not a single praiseworthy literary achievement; journalism throughout the whole glorious empire is null, the clever heads discouraged, under suspicion, very often exposed to the most stubborn persecutions in consequence of slanderous denunciations. . . . . Such writers as Gibbon, Robertson, Hume, were partly forbidden and all the geniuses of Germany (Goethe, Schiller, Johannes Müller, Herder, Lessing, Jean Paul) were totally or partly suppressed.

It became an axiom of the system that people *read themselves into criminals*. No wonder that they regarded censorship as the most important instrument against criminality. This atmosphere became the death of all true talent, and the passionate cry of Grillparzer, the greatest Austrian poet of this epoch: "despotism has destroyed my literary life," may be regarded as the cry of pain of the best of a whole generation.

A real drive was started against all those scientists who, as rare exceptions, represented a freer type of spiritual investigation. They were constantly persecuted, often ousted from their positions, as the famous Bolzano, professor of religious philosophy in the University of Prague. This educational system which put science into the service of the dynasty and of Catholicism naturally made all inquiries into political and social matters impossible. Sealsfield complained:

Free spiritual creation or investigation is completely unrealizable, nay, it is strictly forbidden to the professors. During his studies the student is severely watched over and his professors are official spies. The teacher of religion must hold a confession with the students six times a year. The inclinations, the good and bad qualities, every emotion of the young men, are observed and noted in catalogues from which a copy is sent to the Court Commission for Studies in Vienna, a second to the governor's office, and a third remains in the school archive. This sharp supervision is augmented in the upper years. . . . .

After finishing their studies, those who are graduated, both jurist and theologian, are entirely in the hands of the government. Their past and moral curriculum are the measure of their career.

The German national student movements, the activities of the *Burschenschaften*, especially the excitement of the *Wartburgfest* (1817), an outburst of the patriotic feelings of the students and the killing of a Russian spy, a widely known playwright of the epoch,

Kotzebue by a German youth only strengthened the exacerbated struggle of the system against the ghost of revolution. The ill-famed decisions of Karlsbad put all the universities under police supervision and the censorship was intensified. But the system did not consider the police and the organization of the spies sufficient for the mainte- nance of its power. Its alliance with clericalism became more rigid and outspoken. They tried not only to check political ideas but also the so-called *Deist venom*, the spirit of a Kant, a Fichte, and a Schelling. Religion was considered as the most important part of secret police activity and the complot and hidden intrigues of bigoted archduch- esses with the reactionary monastic organizations began to influence the whole machinery of the state. The Josephinist traditions, how- ever, of the dignity of the state counterbalanced to some extent in the person of the Emperor and his chancellor these tendencies. But when the fourth wife of the Emperor, the Bavarian princess, Caroline Au- gusta, appeared in the political arena, the attack of clericalism be- came more vehement and successful. The new Empress brought from Munich her Jesuit confessor and at the court a well-organized coterie was created, called the "pious party," which was able to bend the Em- peror to its will. The Order of the Liguorians obtained an asylum in Vienna to the great astonishment and fear of the more liberal, Jo- sephinist circles, who saw in them precursors of the Jesuits. And indeed very soon the Jesuits themselves were officially readmitted into the country and the influence of Rome became manifest. In 1819 the im- perial couple made a trip to Rome which signified the triumph of the ultramontane influences. Sickness and age made the Emperor more indulgent and the Empress herself supported energetically the fight of her husband against the "Aufklärung." She opposed even the work of the Kindergarten because she feared they would foster too much "enlightenment" among the lower classes. She used to say that she would prefer to be hanged rather than to contribute something to the unhappy trend of this unstable period. To this same circle belonged Archduchess Sophie, the Empress' sister who later became the leading motor force in bringing her son Francis Joseph to the throne!

The constant terror from the demon of revolution made the sys- tem entirely blind to the real needs of the masses. The grandiose be- ginnings of Maria Theresa and Joseph II were not only abandoned but a period of open reaction began. The dynasty made a defensive alliance with the most backward elements of the nobility. They no longer dared to touch the chief problem of the monarchy, the emanci- pation of the bondsmen, because they felt that both the social and the national consciousness of a people growing in wealth and culture would be irreconcilable with the leading thoughts and fundamental institutions of their system of stability. Quite symbolical is the an-

swer which one of the leading adherents of Metternich, Frederick
Gentz, a brilliant publicist, gave to Robert Owen, the great English
philanthropist who tried to convince the Austrian government of the
necessity of certain reforms in the interest of the working people.
This assistant of the great chancellor was quite outspoken on the subject: "We do not desire at all that the great masses shall become well
off and independent. . . . . How could we otherwise rule over them?"[2]
A corollary axiom of the system was that "Mankind needs from time
to time a radical bleeding or else its situation will become inflammatory and the liberal frenzy immediately bursts out." Such a state
philosophy regarded every manifestation of the modern spirit as its
enemy. When, on one occasion, the plan of a new railway was submitted to Emperor Francis he received it with the greatest distrust:
"No, no, I will have nothing to do with it, lest the revolution might
come into the country." And the Emperor was perfectly right from
the point of view of his system: Any development of the techniques
was irreconcilable with his policy which tried to maintain rigidly the
absolutist patrimonial monarchy.

But that which exasperated the system most in the new world-
order was, in the first place, the desire for a written constitution and
—the logical corollary of this—the idea of national self-determination. And the destiny of a Tyrolese deputation which went to Vienna
before the Emperor in order to make a humble petition for the restoration of the old constitution of the country tells us more about the
real system of the Emperor than many volumes could. It must be no-
ticed that the Tyrolese people were the most loyal and most faithful
element of the monarchy which in the struggles against Napoleon under the enthusiastic and brave peasant leader, Andreas Hofer, stood
heroically by the Habsburgs as a symbol of their ardent Catholic
feelings and their vehement Tyrolese local patriotism. These very
humble and very conservative people, when after the Bavarian occupation they were reattached to Austria, seem to have caught something from the pulsation of the Napoleonic period, for they appeared
before the Emperor for the betterment of their constitutional position. Even the word constitution irritated the Emperor very much
and he received his most loyal Tyroleans in bad humor and gave them
the following lesson from civic education:

So, you want a constitution! . . . . Now look, I don't care for it, I
will give you a constitution but you must know that the soldiers obey me,
and I will not ask you twice if I need money. . . . . In any case I advise
you to be careful what you are going to say.

To this imperial decision the good Tyrolese answered: "If thou (it
was a privilege of the Tyrolese to address the Emperor in this form)

[2] Bibl, *op. cit.,* I, 157.

thinkest thus, it is better to have no constitution. . . . ." To which the Emperor replied "That is also my opinion."[3] This attitude distrustful toward the people, but gladly accepting the alliance of his former enemies, the feudal estates (which now became harmless), found an almost classic expression in another utterance of the talkative Emperor when in 1820 he gave the following admonition to the Hungarian magnates at Pest: *Totus mundus stultizat et relictis antiquis suis legibus constitutiones imaginarias quaerit. Vos constitutionem a majoribus acceptam illaesam habetis; amatis illam et ego illam amo et conservabo et ad heredes transmittam* ("the whole world has gone crazy, and abandoning its good old laws, is searching for idealized constitutions. You have a constitution which you have received unimpaired from your ancestors. You love it and I love it. I shall cherish and defend it and hand it down to my descendants"). The harmony between autocracy and feudalism was, at least seemingly, complete.

Such a mode of thinking naturally could not understand (it could only hate and persecute) the most important revolutionary force of the period: the thought of national unification and self-determination. The conception of Metternich and of the whole system is very important at this point, because their policy was the issue upon which the old Austrian world came most severely and fatally into conflict with the spirit of the times, and from this time on it remained a problem of life and death until the final collapse of the monarchy. Many— not only foreign observers—often misunderstood completely the point of view of the *ancien régime* as regards this all important question; its attitude is often interpreted as if it were directed against all manifestations of the national idea in the spirit of an intolerant and ferocious Germanization. This opinion is completely erroneous. The truth is that the system hated German nationalism no less than the Hungarian or the Italian (which were at this period the most highly developed) but it had no objection whatever to permitting every people to speak, cultivate, even develop its own language in its local sphere. Those elements of the national idea which especially exasperated the system were the aspirations to overthrow the former status of the European state system and the attempt to rebuild the national territories on a unified basis. Or to put the thesis in the words of the most reliable interpreter of Metternich, the Austrian historian already quoted:

Regarding things more closely, the revolutions are directed both against the throne and the people which latter can have no advantage from the levelling which is the purpose of the middle classes. That is the reason why the masses remain indifferent to the national movement for unification: In Italy the productive element in city and country wishes to have nothing in common with the machinations of the nobility, of the at-

[3] C. Sealsfield, *op. cit.,* p. 115.

torneys and physicians without occupation, of the half-cultured *litterati*. In Germany the real German people are indifferent toward what is called by the national chauvinists *der Deutsche Sinn* (the German spirit) and they are similarly apathetic towards the troubles which have their center in the cabinets incapable of governing and in the middle classes.

According to this point of view Italian unity is a pure phantasm: "Nationalism does not fit Italy, for Italy is a purely geographical idea" which has no foundation, neither in history nor in the soul of the people. The same was the opinion of Metternich concerning Germany. German particularism emanated from the very spirit of the people. It was a political axiom of Metternich that "No Bavarian will become an Austrian, no Austrian a Prussian, no Prussian a Bavarian, no Bavarian a Würtemberger and no one in any of the German countries will become a Prussian who was not one before."

Those who so completely failed to comprehend the fundamental nature of the national movements for unification were almost organically incapable of applying an adequate policy concerning these aspirations. Their unique political aim remained the same to the end: to withdraw the national demagogy in order to maintain the nationless vegetative unity of their empire in the same rigid unchangeability as the system of absolutism. And what the chancellor expressed in a pretentious style, based on a very extended reading, was propagated by Emperor Francis in his despotic crudeness and in his petty bourgeois gossip. I know, for instance, no more characteristic expression of his nationless attitude than when he explained his own policy to the French ambassador as follows:

My peoples are strange to each other and that is all right. They do not get the same sickness at the same time. In France if the fever comes you are caught by it at the same time. I send the Hungarians into Italy, the Italians into Hungary. Every people watches its neighbor. The one does not understand the other and one hates the other. . . . . From their antipathy will be born order and from the mutual hatred, general peace. . . . .

It will be instructive to compare with this naïve but sincere utterance the following from the French *Déclaration des Droits* of 1795:

All the peoples are independent and sovereign whatever may be the number of individuals constituting them and whatever may be the extent of the territory occupied by them. This sovereignty is inalienable, every nation has the right to organize and to change the forms of its government. No people has the right to interfere with the government of other people. An attempt against the liberty of any people is an attempt against all others. . . . .

Two diametrically antagonistic conceptions of state solidarity speak to us from these declarations, and the struggle of these principles determined indeed the history of the whole subsequent century and even an important part of the struggles in the present. In this struggle the Emperor and Metternich were not only "the Don Quixotes of legitimism" but also of medieval nationalism which emphasized national particularism to the detriment of a national unity. In this system the idea of a modern patriotism always remained unknown. When on one occasion someone was recommended to Emperor Francis with the explanation that he was a clever and ardent patriot, the sovereign replied distrustfully, "I hear he is a patriot for Austria. But the question is whether he is a *patriot for me*." This patrimonial conception of patriotism remained unchanged until the end of the monarchy and became, as we shall see in detail, the deepest cause of its dissolution. The same force which, in the great national states, was the real fundamental of state cohesion and which, directed by prudent sovereigns, proved to be an eternal source for the sacrifices of the people: the same force remained in the Habsburg monarchy not only unused but it was drawn back and even insulted.

The cruel persecutions against the German "Jacobins" have already been noted. At the same time in Hungary, too, under the protection and denunciation of the reactionary aristocrats, the cultural rather than political movement to propagate liberal ideas, led by the Abbot Ignatz Martinovics, one of the freest spirits of the epoch, was distorted into a dangerous complot, and with the help of a corrupt tribunal seven of the best men of Hungary were executed. At the same time many of the leading figures of the Hungarian literary renaissance suffered many years of imprisonment in the ill-famed jails of Spielberg, Kuffstein, and Munkács. But the brutality of the system culminated in Italy where Austrian troops were penetrating as far as Naples and Sicily in order to annihilate the new constitutions of the peoples. In the Austrian and Italian provinces a drive was made against all the Italian patriots and liberals. Among these Count Confalonieri and Silvio Pellico, the poet, were sentenced to death but by "imperial grace" the penalty was commuted to imprisonment. Their experiences in the fortress of Spielberg were of such a terrible nature that the later memoirs of the poet *Le mie prigioni* and the revelations of the count drew upon the Viennese government not only the indignation of contemporaries but even aroused the anti-Austrian feelings and politics of later generations. It is quite natural that under such a system and practice Machiavellian measures were often attributed to the government of Metternich, perhaps, in cases where it was not true. For instance, when in 1846 the Ruthenian peasants killed one hundred and forty-six Polish nobles and carried the corpses together with a large number of wounded in a long train of carriages into Tarnow before the edifice of the imperial district office, this terrible peasant upheaval aroused the general conviction in the society of the

Polish nobles that the whole rebellion was inspired by imperial agents in order to check the Polish nobility which at that time was imbued with revolutionary ideas.

This system would have been dangerous and impossible even if it could have been carried on with a Jacobin dogmatism and with a fanatical purity devoted exclusively to abstract ideas. But the system did not have such a moral foundation. Its leading men represented, in the first place, their own interests. Grillparzer wrote about Metternich:

If a chief permits his subordinates to accept presents, he is ordinarily not meticulous in his own dealings. And the colossal expenses of the prince who took over the legacy of his father in a bankrupt state, his buying of estates, points clearly to diplomatic *pour boire.* . . . .

And when in consequence of the frenzied military, diplomatic, and police squanderings, a state bankruptcy was proclaimed in 1811, reducing the price of money to one-fifth, Viennese public opinion was convinced that the Emperor utilized this catastrophical financial crisis of his subjects to his own enrichment. This accusation was so persistent and general that the sovereign tried to appease exasperated public sentiment by a stammering and hypocritical declaration in the official paper. This spirit of hypocrisy permeated the whole system of Emperor Francis who with his artificially created public opinion endeavored to mask his bloody despotism in the colors of a jolly *bonhomie* and of a *petit bourgeois* joviality. He knew the dialect of the suburbs and loved crude jests. He often mixed with the people of Vienna and one of his wives was a frequent guest at the Viennese dance halls. He was always extremely busy with the enthusiasm of an accountant over the smallest affairs of his subjects to such an extent that his bureaucratic fervor made a real governmental function quite impossible. With the system of spies and jails he formed his society as efficiently as he did by assuming the pose of a *Landesvater* and a *Familienvater* (the official press applied to him the phrase "father of the country," ascribed to him paternal affection possessed by the head of a family). The spirit of his government penetrated public life and society to such an extent that the so-called *Biedermeier* style of his epoch is the very expression of the pulsation of a society which, turning aside from all great and general interests, exhausts itself in the voluptuous enjoyment of the petty pleasures of existence and which varnishes its greedy sensualism by a Philistine formalism. Not without reason, Francis was called the *Tiger im Schlafrock* ("the tiger in the night gown").

One could not survey better the whole intellectual and moral face of this system than in the picture which Grillparzer gave us with such an artistic intuition, in his diary:

The emperor has died. Whereas the papers spoke during his life of the almost idolatrous veneration of his subjects concerning the person of the fatherly monarch, of all this not a single trace was manifest after his death. All went to his burial with a serene face, as if they were going to a carnival dance. . . . . The reason is that he was not at all adored and that the papers lied. . . . . In ordinary times his nature was not bad, not stupid, not even feeble, not base, even vulgar would be too hard; it was common. There was no elevation, no kind of sublimity in him. He was just concerning material mine and thine; had he the slightest idea that there were also spiritual goods, perhaps his justice would have extended also to them; but his spirit was closed and barred. He esteemed arts and sciences only as far as they bring accountable and ponderable utility or as they furnish the spirit, not as they strengthen it. His religiosity was a custom. . . . . If he himself would have become in a night a Turk under the pressure of the necessity of the state, the next morning he would have considered a rebel anyone who still believed in Jesus Christ. Those nearest to him indulged in the vilest debauches; he knew it and tolerated it for one secretly dissolute was more sympathetic to him than a morally elevated man. Of his promises he held those given as a private man scrupulously (as a nobleman holds his debts contracted in game); as sovereign, he had no hesitation in breaking the most formal ones. . . . .[4]

After the death of Emperor Francis when Ferdinand I (as Hungarian king, Ferdinand V), an imbecile and epileptic, came to the throne (1835–48) all the reactionary and clerical tendencies of the system developed unchecked to full maturity. The system became almost its own caricature. The Josephinist traditions disappeared completely and Metternich becoming old was more and more subservient to Jesuit influences. This "absolutist monarchy without a monarch" was dominated by a clique which an acute observer of the period called a *theologisch- diplomatische Weiberzunft* ("a theological diplomatic female guild"). Clericalism and absolutism attained its climax in Austria. The Jesuits taught according to their own order of studies, the so-called *ratio studiorum* and their spirit infiltrated all the strata of social and cultural life. The Spanish spirit of the Counter Reformation reappeared. Some four hundred Protestants of Zillertal were driven out from their mountains in the fourth decade of the nineteenth century in order not to irritate their Catholic rulers.[5] Austria lived medieval days in a time when the third French Revolution was rapidly approaching.

[4] *Grillparzer's Werke.* Herausgegeben von Stephan Hock. II Teil, pp. 94–95.

[5] Georg Loesche, *Geschichte des Protestantismus in Österreich* (Tübingen u. Leipzig, 1902), pp. 214–22.

CHAPTER XIII

REVOLUTION AND MILITARY ABSOLUTISM

The system of Emperor Francis developed by Metternich into its last consequences piled up an immense mass of discontent in the whole monarchy. This situation was the more dangerous as, since the beginning of the forties of the last century, the advance of mechanical industry in the manufacturing districts of the monarchy, especially in Bohemia, led to a serious crisis in economic life. A large part of the former handicraftmen could not suffer the competition of the big plants and they swelled the ranks of the proletariat. The seriousness of the social conditions was still more aggravated by the intensification of the difficulties of the bondsman problem not yet solved. In many places the peasants refused to comply with feudal taxations and here and there serious upheavals arose which could be suppressed only by military force. The crisis in agriculture enhanced the danger of the industrial. The famine year of 1847 envenomed still more the tense social conditions. The rabble proletariat of Vienna attacked and plundered in several districts the baker-shops and the whole imperial city was full of alarming news. This misery was not restricted to the laboring-classes in a proper sense but choked the poor intelligentsia also. Especially the wretchedness of the university youths (particularly that of the Jewish students) created an intellectual strata full of revolutionary dissatisfaction. The exacerbation of the masses ran so high that some official reports of the epoch speak of the danger of communistic ideas. Against these revolutionary disaffections the police became impotent because their activity was so completely absorbed by the great policy, the "ramifications" and ferreting out of complots, which was at that time extended to the police control of the newly established Scientific Academy, that the system had not sufficient officials and soldiers to maintain internal order.

But Metternich would not make any concession even now in spite of the fact that the waves of the February Revolution of Paris aroused Austrian public opinion to the boiling-point. He contracted a loan of six million silver rubles from the Tsar for the renovation of his dilapidated "bulwarks" and announced in his official paper that Austria was sufficiently strong to defeat all revolutionary movements. But some days later bloody rebellions started at Vienna in the face of which the court did not dare to retain Metternich; and his system of forty years suddenly broke down accompanied by the jubilation of the people. Absolutism completely lost its head and accepted from one day to the next the entire independence of Hungary without having a clear understanding of the significance of this new constitution, without making any serious effort to bring this new constitution into harmony with the other parts of the monarchy. Similarly it tried to appease the Czechs by the so-called Bohemian charter, by the far-reaching promises of an imperial decree which assured to the crown of Wenceslaus almost the same independence which it bestowed upon the crown of St. Stephen. Every act of the government showed the stamp of headlessness and insincerity: the catastrophical aggravation of the Italian problem and the fight for liberty carried on by King Charles Albert, shook the very foundations of the Old Austria and forced it to compromises with its own peoples. But instead of a serious effort to place the empire on a new democratic basis and to create a workable compromise among the evolutionary possibilities of its various nations and peoples living on such different cultural levels, from the first moment of the constitutional concessions the old absolutist militarism and police system lay in wait in order to annihilate the new liberties of the peoples and to restore the old autocracy.

The sins of the past continued to live not only in the fact that the petrified absolutism was entirely incapable of accommodating itself to the spirit of a constitutional life but also because another no less dangerous situation which consisted in the lack of organization and immaturity of the democratic public opinion. The absolutism of many centuries so completely choked all movements of the popular forces and eliminated so entirely all political criticism and civic education that those peasant, citizen, and intellectual elements which now appeared for the first time on the scene of public life were lacking in all political preparedness and in all systematic effort toward the realization of those great aims which they suddenly faced. They sought in confused, disordered, and purely sentimental ideological conceptions, not seldom in unrealizable dogmatic exaggerations, the way of solution instead of embracing the only possible task, to remold the old feudal absolutist state with the help of necessary compromises into a new form of constitution apt to guarantee the free development of all the nations of the monarchy. There was almost wholly wanting in the empire, except among the Germans, an educated and self-conscious bourgeois middle class which could have undertaken the work of reconstruction with hope. Nay, even this German middle class was almost blind toward this purpose for in its haughty German hegemonial consciousness it could not realize the Austrian problem, but it visualized only the unity of the German empire as it became manifest in the *Paulskirche* of Frankfurt among brilliant ideological declamations, but with little real political insight. At the other extreme there was the street, the pressure of the violent demagogic agitation, the politicians of the petty bourgeois coffee-houses and restaurants whom the system of Metternich had estranged from all reasonable political thinking. As a sharp observer of the period said, "They feasted now in street demonstrations and hootings and howlings as they formerly revelled in roast chickens and the waltzes."

But there was also a third fatal heritage of the Metternich system which impeded, almost hopelessly, the efforts of the democratic public opinion of 1848 from establishing adequate reforms. This opinion was divided into as many parts as there were nations spread over the whole area of the empire, and none of the nations had the slightest idea of the aspirations of the other peoples living outside the narrow limits of its own territory. For instance when Count Stadion drew public attention for the first time to the deplorable state of the Ruthenians of Galicia in many political circles it was asserted that this people did not exist at all, and that they were purely the invention of the statesman to counterbalance Polish influence. In such an atmosphere, where the second greatest nation of Galicia was not even known, it might be expected that each people would regard the problem of the revolutionary unheaval from the narrow point of view of its local country. With the exception of some clear-sighted spirits, general public opinion did not realize that the monarchy was based on the co-operation of ten nations and many smaller nationalities but each nation was busy only with its own existence and problems. The ruling German nation was occupied chiefly with the problem of German unity and with plans to safeguard the German hegemony both in the Reich and in Austria against the growing pressure of the awakened Slav peoples. Though Emperor Francis, amid the storms of the Napoleonic Wars, took the title of an emperor of Austria in 1804 and, two years later under the pressure of the *Rheinbund*, he abdicated the German imperial sovereignty: the leading Germans of Austria remained still under the sway of the old unified conception and the central committee of the Viennese estates accepted, in April, 1848, a resolution in favor of the German character of Austria. Both the liberal nobility and the bourgeoisie cherished the plan to give to Lombardo-Venetia, to Hungary, and to Galicia an extended autonomy, retaining them only in a loose connection with the monarchy in order to maintain the German hegemony in Austria against the growing preponderance of the northern and southern Slavs. It is significant to observe that the Austrian Germans, from the first moment of their revolutionary awakening and relative liberty, felt their solidarity with their brothers in the German empire more clearly and intensely than their historical connection with the other peoples of the Habsburg monarchy. (Even then the idea of the *Anschluss* was far stronger than the idea of a confederation toward the east.)

The aspiration of the Magyars was even more manifest. The only idea by which they were dominated in the revolutionary period of 1848–49 was the idea of their total independence from Austria and the effort to build up a unitary national state by the assimilation of all the nations living on Hungarian territory. It is similarly beyond doubt that the Italians felt nothing in common with the Habsburg empire and their chief desire was to get rid of the Habsburg yoke. The tendency of the Slav peoples of the monarchy was not so clear and precise. The great Slavic Congress in Prague (May, 1848) which was a reply to the German National Assembly in Frankfurt and which gathered almost all the Slav tribes of Europe, was so mixed in its composition, so heterogeneous in its political and social consciousness that there was no really unified conception or common point of view among them, the less so because the representatives of the various Slav nations had serious linguistic obstacles in the way of understanding each other, even if the anecdote may be untrue, often reported by German sources, that these Pan-Slavs, ardently remonstrating against German supremacy, were often constrained to use the German language as a vehicle of their deliberations. In spite of all these difficulties, in this memorable assembly which contained such diametrical antagonisms as the conservative Palacký, the great historian of the Czechs and Bakunin, the Russian revolutionary anarchist, two fundamental agreements grew out of the aspirations of the Slav peoples. The one was the dawning consciousness of the Slav solidarity, the feeling that the Slavs have a special historical mission in Europe; the other, that, in face of the growing military and cultural expansion of the Germans, the Slavs must defend the integrity of their national cultural evolution.

What interests us most in this connection is the fact that the existence of historical Austria was not a really important issue for the peoples of the monarchy in these overflowing days of their revolutionary nationalism, but that each of them regarded its own national problems. These centrifugal forces were even more enhanced by the renaissance of the *Ländergeist*, the spirit of the old local particularisms of the various crownlands and countries. The diets showed everywhere a perfect indifference toward the problems of the whole empire. The few Austrian patriots regarded almost with terror this audacious trend of national and local patriotisms against the state, and one of them exclaimed—and his exclamation became a slogan: *Ein Königreich für einen Österreicher!* ("A kingdom for an Austrian.")[1] This feeling was so strong even in German liberal circles that when the first rumors came that Marshal Radetzky, the imperial army chief, won decisive victories over the Italian troops (which was a victory of Austrian absolutism not only over feeble Italian liberty but also over the fresh freedom of the peoples of the monarchy) Francis Grillparzer,

---

[1] Richard Charmatz, *Österreichs innere Geschichte von 1848 bis 1895* (Leipzig u. Berlin, 1918), I, 10.

the leading poet of the epoch, glorified him as the hero of the Austrian unity in the following often quoted verses:

> Glück auf mein Feldherr, führe den Streich!
> Nicht bloss um des Ruhmes Schimmer,
> In Deinem Lager ist Österreich,
> Wir andern sind einzelne Trümmer.
> (Good speed, my general, strike the blow!
> Not only for the splendor of glory,
> In thy camp is Austria,
> We others are only isolated ruins.)

The men did not perceive that the enthusiastic ode of the poet was in reality not the trumpet of victory but rather the epitaph of the Austrian state because it emphasized with an almost symbolical force the fatal fact that the army of the monarchy and the peoples of the monarchy were fighting for different ideas and that the unity of the empire remained a militaristic unity opposed to the antagonistic aims of its peoples. In any case the specter of the dissolution of the monarchy pressed very hard on the contemporaries.

Curiously enough, if one penetrates more deeply into the national and social structure of Austria during these years, one cannot share this boundless pessimism. There were still great and powerful forces in operation which could have saved the monarchy. The might and prestige of the imperial house based on the army and the bureaucracy were at that time not seriously attacked. Even Louis Kossuth the leader of the radical Hungarian opposition expressed his loyal expectations concerning the person of the young king, Francis Joseph. He and his followers did not think of a real severance of Hungary from the other parts of the monarchy and the *Pragmatica Sanctio* was not attacked. Only a complete constitutional freedom was claimed for the country. The non-Magyar population of Hungary were distinctly in favor of the maintenance of the imperial unity because they saw in it their only safeguard against the more and more vehement and intolerant attacks of Magyar chauvinism. At the same time the most influential elements of the Germans in Austria (in spite of some pan-Germanistic sentimentalism) stood firmly for the maintenance of Austria. And what is still more important: the large Slav majority of the monarchy was emphatically loyal to the Habsburgs because, in spite of a vague Pan-Slavism, it clearly felt that it needed a state which would and could guarantee its national development against both the German and Russian pressure. Not only Croats and Serbs defended with their blood the cause of the dynasty but even the leading elements of the Czechs were of the opinion that they were deeply interested in the safeguarding of the monarchy. In that memorable letter in which Francis Palacký, the generally accepted leader of the new Czech nationalism, repudiated the invitation of the Parliament of

Frankfurt, as a protest against German unity, intended to absorb the Slav nations, he gave a real program of a new Austria fit for the aspirations of her Slav peoples. He emphasized very distinctly the historical necessity of Austria as a shield and shelter for the smaller nations of the Danube basin (Slavs, Rumanians, Hungarians) against the growing pressure of a despotic Russian empire. "If the Austrian empire had not existed during past centuries, it ought to have been created in the very interest of Europe and of humanity."[2] Not for the destruction of Austria but for the remolding of the empire was the struggle of the Czechs and the Jugo-Slavs carried on almost until the outbreak of the World War. The conception of Palacký was corroborated by the Slav national convention at Prague with an imposing force in spite of the ideological chaos of this assembly. The Slav Congress elaborated a proclamation to the nations of Europe which delineated very strongly its standpoint concerning the Austrian problem. This manifesto emphasized the peaceful intention of all the Slavs and at the same time their right for self-determination and national independence. They were not hostile to the empire but they intended to remold the old monarchy into a confederation of nations equal in their rights, maintaining the necessary unity of the whole monarchy. They claimed especially the same constitutional position which the German and the Hungarian element possessed. The Congress made an appeal to the Hungarian government to do away with those revolting coercive measures which were directed against the Slavic tribes of Hungary, especially against the Serbs, Croats, and Slovaks.

Even more clear and significant for the moral atmosphere of the Slavs was a memorandum, drafted by the Congress, to the Emperor to inform him of the real aspirations and desires of the Slavs. The aim of this memorandum remained in many respects the foundation of the Slav policy also for the future. This document emphasized the fact that the system of centralization could only keep together the loose masses of the various nationalities of the monarchy by the means of absolutism, whereas the real future of Austria and its rôle as a great power depended on whether it could guarantee to the Slav nations of the monarchy, hitherto oppressed, a real autonomy for national development. The only constitution which could secure this aim would be one which remolded the centralized monarchy into a federative state.[3]

In this historical constellation Francis Joseph, 18 years old, occupied the throne (1848–1916) in consequence of a court complot which eliminated the feeble-minded Ferdinand. The young Emperor himself attached to his name Francis the name of his great popular

[2] Dr. Alfred Fischel, *Der Panslavismus bis zum Weltkrieg* (Stuttgart u. Berlin, 1919), p. 254.

[3] Alfred Fischel, *op. cit.*, pp. 284 ff.

predecessor Joseph, and there were people who saw in this fact an
almost symbolical action because according to their judgment the
long reign of Francis Joseph was a curious mixture of the reactionary
principles of Emperor Francis and of the revolutionary methods of
Emperor Joseph. This point of view is not without a certain truth
but it seems to me that what was really Francisist in his system was
spontaneous, emanating from the very character of the sovereign,
whereas its Josephinian elements were rather superficial, artificial
compromises forced on the Emperor by the necessities of a given situation. But however unstable and changing his method of government
may have been, there remained always constant and unaltered in his
profound distrust of his peoples, of the constitution, of democracy,
and his conviction that the only real foundation of his rule must be
his army and his attachment to the feudal aristocracy.

It was a real misfortune for the whole monarchy that the young
Emperor with his eager energy for work, his vivid sense of administrative duty (he might be called without exaggeration the first *Hofrat* of his monarchy, so fervent for bureaucratic work, so amazing in
his *Kabinettsfleiss*, and so lacking in any real broad conceptions),
occupied his throne under the terrifying experiences of a world-revo-
lution when he saw his power vacillating amid the menacing clamor of
the street, when twice he witnessed the flight of the imperial court
from Vienna, and always stood under the sway of his rigid generals,
Windischgrätz, Jelačić, and Radetzky, who were rooted deeply in the
ideas of the old autocracy. It is no wonder under such conditions that
the youthful emperor did not realize the one fatal problem of the monarchy which consisted in giving free opportunities for the development of so many fragmentary peoples between the two millstones of
German and Russian imperialism. He visualized only the old problem
of the Habsburg *Hausmacht,* how to augment its international splendor, how to overcome its Prussian rival, and enhance its influence in
the Balkans against the Russian protector of the Slav nations.

The great fatal problem of the monarchy, the problem of nationality, appeared to him still in the old narrow-minded conception of
Metternich in the spirit of the *divide et impera.* In spite of all his real
and seeming concessions which he made to the necessities of the changing historical situation, he remained rigidly attached to a system of
centralization until the end, disregarding the fundamental national
claims.[4] This attitude was not motivated by any national bias, he did

---

[4] The Emperor never took the idea of a national compromise between the Czechs
and the Germans seriously. In his new important work *(Kaiser Franz Joseph von
Österreich,* Berlin, 1928), Joseph Redlich narrates that it was a widely accepted
public opinion among the Austrian parliamentarians that the Emperor did not
favor such a compromise because, according to a statement of his daughter, Archduchess Marie Valerie, "if Germans and Czechs should make a compromise, the situation would become the same as in Hungary—the Emperor would lose his power
there too."

not hate the various non-German nations of his monarchy, nor did he particularly love the Germans whose language was the vehicle of his army and bureaucracy. On the contrary every conscious manifestation of German nationalism disgusted and alarmed him because he feared a gravitation toward his later ally and, subconsciously always, his hated rival, the Hohenzollern. But he remained unaltered, a rigid autocrat in all the questions pertaining to the interests of his imperial will. In his state ministers he always saw a kind of court lackeys and he said repeatedly to Conrad von Hötzendorf when he was the Chief of the General Staff: "Believe me, the Monarchy cannot be ruled in a constitutional manner." And he was perfectly right in this because, with those two systems with which he experimented during his long reign, with the system of the rigid centralization, and later with the dualist system based on the German-Magyar hegemony, an honest constitutional government was really out of the question.

This attitude was the more fatal for in spite of the first chaotic movements in the early days of the revolution of 1848, the more careful observers could distinctly see that this vast popular movement was not only directed toward the destruction of the old régime but that it also contained powerful constructive forces. So even Hungary, the country of rigid feudalism, also, under the leadership of a very able and enthusiastic group of her revolutionized nobility, undertook the first decisive steps toward the elimination of the feudal privileges and the rebuilding of the country on a democratic platform. It is true that in the most important question, in the problem of nationality this new liberal public opinion completely misunderstood the real spirit of the epoch, but by a prudent, humane, and loyal policy, the Habsburgs could doubtless have been successful in adjusting Hungarian democracy amid the newly liberated co-operation of the other nations. For the very leaders of the Hungarian movement for independence in September, 1848, knocked at the door of the Austrian popular assembly inviting it to undertake the rôle of mediator in the fatal controversy between the Emperor and the Hungarian nation. But far more than this happened. The parliament of the Austrian people, which the military reactionary rulers after the second Viennese rebellion had interned at Kremsier, a little remote Moravian town, recovering from the feverish revolutionary dreams, undertook the task with remarkable energy and sagacity of giving a new constitution to the peoples of Austria. After the absolute rule of many centuries the nations of the Austrian half of the monarchy met for the first time in order to discuss face to face their mutual national and cultural problems and to find a solution for all. The antagonisms were very great and, at the beginning, the spirit of the old distrust dominated. The rigid centralism of the Germans and the radical federalism of the Czechs clashed vehemently. The plan of the Czech leader, Palacký, was to rebuild the monarchy entirely on the basis of the principle of nationality and to divide the whole monarchy into a German-Austria, a Czech-Austria, a Polish-Austria, an Illyrian-Austria, an Italian-Austria, and a Jugo-Slav-Austria, and also to form separate territories for the Magyars and the Rumanians. (It is worth while to notice at this juncture that this platform of the Czechs was later radically changed when they accepted the old feudal basis of the historical right, claiming the integrity of the whole territory of the former crown of Wenceslaus without taking into account the diversity of the nationalities living in Bohemia, Moravia, and Silesia.) This plan hurt not only the German centralist consciousness but the very developed traditional feeling for independence of the single countries. The Tyroleans, for instance, had already previously emphasized that they must have a proper government and would have nothing to do with the Viennese ministry.[5] Similarly the Poles refused vehemently the idea of dividing Galicia into a Polish and a Ruthenian territory. The Istrian and the Dalmatian particularism clashed and the antagonism was very great between Carinthia and Carniola, while the historical individuality of Vorarlberg, Salzburg, and Görz revolted energetically against all plans of territorial dismemberment.

Under such auspices the chances for a compromise looked very unfavorable. But the natural wisdom of the various peoples soon became victorious. The parliamentary reporter of the constitutional committee understood the dangers of the situation very sharply and he admonished the representative in a powerful speech that in the present controversy, only those dragon teeth are shooting up which Metternich had sown during his long régime. Now the liberated nations must get rid of this spirit and, as the great principle of national equality appeared in world-history, it should not be transformed into the emancipation of the Slavs. If it is true that the German was previously the master and the Slav the servant, this proposition can only be accepted with the qualification that the former government was German and enslaved both nations. Those who transmit the hatred of the Slavs against government and bureaucracy to the German people continue in the old policy of *divide et impera* of Metternich. The constitutional committee also emphasized the dangers which a radical annihilation of the old constitutional frames would have caused (as Palacký proposed it) and offered a solution which would avoid centralization, the death of the single provinces, but at the same time a loose federation which would make all central government impossible.

Indeed, the compromise delineated in this manner was successful and the Parliament of Kremsier adopted a solution along the middle line reconciling the centralist and the federalist ideals. It main-

[5] Viktor Bibl, *op. cit.*, II, 179–80.

tained the historical kingdoms and countries but it divided the larger territories into *Kreise* (districts) the establishment of which was arranged according to the ethnographical settlements of the peoples. In the administration of the individual countries local governors were planned responsible to the particular representative bodies in order to secure a true self-government against the possible abuses of the central power. The principle of national equality was pronounced as the basic institution of the new constitution and provisions were made that, in territories where mixed nationalities lived, tribunals should be erected on the footing of equality for the settlement of all disputes concerning national issues.

Unfortunately the limits of the present work make it impossible to outline in detail this remarkable draft of a constitution though its significance from the point of view of the history of ideas is considerable and at the same time a powerful argument for the force and fertility of the democratic principle. Behold! after three hundred years of absolutism and militaristic centralization, in spite of the envenomed past, it sufficed to bring these peoples together and to secure for them the right of free discussion and a new spirit and a new will was triumphant over the old spirit infested by feudalism and absolutism. *Here for the first time a consequent and logically consistent attempt was made to rebuild a large empire on the basis of a supranational unity and to codify the great principle of national equality in all the walks of public life.* In this manner the first freely elected representative body of Austria solved or at least brought nearer to solution a problem which the periods of absolutism did not even distinguish. Particularly imposing is the clear-sightedness with which the makers of the constitution realized the basic importance of the principle of self-government for the solution of the national problem. The speakers of the national assembly emphasized continuously that France, in spite of her repeated revolutions, could not be regarded as a free country because she had no municipal liberties. *Free local government is the basis of the free state!* At the same time the work of Kremsier remains a memorable document of that high spirit of humanism which animated the generation of 1848, both the Germans and the Slavs. And it is no exaggeration when Joseph Redlich, the keenest analyst of this constitutional draft, asserts that *"measured both by moral and intellectual standards this document is the only great political monument of the common will for the State which in imperial Austria the peoples have created through their own representatives. . . . ."*

But Francis Joseph and his councilors did not care for the work of Kremsier, they did not care for those mighty popular energies which were manifested by it. The cynical words of Prince Windischgrätz which he uttered according to tradition when he heard that the

popular representation refused to give to his Emperor the old title
"by God's grace": "If they will not hear from God's grace then they
must hear from cannons' grace . . . ." may be true or later invented,
they express at all events the spirit and practice of the military counter-revolution. That was the reason why the constitutional assembly
of Kremsier was dissolved by armed force when absolutism became
sufficiently reinforced by the conquest of Vienna, by the Italian victories of Radetzky and by the armed occupation of the Hungarian
capital. And, though after Kremsier they made a new experiment
with an arbitrary sham constitution which restored the full power of
the centralistic system, they simultaneously continued with great energy their campaign for the military subjugation of the rebellious
peoples and the supreme aim was quite manifest: the complete restoration of the old régime. Already under the feeble-minded Ferdinand, there began the work of the "pacification" of Hungary, the
armed struggle against a constitution to which the Emperor himself
gave sanction and the perfidious game with the Jugo-Slavs exasperated by the Magyarizing policy of the Hungarian government. Jel-
lačić, the Croat Ban, became the obedient instrument of the Viennese
camarilla for the destruction of the Hungarian constitution and the
world witnessed a very stupendous political drama of which it was said
by a contemporary: "The King of Croatia declared war on the King
of Hungary and the Emperor of Austria remained neutral and these
three monarchs were one and the same person." This treacherous
game, which, after the victory of Radetzky at Custozza threw away
its mask definitely, drove the Hungarians into despair and, when the
new arbitrary constitution abolished quite openly the independence
of the country, the national assembly accepted the proposition of
Louis Kossuth and dethroned the Habsburg dynasty at Debreczen
(April 11, 1849) exactly in the same manner as more than a century
before, the Diet of Rákóczi had done. The declaration of independence
adopted by the national assembly is a long enumeration of the historical crimes of the Habsburgs committed against the constitutional
and personal liberties of the Hungarian people. They are accused of
plotting
with the enemies of the country, with robbers and rebels for the suppression of the Hungarian nation; of attacking the legally sanctioned constitution by armed force; of dismembering the territorial integrity of the
country which they had sworn to maintain; of employing foreign military
power for the murdering of their own subjects, and for the annihilation of
their legal freedom. . . . .

The constitutional accent of the rebellion of Rákóczi and the revolution of Kossuth was the same, but whereas the former did not surpass the limits of feudal rebellion the latter was no longer the private
affair of some malcontent feudal lords and of a wretched serfdom attached to them, but a distinctly national and democratic movement in

which not only the liberal wing of the nobility but also the new middle classes and the whole peasantry, liberated from the yoke of feudalism, took up arms for the defense of their young freedom. That is the reason why Vienna was incapable of suppressing it as it formerly suppressed the rebellions of the feudal exiles and the *kurucz* forces. The Habsburg power, victorious over revolutionary Vienna and Prague, was incapable of conquering the Hungarian revolution in defense of the Constitution of 1848. The later dualistic structure of the monarchy was an expression of this historical fact. But in 1848 the dynasty was not inclined to any just compromise though before the dethronement of the Habsburgs very influential Hungarian circles were in favor of an honest peace but Prince Windischgrätz haughtily refused the representatives of the Hungarian national assembly with the words which became fatal: *Mit Rebellen unterhandle ich nicht!* ("I will not negotiate with rebels!") Therefore later when the Hungarian armies became victorious the dynasty had no other choice than the unheard of humiliation of asking for the assistance of the Russian Tsar who sent a mighty army for the pacification of Hungary. General Görgey, the great Hungarian war-leader, acknowledging the futility of the struggle and in order to save the last remaining force of the unhappy country, surrendered not into the hands of the Austrians, but into those of the Russian general Paskiewicz, who, as the Hungarian tradition tells, announced proudly to the Tsar: "Hungary lies at the feet of your Majesty."

But Habsburg proved to be not only a ferocious enemy; it was a cruel conqueror thirsty for revenge at the same time. The same terrible method which the victorious Austrian army applied in Lombardia and Venetia when the Habsburg foreign rule was again restored by terror tribunals, by war taxes, by the imprisonment of thousands of suspicious men, and by the most carefully selected brutalities (General Haynau, called the "Hyena of Brescia," whipped the women in the open streets): the same method was introduced, as so often in the past, into unhappy Hungary unconquered by the Austrians. The bloody hangman of the Italian people, General Haynau was sent to Hungary to create order there. Indeed, the "punishments" inflicted by the conquerors were so without parallel that the Russian Tsar and his chief of staff felt themselves impelled to ask in Vienna for the mitigation of their measures. And this system was not the accident of some officers breaking away from discipline but the deliberate policy of Prince Schwarzenberg, the Austrian premier who when he was advised to follow a policy of grace and conciliation toward Hungary, repudiated the offer with the following remarks: "That sounds all right but before all we wish to hang a few." No, the Viennese camarilla wanted to establish a terrifying example, and on the anniversary of the same day that the Viennese populace killed the war minister, Latour, thirteen Hungarian generals were executed in Arad (nine of them on the gallows). Their only crime was that they defended the constitution to which they had sworn in the name of the King. A great number of other officers were given heavy penalties in jail. According to Hungarian tradition, which was held three generations, the various terror tribunals handed down 114 death sentences and imprisonment was resorted to in 1,765 cases. The later official historians have tried to mitigate the poignant memory of these horrors by affirming that the young emperor had no knowledge of these judicial murders but later investigations demonstrated that Francis Joseph had previous information of the execution of the Hungarian generals.

But the revenging arm of Haynau and his men struck not only the rebels of the army but all those who were in contact with political life in that stormy period. Bishops and ministers encountered harsh imprisonment and several leaders of the Hungarian revolution were hung in effigy. And on the same day when the martyrs of Arad ended their lives, there was executed in Pest one of the most excellent and most moderate Hungarian statesmen, the premier of the first Hungarian constitutional government, Count Louis Batthyányi. Thus the whole monarchy was pacified by the old Spanish methods of blood and iron. The jovial people of Vienna, the successors of the Hussites in Prague, the Italian patriots, and the Magyar "rebels," all succumbed to the bloody arms of the Habsburgs. No wonder that these events profoundly impressed the public opinion of all those peoples who suffered by these terrible methods. That is the reason why I try the patience of the reader with an enumeration of all these details. *For these facts are not only facts of the past in the Habsburg drama but they were direct causes of the process of dissolution.* These bloody facts created such a psychological state among the masses, for instance, in Hungary, that it influenced most powerfully the whole political life of the country. The slogan of the *accursed Austria-Vienna* remained always a kindling symbol in the imagination of the masses. "Vienna" remained always equivalent to the wailings of the Protestant galley slaves, to the insurrections choked in blood, and above all to the constitution stolen by the help of the Russian bayonets. In the face of this emotional complex all rational argumentation broke down. Habsburg remained hated and abhorred even when he tried to give rights and liberties to the people. *Timeo Danaos* . . . . "We accept nothing from the *Viennese camarilla,* not even the good." That feeling was so intense that ten years after the catastrophe when Count Stephen Széchenyi, the great conservative statesman, was placed with broken spirit in a Viennese asylum shortly before his tragic suicide, he gave in his diary to Francis Joseph the epithet of "the apostolic usurper" and he called the gallows the "pillars of Francis Joseph."[6] And even

---

[6] *The Literary Legacy of Döbling of Count Stephan Széchenyi.* Edited by Dr. Arpád Károlyi (Budapest, 1921), II, 40, 84, 86. In Hungarian.

in the last decade of the monarchy when attending public meetings, I often observed that the memory of "the thirteen of Arad" swayed the masses as the wind does the standing grain. That is what many Austrian and Hungarian statesmen never realized. They did not understand how insignificant demagogues could excite the feeling of the masses into paroxysms against institutions which, as the free-trade policy or the Austro-Hungarian bank, could serve the very interests of the Hungarian majority too. They did not understand because they always used rationalistic methods and they did not know that the masses are led more by old memories and semiconscious ancestral sentiments than by the rational calculations of economic motives. All political dissatisfaction and all social discontent could be easily directed against Vienna in such manner. And I think I am quite safe in believing that the same mental processes were going on in the soul of the Czech, of the Polish, and of the Italian masses. What Arad was to the Hungarian, the scaffold of Prague was to the Czech, the jail of Spielberg was to the Italian, and the bloody parade of Tarnow was to the Pole.

CHAPTER XIV

THE STABILIZATION OF ABSOLUTISM: THE SYSTEM BACH

After the "settlement" of the Italian and the Hungarian difficulties the system sat more and more haughtily in the saddle of absolutism; it could do so with a reassuring complacency since in the face of its reinforced military power, its Prussian rival got himself into a position of humiliation. The struggle of Premier Prince Schwarzenberg for German hegemony was temporarily successful: the old loose *Bundestag* was re-established. Though without the title of a German emperor, Habsburg became again at least seemingly the leading power of Germany. There was no further obstacle to a new reign of the old absolutism. The second enlarged edition of the Metternich system began which culminated in the so-called "system Bach," named after the Minister of Interior, Alexander Bach, who from a champion of the March revolution transformed himself into the incarnation of the new reactionary system. The Bach system agreed with the system of Metternich on three substantial points. One was the Germanizing centralization which now was extended without any check to Hungary. Bach shrewdly constructed his ill-famed *Verwirkungstheorie* according to which Hungary has forfeited her former constitutional liberty in consequence of the Revolution. The country with complete disregard for its historical evolution and for its local municipal life was divided into quite mechanical administrative districts which got all their directions from the imperial government. At the same time a veritable army of German and Germanized Czech officials flooded the country, called in the popular language the "Bach hussars," and received by the public opinion of the country with distrust and hatred. "A swarm of locusts covers the country to eat it up," said the contemporaries. And though the system was equally served by many hundreds, nay, thousands of the nobility trembling for their jobs, it remained until the end a strange and hostile power in the country.

The second point in which the old absolutism continued was the extension of the former police and spy system over the whole country and was pushed so far that the very chief of the system, Alexander Bach, came under police control. The extent of the police system may be sufficiently characterized by the following episode, narrated by Heinrich Friedjung, the historian of the epoch: Once the archbishop of Vienna made a reproachful remark to the head of the police, concerning the moral conduct of the officers of the gendarmes, of whom many lived in concubinage; to which the chief of police replied that the archbishop would do better if he would control the relation of his clergymen to their cooks. Several days later the police handed over to the cardinal a long list containing many canons and other clergymen with a precise statement of their mistresses. This same police minister established a curious type of herbarium in which every man somewhat known in the political field was classified according to genus and species. In this herbarium Bach himself did not enjoy a very white sheet.[1] But the enormous police force was not sufficient, not even the ordinary troops put on a war footing, but the organization of the *gendarmery*, a kind of military police, was created whose colossal proportions amazed even an expert of the Tsar.

The third point in which the system of Bach continued and surpassed the system of Metternich was the total surrender of the empire to Catholicism and especially to the Jesuits. The Concordate of 1855, this *"printed Canossa"* appeared before the liberal and Josephinian intelligence as a vassal treaty with Rome which stifled the spirit of the youth delivering the whole educational system, the whole spiritual production, and the whole matrimonial jurisdiction to the representatives of Rome.

These were the most outstanding features of the system of Bach which pressed heavily not only on the "rebellious" Magyars but also on the other nations of the monarchy, even on the Croats and those Hungarian nationalities which were the chief pillars of the Habsburgs in their fight against Hungary. The same system of centralization, Germanization, and spy control tortured the loyal nations exactly in the same manner as the Magyar revolutionaries. The leaders of the Slovak movement, Stúr and Hurban, and the Rumanian hero, Jancu —though in the revolutionary period they were obedient instruments in the hands of the Viennese court—could now enjoy the famous "gratitude of the Habsburgs" because they were captured and interned in the same way as many leaders of the Hungarian renaissance, among them the greatest poetical genius of the period, Michael Vörösmarty. Under such circumstances with a well-motivated irony a Magyar nobleman could say to his Croat colleague, "What we received as punishment you got as recompense."[2]

This system was an absurdity not only from the moral point of view but also from the national. In a period when national consciousness was already developed, after the transitory realization of the Hungarian independence and after the popular parliament of Krem-

[1] Heinrich Friedjung, *Österreich von 1848 bis 1860*, II Band, I Abt. (Stuttgart u. Berlin, 1912), pp. 193–94.

[2] Many interesting details concerning the dissatisfaction of the non-Magyar nationalities under the Bach system can be found in Albert Berzeviczy's book, *The Period of Absolutism in Hungary, 1849–65* (Budapest, 1922), I, 144–63. In Hungarian.

102 DISSOLUTION OF THE HABSBURG MONARCHY

sier, it made a desperate effort to maintain the absolutist state, disregarding the national principles, with the help of ecclesiastical and police auxiliary troops. The Bach system was truly characterized by a former comrade of his in the revolution, the deepest political thinker of the period, the noble and clear-sighted Adolph Fischhof: "A standing army of soldiers, a sitting army of officials, a kneeling army of priests and a creeping army of denunciators."

The Bach system, however, was not at all a simple copy of the traditions of Metternich, because it also contained important Josephinian elements. One might even say without exaggeration that this absolutism realized such revolutionary reforms in that period still dominated by feudal influences which a constitutional government could scarcely have accomplished. Alexander Bach, the renegade, remained indeed on one point a revolutionary: he took the liberation of the serfs very seriously and carried on the great reform against all resistance and laid the foundation of the modern state in administration and in economics. For, however incomplete, dull, slow, and servile the bureaucracy created by him may have been, it was undoubtedly a great advance compared with the former inefficient administration of the nobility. New railroads and new highways were built in all the countries of the monarchy. A unitary custom barrier guaranteed free trade between Hungary and the other parts of the empire. The legal system and the judiciary became modernized and unified.

But this very cultural and economic renewal made the system more and more oppressive and hated. The growing spiritual and material energies of the nations were increasingly opposed to foreign domination. Besides uncontrolled absolutism was almost limitless in squandering the money of the treasury of the country. Immense sums were spent for useless military fortifications in Lombardy and Venetia and the provisional occupation of the Danubian principalities cost two million florins and the lives of forty thousand men. This adventure was not only futile but of very disastrous consequence. The leading Russian circles were exasperated by the perfidy of their former ally during the vicissitudes of the Crimean War and the door was open for the Pan-Slav propaganda. *Der Weg nach Konstantinopal führt über Wien* ("The road to Constantinople leads through Vienna!")

CHAPTER XV

EXPERIMENTATION IN CONSTITUTIONALISM: THE "DIPLOMA" AND THE "PATENT"

The more one digs into the history of the monarchy the more clearly does one realize the long series of faults, errors, and crimes which drove it into dissolution. Opposed to this point of view, the leading German and Magyar circles always try to show that this process was a fatal one and nobody could foretell the consequences of various measures into which the monarchy was pressed under the weight of external conditions. It cannot be sufficiently emphasized, however, that in no important issue of the monarchy were there wanting men who predicted with an amazing insight the consequences of a policy motivated by a criminal light-mindedness. That was the case in face of the absolutism of Metternich. The same was now true in regard to the neo-absolutism of Francis Joseph. I could quote, if space would allow me, a long series of eminent men who understood that this centralization, based on the imperial bayonets, must lead to collapse and only a system of a well-balanced federalism which would satisfy the national aspirations of the various peoples of the monarchy could maintain the state. But federalism without local government is an empty word. It is perfectly clear that the system of absolutism was entirely incapable of solving the problem of the monarchy. It was even unfit half a century before in the hands of such a genius as Joseph II, who at least knew what he wished to accomplish and who tried to remold the empire on the basis of a vast and logical (though an essentially erroneous) scheme. But how much more was the system of Francis Joseph, which tried to apply the old methods of his ancestor without any true conception, without any ethical ardor, sentenced to a fiasco in a period when even the most modest popular fragment of his monarchy reached the totality of national consciousness.

If we look over the seven-decade reign of Francis Joseph, we are unable to find in his governmental system—in spite of his proverbial energy and feeling of duty—anything which could be called a standpoint based upon principle, a systematic endeavor, or even a modest program looking to the future. The only real motives of his system were military power and diplomatic prestige. What later Premier Taaffe called, with open cynicism and with an untranslatable word, *Fortwursteln* ("blundering along the old rut," perhaps), meaning the petty compromises from day to day, the concessions without principle, the sacrifice of all true political conceptions for the momentous exigencies of opportunism—this policy was not an invention of the

Kaiserminister but the old historical tradition of the empire. There was no spontaneous initiative in this system. The great changes were not the results of statesmanlike aims but only adaptations of a purely mechanical nature under the pressure of the events of the outer policy. However manifest the unfeasibility and the demoralizing effect of the Bach system became, it would have been continued without doubt, if on the battlefields of Magenta and Solferino (1859), the Habsburg absolutism had not received a mortal blow, being constrained to surrender Lombardy, through Emperor Napoleon, to the King of Sardinia in order to save at least his endangered German hegemony.

The entire lack of a clear political conception was also demonstrated after Solferino, when haphazard experiments were made in replacing absolutism by a form of moderate constitutionalism. In October, 1860, the Emperor issued the so-called "October Diploma" which he qualified as a "permanent and irrevocable fundamental law." This new constitution signified a rupture with the Germanizing centralism and an essay to gain the more active co-operation of the feudal nobility of the various countries. The special purpose was the reconciliation of the Hungarian conservatives for whom the feudal constitution before 1848 was re-established. But this half-measure could not gain the more liberal public opinion in Hungary. In this manner the Diploma satisfied only the feudal elements of the Slavs to whom it gave the possibility of reorganizing their forces on the basis of a larger local autonomy.

As the general dissatisfaction was growing the Emperor dismissed the author of the Diploma, the Polish Count Goluchowski, as early as December of the same year and two months later casting aside the "permanent and irrevocable" October Diploma (though under the pretext that it would only be reinterpreted and supplemented), gave to the monarchy the so-called "February Patent" (1861) which, in the hand of Anton Schmerling, the former president of the Parliament of Frankfurt, became an instrument to carry on a conception diametrically opposed to the Diploma. If the Diploma—as it was rightly characterized—may be regarded as a *coup d'état* of the aristocracy against the reigning German bureaucracy of Vienna, the Patent signified the continuation of the German bureaucratic centralization. The only difference was that the absolutism got a fig leaf by the so-called "Curia System" which played a preponderant rôle in Austrian political life before the introduction of universal suffrage. Under this system public life was represented by four groups of interests. The big landed estate, the chambers of commerce, the towns, and the villages sent their deputies into the *Landtags* or the diets of the single countries; and the diets sent their representatives into the *Reichsrat*, the central parliament. (Only later, in 1873, was the *Reichsrat* directly elected by the electorate on the basis of the same Curia system.) This very artificial procedure was established to secure the rule of the wealthy and highly cultured German minority above the Slav majority.[1] It is clear that this constitution was only a continuation of the old feudal diets, and a leading publicist of the period wittily called the new system "provincial diets strengthened by a few attorneys and manufacturers." The moral weakness of this pseudo-parliamentarianism after the experiment of Kremsier soon became manifest and the "theater of Schmerling" was boycotted not only by the Magyars, but also by the Czechs, and the Poles soon abandoned it, exasperated after the short Slav intermezzo of the Diploma by the new régime which again continued the German centralization of the Bach system with a small parliamentarian show window. The best criticism of the system was given by Count Julius Andrássy, the later Hungarian premier and foreign minister of the monarchy, who declared:

Messrs. Bach and Schmerling committed not only a political but also an arithmetical fault. They put the monarchy on a basis on which there were six millions against thirty millions: they put the pyramid on its head.[2]

Golden words indeed, but a few years later the same arithmetical fault was committed by Andrássy himself who, with the help of Francis Deák won the Emperor for the compromise of 1867, creating the dualist system which maintained the pyramid further on its head with the small correction that they heightened the basis from six to twelve million by the addition of five million Magyars and a million Hungarian-Germans. This new basis was manifestly very unstable against the will of eighteen million people, the more so as the Germans and the masses of the Magyar people (as we shall see later in detail) felt the new connection rather as a burden.

[1] An acute analysis of the Curia-System is given by R. Charmatz in his able book, *Österreichs innere Geschichte von 1848 bis 1895, op. cit.*, I, 50–52.

[2] Quoted by Victor Bibl, *op. cit.*, II, 274.

CHAPTER XVI

THE PERIOD OF SHAM-CONSTITUTIONALISM:
THE DUALIST SYSTEM

As all great constitutional changes in Austria, the system of Dualism, too, was the result of a historical catastrophe. The dualistic system was born on the battlefield of Königgrätz, July 3, 1866, when Austrian absolutism definitely collapsed under the stroke of its more national and more liberal Prussian rival. The crisis of the Habsburg empire was so deep that it was compelled, in the Peace Treaty of Prague, to abdicate not only its claims toward the German empire but also, in spite of its successes on the Italian battlefields, to surrender Venetia to Italy. That was perhaps the greatest crisis and the most fatal turning point of the monarchy. Now locked out from the German imperial connection and having lost its Italian properties, the traditional *fata morgana* of the Holy Roman Empire was dissolved and the road was open to the historical mission of Austria which would have consisted in giving a home, shelter, and defense, the possibilities of a national development for all those smaller nations which lived in central Europe either in a complete isolation or divided from their co-nationals.

Unfortunately the political atmosphere was not propitious for a really creative policy. The masses became apathetic and cynical by the long absolutism. It makes almost a ghastly impression when we read that the very day when the news of the disaster at Königgrätz arrived at the imperial city, many thousands of Viennese were united in a dance in fancy costumes and they sang and drank merrily in the gardens of their jovial inns. Even the leading German bourgeoisie stood hesitatingly, and in frozen despair, at this fatal crisis. This attitude was symbolically characterized by Grillparzer in the pathetic question: "I am born as a German, am I still one?" and he shouted to the victorious Prussians: "You believe you have given birth to an empire, but you have only destroyed a people!"

The Magyars, too, saw only the problem of their own national state and they did not grasp seriously the consequences of the new situation and did not ask what would happen with the many countries and nations of the monarchy with which they were connected by the ties of the *Pragmatica Sanctio*. According to a tradition, when Francis Deák, the great liberal Hungarian leader, heard the first news of the Austrian defeat, he exclaimed, "We lost the war! . . . . we are now victorious." Similarly in the Czechs flamed up again the consciousness of the independence of their holy crown. The recent war events accentuated very much the patriotic feelings in both countries. The Hungarian Legion of General Klapka, supported by Bismarck, had made a common cause with the Prussian armies against the hated Austria and the Prussian proclamation to the peoples of "the glorious Czech Kingdom" poured new oil on the fire of Czech nationalism.

This situation was further endangered by the fact that the dynasty and the ruling circles still considered nothing else but the old problem of the Habsburg patrimonial power and their chief endeavor was not to establish a new and better balanced order in Austria but rather to prepare a war of revenge against the victorious Prussian rivals. That was the reason why after the defeat of Königgrätz Baron von Beust, the former Saxon antagonist of Bismarck, was nominated foreign minister of the monarchy. He abandoned the federalistic tendencies of Count Belcredi (for, after Schmerling, there was again a Slavophile political experiment) and opened the way for the dualistic compromise. To make a policy of revenge possible a compromise with the Magyars seemed inevitable.

The burning desire for revenge against Prussia, the uncertainty of the international situation, the untenableness of the Hungarian conditions, and the effective intervention of Empress Elizabeth (called the "beautiful Providence" by the Magyars), in favor of the Magyar standpoint were victorious over the resistance of the Emperor who at last accepted the restitution of the Constitution of 1848, the platform of Hungarian independence, the division of the empire into two countries, in a word, that whole program against which he carried on a bloody war and pressed during two decades the nations of the monarchy into the Procrustes-bed of the unifying and Germanizing absolutism. In opposition to this policy the dualistic constitution was a definite attempt to secure the leadership of the Germans in Austria and of the Magyars in Hungary. At the moment of its birth this new equilibrium was, at least temporarily, possible, for the German economic and cultural hegemony was still preponderant in Austria, whereas the Hungarian nobility was an almost absolute master of the political and municipal life. In spite of this fact in a true constitutional way the dualistic platform would never have gained a majority either in Austria or in Hungary. Only on the basis of a parliament emanating from the artificial machinations of the Curia-system, did the new constitution become a law in Austria. But even that pseudo-majority did not have an opportunity for fair discussion because it was put before a *fait accompli*. The whole dualistic compromise had already been practically settled by the Emperor—the Hungarian king—and the Magyar upper classes. The Austrian parliament was under the strict necessity of accepting the will of the Emperor. It is true that it was the loyal conception of Francis Deák that Hungary could only accept a connection with a constitutional Austria, and really the German liberals received as a kind of a political present the December Constitution of 1867 which introduced a series of legal guaranties. But in reality no true constitutional life was possible on the basis of the purely artificial German majority, the less as paragraph 14 of the new constitution established the right of the Emperor to issue, in cases of emergency, decrees which were under the competence of the parliamentary representation. (This right was exercised between 1897 and 1904 in seventy-six cases.) Also in Hungary the situation was that of a pseudo-constitutional device because the masses of the nationalities and of the laboring-classes had never (as we shall see later in detail) an adequate share in political and municipal rights. Therefore, the compromise of 1867 and the dualistic system based on it, appeared before public opinion as the compromise of the Austrian Emperor with the Hungarian feudal classes which the liberal German high bourgeoisie accepted, though not without serious hesitations, in order to secure its own hegemony against the will of the Slav majority.

The Slavs of the monarchy knew very well from the beginning what dualism meant for them and though the new constitution was prepared in a rather hidden way, the Slavs expressed repeatedly their exasperation against the dualistic plans. Francis Palacký, the same Palacký who announced the Habsburg monarchy in 1848 as a historical necessity for the Slav peoples, on the first rumor of the dualistic *pourparlers* which had already begun before Königgrätz, declared in 1865 that "the day of the proclamation of the dualism will become with an unavoidable necessity at the same time the birthday of Pan-Slavism in its least desirable form." And he added, "We Slavs will face it with an honest suffering but without fear. We have existed before Austria, and we shall exist after it." The Slavs knew very clearly what they wished. Immediately after Königgrätz the so-called second Slav congress at Vienna made a decision in favor of a pentarchical constitution for the monarchy which set against the Hungarian conception of dualism a plan of federation among the five big national groups of the monarchy. And in the same month, when the draft of the dualist compromise was put before the Austrian parliament, a considerable number of Czech, Croat, Ruthenian, and Slovenian politicians under the leadership of Palacký and Rieger, the Czech leaders, made a pilgrimage to Moscow to express their belief before the public opinion of the world that after the triumph of dualism the Slavs had their only hope in Russia. The German Liberal "majority" of the Parliament soon remained alone, all the other nations deserted the assembly which they regarded as incompatible with their national liberties. Only later they came back when the "permanency" of the Dualistic system became manifest.

So the emigration of the Slav souls from the monarchy began early and the conviction grew that their fate could be alleviated only by an international complication. These feelings were strengthened not only by the romantic Pan-Slavism of the epoch, but the Czechs, exasperated by the dualistic system, soon found an effective protector in French public opinion. A series of enthusiastic and brilliant French writers became patrons of the Czech cause and their sympathy was not only due to the successors of the Hussites but it was also in accord with the French *Realpolitik* which knew very well that the German-Hungarian dualism against the Slavs must inevitably lead to a bulwark of a Pan-Germanist imperialism whereas a federalized monarchy would be incapable of carrying on any kind of an aggressive German policy.

Not only was the hatred of the Czechs aroused under the injustices of the dualist constitution against Austria but even in the ranks of the hyper-loyal southern Slavs a growing distrust became manifest in consequence of the fact that simultaneously with the Austro-Hungarian compromise, a new Hungarian-Croat compromise was forced on the Croatian nation which, according to southern Slav public opinion, made a constitutional development of the Croats and Serbs impossible. Thus the Austrian and the Hungarian pseudo-constitution was completed with a Croatian pseudo-constitution which got an artificial majority only with the help of a packed diet in Zagreb. From this time Croatian public life was always in an open or hidden state of absolutism which under the twenty years régime (1882–1903) of Count Khuen Héderváry applied the worst methods of the Habsburg *divide et impera* system, fomenting national hatred among the nearly related Croats and Serbs.

Among the Slavs of the monarchy only the Poles became real beneficiaries of the dualistic system because the Austrian government urgently needed their help to get a workable majority in the Austrian parliament in order to renew the economic and military compromise with Hungary every ten years. In order to secure their assistance Galicia gained, if not a jural, at least a *de facto* state independence: the Polish *Szlachta* (the noble class) got an almost unlimited opportunity for the development of Polish cultural life and for the economic and political exploitation of the Ruthenian half of the country. In this manner the dualistic constitution—according to the plastic expression of Professor Schücking—created two *privileged* nations (the German and the Magyar) two *mediatized* nations[1] (the Polish and the Croatian, which in spite of its pseudo-constitution, still had a sufficiently extended local autonomy). In face of these aristocratic nations

---

[1] Mediatized is the term applied in the old German public law to those territories which stood not directly under the control of the empire but only indirectly through the intermediary of their feudal lords.

the other nations of the monarchy played only the rôle of third-class peoples which did not even have a proper name in the constitutional frame but figured as a somewhat confused conglomeration under the anonymous title *die im Reichsrate vertretenen Königreiche und Länder* (kingdoms and countries represented in the parliament).

But not only the Slavs felt as a heavy burden the pressure of the dualistic system; the nations of first rank themselves entered with very mixed feelings into this marriage of political interest. The liberal Germans, the most cultured element of the monarchy in those times, distrusted from the beginning the dualistic system. The more thoughtful elements of the Austrian-Germanhood understood very well indeed, that they won only a pyrrhic victory in the dualistic compromise. Ignatz Plener, one of the outstanding leaders of the German liberals, called the new constitution a monarchy on short notice *(Monarchie auf Kündigung)* and another liberal talked of the *Königgrätz of the parliamentary system* thinking of the anti-democratic institution of the so-called Delegations. And the compromise was not yet settled when in an anonymous and sensational booklet a "German-Austrian" predicted the dissolution of Austria as a consequence of the dualist constitution. For the very moment in which all the other nations would be surrendered to the Magyars in the eastern half of the monarchy, the bloody events of the Revolution of 1848 would repeat themselves: against the unjust supremacy of the Magyars not only the nations of Hungary would rebel but also the Czechs, the Poles, and the southern Slavs, who would demand the same constitutional independence as the Magyar upper classes possess. Under such conditions the historical necessity of Austria would become a senseless slogan. On the contrary the life and peace of the nations and states of Europe would depend on the dissolution of Austria.

And two years after the toiling through of the dualistic system Adolf Fischhof, the great independent political thinker previously quoted, called by his contemporaries the sage of Emmersdorf, with the whole force of his political wisdom, admonished the leading circles of the dangers of the dualistic policy. He wrote:

None of the great nationalities of Austria could secure in itself the existence of the monarchy but each of them can endanger the Empire by its resistance. Every one can act destructively but *to proceed constructively can be done only with all united.* . . . .

The existence of Austria could only be based on the principle of justice.

It is therefore a vital interest for a state of nationalities to spare the feelings of its peoples, and to keep away from them everything which would give the impression of a domination of strangers, and it would be advisable to comply with their desires as far as its own safety permits. The state therefore must give them the guarantee that one nation will not be subordinated to the other but each will be coordinated in order that they should not march as parties against one another but as allies side by side in a common cause, for national unity in a Nation State is the harmony among nations in a Nationality State. . . . .

Such a supra-national state would also be in the well-comprehended interest of the Germans. And the great prophet admonished his contemporaries to regard the example of Switzerland. He recalled the truth, already announced by some German liberals several decades previously, that Switzerland is a republican Austria in miniature whereas Austria is a monarchistic Switzerland enlarged. But what a difference in the inner social and cultural life of the two countries!

However, in addition to considerations of the inner policy, international points of view demanded also the up-to-date remolding of the Monarchy not in the spirit of force and constraint of the Dualistic system, but according to the principles of a popular federalism which alone could achieve peace among the nations. The real mission of the monarchy would be toward the East. This mission could not be accomplished by a centralized Austria. Every growth in power of such a monarchy at the lower Danube or toward the southern Slavs could only paralyze the more advanced nations living in it, without giving an advantage to the uncultured peoples with which it would come in contact. The situation would be quite different when the monarchy would become federalized and would thus give the opportunity to the peoples outside the monarchy to join their kindred nations already living within its boundaries. Never was the Austrian problem presented with such lucidity to public opinion, and the axiomatic proposition of Fischhof, ". . . . *centralization only makes the nations centrifugal; let us decentralize and they will become centripetal . . . . ,*" may be regarded as the veritable key to the Habsburg problem. The neglect of these principles, in the last analysis, ruined the monarchy.[2]

Not only in the ruling German nation were mighty currents opposed to dualism, but also in Hungarian public opinion (though the leading classes of Hungary enjoyed most of the advantages of the new system) there was a growing party which abhorred from the beginning the dualistic constitution as unfit for the complete independence of the Hungarian state. However, not only national chauvinism fostered this conviction but there were far-sighted men who feared the artificial nature of the dualistic system. The great leader of the Hungarian Revolution of 1848, Louis Kossuth himself, made an ardent protest from the solitude of his exiled life against the new constitution which would inevitably arouse the wrath and hatred of the Slavs against the two privileged nations. At the same time he repeatedly

[2] This prophetic book, *Österreich und die Bürgschaften seines Bestandes* (Wien, 1869), should be read by all the students of the Habsburg problem.

admonished Hungarian public opinion that Hungary's independence
from Austria would remain a dead letter as long as the Hungarians
would not guarantee equal freedom to all the other nations living
with them. This chief dilemma of the Hungarian national policy will
be treated elsewhere. I would only emphasize at this juncture that
from year to year it became more difficult to maintain this constitution and every critical observer could clearly see that it could be
maintained only by a corrupt and restricted electoral system, by open
ballot, and by terroristic procedures in the administrative and military machine. Nay, at the beginning of our century this anachronistic sham parliamentary system itself proved to be incapable of safeguarding the dualistic order. When a majority came into the Hungarian parliament with a program to give a more ample sphere to the
Hungarian national army the sovereign, called by the servile press of
the country the "most constitutional Emperor of Europe," did not
hesitate to dissolve the legislature by armed force (February, 1906).
It became manifest that the dualistic system could be maintained only
by open absolutism against the overwhelming majority of the people
of the monarchy. The pyramid on its head became more and more
unstable and not only the base but the apex as well began to revolt
against the system. The ruling Magyars attacked it even more vehemently than the Slavs outside the constitution.

The psychology of this strange phenomenon (which became one
of the deepest causes of the dissolution of the monarchy) will be analyzed later. Here I wish only to observe that there were from the beginning keen observers in the surroundings of the Emperor who foresaw the catastrophe which the dualist constitution would bring into
the monarchy and who made a desperate effort to put the decaying
pyramid on a new basis. This endeavor was further corroborated by
the conviction that the German unity in the Reich could influence in a
dangerous manner the German people of Austria. Victor Bibl writes:

> It became a conviction of most members of the dynasty that it was to
> the very interest of the existence of the monarchy to divide the Germans
> in two halves and to commit their tribe in the Sudets [mountains between
> Prussia and Bohemia] to the reliable custody of a Bohemian-Czech state.
> In this manner the possession of the Bohemian countries should appear
> by their Slavization less desirable to the Hohenzollern state.

But as always under the rule of Francis Joseph, a new emergency
in the external policy was needed to enforce a new turn to the internal
policy. In February, 1871, fourteen days after the proclamation of
the German empire, Francis Joseph appointed Count Hohenwart as
his premier, who, with the co-operation of Albert Schäffle, the brilliant
German economist and sociologist, tried to take a definite step toward
the federalization of the monarchy. Since the German hegemony was

definitely lost for Austria after the final triumph of Prussia, Habsburg renewed his Slav sympathies. To prepare for this achievement, the electoral law was extended. The government lowered the property qualification for the franchise and, with the help of the so-called *Zehnguldenmänner* (the ten-florin men), the way was open toward political assertion to new masses of citizens, with the clear understanding that the enlargement of the franchise was equivalent to the destruction of the German hegemony. For the beginning the chief endeavor was the reconciliation of the Czechs, and indeed Schäffle was successful in making a compromise in his famous *Fundamentalartikel* with the Czech leaders as a result of which the Emperor, in his solemn decree, , promised to the Bohemian Diet to lay down the coronation oath as a symbol of the acknowledgment of the rights of the Czech crown. And the ninth point of the articles delineated these rights in the following manner:

All the affairs pertaining to the Kingdom of Bohemia which will not be declared as common among all the kingdoms and countries of the empire belong in principle to the legislation of the Bohemian Diet and will be administered by the Bohemian authorities.

At the same time a draft of a nationality law was presented to the diet guaranteeing the full equality of the German and Czech people in the kingdom. It was announced as a cardinal proposition that in the future only such officials and judges as speak and write both languages will be appointed. And lest the national equality should not remain a dead letter, provision was made that the diet should be divided into national sections.

These fundamental thoughts carried out in detail and combined with an appropriate revision of the dualistic compromise would have signified without any doubt a new period in the history of the monarchy. By them the door would have been opened toward the federalization of the empire under the maintenance of the community of those affairs which touched the common interests of all the nations. But the Germans were so much imbued with the thought of their hegemony and they felt the planned bilinguist administration to be such a burden that they considered the reform plans of the government an attack on themselves; the Fundamental Articles were called "Destructive Articles" and Vienna was stirred to an almost revolutionary mood. This current alone would not have been sufficiently powerful to oust Hohenwart but at the same time the Hungarian leaders, trembling for the Dualistic System and allied to Beust, made such a vehement resistance against the new constitutional scheme that the Emperor lost heart and abandoned the whole plan of reconciliation by dismissing the Hohenwart cabinet. In vain Schäffle demonstrated in the conference, presided over by the Emperor, how modest and cautious his issues were, and how remote they were from the Swiss or American plan of confederation. Even a faint approach toward a mild scheme of federalization aroused the nervous indignation of the privileged nations.[3] So, ultimately, the Prussian victory over the French gave a final stabilization to the Dualistic Constitution and Count Michael Károlyi is right in his assertion that the System of Dualism was the consequence of two battles: *Königgrätz* laid the foundation for it; *Sedan* consolidated it.[4]

This short-lived Hohenwart-Schäffle intermezzo was the only serious and broad-minded attempt, since Kremsier until the dissolution of the monarchy, which, in the petty atmosphere of the Habsburg policy, without principles and without moral scruples, showed a real path toward the solution of the national problem. Its failure was a fatal misfortune for the monarchy not only because it did not attain its purpose but because the Emperor with his light-minded promises drove the Czechs to exasperation and strengthened their anti dynastic feelings. From this moment until the last hour of the monarchy the sheer struggle of interests among the various nations made a real constitutional life impossible because every nation felt it more important to gain for itself the so-called "national advantages" (the establishment of new schools and universities or the acquisition of administrative jobs) than to defend the common constitution. On the contrary, the nations were not unwilling that the Emperor should apply paragraph 14, his right for emergency decrees, by neglecting parliament, supposing that they would get for their indulgence certain national recompensations. As a matter of fact the general tendency of evolution could not have been other than to strengthen the power of the Slav majority to the detriment of the former German hegemony. The economic development of the various nations, their cultural expansion, and every extension of the franchise necessarily broke a stone each time from the citadel of the German hegemony. This inevitable process led toward Pan-Germanistic and anti-Semitic mass currents, the more so as the German liberal party during its long government sacrificed entirely the social interests of the big masses to the leading financial groups, mostly Jewish, a tendency which resulted in the formation of a Christian socialist anti-Semitic party under the energetic leadership of Karl Lueger, the later mayor of Vienna (1897–1910).

The lack of any constructive aim in the national policy found a cynical expression in a saying of Count Taaffe who, during fifteen years, was the leading exponent of a policy of slow Slavization that

[3] The details of this significant episode were stated with great moral sincerity by A. E. F. Schäffle himself, *Aus Meinem Leben* (Berlin, 1904), two volumes.

[4] *Fighting the World* (New York, 1925).

"all the nationalities should be maintained in the same well-tempered dissatisfaction." This was the new addition to the old policy of the *divide et impera* in the era of sham constitutionalism. But the most dangerous consequences of this sham constitutionalism became manifest in the direction of the foreign policy, which, closed from all popular opinion and true parliamentary control, put the nations of the monarchy before a *fait accompli* in the most important issues. Among these diplomatic chess moves nothing was more fatal than the occupation of Bosnia-Herzegovina (1878) and its final annexation (1908) which made the dual monarchy the most hated enemy in the opinion of the southern Slav peoples. By this policy the Habsburg monarchy became *an openly anti-Slav power* and this change found immediately its diplomatic expression in the defensive alliance concluded between Austria-Hungary and Germany (1879) which in four years was extended to the Triple Alliance. This policy which later the Serb custom war, initiated by the big landed interests of the monarchy, and the artificial establishment of the impotent Albanian buffer state, envenomed still further, made the Habsburg monarchy the chief obstacle of the Jugo-Slav efforts for unification. The haughty and imprudent words of Count Andrássy after the Congress of Berlin: "The doors of the Orient are now opened for your Majesty," clanged in the ears of the Jugo-Slavs like an insult and aroused the jealousy of Russian absolutism. Immediately after this "diplomatic triumph" of the Hungarian statesman, the acute eyes of Adolph Fischhof detected the real significance of this event which he compared with the catastrophe of Königgrätz. He wrote:

Andrássy is our political Benedek [the general who lost the battle against the Prussians]. Covered by the fog of his preoccupation, as his unfortunate compatriot by the fog of Chlum, he was enveloped and attacked by the enemy in the rear, without even divining it. And this diplomatic defeat is far more menacing than the former military disaster; for this diminished only our power, but the latter endangers our existence.[5]

And to the extent that the dissatisfaction of the Slav peoples of the monarchy and of the Hungarian nationalities grew, it was further nourished in the same measure by this general excitement which the anti-Slav foreign policy of the monarchy aroused. I shall devote a separate chapter to a more detailed analysis of this connection because this fatal convergence of the outer and inner policy in the southern Slav question which foreshadowed its terrible dangers during the last three decades of the monarchy led with inevitable logic to the catastrophe of Sarajevo and to the World War. Francis Joseph

[5] Quoted by Joseph Redlich in *Kaiser Franz Joseph*, p. 351.

was undoubtedly not entirely unconscious of these dangers, for the war party of the monarchy under the energetic leadership of Conrad von Hötzendorf often alarmed him with the desperate accentuation of the necessity of a preventive war with Serbia and Italy. These same circles admonished the Emperor that the military coercion of the enemies of the monarchy alone would not suffice if, at the same time, the monarchy would not receive a new constitution in the spirit of federalization. But the Emperor was incapable of deciding himself either for war or for any important constitutional issue though he considered a future conflict inevitable. He could not realize the extreme gravity of the southern Slav question for Austria and the growing dissatisfaction of all the nations with the dualistic constitution. The crowned bureaucrat and enthusiastic officer became too old to comprehend the real vital issues of his peoples. In this manner *Schönbrunn*, the residence of the senile Emperor and his court, came in a more and more vehement conflict with *Belvedere*, the residence of the heir apparent, Francis Ferdinand.

The long reign of the Emperor, covering the lifetime of three generations, became a veritable fate of the monarchy. In the last decade of his life he was transformed into a rigid dualistic state-machine incapable of understanding or even of hearing any new or opposite political conception. The word of Trialism (a tendency to remold the dualistic monarchy into a trialistic structure by building up a Jugo-Slav state) was not even allowed to be mentioned in his presence. Similarly the dissatisfaction of the Hungarian nationalities were entirely disregarded among his intimates and it was assumed that they were perfectly happy. Generally speaking all disagreeable news were consistently held back from him. He never had an intimate conversation aside from the highest members of the aristocracy and of the military staff. He regarded his ministers as lackeys of a higher rank with whom he had intercourse only under the strictest formalities. His hostility and contempt for the press, which he regarded as a dirty business, was proverbial. In the last years of his life his entourage held him so strictly under its sway that sometimes (as I know from a reliable source) extra copies of the newspapers he read were printed lest the true news should excite his majestic nerves. And the older he became the more the hereditary qualities of absolutism became manifest as against the superficially acquired qualities of constitutionalism. General Baron von Margutti, who worked in his cabinet, noted many intimate traits of that rigid Spanish atmosphere which surrounded the Emperor.[6] When he was compelled to abandon the Lombardy, even in those hours of the catastrophe he did not forget to secure the

---

[6] *Kaiser Franz Joseph. Persönliche Erinnerungen.* (Wien, Leipzig, 1924).

right to appoint during his lifetime the cavaliers of the Iron Crown, the symbol of the lost province. If he wore the uniforms of his foreign regiments, he applied meticulous care that they should correspond to the latest prescriptions. This scrupulousness sometimes approached the comic. For instance, when his daughter Gisela, the Bavarian princess, appeared at the imperial table, the Emperor wore the star of the Bavarian order of Saint Hubertus and he expected his staff to wear their Bavarian distinctions. This mentality was manifestly very remote from reality and the deep necessities of modern life. His one-sidedness was further augmented by his greatly developed susceptibility against the disagreeable reminiscences of the past and by his almost inhuman rigidity toward the sufferings of common beings. A short story narrated by the private secretary of Francis Ferdinand in his memoirs throws a gleam of light on the whole psychology of the Emperor. A colonel who lost his leg at Königgrätz came before him for an audience asking for an official appointment, being incapable of providing for his large family with his modest pension. The Emperor received him gracefully and asked him where he lost his leg. The colonel answered, "In the battle of Königgrätz," to which the Emperor rudely remarked, "Well! sir. We lost that campaign and you will be remunerated for it!" A man of such a moral atmosphere, how could he understand and rightly measure the sentiments and aspirations of the subjugated national minorities?

But the quality which made his individuality entirely unfit to understand and appreciate the real character of all mass problems was his rigidly anti-democratic personality. The people and the middle classes were entirely alien to him as men of a minor rank and only of incidental importance. The following episode, reported by the same author, speaks more than volumes about the true atmosphere of his period and about his so-called correctly constitutional attitude so much vaunted during his life by the leading articles of the newspapers of his realm. According to the court etiquette Doctor Kerzl, his physician in ordinary during many decades was required to wear a frock coat on every occasion in which he met his imperial patient. One night the Emperor had a serious catarrh and suffered under great respiration troubles. His old lackey ran very anxiously for Dr. Kerzl. The doctor in his excitement took only his lounging coat and ran to the Emperor. But the patient as soon as he observed his doctor, though scarcely capable of taking his breath and with a face almost blue from the coughing-fit, with a final effort made a rejecting gesture toward his physician and shouted the single word, "*Frack!*" (frock coat).[7] In

[7] Paul Nikitsch-Boulles, *Vor dem Sturm. Erinnerungen an Erzherzog Thronfolger Franz Ferdinand* (Berlin, 1925), pp. 47–48.

this single word we realize the pulsation of the whole atmosphere of absolutism and at the same time the feeling, not without grandeur, of that grace-of-God origin which defies death rather than transgress the rule of Spanish etiquette.[8]

[8] Since the completion of my manuscript three monographs were published on Francis Joseph by Eugene S. Bagger (New York, 1927), by Joseph Redlich (already quoted) and by Karl Tschuppik (Hellerau, 1929). These important and very different contributions, both in conception and personal attitude, did not alter my understanding and evaluation of the rule of Francis Joseph in the main things. The trait which mostly strikes the reader in the biographies of Redlich and Tschuppik is the fact that the Kaiser became so much a governmental institution and organ that his personality almost disappears. In spite of the monumental and comprehensive quality of Redlich's work and in spite of the journalistic acuteness of Tschuppik, one scarcely feels a human being behind his "state-life"—without conceptions, without principles, entirely devoted to the traditional dynastic interests. And this presentation is not the fault of the authors, but it rather clearly expresses the pathological rigidity which the "Habsburg structure" has assumed in its last true representative. And when Bagger tried to humanize this figure with the help of more intimate anecdotes and reminiscences, one has the feeling that in spite of the method of the psychology of Adler which he sometimes brilliantly applies (see the relation of the Kaiser to his tragic brother Maximilian) the picture of his intimate character does not become clearer, but sometimes assumes an almost grotesque, inhuman, and sinister quality which he scarcely possessed.

CHAPTER XVII

DAMNOSA HEREDITAS

Perhaps on some pages of the previous analyses the reader may have the feeling that, in the reconstruction of the historical atmosphere, I was too much impressed by my personal experiences during the catastrophe of the monarchy and projected them in an undue manner upon the remoter past. In proving my point of view I shall now adduce two crown witnesses in a true sense: the two heirs apparent of the monarchy, Rudolph and Francis Ferdinand, both tragic heroes of those historical forces which were developed from the products of the envenomed methods of the Habsburg polity.

The details and true causes of the love-tragedy of Mayerling (which put an end to the young life of Crown Prince Rudolph) are still not sufficiently elucidated and are contradictory. This fact itself is highly symptomatic. The spirit of the secret police was so strong in the monarchy, the publicity of the press so weak, and the prestige and the will of the court so feared that an event of such enormous consequences which shook public opinion in the monarchy and all around the world could be veiled until the end and held back from a historical criticism. But the fact that such a keen spirit and well-intentioned will as the late royal son had, perished amid the joys of a crude revelry or after it, or in a common suicide with his mistress, or by a foreign hand: this fact alone shows very clearly how a personality of a greater caliber was without a sphere of activity and without creative hope in the vast realm of the Habsburgs, and how he was abandoned to his disorderly passions.

Crown Prince Rudolph, the intimate friend of liberal publicists, scholars, and politicians, was a typical *libre penseur* of the last decades of the nineteenth century who considered a wealthy bourgeois class as the real foundation of the state, who sympathized with the Jews, and who had a certain aversion against the Slavs as supporters, in those times, of a clerical policy. He was an ardent enemy of feudal aristocracy because he realized that this class was becoming more and more a parasite caste, performing no serious work in the interest of the state. As every Habsburg, he laid the utmost stress on his army and was a passionate antagonist of the Hungarian aspirations for independence, though he liked the Magyars and he felt comfortable in the society of Magyar aristocracy. In the time of the vehement manifestations in consequence of the Hentzi affair (when Magyar nationalistic feeling was very tumultuous) in 1886, he advised a military demonstration against Hungary. The Hungarian problem as a social

problem too occupied his attention very much, and in connection with
some anti-Semitic outbursts in the eighties of the last century, he
wrote the following clear-sighted lines:

> Poor Hungary. We stand before an epochal crisis. Things cannot go
> on in this manner. The so-called Jewish persecution and the Croatian com-
> plications demonstrate that the Slav problem becomes more and more pres-
> sing. Hungary is badly administered. It has no good bureaucracy, it has no
> solid basis. This is a country like Russia or Turkey. Like those countries,
> it also lacks a rich and cultured middle class. It has only a wretched offi-
> cial class, it has many Israelites and poor people, impoverished peasants,
> and a big populace. The real basis of a modern state, an extended bourgeois
> class, is absent. Opposed by Croatia, such a country will not be capable
> of undertaking the struggle with success, and to solve the inner situation
> there is wanting the necessary state power. Hungary faces a complete state
> decay, and the time will come when we shall be compelled to interfere from
> Vienna.[1]

Aside from the uncertainty of the inner situation, the Crown
Prince felt equally certain that the monarchy would come into una-
voidable conflict with Russia. Oscar von Mitis, the able biographer of
Rudolph, writes:

> A deep anguish took possession of him at the thought of the approach-
> ing great war and he always complained—here he was again entirely mili-
> tarily motivated—when an occasion was omitted to strike the future
> enemies separately.

Though he disliked the Prussians and though his entire sympathy was
for French culture, his fundamental political thought remained still
that the monarchy could not be maintained without the protection of
Prussian bayonets. For there must come a final reckoning with Russia in order to open the way toward Saloniki, the expansion toward
the Balkans being the special mission of the monarchy. And in this
connection the Crown Prince favored more an economic and a cultural than a political expansion. That such a tendency would be un-
reconcilable with the old constitution and structure of the monarchy
seems to have been sufficiently realized by Rudolph. The mission of
Austria should be to carry on the culture of the West toward the
East, German culture, but not German force. On the contrary Austria should protect in their national aspirations the southern Slavs
as peoples who came last into the sphere of Western culture and to
whom belonged the future.[2]

[1] Other acute observations will be found among his letters published under the
title, Kronprinz Rudolf: *Briefe an einen Freund, 1882–1889* (Wien, 1922).

[2] Mitis, *Kronprinz Rudolph,* Neue Österreichische Biographie (Wien, 1925),
Vol. II. Since I wrote this sketch of the figure of the Crown Prince a more complete
biography has been published by the same author (*Das Leben des Kronprinzen Rudolf,* Leipzig, 1928). His more extended researches only corroborate the main lines
of his provisional biography. It is now very probable that his death with his mistress

Almost a generation later the same problems were faced by the other heir-apparent, Francis Ferdinand (the nephew of the Emperor), however, no longer from a liberal but what later was called in the monarchy a Christian-Socialist point of view. He was a deep-dyed absolutist, almost on the verge of atavism. He inherited the distrustful melancholy of Emperor Rudolph II, and the signs of a mental disorder were soon manifest. He despised liberalism and progressive intellectualism; his only confidence was in his army, in his church, and in the loyal part of feudalism, but at the same time he keenly understood that his throne could not be maintained without satisfying the social and particularly the national aspirations of the broad masses of population. He hated the old governmental and military system of Francis Joseph because he saw that the dualistic constitution swelled up from day to day the centrifugal forces of the monarchy and forced it into a struggle of life and death with the Slav peoples who were coming more and more under a Russian protectorate. Also, from strictly personal points of view, he pitilessly despised the court of his uncle which exposed him and his morganatic wife, Countess Sophie Chotek, the later Duchess of Hohenberg, to a long series of humiliations and which forced on him a renunciation under oath of all the rights of his children to the throne. It was a widely known fact that often very vehement conflicts arose between him and the old Emperor. Not seldom he burst forth that he had "no more value than the last lackey in Schönbrunn" and he said among other sinister presentiments that "sometime I will atone for the faults of the governmental system."

But his more ardent hatred was directed against Hungary, because in the Hungarian problem he perceived little else than the Magyar chauvinistic policy which suppressed the non-Magyar nationalities and which, denouncing every endeavor for federalization as high treason against the fatherland, barred the way toward the solution of the southern Slav question. That this Magyar megalomaniac policy was only a result of deeper social causes, especially that it was a consequence of that feudal and clerical system of the monarchy with which Francis Ferdinand was in complete sympathy, this connection did not stand clearly before the protector of oppressed nationalities. But he saw one point with an almost terrifying lucidity,

---

was a double suicide similar to one which he contemplated in 1888 with another woman. An though a hereditary burden in his nervous and moral character is evident, the new analyses of von Mitis make the political factors in his tragedy even more manifest. The spectre of the approaching Russian war, of the necessity of a preventive war with Italy, of the dissolution of the monarchy, of the irreconcilable antagonism between the two parts of the empire (which implicated him, as it seems, in a secret plot with the Magyar feudalism), his growing exasperation against the petrified policy of his father . . . . all these dangers of the empire undermined his frail nervous system and pushed the liberal atheist into a kind of sensuous nihilism.

namely, that if he should not be successful in solving the Jugo-Slav problem of the monarchy, giving full guaranty of national development for the southern Slavs, then this problem would destroy his whole empire. At the same time he perceived very distinctly that the chief obstacle to any reasonable solution was the dualist constitution which gave to the Magyar ruling class great privileges detrimental to other peoples. Under the sway of this conviction he threw more and more passionately and demonstratively into relief his point of view as protector of the Slavs and of the other oppressed nationalities and in every single cause he accentuated this attitude. For instance before the delegation of a small nationality of the monarchy, he expressed his surprise that there was any trace of loyalty left toward the throne when the government was tolerating the unjust procedures toward this people.[3] When the Cuvaj absolutistic régime threw Croatia and the whole Jugo-Slav world into despair and exacerbation, he used vehement utterances against the system. He denounced repeatedly Magyar supremacy and declared that Hungary was maintained in quite medieval conditions by a small oligarchy and that the Magyar nobility was working continuously against Austria and the monarchy as a whole. This attitude of his was so sincere that it proved to be more powerful than his greatest passion, his strictly Catholic conviction. When, in 1913, the Greek Catholic bishopric of Hajdudorog was established by the Roman Curia in accordance with the intention of the Hungarian government, and against the Rumanian desires, as a religious instrument for a policy of Magyar assimilation, Francis Ferdinand wrote a sharp letter to the papal nuncio in Vienna in which he uttered, among others the following statement:

I am surely a good son of the Roman church but when the issue concerns the most elementary rights of the peoples, whose destiny I shall lead some day with God's help, I pay no heed to anyone and I do not abstain from severing my connections with the Holy Father, if he should exercise his powers in a direction which would run contrary to my intentions, devoted to the welfare of my future *Landeskinder*.[4]

Francis Ferdinand was indeed a tragic personality. If his character in his narrow fanaticism, in his sometimes petty and greedy business transactions, in his rigid haughtiness (all his kindlier feelings were exhausted in his marital and family relations), in his almost pathological hunting passion, near to bestiality, cannot arouse our sympathy, still, any observer striving for justice will acknowledge that he became a martyr of a world problem, the importance and fatal conse-

[3] Other characteristic details concerning the motives of the Archduke will be found in R. W. Seton-Watson's book, *Sarajevo: A Study in the Origins of the Great War* (London, 1925).

[4] Albert Freiherr von Margutti, *Vom alten Kaiser,* pp. 123–24.

quences of which he grasped more clearly than any of his predecessors and to the solution of which he wished to sacrifice his whole life and energy. In the interest of this supreme aim he was even inclined to experiment with universal suffrage and democratic reforms, in order to overthrow Magyar feudalism which he hated not so much for its anti-social as for its nationalistic and particularistic character. As a matter of fact the moral and political structure of this revolutionary protector of the nationalities cannot be portrayed in too reactionary a light. The director of the war archive of Vienna, Colonel Glaise-Horstenau, gave us a vivid and impartial picture of his atavistic and unbalanced personality. He considered universal suffrage a sheer absurdity. He regarded the ministers as private employees of the sovereign who could be dismissed when he liked. He had a distrust for strong and independent personalities. He persecuted corruption but he had no scruples against building roads for the benefit of his private property with state money. He threw over the railway schedules according to his mood and closed important highways to the public in order to satisfy his hunting passion. He hated the Jews, the liberals, the Free Masons, and the Socialists. He used the words "to make order," "to put down," "to shoot," and other similar menaces as extensively as William II did.

In this moral and political atmosphere he did not hide his intention to overthrow the dualistic system and the Magyar hegemony as soon as he came to the throne, and to be willing to apply force should it be necessary. Colonel Brosch, one of his intimates, the director of his military bureau, had elaborated the minutest details of a plan to establish order by armed force in the monarchy, especially in Hungary, should his anti-constitutional measures arouse a revolutionary excitement. He was determined not to take the Hungarian coronation oath as long as he would not be capable of putting the constitution in harmony with his conviction. All these details were widely known during his life. But what public opinion, even well-informed opinion, became acquainted with only after his death and which makes his fate almost symbolically tragic is the fact that a few months before the catastrophe of Sarajevo he had in the drawer of his writing-table a fixed plan of a manifesto which he intended to publish the very moment when he should occupy the throne of Francis Joseph. In this manifesto, obviously influenced by the constitution of the United States, he gave a solemn declaration of faith in favor of the principle of national equality in the monarchy.

This promise was an open and decided determination against Dualism and the details of this plan were recently published by an intimate of the dead prince. Francis Ferdinand contemplated a federation of the nations of which members of equal right should be the

Germans, Magyars, Czechs, Slovaks, Poles, Ruthenians, Rumanians, Croats, Slovenians, and Italians. Where the linguistic frontiers were doubtful, there a plebiscite based on a very simple and just criterion should decide to which state group the various popular elements should belong. "The economic freedom of the individual, the political freedom of the nations, or mutual dependence in the economic sphere . . . . independence in the political sphere . . . ." these would have been the leading ideas on which the United States of Great Austria would be based.[5]

And if one may legitimately doubt whether such a dismemberment of the monarchy on a strict linguistic line was a workable plan and whether the strictly feudal and militarist environment of the archduke would have been capable of the realization of such an immense conception, nobody can deny the truly Napoleonic measure of this construction (and really Francis Ferdinand had an enthusiastic veneration for the Corsican dictator, whereas he regarded Metternich as the bad spirit of the monarchy). But, what makes him a true tragic hero, is the lethal irony of destiny that he was killed by the same southern Slav world the emancipation of which was his chief endeavor. At the same time the attempt at Sarajevo is symbolical from another point of view. It was the old Emperor, the representative of the rigid antiquated structure of the monarchy, who sent to death—though unintentionally—the representative of the new spirit, the hated presumptive heir of his throne whom he did not understand at all. According to the careful analysis of Victor Bibl, an impartial authority on this subject, the heir-apparent had been admonished from different sides that because of the intensity of the Jugo-Slav revolutionary movements, he would risk his life if he should attend the maneuvers in Bosnia. Not only the traditional hatred against Austria was at the boiling-point but the visit of the Archduke at Sarajevo which was previously made public and which coincided with the national holiday festival of the Serbs, the Vidov-Dan (St. Vitus's Day) had the effect of a provocation to Jugo-Slav public opinion. Indeed, the heir-apparent did not remain untouched by these admonitions. He even expressed his scruples before the throne itself but there an appeal was made to his sense of duty and the performance of the task was resolutely demanded. Mr. J. N. Jovanovič himself, the Serbian minister at Vienna, informed Ritter von Bilinski, the joint finance minister, of the perils of the contemplated military enterprise. The maneuvers in Bosnia were regarded by the Jugo-Slav public opinion as simply the rehearsal for an attack against Serbia as the mortal enemy of the monarchy. And what makes the Viennese plan even more strange and startling is the

[5] Johann Andreas Freiherr v. Eichhoff: *Die geplante Gründung der "Vereinigten Staaten von Grossösterreich"* (Reichspost, March 28, 1927).

fact that the military authorities of Bosnia and the secret-police organization made such insufficient preparations for the protection of the Archduke and his wife that seven would-be murderers were counted at the criminal investigation after the catastrophe, and Archbishop Stadler of Sarajevo was really justified in saying that the Archduke was sent into a regular avenue of assassins. General Margutti, the intimate of Francis Joseph, said that the inadequacy of the precautions in Sarajevo "baffled every description." And one of the Archduke's Hungarian adherents, Joseph Kristóffy, a former minister of interior, wrote that when the Emperor had come to Sarajevo there was a detective behind every tree and when the Archduke came, there was an assassin behind every tree.

The events after the murder were also very strange and disconcerting. One of the first declarations of the Emperor after hearing of the catastrophe were the stupendous words: "In this manner a superior power has restored that order which I unfortunately was unable to maintain,"[6] (that was surely an allusion to the morganatic marriage of the prince and to the dangers that the order of legal succession could have been altered by his will in the future). At the same time his chamberlain, Prince Montenuovo, took such measures concerning the burial, as came near to an insult to his memory and his dead wife, the courageous comrade in his deadly adventure. The circle of the Archduke was so exasperated by this and similar rude procedures that General Auffenberg called them "a fanatical attempt to eliminate the dead Archduke as speedily as possible from the sphere of his former activity and, if this could be attained, from the memory of his contemporaries." On the other side the enemies of the dead prince both in Vienna and in Budapest laid not the least restraint on their joyful feelings over the event, which seemed to liberate themselves from many political cares.

Under the sway of these and many other similar facts some observers both in Vienna and in Budapest held the opinion that an influential court camarilla which hated the Archduke sent him intentionally to death. As far as I can estimate the situation, this hypothesis is as erroneous as the other which regards the Sarajevo plot as the criminal work of the Belgrade government. The truth is that on both sides the person of the Archduke was equally hated (the old Austrian dualistic gang hated in him the daring reformer; the Serb nationalistic revolutionary organizations, the man who was determined to solve the Jugo-Slav problem not on a Great-Serb but on a Great-Croat basis, not outside but inside of Austria) and perhaps this latent subconscious attitude corroborated the traditional *Schlamperei*,

---

[6] *Vom alten Kaiser*, pp. 147–48.

this Balkan slovenliness which was not only confined to the Balkans but began at Vienna.[7]

All these facts, however, have only a symptomatic interest for us as the outburst of the old struggle between Schönbrunn and Belvedere, between Dualism and Federalism. For we should not overemphasize the importance of Sarajevo as the immediate cause of the World War. Every competent observer of the situation will agree, I think, on the point that if the catastrophe of Sarajevo had been avoided June 28, 1914, it is more than probable that the unsolved problems of the various irredentas would have led earlier or later to other outbursts and the world-conflict would have arisen from another incident. One can affirm without exaggeration that Francis Ferdinand was a man sen-

[7] The admirable work of Professor Fay on the *Origins of the World War* (New York, 1928) did not change my opinion concerning the responsibility of the leading Viennese circles in the catastrophe. He dismisses, it seems to me, too easily the charge of criminal negligence, raised against the Sarajevo authorities. Not only the intimate circle of the Archduke was shocked by their behavior, but also such men, whose objectivity cannot be doubted, as the German Ambassador von Tschirschky, General Margutti, General Auffenberg, Colonel Glaise-Horstenau, Victor Dihl, and others expressed similar opinions. Many newspapermen who ran to Sarajevo immediately after the murder were quite emphatic on this point. One of them, the brilliant Hungarian correspondent to *Az Est* gathered a long list of facts for the demonstration of the *mala fides* of certain governmental organs and intended to write a whole book on his experiences, but the World War, the Revolution, and his internment in Russia impeded the finishing of the work. But the chief witness in this matter was Francis Ferdinand himself who, after the first attempt against his life, accused passionately the mayor of Sarajevo. I feel that Professor Fay wrote an almost exclusively diplomatic history, whereas the social and moral atmosphere of the period is somewhat neglected.

At the same time he overstates the responsibility of Serbia though there can be no doubt that some officials and officers of the Serb government were involved in the plot. However, he overemphasizes the artificial character of the assassination and does not take sufficiently into account the overheated revolutionary atmosphere and the wild southern Slav temperament for which life does not count very much. (See the murder of King Alexander and his wife and the recent tragic case of Mr. Radić and his followers!) He accepts willingly the demonstrations of loyalty to the Archduke, knowing not how such manifestations were arranged. He accepts, somewhat too credulously, the Protocol of the military tribunal of Sarajevo as an entirely authentic document. After the scandalous experiences of the Friedjung, and Zagreb trials in time of peace, it is scarcely critical to suppose that during the excitements of the war and when the Austrian militarists were seeking for the justification of their war, a fair trial could be expected. Finally, he underestimates the admonition given by Ambassador Jovanović to the Austrian minister of Finance, Mr. Bilinski, because he spoke only of the possibility of an outburst of disloyalty in the army and did not mention the danger of private assassins. Professor Fay forgets that such an announcement on the part of the Belgrade government would have aroused such indignation among the super-excited nationalists of Serbia and especially in the menacing organization of the *Black Hand* that the position of the Pasić government would have immediately become untenable, perhaps even the lives of the ministers endangered. Besides the declaration of the Serb minister at Vienna was not a hiding, but an overstating of the dangers. For in a country where the loyalty of the imperial army becomes doubtful, it is manifest also that the danger of anarchistic elements must be guarded against. One should not forget that the revolutionary outbursts against oppressive Austria became so vehement that the German Kaiser did not dare to attend the funeral of his murdered friends at Vienna due to the warnings of Count Berchtold.

tenced to death by volcanic social forces, and the ghost of plots and attempts persecuted him and his environment almost constantly. That this opinion is not a gratuitous a posteriori assumption but is founded on facts will be evident from an episode which demonstrates that only by a hair did he escape death in 1906, in a plot prepared by another irredenta. In the issue of July 25, 1926, of the *Neue Freie Presse* an eyewitness narrates the following incident: When the last part of the *Wocheinerbahn*, the second railway communication between Vienna and Trieste, was opened to the public, the Archduke was charged with the representation of the Emperor at the festival, because, considering the vehement Slovenian and Italian irredentist agitations in these parts of the country, the council of ministers vetoed the original plan according to which the Emperor personally was to assist in the solemn opening. The correspondent writes:

During the trip Francis Ferdinand was in a state of great excitement. He was continuously nervous and sought to master his uneasiness by a forced cheerfulness and by harmless stories, as if he had forebodings of his end. He lived in a constant fear of attempts, which was further heightened by the plot against the life of the grand duke of Russia committed several days before. With a definite forethought, in the dailies and in the several localities where the train was stopping the precise hour of the arrival and departure of the train was announced. Exactly on time a special court train went through the stations . . . . but it was occupied only by some police organs. The train on which Archduke Ferdinand and his suite traveled followed many hours later, and this precaution was well motivated indeed. Though the track was rigorously guarded, a bomb exploded in a great tunnel which the empty special train passed through and killed four gendarmes. This is a fact, which in those times was strictly concealed and which remained unknown to the public until now. . . . .

But the catastrophe could have reached him not only here but during the later festivals at Trieste. The same correspondent narrates that there, too, they did not dare to arrive on time, but only several hours late, when darkness had begun to fall.

The police of Trieste took almost Tsaristic measures of precaution. From the railway station along the embankment to the palace of the governor where the archduke took lodging, every house was crowded with policemen who were ordered to keep all the windows closed from the early morning through the whole day, and to hold every person at home behind closed doors after two o'clock in the afternoon. There was a constant fear that from one of the windows a bomb could be thrown. The governmental edifice was full of secret police. The widely opened windows of the state apartment looked down on the piazza. Suddenly a crowd of a hundred people marched there and began to sing irredentistic songs and to shout: "Abasso Austria, Abasso Habsburg, Abasso il Principe!" ("Down with the Prince.")[8]

[8] Ludwig Klinenberger, *Die Eröffnung der neuen Alpenbahn nach Triest.*

The situation remained unchanged or got even worse during later times. In almost every part of the Jugo-Slav provinces, especially among the university youths, were some exalted personalities who were in favor of terroristic acts to attain Jugo-Slav unity.

On the basis of such widespread facts everybody who knows the exuberance of the Italian and southern Slav temperament and those traditional feelings which the Habsburg rule piled up in the consciousness of these peoples, will realize that Sarajevo was not an accident but only a link in a long catastrophical chain of mass-psychological excitements. It was rightly said with a pun not quite adequately translatable that the real cause of the World War was not the young unbalanced Princip, the murderer, but the traditional principle of the monarchy which put under yoke the national aspirations and possibilities for development of the various peoples of the country.

CHAPTER XVIII

A HISTORY OF CONFLICTING SENTIMENTS

One who looks over again dispassionately and without bias all those mass-psychological problems, the hopelessly incomplete picture of which I have tried to present on the preceding pages, will clearly understand that this special something which characterizes most of the history of the monarchy compared with the history of other states is the fact that we do not find a single common ideal or sentiment which could have united the peoples and nations of the monarchy in any political solidarity whatsoever. This history was not a common undertaking of the nations but mostly the struggle of the Habsburgs against the particular national consciousnesses and the struggle of these national consciousnesses among each other.

Regarding the problem of the existence of the monarchy from a mass-psychological point of view, its solution would have meant the establishment of a psychic synthesis which would have been capable of reconciling the special experiences and personal events of the various nations into a superior common unity, of building up a historical Pantheon in which the heroes of all the nations could have shaken hands with each other in the light of some new common ideals which could have reduced to a common denominator the antagonistic experiences and struggles of the various peoples of the monarchy. Such an ideal, however, was totally absent from the history of the Habsburgs and lived only in the consciousness of some few isolated, outstanding spirits who realized it almost personally in their own souls with a distinct sentimental and intellectual accent. Something was felt of this ideal by Joseph II and his enthusiastic collaborators, the Austrian and Hungarian lovers of the *Aufklärung*, and the same ideal in a clearer and more differentiated form later stood before the eyes of such heterogeneous but in this respect equally motivated personalities as for instance Dr. Fischhof, the German revolutionary; Baron Eötvös, the Hungarian state philosopher; Palacký, the Czech historian; Ludovit Gaj, the Illyrian apostle; Jancu, the Rumanian fighter for independence; or in a later generation, Hermann Bahr, the critic; Joseph Redlich, the historian; Karl Renner, the socialist; Baron Szilassy, the diplomat; Conrad von Hötzendorf, the warlord; and Masaryk, the "realist," to mention only some outstanding representatives of this type. All these men felt something of the international solidarity of the peoples of the monarchy and visualized very positively that out of these various energies something greater and

more brilliant, more many sided and humane, could have been formed
than the exclusive ideal of the nation states.

Regarding from this point of view the process of dissolution of
the former monarchy, it could be expressed in the following few words:
*The Empire collapsed because the historic tradition of each nation
stood in a hostile and hateful way against the historical experiences
of the other nations.* The monarchy collapsed on the psychic fact that
it could not solve the problem declared insoluble by a Hungarian
statesman: it could not establish a reciprocity among the different
experiences, sentiments, and ideals of the various nations. Nobody
saw more clearly this delicate connection than Hermann Bahr who
with the intuition of his visionary imagination wrote the following impressive words:

. . . . Elsewhere the descendent has an easy task in entering the heritage of the fathers because it contains a single will and a uniform sense.
In us, however, about a hundred voices of the past, the struggle of the
fathers is not settled, each must decide it anew, each must choose among
his fathers, each must for himself pass through the entire past again. For
the past of our men has this in particular, that none of them was ever
closed, nothing was fought out, the father recedes before his son, but in
the grandson he goes ahead again, nobody is or feels secure, each feels himself divided, our men have too much inborn. Elsewhere one can confidently
follow his fathers, we cannot do this because our fathers, disunited
among themselves, make an appeal to our judgment. *Je ne puis vivre que
selon mes morts,* ("I can only live according to my dead ones."), Barrès
said. But we cannot live according to our dead ones because we would be
torn apart since each of our dead ones tears in an opposite direction.[1]

Indeed this was the problem, but not a single serious step was undertaken to solve it, because it became perfectly insolvable as we
shall see. Under such circumstances only a purely mechanical solidarity, a kind of "vegetative symbiosis," could have been established
among the various nations of the monarchy and every true sentimental, organic connection was lacking. If Renan is right in his famous
definition which he gave concerning the concept of a nation—and he
is right without doubt—: *Or l'essence d'une nation est que tous les
individus aient beaucoup des choses en commun et aussi que tous aient
oublié bien des choses,* then it is manifest that the history of the monarchy is the most opposite imaginable pole of such an evolution: *here
the peoples did not do anything in common and they did not forget
anything.*

[1] *Dalmatinische Reise* (Berlin, 1909), pp. 95–96.

PART III

THE CENTRIPETAL FORCES: THE EIGHT PILLARS
OF INTERNATIONALISM

CHAPTER I

THE CENTRIPETAL FORCES AND
THEIR GENERAL DYNAMICS

After the summary reconstruction of the historical and moral atmosphere of the former monarchy the reader will be enabled, as I hope (however incomplete and rudimentary the picture of the mass-psychology currents may have been), to follow with attention and comprehension the work and development of those forces which determined in the ultimate analysis the fate of the monarchy. These forces may be roughly divided into two big groups. The one is composed of those, which in consequence of their historic structure or social position or their transitory purposes, worked consciously, semi-consciously, or unconsciously for the continuing and the maintaining of the monarchy. These we shall call *centripetal forces.* Into the second group belong those forces which endeavored with greater or less consciousness to relax or to dissolve the imperial tie. These will be called the *centrifugal forces* of the monarchy.

It is manifest that this division, like all scientific classification, is to some extent an artificial and arbitrary one as it severs processes which in reality are closely connected. This inherent artificiality of our division is further corroborated by the fact that each social force in history has a certain particular dialectic movement, by which itself and the institutions created by it receive, in the course of its historical development, such new tendencies as at the beginning were alien to it. For instance, we witness very often that the forces of social conservation exercise revolutionary effects in their later developments or —on the other hand—that the forces, revolutionary at the beginning, later become factors of maintenance and conservation. The somewhat vague and mystical Hegelian dialectics of the thesis, antithesis, and synthesis point toward a connection of social forces which has some analogy to the phenomenon just emphasized. I have here no space to enter into the discussion of this interesting transformation. The only thing which I would like to accentuate at this juncture is that almost all the centripetal forces with which we shall become acquainted in the following analysis, developed in their later course centrifugal tendencies in one direction or another.

The same is true regarding things from the other point of view concerning the centrifugal forces. We shall soon see that the most conspicuous centrifugal forces, the forces of national awakening and integration, were at their first appearance not at all forces of dissolution or segregation but they became such only because, instead of being prudently canalized and utilized in the interest of the state, they were pushed back by violence or fraud and were forced into a direction which was irreconcilable with the unity and development of the old state.

If we now turn to the analysis of the centripetal forces, we shall soon see that they all represented a certain *supra-national* tendency in the old monarchy, that they emphasized the unity and the common aims of the empire in face of the separatist and particularist attitude of the various nations and nationalities. They represented, therefore, common ideals and a solidarity above the nations in that league of nations against its own will, in that race struggle which was called the Habsburg monarchy. They were really international forces amid the national overclaims and individualisms. The dynasty, the army, the aristocracy, the Roman Catholic church, the bureaucracy, capitalism (represented in its majority by Jews), the free-trade unity, and (however strange it may appear) socialism were the real pillars of Austrian internationalism. These pillars incorporated very powerful organizations and vital tendencies. That they proved in spite of their strength to be too weak for the maintenance of the Habsburg structure is due partly to that dialectical movement of which we already spoke, partly to the fact that all these forces did not constitute a united front but stood very often in a desperate struggle with each other. Among the eight pillars of internationalism only the first four (and even these incompletely) were united in a real political architectural scheme. The other four were conflicting with the first four and even with each other on very important points. In this manner the eight internationalisms were rather isolated bulwarks of the Habsburg fortification than a construction directed by the same strategic plan.

We must now consider these pillars in their psychological and sociological structure.

CHAPTER II

THE DYNASTY

What was said in the historical part has already put into sufficient light the fundamental rôle (both from the point of view of initiative and of conservation) of the Habsburg dynasty in the whole drama. In the given historical constellation the political aspiration of the Habsburgs was strictly determined and this ideal remained almost unchanged for four centuries. However different individualities, in value and in capacity, may have been the possessors of the Habsburg throne and however different their method was in the realization of their aims, their purpose in its fundamental character remained the same from Maximilian I until the passing of the last Habsburg. Every keen observer who was occupied with the problem of the monarchy has felt that there was something rigidly constant in the intellectual and moral structure of the Habsburg dynasty. Under the sway of this predominant impression it became a habit to speak of the monarchy simply as of Habsburg: Habsburg did this or that; that was the will of Habsburg; that was the fate of Habsburg; so was the decision of Vienna, etc. Above the single individual, however tyrannical a despot he may have been, there hovered always the spirit not only of the biological but of the social inheritance: the *Habsburg structure* as a quintessence of all those traditional values which led and directed the dynasty and the supreme military, diplomatic, and bureaucratic organizations combined with it (the Austrian *camarilla*, as it was called by its exacerbated enemies, the Hungarian leaders for independence). These almost constant elements of the Habsburg structure from which all the others can be easily deduced are religious mysticism, Catholicism, militarism, and the universalism of the Habsburg dynasty.

In his religious *mysticism* each Habsburg felt himself connected by a special tie with divinity, as an executor of the divine will. This explains their almost unscrupulous attitude in the midst of historical catastrophes and their proverbial ungratefulness. *Der Dank vom Hause Habsburg* ("the gratitude of the Habsburg family") became a widely spread slogan. They broke their most solemn promises very often and cast away their most loyal and self-sacrificing men as squeezed lemons, if, in so doing, they could somewhat alleviate a transitorily difficult situation. When, for instance under the pressure of revolutionary Vienna, Metternich was dismissed and was compelled to flee, nobody in the whole court asked him where he would go and how he could live. Naturally, in the robust naïveté of their dynastic mysticism, they could not even face the problem of whether the interest of their peoples and countries would coincide with the interest of their patrimonial possessions. It was well said by a Slav statesman of the monarchy that the key and the deepest spring of the Habsburg policy was at all times and under all circumstances the eager instinctive desire for *plus de terres*. Beginning with the immense land hunger of Rudolph until the occupation and annexation of Bosnia-Herzegovina, that was always their leading motive, disregarding not only the national interests of the peoples but even the problem of the unity and cohesion of the state. The principle of the *l'état c'est moi* remained until the end the exclusive maxim of the monarchy unmitigated by any other consideration.

This mystical imperialism was completely welded with the ideology and aspiration of Roman Catholicism. After a brief hesitation, Habsburg adhered with his entire force to the cause of the counter-reformation and became its leading power. The spirit of Protestantism emanating from a popular soil, making concession to critical reason, emphasizing at least *pro foro interno* the rights of the individual, hurt instinctively the Habsburg soul in its absolutist and transcendentalist impatience. This attitude was strengthened and matured by the political constellation. In Germany the reformation became the ideological support of the estates and other particularist interests fighting the imperial power, whereas Habsburg in this vehement controversy could not miss that big religious and historical force which his connection with the papacy bestowed upon him. Besides, the Protestant movements (as in Hussitism) often became a religious background for the nationalistic tendencies, giving for the first time to the great masses of the population the Bible in their mother-tongue. And .such a conscious national spirit would have endangered the work of political unification which was the chief endeavor of the Habsburgs.

This endeavor had the character of a political universalism. Among their immense conglomeration of peoples and countries the Habsburgs would not suffer political or religious divisions. All which was local, autonomous, or determined by a particular popular entity appeared suspicious and antipathetic to them as a sign or danger of feudal rebellions. As a matter of fact the Habsburgs felt and thought in a supra-national manner as a consequence of their extremely complicated blood-mixture,[1] of their Catholicism, and of the exceedingly variegated ethnic composition of the monarchy. It is not true as we have already demonstrated that the Habsburg dynasty appeared as

---

[1] In a curious document concerning the pedigree of Francis Ferdinand his 2,047 ancestors are carefully enumerated. Among them are German 1,486, French 124, Italian 196, Spanish 89, Pole 52, Danish 47, English 20, and four other nationalities. *Ahnentafel Seiner Kaiserlichen und Königlichen Hoheit des durchlauchtigsten Herrn Erzherzogs Franz Ferdinand.* Bearbeitet von Otto Forst (Wien u. Leipzig, 1910).

a consciously and consequentially Germanizing power. They were really remote from such a tendency. There were Habsburgs who did not even speak German. Even those Habsburg emperors who sometimes fostered a policy of Germanization were not led in their efforts by any nationalistic point of view, but their measures were dictated by the interest of unification and universalism of their empire.

The spirit of militarism in the Habsburg empire was far more than in the western states an instrument for the maintaining of inner cohesion than of a defense against foreign aggressors. Indeed, from its beginning until its last hour, the solidarity of the monarchy was based on the imperial army and in the case of any serious crisis the Emperor acted with the consciousness that he would always be capable of cutting the Gordian knot of political troubles by the sword of his military power. In two things the Habsburgs never understood a joke, for which they always cast away the mask of the pseudo-constitutionalism of the later epochs, whenever popular will became opposed to them; the one was their autocratic disposition with the army, with *meine Armee;* the other was the direction of the foreign policy which put *faits accomplis* before the so-called "Delegations" of the two parliaments, devoid of any serious sanction. The Habsburg monarchy remained until the end the model state of military absolutism, beside Russia and Prussia, even its power being perhaps more conspicuous here because the feeble force of public opinion, divided in continuous national struggles into eight or ten parts, could not counteract in any serious manner the exclusiveness of the imperial will.

This unchecked force of the dynastic idea found its final and solemn formulation when Emperor Francis sensing the growing fragility of his German-Roman empire took up the title of an Austrian emperor. This state act and two years later in 1806 his final abdication from the German imperial dignity were emphatic formulations of the patrimonial state and of the fatal conception that the idea of the state is identical with the person of the monarch. The whole empire was simply regarded as the extension of the former *Hausmacht*, the patrimonial possessions of the dynasty.

This purely dynastic conception of state found its psychic expression and political incorporation in the Viennese imperial city, the unique splendor of which was more than the center of a sumptuous court life. It was, in a certain sense, the moral synthesis of the whole empire. The most various ethnic and cultural elements met here in the furnace of the imperial life and the old German culture obtained under very strong Slav, Italian, and Magyar influences, a special Austrian color. This cultural synthesis called *Alt-Wien* carried out its effects on the whole monarchy; it became the basis of a general bourgeois culture which attracted into the sphere of its influence the higher nobility and the richer middle classes of all the countries and provinces. Vienna became everywhere the chief leader of fashion and elegant social forms and its unrivaled sway found expression in both the architecture of the churches and public buildings and the castles of the Hungarian, Czech, and Polish nobility. The two most characteristic aesthetic manifestations of this typical Austrian culture, the *Baroque* and the *Biedermeier*, were vivid expressions of the artistic sensibility of two distinct social types: the heroic and the police absolutism. The brilliancy and the grace of the court remained the chief conductor of every talent and ambition for generations. The distribution of nobilities, dignities, orders, this application of the *divide et impera* principle in the social and family field was quite an important support of the Habsburg rule. In addition, it became a custom to establish in the more conspicuous countries and provinces *branches of the imperial court* by the location there of some archdukes who assumed a certain local and national hue, used the language of the country, and became moderated protectors of the local patriotisms. These local Habsburg exponents exercised a smoothing and reconciliatory influence on the recalcitrant national nobility and administered, one might say, *per procura*, the imperial grace.

Beside the homogeneous culture of the higher classes, there emanated from Vienna another powerful factor of spiritual cohesion, the literary German language which had the function of a *lingua franca* among the different nations of the monarchy. From the Czech mountains to the Adria, from Innsbruck to Czernowitz, anyone could travel unhindered with the help of the German language. There were everywhere some officers, officials, merchants, or intellectuals who spoke this language fluently and there was not a single hotel or inn where the traveler would not have been understood in this language. This effect of the German language and culture radiated far into the Balkans and that gave the impression to some superficial observers of a conscious Germanization. But what made the process so general and more and more extended was not a constrained or artificial propaganda but a deep economic and cultural necessity which could only be satisfied by the intermediary of the German language, as a consequence of its historical contacts. As a matter of fact German became the language both of science and of capitalism. The connecting force of the Viennese university which, during generations, had educated the best lawyers and physicians for the monarchy, was very marked until the end as a species of spiritual solidarity. The German language was a veritable bridge which connected Slavs, Magyars, and Rumanians with the Western culture. This unifying force of the German language would have become without doubt even more general and intensive if it had not had attached to it the conception of the Habsburg state coercion, and the struggles of the awakening peoples against German centralization. The truth of this assertion is demonstrated by the fact that many of the leaders of the national *risor-gimento* in the various countries of the monarchy began their liter-ary career in the German language. Also the example of Bukovina strengthens this argument, where the Rumanian and Ruthenian masses were not confronted by larger German settlements and by an artifi-cial German hegemony. Under such circumstances the world-language nature of German could gain prevalence without hindrance and one could witness the interesting situation of the two rival nations adopt-ing spontaneously German as the language of internal administra-tion.[2]

Especially for the more backward peoples of the monarchy who lived under Turkish rule, the Austrian imperial connection was, through long periods, almost the only source of a cultural initiative and social organization. It was the imperial center which introduced the first elements of European agriculture, school, and administra-tion into the barter economy of feudalism, and which erected the first ramparts against the merciless exploitation of the peasant masses. The struggles among the various nations of the monarchy even strengthened the force of the absolutist monarchy. The national idea pushed back in the Austrian half of the monarchy the idea of consti-tutionalism.

This situation created the atmosphere of a hypocritical loyalty in the whole monarchy. Each nation, even the most rebellious, tried to emphasize continuously not only its legal fidelity to the dynasty, but even its enthusiastic devotion to it. We witnessed very often real out-bursts of loyalty paroxysms and loyalty competitions which under-mined both civic consciousness and individual honesty. A character-istic little episode will illustrate the situation. In 1909 the official Hungarian paper wrote the following in connection with the seventy-ninth birthday of the Emperor:

The often severely tried Hungarian nation stands in its fidelity to its crowned Master without example and above all comparisons. No other nation of the universe can surpass the sons of the Hungarian people in their loyalty coupled with self-sacrifice.

This Byzantinism was the more nauseating for all sincere men because a few years previously, if not the Hungarian people, at least the feu-dal parliament continued the most exacerbated struggles against the king in the so-called military questions, and this beloved king did not hesitate to drive asunder this hyper-loyal representation by armed force. Not only the Magyars but also the Czechs and Italians uttered very often expressions of an exaggerated loyalty after vehement and exasperated criticisms when they saw a chance for imperial power to

[2] For details see the highly interesting book of F. Kleinwaechter, *Der Unter-gang der österreichisch-ungarischen Monarchie* (Leipzig, 1920), pp. 171–73.

help or promote their national aspirations. No one had better characterized this basely servile atmosphere than Louis Mocsáry, a close adherent of Kossuth and a brilliant leader of Hungarian independence saying: "In this vast conglomerate called the Austro-Hungarian Monarchy on both sides of the Leitha, countries, provinces, nations, denominations, social classes, groups of interests, all being factors in political and social life, put up to auction their loyalty for the grace of the court."

This tendency, demoralizing public opinion at large, was strengthened by another which was the system of protection and distribution of posts and dignities which the members of the imperial family often exercised for the compensation of their own gang. The recommendation of the smallest archduke had a greater influence in awarding public services than the work and result of a whole life. The luck of the archducal instructors and godchildren became proverbial. This archducal influence was not seldom a derivatory one exercised by certain officials, even lackeys, of the archdukes. There circulated many anecdotes in this connection emphasizing the fact that sometimes the word of an old lackey was more influential than the determination of a state minister.

In spite of all these tendencies, slackening the force of cohesion of the monarchy, one cannot deny that the prestige of the imperial family was until the end more than a purely military or power position but it was based on very widely spread mass feelings in many more traditional parts of the monarchy under the influence of the school and the church.

CHAPTER III

THE ARMY

The most powerful pillar of the Habsburg fortification which from its beginning until its breakdown represented the chief supporter and maintainer of the monarchy was the imperial army. This army from the beginning until the end—however masked it may have been by constitutional veils—was and remained under the autocratic disposition of the monarch uninfluenced in the really important issues by the parliamentary system. This army was the most individual creation of the dynasty, and it was further strengthened and developed from generation to generation. Especially the genius of Eugene of Savoy was a powerful influence in replacing the old feudal and mercenary spirit of the army by a more modern one. However, the patrimonial character of the army continued even in more recent times when the system of general conscription was introduced, carried on by feudal administration. Almost until the constitutional era the procedure of levying remained untouched, especially in Hungary where the conscription could not have been effectuated without the concurrence of the country administration very often in a fight against Vienna. This levying was not at all apt to promote any kind of civic consciousness. So writes the historian of the Austrian state administration:

In the levying places the levyers chose as their headquarters an often frequented inn or an isolated tavern. When a man came in who seemed suitable for military service, he was invited to drink and they tried to make him intoxicated. If he could be seduced to put on a soldier's uniform for the sake of experiment or to wear a military helmet or to pronounce a *vivat* to the emperor he was immediately considered to be enrolled.[1]

It is manifest that such and similar procedures could not augment in the people its love toward the Habsburg army. Especially in the soul of the Hungarian people this practice appeared both as foreign domination and social oppression which popular songs carried further from village to village. One of these plaintive rhymes I heard personally in my childhood from the lips of the peasantry: "Now among us they enlist with a rope. . . . . The poor fellow is carried away by force. . . . . Five or six sons of the rich are undisturbed. . . . . An only son of the poor is captured. . . . ."

But even when the army was put under the semblance of a parliamentary control by the introduction of universal military obligation,

[1] Ignaz Beidtel, *Geschichte der Österreichischen Staatsverwaltung: 1740–1848* (Innsbruck, 1896), I, 64–65.

the army remained in its bulk, in the formations of the so-called *gemeinsame Armee*, "joint army" (in opposition to the local territorial formations, the so-called Austrian, Hungarian and Croatian *Landwehr* which remained in closer contact with the parental soil), the exclusive army of the Emperor and the dynasty, and reflecting their own spirit. Indeed the joint army remained until its end a "dynastic body guard," "a school of loyalty." And whatever our feelings may be concerning this institution we cannot deny that it attained its purpose during a long period. Unfortunately this state solidarity promoted by the mightily consolidated ideology of the army was an exclusively dynastic one, which became more and more confronted by the democratic and national consciousness of the various peoples. The overwhelming majority of the officers remained until the end German, a Germandom, however, which signified no national tendency but similarly, as in the bureaucratic and diplomatic organization, it represented only, so to say, the diplomatic language of the whole Habsburg joint monarchy. This spirit, the spirit of the Habsburg patrimonial state, was not only preponderant among the German element but also among the officers belonging to other nations who followed in a rather unconscious way the principle of Emperor Francis, being the patriots not of their nations but of the Habsburg dynasty. The following anecdote narrated to me by the editor of a great Hungarian daily characterizes very well this curious atmosphere. A correspondent of this paper interviewed Admiral Horthy, the present governor, in the military headquarters during the war, on the occasion of his being wounded. The glorifying report ended with the delicate allusion of the correspondent that manifestly the thoughts of the wounded hero abandoned often the imperial headquarters and returned to the Hungarian fatherland, the old home of his ancestors. When the next day the Admiral read the article, he was very much disappointed by its conclusion and repudiated energetically the imputation of the correspondent, saying to him ". . . . Remember that, if my chief war lord is in Baden, then my fatherland is also there! . . . ."

This spirit was nourished with a suspicious care by the leading elements of the army, especially by the Emperor himself. They visualized perfectly clearly that, while the national struggles of the monarchy were becoming more and more acute, their state could be maintained only on condition that they would be successful in keeping their army immune from the spirit of national quarrels. However dynastically and rigidly separated from the constitution the Austrian army may have been, two of its traits were in advantageous contrast with the general Austrian and Hungarian life. One is that there was less caste and class spirit than in the so-called fashionable offices of the monarchy which were a hotbed of the aristocracy and plutocracy. Especially, after the fatal catastrophe of 1866, the leading circles of the army became aware of the fact that the aristocratic cult of the former army led to a hegemony of incapacities, and the work of purification was carried on with great energy which signified the democratization of the army. In the highest military ranks, with very few exceptions, there were for many years no longer aristocrats. Among the great war lords of the last war their names are absent. "The army was too important for the monarchs to build it up—after the experiences they had—on the connections of aristocratic families. . . . ."[2] (On the other hand these same devastating influences continued in a more indirect but no less pernicious way, as we shall soon see.)

Another trait of the army which might have been a model for the public spirit of the monarchy was the delicate and tactful handling of the national antagonisms. The joint army stood both in principle and in practice on the basis of national equality. As I previously mentioned the German language of command to which the leading circles so tightly clung as the chief dogma of army leadership, was not—at least in the more recent times—a Germanizing measure but the expression of the conviction that the introduction of various languages of command would make an effective war-activity impossible. However erroneous this measure may have been, it was dictated by a national consideration only in one respect: the leading military circles were aware of the fact that the claim for a Magyar language of command and for the Magyar regiment language (which led in the last two decades of the monarchy to a very serious constitutional crisis) became the war cry for a total Hungarian independence inclined only to recognize the joint person of the monarch and serving at the same time the purpose of employing the army as a means of Magyarization. And though, since the compromise of 1867, the Emperor cared practically nothing for his former allies, the nationalities of Hungary, in spite of this, and amid the growing difficulties and dangers of the Austrian nationality struggles, the more far-sighted Viennese circles shrank from the thought that the army should be employed as a means of artificial assimilation in the Hungarian half of the monarchy. As the different national consciousnesses could be tamed more and more by compromises only and not seldom by military force (for the using of the army for the maintenance of civic order belonged to the ordinary methods of the government in Bohemia, in Bosnia-Herzegovina, in Galicia, in the Bocche, and at the electoral campaign in Hungary), it became manifest that in the very moment in which the army would be imbued by the same nationalism as the nations from which it was recruited, the monarchy would break to pieces under sanguinary civil wars. The supreme purpose remained the same, there-

[2] Acute remarks concerning this situation will be found in the excellent book already quoted of F. G. Kleinwaechter.

fore, until the last, and that was to fill the army with an exclusively
Habsburg patriotism and to maintain the nationalism of the members
of the army in a state of an *apolitical nationalism,* in the state of a
linguistic, family, or, at most, of a racial nationalism which would
have nothing to do with the political and state struggles of the single
nations.

This endeavor was really successful for a long period. The joint
army formed a real state within the state, the members of which—
especially its officers and under-officers—breathed first of all throughout their whole life the spirit of their military colleges or their regiments and not that of their mother-nations. Indeed the fatherland of
the officers' staff was the whole monarchy and not the territory of a
particular nation. It was a real educational principle in the army to
move the officers around from one country to another. These men who
lived now in Vienna, now in Budapest, now in Prague and then in
Zagreb, in Galicia, in Transylvania, in Bosnia, or in the Bocche represented a certain spirit of internationalism confronted with the impatient and hateful nationalism of their surroundings. They constituted something like an *anational caste* the members of which lived
even in their private lives ordinarily distinct from their national en-
vironments and spoke very often a special language, the so-called
ärarisch deutsch ("fiscal German") as it was ironically named by the
representatives of the literary German, meaning by it a strange linguistic mixture which does not take the rules of grammar very seriously. During a long period it seemed that this Habsburg solidarity
would remain stronger than the developing ideology of the national
solidarities. It was an interesting symptom of this supra-national solidarity that when in 1903 the Hungarian government, under the pressure of the nationalist opposition, was successful in gaining from the
Emperor the privilege for officers of Hungarian citizenship to be
transferred into Hungarian regiments, more than a thousand officers
of this category (belonging to the various nationalities) tried to
gain Austrian citizenship in order to avoid the change, because they
feared that growing Hungarian nationalism would put them in an
awkward situation from the point of view of their own nations.[3] For
a better understanding of this situation we must note that among the
forty-seven infantry regiments located in Hungary, only five were
purely Magyar whereas thirty-seven were nationally mixed. Among
these latter, in sixteen the Magyars constituted the majority, in two
they were even, but in nineteen they were in a minority. Besides, there
were five regiments in which the Magyars were scarcely represented.[4]

[3] Interesting details concerning the struggle for the army may be found in Paul
Samassa's *Der Völkerstreit im Habsburgerstaat* (Leipzig, 1910), pp. 84–104.
[4] Theodor von Sosnosky, *Die Politik im Habsburgerreiche* (2d ed., Berlin, 1913),
II, 204.

Therefore, the more vehemently Magyar nationalism came upon the stage and the more it endeavored to establish a distinct Hungarian army, or at least an exclusively Hungarian part inside of the joint army which could Magyarize the soldiers of the non-Magyar nationalities by the help of the single Hungarian regiment-language (the tongue employed in the joint army out of service was called regiment-language, playing the rôle of a colloquial, educational, and instructional idiom) and the more the ire of the Magyar opposition became exasperated with the imperial colors and emblems of the joint army the more grew the fear and apprehension of the court and the leading circles over this vehement and reckless movement.

In 1903 the situation became so acute that it assumed the character of an open conflict between the Emperor—that is to say the Hungarian king and the Hungarian parliament. At this juncture the Emperor issued his famous General Order of Chlopy (that is the name of the small Galician village where the headquarters of the maneuvers were) which in its rigid and severe formulation was almost a symbolical expression of the military policy of the imperial absolutism. The chief thesis of this manifesto read as follows:

I shall never waive those rights and privileges which are warranted to the chief war lord. . . . . My army should remain as it is now, joint and united, the strong power for the defense of the Austro-Hungarian monarchy against all enemies. . . . ."

But this rigidity augmented all the more the centrifugal forces of nationalism, for the old imperial army with its Habsburg consciousness came in an increasing antagonism not only with the Hungarian effort for independence but also with the consciousness of the other nations which felt with greater force their national purposes in all the activities of states life. The unsolved constitutional and national problems of the monarchy pressed increasingly upon the conscience of the younger officers and soldiers. The sons of those nations which continued an exacerbated struggle against each other in parliament, diets, and local administration could not co-operate in the anational atmosphere of the Habsburg army which was enveloped with the suffocating atmosphere of an artificial dynastic hothouse.

The dangers of the situation were deeply felt by the more valuable elements of the army. Especially by the head of the staff, Conrad von Hötzendorf, who, as the real conscience of the army followed with a fearful attention the manifestations of this state of mind, chiefly because he understood very well the fatal connection of the Jugo-Slav and Italian irredenta with the inner decomposition of the monarchy. In his memoir, addressed to the Emperor in 1907, he says, among other things, the following:

Relating to the spirit of the army the national problem is the most important. Only in an army in which each of the various nationalities can have the conviction of being regarded as equal in right and value can there be a common spirit and a united attachment to the great Common Cause. . . . . This equality finds its expression above all in the equal right of each nationality to use its peculiar language, in so far as it is not restricted by the necessary establishment of a common language of communication inside of the army. . . . .

But beside this connecting language everywhere the language of the soldiers must be decisive and every officer must know perfectly the mother tongue of his soldiers. And he continues:

The forceful introduction of the Magyar language in the joint army would, therefore, alienate from it all the other non-Magyar nationalities, nay, it would induce them to opposition against the army and undermine its spirit in a grievous way. . . . .

The chief end should be, therefore, according to Conrad, that "the officer, irrespective of where he originates, should feel himself at home in any place in the monarchy. . . . ."[5]

But Conrad saw more than this. He clearly visualized that this spirit could not be established inside the army as long as they did not succeed in remolding the position of the nations outside of the army. Therefore, he advised that the dualist constitution should be changed and the relation between Hungary and Croatia be put on a new basis. For this purpose universal suffrage must be introduced by compulsory means if necessary. Conrad admonished the Emperor not to permit the utilization of the army during the electoral campaign for the terrorization of the national minorities. (A procedure which led sometimes to real massacres, as it happened for instance in Galicia in the village of Drohobycz, where, at the elections of 1911, a volley was loosed upon the electorate which resulted in twenty-seven deaths and eighty-four serious injuries in order that the reign of the Polish Szlachta should be maintained over the Ruthenian peasants.) Conrad was rightly convinced that without the complete equality of the various nations the unity and combative effectiveness of the army could not be safeguarded.

Furthermore, the army not only languished through the growing national antagonisms which vehemently opposed the increase of the military budget (the leading circles spoke always more anxiously of the *Verdorren der Armee*, "the withering of the army"), but the influence of the archdukes, the atmosphere of what was called the Court-Camarilla impaired its situation for very often talentless place-hunters were put above the really worthy elements. This spirit manifested itself in its complete baseness just at the time of the catastrophe of Königgrätz and produced an episode which with the force of a *fait saillant* (as Taine called the really characteristic facts of an epoch) throws light upon the secrets of the Habsburg dissolution process.

[5] *Aus meiner Dienstzeit 1906–18* (Wien, 1921), I, 503–4.

The tragedy of General Benedek, defeated by the Prussians at Sadowa, demonstrated how the private interests of the archdukes were triumphant over the most conspicuous necessities of the state and of the army itself. Benedek was one of the most popular generals after the death of Radetzky, who enjoyed great prestige in the army. The year 1866, when the empire was harassed both by the Prussians and the Italians, found the general in Italy where he had been for several years the chief commander of the Austrian forces. He was really the best leader imaginable for the southern field of operation, who according to his own words "knew each stone and tree in Lombardy," but at the last moment the order came to surrender his post to the uncle of the Emperor, to Archduke Albrecht, and to take over the northern battlefield in Bohemia against the Prussians. Benedek protested desperately against this order, explaining that he "would be an ass in Bohemia" where he did not even know the course of the river Elbe. He was determined to return to Italy but at the last moment such pressure was exercised upon him in the name of the Emperor that he was forced to comply. The background of this absurd order was the presumption that victory over the Italians was certain whereas the fight with the Prussians was very dubious, and under these circumstances they tried to secure the glory of the former to the extremely ambitious Archduke, and the possible defeat to the general. And that is what really happened. The Archduke returned as a hero, and Benedek as the scapegoat of the catastrophe of Sadowa. Against this calumniatory campaign Benedek tried to justify himself, but he was not received by the Emperor. Later Archduke Albrecht requested and received from the general the promise that on his word of honor he would suffer all attacks without a reply in the interest of the monarchy. But scarcely had the general given his vow when an article appeared in the official journal, the *Wiener Zeitung*, which in a perfidious way put the honor of Benedek into the pillory, blackened his whole career as a war lord, and emphasized the humiliation of the monarchy as only a result of the omissions and crimes of the general. The proofs of these defamatory articles were revised personally by the Archduke and by the minister of war. In spite of this Benedek kept his given word and maintained silence. Only in his testament he characterized this procedure as "surpassing his ideas concerning law, justice, and honesty. . . . ." And in order to demonstrate the tragedy of his life, he forbade that his corpse be buried with military honors.

In a country where such dark things could have happened, the corruptive influence of the archdukes did not have a serious obstacle in the army. And though in the last decades of the monarchy, as it was previously mentioned, serious endeavors were undertaken for the purification of the army and for the checking of illegal influences (especially Archduke Francis Ferdinand and his intimate circle were very active in this direction when Conrad von Hötzendorf was chief of the staff), it still remained under the suffocating atmosphere of the autocratic surroundings. The gravity of the crisis became manifest only in the period of the World War when the great majority of the leading generals failed completely. Not without reason did the old Emperor so strongly distrust his generals. The reports of Conrad and of the other more talented generals abound in eruptions against the unfitness of the leading military circles: "All the gravity of our defeat," said General Krausz, "falls exclusively to the share of the highest leadership. . . . . Never was an army, worthy of a better fate, pushed into disaster with such light-mindedness."[6]

Not only the corruptive influences of the court weakened the army, but the spirit of class domination, too, undermined its inner structure. This influence became particularly damaging during the war when all the privileged classes of the monarchy succeeded (naturally with many honorable individual exceptions) in avoiding the dangers of the fronts in a measure which is unparalleled, as far as I know, in the history of any other country. A new kind of class struggle pressed heavily upon the whole public life of the monarchy, a silent but awfully exasperated class struggle: a conflict between those who were driven into the trenches, abused, and their last energies spent, who were frequently wounded and not sufficiently restored; and on the other hand those who, as the result of their social standing, aristocratic, plutocratic, or influential journalistic connections, were successful in dodging the real dangers of the war. They did this chiefly by two methods. The one was the institution of the so-called "indispensability" by which many thousands were without cause retained from the fronts under the pretext that their services were absolutely necessary to the country in economic life or in higher offices or in the influential press. The other was that the youth belonging to the wealthy or aristocratic classes found employment far away from the trenches within the organization of the higher commanders which were relatively seldom exposed to direct war-activity. Everybody who had occasion to come into contact with these higher headquarters during the war had the unanimous experience that many thousands of elegant and perfectly healthy young men found bodily protection in these aristocratic detachments in or near the hinterland. This crude antagonism between the ragged and untrimmed soldiers of the trenches and the well-dressed and polished orderly officers of the higher quarters (the people of the trenches called them with disgust *Etapenschweine* or "swines of the hinterland") was indeed one of those mass-psychological forces which weakened in a great measure the solidarity of the fronts.

[6] Geza Supka, *The Great Drama* (Miskolcz, 1924), p. 359. In Hungarian.

CHAPTER IV

THE ARISTOCRACY

A liberal deputy once said in the Austrian parliament the following words, which became household words of political life:

> The thought was often expressed that there were in Austria some sixty aristocratic families who conducted the state as their private enterprise and attempts were made in an ingenious way to deduce the story of Austria from this proposition. This thought has some truth in it but it is incomplete. Add to these sixty aristocratic families thirty or forty bishops and you will have the whole truth.

The foreign reader might believe that these words belonged to those plastic exaggerations which political enemies so often employ against each other, but they signified in the monarchy the complete reality proved by any careful sociological or historical survey. This aristocracy was the most decisive factor in the monarchy even in times when it lost the majority of its legal privileges. Practically, its power rivalled that of the monarch until the very end of the empire.

As the historical roots of feudalism penetrated the entire soil of the monarchy, and as its effects until the end were more elementary than in any other state of Europe, with the possible exception of Russia, it will be wise to reconstruct with a few traits the genesis of this situation. Ignaz Beidtel, the able historian of the Austrian state administration, says:

> The relations of nobility and feudalism brought about this result that the monarch could regard only a relatively small part of the population as his direct subjects; the other, the far greater part, was only indirectly under his reign but directly under the rule of the feudal estates. With this situation the possessor of several estates was a great lord. Every year he had some hundreds of free peasant lots which he could grant as he liked, and in the eyes of his feudal subjects, he was a more important person than the monarch. Under these great lords or as the people called them between 1720 and 1830, the "Greats," very often stood poorer noblemen as officials or higher servants. . . . .

The possession of fifteen or twenty villages was quite common but it was not a rarity that some mighty lord was the owner of seventy-five to one hundred and twenty villages. These "Greats" had an unlimited administrative and judiciary power over their subjects. Some of them enjoyed an almost semi-sovereign situation. For instance, the Silesian princes had the right to establish a kind of "government." They had a "court" and a regular court session. The prince of Liechtenstein

149

possessed in addition to his Silesian duchies in Troppau and Jägern-dorf, extended estates in lower Austria, in Bohemia, and Moravia.[1]

The noble estates in Hungary played the same preponderant rôle and their social and economic influence was perhaps still greater. According to a calculation, from the end of the eighteenth century the civilian and ecclesiastical lords owned from 31 to 58 per cent of the whole arable land in various parts of the country. Hungarian history is full of reminiscences that one or another feudal lord or bishop acquired immense properties in the country by sheer violence or fraud. Stephen Verböczy for instance, the famous codifier of the feudal law of the country in the first half of the sixteenth century, was capable of gaining possession of more than two hundred villages in almost every part of the country. The kingly riches of Prince Rákoczi, the anti-Habsburg leader, has previously been reported.

After the reconstruction of the whole feudal nobility on a strict Habsburg basis in the entire territory of the monarchy, the power of the aristocracy became even more preponderant because the most outstanding families were bound together by frequent marriage ties and formed, so to say, a single family of small kings. Knowing this we understand the complaints of Prince Rákoczi in his memoirs when he explains the failure of his enterprise by emphasizing the fact that the Hungarian aristocrats had married wives from Austria and Styria and some others educated at Vienna possessed hereditary estates on the borders of Austria, Styria, or Moravia and "therefore they favored with their heart the Austrians and did not wish to expose to hazard their wealth and fortunes." About half of the most splendid families lived always at Vienna and were in a continuous contact with the intentions and order of the Emperor.

It is only natural that this almost semi-sovereign power of the leading families did not cease even in the times when their old feudal privileges were expropriated and the Habsburgs succeeded in building up their own military and administrative organization all over the country. Their social and political predominance remained a fact until the end of the monarchy, based on their colossal landed properties and political privileges in the election of the diets and parliaments.

We shall analyze the economic, social, and political consequences of this colossal power in the modern monarchy in another connection, because directly or indirectly, there emanated from it some of the most fatal centrifugal tendencies which pushed the empire into disaster. At this point we must consider aristocracy from another angle, namely, as the chief representative of the Habsburg state ideal, that most conspicuous social force by which the dynasty tried to carry on its work for centralization and Germanization. The reader will remember those memorable events by which the Habsburgs partly tamed, partly ex-

[1] *Op. cit.,* I, 6–9.

tirpated the native nobility and replaced it with a loyal aristocracy. Such an aristocracy was a vital necessity for the dynasty, because, among pre-modern conditions in the times of a predominant barter-economy and a very primitive means of communication, the system of feudal patrimonial estates was, from the point of view of the Habsburgs, something like an unavoidable evil which could not be replaced by any other institution. Besides, in the reckless anarchical feudal world, Habsburg needed such a preponderant social and political power by which he could easily influence the masses of the smaller nobility and counterbalance the constant danger of feudal intrigues or peasant revolts. The political unity established by the dynasty would have been unimaginable without their help and concurrence, for instance the *Pragmatica Sanctio* in Hungary and in Croatia was chiefly their work.

But the more the structure of the monarchy changed with the evolution of economic and intellectual life and the more Austria became democratized by the more conscious rôle of the bourgeois and peasant masses (this process was in Hungary far more slow and therefore the latifundistic hegemony remained almost unshaken), the more feudal aristocracy lost its roots and became an isolated body in national public opinion. The overwhelming majority of the Austrian aristocracy remained a stranger in the soil where it was planted by the donations of the Habsburgs. Kleinwaechter, the acute analyzer of the old Austria already quoted, says:

It lost the ground, its roots did not draw their energy from the native soil, but they climbed around the trunk of the ruling house, getting nurture from its juice. And doing this the Austrian nobility surrendered itself to a singular delusion. The creeping plant which clutched tightly around the tree without which it could not live, regarded itself as the supporter of the tree. And what was a still more singular delusion: the tree itself considered the creeping plant as its powerful supporter.

But with one exception. Crown Prince Rudolph felt very distinctly that the aristocracy had outlived itself and that his empire could not be maintained on such a basis. In 1878 a book was published in Munich under the title *Der österreichische Adel und sein constitutioneller Beruf, Mahnruf an die aristokratische Jugend, Von einem Österreicher* ("The Austrian Nobility and Its Constitutional Mission: An Admonitory Appeal to the Aristocratic Youth. By an Austrian"). The author of this sensational pamphlet was the Crown Prince himself who wrote this document in collaboration with his professor and friend, the brilliant Austrian scholar, the founder of the so-called Austrian school of economy, Charles Menger. One can say without exaggeration that the reigning Austrian caste has never been analyzed in a deeper and more just way either before or after this publication. The author emphasizes the fact that nobility neglects both the administrative and the military service of the state. It proved to be unfit for military service because the military catastrophe of the monarchy (allusion to Königgrätz) was caused by the very fact that it occupied in that period all the leading positions. This nobility was courageous but entirely incapable of keeping pace with the military sciences.

The only speculation and aspiration of the aristocratic commanders was directed towards an easy, chivalrous tone in the officers corps and to educate excellent horsemen. But all organic reforms were carefully avoided. . . . . The bravest sons of Austria bled on the Bohemian battlefield as victims of this delusion. . . . .

And when a severe order of study and examination was introduced in the army, the noble youths lost all interest in the cause of national defense. These noble youths endeavored not to be accepted for military service by the recruiting officers. These youths avoided the army not only because "where the law puts the nobility on a completely equal footing with the other classes, this latter cannot serve joyfully" but also because of its "unlimited laziness" which makes them incapable of any more serious effort or examination. In the same manner nobility proved to be unfit for all such administrative functions the performance of which needs a special expertness. The same is the situation in the constitutional life, in spite of the fact that the nobility dominated the house of the magnates in consequence of their feudal privileges. Partly, because it has an antipathy for constitutional institutions, and partly, because it has inadequate faculties for it. The Crown Prince drew the conclusion that the fate of conservative thought is not in the right hands.[2]

What is the reason for this apathy and for this lack of talent? In order to discover the answer, Rudolph gives a careful analysis of the standard of life and the social customs of the nobility. He describes their life spent in revelry, concentrated around hunting and dancing parties. A life having nothing in common with the more serious problems, into which there does not penetrate either science or a more noble art. They have not even the slightest idea of the earnest struggles and aspirations of the other professions.

Another cause of the bankruptcy of the aristocracy consists, according to Rudolph, of the Jesuit education which fills the youth with the ideology of past times. From this school the young men came as strangers into life permeated not even by conservative ideas or by the love of the historical but developed abhorrence against existing legal institutions and against all cultural progress.

The conclusions of the Crown Prince and his professor were veri-

---

[2] The same thought was asserted already a generation earlier by Prince Felix Schwarzenberg, the Austrian premier, restorer of absolutism, who used to say that "there were not four men of the high nobility who would have the quality to justify the establishment of a House of Lords in Austria."

fied by the consequences almost to the last word. In the later decades
the old aristocracy was eliminated more and more from all those positions for which real work and qualification were required. After the
introduction of universal suffrage in Austria (in Hungary the old
corrupt electoral system continued), the Austrian nobility was almost
entirely turned out from parliament, in which in former times it played
a considerable rôle. Among the five hundred and twelve deputies there
were only one duke, one prince, and four counts. Also in the state departments they became rare. Only in the foreign ministry and in diplomatic service (for which, though a very high qualification was required, this examination served only as a bulwark against undesirable
bourgeois elements) remained the old hegemonic rôle of the aristocratic element. The almanac of the foreign service from 1914 on gives
the impression of the almanac of Gotha (the annual list of aristocratic families) : in the higher ranks one will not find a single member
of the middle classes.

As time passed the aristocracy became more and more dangerous-
ly the supporter of the Habsburg state idea. Its overwhelming majority developed into a leisure class, purely decorative, intriguing,
and pleasure-seeking, hermetically closed from the real interests of
the country. Whereas a smaller part of it became so fond of the constitutional order of the various countries and crownlands in which
feudal nobility had such outstanding privileges that it was the most
obstinate defender of local patriotisms. Though the ancestors of
many of them were strangers in the country, obedient creatures of the
Habsburgs, in a few generations some of these families embraced so
completely the atmosphere and ideology of the respective countries
that they often fought bitterly the central power in order to defend
the old local constitutions. For instance the ideology of the Czech
crown which was a mainspring of the troubles of the monarchy was the
very creation of the feudal aristocracy of that country.

A further pathological consequence of this undue preponderance
of the nobility was the fact that they infected with their archaic ideology the other classes too. The spirit of snobbishness and social
climbing emanated from them throughout the whole monarchy. "Man
begins with the baron." These winged Austrian words rightly characterized a society where a middle-class consciousness was entirely lacking. The higher officials after the lapse of a number of years of service were raised to the nobility; the most important of them even
acquired the baronate, and though this new nobility not backed by
landed property never had a real social prestige, it was still instru-
mental in bringing the more ambitious elements of society into a
species of moral vassalage to the feudal classes.[3]

[3] That is the reason why in the new Austria there is no liberal party and no single representative of a self-conscious bourgeois class can be found in the Austrian
parliament. The situation is almost the same in the new Hungary if one knows the
real ideology of the parties under the political show-windows.

But the most dangerous consequence of this exuberance of the nobility was that it kept the sovereign rigidly isolated, especially Francis Joseph, by the system of the stiff court ceremonials, from popular public opinion. The Emperor practically never had the opportunity to come in touch with the middle classes or the people who were never accepted by the court as equals in rights and distinctions. And on the few occasions, when, after an official dinner or reception, the Emperor was compelled to exchange some words with the representatives of the higher bourgeoisie, his so-called *cercles* (the ceremonious interrogations) moved always on the verge of the comic in their ceremonial rigidity. It never occurred that, outside of his magnates and generals, the monarch had a serious conversation with members of the other classes. I do not know of a single case where he was anxious to know the opinion of a scholar, an artist, or a leading man of industry. The very idea of the people was for him like a metaphysical conception devoid of life and blood. The awfully intricate mechanism of the court ceremonial, the sphere of influence of the orders and dignities calculated with an almost microscopic care signified in the hand of feudal aristocracy a tendency to keep back the monarch from all modern currents of ideas, from all really popular wishes. In this hothouse atmosphere, aristocracy became a really artificial creature in the state which became quite manifest in the days of the catastrophe of the monarchy. This almighty, overwealthy, and haughty class did not make even the slightest effort to maintain the sovereign, the unique source of its privileges, when popular public opinion after the collapse embraced the idea of the republic. On the other hand from day to day it was itself eliminated from the blood circulation of the new democracies, even in Austria where their feudal estates were not expropriated. Only the Hungarian, and to a certain extent the Polish feudal nobility, were capable of retaining their former leadership. The cause of their different fates was partly the fact that they were more connected with the national struggles of their countries, partly because the difference in social and cultural power among them and their backward peasantry was far greater than in the other succession states, and partly because a conscious middle class was entirely lacking in their countries. Besides, both in Hungarian and Polish society, there was also a very extended middle noble class which in face of the Habsburg aristocracy represented the ideas of national independence. This Hungarian noble middle class (the so-called *gentry*) had a preponderant rôle in the creation of the anti-Austrian separatistic movement. Therefore, it is better that its rôle be considered when we shall analyze in detail the dynamics of centrifugal forces.

CHAPTER V

THE ROMAN CATHOLIC CHURCH

Aside from its army the Roman Catholic church was the most solid pillar of the Habsburg dynasty. The Habsburg dynasty, as we saw in our historical survey, helped the church with its entire political and military force and by the most brutal instruments in the execution of the counter-reformation and in reconquering the countries which had become to a large extent Protestant. On the other hand, Rome becoming again victorious, put at the disposition of the Emperor without reserve its own spiritual, moral, and political forces in making the empire united, centralized, and loyal. In periods when the church represented almost exclusively the higher spiritual culture, its assistance had a paramount importance for it held in its hands the whole spiritual and educational organization. But even later when general lay-culture became preponderant or even when the state tried to push back the power of the church in legal and educational matters (for instance, under Joseph II or in the sixties of the last century when the Concordat was abolished in Austria and a long series of liberal reforms introduced; or in Hungary in the nineties of the last century when important laws such as civil marriage and marriage between Jews and Christians were passed in the field of church policy), the political and moral power of the Roman church did not suffer any real damage. Nay, those attacks of militant liberalism led rather to a more conscious and efficacious organization of the clerical forces.

This immense power of the church was based on several factors. The backward cultural condition of the rural masses; the colossal donations given by the dynasty which made the Roman Catholic church of the monarchy the most opulent in Europe; the imposing splendor of the Church which developed a great religious art, the brilliancy of which constitutes even now the greatest heritage of the artistic past of the empire; the establishment of humanitarian and educational institutions in times when state activity did not embrace those fields; its constitutional privileges by which it influenced, to a large extent, the legislature; the broader and more international perspective of its leading elements which far surpassed the mentality of the representatives of the Protestant churches were factors which with others, contributed to the exceptional power and authority of the Roman Catholic church.

Generally speaking one might say that ecclesiastical feudalism combined all the material powers of lay feudalism with the force of spiritual culture and with the spell of a transcendental authority.

155

But the bulk of its powers was still based on its immense landed estates which held the widest strata of peasant populations in its material and moral dependency. It is therefore quite natural that such an enormous historical and economic power had a paramount leading rôle above the masses. This power continued almost unaltered even in modern times; but feeling its unrivaled forces and privileges, it became more and more mechanical and ceremonial. It increasingly developed into a political and powerful organization, into a *political antidote* of the Habsburgs, against the rising classes of society, an organization which drew its energies less and less from the popular soil but almost exclusively from the riches and jural privileges imparted to it by the Emperor. That the majority of the social democratic working-people of the monarchy grew not only anti-clerical but outspokenly atheistic was manifestly connected with this attitude of the church. At the same time its moral influence, taken in a subtler sense, was negligible even on the masses which stood under its exclusive sway. Negligible even in fields the significance of which was overemphasized by the church. Though it carried on a constant fight against illegal sexual relations and for the indissolubility of marriage and though it was supported in its endeavor by the ideology of the court nobody could assert that the church was really successful in the raising of the moral atmosphere. At the same time when, in the first decade of the present century, it was capable of subscribing 4,500,000 names against a petition which favored dissolving marriages under certain conditions, the proportion of illegitimate births in Austria was the worst in all Europe and record figures were reached in those regions of the monarchy where the moral authority of the church was the most uncontested. Similarly the dogma of celibacy was very incompletely fulfilled by the church itself and the illegitimate family life of the country clergy was proverbial and the rôle of the clergyman's cook was a standing cheap joke in all the humorous papers.

Also in the higher spheres of education the function of the church was not favorable to the building up of a modern type of civic education. The famous Jesuit colleges in Kalksburg and Feldkirch, where the offspring of the aristocratic and wealthy classes were educated, produced a type of man characterized by a certain feudal rigidity with not much sympathy toward the modern democratic and social problems. Those older and richly endowed orders, which as the Benedictines, the Cistercians, and the Augustines represented a freer and more worldly spirit, came into a growing conflict with a very influential current of the church, led by the Jesuits who fought both the looser discipline and the outspoken German spirit and culture of these orders.

For, if we disregard certain individual exceptions which can be motivated by individual interests or predilections, we witness that the

Roman Catholic church as a whole was remote from any German nationalist tendencies and was rather inclined toward a Slavophile policy. This attitude of great consequence had several causes. Before all, the universalist spirit of Catholicism was not in favor of accentuating the differences between national particularisms. A further cause was the clear intellectual vision of the fact that to Austria, having a Slav majority, the idea of a Habsburg united monarchy of which the church was its main moral exponent was irreconcilable with the neglect or repudiation of Slav intellectual and cultural endeavors. Another factor which worked in the same direction was that the Germans, as the most cultured element of the empire, did not remain so much in the tow of the church as the Slav, Polish, Slovak, Croat, and Slovanian masses who were on a lower cultural standing and who continued to be unchanged vassals of the church power.[1] But there was another cause, perhaps even more important, which explains this pro-Slav attitude: the national liberalism of the church was only an expression of that traditional antagonism and antipathy which divided Catholic Austria from its rival, Protestant Prussia. We witness indeed that the church tried to smooth the national divergencies in the monarchy in a Slavophile direction, the more so because, until the eighties of the last century, the German hegemony was not seriously endangered in Austria. But even at the times when the struggle between the Germans and the Slavs became very acute and, when under the régime of Count Taaffe, the so-called process of Slavization began, the German clericals were the most outstanding supporters of that *Eiserner Ring* (iron circle) which made this policy workable, a coalition between all the clerical and feudal elements of Austria. Even the author of that ill-famed *Lex Falkenhayn* which in 1897 (when the linguistic decrees of Count Badeni aroused the vehement opposition of the Germans) tried to break down the obstruction of the Germans by force, was the German clerical deputy, Count Falkenhayn.

We must not forget in this connection that the German elements were always the *beati possidentes* of power and it is a well-known psychological fact that the defenders of antiquated privileges never reach the moral enthusiasm of those who fight for a newer and juster compromise. Therefore, the German elements of the clergy were of a cooler and more sober mind, whereas some Slav members of the Roman Catholic church became really the most outstanding leaders of their people in the fight for national emancipation. Briefly stated, the German Catholic clergy was solidly but not aggressively conservative, the Slav impatiently nationalistic. Without the imposing personality of

---

[1] The unique exception from this vassalage were the Czechs who, under their Hussite traditions and fighting their Catholic aristocracy of a German origin allied with Vienna had a very cool attitude toward Rome which was returned with suspicion and distrust.

the Croatian bishop Strossmayer, without his continuous and strenuous effort for the cultural elevation and national enlightenment of his people, Jugo-Slav unity is almost unimaginable. Similarly the Slovenian Roman Catholic priest, Janez Krek, played an almost apostle-like rôle not only in the national field but also in the economic and social walks of his nation. Even in Hungary where the strongly nationalistic Magyar spirit checked to a large extent the international tendencies of the church, we find a series of Roman Catholic or Greek United priests who became the chief fighters for the claims of their national minorities and some of them even dared prison for their convictions (the Slovak priests Hlinka and Juriga).

The Slavophile tendency of the Roman church was so manifest that, in 1898, Prince Lichnowsky, when he replaced the German ambassador in Vienna, in one of his reports, drew the following characteristic picture of the national and moral situation of the dual monarchy before the German chancellor.

Outside of the clerical and feudal camp there are now few Germans in the Ostmark [How significant, that in the eyes of the Prussian diplomat Austria remained still the Ostmark, the eastern bulwark of the German empire!]. Without the companionship in arms of Mr. Wolf and his comrades [this group was in those times the most vehement exponent of the Austrian German nationalism, operating with an extreme nationalistic and anti-Semetic demagogy] Germandom would be hopelessly lost in face of the Slavs and their lay and clerical protectors.

Lichnowsky emphasized the fact that this conviction has an ascendancy also in the more moderate German circles and therefore the idea of an Austro-German unification would become inevitable to which only the court and the ecclesiastical circles are opposed. Then he continues in the following way:

By what could the national state idea of the Czechs, so full of strength, be counteracted if not by another national ideal? The entirely bloodless Austrian state-idea represented only by a pitiful old man and his unruly nephew and by a Roman Slav clergy does not suffice in any case. . . . . [2]

The picture, however, drawn here by the German diplomat, was at that time too exaggerated and biased by a Pan-German point of view. The truth is that the militant Pan-German nationalism under the leadership of the talented Georg von Schönerer, was never capable of obtaining more serious results. At the end of the last century, terrified by the growing influence of the Czechs and, as a reaction against the Slavophile policy of Badeni, the German nationalists initiated the so-called *Los von Rom* ("away from Rome") movement by which Austrian Germans were invited to abandon Catholicism and to adhere to

---

[2] *Die grosse Politik der Europäischen Kabinette 1871–1914.* Sammlung der diplomatischen Akten des Auswärtigen Amtes (Berlin, 1924), XIII, 118–19.

Protestantism. That was intended as a demonstration against the Slavophile tendencies of the Catholic church and at the same time some manifestation of sympathy toward the Protestants of the German empire. But it was an open secret that the movement had in its ultimate resort an anti-Habsburg character. If the nine million Austrian-German Catholics should become Protestants, then Germany would have no further apprehension against the admission of Austria to Germany. In this manner the propaganda for *Los von Rom* assumed more and more the character of a *Los von Habsburg* but, in spite of the extreme demagogy with which it was carried on, it was incapable of capturing the greater masses of population. During a whole decade only 60,000 to 70,000 men abandoned Catholicism and became Protestant or partly so-called Old Catholics (a sect which severed its connection with Rome).

Of a far greater importance was another mass movement of a religious character which utilized the social discontent of the German small bourgeoisie and which, by means of strongly dynastical and Greater Austrian slogans, was really successful in pushing back German separatism and in fructifying its anti-Semitic tendency in quite another direction. The real soul of this movement in the eighties of the last century was Karl Lueger, the later Viennese Mayor, who combined skilfully his enthusiastic Catholicism with the interests of the dynasty and of a so-called Christian Socialism, the edge of which was mainly directed against the Jewish better middle classes the financial and political preponderance of which pressed heavily on the working-people and small bourgeoisie of the bigger cities, especially of Vienna. Lueger and his comrades succeeded, to a large extent, by maneuvering cleverly with the anti-capitalism and anti-Semitism of the masses, in creating a loyal German dynastical movement on a Catholic basis, which became the most solid bulwark of all the efforts for a united monarchy and from which was recruited the most reliable and capable staff of Archduke Francis Ferdinand when he endeavored to rebuild the monarchy on the basis of the *Gesamtmonarchie* ("United monarchy"). The movement of Lueger encountered at the beginning the vehement attacks both of the so-called liberals and of the official clericals. The former hated the anti-Semitism of the Christian Socialists and their endeavors to replace private capitalism in the field of public utilities by municipal ownership. The latter, in its feudal and courtly atmosphere, was terrified by the effort of Lueger to make the social discontent of the masses conscious and to organize it. The fear and hatred against the new Catholicism of Lueger was so great that though the people of Vienna elected him four times as mayor, the Emperor refused to give his sanction to the election. But Lueger succeeded in destroying both fronts fighting against him: Austrian liberalism and orthodox Catholicism. Christian Socialism became, both in parliament and in municipal life, a leading factor which always force-fully emphasized the unity of the state and of the army. And though the party in consequence of its closer co-operation with the popular masses was forced occasionally to play more nationalistic tunes, nevertheless, it was characterized by a certain supra-national attitude and Lueger tried to avoid national controversies in his camp. The words which he uttered on one occasion: *"Lasst's mir meine Böhm' in Ruh"* ("Leave me my Czechs in peace"), expressed with the force of a slogan his attitude toward the problem of nationality.

In spite of this with the growing national differentiation among the peoples of the monarchy, the unity of clericalism also became imperiled. It became more and more impossible that German clericalism should play the rôle of an appendix of the feudal and Slav coalition. It is characteristic that in 1909 the great Austrian-Catholic convention could not take place because the leaders of the clerical parties in the various countries felt themselves not sufficiently sure of keeping national controversies out of their discussions. But in 1912 the Viennese Eucharistic Congress became a real apotheosis of the Emperor and of the dynasty.

On the other hand the imperial house, too, remained loyal to its reliable spiritual bodyguard until the end. Everyone could assert that the more the national decomposition of the monarchy progressed, the more the sentiments of the dynasty became intense toward its Church. After the short-lived anti-clerical episode in both states of the monarchy, we witnessed a revival of clericalism, its more efficacious organization, and a systematic checking of all freer manifestations in public education and in social life. If Francis Ferdinand had reached the throne, this tendency would surely have culminated in the atmosphere of his highly bigoted wife.

The picture which I drew on previous pages of the force and tactical position of Catholicism applies chiefly to Austria. The religious situation in Hungary was somewhat diverse. That was the consequence in the first place of the difference in the numerical forces of Catholicism in the two countries. In Austria there was an overwhelming Catholic majority of 78.8 per cent which reached the total of 90.8 per cent by including the Greek Catholics. The Greek Oriental church constituted only 2.3 per cent of the population, whereas the Protestants did not reach even this figure (2.1 per cent). The Jews, with a total of 1,300,000 (4.6 per cent), lived far too remote from Christian society to influence its general religious texture. In Hungary proper, on the other hand, the Roman Catholic church constituted only a minority of 49.3 per cent which became only a majority of 60.3 per cent by including the Greek Catholics. This Greek Catholic element, however (mostly Rumanians and Ruthenians), at least in its bulk, constituted a distinct national entity which could not be regarded as a firm pillar of the Roman church. The monopolistic position of the Roman Catholic church was further counterbalanced by the fact that the Counter-Reformation was not as entirely successful in Hungary as in Austria and a Protestant minority of 21.4 per cent (14.3 per cent of them Calvinists of a purely Magyar stock) had a great influence both in political and social life and represented a freer and more liberal current of opinion. At the same time a considerable minority of Greek Orthodox, 12.8 per cent, mostly Rumanians, formed a world the ideology and aspiration of which were neither in contact nor harmony with the ruling Catholicism. Finally a Jewish minority of 5 per cent was a very active element in all the intellectual spheres of Hungarian society.

In spite of these differences in the religious surroundings the Hungarian upper clergy of the Roman church was in its great majority a no less obedient instrument of the dynasty than in Austria. Every attack of the Viennese central authority and absolutism against Hungarian independence, and every plan for the creation of a joint state was always supported by the majority of the higher clergy and the loyalty of the church toward the throne remained always exceedingly emphasized and declamatory. The maxim: "God, King, and Fatherland" continued to be a symbolical expression of its attitude in this characteristic sequence. It must, however, be emphasized that after the compromise of 1867 when a distinct Hungarian state was acknowledged by the Emperor and when the government of the Hungarian state came under the exclusive control of the Magyar upper classes, the Catholic church also assumed more and more the Magyar colors. Some of the prelates were animated by true patriotic sentiments, others were making necessary concessions to the growing tide of Hungarian nationalism and chauvinism. Taking it as a whole, the Hungarian Catholic church remained far more feudal and imbued with class spirit than the Austrian. The cause of this phenomenon lay in the fact that the greatest masses of the Hungarian population had no political rights at all and, therefore, the Catholic church had the same aristocratic and anti-democratic spirit as the Austrian church had before the constitution of a modern Christian Socialist party. The Hungarian church was not only the chief pillar of the dynasty but of Magyar feudalism too. The Catholic church did not feel the necessity, as it did in Austria, of becoming a protector of the oppressed national minorities though we here witnessed also isolated efforts in this direction. So for instance Count Ferdinand Zichy, a very influential Catholic magnate, and his group, under the sway of Christian Socialist principles, energetically defended the elementary rights of the Slovak people and some of the bishops in the Slovak territory (especially the very gifted Fischer-Colbrie) saw clearly that the policy of Magyarization would cause serious difficulties from the point of view of the church. But these currents remained almost without influence, partly because of the feudal spirit of the church.

The factor, however, which made the religious atmosphere of Hungary so distinct from that of Austria was the existence of the powerful Protestant minority to which I just alluded. This minority, especially its Calvinistic branch, was so intimately interwoven with the most energetic part of the Magyar small and middle nobility and peasantry that it was regarded by public opinion as a specific "Magyar religion" and as such it was one of the most fruitful sources of the Hungarian efforts for independence. This Calvinistic spirit counteracted very efficaciously Habsburg clericalism because the Catholic church did not dare to oppose seriously the nationalistic and chauvinistic tendencies lest it should lose the sympathy of patriotic public opinion to the advantage of the Protestant religion.

CHAPTER VI

BUREAUCRACY

In its work for centralization and unification, there was a secular effort of the Habsburg dynasty to create everywhere in its empire an absolutely reliable and loyal bureaucracy entirely under the control of its will. This effort was totally successful in the Austrian half of the monarchy, nay even in Hungary under the Germanizing centralization of the Bach system, absolutism was already very near to accomplishing the task of uniting the whole empire under the sway of a German administrative staff.

This administration, I repeat, was the most personal work of the Habsburg dynasty and aimed to eliminate all national particularism and all serious local autonomy. If the army could be called the military bodyguard of the Habsburgs and the Catholic church its spiritual bodyguard, then, the bureaucracy played the rôle of an official and police bodyguard. In the atmosphere of the *ancien régime* so full of feudal intrigues, treasons, and local interests, it was not an easy task to establish such a reliable bureaucracy and, therefore, the dynasty as a matter of fact employed by preference foreigners, very often adventurers, who sought for bread and glory in the imperial service. This historical structure of the older Austrian bureaucracy was pictured in a vivid manner by Hermann Bahr the able critic whose little book *Wien*, published in 1907, already mentioned, was immediately confiscated by the Viennese police. His most characteristic description is the following:

It became urgent to discover creatures into whom the semblance of a living force could only be blown by the breath of the imperial grace and which could be extinguished whenever wished. People nowhere at home, without fatherland, rooted nowhere, yesterday nobody but suddenly lifted up by an unseen hand, suspended in the air, as it were, in constant fear, almost on the gallows of the imperial grace. Runaways, vagrants, outcasts, forlorns, stablemen, adventurers, alchemists, astrologists, bastards, fortune-hunters, lackeys, penmen, and outlawed fugitive folks of the streets, unbound, nowhere adjusted to a social structure, everywhere at home where they had a chance to be fed. . . . . And they know always that they may be hanged tomorrow. . . . . Out of such people emanate the new races. And here was also a new colony, the colony of the imperial house. Here originated, too, a new race, the "patriots for me" of Emperor Francis. . . . . They were artificial in their thoughts and sentiments, nay even in their language. A special Austrian-German was invented, an idiom still used in our administration and by Jews who do not wish to be Jews. They were, one might say, imaginary men created from above. This people have maintained state and society through two hundred years. . . . . The nation of the Holfräte [court councillors]. . . . .

But even in modern times when bureaucracy was no longer a foreign body in the state but the accustomed career of the sons of Austrian nobility and high bourgeoisie, this caste character of the organization continued. The acute analyst of the pre-war Austrian society, Kleinwaechter, who passed his life in the Austrian bureaucracy, describes in the following manner the type of an official whom the Habsburg spirit tried to develop:

The ideal of an Austrian official was a man who had a perfect command of the German language but having no kind of national consciousness, not even a German if he happened to be a German; a man who was devoted to the dynasty as a blind instrument without a semblance of criticism. . . . . Naturally this ideal was not reached to a large extent. It flourished most outstandingly in the old official and noble families in which the national feeling was stunted by transferring them from one country to another and so eradicating their own soil from them. These men sought to find a poor substitute for the missing idea of a nation and of a state in the ideal of the so-called Austriandom. . . . . Just the best among them came through it into the heaviest inner conflicts. They detected very soon that what they called Austriandom was not at all a state consciousness which offered a place for patriotism but in its essence only a mechanical fashion, signifying a loyalty to the dynasty untouched by any state or national sentiment. . . . .[1]

This imperial bureaucracy pressed heavily on the various peoples of the monarchy. Always renewed complaints were made because of its pedantry, of its servile and thoughtless routine, of its haughty incompetence, from Joseph II through Baron Andrian to Joseph Redlich. The great Emperor in 1765 wrote:

It occurs that nobody does work and that among the hundred reams of paper which are consumed in eight days in the offices of Vienna, you would not find four pages of spirit or a new or an original idea. . . . .
Two generations later Sealsfield made a vehement attack against the ridiculous laziness, dilatoriness, and orthodoxy of the imperial bureaucracy. "Eight hundred miles from the capital an old school bench cannot be mended without the authorization of the prefect of the district." And Andrian writes ironically: "If our ideas concerning China are correct then Austria is in Europe the same as China is in Asia. . . . ." Redlich wrote a monograph and delivered a powerful speech against the anachronistic spirit and practice of the Austrian bureaucracy and the pathological exuberance of this organization.[2]

[1] *Op. cit.*, pp. 107–8.

[2] *Verfassung und Verwaltungsorganisation der Städte.* Band 6: *Österreich* (Leipzig, 1907). *Zustand und Reform der österreichischen Verwaltung* (Wien, 1911).

The situation was made worse by the fact that not a bit of public control reached the imperial offices, the rigidity and secrecy of which was so great that cases were narrated when even the will of the Emperor was frustrated by the administration. And though this system was somewhat mitigated by the traditional Austrian *Gemütlichkeit* ("joviality"), the spirit of patriarchialism enforced on the people checked the best energies of public life and it is no wonder that at the time of the popular reawakening of 1848 many complaints of the most vehement nature were made against this rigid centralizing absolutism. But this hurtful spirit survived victoriously the revolutionary period and remained almost unaltered until the collapse of the empire. It was characterized by Victor Adler, the great Socialist leader: *Ein Absolutismus gemildert durch Schlamperei* ("an absolutism tempered by slovenliness").

This rule of bureaucracy was made more oppressive by other factors. The favoritism exercised by the court and the higher nobility put many unfit men into public service. The whole organization was connected by a hundred ties with the so-called good society and one could often hear when a more influential man had some difficult affair with the authorities the hopeful remark, *Ich werd's mir schon richten!* ("I'll fix it up!"). In a later period the bureaucracy came into a certain dependence upon the great industrial and financial enterprises. By this statement I do not allude to any corruptive influences but to a connection of quite another nature. When the big capitalistic concerns began to dominate the industrial life, their leading offices meant a far more splendid financial position than the badly paid state offices. Under such circumstances the more capable and energetic public servants preferred to go over into capitalistic employment. It was quite natural and human that these gentlemen utilized their former connections with their colleagues in the higher state bureaus in the interest of their new connections and were often capable of securing such advantages as ordinary business people could not attain.

Another factor which poisoned the atmosphere of bureaucracy was an entire lack of clear political aims and the absence of any true ethical motives. The officials who were sent to the various parts of the country were not prompted by any real national or social solidarity toward the population to which they administered. Gustav Strakosch-Grassmann, to whom we are indebted for an excellent history of Austrian public instruction, emphasizes this trait of the Austrian bureaucracy as one of the chief obstacles in the building up of an efficient school administration. He writes:

The lack of acquaintance with country and people of those officials who are sent into the provinces to administer them is an item of great consequence. Without any or with only the scantiest knowledge of country and people, without a knowledge of the language, but with much self-assertion (one must make the acquaintance of these elegant gentlemen in the political administration who with so much poise always play the fine cavalier and emphasize their superiority) came the young and older representatives of the political authorities into the province. Behind their glittering and supple appearance there was nothing in their kernel but bottomless ignorance. Whereas in Switzerland the men of the civic administration fulfilled their duties with a relentless energy and with a calm modesty, in the higher bureaucracy of Austria there rules the spirit of aristocracy and the officials of a bourgeois descent try to copy in their exterior forms, in their demeanor, and in their social life the manners of the aristocracy. . . . .[3]

Another detrimental factor in the work of Austrian bureaucracy was the continuance of the old police spirit and one can say without exaggeration that Austria always remained in its essence the same old *Polizeistaat* that it used to be in the times of Metternich or Bach. In this respect H. W. Steed proved again to be an acute observer when he said:

At moments of crisis the colors revive automatically and render the resemblance or rather the identity more apparent. In normal circumstances, however, the action of the police is not obtrusive. The stranger is unaware that the porter in his house is a *confidant* of the police, and that his goings and comings, his manner of life, the number and names of his friends, and all personal details are carefully communicated by the porter to the police who preserve them in a *dossier* ready for communication to the political or fiscal authorities as occasion may require.

The picture which I drew above of the Austrian bureaucracy would be, however, very one-sided, if I did not emphasize strongly that in spite of its shady sides mentioned above this bureaucracy and the administration accomplished by it was not only far superior to the former feudal administration to which it succeeded, but, compared with Eastern and Southeastern Europe, it represented a very honorable degree of order, accuracy, honesty, and humanitarianism. Especially in the last decades of the monarchy, under the influence of Socialism and Christian Socialism, a great deal of social spirit penetrated into this administration. And what is still more important, this administration in its bulk remained intact from all corruption, and it could seldom be accused of brutality toward the poor and the oppressed. Besides, some representatives of this bureaucracy were really gifted men, often with great erudition. Especially in all state departments we meet the well-known type of the *Sektionschef* ("head of the chief division") who, in spite of the state ministers, harassed in general by party and national struggles, represented very often the constancy, the objectivity, and the higher points of view of justice, not seldom with great energy and success. Perhaps such an evaluation of Aus-

[3] *Geschichte des österreichischen Unterrichtswesens* (Wien, 1905), III Buch, IV Abschnitt.

trian bureaucracy would have seemed, fifteen years ago, to many people as an exaggeratedly optimistic and indulgent judgment. But anybody who experienced that new administration and police which supplanted the old in the succession states could not fairly deny the advantages of the imperial bureaucracy which I have described.

The deterioration of the spirit of the administration of the monarchy began, however, not with the World War, but the signs of dissolution as in the other fields of state activity became manifest much earlier. This process may be recapitulated in a few words by saying that the lack of a state principle and the confronting growth of the particularistic national ideas corrupted this administration both from the intellectual and from the moral point of view. The national consciousness of the peoples of Austria came gradually more and more decidedly and hostilely into collision with the old Habsburg state idea. In connection with this struggle, there went on that ill-famed *politischer Kuhhandel* ("political cow-bargaining") by which state ministers or governors opened the doors of administrative positions to the sons of those nations which gave them the greatest difficulties in their political fights. Under the premiership of the very gifted Ernest von Körber (1900–1904) this tendency became almost a system as specific as the Metternich or Bach systems were. Under the cover of an elastic "liberalism," even of a flirting with socialism, a bureaucratic absolutism was built up which corrupted the press and the political leaders and made continuous secret "national" compromises with those thundering political orators who openly paralyzed parliament by their continuous obstructionism. But even disregarding this political corruption, the very process of the growing national consciousness had the result of making the old German imperial bureaucracy more and more impotent and unable to deal with the administrative problems of the whole monarchy; and there was an increasing need for more bureaucrats, employing the Czech mother-tongue, in Bohemia, the Polish and Ruthenian tongue in Galicia, the Rumanian and Ruthenian in Bukovina, and the Croat and Slovenian in the Jugo-Slav territories. This process would have been in itself completely normal, nay, wholesome, if this natural, national differentiation of the monarchy had been followed by a corresponding federalization of its constitution. But by maintaining the system of a rigid centralization, the newly formed intelligentsia of the various nations got into the imperial offices, one might say, by the back door, often through the conspiring means of the Trojan wooden horse. This new officialdom on a national basis had nothing to do with the old Habsburg state ideal. At the beginning it treated it, with masked and hypocritical sentiments, but later with the growing national tendencies, it left its bureaucratic reserve and went openly into the camp of national struggles. On the other hand, the spirit of the older German bureaucracy still remained the Austrian patriotism without any national color, which began to lose all its reality and which survived only in the minds of the court and the old-fashioned *Hofrat* type. But this Habsburg patriotism became something imaginary, "a pure relation of loyalty, like that of the mercenary to his war lord, which could flourish independently of space and nowhere" (Kleinwaechter). It is only natural that this bureaucratic bodyguard of the Habsburg state idea could not long withstand the attack of the officials belonging to the rising nations whose intolerant vehement nationalism thought more and more of the hour of final liquidation when their own nations would build up their own independent states and national bureaucracy.

This situation led more and more to a complete administrative deadlock. The single nations were already so filled with their national aspirations, all purely administrative problems became so much infiltrated with politics, the various national parties fought each other so bitterly in the provincial diets and in the parliament, that the leading statesmen adopted the principle of *quieta non movere*. Naturally the best elements of the bureaucracy were constantly harassed by this condition, for they saw that no earnest work of reform was possible. On the other hand this situation encouraged all climbers who in a pretended strenuousness possessed merely sufficient ability to do administrative routine work. The consequence was that centralism not only destroyed the efficiency of administration but corrupted also its public morality.

As already mentioned, the description given above, pertained exclusively to the Austrian half of the monarchy. In Hungary the situation was entirely different. Since the compromise of 1867, there had been no Habsburg administration in Hungary. The whole bureaucracy, both that of the state and of the local administration, stood exclusively in the service of the so-called Hungarian state idea, as this idea was interpreted by the leading class in the state, by the great landed interest and the financial powers attached to it. This state idea had, as we shall later see in detail, two fundamental dogmas. The one was that it did not recognize a connection with the Austrian half of the monarchy other than that based on *ad hoc* contracts, and it denounced as treason to the country any effort which tried to build up a common state organization above the two halves of the monarchy. The other was a rigid clinging to the Magyar national character of the state, repudiating as high treason all endeavors which aimed at the bringing into a confederational relation the non-Magyar nations of Hungary with the Magyar nation and the nations of Austria. Instead of such a policy, the Magyarization and assimilation of the non-Magyar nations of Hungary remained the fundamental effort of the Magyar policy of an almost sacramental character which was hidden from foreign public opinion but which was followed constantly with the most passionate perseverance. The Hungarian bureaucracy, all the leading positions of which were occupied by Magyar higher and middle nobility, the so-called *gentry*, and by some entirely assimilated elements of the other nationalities, became the chief supporter of this state idea. This bureaucracy developed into one of the chief centrifugal and separatist forces of the monarchy, and, therefore, I shall analyze its effects in the next part of the book.

CHAPTER VII

CAPITALISM AND THE JEWRY

One of the most powerful forces which upheld the Habsburg monarchy was, without any doubt, the growing capitalistic penetration of its economic organization.[1] This process began with full force as early as the sixties of the last century in the Austrian part of the monarchy. The bearer and leader of this capitalistic evolution was, as a matter of fact, the German bourgeois class. Its power emanated from Vienna and the Bohemian industrial regions throughout the entire monarchy, and had many representatives, branch members, and affiliated enterprises in all countries and capitals of the empire. To this vast German industrial and financial capitalism, the backward, agrarian countries of the empire played for a long time the same rôle as the colonies beyond the seas did for the western states; and indeed Austrian capitalism employed very often in its own countries the unscrupulous methods of colonial capitalism.

This capitalism, proceeding with growing energy and assuming more and more an outstanding Jewish color, became a very efficacious force in the unification and cohesion of the monarchy. The empire gained through it a unity of economic life, a more complete division of labor, and a more efficient credit system. It is one of the most interesting problems by which foreign observers are often startled, as to

[1] In order to visualize this process of growing industrialization some few figures will not be out of place. The value of the general trade of the Austro-Hungarian Custom Union rose between 1876–1913 from 1,660 million crowns to 6,400 millions. The value of the whole Austrian foreign trade (1900–1913) from 5,044 million crowns to 8,539 millions. The output of the coal production between 1876–1913 rose from 118 million quintals to 437 millions. The length of the railway tracks was in 1865, 3,698 kilometers, in 1913, 22,981 kilometers. The mass of the transported goods rose between 1877–1913 from 46 million tons to 159 million tons, the number of passengers from 32 millions to 301 millions, the number of pieces of mail (1865–1913) from 81 millions to 2,049 millions. The percentage of the people occupied in agriculture dropped between 1890–1910 from 55.8 per cent to 48.4 per cent.

Also in Hungary the process of capitalization was a rapid one. The length of the railways which was in 1846 only 35 kilometers, grew between 1867–1913 from 2,285 kilometers to 22,084 kilometers. In the years between 1867–1913 the number of passengers rose from 9 millions to 166 millions, the number of pieces of mail from 38 millions to 828 millions, the merchandise tonnage from 9 millions to 87 millions, the output of coal production from 7 million quintals to 91 millions, the value of foreign trade (1882–1912) from 1,763 millions of crowns to 4,174 millions. The percentage of people engaged in commerce and industry rose between 1869–1910 from 4.9 per cent to 25.1 per cent, whereas the percentage of the agrarian population dropped to 62.4 per cent.

For more details, see the highly interesting study of Paul Szende: "Der Staatshaushalt und das Finanzsystem Oesterreichs und Ungarns" in *Handbuch der Finanzwissenschaft,* Tübingen, 1928.

why these powerful economic advantages were not able to maintain the unity of the monarchy, and why the capitalistic forces of integration did not become victorious over the forces of national particularisms. These connections are so important that I shall consider them in a separate chapter, for it seems to me unquestionable that among all the centripetal forces of the monarchy the policy of free trade was the most decisive and efficient, or one might better say, *it could have become so* if other causes, both economic and political, had not counteracted its work and intensity.

In the present chapter I would like to treat another aspect of the problem: the leaders of capitalistic forces and their influence on the social and national problems of the monarchy. In this respect the most outstanding fact which we must emphasize is this: that in no one of the states of the monarchy arose a truly self-conscious bourgeois class creating its own political and social style, capable as in the great Western states of directing the evolution of the state. The sharp eyes of Sealsfield had already detected this fundamental difference which became one of the chief causes of dissolution when he characterized the economic life of Austria in his own period as follows: "Austria knows only the colossal feudal estates and the petty peasants. Between the two extremes of wealth and culture, poverty and illiteracy, there is no middle class as a connecting link." Austria remained in its structure a hidden feudal state, the tradition and ideology of which pressed heavily on the middle classes, and so they did not become the leading element of political emancipation as in the western states. Not only in the backward agrarian provinces of Austria and in Hungary did the new bourgeois class remain a class without prestige and distinction, but even in upper and lower Austria and in Bohemia where a strong manufacturing and financial organization was established, the bourgeois class always stood under the sway of the feudal and court atmosphere. What was called liberalism in the monarchy was only an artificial plant, introduced by the revolutionary nobility and intellectuals of 1848 and gradually faded away in the hands of the later bourgeoisie. One who studies the history of this liberalism will see that it adopted rather the exterior decorations and rhetorical formulas of the great Western models but it never was in real contact with the popular forces of society. Austrian, and, even more, Hungarian liberalism exhausted itself in the formal guaranty of the constitution and in the struggles against ecclesiastical preponderance for which many elegant and scholarly discourses were pronounced, but it had no real sense for the interest of the great masses of population. Neither the agrarian problems of the landless peasantry nor those of the industrial proletariat and of the decaying small artisans existed for it. On the contrary the rule of the large financial interests controlled the state without any scruple in the so-called liberal periods. In the seventies of the last century, a real era of *enrichissez vous* could be observed, the leading men of which belonged to the so-called liberal circles, the greedy and unscrupulous business activity of which led to a financial bankruptcy, the ill-famed *Wiener Krach* in 1873.[2]

Austrian capitalism, the leading elements of which were intimately connected with the liberal movement, gained a special color by the fact (and in Hungary this feature was even more outstanding) that among its members and especially the ruling financial powers, the Jewish element was predominant. This phenomenon had two historical causes: the one was that, until the modern constitutional era, the Jews were excluded from all other than financial activities. The other shows us a continuous migration of Jewish capitalists from west to east, due to the fact that a national capitalism was developed in the Western countries which tried to oust their Jewish rivals. As William Roscher, the great German economist, characterized this process, "For many centuries the Jews were commercial trustees of the newer nations, also to the advantage of these latter. But every tutelage becomes burdensome when it lasts longer than the immaturity of the pupil." That is the reason why a considerable part of Jewish capitalism moved toward the east where it found an unrivaled opportunity in exploiting the almost virgin resources of the younger states. Under these circumstances all the abuses of capitalism and its political representatives appeared before the uncritical mass-mind as the abuses of "Jewish" capital, the more as the leading daily press stood largely under the control of the financial powers. In Austria this situation led to an acute anti-Semitic movement under German nationalist and Christian Socialist flags. All the shortcomings and abuses of the capitalistic system were demagogically denounced as crimes of "Jewish liberalism." Especially since the great crisis of the stock exchange of 1873 which followed the bogus activity, this tendency assumed dangerous proportions and finally swept away the liberal party from Austrian public life. In vain the widely spread co-operation of the feudal classes in the financial scandals was demonstrated. In vain it was pointed out that in the most outstanding "Jewish" enterprises 13 princes, 64 counts, 29 barons, and 21 nobles were participating, who lent their aristocratic names for opulent profits to the hazardous business men: public opinion saw only the Jewish capitalists and their press as the real responsible parties. But even later when the political predominance of the German-Jewish upper bourgeois class was eliminated, and a feudal clerical coalition got into power, the abuses of certain capitalistic monopolies often alarmed public opinion. For instance the extension of the privileges of the Nordbahn Company

---

[2] Interesting details concerning this big bogus company swindle are given by R. Charmatz, *op. cit.,* II, 11–13.

aroused a real storm of public indignation, a scandal in which even the authority of the Crown was involved. In this manner Austrian capitalism developed serious centrifugal tendencies by fomenting racial and national struggles.

The situation was quite similar in Hungary where capitalism, owing to the feudal tradition of the country which despised industry and commerce, was almost exclusively in Jewish hands with the friendly participation of the aristocracy and the gentry which received splendid salaries for the fructification of their titles. In spite of this fact, anti-Semitism played a far smaller rôle in Hungary than among the Austrian population until the World War. This interesting antagonism had several reasons. One was surely the sober and benevolent character of the Hungarian peasants, devoid of any religious or race fanaticism, somewhat analogous to the Confucian type of philosophy, which was based on agriculture, order, and tradition. Another reason was the backward political and social differentiation of the country. The large popular masses were almost entirely unorganized, whereas the beginning social democratic movement tried to keep aloof all anti-Semitic tendencies from the party in which the entirely poor Jewish element had a considerable influence. Finally, the power of the government, in consequence of the restricted franchise and the overcentralized bureaucracy, was so absolute that it could suppress any movement which was disagreeable to it. And as long as the liberal traditions of such statesmen as Deák and Eötvös continued, the Magyar ruling class accepted very gladly the co-operation of the Jews not only for financial reasons but also as an instrument of assimilation against the non-Magyar nationalities of the country.

This identification of Jewry and capitalism envenomed not only the social struggles with a demagogic color, which in the economic life of the Western countries never became so accentuated, but augmented the acuteness of the national struggles too. The Jew was not only the chief representative of the capitalistic system but also that of the Austrian state idea, because, wherever he settled, he took with him the German language and culture if only in the form of the German-Jewish jargon. This exclusive German character of the Jews, however, ceased in the later periods, though the German language remained in the majority of cases their family language. With the growing national consciousness of the various nations of the monarchy, the Jewry became more and more assimilated with the language and customs of those nations among which it lived as *diaspora*. And when these nations became the leading powers in the state (as in the case of the Magyars and the Poles) the Jews served the new idea of the state with the same ardor as the former Austrian state. This attitude was to some extent determined by material considerations and by the traditional fear complex of the Ghetto. But to a larger extent a natural process of assimilation was taking place in all the countries in which the Jews acquired an appropriate opportunity for material and cultural development. This process of assimilation was enforced by their inherited faculty for adaptation and by the lack of a national tradition in a proper sense. Besides, in the national struggles between the ruling nation and the subjected nationalities—as in all struggles—the average Jews had a tendency toward the extreme points of view and they were always inclined, in their intellectual rationalism unchecked by national traditions and the instinctive attachment to the soil, to exaggerate and to put in the most glaring colors their newly accepted standpoint. There is another point which explains the extreme ardor of the Jewry in serving their new state idea. It is the greater mobility and elasticity with which they adopted more quickly and completely certain superficial elements of the new culture than the clumsy peasant and artisan elements of the native race. This interesting aspect, however, was not restricted to the Jews, but it is only a part of a more general psychology of the renegades. I observed many times, for example, that not only assimilated Jews but also Magyarized Germans and Slavs very often became the loudest and the most intolerant representatives of Magyar nationalism.

Be that as it may, it is certain that the reigning German and Hungarian states possessed an extremely passionate, loud, and bigoted Jewish bodyguard which extended far beyond the circles of capitalism. This attitude of the Jews augmented the exasperation of the oppressed nationalities against the state and sanctioned at the same time the anti-Semitic currents increasing, in a pathological manner, the centrifugal forces of the monarchy. So, for instance both in Austria and in Hungary, the Jewish capitalistic press took the crudest jingoist attitude in the national struggles and was a chief obstacle to a reasonable compromise among the rival nations. This press denounced all serious efforts toward compromise and was the loudest in Hungary in the unveiling of the so-called "treasons of the nationalities" and in fomenting the trend of national chauvinism against Austria and the joint institutions of the monarchy. This attitude, especially in Hungary, was so manifest that Lueger and his anti-Semitic friends liked to declaim on the terrorism of "the Judaeo-Magyars." Speaking generally, the large majority of the daily press both in Vienna and Budapest and especially the so-called liberal press, became an unscrupulous instrument of feudal and financial class-domination under the slogan of a German and Magyar hegemony. None felt the immense moral danger of this situation more vividly than Karl Kraus, the able critic and poet, who for decades fought a solitary and desperate fight in his *Fackel* against the ruling press-oligarchy of Vienna.

This intolerant nationalism and chauvinism of the Jews which ac-

cepted blindly and without criticism the most extreme ideology of the
foreign nation by which they were assimilated (a specific Jewish nationalism or Zionism was in those times only in its earliest formation)
aroused an acute and envenomed moral situation between the Jews and
the intelligentsia of the nationalities.

The same fatal antagonism was reported by an eminent Slovak
leader, Dr. Anton Štefánek, now minister for public instruction in
Czechoslovakia, in the third year of the World War in answering a
questionnaire which I addressed to many eminent leaders of Hungarian public opinion (to representatives both of Magyars, and the nationalities, and of the Jews), observing the more and more envenomed
state of the Jewish problem. Dr. Štefánek wrote:

As the Slovak question is eminently a village question, the Slovak-
Jewish antagonism is the most manifest there. How does the village Jew
live and what is his social situation? He is the merchant and the innkeep-
er of the village. He constitutes a distinct community with his co-religion-
ists, a community tied up by religion and even more by common economic
interest. The Jew lives quite apart from the people. He has only on the
economic terrain an intercourse with them and has not the slightest sympathy with their religious and social endeavors. . . . . The more the
schools progressed in the field of Magyarization, the more aggressive and
active the Jew became in party politics, and the deeper the antagonism
grew between him and his surrounding people. Today they are considered
as the exponents of the Magyars, as an auxiliary troop of the sheriffs, of
the village officials, and the gendarmerie and they are feared everywhere. . . . .

The Slovak leader emphasized the fact that the relation became worse
during the war when the Jew was victim of the war paroxysm and a
blind instrument of struggle against "Pan-Slavism," even in a greater
degree than the Magyar intelligentsia.[3]

The cause of these phenomena, as I observed them, should be
sought not so much in the economic interests and the desire for power
of the Jews as in the uncertain equilibrium of the Jewish soul in consequence of its half-assimilation. This uncertain equilibrium made them
extremely labile in things political and inclined toward exaggerations
and intolerance. Besides, the accusers of the Jews forgot very often
the fact that there was an important Jewish minority which took the
liberal ideas seriously and was sympathetic with the national struggles of the minorities. At the same time the social democratic parties
of the monarchy which counterbalanced efficaciously the chauvinistic
currents had a Jewish majority in their leadership.

In this manner capitalism and the Jewish problem intimately connected with it contributed very much to the growing acuteness of na-

[3] In the monthly magazine, *Huszadik Század*, July–August, 1917. In Hungarian.

tional struggles. This increasing anti-Semitism impaired in the first place the tactical position of the Germans as the Jewish citizens were excluded later from the German national parties. This fact is the more striking because, as we saw, the Jews in Austria were largely German and represented German interests ; many of their middle-class families were permeated with the most refined German culture ; they produced many excellent German writers and scientists who, as for instance Dr. Friedjung, the known historian, played a leading part in the foundation of a greater German ideology. This attitude was the consequence partly of the extension of the new racial ideologies among the German middle classes, partly of the fact that in the consciousness of the small bourgeoisie, as has already been emphasized, even the economic struggles got a false theoretical explanation. Not only the abuses of the big financial capitalists were qualified as Jewish abuses but also that whole painful process which small artisanship and small commerce suffered by the preponderance of the great industrial enterprises and which led to the catastrophe of many thousands of independent economic existences.

But all these centrifugal tendencies of the capitalistic evolution were surpassed in significance and consequences by a tendency which emanated from the very nature of capitalism. I mean the tendency that capitalism led inevitably toward the strengthening of the national feeling and consciousness of the masses and by it made national struggles more acute. It was emphasized by some of the leading socialist thinkers that the national movement is only the other side of the capitalistic evolution and that national hatred is in its essence a transformed class struggle. However exaggerated and simplified this theory may be, we shall see that capitalism was a really dominant factor in arousing national consciousness and particularism.

CHAPTER VIII

SOCIALISM

"Nothing can show more clearly the abnormal state condition of the Danube monarchy than the fact that the strong parliamentary progress of Socialism could be regarded as a gain for the state."[1] This remark of Rudolph Kjellén points rightly to one of the most efficient centripetal forces of the monarchy but his surprise shows that he did not completely understand the relation between the national and the Socialist thought. Socialism as the solidarity of working-people and an effort for their economic and cultural elevation must naturally strengthen the basis of the state though it tries to check the militaristic and imperialistic elements of government. The ideological internationalism of Socialism does not signify, because it cannot, the repudiation of national solidarities, but their spontaneous and harmonious adjustment into a superior unity.[2] It cannot be denied, indeed, that not a single class of the former Austria realized so clearly the fateful problem of the monarchy as the Austrian Social Democracy.

But Austrian Socialism was not always that unifying force which it became later. In the frames of the old absolutist, militaristic, and police state, the labor movement could not have its legal place. Nay, even later when a so-called liberal bourgeois government ruled in the country, in the sixties of the last century, the state power was brutally opposed to the working-class. When a labor delegation asked for the introduction of general suffrage, one member of the government said to the workers: "You should not believe that we would be inclined to introduce mob rule into Austria for a proletariat, with the cap on its head and the pike in its hands to run into the council hall." By this governmental spirit the labor movement was constrained to adopt underground methods and used more and more revolutionary and anarchistic means. The situation became very acute in the eighties of the last century and some political murders greatly corrupted the atmosphere of the proletarian movement. In 1886 the Emperor sanctified the ill-famed *Law Against the Anarchists* which eliminated the jury in case of political offenses. The labor movement now enlisted the extremist elements and lost touch with the real problems of the state and society.

[1] *Die Grossmächte und die Weltkrise* (Leipzig u. Berlin, 1921), p. 16.

[2] The relation between Nationalism and Socialism was analyzed more clearly perhaps than by any other author, by Henry de Man in *The Psychology of Socialism* (New York, 1928).

177

In this critical situation Austrian socialism found its savior in a man of remarkable insight and of a pure unselfish attitude, Dr. Victor Adler, who through long and laborious propaganda united the various labor factions into a common organization on the basis of a reasonable and workable program. From this time the Social Democratic party made rapid progress and in 1897 an electoral reform was carried on which added a fifth Curia to the four already existing in order to open the doors of parliament to the Proletarian elements. The representatives of the working-class appeared for the first time in the Austrian parliament. The national problems of the monarchy greatly aroused the interest of the party because its leaders realized perfectly the danger which menaced the unity and efficiency of the labor movement in consequence of the national differentiation of the proletarian masses. The leaders of socialism regarded as the essential element of this antagonism the scuffling of the bourgeoisie for economic and political jobs, and tried to elaborate a national program fit for the particular interests of the working-classes. In their theory the interests of the proletariat were in harmony with the well-understood interests of the state, because the socialist considered the elimination or at least the mitigation of national struggles as a paramount condition for social and cultural progress. The socialist movement of Austria produced indeed some remarkably gifted and scientific thinkers in the field of the theory and practice of national movements, who introduced new and original points of view in the old vexed problems. These points of view united in a solid system, especially by Dr. Karl Renner and Dr. Otto Bauer, gained a European reputation and may be summarized as follows.

1. The national struggles of the bourgeoisie have a tendency to become submerged into a sheer demagogy and form the chief obstacle to serious parliamentary work for economic and social reconstruction.

2. These national struggles cover bourgeois class interests against which the solidarity of the proletariat belonging to the various nations must be emphasized.

3. First of all, the economic and political unity of the state must be safeguarded in order to secure a wholesome capitalistic evolution as the precondition of Marxist socialism.

4. Therefore, the chief endeavor of Austria, composed of so many nations and nationalities, should be to establish an appropriate scheme of local governments by which the reasonable content of national aspirations (educational system, cultural associations, administration, and judiciary in the mother-tongue) could be achieved without the dismemberment of the unity of the state.

In order to attain these aims Dr. Renner elaborated a new and ingenious system of national autonomy on the basis of what he called the *principle of personality*, in conscious antagonism with those efforts which tried to solve the problem on the basis of the *territorial principle*. This latter endeavored to divide the monarchy into various political territories based either on the historical rights of the various countries or on the natural settlements of the various nations. All these distinct territorial governments should be combined into a kind of confederative state. The principle of personality advocated by the socialists rejected this conception of distinct national states. They were not willing to establish a distinct Czech, Polish, Jugo-Slav, or Rumanian state inside the monarchy, but tried to give to the old state an international or, better say, *supra-national organization*. As two generations previously, Louis Kossuth among the plans of his exiled life cherished the idea of solving the national problem on the model of religious autonomy, so now Dr. Renner (without knowing the political speculations of the Hungarian statesman) adduced an analogous scheme. He based it on the conception that just as the religious controversies could not be solved on a territorial basis because the principle of *cujus regio, ejus religio* led to incessant warfare, so the national problem could not be answered by a territorial dismemberment of the old state but the same principle of personality should be introduced here too. Following this principle, all the members of each nation should be entitled to form local, intermediate, and central national associations, so-called "National Universities," endowed with a state-like jurisdiction in all matters pertaining to cultural life and educational system, disregarding the territorial divisions of the whole empire. In this manner all the Germans, Czechs, Poles, and the other nations of the monarchy could have been united from a national point of view without establishing national state divisions inside the empire. According to this program the joint state should be doubly organized: first, from a national standpoint; and second, from an administrative standpoint. The national organizations would not coincide with the administrative divisions which would be determined not by national but by economic, financial, and trade considerations. National considerations would be acknowledged only so far as the local administrative unities should form, when possible, homogeneous national settlements. By the establishment of such administrative districts on a local national basis, public government could be carried on in the maternal tongue of the various nations.

This plan of Dr. Renner which may be regarded as an enlargement of the principles of the Kremsier constitution (with the difference, however, that he would abolish the antiquated crownlands and substitute for them a fourfold division: Inner Austria, the country of the Sudets, the Littoral, and the Carpathian provinces) had a great influence on the Austrian proletariat which accepted these principles as the solution of the national problem, in the so-called "program of

Brünn" (1899).[3] This program asserts that the national problem can be solved only "in a strictly democratic community, based on universal, equal, and direct suffrage in which all the feudal privileges in the state and in the provinces are eliminated. . . . ." It attacks equally the bureaucratic centralized state and the feudal autonomy of the crownlands and designates the democratic "Confederation of Nationalities" as the state ideal of the Austrian working-classes. Instead of the old nation of a territorial basis, a new nation should be constituted as a purely cultural association. It acknowledges emphatically the right of all the nationalities for cultural self-expression and admonishes the workers of Austria that "the peoples can only achieve progress in their culture through a firm solidarity with each other and not in petty strife against each other."

It is manifest that this program and especially its driving ideology[4] was the most complete affirmation of the idea of a greater Austria and indirectly (though not outspokenly) of the German hegemony inside of Austria. The plan of Dr Renner would have strengthened the leading economic and political rôle of Vienna. Even his last book published immediately before the collapse of the monarchy and in which he restates his plans of reform *(Das Selbstbestimmungsrecht der Nationen in besonderer Anwendung auf Österreich)* is the description and recommendation not of a real confederative state but of something which he called *Staatenstaat*, a supra-national synthesis which tried to satisfy the nations with a cultural autonomy.

In a period which heated the German, the Magyar, the Czech, the Polish, and the other national consciousnesses almost to the boiling-point and when the idea of a nation was no longer a simple cultural and ethnographical connection but an effort to unite the traditional national settlements into an independent state, the imagination of Renner was manifestly too schematic and too bloodless in the eyes of the fighting nations. These nations would have perhaps been inclined to combine their independent states with the others in a confederation but they refused to accept the competency of a super-state even in matters which they felt not strictly national.

In spite of its Utopian elements, the socialist ideology of state unity—*free nations in a free state*—became a very important connec-

---

[3] It is worth while to notice that the brilliant solution of the nationality problem in Esthonia and Latvia is due to an arrangement which is animated by the very principles of Austrian Socialism.

[4] The main ideas of the Austrian Socialists concerning the problem of nationality are contained in the following books: Karl Renner (Synoptikus), *Staat und Nation* (Wien, 1899). Karl Renner, *Der Kampf der österreichischen Nationen um den Staat* (Wien, 1902). Karl Renner, *Grundlagen und Entwicklungsziele der österreichisch-ungarischen Monarchie* (Wien, 1906). The last two named, under the pseudonym of Rudolph Springer. Otto Bauer, *Die Nationalitätenfrage und die Sozialdemokratie*, Zweite Auflage (Wien, 1924). Otto Bauer, *Die österreichische Revolution* (Wien, 1913).

tive link in the last decades of the monarchy and at the same time a strong admonition that without the democratization of the empire and especially without the establishment of a system of local autonomy, the monarchy was sentenced to death. At the same time the socialist conception emphasized most vividly the basic significance of the economic unity of the monarchy. It is very interesting to note that the chief defenders of this unity were not the real beneficiaries of this connection, the German high bourgeoisie and the Magyar landed interests, but the leading theoreticians of socialism who denounced the Magyar movement for independence (which aimed at the economic and military severance of the monarchy) as damaging important interests of the working-classes. And when the crisis of the constitution became the most acute between the Crown and the Hungarian opposition in 1905, it was the Austrian-German socialists who led the most vehement fight against Hungarian separatism. So, for instance, Dr. Renner chastised the cowardice of the Austrian bourgeoisie who began to acquiesce in the separatistic plans of the Magyars, though "the Hungarian market is incomparably more significant for Austrian capital than Moroccan is for the German," which German foreign policy defends so energetically. In the claim for an independent Hungarian customs territory, he saw nothing else than the clamoring of city sharks, swindlers, and political demagogues, against the very interests of Austrian industry, of the Austrian working-classes, and of the Hungarian agricultural population. And even Dr. Otto Bauer, though he realized that there were more serious interests behind the claim for a Hungarian economic independence, refuted these separatistic efforts emphatically; nay, he did not hesitate to advise military intervention against them in a memorable passage of a popular book:

To curb the country, split by class and national antagonisms [he refers to Hungary], by sheer military force, in the period of the Russian revolution, nobody will dare. But the inner conflicts of the country will give to the Crown other opportunities which it will be constrained to utilize if it cannot endure the fate of the Bernadotte dynasty: it cannot remain the organ of two distinct wills and still rule both Austria and Hungary. Therefore, it must take care that Hungary and Austria should have one will, and should constitute one empire. The tattered conditions of Hungary give a possibility to this unity. The Crown will not hesitate to send its army to Hungary in order to reconquer it for the empire, but it will write on its flags: Unadulterated, universal suffrage and secret ballot! Right of coalition for the agricultural proletariat! National autonomy! It will oppose to the idea of the independent Hungarian national state the idea of the United States of Greater Austria, the idea of a confederative state in which each nation will administer independently its national affairs and all the nations will unite in one state for the protection of their common interests. Necessarily and inevitably the idea of a confederation of nationalities will become the instrument of the Crown because the dissolution of dualism menaces it with the destruction of its empire. . . . .[5]

I scarcely know a document more significant for the elucidation of the inner crisis of the monarchy than this declaration of the socialist leader in 1907. Behold, this cool man, of uncommon intellectual penetration, an international socialist, and an anti-militarist, here gives counsel to the Habsburgs, to make a new effort for the armed coercion of Hungary and for its assimilation into the empire. What could demonstrate more clearly than this the bankruptcy of the centripetal forces and the menacing dissolution? For Bauer understood perfectly well that without the solution of the national problems the monarchy could not be maintained, and that its dissolution would signify an enormous crisis for its working-classes. For this reason, he advised this desperate method, showing that he regarded the problem very likely as Francis Ferdinand did: only by an operative interference did he think it possible to give a federative constitution to the monarchy against the will of Magyar feudalism. This federative state appeared also to him more as a superstate than a federation of national states: "If Austria should continue to remain, a national autonomy will be established."

This ideology of Austrian socialism represented with great brilliancy and dialectical force was felt beyond the ranks of the proletariat, and made a profound impression on many high officials and officers even in the entourage of the Emperor, who accepted more and more completely the doctrine that the envenomed national struggles of Austria could be checked only with the help of social, even socialist, forces. A kind of a neo-Josephinist policy began and the old Emperor himself became the chief protector of universal secret suffrage. It was the fashion in the camp of the enemies of democracy to speak ironically of *Burg socialism* ("socialism of the Court") and the gifted leaders of socialism adroitly utilized this disposition of the leading circles.

This social turn of the dynasty started in Hungary when the Crown was confronted with a nationalistic majority in parliament. Then it happened in 1905 that the minister of interior of the Fejérváry cabinet, Joseph Kristóffy, attacked vehemently by the whole chauvinistic public opinion, promised to a socialist deputation the introduction of universal suffrage. This promise, later indorsed by the Crown, had the effect of a bomb on the Magyar feudal classes who were perfectly aware of the fact that a popular parliament would put an end to the latifundist system and to the so-called Magyar national supremacy. Therefore, they provisionally abdicated from their claims

<hr>

[5] *Die Nationalitätenfrage und die Sozialdemokratie* (Wien, 1908), p. 373.

concerning the army, whereas the Emperor under the pressure of the annexation crisis (when Bosnia and Herzegovina were definitely incorporated into the monarchy) in order to gain the assistance of the Magyar upper classes, abandoned universal suffrage. The stone, however, thrown by Habsburg caused a tremendous political avalanche which descended upon the public life of Austria. Austrian Social Democracy utilized, in a skilful way, the Hungarian situation and demanded for Austria the universal suffrage promised to the Hungarian people. And indeed the action here led to success. In January, 1907, the electoral reform received the sanction of the Emperor, and in June of the same year the first parliament was convened on the basis of a universal, an equal suffrage, and a secret ballot.[6]

It has often been asserted that this experiment with the democratic forces refuted the hopes of their advocates because the parliament of the people continued the national struggles in the same manner as the parliament of the antiquated Curias, and that even the spirit of obstruction reappeared. These were really the facts, but the conclusion drawn from them seems to me still erroneous. On the contrary, one who had a clear vision concerning the fundamental forces of national movements could foresee that the masses are not less nationally motivated (though in another way) than the privileged classes, and that the problem of nationality could not be quieted until institutions are established satisfying all the reasonable national claims of the large masses of population. For this work, the forces of democracy were absolutely necessary. To believe—as many reactionaries did—that this work could have been carried on by the sheer force of military absolutism, over the heads of some twenty countries and ten nations, is a militaristic Utopia in which I cannot believe. On the other hand, however, to believe that democracy in the very moment of its birth would be successful in repressing the national fanaticism of the past is not less utopian. Besides, the new democratic constitution became only the basis for the election into the central parliament whereas the diets and the local administrative assemblies remained unaltered in their feudal atmosphere. And as the power of Magyar

[6] By this coincidence of events Joseph Kristóffy, a former sheriff and later member of parliament, closely attached to the Tisza administration, became the man who gave the first impetus for the realization of universal suffrage in Austria. By this he acquired an almost mythical prestige in Austria, as a man of exceptionally bright ideas. (Even Joseph Redlich accepts this legend.) The truth, however, was that his intellectual and moral horizon did not surpass that of the average Magyar *szolgabiró* ("county sheriff"). He utilized the weapon of universal suffrage not as a real reform idea for his people, but as an instrument against feudalism for the benefit of the Emperor. The real author of the far-reaching plan was Mr. Charles Méray-Horváth, the distinguished sociologist who, twenty years before Oswald Spengler in a remarkable book which Spengler possibly did not read, diagnosed in the sharpest way the decline of the Western civilization (*Die Genesis des Kommenden Tages,* Budapest, 1901). Mr. Méray elaborated the whole plan for Kristóffy and made it acceptable to him. I was informed of their discussions, so to say, from hour to hour.

feudalism was not checked by the crisis of the constitution, and the Dualistic System was not even discussed, only political dreamers could hope that this half-measure tardily introduced could really solve the national problem.

The national aspirations, indeed, manifested themselves more and more vehemently not only in the bourgeois society but also in the masses of the proletariat. From the beginning the Austrian Social Democratic party was organized in various groups according to the mother-tongues of the population and combined into a unified system. But from 1907 the party was transformed into an association of national parties. In 1909, however, not even this loose unity could be maintained; and there arose an embittered fight between the German and Czech socialist parties, which latter would no longer accept the Viennese administrative and financial centralization. This struggle led to a disruption of the unified trade-union movement. The Czechs, disregarding the protests of their German comrades, began to build up their own trade unions. The international congress of Stockholm (1910) was unable to restore the unity of Austrian socialism. At the election of 1911 for the Reichsrat the autonomist and separatist wing of the Czech Social Democracy gained a large majority over the united party. The socialist movement, which always asserted very proudly that it possessed the panacea of national struggles, was incapable of uniting the various nations in a single party, even in its class-conscious camp. *The truth is that national solidarity vanquished class solidarity.* The centrifugal forces were victorious even in the labor movement. The crimes of the past had a greater effect than the tardy half-reforms of the present.

CHAPTER IX

THE TRAGEDY OF FREE TRADE

It has already been emphasized that one of the most outstanding centripetal forces of the monarchy consisted in its free-trade policy which made so many peoples and territories a complete economic unity. There can be no doubt that, if all the possibilities of the free-trade policy had been utilized in the right way, the centrifugal and particularistic tendencies could have been checked by the growing economic solidarity of the various nations and countries. Even under the shortcomings of the actual policy, which we shall consider in detail, its advantages were always emphasized by the supporters of the customs union. They employed the classical arguments of Cobden and Bright, saying: "Behold the Habsburg monarchy gives the privilege and opportunity to many peoples and countries different from each other in natural conditions, in language, in culture, in economic development to trade with each other without the obstacle of custom barriers and, therefore, to complete each other in the most harmonious way. Bohemia, for instance, can freely communicate with Transylvania, Styria with Galicia, Silesia with Dalmatia. How advantageous and progressive this free trade is!"

Recent political developments seem to corroborate this argument. In 1919 the Austro-Hungarian customs union was broken into seven parts and each of these seven parts is today much poorer economically, and much less efficient than in the flourishing period of the old connection. Besides, there can be no doubt that the present economic distresses of Czecho-Slovakia, Jugo-Slavia, Poland, and Rumania were caused to a large extent by those economic changes which were a consequence of the new custom barriers, not to mention the Austrian Republic and Hungary mutilated almost into a torso. It is now the general opinion both in Europe and America, expressed by the International Manifesto of the leading bankers, that the dismemberment of the Austro-Hungarian customs union was a great disadvantage to all the peoples concerned. That is also the chief argument for all those efforts which endeavor to use propaganda for the re-establishment of the Habsburg empire under an economic disguise.

Under such circumstances it is worth while to study whether the advantages of the customs union were really so overwhelming for the interests of the peoples who constituted it, and whether its dismemberment is really so detrimental to the future development of the various national economies. It is a firmly established fact that, since 1919, the succession states of the monarchy suffer more under the general economic depression which followed the World War throughout Europe, than the Western countries of Europe. But this fact alone does not decide the problem. The peoples who lived in the Austro-Hungarian monarchy were economically less developed and more feeble than the Western nations, and a weaker economic organism has more difficulty in restoring itself than a stronger one. If we speak with the bankers of the newly established states, we find that they are not pessimistic at all: "Should we once pass the evils caused by the *Umstellung* ["transposition"] then we shall reach greater results than possible in the territory of the old customs union. . . . ." This argument sounds somewhat strange because we are accustomed to accept the truth of free trade and its beneficial results without any qualification.

The careful investigation of this process is the more important because the free-trade argument regains vigor in Europe, and also the Pan-European movement emphasizes the importance of economic unity. All these movements try to reconstitute something which was already a living reality in the old Dual monarchy. Therefore, the discussion cannot be carried on as in the times of Cobden and List, some eighty or ninety years ago, exclusively on the basis of the general arguments for free trade or protection, but we must put our questions in a more concrete way: What are the real conditions of free trade? What are the conditions under which free trade can be really operative and advantageous for all the peoples and territories concerned?

A. THE NATURAL AND OTHER CONDITIONS OF ECONOMIC CO-OPERATION IN THE HABSBURG MONARCHY

The Austro-Hungarian customs union was established in 1850 by an imperial decree of victorious absolutism. In the previous period there were customs barriers between Hungary and the Austrian provinces. These customs barriers were an instrument in the hand of the imperial policy for the colonial exploitation of Hungary in the interest of the imperial treasury and of the more industrialized regions of Austria. (As was previously mentioned, the chief cause of this measure was the fact that the nobility of Hungary, the only prosperous class of the country on the basis of its feudal privileges, was unwilling to pay taxes and, therefore, the indirect way of customs duties was the only expedient to break their resistance.) In those times it was the constant claim of the feudal estates that trade should become free and that exports and imports should be regulated on a basis of strict parity. Later in the two decades before 1848, a customs union was the chief demand of the Liberal Hungarian opposition. "This idea had also its supporters at Vienna," says the noted Hungarian historian, Acsády, already quoted, "but only for the reason that they realized that the economic separation was the chief obstacle for the assimilation of Hungary." But immediately before 1848 the most advanced group of Hungarian opposition—under the leadership of Louis Kossuth—had already abandoned the claim for the customs union (especially under the sway of the doctrine of Frederick List, the great German economist), and on the eve of the revolution the demand for a complete economic independence of Hungary became loud. This growing tendency for the economic and national independence of Hungary was the chief cause which induced the Habsburgs, after the defeat of the Hungarian revolution, to establish in 1850 the customs union as the most efficacious means to oust all particularistic tendencies. The compromise of 1867 only confirmed and sanctioned the previous situation.

It is evident from these historical antecedents that the Austro-Hungarian customs union was already in its origin a great historical experiment, the experiment of a conquering army and of a victorious emperor to unite economically by force the various national territories of the whole realm. Against this experiment more and more vehement reaction became manifest. The most important group of those reactions was, as we have already emphasized, of a sentimental nature. The nations fought bitterly against all endeavors in which they supposed there was a purpose in the unifying absolutism.

In order to see the situation more clearly we must, therefore, investigate all those conditions which determined the success or the failure of the free-trade policy in the frames of the Habsburg monarchy. Let us begin with the natural conditions.

The more two or several economic territories can offer to each other, the more they complete each other, the more advantages free trade promises to them, the more disadvantage if tariff walls separate them. For instance, a mountainous country, rich in forest and pastures and producing wood and cattle, is the natural complement to a plain region abundant in grains. A region of moderate climate and of cold winters, exporting milk, beet sugar, and potatoes, is a complement to a southern district abounding in southern fruits, cotton, and oils.

Regarding the separated parts of the monarchy from this point of view, we come to the conclusion that the natural completion of the various regions was not so conspicuous as to render their economic union particularly advantageous or their severance particularly detrimental.

In mineral resources the Habsburg monarchy was not rich. The raw materials produced by the mining industries in the year 1907 amounted in value to 1,845 million marks in the German empire, 274 million marks in Austria, and 85 million marks in Hungary.[1] These

---

[1] For this and other points of the argument the reader will find reliable information and a wholesome criticism in the book of Friedrich Otto Hertz, *Die Schwierigkeiten der industriellen Produktion in Österreich* (Wien u. Leipzig, 1910).

figures make it manifest that the Austro-Hungarian monarchy, compared with the German Empire, was poor in minerals. And what made the situation even more difficult was the fact that the places where these relatively small mineral resources were found, as well as the other natural treasures and motive powers important for the industry, were not concentrated in certain regions of the monarchy but were divided, so to speak, among all the countries and provinces.

One of the chief conditions of modern industry consists in the motive powers: coal, crude oil, natural gas, water-power, and wood (partly as sources of energy, partly as raw materials). Among its modest mineral resources the monarchy was relatively rich in coal and petroleum, in water-power and in wood. But from the point of view of a natural division of labor, it must be noted that in water-power the Alpine provinces are most abundant, but there is water-power also in the Carpathians, in the Bohemian mountains, and in the Jugo-Slav territories. Similarly, the forests were distributed over many parts of the monarchy. The chief deposits of petroleum are in Galicia, of coal in Bohemia and Moravia, but coal could be found also in many regions of the monarchy, and in Transylvania are important resources in natural gas. That is partly the reason why the succession states of the dismembered monarchy are not lacking in those energy powers which are essential for industrial exploitation.

But still more important from the point of view of division of labor between the various territories of the former monarchy is the situation of agriculture. A region of warm climate where the olive and southern fruits were growing was only a very restricted territory, the littoral of the Adriatic, Istria, the Croatian littoral, and Dalmatia. The preponderant part of the monarchy furnished the articles generally produced in the temperate zone, and in this respect the differences in the monarchy were not great or decisive.

From the point of view of the foodstuffs, the interdependence of the cattle-breeding mountainous districts and of the grain-producing plains and hills had the greatest significance, but mountains, plains, and hills were so distributed throughout the monarchy that two or three of these terrains could generally be found within the limits of any one country. When the Habsburg monarchy was dismembered Czecho-Slovakia, Poland, Jugo-Slavia, and Rumania got both mountainous and plain regions from its ancient territory.

But let us now return to the mineral resources. How far they can serve as the basis for industrial development depends not only on their quantity but also on the cost of mining coal and ore per cubic yard, and further on the cost of transportation from the mining-place to the place of manufacture. For instance in England, where coal and iron-ore are mined often in close neighborhood or in the vicinity of waterways, an iron industry could easily establish itself. Just the opposite was the situation in this respect in the territory of the former Austro-Hungarian monarchy where the deposits of minerals were generally far removed from each other and from the waterways. For instance, the smelting furnaces of the *Alpine-Montangesellschaft*, which stand in the neighborhood of the Styrian iron-ore mines, were obliged to transport coal from the region of Mährisch-Ostrau at enormous expense.

The consequences of this geographical situation were that only a comparatively small industrial development took place and even this was concentrated in various parts of the monarchy, namely in north Bohemia, in the neighborhood of Vienna and in Styria, around Graz-Leoben. This comparatively weak and dispersed industrial development could not create such an interdependence between the manufacturing and the agricultural regions as would have been sufficiently strong to counterbalance the centrifugal tendencies that had arisen within the territory of the customs union.

The industrial development was further weakened by the difficulties of transportation. It was comparatively costly to ship commodities from certain parts of the monarchy into other parts. This situation was intimately connected with the very origin of the Habsburg empire. We must remember that the monarchy was not the outcome of a natural economic evolution which united territories on the basis of economic advantage, but the artificial creation of the Habsburg dynasty. The frontiers of the monarchy cut here and there the ties of natural interdependence. For instance, Bohemia was connected with Vienna by political boundaries whereas its natural outlet would have been the valley of the Elbe, leading toward the northwest, toward Germany and the North Sea. Or, to take another example, Galicia sloped toward the Baltic, partly toward Poland, and was separated from the bulk of the monarchy by the mountainous chains of the Carpathians. These natural obstacles made the building of railways and their operation very costly. At the same time the various regions were not sufficiently connected by navigable waterways. Generally speaking, there were few navigable waterways in the monarchy.

Not only from the point of view of internal waterways but also from the point of view of connection with the sea, the former monarchy was in a disadvantageous position. The basin of the Danube is separated from the Adriatic by the arid mountainous chain of the Karst, whereas the Danube empties itself into an isolated and economically abandoned bay of the Black Sea. It was characteristic of transportation conditions of the monarchy that a Viennese plant was occasionally able to ship its products from Vienna to Argentina by way of the Elbe and through Hamburg cheaper than from Vienna to Bukovina.

These disadvantageous conditions of transportation were further aggravated by the lack of unity in the economic administration. The Austrian, the Hungarian, and the Bosnian railways stood under separate, independent control, and each government could establish a railway tariff system according to its own taste. For instance, in 1880, it was stated in the Hungarian Parliament that the comparatively expensive railway rates of the Austrian administration impeded more the export of Hungarian grain into Germany than the German agrarian custom duties then in operation. This possibility of influencing in a certain sense the traffic between the various regions of the monarchy by an artificial system of railway rates, was largely utilized equally by the Austrian, the Hungarian, and the Bosnian governments. The transportation policy of the Austrian government tried to exploit the Hungarian producer in the interest of Austrian industry. For instance, there were higher railway rates on Hungarian grain than on Rumanian or that originating from other Balkan countries.

This policy of influencing Hungarian economic life by the way of transportation rates was easier for the Austrian government because its control also extended over Hungarian internal navigation. Namely, the Austrian government had the complete direction of the Austrian societies of Danube navigation, and the Austrian concerns compelled the only greater Hungarian navigation company to ally itself with them. On the other hand the Hungarian government which controlled directly almost the whole railway system of Hungary, was capable of securing very important rate privileges for the Hungarian industry. Similarly the Bosnian government employed the same measure on its own territory.

National and state jealousies heightened even more the difficulties of transportation. A startling example of this was the case of the Dalmatian railways. Dalmatia was an Austrian province, but Hungary made a legal claim upon it based on the historical right of the Crown of St. Stephen. Dalmatia was separated from the other Austrian provinces by the wedge of Croatian territory belonging to the Hungarian kingdom. Therefore, a railway which would have connected Dalmatia with the other Austrian provinces could only be effectuated through Hungarian territory, but the building of such a railway was always opposed by the Hungarian parliament lest it should make the possession of Dalmatia easier for Austria. In consequence of this conflict the goods from Austria to Dalmatia were transported by railway to Trieste and from there they were transferred to ships and perhaps again loaded on a train from a Dalmatian seaport.

As revenge for this policy the Austrian government refused the claim of Hungary for a direct transportation of its goods toward Prussian Silesia and Berlin. The Austrian government could molest the business traffic between Hungary and Germany on many pretexts. This quite artificial obstacle of transportation, for which bitter diplomatic struggles were fought for years between the two countries under the name "the Junction of Annaberg," was sometimes detrimental to the economic interests of Hungary.[2]

The traffic in goods had other obstacles also in the territory of the customs union. On the basis of old historical rights Tyrol collected customs duties and Dalmatia the so-called *Dazio consumo* on their borders upon grain or flour imported from the other parts of the monarchy. At the same time economic boycott movements were arranged by the rival nations of the monarchy against each other. Already Louis Kossuth initiated such a movement, the so-called "Protective Association" which had interesting analogies with the recent movement of Gandhi against the English manufactured products. In the nineties of the last century a similar movement was inaugurated in Bohemia in nationalistic circles against the consumption of Hungarian flour. Similar to this was a Magyar nationalistic movement, the so-called "Tulip Movement"[3] in 1906 which made it a duty for the consumers to buy exclusively Hungarian manufactured products.

From all that has been said it is manifest that the principle of free trade was considerably hampered on the territory of the custom union. At the same time we realized that the natural conditions of the monarchy were not very favorable for the mutual interdependence of the various territories. In spite of these facts a sufficiently considerable traffic in goods was established between 1850 and 1914 on the territory of the Austro-Hungarian custom union. The reason was that the process of industrialization went on in various times and in various measures in the different parts of the monarchy.

Speaking generally, Galicia-Bukowina, Hungary-Transylvania, and the Jugo-Slav parts of the monarchy were no less fit for the development of big industry than Bohemia-Moravia or the Alpine provinces. Nevertheless in 1850 when the custom union was decreed, the latter regions were already manufacturing to some extent whereas the former were exclusively agrarian. Approximately until 1890 the industrial development did not even start in the eastern and southern parts of the monarchy, whereas until the same time Bohemia-Moravia, Silesia, Lower and Upper Austria, and Styria made a great advance in industrialization. About 1890, therefore, the difference between the industrial and the non-industrial regions became even more conspicuous. The causes, however, which created this interdependence were of a transitory nature. As a matter of fact the difference and interdependence between the industrial and the agrarian regions lessens in

[2] This and other grievances of the Hungarian economic life were enumerated in detail by Joseph Vágó in his *Memorandum concerning the Renewal of the Austrian-Hungarian Customs and Commercial Treaty* (Budapest, 1916). In Hungarian.

[3] The promoters of this movement wore tulips in their buttonholes.

the long run in the same measure in which the latter advances in industrialization. Therefore, the dependence of the eastern and southern agrarian parts of the monarchy on the industrialized west must have lessened, in a certain measure, when the agrarian territories began to establish their own industries. That was really the case: there was a tendency toward a diminished interdependency in the last twenty-five years of the existence of the Austro-Hungarian customs union.

For instance, if space would permit me, I could demonstrate by statistical figures that coincidentally with the strong absolute growth of foreign trade—both in the foreign trade of Hungary and of Austria—their trade with each other had a comparatively smaller significance and their trade with foreign countries, a comparatively greater, in 1910 than in 1890. That is to say, the tendency of economic evolution was toward the emancipation of the two countries. A similar tendency was also operative among various territories of Austria, the Alpine, the Sudet, and the Karst provinces.

But there is also another factor which we must take into consideration. It is evident that the more primitive means of production the population of a given territory employs, the less productive its work is and the poorer the standard of living of their working-masses, the more insignificant is the rôle which the exchange of their products plays in their economic life. The primitive peasant communities of the Middle Ages produced the largest part of the commodities which they needed; whereas the part which they were compelled to exchange on the market was reduced to a minimum. In those times, Europe was divided into an immense number of petty sovereignties, under greater or smaller feudal lords who were at constant war with each other. In spite of this situation, economic life went on in these small, isolated territories because life was very crude, mostly independent of any economic exchange. In the course of the European historical evolution, roughly speaking from 1000 to 1871, the small feudal territories of the Middle Ages were integrated into principalities, and later into vast patrimonial, then into national states. The driving force of this integration was the growing productivity of labor which lessened the poverty of the broad masses of population. This comparatively growing welfare of population augmented economic needs and made them more varied: it heightened the division of labor and the necessity of co-operation.

Now regarding the Austro-Hungarian customs union, we are impressed by the fact that it was constituted of human masses employing very primitive instruments of production and the great majority were living in very great poverty. Therefore they needed comparatively little exchange of their products. The barter economy (the *Naturalwirtschaft* in the German terminology), which accompanies the primitive methods of production, plays even now a far more preponderant rôle in the villages of the former Austro-Hungarian monarchy than those who regard and judge the degree of the culture of the former empire by the facades of the palaces of Vienna, Budapest, and Prague would imagine. According to the report of the inspectors of industry, in 1901, in Styria, Salzburg, Tyrol, and the northern parts of Lower and Upper Austria, the flax, hemp, and wool produced in the villages were spun into yarn and woven into cloth by each family or by the help of traveling weavers.[4] Now, if in the villages of the most advanced western parts of the monarchy the old family economy still existed in such a measure, we can imagine how conditions were in the backward eastern and southern parts—in the Ruthenian, Rumanian, Serbo-Croat, and eastern Slovak regions or even in the intermediary Polish, western Slovak, Hungarian, or Slovenian territories, which are less advanced in economics and culture than the Austrian-German and Czech parts of the west and north. Generally speaking, in the eastern and southern parts of the monarchy, the rôle of the traffic of goods was relatively so small that we met there certain survivals of the age-old tribal communism. For instance, the pastoral communities of the Rumanian mountains and the so-called Zadruga settlements of the Jugo-Slavs, uniting some dozens, not seldom sixty to eighty people in a semi-communistic life, restricted modern trade to an insignificant place.

This situation had also another important aspect. A higher productivity of labor means an extension in the traffic of goods not only because it creates well-being and in connection with it many new needs, but also because a higher productivity is dependent on a growing differentiation of the whole process of production. There is a demand for an immense variety in raw materials and technical implements in order to maintain a higher productivity and a more developed type of production. A high productivity of labor, therefore, can only be the result of co-operation between numerous millions of men and many different geographical areas.

But the greater the rôle of the exchange of products in the life of a people, the more important for it is the system of free trade. That is the reason why peoples on a higher cultural and economic level aspire, if not for free trade, at least for the creation of big customs unions. That is the reason why countries with a small population, if their economic life is developed, cannot suffer at their frontiers high custom tariffs, but are under the necessity of accepting, if not the policy of free trade, at least low protective duties. The truth of this proposition is demonstrated by the examples of Switzerland, Belgium, the Netherlands, and Denmark. On the contrary, the succession states of the former Habsburg monarchy—Czecho-Slovakia, Hungary, Ruma-

[4] Friedrich Otto Hertz, *Die Schwierigkeiten der industriellen Produktion in Österreich*, pp. 33–36.

nia, and Jugo-Slavia—though they are small states, can endure the system of high protective tariffs because their economic life is comparatively undeveloped.

Briefly speaking *the Austro-Hungarian customs union satisfied an economic need which was not yet sufficiently developed in the peoples living in its territory*. Therefore when in 1850 the imperial power, anxious for the unification of its empire, dictated to the peoples of the monarchy the system of free trade, they did not yet have a serious economic motive for it. They could have existed in nearly as good a condition with customs barriers between their national territories. For instance, in Hungary, before 1850, many people got their livelihood from small artisanship which satisfied tolerably the primitive needs of the country in that period. This small industry was destroyed after 1850 by the competition of the big Austrian-German and Czech industrial plants, so that the introduction of the customs union led to the bankruptcy of a not unimportant strata of the small bourgeoisie. That is the reason why the propaganda of Louis Kossuth and his followers for political and economic independence found its most ardent supporters among the smaller bourgeoisie of the Hungarian towns, large and small. Only a constant economic growth of all the peoples of the monarchy could have been the real unifying force of the customs union and which could have filled, with a real content, the economic framework created by the despotic will of the Emperor.

But at the same time there was the danger already alluded to that the economic development through the work of industrialization would have lessened the economic interdependence among the various parts of the empire not held together by the ties of a natural international division of labor. That is to say that economic progress has produced simultaneously two antagonistic tendencies on the Austro-Hungarian customs union: one connecting, the other dissolving. We shall see their work now in detail.

B. THE DISSOLVING FORCES

a) THE AGRICULTURAL POLICY OF THE FEUDAL CLASSES

We saw that the most important condition for making the customs union indispensable for all the peoples of the dual monarchy would have been to raise them to a high level of development. It is therefore manifest that the chief effort of all those who aspired for the consolidation and maintenance of the empire should have been the propagation of culture, productivity, and economic welfare among all the people in the shortest possible time. This idea was not entirely absent in the historical evolution of the monarchy. Few of the more clear-sighted emperors, as was emphasized in our historical part,

clearly understood that only a general economic and cultural progress could have been a real tie among such various territories and
variegated populations. This policy was energetically advocated by
the socialist adherents of "Greater Austria" in emphasizing the necessity for economic and cultural progress on the basis of national
emancipation in order to maintain the monarchy. But this very conception of an economic progress and thoroughgoing democratization
was, since the times of Maria Theresa and Joseph II, always opposed
by the big feudal aristocracy of the monarchy which knew very well
that such a policy would ultimately undermine its social and political
privileges. Against this overwhelming force the imperial power could
not adequately represent the interests of the great masses of the population. It is the very essence of autocratic power that it cannot
adopt seriously and consequentially a policy of alliance with the lower

TABLE I

	Total Population in Thousands	Total Engaged in Agriculture in Thousands	Agricultural Percentage
Austrian provinces...........	28,572	13,842	48.5
Countries of Hungarian crown	20,886	13,470	64.5
Bosnia and Herzegovina.....	1,932	1,674	86.6
Total.................	51,390	28,986	56.4

classes of the population. There is a limit where it must check inevitably the growing trend of democratic and constitutional progress.

This truth is distinctly shown by the very history of the Austro-
Hungarian monarchy. Disregarding short episodes, the harmony was
complete between the dynasty and the feudal aristocracy of its empire. The government appointed by the emperors represented in all serious issues the aspirations and interests of the leading feudal classes.
Therefore, the government served the cause of economic progress only
so far as it was not opposed by the interests of the great landed proprietors.

Now under the given conditions, economic progress could only
start from the progress of agriculture. The reason is (besides the
causes which we shall discuss later) that the greater half of the population was occupied in agricultural work. Table I indicates the numbers engaged in agriculture in 1910.

On an average, therefore, the agricultural population constituted
the majority of the monarchy, but naturally the agricultural or industrial character varied largely in the different parts.

Generally speaking the western and northwestern industrialized
parts were confronted by the other territories consisting chiefly of a

small, backward peasantry and by a wretched agrarian proletariat. The industrialized and more progressive areas did not amount to a three-tenths part of the whole territory of the monarchy, whereas the other seven-tenths were populated by poor peasant masses, almost on the level of slow starvation, as we shall see in the chapter devoted to the *morbus latifundii*. In consequence of these circumstances, on the large territories mentioned above, no other real economic progress was imaginable than the heightening of the standard of life of the agricultural population.

The next method for this purpose would have been the raising of the productivity of agricultural labor and the growth of the crops. It would be unfair to say that nothing happened in this direction. On the contrary, between 1850 and 1895, the agricultural production of the monarchy made very considerable progress. Especially in Hungary, the agriculture of which was very primitive before 1848 and where the pastoral system was predominant, great improvements were made in the technique of agriculture and consequently in the productivity of labor. The rudimentary wooden plow was supplanted by the iron plow, and the pastures shrank to a small amount of the agricultural territory.[5]

An agricultural advance in the same direction—though in a far smaller degree—went on between 1850 and 1890 in Croatia and in the Austrian provinces. Generally speaking, the Austro-Hungarian monarchy as a whole made a considerable advance in economic wealth until the end of the nineteenth century. The chief driving force of this economic progress, starting in 1850, was the great landed property. In all the improvements of agricultural technique the great landowners took the lead whereas the smaller and bigger peasantry only imitated the new methods introduced by them.

An eminent agrarian expert, Arnold Dániel, was able to demonstrate that the landlords of Hungary, in the period from 1850 to 1890, were deeply interested in the increase of their agricultural production,[6] partly because in 1850 the customs barriers which formerly impeded the exports to Austria ceased to exist, partly and chiefly because the world-prices of wheat stood at that time on a very high level. In this progress the customs union was manifestly a factor, but the chief cause was the price situation of the world-market. Austria and Hungary together produced more grain than they consumed, they sold part of their crops to foreign countries, and the price situation of these countries (for instance, in southern Germany or in the states

[5] A careful discussion of the agrarian situation was given by Arnold Dániel in his important essay, "Towards the Economic Revolution of Hungary," *Huszadik Század* (1909), Vol. I. In Hungarian.

[6] For this and other connected data see his remarkable book, *Soil and Society* (Budapest, 1911). In Hungarian.

around the Channel) determined the price of the grains inside of the customs union as well. Therefore, as before 1885 the high prices of the world-market were an incentive for the Austrian and Hungarian big and middle landed interests to increase their production: the falling of prices in the later period was answered by them by ceasing to increase their outputs. Instead of trying to intensify their agricultural production by the introduction of the new methods of agrarian technique, and especially by the adoption of processes of irrigation, the big landowner class of the monarchy did not choose the road of progress but took quite the opposite course.

I must emphasize at this juncture that the Hungarian feudal aristocracy had a prominent, almost decisive rôle in the direction of the agrarian policy of the whole monarchy. The only solidly organized part of the population was the big landed interest, that is to say, that part of the agriculturists that lived on their rents and the leading element of which was constituted by the old feudal aristocracy. Among this aristocracy there were several groups: an Austro-German, a Czech, a Polish, a Hungarian, and a Croat. These last two had a more intimate cohesion and formed almost a unitary group, exercising a kind of hegemony over the other groups. Though the various groups of the feudal aristocracy were rivals of each other for the most outstanding offices of the state (in which competition generally the German and the Czech aristocracy were victorious, being the most intimately connected with the Court), they formed a united front in all cases when the economic interests of the big estates were questioned. Therefore, if the leading Hungarian aristocracy tried to carry on some measures in the agrarian policy, it could be perfectly sure of the solidarity of the other national groups.

This was the situation in the nineties of the last century when there occurred a considerable change in the agrarian policy of the big landed interest in Hungary. This agrarian policy was previously in favor of protective tariffs, but at the same time it tried to develop agricultural production. But around the year 1895 the chief effort in the agrarian policy of the Hungarian landlords became the tendency to increase as much as possible the agrarian customs duties on the frontiers of the monarchy, and at the same time to check agricultural production within the boundaries of the customs union. The cause of this change was a simple result of the factors already mentioned. It became manifest that, if the population of the Habsburg empire should continue to increase and therefore the internal need for foodstuffs of the customs union should constantly grow, a day would inevitably come when the monarchy would no longer export grains but, rather, would be compelled to import them.

Now if in a customs union there is grown substantially more grain than the population consumes, it is useless for the state to limit importation through high customs duties. These duties will not raise the price of the grain a single cent. On the contrary if there is, within a customs union, a substantial lack of grain, the customs duties will raise the price of grain to the full extent of the duties above the world-market level.

This situation was perfectly well understood by the large landed interests of the monarchy. Count Stephen Tisza, the most class-conscious representative of the feudal aristocracy, wrote a book in 1897 under the title of *Hungarian Agrarian Policy* in which he anticipated with great vigor this effect of the customs duties. "The greater the export of the crop is," so wrote the agrarian leader, "the less we can hope from the protective tariff; the smaller this export is, the more we shall enjoy the full realization of the custom duties." On the basis of statistics, Count Tisza demonstrated that "unfortunately it is not true that the customs union needs imports in grain but it is quite true that our exports in the last four years have, on the average, fallen to quite an insignificant amount." Considering this fact and, the one that the population of the monarchy was growing year by year approximately by 400,000 souls, "which increases the internal consumption exactly in the same ratio," he gave the following cheerful message to his class: "Therefore we can reasonably hope that the customs union will, in a few years, enter into the class of those countries which have a deficit in wheat and that tariff protection will be realized completely by our farmers."[7]

This meant that, at the end of the nineties of the last century, a new chance appeared for the agrarian aristocracy to raise their rents by increasing the price of the grains through the help of tariff protection. This policy was highly desirable for all the national groups of the big landed interests as it offered an opportunity to sell their grains for sixty or eighty crowns higher per ton than the world-market price. It is natural, however, that in the customs union which in 1897 still exported grains in a small measure, a lack of grains could occur only, if, on the one side, the internal need should increase and on the other, the development of production would cease or at least lag behind the inner demand. Therefore, all those who in consequence of the new situation, arisen since 1895, were desirous of seeing the prices of the grains raised by the customs duties, were impelled by the very logic of their efforts to take measures which would impede any considerable augmentation of agricultural production within the boundaries of the customs union.

This consequence was really drawn by the leading landlords of the monarchy. Since 1890, an agrarian policy was followed, which was unsympathetic toward the progress of agricultural production.

[7] The book was written in Hungarian, and later a German translation was published.

And it was in the power of the leading elements of the big landed interests to check, if not entirely at least to a large extent, the development of production. They dominated the agricultural societies and dictated to the ministers of agriculture the kind of agrarian policy that should be adopted. It was highly characteristic of the agricultural administration of both states of the monarchy that agricultural instruction of the many millions of peasant population was entirely neglected, with the exception of some sham measures intended only to placate democratic public opinion. In former times the new improvements of the agricultural technique were formally initiated by the big landed interests, and the masses of peasantry followed their example slowly. Now as the leading landlords abandoned the course of agricultural progress, the small peasantry remained without any guidance and incentive toward useful and necessary reforms. This tendency was further strengthened by the fact that a rather conspicuous part of the monarchy was occupied, as we shall see later in detail, by *fidei commissa* and by ecclesiastical and state properties excluded from free circulation.[8]

Generally speaking, that was also the tendency of the agrarian policy in Austria. Here, too, the conservative forces—though perhaps less intentionally—did not favor any serious progress in the agricultural system. However, not only the selfish interests of protection, but also the whole feudal and backward atmosphere of the country and the anachronistic distribution of landed property was highly detrimental to economic progress. Under the pressure of all these circumstances the agriculture of the monarchy had a definitely stagnant tendency since 1895.

What Count Stephen Tisza, and with him the whole big landed interest, was anxious to obtain, even before 1897, was the transformation of the monarchy into a territory needing the import of grains, in which custom duties have a price-raising tendency. This situation arrived step by step. In 1907 the point was reached from the beginning of which protective tariffs had a constant effect. It is, therefore, quite natural that the big landed property owners were extremely anxious not to increase their production. Especially in Hungary where the power of the big landlords was uncontested, their leaders dared to express publicly their antipathy against the increase of the agricultural output. When in 1911 a new minister of agriculture, Count Béla Serényi, emphasized the necessity of augmenting agricultural production on the basis of the financial interest of the state, the agricultural societies openly fought his point of view and compelled the government to

[8] This conspiracy against the raising of the agricultural output of the country was unveiled in all its details by Arnold Dániel in his essay: "Custom-union, Agriculture and Industry," in the review *Huszadik Század* (1915), Vol. II. In Hungarian.

adopt their conception, sabotaging agricultural progress. Even more significant is another episode: In 1910 Gideon Rohonczy, a great land-owning nobleman, playing a prominent rôle in parliament, fostered publicly the plan that the Hungarian state should lessen by coercive measures the production of grains, and so make the import of grains necessary, lest the grain duties should lose their price-raising effect. His plan was manifestly too shameless to be accepted openly by the government, but it illuminated with the light of a caricature the agrarian conception of the big landed interests of the monarchy.[9]

Never was the system of protective tariffs reduced so much ad absurdum as in the former Dual Monarchy. Frederick List, the father of the protective tariff, said that protection is necessary in order to develop and raise the inner production. In this conception protective tariffs were only a means, the aim was the augmentation of production. This principle was applied in a diametrically reverse direction in the agrarian policy of the former monarchy. Here protection, that is to say, its effect in raising the price, that is the rents, was the aim, and to this aim they sacrificed the increase of the production.

This policy was not only clearly emphasized by the leading landed interests, but the more the date approached when the monarchy was changed from an agrarian export territory into an import territory, the more aggressive became the land barony, and the more ruthlessly it abused its influence on the customs policy of the country. Already in 1901 it forced a very narrow-minded measure, the suppression of the so-called "milling regulations." Previously the mills were authorized to import grains without duty if they exported a quantity of flour equivalent to the imported grains. As the mills exported the finer and more expensive types of flour, while the cruder varieties remained in the country, the milling regulations had a tendency to increase the price of the finer varieties but to lower that of the coarser types consumed by the poor population. Therefore, the elimination of the milling regulations made the bread of the poor man more expensive without being seriously useful to the big landed proprietors.

Far more disastrous in its consequences was the policy of the landed oligarchy directed against the import of animals from the

[9] How exclusively considerations regarding their agricultural profits determined the general policy of the Magyar feudal aristocracy (even in its so-called "patriotic field") recently found an almost comical a posteriori verification in a speech of Count Joseph Károlyi, the leader of the Magyar legitimists. The Count attacked the propaganda of Lord Rothermere for the revision of the Trianon Treaty on the ground that a correction of the frontiers suggested by the English lord and his Hungarian adherents "would add only 2,000,000 consumers but so much agricultural terrain that to maintain the price of grain Hungary would be driven to enter the customs union with Austria and Czechoslovakia." This exposed him to the retort from the Hungarian Socialists that the slogan of the Legitimist aristocrats is "Long live dear grain and King Otto!" (See for details *The New York Times,* March 17, 1929.) But that is not a joke, it is simply the continuation of the traditional agrarian policy of the big landowners initiated by Count Stephen Tisza.

Balkan states which, beginning with 1906, made the customs quarrel permanent between the monarchy and Rumania and even to a greater extent Serbia. The customs war following this policy was highly detrimental to Serbia for which the market of the monarchy was almost a condition of existence and became a chief cause of the Jugo-Slav upheaval as we shall see in detail in a following chapter. At the same time this usurious policy made the alimentation of the monarchy more expensive and therefore checked further economic progress.

The chief result of our inquiries concerning the agrarian policy of the monarchy is this: progress in agricultural production would have been the chief condition for raising the economic and cultural interdependence of its various nations and territories. By checking agricultural progress, the landed oligarchy weakened the centripetal forces of the monarchy and at the same time increased the dissolving tendencies.

b) THE DEVELOPMENT OF INDUSTRY AND USURIOUS CAPITALISM

When the feudal aristocracy of the monarchy, by its agrarian policy above described, limited the growth of agricultural production in the Austro-Hungarian customs union, it restricted by this measure not only the social progress of the working agrarian masses but at the same time it damaged to a large extent the development of industry. A significant industrialization on a Western pattern could not arise in the Austro-Hungarian customs union and generally speaking had a rather east-European than west-European character. This comparatively small productivity of the agricultural system was a serious check to the development of industry. As the agrarian population had a small production, on the one hand, it furnished few raw materials to industry; on the other, it consumed restricted quantities of industrial goods.

It was only a corollary of the relative poverty of the agricultural population that there was a lack in the accumulation of capital which could have served as a basis for the development of big industrial plants. This connection is demonstrated by the fact that, in many parts of the monarchy, great natural resources remained unexploited partly because there was not a sufficient amount of working capital. Frederick Hertz complains concerning the wood industry:

The industrial utilization of wood is absolutely disproportionate to our riches in forests. Colossal forest territories cannot be utilized at all because of the absence of the most necessary means of communication, so that valuable supplies of wood are entirely rotting.[10]

Generally speaking, in consequence of the existing relations between powers, an inconsistent and irregular economic policy has been

[10] *Op. cit.,* p. 18.

followed: On the one hand, the governments pursued a conservative agrarian policy and refused to broaden the agricultural basis of industry; on the other hand they tried to develop an industry by customs tariffs, subventions, railway, and other privileges on the existing narrow agricultural basis. Even this half-hearted policy had certain results because in the Alpine and the Sudet provinces a comparatively more developed agriculture and other natural conditions gave a broader basis for the development of industry. Not only here, but in the other parts of the monarchy, especially in Hungary, in Croatia, in Galicia, and in the Austrian Karst provinces, certain beginnings of industry were established.

Though the chief places of industry remained in the Alpine and Sudet countries, there arose also in the eastern and southern agrarian regions of the monarchy an industry and commerce sufficiently developed to give existence to millions and millions of peoples. On these agrarian territories—in Galicia, in Bukovina, in the Austrian Karst regions, and in the countries of the Hungarian crown in 1910 there lived 7,161,000 peoples on industry, commerce, and transportation. At the same time in the Sudet and Alpine provinces the same occupations were represented by a population of 8,869,000. That means that in 1910 these two latter regions contained only 55 per cent of the whole industrial and commercial population, whereas 45 per cent were already located on the agrarian territories just mentioned.

At the beginning of the twentieth century there was already in each national territory of the monarchy a population engaged in industry and commerce which, concentrated in smaller and larger cities, was inclined and able to defend their particular interest. And now all these industrial workers and merchants living in the Hungarian, the Polish, the Czech, and the Jugo-Slav territories had their own interests which brought them into antagonism with the chief economic powers of the monarchy.

Of what nature were these particularist interests? In order to clearly understand the situation, we must see the main traits of the industrial organization of the Habsburg empire. The most developed economic territory of the Austro-Hungarian monarchy was the settlement of the ten millions of Austrian Germans, that is to say, the Alpine provinces and the Czecho-Moravian-Silesian German regions. Now it belongs to the natural economic order that the region more developed utilizes the less developed with which it constitutes a customs union as a colony. And so it was from the beginning in the Austro-Hungarian monarchy. Hungary, Galicia, the southern Slav territories—and at the beginning the Czecho-Moravian Slav territories too—were nothing else than colonies of an agrarian character which bought industrial products of the Austro-German regions. Later, when in the Hungarian, Slav, and Rumanian territories conditions arose which permitted the establishment of a manufacturing industry to a greater or smaller extent, the Austro-German banks furnished in a large measure the capital necessary for those industrial plants. The Austro-German capitalists founded these factories in the non-German territories, partly because their investments there were more lucrative, finding cheaper raw materials or labor, partly because when in the Slav-Hungarian-Rumanian regions the development of industry became more advanced, Austro-German capital participated in these enterprises in order to secure for itself a considerable part of the profits.

Almost every plant, factory, or mine in Galicia, Bukovina, or in the Austrian southern Slav territories was the property of the Austro-German capitalists or at least controlled by them. The situation, though not the same, was nearly akin in Hungary, in Transylvania, and in Croatia, though the political government of these territories utilized the Hungarian state power as far as possible to make industry independent of Austria. In spite of this, the Hungarian, the Transylvanian, and the Croatian industry were to a large degree dependent on the Austrian capital as a result of the "bank rule" which characterized the whole industrial and commercial life of the Habsburg empire.

In general the Austrian industrial enterprises were poor in capital and to a large degree subservient to credit. Therefore the industrial plants were compelled to depend upon the credit of the banks. If the plant had the form of a joint stock company, the majority of its shares was owned—directly or indirectly—by a bank.[11] And as the smaller banks were dependent on the large ones, in the Austrian provinces the few great banks controlled the whole industry. The situation was even more acute in the Hungarian countries. In many cases big Austrian and, in still more, big Hungarian banks were the masters of the Hungarian industrial plants. For instance, a single big Hungarian bank, the Hungarian Commercial Bank of Pest, had in 1910 the major part of the shares of seventy-five important mines and smelting-furnaces, textile and machine plants, mills, transportation companies, and similar undertakings. The invested capital of all these enterprises amounted to 500 million crowns and their reserve funds to 109 million crowns, a sum relatively colossal under Hungarian conditions, though in this sum there are not included other smaller plants or those directly controlled by this bank.[12]

It was said above that the Hungarian industrial and mining enterprises were mostly under the control of the large Hungarian banks.

[11] The financial situation of the industry was keenly analyzed by F. Hertz in his book already quoted.

[12] For this and other reliable information on this subject see the book of Eugene Varga, *The Hungarian Cartels* (Budapest, 1913). In Hungarian.

But this does not signify that they were independent of Austrian capital. On the contrary, the leading Hungarian banks (popularly called "big banks") utilized chiefly Austrian capital; in most cases they were nothing else than the Budapest exponents of leading Austrian banks. For instance the Viennese Rothschild group or the *Wiener Bankverein* controlled several of the most influential Budapest banks.

Wilhelm Offergeld who wrote an excellent study in 1914[13] of the development of Hungarian industry, made manifest that this industry, though not a sheer puppet of foreign countries, was largely dependent on foreign capital, that is, on Austrian capital. I remember in 1909 that a friend of mine, a high official in a Hungarian state department, stopping on the middle of the suspension bridge at Budapest and pointing out the many factory chimneys to the north and south, told me: "All the factories you see from here are the property of foreign and chiefly of Austrian capital. If, in Hungary, the state would socialize the factories, this would mean a national policy conducting Austrian property into Hungarian hands." Similar words in the same sense could have been uttered in Zagreb, in Laibach, in Lemberg, in Cracow, and even with a certain right in Prague too, though the Czecho-Moravian Slav region succeeded since the end of the nineteenth century in emancipating itself to a considerable extent from the domination of Viennese capital.

Broadly speaking, the industrial organization of the former Habsburg monarchy was the following: the industrial enterprises were ruled to a far larger extent than anywhere else by this type of capital which R. Hilferding, the able Socialist economist, called "finance capital," which lends the money but does not participate actively in the production. And the Viennese financial capital was the center to which ran all the ties of the industrial organization of the monarchy. Beside, there were two smaller foci, the finance capital of Budapest and Prague. But these smaller centers were not independent being, one might say, vassals of the Viennese. This predominant position of Viennese capital was due not only to economic causes and to the circumstance that Vienna was the oldest and richest center of the accumulation of capital, but also to its many intimate connections with the government, the armed force, and the whole administrative machinery of the monarchy. The long hand of Viennese capital reached all points of the empire: through Budapest and Prague, even the Hungarian and Czech territories. It could foster or impede the building of railways according to its own interest. It could influence the officials of the empire from the ministers to the last local authority. Let this be illustrated by a very characteristic and not at all exceptional case: in the southeastern Carpathians, in the county of Krassó-Szörény (belong-

---

[13] *Grundlagen und Ursachen der industriellen Entwicklung in Ungarn* (Jena, 1914).

ing now to Rumania), the Austro-Hungarian State Railway Company with headquarters at Vienna had important coal mines at Anina and Resica, and large surrounding territories under "closure," which made further exploitation of coal impossible. But later, not far away from it, another important coal basin was discovered. Here a smaller Hungarian group of capitalists tried to buy the right of exploitation from peasant owners. This action, however, was unsuccessful because the sheriff of the district intervened by simply arresting the attorney of the Hungarian capitalists and expelling him from the district. The victorious railway company then bought the right of exploitation for a ridiculous price.[14]

It was quite easy to monopolize the industrial and mining production by means of trust-like organizations called "cartels." It was characteristic of these conditions that no less than fifty-six special Austro-Hungarian cartels were functioning in the customs union, not taking into account the international cartels and many local similar concerns of Austrians or Hungarians alone. The cause of this phenomenon was that on the one hand, the finance capital enforced high protective duties, and on the other, it formed cartels in order to monopolize the advantages of protection.

This monopolistic system of industry concentrated around the Viennese finance capital had two great detrimental effects—two results which contributed to the undermining of a veritable free-trade policy. The one damaging result was the checking influence of the cartel system upon industrial development. In the evolution of capitalism we can well discriminate between a lower and a higher stage. The lower, the primitive type of capitalism, is characterized by the effort of the capitalists to get high profits without productive investments by usurious loans. Or, if they are compelled to make productive investments, they try to gain big returns not so much by increasing production as by raising the prices and lowering wages. The other, the more evolved type of capitalism obtained its highest expression in the American Fordism, the basic principle of which is high wages, expansion of production through the cheapness of the products, and a very high efficiency of labor. The capitalism of the former Austro-Hungarian monarchy belonged to the lower primitive type of capitalism. This usurious tendency of Austro-Hungarian capitalism was partly a result of the shortage of capital and of the high rate of interest. But it was still more accentuated by the system of protection, and the cartel monopolies.

At the same time the cartel system impeded the development of industry in another direction. When the ruling "big banks" estab-

---

[14] This and many similar cases were narrated by V. Aradi, "Notes on the Pathology of the Hungarian Industry," *Huszadik Század,* July–August, 1912. In Hungarian.

lished their cartels, they took care that inside of the customs union no new enterprise should be created which could rival their plants. And as their more important industries were originally located in the Alpine and Sudet territories, their cartel policy damaged in the first place the eastern, middle, and southern parts of the monarchy, the agrarian population of which was yet unable to develop a national industry. In this manner many natural resources of these territories remained undeveloped.

This narrow-minded monopolistic cartel policy of the Austro-German finance capital and of certain Hungarian groups connected with it controlled almost all branches of industry. It was an economic tyranny which hindered progress in the Hungarian, Slav, and Rumanian territories of the monarchy and which thereby obstructed the well-being of the population. It is, therefore, quite natural that the working-people and certain parts of the intelligentsia who suffered most under the economic depression, should regard with growing dissatisfaction, even with hatred, the leading Austrian financial powers. These financial powers were even capable of oppressing the political manifestation of this dissatisfaction. The corrupt electoral system and especially the open ballot in the Hungarian countries permitted them to exercise an economic pressure, through the smaller banks dependent on them, on the great masses of the indebted peasantry and small bourgeoisie. This pressure was so keenly felt that the intelligentsia of the various nationalities regarded as their chief aim the obtainment of financial independence by the creation of national banks under their own control. The Czechs were entirely successful in this endeavor, and the greatest Czech national bank, the *Živnostenska Banka* became, even before 1914, the leading financial institution in the Czech territories. The Hungarian efforts for financial independence were less successful because the more backward state of Hungarian agriculture made Hungarian economic life far more dependent on Austria. The Hungarian party of independence put in its program the establishment of a distinct Hungarian bank of issue, though the Austro-Hungarian bank of issue was a model institution. The national claim, however, was not a purely sentimental one, because the Austro-Hungarian bank was largely controlled by Austro-German capital and served the monopolistic interests of the big cartels. A Hungarian enterprise troubling the interests of the Rothschild group could scarcely obtain a loan.

Now this whole monopolistic industrial, and financial system injured the Hungarian, the Slav, and the Rumanian territories not only by hindering their economic progress but also in another direction. Austrian capital with the help of its cartel policy extracted enormous sums from the Hungarian, Slav, and Rumanian regions of the monarchy, and surrendered these sums mostly to the Austro-German regions and later to a smaller extent to the Bohemian-Slav territory.

As a result of the comparatively high cartel prices and comparatively low wages, the majority of industrial enterprises gained big returns and the lion's share of these returns went into the treasuries of the Austro-German capitalists. This situation damaged with a kind of absenteeism the bourgeoisie and the working-classes of those territories.

In the eighteenth century when there was scarcely any capitalism in the Habsburg empire and when the landed aristocracy was the only ruling class, the proprietors of the big latifundia in the Hungarian, Slav, and Rumanian regions did not generally live on their estates but in Vienna. They spent the revenue from their estates in the splendor of the Viennese court. The consequence of this situation was that the regions named, covered with large estates, became even poorer and had no chance for industrial progress, whereas in Vienna and in its surroundings, there arose a comparatively significant fancy industry which gave a livelihood to several hundred thousands of working-men. That is to say the absenteeism of the great landlords tending toward better living conditions for the Austro-German population in Vienna diminished at the same time the sphere of existence of the population living on the regions of the feudal estates. This effect was almost symbolized by the grain ships and the cattle herds which were furnished from the regions of the latifundia to Vienna. This feudal absenteeism was analogous in its consequences with the new one which carried the profit of the manufacturing plants in the Hungarian, Slav, and Rumanian territories into the safes of the Austro-German "big banks." The share-holders of these leading financial institutions (not to mention their officials and directors) lived for the most part in the Austro-German regions where they spent their incomes, the source of which lay in the Hungarian, Slav, and Rumanian territories, and their expenditures created a market in the German territories for many greater and smaller entrepreneurs and for the work of a considerable number of working-people.

These advantages give us the reason why the Austro-German labor movement favored, as a whole, the maintenance of the Habsburg monarchy, and why the ideology of a Greater Austria expounded by Karl Renner has emanated from these circles. But on the other hand that new urban population, which has evolved in the last decades of the nineteenth century and at the beginning of the twentieth in the Hungarian, Slav, and Rumanian regions of the monarchy, observed with growing dissatisfaction that the Austro-German urban population was progressing far better than itself. And though it did not know the real economic connection delineated above, or knew only a small and rather superficial part of it, the smaller bourgeoisie and the working-classes of those regions became ardent supporters of the nationalistic movements and of the separatistic tendencies from Vienna.

It is quite sure, as we shall see in detail, that purely idealistic motives had a preponderant rôle in the national movements. But it is equally sure that very real economic interests were unconsciously fostering them: the aspiration to liberate the industrial development from the pressure of the cartel policy and to put an end to the absenteeism of the capital.

C. THE ENTRANCE OF THE AUSTRO-HUNGARIAN CUSTOMS UNION INTO THE DANGER ZONE

We saw in the foregoing considerations that the economic development strengthened, in some respects, the forces of separatism and secession in the Austro-Hungarian customs union. But at the same time this same economic evolution produced forces tending toward cohesion and integration. Under propitious circumstances these unifying forces could have become sufficiently strong to counterbalance and paralyze the dissolving tendencies. Among these integrating forces was the very important fact that a market counting fifty million peoples gives a far greater possibility for the specialization of production than a market of only ten millions. This advantage, however, under the given conditions, was not so conspicuous as it might have been.

The Austro-Hungarian monarchy consisted of some ten or eleven distinct ethnographical territories. The populations of all these territories stood on different cultural levels and produced and consumed according to different habits and traditions. As a result the market was very much disintegrated. For instance, in the field of the cloth industry the Austrian manufacturer was compelled to produce a great variety of hats, bonnets, cloths, aprons, and handkerchiefs, because, in every national region, the people dressed according to a different style. Not only the objects of consumption, but also the instruments of production were different to a large extent in the various regions: the tools, the plows, the carriages, etc. Besides, the manufacturers were obliged to advertise and carry on business propaganda in ten different languages. These and other difficulties compelled many firms, especially those engaged in mass production, to decentralize their establishments among the various territories. Frederick Hertz has shown how this procedure made production more expensive and specialization more difficult.

This splitting-up of the market could have only one remedy: growing well-being and culture. Between the standards of life, clothes, tools, and consumption of an average Englishman, an average Frenchman, or an average north German, there is an incomparably smaller difference than between the standards of life and consumption of an average Pole, an average Serb, or Rumanian. Therefore, only a higher popular culture and welfare could have made uniform the consumption of the various nationalities of the monarchy. In this case the geographical and national differentiation of the various regions of the monarchy would not have been a disadvantage but a real advantage from the point of view of industrial specialization.

But such a propitious development had no place in the monarchy under the injuries and hindrances of its agricultural policy, its customs policy, and monopolistic cartel policy. In consequence of the low standard of life of the masses, the division of labor, and the interdependence of markets, local specialization remained very incomplete in most parts of the customs union. The result was that the forces of dissolution were more powerful than the forces of unification.

This dissolving tendency became particularly evident after 1907, when the feudal aristocracy attained the aim of its policy by checking agricultural production and the raising of prices of foodstuffs. The growing importation of grains and other foodstuffs and raw materials, under the heavy protective tariffs, made the life of the working-classes more expensive and had another dangerous consequence. For the imported grains and other raw materials the monarchy was obliged to pay with something. Being not a creditor but a debtor country, the monarchy as a whole could not pay for the raw materials otherwise than by the export of industrial commodities. The agrarian policy of the feudal aristocracy, therefore, compelled the peoples of the monarchy to enhance the export of industrial commodities after 1907.

The time when this happened was very unfortunate. For, just at the end of the first decade of the new century, as a result of the growth of population in Europe and in the northern parts of America, the food supply of these continents became less abundant than they had been between 1885 and 1905. This resulted in rising prices in foodstuffs and in a diminishing demand for industrial commodities. Since 1907 industrial competition had become very keen in the world-market.[15] England and the small free-trade countries (Belgium, Holland, Switzerland, and Denmark) had an advantage in this competition due to the free import of grains; their industrial system was aided by comparatively lower costs of production. The German Empire had protective tariffs for its foodstuffs but in spite of this competed successfully because, with its very efficient agricultural system, it was able to create a powerful and from the standpoint of technique extraordinarily developed industrial system. Austria-Hungary, however, in the customs union of which the price of the foodstuffs, and, therefore, the costs of industrial production, became very high and which in consequence of its backward state of agriculture could not develop a sufficiently efficient industry, became unsuccessful in the keen industrial competition. Its industry lost a comparatively large number of markets, not only

[15] An interesting analysis of this situation will be found in the book of Arthur Feiler, editor of the *Frankfurter Zeitung, Die Konjunkturperiode 1907–1913* (Frankfurt am Main, 1914).

outside the customs union but also inside. The German, the Belgian, and the English plants, in some of their branches, were able, in spite of protective tariffs, to offer their products on the Viennese market cheaper than the Austrian plants. Therefore, the increase in the imports of foodstuffs and the imports in industrial commodities rose simultaneously, and these imports could not be counterbalanced by an increase in exports. As a result of this situation, the commercial balance became very unfavorable. Table II clearly shows that this unfavorable balance coincided with the rising prices in foodstuffs.

In this situation the Austro-Hungarian monarchy, as a debtor country, could only pay for the excess of imports by contracting new

TABLE II

Years	Price of Wheat per Ton in Budapest in Crowns	Positive (+), Negative (−) Trade Balance in Million Crowns
1886–90*................	161	+319
1891–95*................	163	+209
1896–1900*..............	184	+127
1901–5*.................	170	+164
1906....................	157	+ 39
1907....................	201	− 45
1908....................	240	−143
1909....................	289	−427
1910....................	234	−434
1911....................	238	−787
1912....................	232	−823
1913....................	222	−627

* Average.

debts or loans in foreign countries. Such an economic system, however, must sooner or later encounter serious difficulties, if not economic catastrophes. A debtor country incapable of producing an active balance cannot maintain its position. Therefore, in 1913, the Austro-Hungarian monarchy was already a defeated empire from the economic point of view, and as such it went into the World War in 1914.[16]

[16] In his remarkable essay, already quoted, on the financial system of the former Austro-Hungarian monarchy, Paul Szende has drawn the following important conclusions which supplement the picture given here: "The financial story of Austria is the true reflection of the fatal development of the Habsburg Monarchy, a function of the dynastical imperialism. . . . . The Habsburg Monarchy differed from the great national states in this: that with every grave conflict in the international policy she stood before the question of be, or not to be. Her wars served dynastic interests exclusively. . . . . In no other state did the army so decidedly influence the evolution of finances as in Austria. One who writes the history of her army-organization gives at the same time the outlines of her financial history. . . . . Nothing demonstrates more conclusively that the Monarchy was doomed to collapse than the military budget between 1902–1914. One really has a ghostly feeling when one sees how the monarchy was approaching her end, and how she executed her own death sentence. From the overstraining of her military expenses, from this vicious circle there were only two ways out: *Bankruptcy or War*" (*op. cit.*, pp. 191–92, 200).

Of this growing indebtedness there were many symptoms within the frontiers of the empire. Among others were many new loans on the lands and buildings the bonds of which were sold in foreign countries. After 1907, the annual amount in loans contracted on immovable properties rose conspicuously. This indebtedness is shown in Table III, which covers the whole monarchy. (The sums paid on the earlier loans are subtracted.)[17]

Taking the situation as a whole, and excepting brief periods of improvement, the economic life of the monarchy was characterized after 1907, by the symptoms of decay: high cost of living, bad market conditions, and growing indebtedness. That this situation was chiefly caused by the agrarian protective duties was clearly understood by a large strata of the people who had become enlightened through propaganda of the industrial associations, chambers of commerce, and other organizations. But whether or not they recognized

TABLE III

Years	Million Crowns
1891–1900	435
1901–5	602
1906	752
1907	945
1908	1,013
1909	1,244
1910	1,721
1911	1,684

all the factors in their true relation to cause and effect, the pressure of circumstances was deeply felt by everyone, not only by the industrial population but also by the small peasantry and the landless proletariat. Therefore, the intense dissatisfaction of the great masses was constantly growing. Under these circumstances it was quite natural, in consequence of the national structure of the monarchy, that this dissatisfaction under the sway of the particularist propaganda was directed not against the economic and tariff policy, carried on in the customs union, but against the customs union itself. Joseph Grunzel, in an important book on the commercial policy of the monarchy,[18] published in 1912, characterized the dissatisfaction with the customs union as general in all parts of the monarchy. The consumers fought the customs union from economic motives, and the particularists, especially the independent party of Hungary, from political motives. The hatred of the masses against their oppressors was directed simultaneously against the customs union. For they saw that the big

[17] Calculation based on the official data of the *Österreichisches Statistisches Handbuch* and the *Hungarian Statistical Yearbook*. The Austrian figures for the years 1912 and 1913 were not published.

[18] *Handelspolitik und Ausgleich in Österreich-Ungarn* (Wien, 1912).

landed aristocrats, who raised the prices of their bread and other foodstuffs, and the usurious "big banks," which by their cartels artificially raised the prices of their fuel, petroleum, dwelling-places, and necessities, were the chief defenders and pillars of the Austro-Hungarian customs union.

And, if we think over the situation, we must acknowledge that the customs union against which these general dissatisfactions were directed could scarcely be regarded any longer as a free-trade organization. For we should not forget that, on the basis of the free-trade ideal, there was the fundamental postulate of cheap bread. This postulate is organically connected with the essence of free trade. The ultimate aim of the free-trade policy is the increase in the productivity of labor. But to make bread artificially more expensive is an attempt against the very principle of a higher productivity. From 1850 until 1900, the Austro-Hungarian customs union was a free-trade organization, at least in the sense that it did not make the bread of the masses more expensive. After 1900 and especially after 1907 this feature of free trade ceased to exist. *The Austro-Hungarian customs union became more and more a pseudo free-trade organization, an instrument for economic exploitation, for checking economic progress, and was injurious from the point of view of the laboring classes.* The economic dissatisfaction of the masses became one of the chief driving-forces of national separatism and of the growing trend of irredentism.

D. WHY FREE TRADE FAILED

If we review again this negative experiment in free trade we come to the conclusion that such a policy could only be durable on the basis of a spontaneous co-operation among peoples; and then only when the allied peoples are of equal strength or when there is at least sufficient guaranty that the stronger nation will not exploit, by a system of monopolies and political supremacy, the weaker nations. Besides, only nations economically highly developed which have a strong need for the mutual exchange of their products, that is to say, nations with strongly differentiated production and consumption, will have a durable interest in the maintaining of a free-trade policy.

This strong differentiation in production and consumption can be only the result of a great productivity of labor and of an abundant supply in food materials. If a free-trade community does not promote these basic conditions, free trade must inevitably collapse. That was exactly the case in the Austro-Hungarian Monarchy. In this way the most powerful of the centripetal forces which could have built up a real cohesion of the Empire developed more and more distinctly centrifugal tendencies.

PART IV

THE CENTRIFUGAL FORCES: THE DRAMA OF
THE GROWING NATIONAL DISINTEGRATION

CHAPTER I

THE BOOKS OF SIBYL

From the foregoing analysis it is obvious that in its ultimate result the Habsburg monarchy fell down on the national problem through its inability to solve it. All the centrifugal forces were national or at least they appeared under this mask, as the particularism of feudalism, the struggle of the bourgeoisie for administrative jobs, or the land hunger of the peasants. The economic and political analysis of these movements is a comparatively easy task. But anybody who studied these movements carefully felt distinctly that they were not exhausted by purely economic and political motives but that certain irrational and imponderable elements were attached to them.

Something mysterious, something religious, always surrounded the national aspirations, the immense creative force of which was clearly understood by the great theorists of these movements, such as Herder, Mazzini, and Fichte. That is the reason why they were capable of giving a clearer diagnosis of the national movement and its probable consequences than those thinkers as, for example, Marx and Engels, who saw only the political and economic side of these problems. The German efforts for unity, the struggles of the minor Slav peoples for emancipation, seemed to them only secondary issues. Perhaps nobody emphasized more vigorously the irrational character, the deeply sentimental and traditional nature of these problems than the eminent Transylvanian statesman, novelist, and political thinker, Baron Sigismund Kemény, who lived through the Hungarian revolution of 1848 and the bloody drama of the national struggles. This writer likened the national problem to the books of the Sibyl, remembering the Roman legend according to which the prophetess offered twelve holy books to the king Tarquinius for a certain price, and when the king found the price too high, she threw one-half of the books into the fire and asked for the remaining half the same price, and when the king continued to hesitate she threw into the fire all but one of those left, for which the king was constrained to pay the same price as she asked for the twelve. Remembering this ancient legend, Kemény made the following statement concerning the national movement of his age:

We understand that national claims have arisen which ask for solution and have this in common with the books of the Sybil, that the later the attention is drawn to them, the more heavy the price will be which we must pay for them, and the less will be the advantage secured for the public will. . . . .

Indeed the leading circles neglected terribly all the national problems of the monarchy; they misunderstood them completely, treated them in a narrow and frivolous way. It would not be too much to assert that the national question appeared with the force of a mass psychosis, the real nature of which was rarely understood, either by its leaders or by its antagonists. The struggle was carried on often for slogans and sentimental symbols which belonged more to the sphere of a religious creed than to the normal party and class struggle.

The real gravity and content of the problem was darkened in the first place by the rigid habits and judgments of value of those who held the power. The reigning nations regarded only themselves as true nations, whereas those under their rule were only second-rate nations. These so-called "state-sustaining nations," the German bourgeoisie and bureaucracy in Austria, the nobility in Hungary, in Croatia, and in Galicia were so imbued by the consciousness of their leading rôle that they felt the national awakening of their former bondsmen masses as almost a social impossibility. They viewed, until the very moment of the collapse, all these historical processes through the spectacles of their ideology of supremacy. Generally speaking, the reigning classes were entirely incapable of a sympathetic understanding with the national aspirations of the oppressed peoples. Whereas the national minorities lived mostly in an almost ghetto-like seclusion, isolated in language, in customs, and very often in religion from the ruling society.

The danger of this prejudice was heightened by an absolute theoretical blindness concerning the nature and origin of national movements which characterized the members of the upper classes with very few exceptions. This blindness became fatal when the absolutistic state was replaced by the democratic forces. The leading circles did not try to solve the problem but rather to maintain their former national privileges which they simply identified with the very interest of the state.

In a time when superficial observers could already see that the German-Magyar hegemony, the dualistic constitution, had definitely collapsed in the turmoil of the World War, the Germans leaders continued their adventurous plans in their often-quoted memorandum, the so-called *Belange*, to guarantee the German character of Austria and its centralist constitution by the elimination of Galicia, and utilizing the absolutistic means of the seemingly victorious militarism. At the same time Magyar feudalism firmly opposed all efforts which tried to reform the constitution in a spirit more favorable for the Slavs until the last moment of the monarchy. Quite symbolically characteristic of the rigidity and haughty intolerance of this point of view, is the visit of Count Stephen Tisza in Sarajevo on September 14,

1918, where he was sent by the Emperor as *homo regius* in order to seek a possible expediency in the southern Slav question, the extreme gravity of which became manifest. In this conference of an awful consequence, the most powerful statesman of the monarchy, rightly regarded as the dictator of Hungary, manifested a behavior which the reader could not understand without the knowledge of that chauvinistic dogmatism and petrified ideology of power which always characterized the Magyar upper classes. I feel it necessary to narrate this interview somewhat in detail, as it was reported by the Slovenian deputy, Mr. Korošec, the later prime-minister of Jugoslavia, in the session of the Austrian parliament of October 2, 1918, because it speaks more clearly for the psychology of the dissolution of the monarchy than any theoretical analysis. It occurred at a time when the whole Jugo-Slav world was in a revolutionary fervor and when the victory of the Entente was already undoubted even to the average man on the street, six weeks before the final collapse of the monarchy. Deputy Korošec gave the following report of the *pourparlers* of Count Tisza, based on the information of his co-nationals at Sarajevo, which was later corroborated from several sides:

That Count Tisza traveled as a *homo regius* became evident from the speech of General Sarkotić (the military governor of Bosnia-Herzegovina) and also from other signs of his trip. How did this *homo regius* behave himself in Sarajevo and how did he receive the politicians? He did not even offer a seat to them. They were obliged to stand before him as schoolboys. Count Tisza said that the memorandum of the deputation was wrong and called the right of self-determination of the nations a counterfeit. Then he made the following declaration, "It may occur that we must perish. But before we perish, we shall have enough power to smash you." Tisza, who appeared in the uniform of a colonel, lashed his horseman's whip against the memorandum, which he termed a stupidity. He even said that if the Jugo-Slavs were in Hungary he would cast them off. The Jugo-Slavs will always be grateful that the Emperor and King had sent such a man to them. . . . .

It also became public later, from this memorable interview, that Count Tisza was very much surprised by the affirmation of one Mohammedan member of the deputation, of Dr. Mehmed Spaho, according to which antagonisms had entirely ceased, which formerly existed among Serbs, Croats, and Mohammedans. The most powerful statesman of the monarchy again did not know important mass-psychological facts, with which every Jugo-Slav student was acquainted. That such and similar things were possible can be explained only by that ideology of power already referred to, and by another outstanding psychic feature of the system, namely, that the former Emperor and his dualistic staff, with a kind of moral repulsion, kept themselves aloof from all facts and incidents which could trouble their interests and traditional point of view. Again the powerful but narrow-minded personality of Count Tisza is a chief witness for this tragic ostrich-like policy. One of his great admirers, Benedict Jancsó, the well-known Hungarian publicist, by accident got possession, October 18, 1918, of the fourth paragraph of the treaty which the Rumanian government had made with the representative of the Entente at Bucharest (in August, 1916) and which fixed the future frontiers of Rumania. Jancsó ran with his announcement into parliament, and showed to Tisza the point of the contract. Tisza read it, and answered: "That is impossible, that is absurd! And you, Professor, do you believe this?" "As I am a Catholic, my device is, *credo quia absurdum,*" answered Jancsó. Tisza laughed and asked his informer to note the new frontier on a map, and after having seen the new boundary, he exclaimed "Oh! In this case Geszt, too, falls within the new boundary!" (One must know that the great estate of Tisza was in the village of Geszt.) To this Jancsó replied: "Yes, Excellency, Geszt falls within the boundary, and you will protest in the parliament of the future greater Rumania against the peace treaty, *comme un député protestaire. . . . .*" Tisza smiled again.[1] In this manner the traditional atmosphere and moral values of the estate of Geszt which determined his whole policy pressed with such a demoniac fatality on the soul of this "super-man" even in the moment of the agony of the monarchy.

But the mental and moral structure of the rising nations, too, was no more propitious for the solution of the national problems and for the right settlement of the serious conflicts than that of the ruling nations. The great majority of these peoples came without any transition into political life after the exploitation and immobility of their serf-existence of many centuries. Even the most modest beginnings of a civic education were entirely lacking among them. Living without any material or moral independence during many generations, as passive instruments of the landlords and of the official authorities, led by a superstitious rather than a moral religiosity, it is only natural that these masses were devoid of any thoughtful and rational national program. On the contrary, their national efforts were full of age-old emotional elements partly of a social and partly of a mystic origin.

It is no wonder if, in such surroundings as economic oppression, political impotence, illiteracy, the chronic semi-starvation of the masses (the *faim lente* of Proudhon was a regular aspect of social life in the backward parts of the monarchy), and a superstitious emotional and formalistic religiosity, every mass-movement had the tendency to become extremist. There was a credulous mysticism in the great masses of the population, legends originated easily, and had a wide repercussion, arousing the fantasy of the people. We saw, for

[1] Quoted by Dr. Géza Supka in the collective work of some liberal leaders, *After Five Years* (Budapest, 1923), p. 163. In Hungarian.

instance, that the popular reforms of Joseph II led to bloody explosions. Later around the tragic death of Crown Prince Rudolph new legends originated which had even a certain rôle in the drama of Sarajevo. In wide circles of the Jugo-Slav population a fantastic and absurd tale had easy currency, namely, that the murderer of Francis Ferdinand, Gavrilo Princip, was actually the illegitimate son of the wife of Rudolph, Crown-princess Stephanie, whom the royal lady had educated for revenge on the murderer of her husband, Francis Ferdinand. The reader will realize that with masses on such a low level of critical power it was scarcely possible to carry on a rationalistic policy in a modern sense.

Another circle of legends among the adherents of the Greek Orthodox and even in the Greek United church was related to the person of the Tsar, as the head of the orthodox church, who was worshipped by the backward population of many remote villages, and the picture of whom could be seen in the wretched cabins of the Ruthenian peasants. Naturally, these bigoted cults of the unknown Tsar remained not on a religious ground but sometimes assumed a semi-national ideology, fructified by the Russian political emissaries in order to create a pan-Slavistic feeling.

If all the statesmen in the Danubian empire had been men of the caliber of Comenius or Pestalozzi, even then the problem which was to educate every people in its own special national culture without disruption of state solidarity would have been one of the most difficult with which statesmanship was ever faced. But in the dual monarchy there were very few men led by common interests and humanistic points of view in the state and local administration, but as we shall see in detail, the machine of the whole state was moved in the first place by the rigid class interest of the feudal nobility and the financial capitalism attached to it. This feudal atmosphere envenomed the whole intellectual, moral, and political background of the monarchy and became the focus of all centrifugal tendencies.

CHAPTER II
MORBUS LATIFUNDII

When we treated the centripetal forces of the monarchy, we saw that the outstanding feature of the Habsburg structure consisted of the preponderance of aristocracy and the high clergy as the chief maintaining elements of the absolutist power. The old particularist feudalism was replaced by a loyal and dynastic one, but the history of the monarchy remained from the beginning until the end a typically feudal history in the sense that aristocracy and church, based on their immense estates, were almost equal in power and influence to the will of the crown. The preponderant rôle of Austrian feudalism has already been emphasized several times and demonstrated by many examples. This picture must be supplemented with another trait. This is the long series of peasant revolts in Austrian history. The fatal antagonism between the opulent feudal aristocracy and the wretched peasantry ran like a red thread through it. The bloody waves of the great German peasant war in 1525 disturbed also many Austrian provinces. In the Alpine provinces, for a time the peasants became masters of the situation but soon they were cruelly suppressed. The exasperation of the peasantry broke out almost with the force of a sociological law, in the subsequent centuries too. Now here, now there, the fire of peasant revolts burst out. Particularly conspicuous was the peasant revolt of the upper-Austrian regions in 1626. Only with the help of serious military operations and utilizing the whole power of the state, could the feudal classes triumph over the serf insurgents. The last great peasant upheaval took place in Galicia in 1846, and its repercussion was so vehement that it became one of the chief incentives for the liberation of the serfs in the monarchy.

Even more preponderant was the feudal character of the state in the other half of the monarchy, in Hungary, where the essence of social life remained always agricultural. One can say without exaggeration that, with the exception of Poland before its partition and of Tsarist Russia, there was no other country in Europe in which the feudal church and nobility had such power. Whatever period of Hungarian history we may investigate, the sounding lead of the historian will always run onto the sand of feudalism.

It has already been mentioned that the very expansion of the Habsburg monarchy over Hungary was intimately connected with this feudal anarchy. The catastrophe at Mohács which led to the dismemberment of Hungary, to the death of King Louis II, and to the acknowledgment of the Habsburgs is in a manifest causal connection with the insurrection of the crusaders of George Dózsa against their feudal oppressors. This vehement upheaval could be suppressed only by the utmost force of the feudal classes. The frenzied wrath of feudalism started a sanguinary punitive expedition against the peasantry in 1514. Dózsa himself, a man of the middle nobility of the country, was seated on a red-hot iron throne, a red-hot crown was placed on his head, and a red-hot scepter forced into his hand. His peasant companions frenzied by famine were compelled to eat from the corpse of their leader. The law of migration of the serfs was annulled and the Hungarian peasants became *de facto* slaves. That was the reason why the resistance of the country against the invasion of the Turks collapsed. I. Acsády writes:

The peasant upheaval was extinguished. The number of its participants was estimated by contemporaries at 100,000 men and that of those killed at 70,000. These figures may be exaggerated. But it is perfectly certain that the number armed was so large that Hungary could have been protected against all foreign enemies of that time.

Indeed, a decade later this internal crisis of Hungarian feudalism led to the catastrophe at Mohács: the Turks broke down the feudal anarchy without any serious resistance. What happened at Mohács was not a surprise, neither an accident. The reports of the Papal Nuncio, Burgio from Hungary, concerning the events immediately before the catastrophe demonstrate that the acute Italian observer perfectly realized the economic and moral bankruptcy of the whole system. "If Hungary," he writes in a report a year before the catastrophe, "could be saved from this great danger with three florins, I don't believe that three men could be found who would give these three florins. . . . ." The Italian diplomat observed also very keenly that one part of the feudal nobility plotted with the Turks against the King, the life of whom he saw endangered and predicted the final collapse of the country, which could be prevented only by a miracle of God.

This feudal anarchy, this envenomed antagonism between the big feudal estates and mass misery, always gave a sinister color to Hungarian history. The great Czech philosopher, Comenius, who taught in a Hungarian college between 1650 and 1654, in his memoir dedicated to the Prince of Transylvania, gave a terrifying description of the backward state and of the wretchedness of the people. He points out that Hungary could be the happiest country in Europe because its soil is one of the most fertile on the continent. In spite of this, the people are starving and plagues and epidemics devastate the country. *(Abundamus mendicis et squalore.)* They do not work in peace and, therefore, they cannot sustain war. The great educator writes:

If there is a place under the sun where envy and mutual jealousy reign, and where men fight each other with hatred and strife, where nobody respects their fellowmen, and every one is disloyal to another, that place is here. . . . .

All in all, Comenius prophesied the approaching end of the country, and lays against it the heaviest accusation of the Old Testament, saying: "Hungary is a country which devours its own inhabitants. . . . ."[1]

Such and similar observations and statements are abundant also in later periods, from the pen of unbiassed foreign travelers, all emphasizing the feudal structure of the country and the acuteness of class antagonism. Suffice to remember the notes and memoirs of Emperor Joseph II which described in a dramatic way mass-misery and feudal oppression.

A. THE FEUDAL ECONOMIC STRUCTURE BEFORE THE WAR

This feudal atmosphere of the monarchy remained until the end. Though the revolution of 1848 and its absolutist liquidation by the system of Bach destroyed feudalism from the point of view of law and gave landed property to a part of the peasantry, the power of the leading feudal circles still continued in the economic order, in the political structure, and in the moral values of society. This situation was based on the feudal division of landed property. The emancipation of serfdom liberated only a part of the peasantry, but the other part became freemen only juridically and remained in economic dependence, lacking private property, on the big landed estates. With the growth of population, there arose a continuously swelling agricultural proletariat and a dwarfish peasantry, which could only continue their miserable lives as tenants and wage-earners of the landed aristocracy.

The reign of the big landed estates was luxuriant in both parts of the monarchy and assumed a really pathological extension in the Hungarian countries. In 1913, in Hungary proper, with the exclusion of Croatia, a very small number of large and extremely large estates (the so-called *latifundia*) comprised 40 per cent of the total area of the country. The medium sized properties between 142 and 1,420 acres included a smaller area, but this category together with the great landed estates covered 54.4 per cent of the total territory of the country. Only 45.6 per cent of the country was in the possession of smaller farmers owning properties under 142 acres. The picture becomes even more gloomy if we know that only 34.5 per cent of the Hungarian territory belonged to those who personally cultivated their land. If we take into consideration that about one-tenth of this category did not own but leased their property, we come to the conclusion that *such farmer-families which cultivated personally their properties* (or with a little outside help) *did not even own one-third of the territory of the country!*

The sinister significance of this fact will perhaps not be realized by the foreign reader. He will possibly say that the division of landed

[1] Béla Obál, *Deprecatory Speech* (Eperjes, 1911). In Hungarian.

property in Great Britain was not a more propitious one and, in spite of this fact, England could obtain the highest standard in economic and social development. But the unfortunate division of landed property signified quite a different thing in Hungary than in Great Britain. This latter is the most industrialized country of the world with an immense colonial dominion, whereas in Hungary industry was small and two-thirds of the population could not live otherwise than from agriculture. An agriculturist, who had not sufficient property to get his livelihood, was compelled to work for some greater landowner. And under the very keen competition between the landless masses, this situation meant low wages and low social standards. In Hungary proper, without Croatia, there lived 2,280,000 farmer-families. According to the most optimistic calculation only 460,000 families had a property on the average above 20 acres, guaranteeing an independent livelihood, whereas 1,820,000 families, that is to say four-fifths of the agricultural population, had less than 20 acres, and most of them possessed only so-called "dwarf" properties or no property at all.

In other words: 1,820,000 families, that is to say (counting five persons to a family), 9,100,000 people, four-fifths of the agricultural population and one-half of the total population, did not possess one-third of the acreage which would have been necessary for their livelihood. Everyone can imagine how dependent this colossal, half-starved population was on the medium and large estates possessing the overwhelming part of the landed area.

This situation was further aggravated by the fact that a considerable part of the large properties, not less than 16.4 million holds, 33.6 per cent of the whole area, was entailed estate, *fidei commissa* or otherwise exempted from free circulation. That is a ratio surpassed only by Russia before the revolution, by Spain, and Great Britain. But what made the situation even more pathological is the fact that these entailed estates represented, in many cases, mammoth farms, the so-called *latifundia*. The 324 biggest landed properties occupied 19.3 per cent of the whole area, or 9,445,000 holds, which is to say, each of these large estates had an average size of more than 29,000 holds or 41,000 acres. But there were several of them which rivaled the territory of a smaller German principality. For instance, the *fidei commissum* of Prince Eszterházy contained 402,820 holds or 570,000 acres; of Count Schönborn, 240,858 holds or 340,000 acres; of Prince Coburg-Gotha, 147,296 holds or 209,000 acres; of Archduke Frederick, 145,476 holds or 206,000 acres; and that of Prince Festetich, 131,374 holds or 186,000 acres.

But outside of the five greatest, I could enumerate several others possessing smaller but still gigantic territories. The series of lay *fidei commissa* was completed by the entailed estates of high-church dignitaries and ecclesiastical corporations. Following is an enumeration of

only the biggest of them: the property of the Roman Catholic Bishop
of Nagyvárad contained 187,000 holds or 266,000 acres; that of the
Greek United Bishop of Nagyvárad, 140,000 holds or 200,000 acres;
of the archbishop of Esztergom, 96,000 holds or 136,000 acres; of the
archbishop of Kalocsa, 95,000 holds or 134,000 acres; of the bishop
of Veszprém, 65,000 holds or 92,000 acres; and that of the Chapter
of Eger, 116,000 holds or 165,000 acres.

The reader can imagine what such colossal *latifundia* and other
big estates meant in a country where many millions were without any
landed property at all and without the opportunity to get industrial
jobs.

The distribution of landed property in *Croatia-Slavonia* was analogous to Hungarian conditions. Fifty and eight-tenths per cent of
the whole area was comprised by properties above 1,000 holds (1,420
acres) and by "forest and pasture properties" (so-called by the official statistics) belonging with few exceptions to large estates or *latifundia*. On the other hand from more than two million agriculturists,
which is to say from 415,000 families, only 75,000 owned, on the average, a property above 14 holds (20 acres), whereas the other 340,-
000 families, four-fifths of the agricultural and two-thirds of the total
population, possessed only on the average 5.2 holds (7.3 acres). This
oppressive situation was further aggravated, as in Hungary, by the
excess of entailed estates amounting to two million holds, or 27.3 per
cent of the whole area.

The distribution of property in Austria varied to a larger extent
from that in Hungary. In Austria properties above 100 hectares
(247 acres) included only 33.1 per cent of the entire territory. In
spite of this conspicuous difference, the distribution of landed property in Austria, too, was not at all favorable, partly because the system of *latifundia* was also prominent in Austria, though in a smaller
measure than in Hungary.

According to the official figures the 232 biggest landowners occupied 2,370,000 hectares, which is to say, one proprietor in this category owned, on the average, 10,172 hectares or 25,325 acres. Among
these big estates we find real mammoth farms, *latifundia*, as in Hungary. For instance, among the great landlords of the former Bohemia, an official census showed the following data: Prince John A.
Schwarzenberg owned 177,000 hectares or 437,000 acres; Count Joseph Colloredo-Mansfeld, 57,000 hectares or 141,000 acres; Prince
Egon M. Fürstenberg, 39,000 hectares or 96,000 acres; Prince John
Liechtenstein, 36,000 hectares or 88,000 acres; the Emperor, 35,000
hectares or 86,000 acres; nine other princes and counts averaged 20,-
000–30,000 hectares or 49,000–74,000 acres; the Archbishop of

Prague, 23,000 hectares or 56,000 acres; and the Order of Premon-
stratensians, 21,000 hectares or 52,000 acres.

Similar lay and ecclesiastical *latifundia* could be found also in
other provinces of Austria.

These *latifundia* formed entailed estates. The formation of *fidei
commissa* was even more excessive than in Hungary because many of
the middle-sized properties likewise formed entailed estates. The size
of such a *fidei commissum* was on the average smaller than in Hungary. (In Austria 3,900 hectares or 9,600 acres, in Hungary 14,660
hectares or 36,200 acres.) But the total number of *fidei commissa* was
three times as great as in Hungary, and their total extent was not
much smaller. According to an estimate the entailed estates of Austria covered 6.4 million hectares which is to say 21.3 per cent of the
total area.

Generally speaking, the division of land in Austria, taken as a
whole, was not much better than in Hungary. According to an average estimate among the 2.8 million peasant families living in Austria,
only a half-million possessed property giving an independent livelihood, whereas 2.3 million families (11.5 million people) constituted a
class of "dwarfish" farmers or of a proletariat without any property
at all.

The wretchedness of the agricultural population varied in the different parts of Austria. It was most acute in the Carpathian and
Karst provinces, in the Sudet countries the situation was not worse
than in Hungary, whereas in the Alpine provinces it was substantially
better.

That our picture of the division of land in the former monarchy
may be complete, we must take into consideration the situation in
Bosnia and Herzegovina, which was rather a colony than a real part
of the Habsburg empire. In this province the old type of feudalism,
already annihilated in Western Europe in the eighteenth century by
the French Revolution, was still a living reality in 1914. In 1878,
when the monarchy occupied these provinces, their population lived
almost entirely on agriculture, and the greatest bulk of it with small
exception formed a class of landless serfs. After the occupation these
serfs called *Kmets*, tried to liberate themselves from the yoke of their
Mohammedan landlords. Since 1883 the Austro-Hungarian government—though very slowly and unwillingly—gave way to these efforts
and took into its hands the liberation of the Kmets. But its measures
were inadequate and the financial obligation placed upon the Kmets
were so burdensome that the "liberated" Kmet became in most cases a
slave of private usurers or usurious banks. According to Dr. Mehmed
Spaho, a native expert, the burden of the bank loans was greater than
the value of the services which the Kmet previously furnished to his
landlord. But even this "liberation" was continually hampered and

checked partly because of the conservative tendency of the Austro-Hungarian administration, and partly because of the anti-Slav tendencies of the ruling circles, the Balkan policy of which favored the economic rule of the landlords in Bosnia-Herzegovina which were Moslem to a great extent. The servitude of the Kmets was, therefore, an instrument of the anti-Slav policy. During its reign of thirty-six years the Habsburg monarchy would not or could not attain the liberation of the agricultural population.[2]

The works of Professor Karl Grünberg and of Dr. Mehmed Spaho demonstrate how incomplete and inadequate this work of liberation was. Bosnia-Herzegovina remained until the end the most feudal province of the monarchy.[3]

B. THE POLITICAL POWER OF FEUDALISM

This economic exuberance of lay and ecclesiastical feudalism naturally influenced very deeply the constitutional structure of the monarchy. The upper houses of the Austrian and Hungarian parliament (*Herrenhaus* in Austria, *Förendiház* in Hungary) decided the fate of each bill because their consent was necessary after the lower houses had passed it. Both upper houses were the political organization of the feudal aristocracy, both lay and ecclesiastical, their members having been the archdukes of the imperial family, the heads of the aristocratic families, and the chief ecclesiastical dignitaries. Though some of their members were nominated by the Emperor-King from the representatives of the higher bourgeoisie and intelligentsia, these elements never had a real importance.

This atavistic nature of the upper houses was counterbalanced only in Austria by a democratic lower house recruited by universal and secret suffrage. Unfortunately this true popular representation was not introduced until 1907, so that it was only a belated experiment with democracy at a time when the centrifugal tendencies of the monarchy were already fatal. Formerly, as previously mentioned, the Austrian parliament was based on a highly artificial kind of representation, the so-called system of the *Curias*,[4] properly speaking, a continuance of the old feudal representation.

Nevertheless after the introduction of universal suffrage and the elimination of the *Curia* system, Austria showed the growing influence

[2] In a letter of May 28, 1913, General Potiorel, the military governor of the provinces, opposed the reform plans of the joint-finance minister, Bilinski, especially the obligatory liberation of the Kmets. He announced the principle that the Serb agricultural population "should be maintained also in the future in their lethargic state of mind." (Quoted in *Der Krieg,* June, 1928.)

[3] Karl Grünberg, *Die Agrarverfassung und das Grundentlastungsproblem in Bosnien und der Herzegovina* (Wien, 1911); Mehmed Spaho, "The Bosnian Agrarian Problem," *Economic Review,* May, 1912. In Hungarian.

[4] See pp. 104-5 of the present book.

of the democratic currents and the ballot being in secret a forceful intimidation of the electorate, was quite exceptional and occurred only in the most backward provinces (Galicia!). Whereas the lower house of the Hungarian parliament was scarcely less a feudal body than the upper house (only its voice was louder and its manners less aristocratic), and it was in every important issue an ardent supporter of the claims of the big landed interests. There were before the collapse in the lower house about fifty aristocrats, the others were the attorneys and the officials of the big landlords or belonged to the richer middle nobility, called after the English pattern the "gentry," a class the interests of which were intimately connected with those of the aristocracy. Generally speaking, the Hungarian parliament remained until its end a representation of what was called in the medieval terminology the *una eademque nobilitas*, signifying the unity and the theoretical equality of the upper and lower nobility. This situation was expressed by the custom that the members of the parliament addressed each other in private intercourse in terms of "Thou" which was a symbol of membership in the so-called "good society," "the society of gentlemen." Representatives of the peasantry and of the smaller bourgeoisie were very rare in this aristocratic corporation and not a single deputy of the city workers and agricultural laborers ever sat in the Hungarian parliament. In the country of an immense landless proletariat and of a "dwarfish" peasantry, such a parliament could naturally only be maintained by an excessively restricted and artificial electoral system. In 1914 only 6.5 per cent of the population held the franchise whereas 54.5 per cent of the farmers, 59 per cent of the artisans, 44.2 per cent of the merchants, 58.5 per cent of the employees of the state, 69.6 per cent of the private employers, and 98 per cent of the workers were excluded from the franchise. But this very limited franchise alone was not sufficient to guarantee a parliament fit for the interests of the feudal classes. Therefore, some other instruments were needed for the falsification of popular opinion. These were open voting, an excessive gerrymandering, official pressure, corruption, and the utilization of the armed force for the intimidation of the electorate. Among these guaranties of the feudal constitution the most important was the open voting because, by this means, the poorer electorate could be easily terrorized by the local administration which was entirely under the control of the feudal circles. This administration could punish the voters of the opposition by an intricate system of fines shrewdly managed and remunerate the chief bosses of the government by a series of administrative favors. At the same time an extensive network of usurious banks, entirely dependent on the local administration, could influence in the same direction the recalcitrant electorate by threatening to recall their loans. Though the opposition to this system became in the last decades of the monarchy very embittered and vehement and though, as previously mentioned, the crown itself promised the introduction of universal suffrage, in its struggle against the feudal parliament which menaced the unity of its army, the ruling classes astutely frustrated the parliamentary reform to which they were bound by a compromise made with the king in 1906.

Count Julius Andrássy, then leader of the feudal Coalition, was successful, as already mentioned, in utilizing the difficulties of the crisis concerning the annexation of Bosnia-Herzegovina to induce the monarch to abandon universal suffrage and to give his consent (the so-called "presanction") to the falsification of the plan by introducing a bill based on plural voting and the open ballot (1908). Andrássy motivated his reactionary measure as a defence against the nationalities of the country and a safeguarding of the "national character of the state." But the real motive was his hatred and distrust of the Hungarian peasantry at large on whose economic exploitation the whole system was based.[5]

This attitude of the ruling classes remained unchanged. In 1912 Count Stephen Tisza carried on a sham reform maintaining unaltered the former system in its worst aspects, after a bloody suppression of the general strike of the workers at Budapest which tried to enforce the solemn promise of the Crown for the introduction of universal suffrage. Even during the war, immediately before the catastrophe, when the young king experimented again with popular reforms, a so-called democratic member of the cabinet, Dr. William Vázsonyi, elaborated a bill with the outspoken aim of depriving the masses of the national minorities of suffrage.

Not only the parliaments, but also the control of the provinces and the local administration were directed by the feudal interests and

[5] Andrássy tried to convince the Socialist leaders of the desirability of his plan and that they should abandon the claims of the peasantry. One of the leaders, Dr. Sigismund Kunfi, later minister of public instruction in the cabinet of Count Michael Károlyi, who discussed the matter with the Count, has recently narrated his whole argument. His motivation is so characteristic of the whole period that I cannot refrain from quoting it: "You do not know, gentlemen, what a malevolent creature such a peasant is, filled with hatred for the towns, the culture, the industrial proletariat. I know their life, their character from direct experience; I live as landlord in the country; I know the physical and moral dirtiness in which they are living. You as Socialists, you wish laws for the protection of the workers. Do you believe that the peasant would favor such measures? You wish a city culture, good elementary schools. You are anti-clerical. The peasant is illiterate, would not give a farthing for social or cultural aims, he is clerical and anti-semitic. Universal equal suffrage would unleash this flood of barbarism upon the whole country and the very interests of the social-democratic workers whom we consider as an element of the national culture would be submerged in this ocean of illiterate, clerical, anti-semitic and anti-social peasants. . . . ." The Socialists asked the minister whether he would be willing to advocate these principles publicly for he always used to extol the high qualities of the Magyar race (the purest element of which was this peasantry so despised by him). To which the conservative leader answered with a defensive gesture: "Well, are you of the opinion that the task of politics is to tell what one really means?" (In the *Arbeiter-Zeitung*, Wien, November 11, 1928.)

the groups connected with them. In the provinces of Austria, in the election of the *Landtag*, the old system of the *Curia* continued which was in some of the provinces even more anachronistic than the former parliamentary electoral procedure. In many places the indirect representation of the village Curia was maintained. So in Galicia, in Bukowina, in Silesia, Dalmatia, Tyrol, and Vorarlberg the leading rule of the big proprietors was secured not only by their distinct Curia but also by the pressure which they could exercise on the Curia of the villages. In some of them the influence of the clergy was preponderant. There was no possibility for the manifestation of popular will. Only the uniting and controlling force of the imperial bureaucracy checked to some extent the exuberance of particularist interests. Besides, the growing influence of the industrial and commercial classes counterbalanced sometimes the feudal hegemony, but there was nowhere an opportunity for a true, local self-government.

In the Hungarian half of the monarchy the so-called self-government of the county *(Vármegye)* had even less connection with the interests of the people. The Hungarian county organization, the basis of self-government, remained unaltered as it used to be for centuries, an organization of the upper and middle nobility with the exclusion of all other interests. The officials of the counties and of the districts were elected by a central committee. One-half of this organ was recruited from those who paid the highest taxes (elements belonging almost exclusively to the sphere of interest of the great landed property), the other half was elected on the basis of the same restricted franchise and open ballot as was parliament. Naturally the county elections were controlled even more efficiently by the landed aristocracy than the national elections, because the noble proprietors regarded their county as a kind of family estate. Especially for the middle-class nobility, the gentry, the control of the counties was an excellent opportunity to give elegant and remunerative jobs for their less talented members or for those who squandered their patrimonial possession. One can say without exaggeration that, in most of the counties, three or four leading families disposed of all the desirable offices, filling them with their relatives or intimate friends. This character of the counties, as nurseries of the nobility, became more and more unbearable, so that the better elements of the nobility themselves began to fight the institution and to ask for its secularization. The roughness and the corruption of the county officials was almost proverbial and their own press organ wrote repeatedly that the Hungarian administration was "sick and impotent . . . . eternal obstacle to the development of the nation, to the building up of the modern Hungarian state."

Liberal and socialist public opinion regarded the county administration as the hotbed of political and social reaction. And even the more far-sighted elements of the landed aristocracy realized that the agrarian socialist movement, which became dangerous at the end of the last century, was caused by it to a large extent. For instance, a very conservative statesman and a leader of the feudal interests, Count Joseph Majláth, who was very much impressed by the agrarian Socialist upheavals in Hungary, wrote in a book published (1905) in German for the information of foreign opinion, the following criticism of this administration:

The administration is very defective and is generally apt from all points of view to foster dissatisfaction and to make the people receptive to doctrines which attack the administration. . . . . The people see the representatives of this administration only when taxes or fines must be paid or last, but not least, on the occasion of the various elections. . . . . No wonder that the organs of the administration are not liked.[6]

Another outstanding leader of the great landed interests, a notorious enemy of Socialism and the secretary general of the leading agrarian association of the big estates, Julius Rubinek, characterized as follows the Hungarian administration in his book devoted to the dangers of agrarian socialism:

The inefficiency, the unreliability and the corruptness of the administration became colloquial in the past. Not only in the Hungarian plains [the chief center of the agrarian troubles], but all around the country such complaints abound. It became almost a principle that the peasant can never be right and, therefore, he seldom appealed to the justice of the administration, knowing that he would always be wrong. . . . .

This dangerous situation was not mitigated as in Austria by a more objective and just attitude of the central administration, which very often checked the abuses of the Austrian provinces. In Hungary, the central administration itself was controlled by the same aristocracy and gentry which dominated the local administration. One can say in fairness that all the more influential officials of the country were related to each other by family or by marriage ties. This situation had a symbolical expression in the fact that all the leading officials were members of two very exclusive national clubs, one belonging to the gentry, the other to the aristocracy. It was generally known that the will of these two clubs, especially that of the aristocrats, constituted a power to which every government was tributary.[7]

C. THE SOCIAL AND ECONOMIC STANDARD

It was a natural result of this economic, political, and administrative situation that in no state of Europe (with the possible exception

[6] *Studien über die Landarbeiterfrage in Ungarn.*

[7] A vigorous description of the situation may be found in Joseph Diner-Dénes' book, *La Hongrie, Oligarchie, Nation, Peuple* (Paris, 1927). The main thesis of the book, however, which tries to justify the conspiracies of Transylvanian feudalism with the French autocracy, seems to me erroneous.

of Russia) did the antithesis become so acute between the unheard of luxury of a small group and the boundless misery and ignorance of the masses. I was often told by foreigners of more refined sensibility and taste that they were exasperated by the culinary luxury and the big army of servants and lackeys of the brilliant castles, especially when they visualized the other side of the story, the unhygienic over-crowding of the slums of the agricultural servants in the backyards, and the pallid and underfed peasant children in the village schools. An entire monograph would be necessary to describe the social and moral misery of the backward parts of the monarchy in the Hun-garian plains, in Transylvania, in Galicia, and Bukowina. Here I can give only a few outstanding facts. It was a common complaint of all the social politicians that the standard of life of the population, espe-cially in the districts crowded with *latifundia*, was characterized by a state of slow starvation. For instance, the average yearly income of a Hungarian agricultural laborer before the war varied between 60 and 100 dollars (that of a woman laborer only between 40 and 50 dol-lars). But even this low standard of living was very often debased by a widely spread custom of usury and compulsory labor (so-called *ro-bot*), passionately combatted even by the better conservative leaders. Mr. Rubinek, in his book already mentioned, described these abuses in detail showing how, by the arbitrary curtailment of wages, by stipu-lations of unpaid overtime work, and being forced to furnish draft animals without remuneration, the standard of life of big masses of population became even more precarious.

When the abused agricultural population tried to better their ad-verse conditions by economic organizations, the county administra-tion swooped down upon them and suppressed by fines and imprison-ments all endeavors to form political, professional, or even cultural associations. And, when the agricultural laborers resorted to the in-strument of the strike, during the harvests, in order to secure better labor conditions, the Hungarian government itself established a kind of a "scab" camp. The same ultra-chauvinists, who advocated a scheme of a complete Magyarization of the country by the assimila-tion of all other nationalities, did not hesitate to transport thousands and thousands of Slovak and Ruthenian wage-earners into the Hun-garian plains in order to coerce the purely Magyar agriculturists, by the lower standard of life of these Slav competitors, to accept living conditions unbearable for them. This strike-breaking organization established and controlled by the state was elaborated into the minut-est details under the administration of a minister of agriculture, Dr. Darányi. The situation became so acute that in 1898 a special law was passed "for safeguarding national production." The measures of this exceptional law were so brutal that a magazine of moderate tend-ency, the *Monatschrift für Christliche Sozialreform*, wrote the following judgment about it: "Nobody will be able to suppress the thought that this law belongs to the most barbarous which a human mind has ever excogitated for the suppression of fellow men."

This terribly low level of earning conditions and of the standard of life had its expression in many facts of social and cultural life. The international hygienic and demographical congress held in Budapest in 1894 gave opportunity for several reports demonstrating the slow starvation of the Hungarian agricultural proletariat. The complaint was general that in many regions two or three large servant families were crowded in a single, unhealthful room and that living conditions in general endangered the physical and moral health of future generations. Dr. Eugene Farkas, a hygienic commissioner, made a speech in 1897 in the Hungarian Medical Association demonstrating on the basis of official figures that the elementary conditions of the working-people were in many places of the country under the strictest biological minimum of existence. No wonder that alcohol played everywhere an important part in the food ration of the agriculture workers. Other hygienic experts emphasized the fact that the population of entire regions became degenerated and that trachoma, typhoid fever caused by famine, and pellagra, that sinister disease of starvation, could not be eliminated. The famous statistical inquiries of Charles Keleti, a widely known specialist, gathered from various parts of the country, demonstrated the substantial lack of the Hungarian agricultural population in the most necessary foodstuffs.

The general standard of life was not higher in many provinces of Austria, especially in Galicia, Bukovina, and Tyrol. The pellagra took dangerous proportions. The great majority of the villages of Bukowina was infected with this disease. The supreme hygienic council of Austria, in a communication made in 1909, emphasized that pellagra was still increasing in spite of the measures undertaken by the government. The ravages of tuberculosis on the Hungarian plains always alarmed hygienists and philanthropists. Tuberculosis was also often called *morbus Viennensis* and the records of the infant mortality both in Hungary and Austria ranged among the highest in Europe.

These entirely unsatisfactory economic and social conditions naturally influenced the general cultural standard too. Though the ratio of illiteracy in Austria was not excessively high (according to the statistics of 1910, 16.5 per cent of the population above ten years was illiterate), the cultural level of several provinces was desperate. For instance, in Dalmatia 62.8 per cent, in Bukowina 53.9 per cent, in Galicia 40.6 per cent, and in Istria 39.8 per cent were the respective proportions of illiteracy.

In Hungary, conditions were far worse. The percentage of illiteracy above six years in Hungary proper was 31.3 per cent, and in Croatia, 47.7 per cent. In certain regions the ratio was alarming.

For example, in the county of Mármaros, 78.2 per cent, in Szolnok-Doboka 71.4 per cent, and in Hunyad 64.4 per cent of the population could not read or write. But in this respect the most backward part of the monarchy was also the "colony" of Bosnia-Herzegovina, where 82.9 per cent of the population was illiterate.

There is, however, a field of statistics which demonstrates even more emphatically the economic and cultural backwardness of the monarchy. That is the statistics of emigration. Between 1876 and 1910 more than 3,500,000 men abandoned the monarchy; of these almost three millions migrated to the United States. The greatest emigration was witnessed in the last decade before the war. In this period more than two million people went to the United States. The monarchy reached the sorrowful record that it furnished 24.39 per cent of the total emigration directed toward America, surpassing by this even the emigration rates of Italy and Russia. Besides, there was a strong periodical emigration, especially toward Germany, for the performance of agricultural work. Year by year several hundred thousands of workers were compelled to abandon for months their native soil unable to give them a bare subsistence.

The loss in blood to Hungary was particularly discomforting, because its backward industrial development could not supplant the lacking opportunities in agricultural work. Julius Rácz, a noted economic expert, exclaimed in 1908:

From the countries of the Hungarian crown, 200,000 to 250,000 strong men are compelled to emigrate from the backyard of the *latifundia,* of the *fidei commissa,* and of the episcopal estates. . . . . Since 1890 this unfortunate country lost at least 1,500,000 emigrants. . . . . At the same time in the last decades the state used its power to help the aristocratic families to expand their *fidei commissa* from 463,352 holds to 2,362,822 holds and the ecclesiastical estates to increase their dominions from 1,288,000 to 2,506,000 holds. . . . .[8]

D. THE MORAL AND SOCIAL ATMOSPHERE

Such and similar statistical data which could be easily enlarged to a volume cannot, however, give an adequate conception to the foreign reader of the pressure which the system of the *latifundia* exercised on the whole people of the monarchy. Every careful observer was under the terrifying impression of this situation. The slogan of *morbus latifundii* used by the writer of this book in a public discussion at the Sociological Society of Budapest became winged words in Hungary, shared also by some few of the more enlightened representatives of the aristocratic classes. For instance, Count Michael Károlyi, the

[8] Compare the detailed study of Rácz, "L'état économique et social de la Hongrie au vingtième siècle" in a collective work of Hungarian liberals and socialists, which I edited under the title, *La Hongrie Contemporaine et le Suffrage Universel* (Paris, 1909).

leader of the radical group in the Independent party, and a follower of the Kossuthist anti-Austrian traditions (later president of the Hungarian Republic after the collapse), combined the claims of his group for national independence with those of universal suffrage and the dismemberment of the latifundist system. Unfortunately, the time-old feudal organizations, spread as an immense polyp on the country, and impeded all efforts toward democratic organization and cultural reconstruction. Lord Bryce made somewhere the profound remark that democracy is not so much a governmental form as it is a particular feeling and psychic attitude. Well, such a true democratic feeling and attitude could not be developed in the backward parts of the monarchy under the pressure of feudal absolutism: the castles of the magnates, the local exponents of the latifundist church, and the corrupt administration combined with alcohol shops of the village usurers made the resistance and reorganization of the peasantry and the working-classes impossible.

It is very difficult to describe to foreign readers the specific moral and mental atmosphere of the monarchy, this curious mixture of feudalism, clericalism, and usurious capitalism. Space does not permit me to analyze the situation in detail, therefore, I shall give only two documents which will illustrate it more clearly than would a long array of statistical facts. One is the description by Nicholas Bartha, one of the most brilliant and influential publicists of Hungary at the end of the last century, of the terrible misery, social and moral isolation of the Ruthenian people (of the Ukraine stock) in the northeast of former Hungary, between the mill stones of the estate of Count Schönborn and of the corrupt administration. I must emphasize that Bartha was not only a conservative but an almost reactionary politician who had great responsibility in the increasing acuteness of the Rumanian question in Transylvania in consequence of his ultra-chauvinistic policy. This man wrote a book, in 1901, entitled *In the Land of the Kazars* ("Kazar" was the nickname of the Jewish usurers in this region) which had a great repercussion throughout the whole country. In this remarkable book the author described the true pathology of the Schönborn estate occupying 240,000 holds (341,280 acres). This estate, like a little medieval state, included some two hundred villages. Two constituencies were under its exclusive control and the management of the estate used on every occasion to ask the prime minister whom he wanted to be elected to parliament. Besides, its influence was decisive in other constituencies of the country. Bartha emphasized the fact that the most vital interests of 70,000 Ruthenian peasants were sacrificed to the estate and, therefore, only armed force could maintain this situation.

The fragmentary parcels of land cultivated by the peasants were scattered confusedly beyond the territory of the *fidei commissum*. In

order to reach his tiny property the peasant was compelled to walk
several hours without roads over ditches without bridges. The mammoth forest of the estate pressed hard on the village and projected
into the churchyard. If the calf or the hen of the peasant strayed into
it, he was heavily fined.

The hand of the estate is everywhere. . . . . If the little boy gathers
some faggots in the forest in order to prepare fire because his sick mother
is quivering with fever, that is a grave crime for which he must be sentenced. . . . . If the little girl picks some strawberries or mushrooms, the
inspector catches her, tears off her clothes and takes away her plate. . . . .

The colossal forest served exclusively for hunting purposes. A
forest economy is almost unknown in this primeval forest *latifundium*
of 200,000 holds. Game is the only care of the administration.

The sovereign stag should not be disturbed in its family entertain-
ments. . . . . What is a Ruthenian compared with it? . . . . Only a
peasant! . . . . The hunting periods last two weeks. There come some of
the Schwarzenbergs, of the Kolowrats, of the Liechtensteins, ... they
tell each other their hunting adventures, it was so last year, it was so the
year before . . . . so will it be in the future. . . . . You know? . . . .
Colossal . . . . Magnificent . . . . The villain . . . . Oh colossal . . . .
What a fellow! . . . . You know? . . . . In order that they should tell
each other all this in the smoke of excellent Havana cigars in the flickering
light of the fire place, 70,000 Ruthenians must be doomed to starvation by
the army of the officials. . . . . The deer and the wild boar destroy the
corn, the oats, the potato, and the clover of the Ruthenian (the whole harvest of his tiny lot of half an acre). . . . . Their whole yearly work is destroyed. . . . . The people sow and the deer of the estate harvest. . . . .

It is easy to say that the peasant should complain . . . . but where
and to whom? Those who have the power he sees always together. The village chief, the under sheriff, the sheriff, the district judge, the tax officer,
the forester, the steward, and the manager all are men of the same education, of the same social pleasures, and of the same standard. . . . . They
constitute the one and same society. They form the *intelligentsia.* They are
dependent upon each other. They fraternize, they drive in sleighs, they
play cards together, they arrange baptismal festivals. . . . . All these
things are well known to the injured peasant. . . . . From whom could he
hope for justice?

Such and similar accounts were written based on long personal observations by the Hungarian publicist of a very conservative type. Is
it a wonder if, under such conditions, the wretched peasant was entirely dependent on "Jewish usury" presented by the Hungarian feudalism as the real source of the evils and against which Bartha has directed his chief publicistic energy?

The other document which I beg to quote narrates concerning another latifundist region of the monarchy, the classic land of Polish
estates, Galicia. A Galician member of the Austrian parliament, the

noted Polish Socialist Daszynski, later minister of the Polish Republic, painted a picture of the situation of his fellow-countrymen which caused an acute sensation in the Viennese chamber because the whole speech of the Socialist leader was based on official data or on conservative sources (November, 1898).

Prince Francis Puzina has stated that the Galician peasant employed on the estates receives as his yearly income 900 pounds of bread less than would be necessary to the maintenance of his family. . . . . The people must permit their children to have rickets or they must educate them to be thieves and scoundrels. . . . . It is a well-known fact that the undernourishment of the people became a constant phenomenon not only in particular districts but in the total working-population in Galicia.

This situation combined with the corruption of administration is the chief cause of the cultural backwardness of the Galician people. In the school year 1896–97, 400,000 children of school age were without any instruction and 500 elementary schools already established were closed. Besides usury and alcoholism pressed heavily on the whole peasant population. Daszynski publicly declared that the leaseholders of the liquor monopoly were members of the highest Polish aristocracy, of the Potockis, of the Badenis, etc., who sublet their right to the Jewish innkeepers.

The Jew is the entrepreneur and he often pays to his lords 50 per cent higher rent than those aristocrats pay to the state. . . . . But the great lords understand very well how to divert the odium of the exploitation to the Jewish innkeepers. . . . . The truth is that the Jewish usurers and the Polish aristocrats had the same responsibility for the exploitation and poisoning with alcohol of the Galician people. . . . . The system of concessions, of protection, of corruption, of paying for connections, and of illegitimate family influences, all these corrode the body of Galicia; all these cause the usurers of the villages to feel themselves so powerful in the face of society. Everybody shouts against them, the magistrates were repeatedly ordered to combat them seriously, according to law, but they laugh up their sleeves, hearing about all these persecutions. Why? Because they possess in the nobility, in the *Szlachta,* in this powerful factor of the country their patrons, their born historical defenders. . . . .

And these were not isolated cases. Almost from all parts of the monarchy similar or worse facts could be cited. Hundreds and hundreds of thousands were driven to premature death or to emigration.

E. THE BALANCE SHEET OF THE SYSTEM

In this atmosphere of misery, illiteracy, pellagra, and administrative abuses, a self-conscious and intelligent citizenship remained a rare phenomenon. Practically there was no popular control or participation in government, and entire regions stood under the despotic rule of the feudal administration. Nowhere in Europe with the exception of Tsarist Russia were there so many autocratic men—*legibus soluti*

—who regarded the whole state and the whole administration as their private dominion. I remember, for instance, that in the Hungarian state department of agriculture there went on a double administration: the one carried on the affairs of the upper ten thousand, with an admirable swiftness and courtesy, the other was occupied with the business of the *misera plebs contribuens* in a slow and rigid manner. On the other hand nowhere, Russia again excluded, were there so few intellectually and morally free men.

And feudalism ruled not only by its economic, political, and administrative power, but also by the force of its traditional prestige. A democratic type of citizenship could not develop because, if somebody had arisen from the people or from the smaller bourgeoisie, he regarded as his chief ambition getting nobility or a baronetcy and being accepted into one of the exclusive clubs. In this atmosphere there grew up a real art of commanding and exercising social prestige. The title of a count, the protection of an archduke, or a leading position in the county administration, opened all doors and blew away all resistance. The smile of the feudal lord and the invitation into his castle were honors which few common citizens could resist.

Only in such surroundings could it happen that in the lobby of the most elegant Viennese hotel Archduke Otto could have appeared drunk and absolutely naked, adorned only by his officer's cap, and his sword-knot in order to enjoy the screaming of the terrified ladies of society; that one of the most honored leaders of the socialist party, Engelbert Pernerstorfer, could be attacked in his home by some unknown intruders because he dared to criticize severely in Parliament the heroic exploit of the Archduke, though not mentioning either his name or his title; that Count Tisza, the most powerful statesman, coming too late to the railway station could have the agent order back the train, already started, by telephoning to the next station; that Andrew Achim, a peasant leader of the Hungarian plain, could be shot for political motives by two noble youths who were twice acquitted by the jury. It is quite natural that this almighty social caste could not only carry on its economic and political interests but could also suggest to society its whole scale of values in historical and ideological matters. He was not regarded as a real *Ur* (to translate this word with "gentleman" gives only a pale shadow of the original feudal distinction) who thought in things essential otherwise than the members of the leading clubs. The famous description of Ostrogorski concerning the moral atmosphere of English society before the first parliamentary reform is only a jaded picture compared with the social environment of the former monarchy.

This situation had many consequences which pushed the monarchy into disaster.

The system of the large estates by their antiquated method of production hindered the accumulation of capital and the development of city life.

The dangerous emigration which it created (the law of Francis Oppenheimer, according to which "the emigration of a certain territory grows in direct proportion to the square of the number of the big estates found there" became here a reality) caused the empire to lose its most active, most courageous, most enterprising human material. The emigration to America was a real safety valve for the monarchy which saved the overheated caldron from eruption, thus making a renewal by revolution impossible.

Sapping the economic and moral development of the country, it made impossible that exchange of minds and products without which no real solidarity among the members of a nation could be established.

The beneficiaries of the system impeded purposely the increasing of agricultural production and the exploitation of the chief resources of agricultural land, in order to enjoy more fully the effects of protective tariffs. This policy became the deepest cause of cultural and social stagnation.

For the maintenance of their economic and political privileges, it was an outstanding interest of the feudal system to make national controversies more acute. As an unproductive leisure class, it was compelled to assume the rôle of a "state sustaining element" defending the country against the "high treason" of the national minorities and of a recalcitrant proletariat.

For the increase of its revenues it proved to be a good instrument to exclude the importation of animals from the neighboring states, a procedure damaging heavily not only the economic life of Serbia and Rumania, but also the standard of life of the middle and working-classes of the monarchy. This selfish policy of the ruling classes led to a customs war and became a chief cause of the envenomed acuteness of the irredentist problems of the monarchy.

And when as a natural result of all these activities the nationalistic problems of the empire became insoluble, there was again the big landed interest of the monarchy which gave the final initiative to that adventurous foreign policy which pushed the Habsburg monarchy into the débâcle. Again, during the World War, it was the corrupt cruelty of the feudal administration in the backward parts of the monarchy which fomented despair, exasperation, and hatred against the state and became a chief cause of dissolution. The most popular Magyar journalist of this period, Ladislas Fényes, member of the last parliament before the collapse, received daily 100 to 200 letters from the Fronts in which the soldiers in the trenches made violent complaints against the injustices of the *Hinterland* that their families were starving in consequence of the maladministration of the subsidies guaranteed by the state. According to a rumor widely spread among

the soldiers which I often heard in my capacity as a war-correspond-
ent, one of the village officials told a soldier's wife when she lamented
that she was unable to maintain her family: "If you cannot live, go
to the pasture and graze!" Perhaps this episode is only a legend,
based on a mass-psychosis, but it truly characterizes a situation which
led to the expulsion of 86 per cent of the village officials by the people
at the beginning of the October revolution in 1918. Finally this system led to an unscrupulous bloodshed of the population on the battlefields even in cases when there was not the least chance for any success.
So at the end of September, 1918, when the Bulgarian front collapsed
and the military situation of the monarchy became evidently untenable, two divisions were sent for the "reinforcement of the Turkish
front." In an intimate conversation with a press conference, debating
the situation, Premier Wekerle said with a gesture which could not be
misunderstood: "Yes, we sent two divisions for the reinforcement of
the Turkish front, but we shall never see these poor people again."
The lives of about 20,000 soldiers did not count.[9]

From whatever side the objective observer may consider the history of the dissolution of the monarchy, he cannot fail to see that the
feudal structure and atmosphere of the monarchy partly caused it,
partly made it more acute, and hastened it. Only so can we understand
the truth of the rather intuitive diagnosis of Rudolph Kjellén, the distinguished Swedish scholar: "Like an animal form of the tertiary period, amidst the animal kingdom of the present day, so the Great Power
of Austria-Hungary was a remnant of a previous stage of evolution,
of the territorial state of the middle ages." The skeleton of this political ichthyosaur was formed by the system of the large feudal estates.[10]

[9] This episode is absolutely authentic. It was narrated to me immediately after
the conference by some reliable and honest journalists in a state of great excitement.

[10] A recent writer of the Hungarian counter-revolution, Professor Julius Szekfü,
undertook the task of demonstrating in his book, *Three Generations* (Budapest,
1922), in Hungarian, just the opposite thesis than the one advocated in the present
work. Namely that the chief cause of the Hungarian tragedy was partly an excess
of the liberal spirit of the West and the exuberance of certain racial sins of the
Magyars (vanity, conceit, short-lived zeal, self-deception, megalomany, disregard of
reality, inertia, contempt of productive work) combined with the corrosive influences
of Jewish radicalism and internationalism. The falseness of this interpretation seems
manifest to me. To speak of an excess of liberalism in Hungarian institutions is the
greatest possible self-deception. On the other hand the so-called racial sins, though
really existing, were not the emanation of a mysterious principle but the historical
consequences of the social, economic, and intellectual facts of a war-like feudal society, previously analyzed. And certain detrimental effects of the Jewish influence
(usury, economic exploitation, and reinforcement of the chauvinistic tendencies)
were far less racial problems than the sickness of a society in which the masses of
the peasantry and of the working-classes led a life of slow starvation and mental
decay under the pressure of an anachronistic and cruel class domination.

CHAPTER III

THE STRUGGLE OF THE CROWNS

This feudal world, with which we became acquainted in the foregoing chapter, had its expression in a particular constitutional order whose basis and development influenced very deeply the history and the fate of the monarchy. There were several territorial entities in the monarchy which developed a stubborn resistance against all efforts of a more organic unification of the empire. In the course of its historical evolution every kingdom, every country, and every province defended jealously its own autonomy which gave to the noble classes special privileges in the administration of their territory. In this variegated historical frame due to the eventualities and the accidents of the feudal past, there grew up a kind of feudal nationalism which may be regarded as a precursor of the modern national feeling. There arose a certain solidarity among the privileged classes against the unifying state and its administrative organs. This feeling of solidarity was rather constitutional than national, in the modern sense of this word, as it signified rather a tendency to keep at a distance the central power and to maintain the local organizations and privileges, whereas the modern national efforts as they manifested themselves in the great French Revolution had just the opposite tendency: to eliminate the antiquated feudal structures, to abolish the privileges of the estates, and to unite the whole nation under the same law.

"The principle of nationality," wrote Robert Michels in his pioneer essay in this field, "is an enlargement of the principle of Human Rights with which it is connected both historically and logically. Nay, it is a necessary continuation of the same principle. . . . ."[1] The author of this present volume, too, came to similar conclusions one year before Michels in a book, written in Hungarian,[2] which emphasized the eminently peasant and bourgeois character of the national movement. I tried to demonstrate that the whole ideology of the feudal world cannot be regarded as national in the modern sense because national language, national literature, and national culture had no important part in it. We may even say that it was anti-national because it separated rigidly the nation into classes instead of uniting them, because it identified the nation with the nobility which refused any real economic and cultural solidarity (both *commercium* and *connu-*

[1] "Zur historischen Analyse des Patriotismus," *Archiv für Sozialwissenschaft und Sozialpolitik* (Tübingen, 1913).

[2] *The Evolution of the Nation States and the Problem of Nationality* (Budapest, 1912).

bium) with the people which it ruled and who cultivated its lands as serfs. The great masses of the peasantry were not members of the nation but they were—according to the forceful expression of Otto Bauer—the *Hintersassen der Nation* ("the tenant farmers of the nation").[3] The so-called patriotism of the feudal estates tried simply to conserve the privileges of the nobility both against the kingdom representing more general tendencies and against the masses of the bondsmen anxious for their emancipation. Besides, among the too powerful and too rich representatives of the nobility, there was always a tendency to expand their territorial estates (for in the feudal period each big estate was a real state within the state) if necessary by forceful means against the king and the weaker elements of peasants and nobility. In this greedy desire they did not hesitate to settle armed conspiracies with whatsoever foreign power, if their service meant for them a greater advantage. One who studies the medieval history of any nation will agree with the remark of Michels that the great lords never felt themselves bound to their fatherlands. "History is everywhere full of the treasons of the princes who led the enemies of the country against their own compatriots." Under the impression of the same spectacle I wrote in my book, mentioned above, that "feudal Hungarian history is a history of continuous high treasons" because the great landlords had no scruples about fighting with foreign armies against their own country and even in their upheavals against the Emperor, though called patriotic and national by certain historians, we can always observe purely personal interests in curious mixtures with national claims.

The rampart of this feudal nationalism was each territory in which the estates were successful in building up a political organization in the past. As we saw, the Habsburg monarchy resulted from the conquest, amalgamation, and unification of such territories. These territories were very unlike in size, population, and power, but it was their common trait that they were an organization of the privileged classes for keeping the central powers at a distance and the peasant masses in silence. Even in pre-war Austria there were still seventeen distinct constitutional territories with separate Diets: Lower Austria, Upper Austria, Salzburg, Styria, Carinthia, Carniola, Trieste, Görz and Gradiska, Istria, Tyrol, Vorarlberg, Bohemia, Moravia, Silesia, Galicia, Bukowina, and Dalmatia. The unity of the Hungarian crown was far more real, but also here Croatia-Slavonia could be regarded as a distinct state, and before the constitutional era there were several territories having more or less independent life. Especially in Transylvania the feeling of its independence and distinct historical life was very vivid until the end of the old monarchy. Besides,

[3] A brilliant analysis of the situation is given in his book, *Die Nationalitätenfrage und die Sozialdemokratie,* Zweite Auflage (Wien, 1924).

the county organization of the nobility developed a very strong feeling of local patriotism and many of the Hungarian patriots deplored in their effort for national unification the particularist atmosphere of these "small republics of noblemen."

The bigger territorial unities of the monarchy were in former periods independent kingdoms or parts of such independent kingdoms. The most essential and the most powerful among them was the Hungarian kingdom consisting of Hungary proper and her connected countries under the symbol of the Crown of St. Stephen as a visible sign of the independence and sovereignty of the country. This crown and the traditional ideology attributed to it, played a preponderant rôle in the struggle between the Habsburgs and the Hungarian nation. The doctrine of the "Mystery of the Holy Crown" which, since the fifteenth century was a firmly established theorem, assumed more and more dogmatical influence against the centralizing tendencies of the Habsburgs. The importance of this doctrine was very much exaggerated by the newer school of Hungarian historians because they interpreted it as an expression of a pretended attitude which did not practice the feudal institutions of the western states, and which constructed the state, not from the point of view of private rights, but public obligation. An enthusiastic admirer of this doctrine writes:

The idea of the public power gains in opposition to the individualistic kingly power a concrete formulation in the public right conception of the Holy Crown. . . . . The Hungarian people regarded the state as a society organized in the interests of the whole as an organic entity incorporated in the Holy Crown. It conceived the Holy Crown on the one hand as a sign and symbol of the Hungarian state; on the other, it personifies it as the owner of the public power residing in the Nation and belonging to the King and to the people in a political sense, i.e., to the nobles. Public power is, by a mystery, present in the Holy Crown. Each factor of the state life is in immediate touch with the Holy Crown and receives its function from it. It is the source of all right and all power. . . . .[4]

However, one who knows Hungarian history somewhat more closely will doubt such an interpretation of the mystery of the Holy Crown. During centuries the big landowners developed typically feudal tendencies robbing the properties of the smaller nobility and of the free peasants. They plotted continuously with foreign enemies against the integrity of the country. Besides, until the middle of the nineteenth century, all the working-elements of the country were hermetically excluded from the Holy Crown, the so-called *Totum Corpus Sacrae Regni Coronae*. (Not only the peasantry but the citizens of the town, too, who had only one collective vote against the hundreds

---

[4] This conception is explained in all its juridical subtleties by Akos von Timon, *Ungarische Verfassung und Rechtsgeschichte mit Bezug auf die Rechtsentwicklung der Westlichen Staaten* (Berlin, 1909), pp. 509–42.

of the deputies of the nobility.) What this doctrine really signified was a defensive attitude of the feudal world against the unifying tendency of imperial power. It was an emphasis of the unity and integrity of the country against new administrative divisions and of the legitimacy of the feudal administration against the Habsburg administration. It was, therefore, a symbol of the privileges of the nobility and their effort to retain the feudal estates in case of the dying out of a family as a possession not of the king but of the Holy Crown. At the same time it signified the claim and aspiration for those countries and territories which belonged formerly to Hungary and which could be reconquered in the future by the Habsburgs. (The practical importance of this doctrine became manifest at the annexation of Bosnia-Herzegovina when the dogma of the Holy Crown made a definite constitutional status of these provinces impossible as we shall see in the treatment of the southern Slav problem.)

This strong solidarity of the Hungarian nobility and its rigid state conception was capable of resisting for centuries the unifying work of the Habsburgs who were trying to build up a *Gesamtmonarchie*. In the historical part of this book we witnessed some phases of this struggle of the feudal estates. Sometimes these movements in the hand of remarkable personalities (of a Bocskay, a Bethlen, and a Rákóczi) became real mass-movements when these leaders were successful in combining the cause of their feudal privileges with certain popular claims, especially with the claim of religious freedom.

But not only the feudal society organized under the Hungarian crown felt the foreign dynastical power as a hateful burden; similarly the other great historical constituent parts of the monarchy cherished analogous separatistic sentiments. Though the greatest part of the old Czech nobility was extirpated, the idea of the Crown of Wenceslaus, comprising Bohemia, Moravia, and Silesia, as the symbol of national unity and independence did not die out completely and had a revival in the modern period. The Polish nobility of Galicia, too, did not forget the former splendor of the Polish crown and, though they later enjoyed a complete autonomy in their province, the restoration of the unity of all the Polish territories under the symbol of the historical crown remained an inextinguishable longing in the Polish soul. Similar sentiments were dormant in the Croatian nobility, which, in spite of its secular connection with Hungary and the regular use of the Latin language, clung stubbornly to the fiction of an independent Croatian state, to the tradition of the Crown of Zwoinimir. Even in Lombardy the memory and tradition of the Lombard Crown continued as the symbol of a specific territorial and constitutional solidarity.

The situation was in essence the same in the crownlands in those smaller provinces of the dynasty which never played such an eminent rôle as the kingdoms or former kingdoms just mentioned. In these, too, there survived a more or less clear consciousness of constitutional and territorial privileges, even in those where a German majority was the ruling element. The noble estates felt themselves as the owners of the provinces and opposed the work of unification of the central powers. The *postulata* of the crown were always confronted by the *desideria* and *gravamina* of the estates. The state remained until the middle of the nineteenth century a double state: the unified state of the Emperor and the local petty states of the nobility which developed a specific territorial consciousness. The social atmosphere of these crownlands is demonstrated by the example of Bohemia. Here, until the beginning of the modern constitutional era, were sitting in the Diet four bishops and twelve abbots in the estate of the prelates; in the estate of the lords, sixty princes, counts, and barons; in the estate of the knights about the same number, whereas the citizens of the towns were represented by only fourteen deputies from seven cities who possessed only a single vote though there were in Bohemia at that time 119 cities and 178 smaller towns.[5]

The feeling of this territorial independence and local privileges remained a driving-force even in the modern period when the peasants and the citizens got a larger, though not adequate, share in the local legislation of the provinces. This crownland consciousness was so strong that it resisted successfully all those modern efforts which tried to reorganize the state on the basis of economic and administrative efficiency irrespective of the historical formations. And, when the triumphant absolutism, after the crushing of the revolution, made an energetic effort in the *Bach system* to organize a new state machine on the basis of a mechanical uniformity, Baron Joseph Eötvös, the brilliant Hungarian statesman, one of the deepest thinkers of the monarchy, opposed to this conception of a uniform state the doctrine of the so-called "Historico-Political Individualities" which, cordially accepted by the Czech nobility, played henceforth an important rôle in the constitutional struggles of the monarchy. Baron Eötvös demonstrated with great sagacity that a real Austrian patriotism was entirely lacking as such a feeling was only alive in some isolated strata of the statesmen, of the army and of certain groups of the *intelligentsia*. A common constitutional life and cultural activity would, perhaps, have created in the future a general patriotism, but for the moment nothing could have been built on it. What did really exist, was the local intimate life of the various historical formations. To divide these Historico-Political Individualities into administrative districts exclusively on the basis of linguistic frontiers would not have rendered the state any more fit to live.

[5] Beidtel, *op. cit.*, p. 15.

However anxious one might be to destroy provincial patriotism by robbing it of its object, through the new division of the provinces, the love for Tyrol, for Styria, or for Hungary will probably survive the existence of these countries. And nobody who loves his fatherland now will imagine it otherwise than he did before. History and the present time demonstrate that there is no need for a diplomatic recognition and for an official title that a country should be ardently loved by its inhabitants. It is in the nature of man that where he sees a past he hopes still for a future. The hopes of the love of country can disappear only with its reminiscences, for where a man loves he believes in immortality. . . . .[6]

This theory of Eötvös from 1850 was evidenced by the results of the absolutism during Bach and Schmerling. A rearrangement of the monarchy from a purely linguistic or administrative point of view was unsuccessful as it was opposed by the traditional particularism of the crowns and other historical territories. Many distinguished political thinkers regarded this particularism as a simple resistance of the feudal spirit and were of the opinion that, connected with a complete democratization of the monarchy, the same course would have been the only way out of the difficulties of the empire. It was also the fundamental idea of the plan of the Socialists, already mentioned, that the problem should be solved on the basis of national corporations independent of territorial divisions. Others like A. Popovici and R. Charmatz advocated the scheme of dividing the whole monarchy into distinctly new territories entirely disregarding the historical limits of the states and provinces. All the old historical organisms were to be eliminated and the peoples rearranged in nationally homogeneous territories made by rule and compass inside of a completely united Greater Austria. By such artificial construction they hoped to subdue the resistance of the old nationalistic spirit attached to the traditional feudal territories. They regarded the crowns and the crownlands as the chief enemies of a harmonious co-operation of the nations. These and similar criticisms were not without foundation. Many of the former territorial units became really obsolete for, in the lapse of time, larger economic and cultural unities had developed and the narrow-minded local atmosphere of the crownlands envenomed the co-operation of an ethnographically mixed population. In spite of this, the real essence of these separatistic movements since the beginning of the nineteenth century was no longer the reactionary nationalism of the feudal world but a growing democratic nationalism of the popular masses who were trying to build up a national state in accordance with historical traditions and which was satisfying at the same time

---

[6] Not only in this connection but concerning the problem of nationality as a whole the works of Eötvös may be regarded as one of the deepest expressions of European thought. His most important contributions in this connection were, *Über die Gleichberechtigung der Nationalitäten in Österreich* (Pest, 1850), and *Die Garantien der Macht und Einheit Österreichs* (Leipzig, 1859).

the new economic and cultural needs. Therefore, the real problem of the former monarchy was not the annihilation of all historical individualities and constitutions in the unity of a nationless super-state (as the Socialists and some prophets of Greater Austria imagined), but to give fair opportunity to the nations to build up their own states according to their historical traditions and to combine them as equal members of a confederation.

From the point of view of higher justice and fuller administrative efficiency, a supra-national state would have meant perhaps a more advanced type of political organization but this plan did not take into account the actual existing power relations. In a period of acute nationalism the struggling nations aspired not only toward a linguistic and cultural autonomy but also toward the establishment of their nation states on a traditional basis. The Magyars fought for the Hungarian state, the Czechs for the Czech state, the Jugo-Slavs for their own state, and they were not willing to abandon these ideals in the interest of a bloodless supra-national state. On the other hand, it is true that the historical territories of the various nations included large national minorities and the danger was near (which Dr. Renner foresaw and which has been fulfilled since in a large measure) that these new nation states would oppress their national minorities in the same manner the dominant nations did in the dual monarchy. But the real remedy for this danger would have been, not the Utopia of a nationless supra-state (which would have meant as a matter of fact a centralized German state), but a statesmanship which would have combined the new national organisms in a confederation. The sovereign power of such a confederation could have efficiently defended the national minorities by appropriately uniting them in national districts and in broader organizations on the whole territory of the confederative state.

This was the only way out of the growing difficulties of the monarchy. Unfortunately, both the absolutistic and the socialist supranationalism did not understand this connection. Both were of the opinion that a united monarchy was opposed only by the old feudal spirit of the crowns whereas the new particularism was fomented by a democratic nationalism. *This democratic nationalism was the new force which attacked Habsburg unity at a time when the hydra-heads of the former feudal particularism were already cut down.* And, whereas, the Habsburgs triumphed with comparative ease against the feudal nationalism which represented a lower type of economic and political organization (based on anachronistic privileges and the exploitation of the bondsmen), the new popular and democratic nationalism, which tried to reconstruct the crowns on the basis of popular sovereignty against the nationless absolutism of the Habsburgs, signified a higher principle of political organization which the dynasty

could not conquer. That is the reason why the many plans for a purely mechanical redivision of the monarchy never had a really popular
support. Witnessing the various artificial schemes for dividing the
empire into new ethnographic divisions with political scissors, an
acute German observer, during the war, wrote the following forceful
remarks:

There comes to one's mind the myth of the daughters of Pelias who,
following the advice of Medea, cut up their old father into small pieces and
boiled him in a magic pot in order to rejuvenate him. Unfortunately the
recipe was not successful and the old gentleman died.[7]

Why the feeling of national solidarity conquered all state expedi-
encies and social rationalism, the reader will see more clearly in the
next chapters when we shall analyze the struggles and dynamics of
the national awakening. But the American reader will understand the
situation more clearly if he remembers the statement of Woodrow
Wilson to the effect that "State patriotism was far more strong than
the Union which was only an arrangement."[8] For, if that was true in
the North American states, the comparatively short history of which
was not burdened by the atmosphere of the feudal past and by the
memories of national struggles against each other, how much better
can we understand the virulence of the particularisms and local patriotisms in the Habsburg monarchy the whole history of which was a
series of feudal and national conflicts.

[7] Dr. B. Guttmann, *Öesterreich-Ungarn und der Völkerstreit* (Frankfurt-am-
Main, 1918), pp. 13–14.

[8] *The State: Elements of Historical and Practical Politics* (Rev. ed.; Boston,
1911), p. 464.

CHAPTER IV

NATIONAL AWAKENING

After the suppression of feudal nationalism it seemed for a long time that the Habsburgs would be triumphant in their work of unification and centralization. Dynastical administration extended everywhere, the recalcitrant feudal nobility was replaced by a servile, courtly one and a policy of mercantilism tried to give to the country an economic uniformity. This relative peace and consolidation was only a seeming one. Beginning approximately with the end of the eighteenth century a new social force appears which, originating from small rivulets, became in several decades the torrent of a powerful stream which undermined more and more the spirit and institutions of the dynastico-patrimonial state. This force was the modern national feeling in the name of which each nation of the monarchy, great and small, laid claim to self-expression and local administration, and, several of them, to an independent state life. This new nationalism, in antagonism with the feudal one, was based on broad popular forces, on the millions of the small bourgeoisie, of the peasantry, and of the industrial workers.

A. THE IDEALISTIC INTERPRETATION

Whence did this new type of a democratic and social nationalism originate? We used to hear two antagonistic answers to this question. One was constructed in the spirit of historical idealism, the other in that of historical materialism. The first lays the chief stress on the intellectual and moral forces. Nationalism is nothing else than a growing realization of the consciousness of the human soul which can reach its completeness only in a national existence fulfilling the work which the World-Spirit assigned to every national individuality. All the great representatives of democratic nationalism stood on this platform. Mazzini, Fichte, Palacký, Kossuth, Gaj, Kollár, Obradović, and others regarded nationalism as an irresistible historical force which tries to unify into a moral intellectual and political organization a whole nation previously divided by accident or dynastical domination. These great prophets of nationalism always emphasized the creative forces of spiritual interests. *Mens agitat molem.* In order to attain its liberty and independence, each nation must, above all, cultivate its spiritual and moral forces. As Mazzini said, in his prophetic mysticism to his *Europa Giovane* (1834): "Each nation has its own task by the fulfilling of which it contributes to the general mission of humanity. This mission constitutes its nationality. Nationality is a holy thing. . . . ." Based on these and similar moral values, the founders of nationalism attributed a paramount importance to the reconstruction of the historical consciousness of the nation and to the achievements of its language, art, and literature. "Should we achieve a national theater," sighed the great poet of Germany, Schiller, "we would become also a nation." Economic and military considerations were only means and instruments in the elaboration of the national ideal.

B. THE MATERIALISTIC INTERPRETATION AND "THE NATIONS WITHOUT HISTORY"

Opposed to this idealistic interpretation, were the thinkers of a later age who did not live through the first heroic period of the national struggles or who regarded with a cooler criticism the results and the methods of the national idea, and its consequent shift into an aggressive imperialism. They opposed these purely idealistic constructions, which they felt sentimental and insincere, and tried to give a preponderately economic and materialistic interpretation to the nationalistic phenomenon. The school of Marx and Engels qualified the spiritual and moral structure of the national movement as sheer "ideology" which must be explained by the fact of economic production and distribution of wealth. The significance of this point of view is very great and has a special merit in the elucidation of the process by which the "nations without history" attained a national consciousness. Nations without history were called by Frederick Engels, and after him by Otto Bauer who elaborated most completely the economic background and mass-psychology of this movement, those peoples which like the Slovenians, the Ruthenians, the Jugo-Slavs under the Turkish conquests, or the Czechs under Austrian absolutism had lost their former nobility, either because their leading classes were exterminated or because they were assimilated by a new aristocracy. These nations remained, through the lack of an intellectual leading class, "nations without history," they did not have a conscious rôle in the respective countries, but, purely as peasant and bondsmen masses, they continued throughout centuries a stagnant, vegetative life as passive instruments of a foreign nobility. They became not real nations but simple *Bedientenvölker*, servant-peoples, the language of which lived only as a despised dialect in the backyard slum quarters of the landlords. According to this point of view the main problem of nationality is the awakening of these unhistorical peoples, which, in consequence of the new economic and social order, began to participate more and more as conscious factors in the life of the state and society. The national ideology is chiefly a result of this great economic and political change. The formerly oppressed slaves adopt simply the national ideology of those nations which ruled formerly over them and demand participation in the states as equal factors.

This point of view contains undoubtedly important elements of reality but seems to me too schematic and simplified. The truth is that the same process of national awakening is also to be witnessed in the so-called historical nations, that is, in those which continued an unbroken national existence during centuries. The truth is that the modern national idea is not a simple continuance of feudal nationalism but the result of more general and complicated causes. This process went on also among peoples who had an old historical consciousness, like the Germans, the Italians, and the Hungarians. On the other hand, the so-called nations without history did not lose entirely their historical individuality.

Unable to enter into the full discussion of this controversy, I would only emphasize my point of view, that national awakening was a general movement in all parts of Central and Eastern Europe from the beginning of the eighteenth century and, therefore, its causes must also be general, dominating the whole political and social atmosphere. (In the large nation states of Western Europe, the problem of nationality did not become so preponderant as in Middle and Eastern Europe for, in the former countries, a superior culture of one kind or another was successful in assimilating all the foreign elements in an age which was determined not by national but by feudal and religious antagonisms. But even here the problem of nationality arises everywhere where national assimilation did not become complete and where local particularisms continued to exist, as in the Celtic fringe of England.)

C. A COMBINED INTERPRETATION

To understand and to interpret modern nationalism in its vital essence as the chief factor in the dissolution of the Habsburg empire, we must investigate with equal care both the social-economic and the spiritual side of the problem. Henry Bergson has admirably shown that an exclusively materialistic interpretation of the soul is not a faithful description of the facts but rather their mutilation. "Our consciousness is undoubtedly affixed to a brain but it does not follow from this that the brain decides all the details of the consciousness or that the consciousness would be a sheer function of the brain."[1] The same is also true concerning the social world. Though we can more or less accurately describe and analyze all the economic and social antecedents and concomitants of the national movement, we cannot say that these antecedents and concomitants explain the whole phenomenon. When, therefore, in the following treatment I shall try to disentangle the process to show the various historical elements—both economic and spiritual—the reader should not forget that all these divisions are purely artificial; and, in reality, in the souls of strug-

---

[1] "L'Âme et le Corps," in *Le Matérialisme Actuel* (Paris, 1926), p. 17.

gling men, all these factors co-operated together to make the national movements irresistible.

Broadly speaking we had two different types in the nationalistic movements of the monarchy. One was a movement for the building-up of a complete national state advocated by the more advanced peoples of the monarchy who had a clear and continuous historical consciousness. Such was the aspiration of the Hungarians, of the Italians, of the Czechs, of the Poles, and of the Croats. On the other hand the smaller or less-developed national elements of the monarchy, scarcely awakened from the feudal torpor, were less ambitious in their desires and for a long time they would have been satisfied if a kind of national and administrative autonomy had been given to them. Such was the attitude, almost until the beginning of the war, of the Slovaks, the Ruthenians, the Slovanians, the Rumanians, and the German minorities of Hungary.

However different the concrete manifestations of the various national programs may have been, there was still a common element in them. All these peoples aspired toward a national self-expression, toward the possibility of developing their own culture and language, and of having an opportunity to speak their own idioms in the schools, the churches, the administration, and before the tribunals. That is what I used to call the "minimum program" of all national struggles. This national program is manifestly the precondition for all further economic and cultural development. Regarding the first manifestation of the national movements in the Balkans, Émile de Laveleye, the brilliant Belgian sociologist, wrote the following prophetic lines:

In provinces where half-animal men are living, let us establish schools, let us construct a railway, and tolerate a printing-press. Twenty years later national feeling will be born. After two generations it will explode, if you try to suppress it. In this manner the national question is born out of the very nature of civilization.

The national problem indeed is only another aspect of social self-expression and emancipation. That is what many foreign observers, especially from homogeneous national regions or from America (where the foreign national minorities are living under conditions and motivations just the opposite to those from which they fled to the new world), are often unable to understand. I heard repeatedly opinions of very distinguished foreigners according to which the struggling national minorities were regarded as prisoners of an anachronistic sentimentalism because, instead of promoting their far more important economic, social, and cultural interest, they were always shouting their national grievances and their linguistic and historical aspirations. This and similar accusations were a total misrepresentation of the real situation, and one of the chief causes of the dissolution of the monarchy was the fact that the so-called progressive and liberal public opinion of the leading nations of the monarchy nourished the same opinions as these distinguished foreigners. They forgot that an oppressed nationality which fights continuously for its national self-expression, for its language, school, and administration, cannot have an adequate interest in the so-called higher problems of civilization.

Bernard Shaw once used in this connection the powerful picture that a persecuted nationality impeded in its development is a cancer-patient: he is unable to think even for a single moment of anything but his inflammation. Similarly in the consciousness of an oppressed nationality, the petty problems of the daily national existence occupy a disproportionate share, and the process of a wholesome economic and political differentiation cannot start as long as the most imperative national needs are not satisfied. This situation leads it to a pathological overestimation of all the national considerations. National oppression signifies a kind of psychic obstruction which impedes both individual and social development.

Such really became the situation in the Austro-Hungarian monarchy, the best energies of all the nations were consumed in seemingly useless national and constitutional struggles instead of economic and cultural achievements so bitterly needed by all the population.

D. POLITICAL CENTRALIZATION AND ECONOMIC ORGANIZATION

The process of national awakening was initiated by the Habsburgs themselves though indirectly and unintentionally. In their fight against feudalism and particularism the "enlightened absolutism" of Maria Theresa and Joseph II, as we saw in our historical introduction, clearly felt the necessity of protecting the great masses of peasant population against misery and exploitation. With their eyes turned toward the great Western models and on the Prussia of Frederick the Great, they were convinced that the power of the modern state could be based only on the financial and military efficiency of the whole people. Therefore, they tried to mitigate the burden of the feudal oligarchy and the first steps were taken toward the emancipation of the serfs. At the same time they introduced the first comprehensive system of elementary education. In an economic order which began to eliminate barter economy, which endeavored to supplant the pastures with cultivated lands, which introduced new methods in agriculture, cattle-breeding, forestry, and other useful arts, the old type of illiterate bondsman became an anachronism and a new, more rational, and self-conscious type of peasantry was wanted. This could be achieved only in a system of elementary education in the mother tongue. The school policy of Maria Theresa and Joseph II was perfectly conscious of this necessity. The imperial educational policy had only a Germanizing tendency concerning the inner administration of the country, but the linguistic necessities of the population were everywhere recognized. Generally speaking, we may say that enlightened absolutism made the first serious and comprehensive attack against feudal Latinity under which the national languages became servant languages whereas the Latin remained the social and diplomatic language of the nobility. At the same time the imperial policy was very anxious to educate a sufficient number of officials from all the various nations of the empire because a German administration could only be maintained in the central organs, whereas in the local administration the use of the maternal language of the people was inevitable.

This dynastical patriarchialism created a new generation of bondsmen whose cultural and economic knówledge grew more intensive, and who began to read books in their mother-tongues, who were administered more frequently by their own co-nationals, and who enjoyed the protection of the imperial power against the abuses of the feudal rule. This process of evolution had inevitably a national reaction. The serfs began to think more critically concerning their own situation. The economic and political pressure of feudal society was felt as a national exploitation. The Czech, the Slovak, the Rumanian, the Ruthenian, and the other masses of bondsmen identified the system of feudal oppression with the national oppression exercised by the German, Hungarian, or Polish upper classes. The rebellions of the serfs very often took on a national hue. On the other hand the fear and hatred of the privileged classes against the revolting serfs assumed the form of national prejudice.

In this way the educational and the cultural policy of enlightened absolutism aroused in all parts of the monarchy a certain amount of national consciousness among the backward peoples who began to awake from their nationless dream. This general awakening of national consciousness became a powerful instrument in the hands of absolutism in counterbalancing with it the influence of the more powerful nations of the monarchy by playing up the national aspirations of the oppressed peoples. There began the conscious policy of a Machiavellistic *divide et impera* based on the national divisions of the country. This tendency was so manifest that Ludwig Gumplowicz coined the word, *Konkurrenznationalität* ("a nationality of competition"), as an invention of the absolutistic statesmanship to maintain the autocratic equilibrium.[2] *Aula est pro nobis* ("The Court is with us!")

[2] This policy of *divide et impera,* however, was not an invention of the Habsburgs but seems to be very deeply rooted in some sad instincts of our human nature. In ancient Rome "it was an economic principle to foster rather than to suppress dissentions inside of slavedom. In the same spirit Plato and Aristotle had already warned . . . . not to gather slaves of the same nationality in order not to bring about local alliances and perhaps plots. . . . ." (Quoted after Mommsen by Francis Oppenheimer, *Der Staat* [Jena, 1926], p. 477). And curiously enough, I was recently told by a German foreman of a big automobile plant of Detroit that for avoiding strikes they always divide their workers in such a way that in each section workers of various nationalities should co-operate.

shouted joyfully one of the leaders of the Illyrian movement directed against Hungarian independence as an expression of the protection which the movement enjoyed from Vienna. This connection between absolutism and national awakening of the Slavs was so conspicuous that it troubled even the clear sight of Marx and Engels who, misunderstanding the real nature of the movement, considered it exclusively as a machination of the Viennese reaction against the liberal and revolutionary Hungarian nobility.

The imperial power, however, was soon frightened by the ghost which it awakened because the national movement proved to be a double-edged sword. It was not only an instrument of the *divide et impera* policy, but it became more and more a conscious and irresistible endeavor of all the nations to build up a constitutional type of national government. This tendency could not be reconciled with an absolutist centralized power and that is the reason that, after the short episode of the enlightened absolutism, the system of Metternich and its successors fought national democracy as bitterly as constitutional liberalism. On the other hand, the growing force of dynastical German centralization aroused inevitably a semi-national resistance of those feudal elements which the Habsburg administration menaced in their governmental independence and social privileges.[3]

All these developments, however, were only a prologue in the history of the national consciousness. The movement gets a quicker tempo and a more powerful repercussion only in the period when, in the first half of the nineteenth century, the capitalistic process of production infiltrated more and more into the economic structure of the monarchy. The eighteenth century knew only a capitalized home industry or the combination of individual artisanships in bigger plants, whereas in the nineteenth century the first results of industrial revolution based on the new technical inventions appear. The small artisanship of former times could not generally compete with the big industrial plants and a concentration of factory labor in the towns began. At the beginning of the nineteenth century there was only one steam engine in Austria, in 1841 there were more than 230 with 3,000 horsepower. In 1852 we find 670 steam engines with nearly 10,000 horsepower. At the same time various labor-saving machines were introduced intensifying very much average production. This process, though far more slowly, also went on in Hungary, where another more important factor revolutionized the old economy of the country. It was a transition from cattle-breeding to agriculture, followed by a restriction of barter economy, the extension of the town markets, by the growth of industry, and the arising of an intellectual middle class. Parallel to these changes a fundamental transformation of the system

[3] See the historical part of this book, pp. 65, 72–73.

of communication occurred. The old feudal primitive roads based on compulsory labor were replaced by more solidly built ones, and from the thirties of the last century there began the epoch of the creation of railroads giving an entirely new cohesion to a society in which the countryside was more and more counterbalanced by the influence of the urban agglomerations.

Under the sway of all these circumstances a new, more conscious, and energetic type of citizenship arose. The new nationally motivated middle class attacked the old institutions and aspired for a nation state, or at least for national local autonomy based on the principles of modern democracy. Parallel to this process the social unrest of the peasantry grew more and more dangerous because a higher type of agriculture and a more developed civic consciousness was entirely incompatible with the old institutions of bondage.

Under such circumstances the position of the former feudal elements became precarious. The peasantry assailed their estates and manorial rights, the new middle class in the towns their political privileges and their apathy concerning the new democratic national interests. Already at the end of the eighteenth century vehement complaints were launched against the anti-national attitude of the Czech nobility.[4]

Since the time of Joseph II a similarly hostile literature arose in Hungary against the nobility, chastising its indolence, its parasitic nature, and its remoteness from the aims of the country. This antagonism between the working-elements and the nobility became in the course of the nineteenth century even more accentuated and Alexander Petöfi, the greatest lyrical genius of the period in a satirical poem with the refrain: "I am a Hungarian nobleman" attacked the anachronistic, exploiting, and useless qualities of the feudal classes. But the better and more far-sighted elements of the nobility understood the danger which menaced them, that the continuance of the system of bondage would eliminate them completely from the life of the new society and at the same time give opportunity to the Viennese government and the dynasty to carry on the liberation of the serfs in a manner which would end also the constitutional independence of the country. (A similar method indeed was applied by Russian Tsarism against the recalcitrant Polish nobility: the forcible expropriation of their estates meant at the same time the grave for Polish independence for a long period.) Not only this social pressure, but the whole moral and mental atmosphere of the epoch brought it about that a clever and gifted élite of the noble classes adopted enthusiastically the idea both of national independence and social-political reforms. Everywhere we find a minority of noblemen who accepted the national

[4] Alfred von Skene, *Entstehen und Entwicklung der slawish nationalen Bewegung in Böhmen und Mähren im XIX Jahrhundert* (Wien, 1893), pp. 53–59.

and political theories of the French Revolution. This process was particularly conspicuous in Hungary, the only country in the monarchy which maintained to a certain extent its own historical constitution. At the same time a bourgeois class in the proper sense was almost entirely lacking and, therefore, the liberal elements of the "gentry" became the leaders both of national and political emancipation.

From the many instances I wish only to quote two, which demonstrate how clearly the new revolutionary nobility comprehended the absolute necessity for uniting nationalism with democracy. Baron Wesselényi, one of the most gifted leaders of the national opposition, advocated the liberation of the bondsmen with this significant argument:

The government [he meant the Austrian government] will not carry on this measure. Putting a deceitful mask on its horrid face, it extracts the fat of nine million people and is now awaiting the uprising of these nine millions and would like to undertake the rôle of liberator. . . . . If this would happen, woe to us because we shall be debased slaves instead of free men. . . . .

The same point of view was emphasized by Louis Kossuth in 1846: "The soil of the people must be freed in the whole country and at the same time . . . . lest the nobility will be put to the scythe and this moment will be simultaneously the fatal day of Magyar nationality. . . . ." We witness a curious mixture of aspirations and ideologies. The old privileged elements began to accept the social and democratic claims of the period, while the awakened peasant masses and the new *intelligentsia* adopted the national aims of the former feudal resurrections. One might say: the people entered into the crowns and gave a new color and a new intensity to the previous struggles for constitutional independence.

Another important feature of the new situation was the growth of an industrial proletariat in Austria and its beginning in Hungary too. This new class concentrated in the bigger cities was less dependent in its ideology on the historical traditions of the privileged elements. Its ideology was far more social and revolutionary than national. In spite of this, as a part of the surplus population of the villages, this class, too, had a warm feeling for its native language and customs. In its general radicalism it was inclined to support the claims for a national independence and equality. As a matter of fact the industrial proletariat became a very important element of national struggles. The concentration in the towns, an unavoidable consequence of the capitalistic system, caused an intense migratory movement in the whole monarchy. Great masses of population, which the feudal agricultural system could not employ, gathered in the manufacturing towns and often altered to a large extent their former ethnic composition. For instance in Austria, some of the former cities of a German character lost their homogeneity and important Slav minorities arose. The same process in Hungary rather favored Magyarization because the Magyars with a greater mental elasticity and more oppressed by the latifundist system, became the chief elements of the industrial migratory movement.

Generally speaking, we may assert as a sociological law that the neighboring population of the villages had a tendency to assimilate the urban agglomerations or, as I used to say, the "sea assimilates the islands." Of course this process was often checked and counterbalanced where the ruling class, controlling the state, had carried on a conscious policy of assimilation, putting into the more important industrial centers, state offices, schools, and factories with a national staff (as it happened in Galicia, from the Polish side and in Hungary from the Magyar); nevertheless, it was everywhere the concomitant phenomenon of capitalism that important ethnographic changes occurred in consequence of the migratory movement of the workers. There arose new, more or less compact, national minorities or many urban agglomerations got a new ethnic majority. As a matter of fact, these new immigrants proposed claims for schools and administration in their own tongues. These quite natural aspirations aroused the uneasiness of the former ruling national groups.[5] This antagonism became an important factor in political struggles. The defense of the old national character on the one hand and the establishment of a new school system and administration fit for the new linguistic needs on the other, determined the very essence of national struggles even in regions where national minorities did not aspire to a constitutional state independence.

The social and political facts herewith enumerated seem to legitimize the point of view particularly emphasized by the socialist writers that "the national problem is only the other side of the social problem." It is quite evident that any effort for the extension of political rights, for the heightening of the cultural level of the masses and for the improving of their economic conditions must inevitably have their national repercussions. National feeling grows in equal ratio with political and economic power. There is really no difficulty in grouping these economic and political facts in such a manner that national movements would appear as a sheer reflex or superstructure of these factors. Those, however, who penetrate more deeply into these connections will not be satisfied with this purely economic construction, rather, they will be obliged to acknowledge the autonomous and inde-

---

[5] This attitude of a distrustful and suspicious nationalism found an expression in the fact that Vienna, the Imperial City, never tolerated public Czech theatrical performances though there was within her territory a considerable Czech minority. This was not an open prohibition; it was only confidentially intimated to the theaters that such performances were not desirable.

pendent work of spiritual and moral forces in the evolution of national consciousness.

Digging more deeply into the sources of national movements and analyzing in more detail the world of ideas of those prophets who initiated the national revolutions, we will find that these great precursors were generally very remote from the economic and class interests of the period, but they tried to give a new synthesis for all the manifestations of national life. For instance, one of the greatest geniuses of the national awakening, the prophet of Hungarian self-realization, Count Stephen Széchenyi, though an eminently practical man full of plans for the economic reconstruction of his backward country, did not comprehend the motive of individual profit in his feverish efforts, but all his powerful schemes and projects were only an expression of the ideal to give national content and consciousness to a country weakened in its soul by feudal particularism and foreign domination. One might say that the national idea was a center of spiritual forces toward which gravitated all individual efforts. If we study the intellectual and moral struggles of the heroic period of nationalism, we distinctly recognize that we face not only the introduction of a new method of economic production, but at the same time the establishment of a new scale of moral values.

This whole conception was animated by a new philosophy of history. The ideas of Humanism, one of the chief structures of the new consciousness, were earlier than the changes in the economic system. Especially the influence of Herder, the great German philosopher, was decisive on the awakening peoples of the monarchy, in the first place in the Slavs who called him *praeceptor Slavorum*. Under the influence of the "Law of Nature," emphasizing the born rights of the individual guaranteed by pure "Reason," the German thinker attacked the old patrimonial conception of the state and regarded the peoples as the real factors of the historical process. In opposition to the unifying and centralizing plans of Joseph II, he advanced with great force and powerful suggestiveness the ideal of independent national evolution. He shouted to the old nationless patrimonial world:

Has a people something more precious than the language of its fathers? In it resides its whole intellectual wealth of tradition, history, religion, maxims of life, all its heart and soul. To take away the language of such a people or to debase it means to take its only immortal property. . . . . The best culture of a people cannot be enforced by a foreign language, it flourishes the most beautifully and, I would say, exclusively on its own soil, in its inherited and hereditary idiom.

These new spiritual constructions found further elucidations or continuations from the side of the historical school of Savigny and in the German romanticism. Savigny rejected the theory regarding

law as a simple act of the state, but he considered it as an emanation of the soul of the people exactly in the same manner as language,
art, and customs. At the same time the German romanticists glorified
the intuitive creative forces of the people building up in an organic
and semi-conscious way a new system of spiritual values. "Each significant and independent nation," said Frederick Schlegel, an outstanding figure of the school, in a lecture delivered at Vienna in 1812,
"has a right to possess its own and peculiar literature and it is the
worst barbarism which oppresses the language of a people.[6]

These and similar elements of thought were naturally eagerly received by those peoples who began to feel their national individuality.
In the center of this consciousness, as a supreme symbol, stood the
idea of the national "mission," the conviction that the respective peoples have their special missions in the history of the world attributed
to them by fate. This idea, too, was already clearly expressed by
Herder who emphasized repeatedly the particular nature of the Slavs,
distinct from that of the Germans, glorifying the "Slav spirit," as
opposed to the conquering desire of the Germans, as the spirit of democracy, pacifism, and self-government. Each nation began to for-
mulate its own rôle in history. The Magyars emphasized the struggle
against the Turks, defending Christianity, as their national mission;
the Poles felt themselves as exponents of Western culture against the
barbarism of Russian Tsarism; the Croats regarded themselves as pi-
oneers of Roman Catholicism against Byzantism; the Rumanians
claimed the honor of being the continuers of the Roman Dacia; the
Czechs kindled their national enthusiasm by the memory of Huss, as
the beginner of continental reformation.

We find everywhere a curious searching for historical ancestors.
Every nation tried to reconstruct its past as the most glorious, like a
lost Paradise. This almost frantic desire for "time-honored glory"
received sometimes a comical touch. So, for instance, some Slovenian
writers made an attempt, though without any historical foundation,
to introduce cruel warlike traits into the history of their peaceful nation. One of their popular historians wrote before the World War as
follows:

It was said that the Slovenians are a tame and mild people. That is not
true. They think erroneously who speak of a meek Slovenian people. We
read that the Slovenians have destroyed such a big city as Cilli. The Germans and the Furlans were horrified by the Slovenians. They tried repeatedly to push back the Slovenians, but our neighbors were rather unsuccessful in this. The enraged Slovenians drove them back cleverly, then they
attacked them and robbed extensively in Bavaria and Northern Italy. . . . .[7]

[6] Interesting data will be found concerning the spiritual awakening of the Slavs
in the book of Alfred Fischel, *Der Panslavismus bis zum Weltkrieg*, pp. 24 ff.

[7] Robert Braun, "The Development of the Slovenian National Idea," *Huszadik
Század*, April, 1917. In Hungarian.

One can imagine if the weakest of the peoples "without history" sought so passionately after its past, how enthusiastically the greater and more conscious nations began to investigate their history and to search after what a Magyar poet called "ancestors, ancestors, you glorious ancestors, you great ancestors, you tempests shaking the whole world. . . . ." All the peoples began to discover the forgotten documents of their literature, art, music, and popular customs. Happy was the nation which could show a time-honored document of its past spiritual achievements. This thirst for old literary glory was so overwhelming that some ardent apostles of the national splendor did not fear even falsifications. So, for instance, the Czech, W. Hanka and his companions manufactured old documents and smuggled them into a historical building in order to demonstrate that the Czechs possessed already a powerful epic poetry in a period when their mighty German neighbors slept in barbary. Another of their "discoveries" was an even more daring falsification relative to the archaeological history and customs of the Slavs. And though several of the most authoritative Slav scientists have demonstrated the apocryphal nature of these "historical documents," they had, in spite of this, a tremendous influence in the awakening of the Czech consciousness.

Not only past glory but recent historical events as well contributed to the consolidation of the national consciousness of the oppressed people. The Illyrian state, established by Napoleon in 1809 (combining the southern Slav territories detached from Austria into a national commonwealth by which the great Emperor utilized skilfully the dawning national consciousness of the Croats and the Slavonians in order to separate them completely from Austria), though it constituted only an experiment shorter than a decade, left an inextinguishable memory in the soul of the people.[8]

Later the "Repeal" movement of the Irish kindled the fantasy of the struggling nations of the monarchy. Especially the Czech patriots regarded O'Connell as their ideal and a club under the name "Repeal" was established. At the same time the Irish movement proved to be an excellent method of propaganda for the Czechs in a time when censorship made all political action impossible. So, for instance, Karel Havlíček, a popular leader of the Czech national movement, had a daily column in his paper under the heading "The Irish Repeal Movement" in which he described from day to day the situation of the unhappy island and the growing force of the national movement. Austrian censorship did not recognize that the Czech publicist was picturing under the Irish disguise the national and constitutional efforts of the Czechs and that his hatred toward the oppres-

[8] A good description of the Illyrian experiment will be found in Herman Wendel, *Aus dem südslavischen Risorgimento* (Gotha, 1921).

sors of the Irish people was not directed against the English landlords but against Austrian despotism.

The example of those neighboring nations, too, which were more successful in their national propaganda or in the building up of their nation states as the Germans, the Italians, and the Magyars, exercised a powerful influence on the aspirations of the less happy peoples. So the victory of the Crown of St. Stephen over the united Austrian state, in the stipulation of Francis Deák in the Compromise of 1867, gave a new impetus to the national efforts of the Czechs who tried to imitate the Hungarian example even in details. At the same time a kind of a national inferiority complex arose in those smaller peoples who could not achieve any serious result in their national aspirations. So, for instance, Francis Prešeren, the noted Slovenian poet, wrote as late as the first half of the nineteenth century the following characteristic lines:

> In our country they generally speak German,
> The Lords and the Ladies who command us;
> But Slovenian speak they who serve them.

This glorification of the past made the spirits more daring and, in order to escape the difficulties and the grievances of the present, they fixed their hopeful eyes toward the future. In each of the awakening nations we find a group of exalted prophets and visionaries who, with a real creative imagination, tried to construct for their struggling nations a promising ideal of future achievements. These men felt sometimes with a terrifying lucidity the evolutionary tendencies and elaborated schemes which in their own time were almost lacking any reality in the economic and political facts. The so-called *Realpolitiker* would have called them naïve dreamers, and such they were indeed from the point of view of an immediate realization. But they accomplished a really creative and constructive work because they delineated the first symbols for a national unity. The words of Stephen Széchenyi, "Hungary was not, it will become," gave an analogous impetus to two Hungarian generations to the famous dictum *Italia farà da se*.

Before the eyes of Ludjevit Gaj, the great Illyrian apostle, already in 1835 the picture of Jugo-Slav unity was complete in a time when all the political, economic, and linguistic preconditions of such a unity were entirely lacking and when the Turkish yoke oppressed several units of the future nation. He described this strange and startling apparition with poetical colors. He saw the virgin Europe holding a lyre at her breast. This lyre is Illyria, the triangle between Skutari, Varna, and Villach. Gaj complains that the strings give a false melody. Carinthia, Carniola, Styria, Dalmatia, Bosnia, and Bulgaria lack painfully in harmony. But Gaj was not satisfied with the poetic picture. In order to illustrate his vision, he drew a map which puts geographically the frontiers of the new Illyria. This map coincides approximately with those changes which the World War brought. How seemingly useless a play it is for the rationalist to draw maps of territories whose inhabitants scarcely know anything of the existence of each other! And still there is a kind of political magic in such jokes. The irredentist movements always gave rise to maps which showed a dreamed of, but non-existing reality. Men not inclined to abstract reasoning visualize at once things unthinkable. Young students regarded such maps with feverish eyes in the hours of nightly conspiracies. And this dream of national unity remained not an isolated dream of the prophet. It developed more and more into a mass vision. Already in 1840 at the occasion of a splendid ball in Zagreb, Croatian ladies pinned to their bosoms a star on whose points the names of the Jugo-Slav tribes of the Dalmatians, Croatians, Montenegrins, Slavenians, Bulgarians, and Serbs were engraved. In the center of the star the following words were to be read: "God help us to union!"[9]

The enthusiastic plunging into the past awoke also another movement of fundamental importance in the history of uprising. The maternal tongue became almost sacred, the mysterious vehicle of all the national endeavors. The contemporaries regarded it with shame and astonishment that this great treasure became humiliated and debased by the general use of Latin, and later German. The native language of the Magyars, the Slavs, and the Rumanians, became a servant tongue, the language of peasants and small shopkeepers. The leading elements of society spoke Latin, German, or French. Therefore, the popular languages remained in a very backward condition. Their vocabulary was languishing. They were incapable of expressing modern nuances, the terms of the new economic and jural life, the more refined feelings and abstractions of the human soul. This anachronism of the traditional language was still further accentuated by the fact that, in consequence of political divisions and obstacles in communication, the language was divided in many dialects which became more and more strange to each other. In this manner there was a growing gap between the various branches of the same nation. This process was progressing especially among the Slavs. The Czechs, the Moravians, the Slovaks, or the Slovenians, the Croats, and the Serbs began already to feel themselves as distinct national individualities.

Under such conditions the creation of a united literary language and the supplementation of it by new words from the old antiquated treasury of the language, or *per analogiam,* from foreign languages, became one of the most important national tasks. This movement called the "reformation of language" augmented very considerably

[9] Szilágyi and collaborators, *The History of the Hungarian Nation* (Budapest, 1895–98, IX, 455). In Hungarian.

the sentimental ardor of the awakened national consciousnesses. At the same time it gave a reliable psychological basis for the new economic and political constructions. Without such a language fit for all the walks of national life, modern society would be as unimaginable as without railway, telegraph, or the new credit organization. Now this mighty movement of the reformation and unification of the language, which shook the awakened peoples of the monarchy with an almost religious enthusiasm, was not a sheer reflex of economic transformations, but a parallel and independent achievement of great creative individualities who undertook the difficult task at a time when it was unpopular and unremunerative both from an economic and from a moral point of view. The following statement of the Hungarian historian, Acsády, gives a vivid description of the whole situation and the same things occurred also with small local differences among the other nations of the monarchy: "The gaining of ground of the German and the Latin languages evoked depression, even despair in the nobler souls." They said, terrified, that the Magyar language, which was not developed scientifically and whose rules were unstated, will deteriorate sooner or later. "But slowly, almost unrecognized, there began the glorious process of the reconstruction of the national language." The Magyar language continued to live in the poetry of the people, in its proverbs, and tales, the products of the old literature. It was in the state of recuperation as was the nation itself. Though it was ousted from the castles of the great lords (like the Hungarian dance and popular music which were replaced for the middle classes by the minuet, the gavotte, and by foreign music), it had a modest existence in the dwellings of the lower nobility and of the working-masses. But it lived and became stronger and began the work of reconquering the Latinized and Germanized leading strata. At that time the language of the people was outside the bulwark of the constitution. "There were not only two nations but two Magyar languages: the language of the noble society full of foreign words which was scarcely understood by the peasant, and the popular Magyar tongue in its virginal purity and limitless capacity for development, looked down upon by the lord with pitiful smile."[10]

Only so can we understand the seriousness of a movement in which many today, in the period of a naïve overestimation of the economic factor, see nothing else than a kind of romantic sentimentalism. This movement, with an emphatical ardor, began to study the language of the people and its memories, especially its popular songs, tales, and legends. A real fever caught the contemporaries for popular poetry, music, dances, and customs. The movement at the beginning was rather literary but it assumed more and more political colors. A group of talented and enthusiastic investigators was formed among

[10] Acsády, op. cit., II, 525.

all the peoples of the monarchy who demonstrated the unity and solidarity of the national language in spite of the variegated diversity of dialects.

A romantic type of historicism influenced the souls in the same direction. It was a delightful task for the contemporaries to investigate the memories of remote periods demonstrating the continuity of national feeling and thought. These researches were not always accompanied by an adequate criticism. So, for instance, an enthusiastic Magyar scholar "demonstrated" that, properly speaking, Adam, the first man, was a Magyar. Vuk Karadžić, the first apostle of the great Serb idea, who placed this conception in opposition to the great Croat vision of Gaj, on the basis of "historical" investigations stated the fact that the Serbs were "the greatest people of the planet," that their culture was five thousand years old, and that it included the whole world history. Jesus, too, with his apostles, was a Serb. And Karadžić proclaimed the cultural unity of his race in an epoch when the leaders of the Serb nation, outside of the frontiers of the monarchy, Kara Georg and Miloš Obrenović were illiterate peasants.

Besides the memories of the past, the poetical creations of the present, too, emphasized the glory and solidarity of the awakened nations. We, the children of a more critical and sophisticated period, are scarcely able to understand how this naïve, fantastic poetry, thirsty for glory, and full of megalomania could inflame with enthusiasm the best spirits of the epoch. One of the most representative products of this literature is the creation of the Slovak poet, Jan Kollár, who in 1824 published a series of sonnets under the title, *The Daughter of Slava*. The reception of the poems was so enthusiastic that the poet added new sonnets to the collection. A love idyll gives occasion to the author to combine his personal feelings with passionate outbursts concerning the past, present, and the future of the Slav peoples. Then he flings a score of anathema against the Magyars and the treacherous Germans and denounces the injustices committed against his people. If the various branches of the Slav race were of metal, he would make a unique statue of them. From Russia the head, from Poland the breast, from Bohemia the arms, and from Serbia the legs. Before such a colossus Europe would kneel down. In his later sonnets he described the Slav paradise and the Slav hell. In more than a hundred sonnets he honors the great saints, heroes, kings, and intellectual leaders of the Slavs. A same amount of sonnets chastises the enemies, the debasers of the Slavs and among these several of his compatriots.[11] Rare granules of true lyrical élan swim here in the monotonous sea of dry archaeological and historical facts, and the descriptions of the poet flow sometimes into an unconscious petty bourgeois comic, for instance when in the Slav paradise, the happy ladies drink heavenly cof-

---

[11] For a detailed analysis of the poem see Fischel, *op. cit.*, pp. 102 ff.

fee, whereas in hell the poor criminals walk on pointed pins. . . . .
In spite of this, the dreadful poem proved to be one of the chief stim-
ulants of the period because it was a poetical *revanche* for a national
inferiority complex of many centuries and it was an unheard of pleasure to conquer this inferiority at least in poetical tropes.

Not only language, literature, and history, but also seemingly dry
scientific researches were capable of stimulating the national ardor of
the contemporaries. There was a tendency to seek for relatives and
allies among the European peoples. Especially in the history of the
Slav movements the idea of a numerical supremacy played an important rôle. Once a French revolutionary kindled the enthusiasm of a
hesitating mass by pointing out its numerical force, shouting to them:
Numérotez vous! Some of the Slav leaders understood very well the
sense of safety which their great number offers to the combatants,
and they often played on the chords of statistics. So, for instance,
the Slav ethnography of Šafařik, published in 1842, was the first systematic description of the Slav tribes and their settlements. His detailed calculations, estimating at seventy-nine million the whole number of Slavs in the world and at seventeen million in the boundaries of
the monarchy, contributed very much to the awakening of Slav consciousness and to the conviction that, in spite of all suppression and
adverse circumstances, the Slavs must only wait because their cause is
based on an almost biological foundation.

Besides the factors already noted there is also another which
played a preponderant rôle in the awakening and strengthening of
national consciousness. That is a kind of "fighting ideology" which
called the awaking nations into array against the older and more
powerful nationalisms which surrounded them and by which they were
oppressed. This fighting ideology heightened very much the intensity
of national consciousness, and found symbolic expressions in popular
poetry. For instance, the so-called *Kurucz* songs reverberated all the
despair and hatred of the Hungarian people against German militarism and German taxation at a time when national feeling, in a
modern sense was still dormant. Let us quote only one characteristic
example:

> Magyar, trust not the Germans,
> No matter how or what they protest;
> Naught is the parchment they give thee,
> 'Though it be as large as thy round cloak,
> And though they set a seal on it
> As big as the brim of the moon,
> Spite of all, it lacks all *virtus* (trustworthiness),
> Confound them, Jesus Christus![12]

[12] I took this translation from the book of Arminius Vámbéry, *Hungary in
Ancient, Medieval and Modern Times* (7th ed.; London), p. 366.

On the other hand the Croatian youths sang veritable war songs against the oppression of the Magyars, when, at the middle of the nineteenth century, the tension became great between the Croatian and the Magyar claims. One of the most characteristic of these fighting songs is the following: "Who is born as a Slav is born as a hero. He should swing the Slav flag and gird his sword and mount his horse. Behold the black, wild Tartar has attacked us and trampled our nation with his feet. Let us wash our honor with the blood of the enemy. Each one should cleave a head and our suffering will have an end." The Tartar meant naturally the Hungarians of Turan origin in this song of hatred.

Besides this naïve outburst of popular passion, journalism, and political oratory, too, made national consciousness more acute. Already in 1816 a Czech scholar summarized in a series of lectures, the grievances of his people:

Are not the Germans born in this country and those who join them favored in this country in a hundred important issues? Is not German the language in which all the higher sciences are treated in this country? . . . . And more than this, are not the prominent people of this country, the rich and the prosperous all, born Germans or foreigners or at least such persons who abandoned long ago the Czech language and customs and can be counted among the Germans? Does the Czech-speaking part of the people not live generally in a state of pitiful poverty and oppression?[13]

All the main points of national struggle which filled the whole history of the nineteenth century were here already clearly stated as accusations against the German rule. The improvisations of political oratory gave a new impetus to national consciousness and antagonism. When Francis Deák in the diet of 1840 accused the Croats of Pan-Slavistic plots, Gaj used the following exciting trope against him: "The Magyars are an island in the Slav ocean. I did not create this ocean, nor turned up its waves. But you should be cautious that they should not close over your head and destroy you. . . . ." This survey of the factors of the national awakening, however, would not be complete if I omitted mentioning the enormous influence of "foreign intellectual and moral help" in the elaboration of national consciousness. The benevolent attitude of many distinguished French scholars (beginning with Cyprien Robert, through Saint-René Taillandier, Henry Martin, E. Denis, and Louis Leger, to Louis Eisenmann and others) toward the Czech efforts for independence heightened and strengthened Czech-Slovak national feeling. Similarly, the ardent sympathy of H. W. Steed and R. W. Seton-Watson for the oppressed Hungarian nationalities did more for the growth of their national feeling than the propaganda of their political leaders. And the philippic of Björnstjerne Björnson, the great Norwegian poet, against

[13] Skene, op. cit., pp. 130–40.

the policy of Magyarization of Count Albert Apponyi aroused more indignation in the hearts of the oppressed nationalities than the policy of assimilation itself. The moment of "prestige" in international relations (due to the inferiority complex of the backward nations) is even greater than in the interindividual field.

All these factors had a great effect on the acuteness of national consciousness. Though the founders of the national movement were right in their assertion that the national aspiration of a nation is not to the detriment of the others, nay, it can only promote the general interests of mankind, nevertheless, all national awakenings appear in history as a struggle against other nations. This antagonism between theory and practice has two causes. The one is that all troubling of the national *status quo* hurts old monopolistic positions of privileged groups. And these groups identify their own interests with the interests of the country. The other is that, behind all national efforts, there is a hidden imperialistic tendency if it is not checked by a sufficient political counterpoise, or by a clean moral restraint. All nations struggling for equality at the beginning easily become fighters for domination later, and from the oppressed they become the oppressors. What destroyed the Habsburg monarchy was the crossing of these two tendencies. It was the blind resistance of the privileged nations against the new forces and the exaggerated claims of the formerly oppressed when they became sufficiently powerful to reverse the situation. Then they aspired not for equality but for domination over the former rulers. Behind the dissolution of the monarchy there was a deep moral crisis which could have been avoided only by a civic education in the best sense. In the absence of this, the monarchy was doomed to perish. The dynamics of this process will be described in the next part.

PART V
THE DYNAMICS OF THE CENTRIFUGAL FORCES

CHAPTER I

THE DISTRIBUTION OF NATIONS AND THE GERMAN-MAGYAR HEGEMONY

As we have repeatedly emphasized, the political struggles of the last half-century of the Habsburg monarchy were chiefly determined by the so-called Compromise *(Ausgleich)* which the Dualistic Constitution settled in 1867, the essence of which was the political domination of the Germans in Austria, and that of the Magyars in Hungary. On the one side the "kingdoms and countries represented in the Austrian parliament, *Reichsrat*," the seventeen so-called crownlands *(Kronland)*, under German supremacy, on the other side "the countries of the Hungarian Holy Crown," which phrase included, besides Hungary proper, Croatia and Slavonia as annexed countries and the city and district of Fiume as a "separate body" *(Separatum Corpus)* of the Crown of St. Stephen. We shall discuss later this strange political structure and its grave political consequences.

This is the more important because that process of the national awakening which I outlined in the last chapter of Part VII, did not signify in itself a centrifugal tendency but only the endeavor of each nation to develop its own national existence and culture. This endeavor became centrifugal only by the fact that the other non-German and non-Magyar nations of the monarchy felt the German-Magyar hegemony as a burden and there was a growing conviction among them that under this hegemony they were incapable of developing those economic, intellectual, and moral values which they considered as their national right. This struggle against the German-Magyar hegemony—as we shall see in detail—was complicated by other national struggles also among the so-called "oppressed nations" and what was still more dangerous was the fact that the two leading nations themselves fought each other more and more bitterly.

Another important fact realized by all objective observers was that these national struggles, growing in passionate intensity, showed directly opposite tendencies in Austria and in Hungary: in the former, political evolution went on manifestly in the direction of national equalization and federalization, whereas in the latter—at least seemingly—toward a unitary, unilingual, Magyar national state in which only one political nation was acknowledged as the force maintaining and directing the state. In the following treatment, therefore, we must separate completely the analysis of national struggles in Austria and in Hungary. But, before entering upon the investigation of these two different processes, I would like to point out some important facts which will elucidate the very nature of the German-Magyar hegemony.

Above all there can be no doubt that the Dualistic Constitution was not created out of nothing by the Compromise of 1867, that it was not a sheer excogitation of Beust and Deák for the oppression of the other peoples, but it was only a jural fixation of a historical situation of several centuries. It was a jural recognition of the facts that the Austrian half of the monarchy consisted of a rather mechanical agglomerate of countries and provinces completely conquered and unified by the Habsburgs, deprived of their former constitutional independence; whereas, on the other hand, the Hungarian half constituted a country more or less independent for a thousand years, controlled by a feudal constitution which was successful until the end in retaining, partly by passive resistance and partly by armed insurrection, the unifying and Germanizing attack of the Habsburgs. This meant at the same time that the Habsburgs were incapable of incorporating Hungary into the uniform system of their other countries and territories and of reducing it to the rôle of a simple *Kronland*. This situation found for the last time an almost symbolical expression in the War of 1848–49 between Hungary and the Habsburgs when the latter could only suppress the Hungarian "rebellion" with the help of the Russian Tsar. This issue demonstrated clearly that there was a certain parity of forces between Austria and Hungary, or better, between Habsburg and Hungary. In 1867 the Emperor acknowledged simply this fact in a new jural form. Unifying absolutism capitulated before Hungarian "constitution and independence."

It is not less clear on the other hand that this Dualistic Constitution was not based upon the ethnographical distribution and the numerical forces of the peoples and nations of the monarchy. In order to get an adequate idea of the ethnic forces of the monarchy, we must regard separately its constitutional units. Austria proper, Hungary, Croatia and Slavonia, and the last conquest of the Habsburgs, Bosnia, and Herzegovina (a kind of a constitutional mystery which did not belong, strictly speaking, either to Austria or to Hungary) constituted both from a historical and an administrative point of view distinct divisions inside of which the dynamics of national forces manifested themselves under different forms.

The distributions of the nations of Austria is shown in Table IV. Round numbers only are used for the sake of simplicity.

Table IV clearly shows that in the Austrian part of the monarchy the ratio of the leading German element was only 35.58 per cent and it was confronted by a great Slav majority of 60.65 per cent. Speaking in round numbers we may say that of the total population of Austria less than ten million Germans lived with a majority of eighteen million non-Germans.

The hegemonous rôle of the Germans was further endangered by the fact that as a colonizing element it was present everywhere in the monarchy but it lacked a solid ethnographical central point from which its economic and cultural forces could have radiated throughout the whole territory. Different nations constituted an absolute majority in various provinces: (1) Germans in Salzburg, 99.73 per cent; in Upper Austria, 99.70 per cent; in Lower Austria, 95.91 per cent; in Vorarlberg, 95.36 per cent; in Carinthia, 78.61 per cent; in Styria, 70.50 per cent; in Tyrol, 57.31 per cent. (2) Czech-Moravian-Slovak in Moravia, 71.75 per cent; in Bohemia, 63.19 per cent. (3) Poles in Galicia, 58.55 per cent. (4) Slovenians in Carniola, 94.36 per cent; in Görz and Gradiska, 61.85 per cent. (5) Serbo-Croats in Dalmatia, 96.19 per cent. (6) Italian-Ladins in Trieste, 96.19 per cent.

National particularism was further accentuated by the existence of three provinces where the leading nation constituted only a relative majority. These provinces and their leading nations were: (1)

TABLE IV

Nations	Total Number	Percentage of Total Population
1. Germans...................	9,950,000	35.58
2. Czechs-Moravians Slovaks....	6,436,000	23.02
3. Poles.......................	4,968,000	17.77
4. Ruthenians.................	3,519,000	12.58
5. Slovenians.................	1,253,000	4.48
6. Serb-Croats................	788,000	2.80
7. Italian-Latins..............	768,000	2.75
8. Rumanians.................	275,000	0.98
9. Magyars...................	11,000	0.04

Germans in Silesia, 43.90 per cent; (2) Ruthenians in Bukowina, 38.90 per cent, and (3) Serbo-Croats in Istria, 43.52 per cent.

Generally speaking, Austria had only six provinces which could be regarded as nationally homogeneous: the German Lower and Upper Austria, Salzburg, Vorarlberg, the Slovenian Carniola, and the Serbo-Croat Dalmatia. German hegemony was further hampered by the fact that national minorities lived often not in close settlements but were found in a very mixed population in the various districts, cities, and communities which was a serious obstacle to the formation of homogeneous administrative divisions. For instance, in Carinthia, the settlements of the Slovenians permeated deeply the German regions. Bukowina was a kind of an ethnographical museum where, beside the two chief nations, there lived Germans, Jews, Poles, Magyars, Slovaks, and Lippovans, not only dispersed in the towns, but sometimes in close settlements. Purely German villages were adjacent to purely Magyar ones.

Also two other factors made German hegemony fragile. The one was of a historical nature: the Germans were confronted by peoples of a very developed national consciousness who like the Czechs, the Italians, and the Poles were animated by a more positive state conception than the Austrian-Germans who with their Janus-faced policy could not choose between the Greater German and the Austrian-German state conception.

The other factor was the awkward geographical formation of Austria. Our economic survey has sufficiently proved how ill-founded the theory was (advocated especially during the World War from Austrian-German side) concerning the geographical unity of the monarchy. The truth was that the monarchy contained various mountain and river systems with no organic connection with Vienna. For instance Galicia and Bukowina had no real contact with the other parts of the monarchy, Tyrol projected like a wedge into the Swiss mountains and Upper Austria might have belonged with equal right to Ba-

TABLE V

Nations	Total Number	Percentage of Total Population
Magyars.................	9,945,000	54.5
Rumanians...............	2,948,000	16.1
Slovaks..................	1,946,000	10.7
Germans.................	1,903,000	10.4
Serbs....................	462,000	2.5
Ruthenians..............	464,000	2.5
Croats..................	195,000	1.1
Others..................	401,000	2.2

varia. If Hungary would have been a real and organic part of the empire, there could have arisen some kind of unity. But Hungary itself was a closed geographical unity admired by Elisée Reclus and other experts in geography, the historical consciousness and constitutional scheme of which was rigidly opposed to an Austrian state unity. With such a centrifugal Hungary in its background, Austria was like a fan which had only a periphery without a central part.

From many points of view the ethnographic and geographic basis of Magyar hegemony in the Hungarian countries was of a different nature. In studying these conditions we must separate Hungary proper from Croatia-Slavonia which had a distinct territorial autonomy. According to the census of 1910, Hungary in the restricted sense had an ethnographical distribution such as is shown in Table V.

These results of the official Hungarian statistics were often attacked by the advocates of the national minorities of Hungary by asserting that this numerical supremacy of the Magyars existed only on paper, and was due partly to the pressure and retouching of the administrative organs and partly to the superficial assimilation of the Jews[1] and the renegades of the other nationalities who joined the Magyars *en masse* in order to share the advantages of their domination. This criticism was not entirely baseless but a detailed analysis of the whole process of assimilation in Hungary led me to the conclusion, in my book already quoted, that the results of Table V may be accepted as a roughly adequate description of the situation. Even applying the utmost caution we may accept it as a fact that the Magyars constituted in pre-war Hungary (Croatia-Slavonia not included) though a small, nevertheless an absolute majority. This conclusion is the more important because at the settlement of the *Ausgleich* (Compromise of 1867) the Magyar element constituted only 44.4 per cent of the whole population of the country. The Magyarization of the country made an important step forward. No honest observer will deny that in this process the artificial political assimilation, of which we shall speak later, was not a negligible factor. Nevertheless more important and more natural causes were operative in the growth of Magyar hegemony. I am compelled to enumerate these causes very briefly:

1. The powerful natural unity of the Carpathian basin held together by two large rivers furnishing a natural division of labor between the mountainous peripheries and the Hungarian plain.

2. The Magyar nation occupied the richer plains of the country and, in its central position, it exercised a great attraction on the nationalities of the peripheries. At the same time, the growing capitalism of the country accentuated this process as the leading elements of capitalism were intimately connected with the Hungarian government. These and other factors concurred with the result that the Hungarian towns with a Magyar majority became six times greater in population than they were at the end of the eighteenth century, whereas the towns with a non-Magyar majority could only double their population in the same period.

3. The cultural and intellectual distance between the Magyars and the other nations of the country was far greater than between the Austrian-Germans and their more developed neighbor nations, for instance, the Czechs, the Italians, and the Poles. The greatest part of the Hungarian nationalities, as the Rumanians, Ruthenians, and the Eastern Slovaks were scarcely awakened from their bondsmen stupor, whereas the more developed German minorities (in the first place the Saxons of Transylvania) had a tendency to unite with the Magyars for certain cultural or political privileges against the other nations.

4. While in Austria the capitalistic evolution created a strong

[1] According to the same census there lived in Hungary 911,000 Jews or 5 per cent of the population. Therefore, if the Jews had been treated as a separate nationality, the Magyar majority would have disappeared.

class differentiation in the ruling German nation, and at the same time caused the formation of an important middle class among the non-German nations, in Hungary this process was only at the beginning; the country remained in its bulk agrarian, and the industrial development of the country, even at the time of the collapse of the monarchy, was scarcely more striking than that of Austria in the eighties of the last century. Therefore, the political unity of the historical society remained far more compact and the leading rôle of the feudal classes, animated by the ideology of Magyarization and national unification, far less contested.

5. But all these factors were surpassed in significance by the following: in Hungary there were no crownlands which could foster the particularist consciousness of the various nations. The particularism of the county organization, already mentioned, was not national but only administrative. This organization stood entirely under the sway of the local wealthy nobility, almost exclusively Magyar or assimilated by the Magyars. These feudal elements opposed vehemently all attempts at national organization of the non-Magyar peasantry because they understood very well that the national emancipation of these masses would have meant also their social and political liberation. A natural result of this situation was that, almost until the hour of dissolution, there was in Hungary proper no national minority which aspired to an independent state as was the case of the Czechs, Poles, or Italians in Austria.

This transitory supremacy of the Magyars, however, was weakened by the fact that in three important regions of the country the non-Magyar nations constituted the majority. In the so-called Left River district of the Danube, the Slovaks constituted 58.8 per cent of the population; in Transylvania the Rumanians, 55 per cent, and in the region called the Tisza-Maros angle again the Rumanians had a relative majority constituting 39.5 per cent of the population. A further fateful trait of Hungarian hegemony was that the pressure of the *latifundia* weighed more heavily upon the Magyar small peasantry than upon the non-Magyar.

Even more uncertain will appear the numerical basis of Magyar hegemony when we consider the fact that the settlements of the various nations varied as mosaically as in Austria. It often occurred that Magyar, German, Rumanian, and Serb villages adjoined each other. In such cases generally the chief law of assimilation went on as the process of the sea which determines in the long run the ethnic composition of the islands. In the midst of the large compact popular settlements, the smaller enclaves were swept away by the waves of this sea. The Magyars, as the most intellectual and proletarianized element of the country, moved toward the greater urban agglomerations and Magyarized them. On the other hand in the smaller villages, included within non-Magyar majorities, the opposite tendency was prevalent.

The numerical hegemony of the Magyars appears even more endangered when we consider the entire territory of the Hungarian crown comprising the ethnic conditions of Croatia-Slavonia. Here in opposition to the kaleidoscopic ethnic relations of Austria and Hungary an almost complete homogeneity prevailed. Of the 2,622,000 inhabitants of this country, 2,283,000 were Serbo-Croats, that is, 87.1 per cent of the population. Confronted with this large majority the rôle of the Germans with 5.1 per cent and the Hungarians with 4.1 per cent was quite insignificant the more so as the Germans were mostly town-dwellers, whereas, among the Magyars, the officials or workers sent from Budapest constituted an important contingent. If,

TABLE VI

Nation	Total Number	Percentage of Total Population
Germans..................	12,011,000	23.38
Magyars.................	10,120,000	19.71
Rumanians..............	3,222,000	6.27
Slavs....................	23,416,000	45.59
Others...................	2,585,000	5.05

therefore, we take the whole Hungarian crown into consideration, that is, Hungary proper *and* Croatia-Slavonia, the reader will clearly realize that the hegemonic Magyar element was on this territory a minority similar in position to the Germans in Austria. The ten million Magyars constituted only 48.1 per cent of the whole population, and beside them there were 10,800,000 non-Magyars.

If we remember finally that of the 1,932,000 people of Bosnia-Herzegovina there were 1,823,000 Serbo-Croats, that is, 96 per cent of the whole population, we see that the two hegemonic nations, the Germans and the Magyars, were in a distinct minority compared with the other nations. If we group the chief ethnic elements of the whole Austro-Hungarian empire, we are faced with the figures shown in Table VI which gives the percentages of the total population of 51,-355,000.

Table VI demonstrates that the two hegemonic nations, the Germans and the Magyars together, with 22,131,000 constituted only 43.09 per cent of the whole population whereas the other nations of the monarchy formed a majority of 29,223,000 which is 56.91 per cent of the whole.

Under these conditions the Dual Constitution based on the German-Magyar hegemony was doomed to come into conflict sooner or later with the will of a considerable majority of the nations. In spite of this the constitution was capable of maintaining itself for half a century, and under its rule a conspicuous material and cultural development of the monarchy cannot be denied. It is, therefore, evident to anyone who is not a naïve admirer of the theory of violence that the German-Magyar political hegemony, not based upon the numerical preponderance of the two nations, must have been rooted in other important facts. I have already several times alluded to these facts in the course of this book. The Austrian half of the empire was a result of the German colonization, and the culture which united its economy, administration, and the army was in the main German culture. Similarly in the capitalistic era the new bourgeois class, which exercised

TABLE VII

Nationalities	Population	Number of Universities	Number of High Schools
Germans...............	9,000,000	5	180
Czechs.................	6,000,000	1	83
Poles..................	4,200,000	2	35
Ruthenians.............	3,400,000	0	3
Slovenians.............	1,200,000	0	0
Serbo-Croats...........	700,000	0	6
Italians...............	700,000	0	8
Rumanians.............	230,000	0	0

the economic leadership, was in its large majority of a German-Jewish character. In the Hungarian half of the monarchy we encounter an analogous situation. The feudal structure of the big landed interests which determined the course of the political and social life was the Magyar nobility and those elements of the middle classes and of the non-Magyar nobility which became entirely assimilated in tradition and ideology with the Magyar upper classes.[2]

It is easy to demonstrate, by means of outstanding facts of economic and cultural life, that this historical German and Magyar hegemony was very preponderant until the collapse of the Habsburg monarchy. I shall quote only some facts, almost at random, in order to give a more concrete idea to the reader of the nature of this hegemony. Let us begin with Austria. The Germans constituting only 35.58 per cent of the population paid 63 per cent of the direct taxes in the first decade of the present century. A German paid on an av-

[2] Before the constitutional era there were about 550,000 nobles in Hungary. Among these 466,000 Magyars, 58,000 Germans, and 21,000 Rumanians. The "national" mission of the nobility was recently reassured by Julius Szekfü, *Three Generations* (Budapest, 1922). In Hungarian.

erage twice as much in taxes as a Czech or an Italian, four and a half
times more than a Pole, and seven times more than a southern Slav.[3]

The same preponderance of the Germans is shown in Table VII
by the figures of higher education at the end of the nineteenth century.

The national distribution of officials and officers make the picture
drawn by the figures in Table VIII even more impressive.

No detailed statistics were published concerning the nationality
distribution of the officers in the army, but there can be no doubt that
even in 1910 at least 85 per cent of the officers were Germans. This

TABLE VIII

Nationalities	Distribution among 1,000 Austrians	Nationalities	Distribution among 1,000 Officials
German.........	357	German........	479 (+122)
Czech...........	232	Czech..........	232
Pole............	165	Pole...........	125 (−40)
Ruthenian.......	132	Ruthenian......	29 (−103)
Slovenian........	46	Slovenian.......	32 (−14)
Serbo-Croat	27	Serbo-Croat....	12 (−15)
Italian..........	28	Italian.........	35 (+7)
Rumanian.......	9	Rumanian......	4 (−5)

TABLE IX

NATIONALITIES AMONG 1,000	OCCUPATIONS			
	Agriculture and Forestry	Industry	Commerce and Transportation	Intellectual
Germans....................	335	383	134	148
Czechs.....................	431	365	93	111
Poles......................	656	148	112	84
Ruthenians.................	933	25	17	25
Serbo-Croats...............	869	46	38	47
Slovenians.................	754	134	35	77
Italians....................	501	234	127	138
Rumanians.................	903	27	25	45

fact is the more significant because according to an official record of
1900 there were in the joint army 400,000 Slav, 227,000 German,
220,000 Magyar, 48,000 Rumanian, and 14,000 Italian soldiers.

No less enlightening are the results of the statistical compilations,
shown in Table IX, concerning the professional classes[4] and the manner in which they were employed.

Table IX demonstrates that the Germans were far more active in
industry and commerce than the other nations of the monarchy which

[3] Heinrich Rauchberg, *Die Bedeutung der Deutschen in Österreich* (Dresden,
1908), p. 18.

[4] O. Bauer, *Die Nationalitätenfrage, op. cit.*, p. 209.

explains their economic leadership. At the same time these figures verify the conclusion that national consciousness grows usually in direct proportion to the industrialization and commercialization of the various nations.

It would be an easy task to demonstrate the great economic and cultural predominance of the Germans also in other fields. But the foregoing examples give a sufficiently clear idea of how preponderantly the former Austria of the absolutistic period was a German state, when after the passionate struggles of more than a century, it retained still its German character.

Even still more striking was the economic and cultural hegemony of the Magyars in Hungary proper. I must restrict myself here to a few examples. Among the towns and bigger villages above 10,000 there were 80 with a Magyar, 9 with a German, 8 with a Slovak, 6 with a Serb, and 2 with a Rumanian majority. This signifies that 76.09 per cent of all the urban agglomerations was Magyar. We reach the same conclusion if we regard the ethnic composition of the towns. Table X, according to the census of 1910, gives the percentages of the various nationalities among the total urban population.

TABLE X

Nationalities	Per Cent
Magyars	76.6
Germans	9.7
Slovaks	4.3
Rumanians	3.6
Ruthenians	0.1
Croatians	0.5
Serbs	2.3
Others	2.9

Knowing the intimate connection between the urban agglomerations and the spirit of culture and democracy, we are entitled to draw the conclusion that the distribution of the spiritual and economic forces of former Hungary coincided approximately with the foregoing figures. Other facts will corroborate this hypothesis.

Among the intellectual professions the Magyars, whose percentage of the total population was only 54.5 per cent, show the figures in 1914 as given in Table XI.

TABLE XI

Professions	Per Cent
State Officials	95.6
County Officials	92.9
Judges and Prosecutors	96.8
Lawyers	89.1
Clergy	63.7
Teachers in Elementary Schools	81.9
Teachers in High Schools	91.5
Teachers in Universities and Colleges	93.4
Physicians	89.1

We find approximately the same ratio among the students of the middle and higher education.

Table XII shows the percentages of the various nationalities among the students graduated from high schools or similar institutions in 1913.

TABLE XII

Nationalities	Per Cent
Magyars	82.0
German	7.8
Slovaks	2.1
Rumanians	5.7
Ruthenians	0.1
Croats	0.2
Serbs	1.6
Others	0.5

Similarly among the students in the universities and colleges 89.2 per cent were Magyars in the first semester of the year 1913–14.

Not less conspicuous was the hegemony of the Magyars in the walks of economic life. Whereas, among the independent artisans working without apprentices, the percentage of the Magyars corresponded roughly to their percentage in the general population, among the more prosperous artisans employing apprentices the percentage of the Magyars amounted to 71 per cent. Generally speaking the larger an industrial plant was, the more its Magyar character became prominent.

Among the 2,884 proprietors of plants employing more than 20 apprentices, 2,228 were of Magyar tongue according to the census of 1910. Among 1,657 proprietors of estates containing above 1,420 acres, there were 1,515 Magyars. Of the intellectual leading staff of the larger industrial plants the Magyars held a percentage of 83 and of the qualified workers, 63.

If we compare the taxes paid by predominantly Magyar regions of the country with those paid by the predominantly non-Magyar districts, we find that the taxes of the Magyar counties amounted in 1907 to 101,000,000 crowns whereas the non-Magyar counties contributed only 81 millions. Budapest alone paid in direct state taxes a sum which equalled the financial contribution of the whole of Transylvania and of the Left River district of the Danube, which was the biggest part of the non-Magyar territory.

In order not to burden the reader with other facts, I beg only to emphasize one more outstanding feature of the situation. Table XIII will show the newspapers and periodicals published in 1909 in the various languages of the country.

In connection with these figures it will perhaps be interesting to note that among the ninety-four libraries of the former Hungary which possessed more than 10,000 volumes, there were eighty-five Magyar, six German, two Serb, and one Rumanian.

In these and similar facts we find the real basis of the Magyar and German hegemony. No honest observer of the situation would pretend that all these facts were only a result of the natural development of the social forces. There can be no doubt that the political system and the state administration influenced them to a certain extent. But it is

TABLE XIII

Types of Newspapers	Languages in Which Published				
	Magyar	German	Slovak	Rumanian	Ruthenian
Political........	248	50	5	17	0
Local...........	287	38	1	4	0
Literary........	50	4	2	5	0
Technical.......	771	55	3	18	1
Others..........	21	3	0	0	0
Total.......	1377	150	11	44	1
Percentage..	80.67	8.79	0.64	2.58	0.06

no less manifest that this hegemony was not an artificial one and was not based on sheer force but was a result of a long historical evolution of effects determined by the German dynasty, bureaucracy, militarism, and capitalism on the one hand, and by Magyar feudalism and finance on the other.

The struggle of the other nations was directed against the economic and cultural monopolies of the two hegemonic nations. This could only be accomplished by the transformation of the whole former political structure.

CHAPTER II

THE CHIEF TENDENCY OF THE AUSTRIAN
NATIONAL STRUGGLES: THE MOVE
TOWARD NATIONAL EQUALITY

The struggle, which went on in Austria for more than half a century with growing ardor and bitterness and which led very often to the obstruction of the Parliament and many of the Diets, accompanied by political persecutions, street riots, military sieges, and imprisonments, assumed sometimes the forms of a chronic civil war. For instance, in 1895 the government of Count Badeni made an end to an absolutistic régime in Bohemia which lasted more than two years. During this time 7 journals were stopped, 17 associations dissolved, and 24 papers were put under daily censorship. One hundred and seventy-nine accused were put before exceptional tribunals and punishments of imprisonment were sentenced which totaled 278 years.[1]

This struggle was in its deepest root the fight between two antagonistic principles and world views. The one was the point of view of the *beati possidentes* (those in power), tending to maintain the historical character of the state, the centralized bureaucratic empire under German hegemony. The other was the point of view of those outside the controlling power, of the oppressed or at least second-rank nations tending to remold the old Austria into a decentralized state of nationalities or of equal nations more or less on a confederative basis. Centralization under German hegemony or federalism, conscious of the fact that Austria possessed a Slav majority and therefore, willing to open a way to this majority will—these were the two antagonistic conceptions lying at the bottom of the kaleidoscopical national struggles of Austria.

Naturally this statement is far too abstract and schematic. The struggling masses and even their leaders very often had not a clear comprehension as to the nature and tendency of their fight because, in politics, the contending parties are led less by principles than by the conflicts of daily interests. It is quite clear that the Germans, full of the traditional conception of a German world-empire; or the Czechs, cherishing the brilliant memories of Hussitism and emphasizing more and more clearly the unity of the Crown of Wenceslaus; or the Polish nobility, regarding their nation as "the Christ of the Nations" and continuing the dream of the empire of Jagello from coast to coast; or the Italians, looking always wistfully toward the end of

[1] Richard Charmatz, *Österreichs äussere und innere Politik von 1895 bis 1914* (Leipzig u. Berlin, 1918), pp. 20–21.

the Italia Irredenta had quite another political idea and could use quite other means than for instance the Ruthenian, Rumanian, or Slovenian peasants with their undeveloped historical consciousness and small social differentiation.

But not only was the national consciousness and conception of the various nations radically different, but even inside of the single nations the ideology of the struggle assumed very changing colors according to the classes which appeared in the arena of political life. For instance, in the consciousness of the historical nobility, the national problem appeared in the first place as the struggle of the crowns in an endeavor to maintain the particular life and historical privileges of their countries under their political hegemony. For the bourgeois classes and especially for the intelligentsia the national problem signified first of all a growing participation in the administrative positions and in the economic advantages dependent on state power. The struggle for national rights was in their eyes identical with the claim that not strangers but the national intelligentsia should occupy the administrative positions, both large and small, and that "national" industry and commerce should enjoy the commissions of the state and its facilities in transportation and taxation. And, as this struggle of the second-rank nations was directed as a matter of fact primarily against the leading German bureaucracy and bourgeoisie, it was only natural that the leading classes reacted with a defensive nationalism against the aggressive nationalism of the rising nations. The "maintenance of the German character" of the endangered cities and regions became a passionate shibboleth arousing broad popular movements. That this so-called national struggle signified very often sheer financial efforts of a private character was conclusively demonstrated by the famous Kestranek affair, when this gentleman, the leader of a great German industrial concern, showed before a tribunal in Prague that a state minister and other influential official personages were mobilized against his industrial plant menacing it with an anti-trust legislation, with the lowering of the iron duties, and other important economic measures motivated by the sole purpose of extorting from it cheap raw material for a screw plant which a Czech member of Parliament intended to establish.[2]

Again quite different was the attitude of the small bourgeoisie. In their eyes the national struggle was above all a "struggle for the customer" in order to assure a national clientele for their shops, inns, and artisan enterprises. And when, in consequence of the repeated extension of suffrage, broader circles of small business men and artisans appeared in political life, national struggles assumed a particularly acute and demagogic accent. The "maintenance of the national

[2] Similar interesting facts will be found in Paul Samassa, *Der Völkerstreit im Habsburgerstaat* (Leipzig, 1910), p. 58.

character" or "the reconquest of the old national settlements" were the slogans behind which the class interest of the small bourgeoisie took refuge. In this heated atmosphere, a great number of so-called national cultural associations arose for the "defense and organization" of the endangered national positions. These societies furnished social prestige, and frequently, remunerative jobs to the leaders of the small bourgeoisie who had an outstanding interest in the maintenance of the struggling attitude of their fellow-citizens by fomenting a kind of a fear complex of national aggression. When capitalism became stronger, and, when as its consequence, an industrial migration took place which concentrated the surplus population of the villages in the large industrial centers and created there important enclaves of foreign nationalities which as a matter of fact put forth the claim for schools and administration in their own language, this fear complex grew into an almost hysterical terror which denounced every movement or organization of the national minorities as political plots or "Pan-Slavistic" or similar dangerous schemes. How exaggerated and embittered this public mood had been, was curiously demonstrated by the fact that the pan-German circles of Vienna in the last decades of the previous century were seriously alarmed by the fear that the Imperial City might become Slavicized. The superficial observer, hearing only the political orations and the demagogic utterances in the national-cultural associations and witnessing very often the street riots and the bloody scuffling of the students and the inflamed articles of the leading newspapers, would have thought that one nation would be exterminated by the other or at least its former position would become precarious. Just the opposite was the truth. All these political troubles and harangues scarcely touched the masses of the two nations which worked side by side in complete peace and the traditional national settlements of which remained almost unaltered. For instance concerning the German-Czech situation where the so-called national struggle was the loudest, sometimes even desperate, the careful investigations of Professor Heinrich Rauchberg have demonstrated that the national forces, after the embittered fights of half a century, remained practically the same.[3]

Substantially different was the mood and attitude of the peasant masses concerning national problems. Both the constitutional point of view and the prospect of economic and administrative monopolies were foreign to their simple and very often primitive standard of living, but more important for them was the land problem in regions where the large estates of a foreign upper class checked them in their cultural and economic development. The national struggle, therefore, signified for them a desire for the expropriation of an alien system of

[3] *Der Nationale Besitzstand in Böhmen* (Leipzig, 1905), I, 662.

feudalism. Besides with growing transportation and market economy the peasant masses also became more and more anxious to have popular education and administration in their national tongue.

Finally the appearance of the industrial working-class in economic life and the political struggles gave also a new color and accent to the national problems. The industrial workers of the cities regarded for a time disinterestedly the struggle of the feudal crowns and the fight of the bourgeoisie for administrative positions and economic advantages. These struggles not only did not interest them but they were even irritated by them because the proletariat had the impression that the national struggles signified for the middle classes a sort of "veiling ideology" as it was happily called:[4] the bourgeoisie make national struggles intentionally more acute in order to divert the attention of the masses from economic and cultural issues. This point of view was not without foundation, but in the same ratio in which the working-classes had an increase in the participation of the cultural and political life of their country, they became more and more aware of the fact that the national problem was only another side of the social problem without the solution of which its emancipation could not be achieved. And as very often in many places it occurred that the working-masses were confronted with employers of a foreign tongue, especially with Germans and Jews, class antagonism often assumed the character of national antagonism. Otto Bauer was to a certain extent justified in saying that "national hatred is only a transformed class hatred."

But however many-sided and variegated the nature of national struggles may have been among the various nations and among their particular classes, the essence of the whole process cannot be doubted. Everywhere we witnessed the same tendency: each nation tried to secure its own individuality, and tried to develop its economic, cultural, and political forces in order to attain an *optimum* situation realizable under the given conditions. Baron Eötvös emphasized as the fundamental character of these struggles the fact that every nation feels its own essence, its own cultural and historical conception to be higher and more valuable than that of other nations. I would be inclined to challenge the correctness of this statement. At least one may ask whether the late imperialistic developments of nationalism do really emanate from the genuine sources of the national idea and not from the monopolistic interests of certain groups which were alien to the original conception of national aims? Be that as it may, the aspect of the national struggles in Austria makes it manifest that the program and purposes of the national struggles are in a constant flux and that

---

[4] The political significance of this type of theory was vigorously demonstrated by Paul Szende in his "Enthüllung und Verhüllung: Der Kampf der Ideologien in der Geschichte," *Archiv für Geschichte des Sozialismus*, 1922.

their final limit is, if not domination as Eötvös asserted, at least *equality of rank*. Nations, as individuals cannot in the long run permit themselves to be treated as inferior persons. Even the most modest nation—to use an expression of Napoleon—feels in its knapsack its marshal baton, the idea of perfect national independence.

That is the reason why the nations could not be satisfied and calmed by *ad hoc* advantages and transitory reforms. The difficulty of the national problem in Austria increased exactly to the same extent to which the various nations grew in economic strength, and in political and cultural rights. There can be no doubt that the weakest nation of Austria enjoyed in real life more rights and privileges than the strongest non-Magyar nation in Hungary. In spite of this fact the superficial observer might well have believed that in Hungary there was no national problem, whereas Austria ran from crisis to crisis in consequence of this problem. Paradoxical as it may seem, one may say without exaggeration that *the more the former claims were satisfied, the more the nations felt themselves oppressed*. For example, the national struggle of the Czechs became the loudest in those decades in which they built up their whole educational organization from the elementary schools to the universities and when they occupied many outstanding administrative and judicial positions. The more the former German ruling nation was put on the defensive, the more the Czechs and the other former servant-nations began to feel that their situation was shameful and the more their orators hurled philippics against foreign domination and oppression. In this relation only the situation of the Poles was an exceptional one. The former revolutionary nobles became the most loyal supporters of the Austrian state since, as a consequence of the Compromise of 1867, the Crown and the German bourgeoisie made an alliance with them. The Poles supported the new constitution with their votes, and as the price of their loyalty, they obtained an almost state-like independence in Galicia. Under the protection of this *de facto* home rule the Polish upper class could establish without hindrance its own administrative organization and cultural life and was checked very little in the exploitation of the other great ethnic element of Galicia, in the economic and political domination of the Ruthenians. The Poles of Galicia were perfectly aware of the fact that their condition was excellent compared with that of their brothers in Prussia and in Russia, and, therefore, they were willing to accept Austria "as a tolerable though transitory domicile" until the millennium of the Jagellonian state ideal should be achieved.

But all the other nations did not and could not obtain such a relative equilibrium. Foreign observers have often expressed the opinion that the chief cause of national unrest in Austria was due to the oppressive and Germanizing tendencies of the Germans. This judgment needs at least a strong qualification. Disregarding the episode of the Bach system, we may safely say that there was no conscious Germanization in Austria, and the conception of a unified German nation as the ruler of a nation state was never a political idea as in Hungary where the hegemony of the Magyars was the fundamental dogma of political life. Both in the schools and in the administration the language of the various nations was acknowledged and the state was anxious to develop a bureaucratic class in every nation capable of carrying on state affairs in the maternal language of the population. Paragraph 19 of the fundamental law of 1867, which codified the principle of national equality, did not establish a revolutionary doctrine but rather emphasized a more or less acknowledged practice, saying:

All the nationalities of the State are equals in right and each of them has the inalienable right to maintain and to foster its own nationality.

The equal right of all the languages of the country in the schools, in administration, and in public life, is acknowledged by the State.

As a matter of fact never, not even in the time of the so-called liberal German rule, did we witness any effort to introduce German as the official language of the state or any attempt at the denationalization of the other peoples.

German constraint which the other nations of Austria felt more and more as an unsupportable burden was of a quite other nature. It was a haughty attitude of cultural predominance, the belief that the economic and cultural hegemony of the Germans was a historical necessity for all time. F. Kleinwaechter characterizes excellently this offensive attitude, so dangerous for the Germans too:

The Germans were accustomed to their hegemony based not so much on power as on their cultural superiority through centuries. They were the calm possessors and enjoyers. Such a position gives no opportunity for thinking of struggles. The Czech uprising came, from a historical point of view, with an amazing rapidity. But for those who lived in this period, it came not in a day. From the program of Palacký to the establishment of the Czech University in Prague was thirty-three years. It was a whole generation. For the German contemporaries, therefore, the evolution was very slow and one which only sharp eyes could discover. I spoke with old people who lived at the time when the Czech nation was a quite unimportant factor in political life and who now stood startled before the new developments. This may be understood more clearly when I mention that Prague, in which scarcely a single German word has been heard for many years, was, in the youth of my father, a completely German city. The political possessors of power are under the sway of a curious psychology. They believe that nothing can happen to them. More likely that the Heavens will collapse than that a change in the political powers should occur. The law of inertia dominates also the human soul.[5]

⁵ Der Untergang, op. cit., pp. 139–40.

Under the sway of the same illusion Emperor Francis Joseph, when he visited Prague in 1868, made the characteristic remark: "Prague makes a completely German impression."

This haughty and naïve belief in the unalterable mission of German hegemony, which was further strengthened and developed by the example of the German empire of a united national character, made the creation of a political atmosphere propitious for the fair discussion and solution of the national problems almost impossible. A dangerous situation because the more Austria progressed in its industrial development and the more democratic concessions to the masses became inevitable by the extension of the suffrage, the more as a matter of fact the old German character of Austria crumbled, the more grew the claims of the non-German nations for cultural and administrative self-expression. This natural and unavoidable process, however, was only realized by a small élite of the Germans. The great majority lived in the unshakeableness of their Pan-German hegemony or regarded the national problems from the narrow, local point of view of their crownlands. One could truthfully say that the political leaders of the Austrian-Germans (with the exception of the Socialists and some isolated political thinkers) were unable to grasp until the collapse of the monarchy the fact that the old hegemony of the Germans was coming into a more and more acute antagonism with the very facts of the economic and cultural evolution, and that, therefore, the state could only be maintained by a prudent progression toward federalism, which, as Albert Schäffle said, besides the *unitas in necessariis* would have opened the way for every nation in the realization of its political and cultural life. The reader will remember that Palacký, the great leader of the Czechs, offered the plan in the constitutional committee at Kremsier of dividing the Czech and the German settlements from an administrative point of view in the Bohemian and Moravian territories in order to make a compromise easier. This measure could have eliminated most of the antagonisms between the two tribes and would have made it possible for the German minority to avoid all dangers of future oppression by a complete national autonomy. But in those times the Germans still felt themselves the masters of the situation and opposed the division of the traditional crownlands giving to them an uncontested hegemonial position. This claim became later the chief war cry of the Germans when they assumed the defensive as a minority but at this time the Czechs felt themselves already sufficiently strong to meet the struggle against the *Länderzerreissung* (the dismemberment of the Czech crown) and for the restitution of the historical unity of the Czech territories. Something similar happened in 1871 on the occasion of the so-called Hohenwart-Schäffle experiment when the government succeeded in making a reasonable compromise with the Czechs in the spirit of a very moderate federalism.[6]

[6] See pp. 113–14 of the present book.

This plan of reform could have been a real turning-point in the history of the monarchy. Without doubt it was not yet a scheme of federalism but, by the satisfaction of the historical claims of the Czechs for the constitutional unity and independence of their country, it would have opened the way for the remolding of the artificial scheme of Dualism into the voluntary co-operation of all the peoples of the monarchy. This, however, was exactly the thing which the two hegemonic nations of the monarchy abhorred the most and they left no attack and no intrigue unutilized in order to induce the emperor to break his word given to the Czechs, to overthrow the Compromise, and to offend gravely by a harsh declaration the whole Czech public opinion.

This haughtiness brought the Germans later into a more and more difficult position. As we saw above, the hegemonic nations refused for a long time to learn the language of their former servants and lackeys, whereas the Czech youth and the youth of the other nationalities eagerly learned the German language as an indispensable condition in their administrative career, for the German language, though not a state language in the official sense, played a preponderant rôle in the so-called inner administration of the country. In consequence of this behavior, the German intelligentsia remained in its majority unilingual whereas the Czech became bilingual. The result was that later when, due to the cultural and political progress of the Czechs, the government of Count Badeni issued in 1897 his famous decree concerning the use of languages in the German-Czech territories, according to which after 1901 each official would be compelled to have perfect command of both languages in speaking and writing, this measure, undoubtedly just and fair in itself, evoked a paroxysm of indignation among the Germans. It came to street riots and to ultra-chauvinistic manifestations and made the system of Parliamentarian obstructionism almost chronic, because today the Czechs, tomorrow the Germans (according to the changing tendency of the governmental policy) impeded the legislative procedures not only by long-winded speeches and repeated calling of the roll but very often by automobile horns, by destruction of the seats, by the casting of books and documents, and often by brutal wrestling.

And though every year, the natural development of economic and cultural life made, as a matter of fact, the relation among political powers less and less advantageous for the Germans (for they had already an almost mature national culture, whereas the non-German masses were building their own step by step), their leading elements disliked to face this situation and shoulder its political consequences. Instead of this they forged artificial plans in order to maintain their hegemony, opposed more and more by the facts of real life. So for instance in 1882 they delineated in the so-called "Linzer Program," a picture of an Austria being with Hungary in a purely personal union (the community of the person of the sovereign) whereas inside of Austria, Galicia, Dalmatia, and Bukowina would have obtained a far-reaching autonomy in order to establish in this restricted Austria a compact German majority over the Slavs. Naturally such a plan could not be carried out even in the time of limited Austrian suffrage in a Parliamentarian way, and the keener Austrian politicians realized the dangers of such a procedure. But this same unhappy project, as was already mentioned, reappeared during the early successes of the World War when, in the claims of the so-called *Belange*, the German bourgeoisie would have liked to utilize the suspension of the constitution for the refoundation of the German hegemony. So little had the German bourgeoisie learned even in the last hour from the national struggles of a century and there can be scarcely a doubt that the Crown itself under the Great German influences would have been favorable to such a coup d'état if the sudden outbreak of the Russian Revolution had not terrified the young Emperor and a part of his entourage. This change in the Habsburg attitude was quite openly complained of by a German writer of the Reich during the war in the following characteristic utterance:

The hopes of the Germans for the carrying on of their intentions were again frustrated by their greatest enemy, democracy. In the moment in which it was determined in Vienna with regard to the Russian Revolution to convoke Parliament and to transfer to it the revision of the constitution, any chance for the accomplishment of the German claims disappeared . . . . at least temporarily. . . . [7]

This statement was perfectly true from the point of view of German domination, from the point of view of the dogma of German hegemony. Really, democracy was the greatest enemy of the Germans because the gradual emancipation of the Slav masses was irreconcilable with the rule of the Germans. That is the reason why every enlargement of the suffrage both under Hohenwart and Taaffe and later in consequence of universal suffrage "Slavicized" Austria necessarily and inevitably and undermined more and more the fragile edifice of the Dualistic Constitution. And the evil was not the process itself, as superficial observers announced it, not even from the point of view of the well-understood interests of the Germans. The real evil which shattered the intellectual and moral forces of the monarchy was the fact that this very natural process was undirected, the growing national forces were uncanalized by any statesmanlike conception either in internal or external policy. With the exception of Kremsier and the Hohenwart experiment the national problem was never treated as

[7] Wilhelm Schüssler, *Das Verfassungsproblem im Habsburgerreich* (Stuttgart und Wien, 1918), p. 194.

the most fundamental problem of Austria but only as a matter of tactics. The chief political task never was how, out of the decaying feudal castle a comfortable, modern home could be created for all the peoples of Austria but rather how this unhygienic slum could be further rented with the help of superficial and cheap alterations.[8] The government dared not introduce any reform principle because the smallest issue of a national character would cause its ruin. For instance in 1895 the coalitional government of Prince Windischgrätz fell because it tried to introduce some parallel classes beside the Germans in the mother-tongue of the population in the high school of the small Slovenian city of Cilli. Very often not even compromises of an objective nature (for instance the establishment of a national office or school) were made by the government, but it distributed jobs and economic concessions among the influential personages of the various nations who were capable of mitigating the momentary troubles of the government in the Parliament or the Diets by their personal influence.

A further great difficulty in solving the national problem of Austria was the system of the crownlands, this feudal and plutocratic self-government of the local territories, which came into acute conflict both with the economic and the national claims because they separated from each other peoples and regions which were already unified in culture, economic life, or national affinity. These anti-democratic structures envenomed further the development of the nations by the fact that the spirit of local patriotism pressed upon them which did not see or recognize the general interests of the state. In these crownlands each nation which constituted a majority tried to dominate the nations in the minority and to maintain for itself certain administrative, cultural, and economic privileges. That is the reason that these crownlands became the hotbed of national struggles and rivalries. Whereas in the Parliament of the empire, in the atmosphere of the metropolis, and in the presence of the representatives of all nations, sometimes a tendency toward justice and mutual consideration could be observed, in the atmosphere of the crownlands, in the surroundings of local interests, and of local notabilities the rule of national demagogy was almost unchecked. The nations in the majority, for instance the Czechs and the Poles, held rigidly to the maintenance of the autonomy of their crownlands and the Germans also in those territories where they formed a majority. On the other hand the minority nations, as the Germans in the countries of the Crown of Wenceslaus or the Slovenians and the Italians in their respective crownlands, demanded a territorial autonomy on the basis of the division of the national settlements. National autonomy on the one side and a struggle

[8] Compare with pp. 115–17 of the present book.

against the dismemberment of the country on the other side were the two contending ideologies according to the minority and the majority interests.

One of the best connoisseurs of this system, the later Austrian chancellor, Karl Renner, characterized it as follows:

The crownlands are the inner foe of the Habsburg monarchy. They and no others are the real fostering soil of the *Irredenta,* they create the desperate minorities and the cruel majorities. But just because the crownlands give hope to their national majorities for national domination, are the majorities of all the crownlands and, therefore, that of the Parliament, too, attached to them, the Germans not excepted! The Germans in Northern Bohemia suffocate under the pressure of the Bohemian crown and cry for help, but the Germans in the Alpine countries will remain citizens of Styria, Carinthia, and Tyrol. As long as this spirit of a past epoch, the idol of the country unity, is not buried, we cannot dream of national peace. . . . .[9]

The situation became indeed insupportable and the various crownlands with mixed nationalities became paralyzed by the obstruction in their Diets. The picture became more and more the picture of anarchy and the crownland system was compared by a foreign observer in a witty way with "cages in which wild animals wrestle with each other" (Schüssler).

The situation was still more complicated and envenomed by the fact that not only the non-German nations faced the Germans with hostility but often also acute struggles arose among the so-called oppressed nations. This observation leads us to the darkest point of the national struggles both in Austria and in Hungary. Namely we see that the same nations, which carried on the most exacerbated fights through generations against foreign oppression and the system of a forcible assimilation and which denounced this system as wicked and immoral before the public opinion of the whole world, did not hesitate to apply this same system when the wheel of history turned and they gained the ruling position. The Magyars for instance who struggled for centuries against the Austrian policy of assimilation, when they "got into the saddle" had no scruples against the application of the same methods not only toward the nationalities of the country which they regarded as inferior but also against the Croats, the national distinctness of whom was at least theoretically acknowledged. The Poles who threw the force of their indignation against the cruel system of Russian oppression refused to recognize the national independence of the Ruthenians, and brutally exercised against them Polish supremacy. The Italians, too, who themselves experienced all the sufferings of foreign oppression vindicated on their own account a ruling position over the big majority of the Croats in Dalmatia. The

[9] *Op. cit.,* p. 81.

hatred and rivalry between the closely related Croats and Serbs was for a long time an easy means of domination for Magyar absolutism in Croatia-Slavonia.

We find everywhere the same spectacle: the political morality of an oppressed nation changes completely when it attains a ruling position. The former claim for national equality easily drops into a claim for national supremacy. At the beginning of the struggle we ordinarily hear the vindication of national autonomy. Later when they become a majority they assert the political unity of the country against the former rulers now in a minority. When they acquire still more power, they begin to lay plans for the reconquest of territories for which they have a so-called historical claim but from which they were ousted by foreign rule. From here it is only a step to a naked imperialism when a victorious nation announces as its cultural and historical mission the occupation of the settlements of weaker foreign nations.

It is evident that we face here a very deep problem which demonstrates that the solution of the national struggle is in its essence a moral issue. As in Eastern and Middle Europe it is impossible to dismember the states so as to establish everywhere united national territories but there will always remain in most of the states national minorities: these problems could only be solved in a wholesome and permanent way if the nation having a majority would be animated by a spirit of justice. Without such a moral attitude all technical or jural solution is useless. I scarcely know a more important task in civic education than to inculcate into the souls of future citizens this elementary idea of national justice in states where an ethnographically mixed population is living. Unfortunately, among the so-called statesmen only very few realize that without a new ethical orientation national problems remain practically unsolvable. So in the former Austro-Hungarian monarchy. Only isolated thinkers, like a Fischhof, a Schäffle, a Deák, an Eötvös, a Palacký, and a few others were animated by this higher moral conception. A real historical monument of this new kind of political morality was erected by Albert Schäffle who, when his plan of compromise with the Czechs was undone by the intrigues of the German and Magyar upper classes, wrote the following memorable passage in a letter to the Emperor in which he resigned from his ministry: "Following the general moral law, according to which we should not treat others in a manner which we ourselves would dislike, my conscience does not permit me to have any share in the carrying on of a plan laid down by the state council."[10] (Schäffle refers here to a plan excogitated by the beneficiaries of the dualistic system which made any compromise impossible for the Czechs and maintained the Magyar-German hegemony unaltered.) This incident

[10] *Aus Meinem Leben* (Berlin, 1905), II, 57.

and some other episodes from the history of the monarchy, for instance, the Constitution of Kremsier, the publicistic work of Dr. Fischhof for peace and justice, the humanitarian Slavism of Palacký, and the nationality policy of Deák and Eötvös, animated by a spirit of fair compromise, could have been worthy topics for a civic education eager to inculcate a more humane spirit of justice into the peoples of the monarchy. But I do not know a single textbook or popular writing which fostered this more moral conception of nationality. Civic education was imbued with quite another spirit as we shall see later in detail. The entire lack of a spirit of political fair play was the chief reason why the national problem could not be solved. But such an attitude could only have been the result of a highly developed system of local autonomy. For the national problem is not only a moral but at the same time a "cellular" problem. The centralized, bureaucratic state cannot establish national peace, not even theoretically, because the most important connections of the national struggles are those which are attached to the daily life of the common man. Only a very intense municipal and county self-government could have brought the citizens of the various nations into a peaceful co-operation. But such a real popular self-government was entirely absent in Austria. Under these circumstances, the spirit of the crown-lands swallowed the spirit of the state which existed only in the weak endeavors of the leading bureaucrats. In the lack of real co-operation among the nations the problems of the empire became so complicated that not even the leading statesmen could grasp them. Therefore it is not a rhetorical formula but the expression of reality when one of the most venerable Austrian statesmen of the last decades, Premier Wladimir Beck, sighed because of the pitiful rôle of an Austrian premier who should overcome difficulties such as "eight nations, seventeen countries, twenty Parliamentarian bodies, twenty-seven Parliamentarian parties, two complicated world views, the intricate relation with Hungary and the cultural differences of eight and a half degrees of latitude and longitude. . . . ."

If we look over again all these great and many-sided obstacles, we must be really surprised seeing those considerable results which the growing culture and democracy, the quick development of industrialism, and the more European atmosphere of the Viennese *Reichsrat* achieved on the field of the national problem. In spite of parliamentarian obstruction, passive resistance of various nations, absolutistic measures, press confiscations, patriotic *Bummels* (provocative promenades of the German students on the main street of Prague) followed by the not less patriotic street riots of the Czech nationalists and in spite of the growing demagogy of the daily press and the patriotic associations, Austria made from year to year a considerable step toward the national equality of all its various nations, each of

which attained an honorable minimum of cultural existence, and some
of them, as the Czechs and the Poles, a high cultural standing even
from a more Western point of view. The most fundamental administrative and cultural necessities of the various nations were, almost
everywhere, satisfied in the mother-tongue of the masses. Even a nation which played a rather stepchild rôle in Austria, as the Ruthenians, ruthlessly oppressed by Polish feudalism, progressed considerably in the last decades both from the administrative and the cultural
point of view. An impartial observer writes:

In Eastern Galicia the Ukrainian language was accepted as the official
language, there arose every year new elementary schools and high schools
with instruction in the Ukrainian language and in the University of Lemberg were created Ukraine chairs. Many cultural institutions and scientific
and literary associations were inaugurated. The number of the Ukrainian
officials grew from year to year. In the economic field also they achieved
great results.[11]

But not only in the field of the national daily work (Kleinarbeit)
but also in institutions of a more general importance the Austria of
the last decades achieved substantial progress. The system of the
"National Cadasters" (the national division of the electorate), advocated so strenuously by the socialists, was introduced into Moravia
and Bukowina and the bifurcation of the cultural offices began in Bohemia. And, if the World War had not broken out, in the crownlands
too the anachronistic electoral system of the Curias would have been
replaced by universal suffrage. This really revolutionary measure in
the best sense would have eliminated the feudal and oligarchic monopolies and brought into direct connection the various nations in the
Diets. We would have witnessed, it is reasonable to believe, the revival
of the spirit of Kremsier.

And however great the wrongs against the weaker nations may
still have been and however much the sins of the past pressed upon the
peoples of Austria, there can be no doubt that the Austrian half of
the dual monarchy made gigantic efforts toward the solution of the
national problems, and it was not an exaggeration when certain Austrian scholars emphasized the fact that never in the history of the
world was the principle of national equality in a great empire and under so many different nations carried so far as in former Austria. And
the best expert and theorist of the Austrian national struggles, the
later socialist chancellor of the Austrian Republic, Dr. Renner, was
fully entitled to write an article for an English magazine under the resigned title "Stifled Germs." As a matter of fact the first foundations
of a state based on national equality were laid down in these tempes-
tuous decades.

[11] Jacob Rappaport, "Die Nationalitätenfrage in Polen," Jahrbuch für Soziol-
ogie (Karlsruhe, 1927), Vol. III.

Superficial observers did not realize the meaning of this process. They saw only the continuous crises in Parliament and the Diets, they were aware only of the street manifestations and riots which accompanied the travail of the popular chaos for national emancipation. These observers turned away from the "Austrian anarchy" with a contemptuous gesture and regarded with admiration the other half of the monarchy, Hungary, showing the example of a state advancing toward national unity. Here they did not see dissatisfied nations but they were impressed by a unified, conscious, national will. The glorifiers of the Magyar hegemony became more and more numerous. Only a few keen students of the Austro-Hungarian reality perceived the fact that this so-called Magyar hegemony would become the gravedigger of the monarchy because this was the *rocher de bronze* on which every effort for the federalization of the monarchy broke down. For the advance of Austria in the direction of national equality, without an adequate reform of the general constitution, had an inevitably destroying influence on the state. It is quite evident that the growing culture and consciousness of the non-German nations enhanced unavoidably their aspirations toward a constitution which, on the ruins of the Dualistic system, would have secured the political *Ebenbürtigkeit* (equal dignity) among the various nations. The legal fiction of the unitary Magyar state made such an evolution impossible.[12] Why and how the next chapter will demonstrate.

[12] The fundamental antagonism between the development of the nationality problem in Austria and Hungary was sharply stated in the essay by Friedrich Tezner, "Das staatsrechtlische und politische Problem der österreichisch-ungarischen Monarchie," *Archiv des öffentlichen Rechts, 1913*. The same problem aroused the gravest apprehensions of Crown Prince Rudolph.

CHAPTER III

THE CHIEF TENDENCY OF THE HUNGARIAN NATIONAL STRUGGLES: THE MOVE TOWARD A UNIFIED NATIONAL STATE

The general process of the origins and dynamics of the national struggles, delineated in the foregoing chapter, is further corroborated by the Hungarian example, however different this evolution may have been in its concrete manifestations, colors, and rhythm. Though it is a favorite dogma of the official historiography in Hungary to demonstrate the continuity of the Magyar national consciousness through a thousand years and to force the modern national ideology of the nineteenth century on St. Stephen, the first king of Hungary, on the feudal warfare of the Middle Ages, on the civil wars of throne-pretenders, and on the feudal rebellions against the Habsburgs, there can be no doubt that the modern national idea, the effort toward the unification of the masses akin in language and culture and toward economic and administrative unity, was absent from Hungarian history until the end of the eighteenth century as completely as from the history of the other Central European peoples.

Having scrutinized all those movements of the past which were described until the end of the eighteenth century under national captions by the historians of the noble classes (for in Hungary with very few exceptions the whole study of history was biased by the ideology of the ruling classes in the absence of a bourgeois class in a Western sense) I could easily demonstrate in my book already quoted that all these movements were influenced by economic, class and religious considerations but never by a national conception because in those epochs all the factors were lacking which created later the national movement. In want of an urban culture, a more intensive communication, press and school, national currents could not become manifest for the unification of the country in a common law and culture. The atmosphere of the society in Hungary continued, far into the nineteenth century, to be the spirit of the famous *Opus Tripartitum* codified by Stephen Verböczy, one of the most rapacious oligarchs of the epoch, in the second decade of the sixteenth century. This law book made the upper and lower nobility, the so-called *una eademque nobilitas,* the exclusive beneficiary of all private and public rights. It laid down the conception of "Hungarian liberty," the chief pillars of which were the non-taxation of the nobility, its exclusive right to have landed property, the monopoly of all administrative offices, and the right of resistance of the Crown if it should offend feudal privileges. As a product of feudal reaction against the peasant upheaval of Dózsa, it deprived the peasantry of its right of migration, bound the serfs completely to the soil, which meant the practical introduction of slavery. Acsády writes:

> From this time there were properly speaking two nations in Hungary, the "Hungarian lords" [*Magyari urak*, as they were called in this period], the ruling class and the millions of slaves, the working-classes. The two nations glared with a wolfish hatred at each other, the master did not regard his serf as a man whereas the latter waited like a shackled beast for the occasion of attacking again his tyrant.

This feudal petrification of the Hungarian society was also clearly felt by some keen foreign observers, among them the greatest poet and genius of Germany, Goethe, who in a conversation in 1821 emphasized the total impossibility of introducing useful reforms in Hungary as long as the feudal rule was not uprooted by violent interference.[1]

This old immobile feudal state collapsed only in 1848, or rather under the system of Bach when the liberation of the serfs was practically carried out. This demonstrates that in a society in which, until the middle of the nineteenth century the nobility remained the exclusive owner of the land, and under a constitution which gave all political rights in a population of eleven millions into the hands of 136,000 noblemen, the really democratic and cultural content of the modern national movement could only be expressed in a very rudimentary way. This unified nobility, the political and colloquial language of which was Latin for centuries, made, so to speak, the emergence of the national problem impossible because in the hothouse of the feudal privileges the nobility of the non-Magyar nationalities became entirely assimilated in interests and culture with the Magyar ruling class and regarded with horror any conscious movement of the masses aspiring toward economic and national emancipation. The more wealthy elements of the bourgeoisie and intelligentsia of the towns, mostly Germans, became also permeated by the atmosphere of the ruling nobility or in some parts they lived a hermetically closed life, like the inhabitants of a Greek city-state.[2]

It is quite evident that in such social surroundings the national idea could manifest itself at best as a solidarity with the interests of the nobility, as a tendency toward keeping away foreign bureaucracy and militarism or as a hatred of the serfs, especially those of a foreign tongue. Particularly in Transylvania where the problem of the bondsmen became very acute the idea of the noblemen was closely associated with Magyar rule, whereas among the masses of the serfs there arose a kind of Rumanian affinity and solidarity against the oppressors of

[1] Viktor Bibl, *op. cit.*, II, 416.

[2] Oscar Meltzl, *The Position of the Transylvanian Saxons in Hungary* (Nagy-Szeben, 1878), p. 31. In Hungarian.

a foreign tongue. The hostile ardor of this antagonism was clearly expressed in many popular verses and dicta. For instance the state of mind of the noble manors is well characterized by the following rhymes:

> Under human form, wild animal, murderous Wallachian,
> Old dog, biting Actaeon, snapping at his master,
> Sprung from a mountain rat, suckled by a shabby wolf. . . . .

It must be remembered that the Magyar upper classes used the expression Wallachian *(Oláh)* instead of Rumanian intentionally and in a deprecatory sense in order to repudiate the Rumanian hypothesis of the Roman origin of the Rumanian people. I scarcely exaggerate the situation when I say that this derogatory denomination caused more hatred and suspicion among the two nations than many administrative or cultural grievances.

On the other hand the peasant masses amid the double pressure of the feudal oligarchy and Austrian militarism sighed in the following dicta: "The Magyars hung my father with the *Approbata and the Compilata* [a famous law book of Transylvania], whereas the Germans deprived me of all my possessions by the *Aufnahm' and the Protocol*" (German official proceedings). Nevertheless, it was a time-old tradition of the Rumanian people that their lot was much harder under the Transylvanian princes than under the Habsburgs.

But in spite of this class and racial division there was never in the past a policy on a strictly national line. On the contrary in the peasant upheavals Magyar and Rumanian masses allied with each other against the common oppressors. For instance in the serf riots in 1437 in Transylvania the Magyar element played the leading rôle, while the result of this civil war, which became the very basis of the constitution of Transylvania, the *unio trium nationum* (the union of the three nations), signified the alliance of the Hungarian nobility, of the Székely (a distinct tribe of the Magyar stock) small peasant nobility, and of the Saxon urban citizenship in order to maintain their domination over the Magyar and Rumanian peasant masses. On the other hand foreign aggressors, as the dukes of Wallachia or the Habsburgs, could often mobilize the Székely and Magyar masses against the Magyar oligarchy. And whenever a movement was started capable of uniting the privileged classes, in their struggles against Austria for their independence, with the social dissatisfaction of the masses or with the defense of their attacked religion, as for instance at the time of the insurrections of Bocskay and Rákóczi, the bondsmen without national discrimination followed the flag of the nobility. Among those so-called *Kurucz* songs which are a striking echo of the popular upheavals against Habsburg absolutism, there are many of purely Rumanian origins.

As has already been shown in an earlier chapter, differentiation on a truly national line was a comparatively recent event, belonging to a period when Hungary changed from a cattle-breeding to an agricultural stage, when the first results of more extensive popular education and more efficient transportation became manifest, when the victorious Habsburgs introduced a defensive policy in the interests of the peasants and when the liberal and democratic principles of the French Revolution penetrated into a part of the Hungarian nobility and middle classes. These new ideas and the reaction against the absolutistic Germanization of Joseph II stirred up, in the first place, the semi-dormant circles of the Magyars as the most developed element of the country both from the political and the economic point of view. Beginning with the Diet of 1825 the national consciousness of the Magyars became more and more active. Since the forties of the last century, this national consciousness has assumed decidedly democratic and liberal forms. The growing bankruptcy of serf economy, the thrilling influence of Western ideas, the hatred of Habsburg absolutism, and the chronic danger of peasant upheavals, created a new ideology uniting the constitutional claims for independence of the former feudal rebellions with the aspirations of a modern democratic and national state. This movement was led (in the absence of a conscious bourgeois or peasant class) by the liberal wing of the Magyar nobility which became the real *tiers état* of Hungary. This fact which was in perfect harmony with the structure of the country, still preponderantly feudal, had very important consequences. One of them was that this revolutionary nobility remained as a matter of fact under the stress of the old, inherited anti-Habsburg, *Kurucz* ideology, whereas the new ideal of the French Revolution constituted, in their consciousness, only an acquired character. From the beginning, therefore, we witness a tendency in this revolutionary nobility to weaken the democratic and social content of the national revolution and to safeguard their ancient monopolies as far as possible. At the same time they renewed with the greatest enthusiasm the old constitutional struggle for national independence against the Habsburgs and they were successful in mobilizing, for this idea, not only the smaller nobility but also the great masses of the peasants and of the urban population, which were for the first time emancipated from the feudal yoke. The program of Louis Kossuth and his adherents was the coalescence of the constitutional traditions of the nobility with the claims of Western democracy. The proclamation of the liberation of the bondsmen became the great act of liberalism in the interests of national unification.

Another consequence of the leading rôle of the nobility was that the traditional, purely jural kind of thinking influenced deeply the revolutionary struggles. The paragraphs of the old lawbooks were far more important for them than the technical and social exigencies of the new period, and the more so because these paragraphs were very advantageous to them whereas the modern exigencies were detrimental to their former privileges. The overwhelming majority of feudal society, until the collapse of the monarchy, gloated over the traditional constitutional debates and the interpretation of the ancient codes while they regarded with distrust, nay with a kind of awe, modern economic and social problems. In the Habsburgs they hated not only Germanizing absolutism but also their introduction of the pernicious microbes of state bureaucracy, capitalism, general taxation, and equality before the Imperial law. This constitutional Talmudic method made modern orientation of the nobility difficult. In the independence of the country they saw rather a jural and constitutional problem and not those fundamental economic, cultural, and moral reforms which the genius of Count Stephen Széchenyi had advocated with prophetic clear-sightedness. The ideology of constitutional independence meant always two things for the privileged classes of Hungary. The one was the passionate indulgence in the traditional efforts for national independence against the Habsburgs. The other was a kind of defensive mechanism, a political *Verdrängung*, used for the purpose of diverting the economic and social dissatisfaction of the masses in another direction. By means of this mechanism they were successful in canalizing the popular passions which would have turned more and more against their own privileges and estates, against Vienna and the "Habsburg Camarilla." This explains the military and jural nature of the Hungarian nobility which the keen eye of Bismarck discerned by characterizing the leading Hungarian class as a "nation of Hussars and lawyers."

But it would be an error to thus characterize the whole Magyar feudal class, because the higher nobility and higher clergy were largely created by Vienna or consisted of elements which were obedient instruments to Habsburg power. Therefore the real bearers of the ideology of independence became the middle and small nobility which after the division of the legislature into two houses was also, from the constitutional point of view, a distinct part in the more and more dissolving unity of the *una eademque nobilitas*. This class, which since the eighties of the nineteenth century liked to call itself, after the English fashion "the gentry," comparing proudly on the basis of a superficial analogy its feudal constitution with the English, was in its standard of life, culture, and aspirations totally different from the very mixed and international aristocracy which followed the fashions of Vienna, Paris, and London. This middle and small nobility, the roots of which extended into the upper strata of the peasantry (for during the feudal struggles against Austria some insurgent leaders gave privileges of nobility to entire villages in order to gain them for

their cause), became the real leaven of the anti-German, anti-Habsburg, and anti-Clerical movement. A very considerable part of this
middle nobility and free peasantry was Calvinist. This Calvinist
stratum, recruited from the purest racial element of the country and
called, not without a certain haughtiness, its religion the "Magyar
religion." This Calvinism centering around the big peasant town, the
strong and proud "Calvinistic Rome," Debreczen, was through three
centuries a real bulwark of the Magyar spirit against the Catholicizing and Germanizing tendencies of Vienna and developed a very keen
racial and national consciousness which was sentimentally backed in
its religion by the doctrine of predestination. It seems to me a fine and
intuitive remark of Joseph Redlich when he compared this Hungarian
Calvinism with the Dutch, English, and Scotch Puritanism which in
its haughty religious individualism and independence, felt as God's
destiny, became the kernel of a vast Colonial culture. This strong,
courageous, prudent, and tough race became the real bearer of constitutional independence amidst the noble society. And when, in consequence of the penetration of the democratic world-spirit and the deep
economic changes already mentioned, the old feudal society collapsed,
the rich Habsburgist aristocracy was forced back in leadership by
the middle nobility; and at least in the political arena the significance
of the gentry became preponderant. The outstanding leaders of the
gentry at this time showed a remarkable intellectual ardor and, according to reliable witnesses, it was not a rarity to see in their pockets
a volume of Volney or of Rousseau. The intellectual and moral atmosphere of their manors was very high and exercised great influence on
the bourgeois elements of society. This democratic and liberal atti-
titude of the élite of the nobility, which made a desperate effort to remold in the last hour the old petrified feudal state into a state of law
based on Western parliamentarian principles, made a great appeal
both abroad and at home. It was the time when, regarding the heroic
struggle of the Magyars for independence and democracy, Heinrich
Heine, the great German poet, wrote the enthusiastic rhymes: "Whenever I hear the name Magyar my German jacket becomes too tight,"
and Karl Marx and Friedrich Engels extolled the revolutionary rôle
of the Magyar nobility against the "reactionary Slavs," calling them
tools of the Habsburg absolutism. At the same time at home great
masses of the peasantry joyfully accepted the leadership of the nobility which promised to them their liberation from the feudal yoke
and the non-Magyar elements of the cities (constituting there very
often a majority), the Germans, the Slavs, and especially the Jews
were eager to be taken into the new society of the revolutionary nobles. After the establishment of the Dualistic Compromise this process
continued with even greater intensity and the "gentry" grew into a
far larger concept. It signified a class whose members had accepted

the standard of life, the customs, and the political ideology of the gentry. The possession of a larger noble estate was no longer regarded as the attribute of this class but many German and Jewish elements and also camp followers of the non-Magyar middle classes adhered to it. The custom of the Magyarization of the family names which later gained official sanction made it possible that foreign racial elements could play the rôle of the gentry in the political and social life. By this process the old *Kurucz* ideology of independence acquired a very extensive and heterogeneous following which included besides the historical gentry and the free peasantry also the more ambitious elements of the new bourgeoisie, successful lawyers, writers, the lower clergy, and the more energetic elements of the Jewish intelligentsia.

This leadership of the nobility as a matter of fact dulled the edges of the economic and social claims of the lower classes but reinforced at the same time the constitutional vindications against Austria and the Habsburgs. This situation had a great effect also on the Habsburgist aristocracy which we shall analyze later. At this juncture I must emphasize another consequence of the leadership of the nobility, fatal from the point of view of our problem. That is the relation of the Magyar revolutionary movement toward the non-Magyar nations of the country which the nobility refused to accept as equals. Louis Kossuth himself said at the beginning of the revolution *that there were many nationalities in Hungary, but only one nation, the Magyar.* This point of view, running as a red thread throughout the whole modern history of Hungary, became one of the chief causes which finally destroyed the monarchy. The ruling element of the Magyars was not willing to apply also in the national field, those democratic and liberal principles upon which it tried to remold the state. On the contrary when the Magyar nobility reached the plentitude of its national consciousness and bursting the age-old cloud of medieval Latinity made a wonderful effort for the re-creation of their national language and culture, it was unable to imagine the new state in formation otherwise than of an exclusively Magyar nature. In place of the Latin, and in every relation, it tried to introduce the Magyar language. It was not willing to acknowledge the distinct national individuality of the other peoples. Beginning with the twenties of the last century, a more and more intolerant effort toward Magyarization became manifest which tried to reconstruct the new state emerging from feudalism into a unified and homogeneous Magyar national state. Already at the Diet of 1825–27 when the first efforts were made to make the Magyar the official language of the state together with the Latin, the Croats advocated the same right for the Croat language in their own country, but this claim was flatly repudiated. And when in 1835 the Diet demanded the exclusive usage of the Magyar language, the Croat deputies accused the Magyars of inconsequence for they formally protested against the endeavors of the Russian government to enforce the Russian language on the Poles but now, "they try to enforce the Magyar language upon the Croats."[3] This current captured so fully even the best minds of the period that such a prudent and humane statesman as Francis Deák, commonly called the "sage of the Fatherland," defended the point of view in the Diet of 1839 that the Croats do not constitute a distinct nation and that Croatia has no rights which cannot be dealt with by the Hungarian parliament. In this spirit a law was passed in 1843–44 which obliged all the Croat authorities to learn the Magyar language so that, at the end of a period of six years, all official intercourse between the two countries should be carried on in Magyar. If this was the attitude toward a people, the national independence of which was acknowledged to a certain extent, one can imagine how haughty was the point of view of the ruling class concerning the national claims of the non-Magyar peasant minorities.

This claim seemed to the Magyar ruling class entirely extravagant though at this time the bulk of the Hungarian nationalities (so for the sake of brevity, will I call according to the official Magyar doctrine, all the non-Magyar nations of Hungary in order to distinguish them from the Magyar state-nation) were not animated by any desire for secession and with the exception of the Croats they had no conception of an independent state life. That for which they aspired was no more than an administrative autonomy of their closed national settlements, entire liberty for the development of their languages and cultures and an adequate national representation in the common organs of the state. In spite of this the Magyar leading class felt these claims as entirely unacceptable, as a kind of rebellion or high treason, though in 1787 only 29 per cent of the population was of Magyar stock and even in 1842, according to the calculation of a very conservative author, of a total population of about 13 million, less than 5 millions (4,812,000) were Magyars. They were opposed by 1,600,000 Slovaks, 1,270,000 Germans, 2,200,000 Rumanians, 900,000 Croats, 1,200,000 Serbs, 440,000 Ruthenians, 240,000 Jews, and several other smaller nationalities.[4] Under such circumstances it is difficult to understand how the leaders of the Magyars and among them many eminent scholars and statesmen, equipped with the best culture of the epoch, could imagine that against the will of all these nationalities, forming the vast majority of the country, they would be capable of accomplishing the miracle of rebuilding and reorganizing their state as a unified Magyar nation-state.

This question must be carefully answered because this rigidly

[3] Szilágyi and Collaborators, *op. cit.*, IX, 388–89.
[4] Julius Szekfü, *Three Generations*, p. 171. In Hungarian.

megalomaniac point of view dominated the Hungarian state, with the exception of a unique *lucidum intervallum*, until the collapse of the monarchy. The repulsive attitude of the Magyar upper class against the aspirations of the nationalities originated from several sources. One was the ancient envenomed class struggle between the nobility and the bondsmen. They regarded their serfs, especially those of a foreign tongue as an inferior race, incapable of understanding their thoughts and feelings. That these century-old servants and slaves began now to demand the same national rights as those claimed by the "conquering and state-building" Magyar nation seemed to them as an effrontery, almost as a rebellion. They accepted the necessity of the liberation of the serfs and their equality before the law as a universal claim of the epoch, but that the community of these former serfs should now establish themselves as a nation, and should assume the same national rights as the former omnipotent rulers of the country, this claim after centuries of feudal domination appeared to them as the most daring impertinence. Behind this indignation, however, there were not only sentimental motives but also those of a strict class domination. For the organization of the nationalities as distinct nations, the acknowledgment of a territorial autonomy for them would have signified not only the jural but also the *de facto* cessation of the administrative privileges of the nobility and finally the expropriation of their estates for the benefit of the peasants.

Another source of the hostile attitude of the Magyar nobility against the nationalities of the country was their rigid jural-historical point of view already mentioned which never regarded the most important facts of state life as primarily economic, cultural, and social problems, but as issues of historical rights. From this point of view it could not be contended that the Magyars as the conquering race had special rights over the country beside which the nationalities could have played only a tolerated rôle in state life. The right of conquest, based on the sword, was always hidden more or less consciously behind the doctrine of Magyar supremacy and the unified national state. That the old feudal society at the beginning of the modern era was entirely hypnotized by this historical point of view of force will surprise no one who knows that this conception remained unaltered in the Magyar ruling class until the end of the monarchy and thereafter.[5]

[5] The rigidity of this conception found a characteristic expression in a pamphlet of Dr. John Karácsonyi, a canon of Nagy-Várad, a member of the Hungarian Academy, and an acknowledged historian. (Written in 1912 under the title of *A Hundred Thousand Evils and a Million Woes for an Error.*) According to this distinguished author the whole dangerous Magyar-Rumanian controversy was due to a historical error committed by the Italian scholar Bonfini who, in a famous book written in the fifteenth century at the court of the great Hungarian king, Matthias (himself of Rumanian origin), made the thoughtless remark that the Rumanians of Transyl-

The Magyar conception, repudiating the claims of the nationalities, however, had a deeper and more serious motive, especially in the consciousness of Kossuth and of his best liberal staff. These men (in the same manner as Marx and Engels) felt the rising of the Slav and Rumanian masses as something artificial, as a plot of the Viennese court, trying to counterbalance the liberal and democratic movement of the revolutionary Magyar nobility by the mobilization of the uncultured and reactionary masses of the Slav and Rumanian serfs. In this observation there was indeed an element of truth. The Viennese court, terrified by the revolutionary movement and by the menacing independence of Hungary, embraced intentionally and energetically the literary, cultural, and political movements of the non-Magyar nationalities (some of their leaders were really Austrian agents) because the shrewd imperial bureaucrats understood accurately those powerful forces which slumbered in the national movements and could be directed against the Magyar efforts for unification. Kossuth and his friends, however, saw only, one might say, the tactical part of the problem and did not perceive that the same historical situation which developed the revolutionary nationalism of the Magyars, Poles, and Italians would inevitably arouse the same movement also among the more backward peoples of the monarchy.

Kossuth and his adherents underestimated the national movements of the former bondsmen and were convinced that the Magyar society would easily solve these problems on its own national basis because in the atmosphere of the liberation of the serfs and of democratic rights and liberties, the former feudal particularisms would cease and the masses of nationalities would find an adequate place in the blood circulation of the unified Hungarian State. Kossuth experienced this process in his own life. If he, the small nobleman of Slovak

vania are the remnants of the Roman population of the ancient Dacia under Trajan. The book of Bonfini had a wide circulation and in the eighteenth century fell into the hands of some Rumanian youths who completely lost their heads and, animated by the fallacious myth of having an older and nobler origin than the Magyars, claimed equal rights with them. This doctrine, however, was erroneous because the Rumanians did not come into the country until 1182 and therefore cannot have the same rights as the Magyars. Now Dr. Karácsonyi was convinced that by his important historical revelations the whole Magyar-Rumanian conflict would be eliminated, because the Rumanians instructed by him concerning the real facts, namely, that they were in the Hungarian state only for the short period of 800 years and that they hadn't so distinguished a pedigree as that light-minded Italian had asserted, would be brought to their senses and would recognize that they can have only a subordinate rôle in Hungary.

In this manner this serious and scholarly man and with him the feudal society conceived the complicated economic, social, and psychological problem of nationality struggles to be exclusively an issue of historical right, accepting the naïve theory that the Rumanian went into the Revolution in consequence of the erroneous teaching of Bonfini. (By the way, the historical thesis of Karácsonyi is more than doubtful. Besides, the Slav inhabitants of Hungary constituted the earliest population of the country and therefore the theory of "historical right" expressed by Karácsonyi would have meant a Slav hegemony in Hungary!)

extraction, who, according to a reliable tradition, in his early childhood still read the Slovak prayer book in the church, had become such
a passionate, ardent, and sincere supporter of the Magyar democratic
state ideal, how could he doubt that the Slav peasant masses, without
any culture and historical continuity, and also the other nationalities,
would accept with joy and love the new Hungarian state, offering to
them, on the ruins of the feudal state, a perfect equality before the
law with all the political liberties of the western states? For the reader
should not forget that the eyes of Kossuth and of the other great figures of the Hungarian Revolution were constantly fixed on the historical example of the great western national states, on English and
French constitutionalism in which there was no place for a separatist movement of nationalities. They were perfectly convinced that
the policy of Magyarization signified at the same time a policy of
democratization and that the Magyar cause was the cause of Liberty
and Reason against the claims of the nationalities fostered and directed by the Viennese absolutism. They were perfectly convinced that the
new liberal and democratic state would exert a powerful attraction on
all its citizens, both Magyars and non-Magyars.

And this conception was without doubt not entirely erroneous.
Our history is full of the remembrances of enthusiasm created among
the non-Magyar nationalities by the proclamation of emancipation of
the serfs. There can be no doubt that if, parallel with the economic
liberation of the peasantry, their national claims would also have been
acknowledged and guaranteed in a reasonable way in the cultural policy and public administration (especially in local self-government),
the new Hungarian state could have developed centripetal tendencies,
sufficiently strong to counterbalance all irredentistic currents. The
model economic and geographical unity of the country, the unrivaled
economic and cultural preponderance of the Magyars, the lack of
state formations or provinces inside the Hungarian crown, and the
sober and forbearing character of the Magyar people were factors
which could have made the solution of the nationality problem in
Hungary incomparably more easy than in the other part of the monarchy. There began, however, a more and more energetic process of a
forcible and artificial assimilation which became the chief obstacle to
a fruitful co-operation between the Magyar and the other races.

A. CONFLICT BETWEEN MAGYARS AND NON-MAGYARS

The policy of an exaggerated unification and an artificial Magyarization carried on by the revolutionary nobility led to a fatal conflict between the Magyars and the other peoples of the country. Space
forbids me to illustrate in detail the growing spirit of national chauvinism. I would only quote from a characteristic speech delivered by

Count Charles Zay, general inspector of the Slovak-Lutheran church
and schools at the beginning of the forties of the last century. Among
other patriotic utterances he made the following statement:

Every idea, every aspiration to hinder Magyarization and to spread
other languages besides the Magyar would signify the undermining of the
intelligentsia, of the constitutional principles, nay of Protestantism itself.
The Magyar language is the staunchest defender of liberty and Protestantism in our country. The victory of the Magyars is at the same time the victory of Liberty and Reason. The Magyarization of the Slavs is the holiest
duty of any true Hungarian patriot, of any fighter for Liberty and Reason,
and of any loyal subject of the Habsburg dynasty. . . . .

This doctrine repeated in various forms found its expression not
only in rhetorical formulas but also under the slogan, "the fight
against Pan-Slavism." Professors and students with Slav feelings were
persecuted. The spirit of an intolerant Magyarization penetrated
more and more the whole public life. Naïve and adventurous plans
were in circulation concerning the rapid and complete Magyarization
of the country. Winged words of hatred were used against the nationalities envenoming the social atmosphere. ("Potato is not a food, a
Slovak is not a man. . . . ." "The stinking Wallachian. . . . ."
"The German is a rogue. . . . .")[6]

The danger of this current was already perceived by the keener
contemporary observers, both foreign and Magyar. Count Leo Thun,
an eminent Austrian statesman, attacked the point of view of Francis
Pulszky (one of the most enthusiastic adherents of Louis Kossuth, a
man of broad European culture) according to which "the Slav people
stands on the lowest level of culture, their nobility is Magyar, the chief
pride of their citizens is to appear German even though they were born
Slav and, therefore, only poor Protestant clergymen are interested in
the Slav literature. . . . ." To this attitude characteristic of the
conception of the period, but totally misunderstanding the dynamics
of the nationality problem, Count Thun answered perspicaciously
(manifestly based on the knowledge of the more advanced nationality
problem of Austria) that, even if the Magyars would check the free
development of the Slovaks under their hegemony, "nevertheless the
Slavs would victoriously fight for their cause; but before a final settlement should be reached, how many sorrowful things would happen
on both sides, how much this attitude would hinder the cause of a social and humane progress in Hungary!"[7]

---

[6] The use of such and similar invectives, however, was not a specialty of the
Magyars. Anton Springer gave a long list of nicknames used extensively through
the whole monarchy among the various nations (*Geschichte Österreichs seit dem
Wiener Frieden* [Leipzig, 1865], p. 5. Interesting data concerning the Czech-Slovak
antagonism will be found on pp. 28–29).

[7] *Die Stellung der Slovaken in Ungarn* (Prag, 1843), pp. 4, 5, 18.

Not only a distinguished foreigner but the most brilliant figure of the Hungarian Renaissance, a man who did more than anyone else for the reinforcement of Magyar culture, Count Stephen Széchenyi, observed with despair this advance of a megalomaniac chauvinism and, in a festival address which he delivered in 1842 at the assembly of the Hungarian Scientific[8] Academy, he gave a real philippic against the fatal spirit of an intolerant Magyarization which he called "a current of dementia," accusing everyone of high treason who dared only to contradict this incessant provocation and persecution of the non-Magyar citizens.

Unfortunately this and similar admonitions were useless. The spirit of a forcible assimilation grew rapidly and the situation became more and more dangerous in the proportion in which the antagonism between Habsburg absolutism and liberal Hungary, fighting for its independence, developed more acutely. And when in 1848 events led to a definite rupture between the dynasty and the revolutionary Magyar nobility, the latter found itself bitterly opposed not only by Vienna but also by a great part of the Hungarian nationalities which now made a common cause against the Magyar rule, menacing their independence. The intolerant words of Kossuth against the Serb claims in which he appealed to the sword as the final judge[9] and the general inability of the Magyar revolution to satisfy the national needs of the non-Magyar nationalities exploded in an extremely bloody civil war in which Jugo-Slavs and Rumanians gave ear to the propaganda of the Viennese Camarilla and sustained the claims of absolutism against Hungarian constitutionalism, unwilling to give national independence to the non-Magyar peoples. This civil war became the chief cause of the collapse of the Hungarian Revolution and, at the same time its bloody memories survived until the end of the monarchy, rolling a veritable sentimental rock between the Magyars and the nationalities. Especially in Transylvania these tragic events envenomed the whole social atmosphere.

The leading Hungarian circles realized belatedly that the wrong treatment of the national problem would push the country into an inevitable catastrophe. Only at the last minute did they try to retrieve the sins of the past and Bartholomew Szemere, Minister of Interior under Kossuth, in July, 1849, three weeks before the final collapse in the battle at Világos, introduced into parliament an extremely liberal bill for a nationality law in order to calm the non-Magyar masses.

[8] "Science" in Hungarian does not mean natural science alone, but all kinds of human knowledge.

[9] According to the reminiscences of certain contemporaries, Louis Kossuth, after a hot debate with a Serb delegation (April, 1848), uttered the words: "In that case the sword must decide." Kossuth later, at the time of his emigration, denied the veracity of this statement, but it continued to live in the memory even of subsequent generations.

It is characteristic that even then, at the moment of the approaching catastrophe, it was difficult to get the bill passed. Szemere announced emphatically—writes Michael Horváth, the contemporary historian of the Hungarian Revolution—that "the aristocratic conception of the claims of the other nationalities, if the nation did not abandon it at the last moment, would destroy Hungary. . . . . Under the sway of this brilliant oration the sham democrats and radicals were dumbfounded and humiliated, men who always did lip-service to the liberty of the people but limited it to their own interests." And the bishop-historian added that this law of fundamental importance which

solved radically the nationality problem, guaranteeing complete liberty to each nationality for its natural development without doing any harm to the political unity of the country . . . . had only one fault in its result, namely that it was not created in March of 1848. . . . .[10]

Even more clear than this was the declaration of Bartholomew Szemere himself, one of the outstanding figures of the period, who knew the most intimate details of the inner history of the Revolution. In 1859 he made the following confession in a Hungarian newspaper concerning the real causes of the débâcle of the Magyar Revolution:

In 1848 was finished the great work of national unification, the last obstacle to which [the feudal system] was definitely eliminated. What is the reason that the nation just as it attained its fullest vigor, had lost the battle? The reason was that in the lapse of time, half secretly, half openly, there was born, developed, and matured a new idea, the idea of nationality, the immense power of which in the foreign races we did not realize and, therefore, did not take into sufficient consideration. I know very well the secret and public intrigues of that period and I know equally well the effect of the Russian army upon the historical conclusion: but in spite of all this we must confess that we did not understand the great importance and immense motive power of the idea of nationality which seemed to us to have broken out by accident though it was the result of an inner process of fermentation. We took for an artificial noise what was the thunder of Heaven. . . . . We thought the earth was shaken by the feet of an army when in reality it was a veritable earthquake. . . . . The entire foliage of a forest will never be moved unless there is a tempest which blows. . . . .[11]

B. THE NATIONALITY-PLAN OF KOSSUTH DURING HIS EXILE

The bloody shadows of the Hungarian Revolution and of its suppression by the help of the Tsar weighed heavily upon the souls of the contemporaries during the sorrowful years of absolutism, the centralization and Germanization of Bach. Not only the vanquished Magyars who, according to the Austrian theory, had forfeited their

[10] M. Horváth, *History of the Struggle for Independence of Hungary* (Pest, 1871), III, 315–17. In Hungarian.

[11] Quoted by Benedict Jancsó, *Our Struggle for Independence and the Daco-Rumanian Aspirations* (Budapest, 1885), p. 186. In Hungarian.

right to the Constitution but the former allies of the Viennese Court, the Jugo-Slavs and Rumanians, too, felt themselves deceived and duped by the renewed system of absolutism. All that happened could have given a powerful lesson to the Magyars and the non-Magyar nations in favor of democratic institutions and of a just compromise. Actually we find that the best representatives of the Magyars and the nationalities reached a better conception of the problem.

In the first place the Magyar emigration, under the leadership of Kossuth, acknowledged completely the errors of the past. The chief care of Kossuth was the finding of a policy which would satisfy the interests of the non-Magyar nations and by this to guarantee the independence of Hungary against Habsburg absolutism. This aim led Kossuth to two great political conceptions. The one was his idea of the solution of the nationality problem on the basis of the "principle of personality." In his constitutional plan of 1851 he elaborated a program which coincided in its essence with that advocated by the Austrian Social-Democratic party half a century later. The fundamental thought of this plan has even now an ardent actuality for all those countries which face the nationality problem. Therefore, it will be perhaps not without interest to set forth here its main features. As religion, nationality, too, is a social interest. The state as such, has nothing to do with either. The Constitution guaranteeing the right of coalition, the citizens have a perfect liberty to unite and form associations for their national interests, as well as for other interests, in every village or county or in national corporations exactly in the same manner as the Protestants are united from the point of view of their religious interests in the villages, counties, and districts. But like these religious associations, the national ones also, would have no right to demand state authority in civic administration, they should be restricted to the cultivation of their national interests. But from this point of view, they would enjoy complete liberty, they could elect their chiefs, hold their meetings, and make decisions limited only by law and the Constitution. This principle will be equally applied to the Magyars and to the other nationalities, nobody will have fewer privileges and the government as such will favor no one to the detriment of the others. And as the government, the legislature, the county, and the village need an official language, the principle above stated will be enforced in such a manner that everywhere the majority will decide in what language public affairs should be carried on, but assuring at the same time the right of the minority. The government, too, will be obliged in its intercourse with a county which uses another tongue to attach to all its decrees issued in the official Magyar language a translation in the tongue of the county, and the same procedure should be adopted by the county toward the villages in its territory. In the same manner the county, if its language is not the

Magyar, will attach a translation to its requests addressed to the government. All the laws of the country should be translated and promulgated in all the languages of the country. . . . . But Kossuth did not stop here. In the solitude of his exile, haunted by the memories of the past, he realized that the Hungarian nationality problem was not only a problem of the internal policy of the country but was also dependent on the policy which Hungary should carry on in regard to the neighboring national states, then in formation, which had large numbers of co-nationals in Hungary. All efforts for independence against Habsburg absolutism must remain unsuccessful as long—and this was the second leading conception of Kossuth—as Hungary does not maintain an intensive co-operation with its neighboring states. From this point of view he elaborated the famous program of a *Danubian Confederation* which only a few of his contemporaries could understand, though it was an ingenious anticipation of a historical necessity. Only an economic and political alliance between Hungary and Rumania and Serbia (and later with Bohemia) would be capable of guaranteeing the independence of these smaller states against Pan-German and Pan-Slav pressure and at the same time, in connection with the solution of the nationality problem, to maintain efficiently the peace of Central Europe.

With far-seeing eyes he emphasized the problem which became half a century later really the destroyer of Hungary. He wrote:

We must take into consideration that due to natural instinct among our non-Magyar citizens the Slovaks of Upper Hungary must have an eminent interest in the fights for independence of Bohemia, the Rumanians for those of Rumania, and the Serbs for those of Serbia. Therefore, they must wish with the utmost desire for all which would foster the attainment of this independence. Consequently it is impossible not to perceive that, if Hungary would take a position and follow a policy in harmony with these interests, the nationality problem could be solved without the slightest difficulty. . . . . Whereas, if Hungary would take a position and follow a policy contrary to these interests, the problem of nationality cannot be solved because, maintaining a hostile attitude in the international field against the natural instinct of the national aspirations, even the most extensive administrative concessions could create only a transitory and artificial peace which would collapse at the very moment in which the policy of Hungary would come into antagonism with the efforts for independence of Bohemia, Rumania, and Serbia. . . . .

The scrupulous and thoroughgoing satisfaction of the claims of the Hungarian nationalities and a policy of confederation toward the co-nationals of these people in the neighboring countries, that was the message of Kossuth from his exile, the echo of the catastrophe of Világos in the soul of the great tribune. "The solution lies in the words," he wrote, "Liberty, Equality, Fraternity and, if not in these, then there is no solution."

The new conception of Kossuth in which he abandoned completely his former chauvinistic policy, was as a matter of fact without any effect on Hungary, languishing under the yoke of Habsburg absolutism, especially since the development of the foreign policy, particularly the turn of French diplomacy, destroyed all hope of restoring the independence of the country with foreign help and by revolutionary means. Therefore, only a handful of his closer adherents continued the policy of Kossuth whereas the weight of public opinion felt his plans to be adventurous and utopian. In consequence the leading statesmen of the period tried to find a tolerable compromise with the Habsburg dynasty in the spirit of the Constitution of 1848, restoring the independence of the country, and maintaining intact the political hegemony of the ruling classes. The débâcle of Königgrätz and the policy of revenge of Beust against Prussia made this way practicable (as it was demonstrated in our historical study), and a compromise was made in 1867 which guaranteed the independence of Hungary, with the exception of military affairs and of foreign policy, and put the control of the whole internal policy of the country into the hands of the Magyar ruling classes with entire exclusion of the imperial administration and bureaucracy. The new dualistic order was shaped by Francis Deák, a symbol of constitutional liberalism and of the continuation of historical right.

Immediately after the introduction of the dualistic system, in 1868, a nationality law was passed which reflects in the first place the thought and the ideology of a man unrivaled by anyone in Europe in the study and deep sociological and philosophical conception of the national problem. This law of Baron Joseph Eötvös was one of the most important and original endeavors to solve the national problem. No one could have been better fitted for this task than this great "doctrinaire" in whom the spirit of a scientific analysis was fortunately intermingled with a profound poetic and religious intuition. Bluntschli himself admired his daring perspective. Already, before gaining power in several fundamental works, he admonished his countrymen and the leaders of Austria of the dangers of the nationality problem, of a forcible assimilation. At the same time he was entirely aware of the fact that in Serbia and in the new Danube principalities there had arisen new *Piedmonts* for the Jugo-Slav and the Rumanian races. He wrote on one occasion:

That the various nationalities of the country should lose the consciousness of their nationality, that they should not be filled with enthusiasm for their nationality, this we shall not attain in this way as others did not who had experimented with the same methods against the Magyar nationality. The only result which we could expect would be that the movement, pushed away from the surface of public life, would gain the more in depth and that the antagonism which is turned today against the Magyar language would direct itself against the unity of the country. . . . .

These prophetic words of the great statesman were fulfilled in a few decades.

On the basis of these principles which were in perfect harmony with the point of view of the leading statesman of the epoch, Francis Deák, Joseph Eötvös began his great work of making peace with the nationalities of the country. The task was really not an easy one. At the time of the conclusion of the dualistic system, even according to the most optimistic calculations, in Hungary proper six million Magyars were faced by seven and a half million non-Magyars. These masses of nationalities were already comparatively advanced in their national consciousness, in consequence of the Revolution and of the Bach system. The bloody reminiscences of the Civil War weighed still heavily both upon the rulers and the nationalities. The co-nationals of the Hungarian nations living outside the Hungarian frontiers made great progress in national consciousness and in the building up of an independent state.

The way chosen by the Hungarian statesman, which in his nationality law led to the codification of the whole complex problem, was a compromise between the intransigent standpoint of the nationalities and the conception of the Magyar chauvinists. The nationalities maintained their former platform, originated before the Revolution, according to which the country should be divided into distinct administrative territories on a national basis, the Magyar chauvinists adhered without any change to the conception of a unified Magyar national state. Eötvös repudiated both points of view, and in the spirit of the Diet of 1861 sought a solution which tried to satisfy the administrative and cultural claims of the nationalities without the disruption of the political unity of the country.

In order to attain this aim the law of Eötvös provided that the nationalities should have their own elementary and middle schools and a certain share in the higher education; that they should develop without any restraint their ecclesiastical institutions; that the non-Magyar middle classes should have an adequate participation in the offices of the state; that the local administration in the counties, districts, and villages should be carried on in the maternal language of the native population; and, in general, that the development of their cultural and national life should be unimpeded. The whole conception was based on the idea that the nationalities should not form distinct territorial units or nationally organized corporations, but as individuals should enjoy the same rights and opportunities as the Magyar citizens. According to the official doctrine they became "equal members of the Hungarian nation," and this term "Hungarian" (in the spirit of the feudal centuries which included not only the Magyar but all the other noblemen of the various nations) meant now not only the Magyars but all the citizens of the country.

This point of view did not satisfy the nationalities. Though they accepted the theory of the political unity of the country, they regarded the concessions of the nationality law as not an adequate guaranty for their national life and they aspired for a territorial autonomy. Considering this dissatisfaction, one small group of Magyar politicians, close adherents of the policy of Kossuth, influenced by the idealistic personality of Daniel Irányi, tried to form a new compromise in 1870 with the leaders of the nationalities on the basis of a conception which excluded the idea of a Magyar hegemony.

This extreme point of view, quite in antagonism with the existing relations among powers, had no foundation at all in Hungarian public opinion and in a comparatively short time the nationalities of the country became aware of the fact that the law of Deák and Eötvös was in harmony with their well-understood interests. They perceived it in a period when, after the departure of the great liberal generation of 1848, the ruling circles of Hungarian politics began not to apply and to elude this law. If any one beholds the history of Hungary from a restrospective point of view after those embittered struggles of half a century which in public life and even more in secret and underhanded ways ground up the moral unity of the country, he must acknowledge, if he wishes to be fair, that the compromise of Eötvös signified a point of view which, carried out loyally, could have really solved the nationality problem. For almost two decades I had the opportunity of being in touch with most of the leaders of the nationalities and I knew sufficiently well their attitude as well as the mentality of the popular masses. On the basis of this knowledge I am convinced that, if the Nationality Law had been applied from the beginning without hesitation and without mental reservation, though it would not have been the last word in the solution of the nationality problem (sooner or later it would have become unavoidable to give also some kind of territorial autonomy to the various nations in their local administration) still this liberal and humane law would have surely created that atmosphere of mutual trust and flexibility which would have extracted the aching tooth of the national struggles. This opinion was held not only by the few sincere Hungarian adherents of the policy of Eötvös but also by those foreign observers who studied the Hungarian nationality problems carefully and loyally. For instance R. W. Seton-Watson, in his valuable researches before the war, always emphasized the significance of this law and called it a basis on which the national struggles of the country growing more and more acute could be cured.

Similarly Louis Eisenmann in his classic work on the Austro-Hungarian Compromise stated the following:

The provisions of the Hungarian Nationality Law could have perfectly achieved the result of which Deák and Eötvös dreamed; not the Magyarization of all the inhabitants of the country, a standpoint which Eötvös called "dementia," but their transformation into loyal citizens of the Hungarian state; not an exterior, formal unity but a unification in feeling. . . . .[12]

D. WHY THE NATIONALITY LAW WAS NOT PUT INTO PRACTICE

But this wise law was never carried out, it remained on paper, as a constitutional show-window for international use whereas, at home, a policy was launched which was in flagrant antagonism both with the spirit and the positive statement of the Nationality Law. The nationalities urged in vain the application of the law, but their voices were feeble against the growing noise of chauvinistic nationalism. The Magyar ruling classes repudiated more and more openly the spirit and practice of the law. We must consider somewhat in detail the psychological causes of this change because the understanding of this process is important not only from the point of view of the Hungarian nationality problem, but also from that of the collapse of the whole Habsburg monarchy. One could hear opinions to the effect that the ruling Magyar classes never took this law seriously and that they passed it only to appease certain Viennese circles, with the deep design that later they would not apply it in practice, that the secret point of view of the ruling classes in 1867 was the same as in 1848: the entire assimilation of the nationalities.

This opinion is manifestly false if we consider the standpoint and ideology of the leading statesmen of that period. It is impossible that these men who embraced the best culture of Europe of their day could have upheld for a moment the idea that they would be capable of Magyarizing by forcible or shrewd means the larger half of the country in a period when national consciousness was already high in the monarchy. But Deák and his collaborators were led not only by a clear intellectual vision but also by a scrupulous morality in these questions. Arminius Vámbéry, the great scholar and explorer, narrated to me this episode: on one occasion not long after the Compromise, when he expressed before Deák his concern as to whether the Hungarian state could be maintained against the will of the majority of its citizens who by the force of a sociological law will become more and more conscious of their distinct nationality, the founder of the Compromise answered:

You are right, the country is not yet a true state. There is still lacking that spontaneous co-operation which is absolutely necessary for the mainte-

[12] *Le Compromis Austro-Hongrois* (Paris, 1904), pp. 552–53.

nance of a state. But in spite of this I am not pessimistic. The Magyar must become so magnanimous, so just that those still backward peoples with which we live in an age-old community would look upon us as on an elder brother who will not dominate over them, but lead them on the paths of law and culture. . . . .

And this was his standpoint not only in his intimate circle but in the political arena also. He defended repeatedly, with his whole moral weight, his law in Parliament and urged its loyal application. For instance in a discussion as to whether a Serb theater should get a state subsidy in addition to the subsidy of the Magyar national theater in 1868, Deák advocated the point of view that if there was not sufficient money for the subsidy of both, then neither should have support: "I cannot reconcile with justice that the state which is from the political point of view a united and undivided Hungarian State should expend from the common taxes for the benefit of one single language and people." (What a deviation from this noble sense of justice took place in Hungarian public life in the later period is clearly demonstrated by the fact that the system of protecting Magyar culture alone, so explicitly condemned by Deák, became the common opinion and practice of the following generations. And even more than this, after the burning of a private German theater at Budapest in the nineties of the last century, there was no state minister who would give a concession for its rebuilding—a mere concession, not subvention—in spite of the fact that in this time about 120,000 Germans were living in the capital.)

The former enlightened spirit was not an isolated instance of the leading statesmen, but one could easily gather testimonies to prove that the better elements of the generation of the Compromise realized the extreme importance of the nationality problem and treated it with far more delicacy and justice than did the subsequent generations. According to the happy statement of Louis Mocsáry, the distinguished follower of Louis Kossuth already quoted, the Nationality Law was the codification of the moral atmosphere of the fifties and sixties of the last century, of the ideology of a generation which lived through the dark period of the civil war and absolutism. But this spirit of tolerance was only a transitory one.

Since the death of Deák in 1876 a new generation occupied the political arena, a generation of the "gentry" which forgot the great lessons of 1848–49 and which regarded the situation of the country exclusively from the point of view of their momentary interests. The leader of this generation, Prime Minister of the country between 1875 and 1890, Koloman Tisza, came into power by cynically abandoning his principles advocated against the Compromise of Deák during several years, after having spread vehement propaganda against the common institutions of the monarchy and in favor of an independent Hungarian army. The new ruling party, called the "Liberal Party," a fusion between the parties of Deák and Tisza, had nothing liberal in its character (except its benevolent attitude toward Jewish finance and big business) but was simply an organization for the *à tout prix* maintenance of the Compromise and for the domination of the country by big landed interests. In this political atmosphere a new spirit was developed concerning the nationality problem which, pushing back the meaning and the statement of the Nationality Law, began to propagate, first in a low voice, later more loudly, a policy of Magyarization, the necessity of the creation of an exclusive Nation State as a kind of a *summum bonum* for the realization of which Machiavellian principles were advocated. And as the maintenance of the Dualistic Constitution became more and more difficult against the rising tides of nationalistic feeling, administrative corruption, the distribution of important jobs and sinecures became more and more a governmental principle. (The ruling party was satirically called *The Mamelukes*.) And as the influential positions and offices were comparatively rare, an ideology was needed which excluded the whole middle class of the nationalities from political competition. The so-called self-government of the counties was put more strictly under governmental control in order to secure a reliable majority for the Compromise and at the same time to reserve the administrative jobs for the gentry. Whereas at the beginning of the Constitutional era, following the Bach administration, many representatives of the nationalities occupied important offices in the state and local government, with the arrival of the "Liberal party" these elements were driven out systematically. Parallel with this process the Magyar language was enforced more and more in public instruction, and all the cultural institutions of the country became instruments of Magyar national assimilation.

This current became even more preponderant after the last decade of the nineteenth century when a third generation appeared in public life which, under the sway of a chauvinistic education, knew nothing about the true history of the Revolution and the Civil War, and which in the atmosphere of reactionary nationalism lost its contact with the ruling ideas of Western civilization. Also important economic and social changes augmented the nationalistic and chauvinistic feeling of this new generation. Large strata of the gentry collapsed before the competition of economic liberalism. Unaccustomed to any serious productive work, they were ousted both in the economic and cultural field. The non-Magyar nationalities and the Jews were successful in developing an energetic and prosperous middle class which menaced more and more the leading position of the former noble classes. And as the co-operation of the Jews was for a long time unavoidable for the maintenance of the economic efficiency and intel-

320 DISSOLUTION OF THE HABSBURG MONARCHY

lectual level of the Magyar State,[13] the gentry, which used to call it-self the "historical class of the country," felt a growing antipathy against the middle class of the nationalities and a kind of a "Magyar Monroe Doctrine" was established against the representatives of the nationalities in the field of governmental and local administration. The meaning of this Monroe Doctrine was in the keen formulation of Mocsáry: "You are traitors of the country. Hands off!"[14]

This economic, intellectual, and moral decadence of the former ruling class, saturated with many foreign elements especially of Germans and Jews, had created since the eighties of the last century an imperialistic doctrine of Magyar nationalism. It became a political axiom that either the Magyars would assimilate the nationalities or the nationalities would destroy the Hungarian state; that only united nation states have a future whereas the polyglot Austria is a disgusting example of a nationality state; that all those who refuse to learn the Magyar language are traitors and conspirators; that the establishment of a nation state of "thirty million Magyars" according to the teaching of the leading chauvinistic daily, the *Budapesti Hirlap*, is a possibility of the near future if we would only discard the naïve and sentimental law of old Deák and Eötvös; that there is only one possible culture in the country, the Magyar culture, whereas all the endeavors for fostering the cultures of the other nationalities were only the work of certain intellectuals wishing to fish in troubled waters; that the nationalities abuse ignominiously the unheard of magnanimity of the Magyars, who gave them a home in spite of their right of conquest when they try to establish their own culture and autonomy in the Hungarian state.

This new doctrine accompanied by a more and more intolerant school policy and a demagogically vociferous daily press had become, since the nineties of the last century, the ruling theorem of the Magyar public life, accepted by all the parties and politicians. Even the party which regarded itself as the heir of the political traditions of Kossuth became a victim of this boisterous nationalism, nay it began to utilize them against the parties of the Compromise, asserting that the wicked nationalities were the chief abettors of Vienna in the breaking down of the struggle for independence in 1849, and that only a completely Magyarized Hungary would be capable of carrying on the decisive fight against Austria.

[13] To give only significant data: the number of the attorneys grew between 1890 and 1900 7.2 per cent, whereas those of the Jewish attorneys 68.6 per cent; there were in 1900, 4,807 physicians, among them 2,321 Jews (48 per cent).

Even in the possession of landed property, the advance of the Jews was quite disproportionate. In 1884 there were 1,898 Jewish proprietors retaining a territory of about 1,750,000 holds. In 1894 there were 2,788 Jewish proprietors retaining a territory of about 2,620,000 holds.

[14] *The Balance Sheet of the Dualistic System* (Budapest, 1902), p. 232. In Hungarian.

Not only irresponsible public opinion, the noisy patriots and stump orators abandoned the spirit of Deák and sought the solution of the nationality problem in the methods of an artificial assimilation, but the leading statesmen themselves made more and more dangerous concessions to the jingo ideology. Among them, besides those who, like the politicians of Transylvania, were envenomed by the tradition-al hatred of the Rumanians, a veritable fear psychosis (especially Baron Desiderius Bánffy, a former, and Count Stephen Bethlen, the present Hungarian Premier), there were also some moderate states-men who often preached tolerance toward the nationalities. So, for instance, Coloman Széll, a so-called liberal Premier, who regarded himself as the follower of the traditions of Deák, made in a speech in 1908 the following declaration:

We have only one single categorical imperative, the Magyar state-idea, and we must demand that every citizen should acknowledge it and subject himself unconditionally to it. From this point of view we, all politicians of Hungary, are intransigent. . . . . I shall tell why. Because Hungary has its age-old, holy, and legitimate rights to strengthen the idea of such a state. The Magyars have conquered this country for the Magyars and not for others. The supremacy and the hegemony of the Magyars is fully justi-fied. . . . .

And the same point of view was echoed two years later by Count Ste-phen Tisza though he was very much impressed by the gravity of the Rumanian problem: "Our citizens of non-Magyar tongue must, in the first place, become accustomed to the fact that they belong to the community of a nation state, of a state which is not a conglomerate of various races. . . . ." Behold, four years before the world catas-trophe the most powerful statesman of the monarchy did not realize that Hungary, even according to very optimistic statistics included a 45.5 per cent non-Magyar population and, therefore, could not re-main a unified nation state but was under the necessity of imitating the example of the despised Austria and to remold the old aristocratic state into a confederation of nations.

This total change of Hungarian public opinion concerning the Nationality Law was a very complicated mass-psychological process which cannot be explained exclusively by the moments of class strug-gle referred to above. Space does not allow me a detailed analysis, I must therefore allude only to the most important factors. After the Dualistic Compromise, a comparatively strong economic uprising took place and the natural assimilation of the non-Magyar masses pro-ceeded very rapidly in the economically more advanced regions of the country; the cities and the towns, formerly with a preponderant Ger-man and Jewish element, adopted the Magyar language and culture with a spontaneous eagerness; Magyar officials, judges, industrialists, and educators became the leading elements in all the parts of the country. As a consequence of great railway constructions and regulations of the rivers, the whole territory of the country became a far more real unity than ever before; the Magyar cultural institutions enjoyed exclusively the protection of the state whereas those of the nationalities were intentionally repressed; the whole administration of the country was entirely dominated by the Magyar ruling class or by elements thoroughly assimilated by them; the leading banks of the country, mostly in Jewish hands, were obedient instruments of the government in every effort at Magyarization; the whole economic and cultural life of the country was concentrated at Budapest, the splendor of which obscured all other parts of the country; the growing influence of the industrialization of the country and of the industrial working-class (in 1900 already 20.7 per cent of the total population) was also subservient to the process of Magyarization because the Magyars were the most proletarianized and intellectually and economically the most mobile elements of the country; the whole system of education became more and more an instrument of Magyarization and the great majority of the middle nationality classes wrote and spoke the Magyar language perfectly; the Magyar daily press, the unique beneficiary of financial and state subventions, gained an almost inconceivable ascendancy and under an unscrupulous capitalistic management did not care much for principles but regarded nationalistic demagogy as the best business enterprise; the so-called Magyar cultural associations grew like mushrooms and their haughty nationalistic declamations filled the air with an atmosphere of chauvinistic megalomania.

All these economic and social factors fostered the self-reliance of the Magyar society, strengthened by the spirit of civic education which we shall consider in another connection. The very existence of the nationalities was almost forgotten in the chauvinistic public opinion which regarded them as mute personages in the scene of the glorious national drama. This pathological state of mind was still more envenomed by certain important psychological facts.

The first was an optical illusion according to which Magyar public opinion and also a considerable part of foreign opinion, completely misunderstanding the whole historical process, looked down with a pitying condescension upon Austria, lacerated by national struggles, with its parliament paralyzed by constant obstructionism. On the other hand Hungary showed for a long period the spectacle of a happy unity, of a compact national force with its anti-democratic parliament, exclusively dominated by the ruling classes. What was in reality the mechanical suppression of popular public opinion (with the help of an anachronistic and corrupt electoral system) was interpreted as the sign of national power and cohesion. As a matter of fact the united Magyar feudal parliament became generally victorious in all constitutional controversies against the more democratic Austrian legislative body in which, in consequence of the national struggles, the government was seldom backed by a reliable majority. It became a fashion to put as an example the "united" Hungary before the "sick" Austria, enfeebled by the national struggles.

At the same time the spirit of artificial Magyarization was enforced by the attitude of the Crown itself. The Magyar ruling classes knew very well the ultra-conservative personality of Emperor Francis Joseph who could scarcely imagine a constitution not based upon the Hungarian noble class. This was, by the way, also the attitude for a long time of the Austrian bureaucracy and the German bourgeoisie, because the German hegemony in Austria could only be maintained with the alliance of the Magyar feudal classes. Therefore, both to the Emperor and to his bureaucracy any experiment seemed extremely dangerous which would have tried to replace the Magyar nobility by uncultivated or semi-cultivated Rumanian, Slovak, or Serb peasant masses, the leaders of which belonged to the small bourgeoisie devoid of the higher forms of social life. As a matter of fact the Emperor remained until the end a loyal Hungarian king who was in sympathy with the Magyar noble classes, the standard of life, and the smartness, stylishness, and "chivalrousness" of which was agreeable to his taste. Francis Joseph accepted as an unchangeable political dogma the hidden contents of the Dualistic Compromise according to which the Magyar feudal classes guaranteed to the crown the unity of his army and foreign policy whereas the crown gave to them an absolute mastery in their internal policy and especially in their domination over the nationalities of the country. He repudiated consequently and energetically all the efforts of the nationalities by which they sought his imperial protection against the policy of assimilation of the Magyars. For instance when in 1892, 300 Rumanians came to Vienna asking for an audience in order to present to the Emperor a memorandum concerning their complaints against the Magyar domination, he refused to receive the deputation, sent the memorandum back, and without a word of objection permitted the Hungarian government to subject the undersigners of the memorandum to judicial proceedings and to condemn several of them to heavy imprisonments by a Magyar jury. The official theory was that the initiators of the Memorandum Movement committed high treason because, though Hungarian citizens, they sought the defense of the Austrian emperor against the Hungarian king.

Similarly when in 1903 a large deputation of the Jugo-Slav members of the Austrian parliament from Dalmatia and Istria appeared before the Emperor to protest against the oppression of their brothers in Croatia-Slovania by the Magyar absolutism, he refused to give them an audience. (This episode had a great significance in the growing trend of Jugo-Slav irredentism.) One will scarcely exaggerate the situation in asserting that the Emperor's complete disregard of the non-Magyar nationalities of Hungary was a dominant factor in the process of dissolution. Joseph Redlich himself, though extremely indulgent with the hero of his book, calls this policy of Francis Joseph, "his gravest political sin."

Another factor in the line of Magyarization was the very mechanism of the Dualistic Compromise by which the whole military strength of the monarchy would have backed the Magyar assimilation in case of a revolt of the dissatisfied nationalities. (As a matter of fact the joint army was often applied during the parliamentarian elections as a means of deterring the voters of the candidates of the nationality parties.) Seeing this situation Louis Mocsáry wrote that there is "a system in the dementia of Magyar chauvinism like in the system of the insanity of Hamlet." This system was to abandon Hungarian independence and, as a reward for this sacrifice, accept the help of the Austrian bayonets of the joint army in order to make the work of assimilation more effective. Only after the complete Magyarization of the country could the fight for national independence begin.[15] This situation was bitterly felt by the leaders of the Austrian nationalities because all the Hungarian nationalities were of the same racial stock as themselves and, therefore, their complaints and irritation envenomed the whole atmosphere of the monarchy. Under the growing pressure of these circumstances the Austrian parliament adopted a motion unanimously (December, 1907) the so-called Resolution Šilinger with the following text:

In regard to the recently growing persecution of the non-Magyar nationalities of Hungary the Imperial-Royal government is invited to call the attention of the Royal-Hungarian government as the second contracting party of the Austro-Hungarian Compromise to the fact that the interest of a prosperous co-operation of all the peoples and the strengthening of the whole monarchy demands peremptorily that the Hungarian Nationality Law of December 1868, should be carried out as soon as possible in the spirit of complete freedom, justice, and humanity.

Naturally nothing could be done by the Austrian government in this direction because the chief idea of the Compromise was to establish an absolute Hungarian sovereignty in all matters belonging in the internal administration of the country.

Another factor in line with Magyar supremacy was equally operative: "the rôle of the renegades."[16] The Hungarian upper class was permeated by foreign elements, especially by Germans and Jews. These assimilated races made the ideology of the ruling class more

[15] *The Balance Sheet of the Dualistic System*, pp. 226–27.
[16] The same problem was already treated from another point of view, pp. 174 ff.

acute and intolerant. It belongs to the nature of the renegades to serve the interest which they adopted as their own by loud and showy means. Besides the material and social advantages other motives also contribute to this result. In the first place the renegade wishes to extinguish the memories of his past by overbidding the claims of the ruling class. There is also an almost biological factor in his behavior. The men of the ruling class in the traditional enjoyment of their power are somewhat unaccustomed to fighting, they are more passive and apathetic, more epicurean, and too lazy to carry on a continuous struggle. But the neophyte, or the newly assimilated, belongs generally to the less prosperous classes. Finally, the old, privileged elements live far from real life, mostly in the atmosphere of a closed and antiquated ideology, and they do not know the thousand small and hidden springs of the daily life outside and below. But the proselytes are men of this fighting and ascending world. They know and realize very well the economic and social motives of the ideological currents. Besides the adoption of the ideology of the ruling class signified for them, especially for the Jews, an "attitude of defense." In the eighties of the last century there arose a very loud and demagogic anti-Semitism which culminated, in 1882, in the ill-famed process of Tiszaeszlár where Jews were accused of having killed a Christian girl for the purpose of blood sacrifice. After some hesitation the government took energetically the part of the Jews and suppressed the movement animated by superstitious and unclean motives. This sorrowful episode contributed to the growing Magyar nationalism of the Jews who wished to demonstrate their fidelity to the Magyar state ideal.

But it would be erroneous and unfair to attribute the Magyar nationalistic attitude of the Jews and of other assimilated elements exclusively to considerations of expediency. There can be no doubt that a large mass of these assimilated elements adopted their new ideology quite spontaneously and enthusiastically out of a sincere love of the new fatherland. For a long period the traditions of the liberal spirit of Deák and Eötvös made a powerful appeal on the half-assimilated elements of Hungarian society. Besides, when in Austria a noisy and irritative anti-Semitism dominated the public atmosphere, the Hungarian Jewry was not molested by such a current and their upper elements were even the pets of the government. But perhaps the most important factor in this process of assimilation was the rôle of the capital, Budapest, which with a surprising intellectual elasticity was marvelously active in art, science, and literature. This intellectual splendor of the metropolitan city attracted into its sphere of influence all those elements of the country which were eager to embrace Western culture. Only very few keen observers realized that there was something distinctly pathological in this splendor because this hyperintellectualism and hyperaestheticism of the few thousands was confronted by the unculture and intellectual destitution of the vast majority.[17]

But more important than all these factors animating Magyar chauvinism and nationalism was the psychological attitude of the ruling classes of society. The more unpopular the policy of the ruling party became, the more class antagonism became acute, the more the proletarian and nationality masses agitated the enlargement of the suffrage, the more agrarian Socialism menaced the monopolies of the large estates, the more the middle class of the nationalities claimed a larger share in the administration of the country: the more did the "nationality danger" (the nationality bugbear) become the fittest ideological instrument for social conservation. A doctrine was more and more established according to which a democratic suffrage would be an impossibility in Hungary in consequence of the growing danger of the nationalities. For the same reason must the reign of the system of *latifundia* be maintained and the corrupt county administration be left unaltered. It was emphatically asserted that the idea of democracy and of a Magyar nation state are irreconcilable. At the same time the idea that Hungary should follow the example of Austria and should remold its constitution in the spirit of the Nationality Law of Deák, that the political supremacy of the Magyars should be changed step by step into a cultural and economic hegemony, seemed to the ruling class as a devilish doctrine which could not even be discussed without the flagrant delict of high treason. This fear complex of the nationality danger systematically developed by press and school and by parliamentarian and social oratory paralyzed all the efforts of three generations and made any serious social or economic reform impossible. Only very few careful observers realized that this doctrine was only a bulwark for the maintenance of feudal privileges. (The post-war experiences, however, gave an evident demonstration of this truth. Though the peace treaty of Trianon made of Hungary really a united nation state consisting almost exclusively of a Magyar population, the ruling class eliminated universal suffrage, re-introduced the old corrupt electoral system, and maintained the overwhelming influence of the large estates and the domination of the gentry administration in the counties. The pretext of the nationality danger ceased, but the system of class domination continued. The theory of the "Nationality bugbear" was transformed into that of the "Jewish bugbear!")

In consequence of the causes elucidated a new spirit drew out the liberalism of Deák and Eötvös, a system in which the Magyar nation state and the nationality bugbear became the leading conceptions of

[17] The brilliant analysis of the Jewish Society in Paris given by Romain Rolland in one of the volumes of his *Jean Christophe* shows a startling analogy of the Jewish situation in pre-war Budapest.

the Hungarian policy. The whole parliament and the entire public opinion stood under its hypnosis. It was shouted by the demagogues, defended by the publicists, carried out even by those statesmen who publicly advocated liberalism toward the nationalities according to the principle: *N'en parlons jamais, y pensez toujours.* . . . .

E. THE PROCESS OF ARTIFICIAL MAGYARIZATION

It is impossible here to enter into the details of the process by which the growing chauvinistic spirit of the ruling classes had built up a very complicated machine of artificial and forcible assimilation. Not only space forbids me from doing it but also a kind of moral repulsion at the thought of indulging in the faults and crimes of the past in a period when Hungary under the pretense of a punishment was hard and in many respects unjustly hit, and when we witness that same policy, for which ostensibly Hungary was dismembered, is in many cases continued by those who were its former victims. Therefore, I shall restrict myself to the reconstruction of the general moral and social atmosphere in which the system was carried on and to its most outstanding results. As to the details and technicalities of the process a comparatively large literature has been written which will give to the reader a comprehensive picture of the whole.[18] This literature or at least the greatest part of it was and is still denounced by official Hungarian historians and publicists as a devilish misrepresentation of the facts, and as a literature of traitors or of spys in the

[18] From this literature I shall quote only the most important contributions: Otto Bauer, *Die Nationalitätenfrage und die Sozialdemokratie* (2d ed.; Vienna, 1924); Brote, *Die rumänische Frage in Siebenbürgen und Ungarn* (Berlin, 1895); R. Charmatz, *Der Demokratisch-Nationale Bundesstaat Österreich* (1904); R. Charmatz, *Deutsch-Österreichische Politik* (1907); André Chéradame, *L'Europe et la Question D'Autriche* (1906); Louis Eisenmann, *Le Compromis Austro-Hongrois de 1867* (Paris, 1904); Fr. Guntram Schultheiss, *Deutschtum und Magyarisierung in Ungarn* (München, 1898); "La Hongrie Contemporaine et le Suffrage Universel," published by the magazine *Huszadik Század* (Paris, 1909); Oscar Jászi, *The Evolution of the Nation-States and the Problem of Nationality* (Budapest, 1912). Oscar Jászi, *Revolution and Counter-Revolution in Hungary* (London, 1924); Anonymous, *Die Magyarisierung in Ungarn,* Nach den Debatten des ungarischen Reichstages (München, 1879); Otto Lang, *Das Österreichische Staatsproblem und seine Lösung* (1905); Aurel C. Popovici, *Die Vereinigten Staaten von Gross-Osterreich* (Leipzig, 1906); Stephen Radić, *Die Slavische Politik in der Habsburgermonarchie* (1902); Paul Samassa, *Der Völkerstreit im Habsburgerstaat* (Leipzig, 1910); R. W. Seton-Watson, *Racial Problems in Hungary* (London, 1908); R. W. Seton-Watson, *The Southern Slav Question* (London, 1911); R. W. Seton-Watson, *Corruption and Reform in Hungary,* a study of electoral practice (London, 1911); R. W. Seton-Watson, *Absolutism in Croatia* (London, 1912); Wilhelm Schüssler, *Das Verfassungsproblem im Habsburgerreich* (Stuttgart and Berlin, 1918); Theodor von Sosnosky, *Die Politik im Habsburgerreiche* (2d ed.; Berlin, 1913), Vol. II; M. Spalajković, *La Bosnie et l'Herzegowine* (Paris, 1899); Rudolf Springer (Karl Renner), *Der Kampf der Österreichischen Nationen um den Staat* (1902); Rudolf Springer, *Die Krise des Dualismus* (1904); Rudolf Springer, *Grundlagen und Entwicklungsziele der Österreichisch-Ungarischen Monarchie* (Wien, 1906); Walter Schücking, *Das Nationalitätenproblem* (1908).

service of Pan-Slavism or Daco-Romanism or Pan-Germanism. The psychology of these accusations has already been explained or will be later elucidated. It is very characteristic that, for instance, a man of the moral integrity and scientific objectivity of Mr. Seton-Watson was always described by the Magyar press and politicians as a greedy adventurer or as an idiot misled by the nationalities of the country. Articles could even be found which advised the government to buy off this undesirable foreigner.[19] As to the general value of this literature I must say that, as it was written partly by the members of the persecuted nationalities or by foreigners informed by them, its descriptions are sometimes too gloomy and one-sided but for the most part its facts and demonstrations are correct. I could only repeat in this behalf the statement of a high Magyar official of a large Rumanian county, when I asked his opinion concerning the accusations of the Rumanians. This man who was a solitary admirer of the policy of Deák told me: "Subtract one-third of all the accusations of the Rumanians, exaggerated by hatred or fear, and you will have the entire truth."

Generally speaking I would say that the methods and practices of the Magyar nationality policy were in their essence the same as those applied by all those countries which tried to assimilate their citizens of a foreign tongue by forcible or artificial means. The policy of Russian Tsarism against the Poles, the Finns, and the Ruthenians; the policy of Prussia against the Poles and the Danes; and the policy of feudal England against the Irish reflects the same spirit and methods however widely they may differ in the concrete details.

As a matter of fact in the first place the educational system of the country appeared to be an adequate instrument for the aims of Magyarization. We witness really that each subsequent minister of Public Instruction became more and more impatient in this work. Beginning with the elementary-school law of 1879, continuing with the law of secondary education of 1883, and terminating with the law in regard to the kindergarten education of 1891, there was a continuous and ever growing endeavor to Magyarize the teaching staff, to expand public instruction in the Magyar tongue and to restrict that in the non-Magyar tongue. For this purpose the denominational schools of the nationalities were subjected to a vexatious control and the state established extensively state schools in the Magyar language in the nationality regions to counterbalance the schools of the nationalities which were generally poor and inefficient. At the same time the agricultural proletariat of a pure Magyar stock was being deprived of the most needed elementary instruction because the wildly Magyariz-

---

[19] As a matter of fact this English traveler, the later "Scotus Viator," came into the country as an ardent admirer of Louis Kossuth, with the intention of refuting the "calumnies" of the nationalities against the Magyars.

ing state did not have sufficient funds for them and the amount of illiteracy in some districts of the Magyar plains was terrifying.

A similar intolerant attitude was applied against the secondary schools which were considered as the most important instruments of assimilation because the leading intelligentsia of the country was recruited from them. "The secondary school is like a big engine," said Béla Grünwald, who was not a common demagogue but one of the most distinguished spirits of the period, a great historian and sociologist, "which takes in at one end hundreds of Slovak youth who come out at the other end as Magyars." From this point of view the secondary schools, too, were submitted to severe control and the chief care of public instruction was not so much the imparting of useful knowledge as a sentimental education according to the ideology of the ruling class. And when state control seemed to be not thoroughly efficient the Slovak high schools were closed under the pretext of Pan-Slavistic intrigues and the only non-Magyar college of the country, the German

TABLE XIV

NATIONALITY	ELEMENTARY SCHOOLS		
	Language of Instruction	Number of Pupils	Number of Teachers
Magyar..............	12,784	1,050,579	26,270
Non-Magyar..........	3,712	853,541	5,547

Law School of Nagyszeben, was similarly discontinued. This spirit of distrust and assimilation was so manifest that an acute French observer, Louis Eisenmann, wrote the following characteristic statement:

One would believe that the Hungarian state is continually menaced by a gigantic plot. If its Slovak citizens claim some rights for the Slovak language, they are called "Pan-Slavs." If the Rumanians do the same, they are called "separatists" or "Daco-Romans"! Even the children in the kindergarten are apt to threaten the security of the state and the Hungarian state takes measures of precaution against the rooms of the nurseries. . . . .[20]

By means of these and similar measures they succeeded in augmenting disproportionately the number of schools in the Magyar tongue and in repressing those of the nationalities by manifest violation of the law of nationalities.

Table XIV demonstrates that the Magyar population, compared with the non-Magyar population of an almost equal size, had at their disposition in their mother tongue four times as many schools and five

[20] *Le Compromis Austro-Hongrois*, p. 558.

times as many teachers. The participation of the Magyar students in secondary and higher education varied between 79.9 per cent and 88.8 per cent and that of the Magyar professors was 75.5 per cent.

In spite of these numerical results the real achievements from the point of view of Magyar assimilation were very doubtful. Where the nationalities lived in compact masses and where intercourse with the Magyars was rare, the Magyarizing drill of the elementary schools was only good for learning patriotic verses and songs by rote but the non-Magyar youth paid an enormous price for this instruction: they did not learn adequately either their mother-tongue or the Magyar. "The time spent in learning Magyar," wrote a noted Hungarian expert, "without obtaining the desired end, impedes the relative efficiency of the other branches of instruction."[21] And studying repeatedly the linguistic conditions in the nationality regions, I wrote (1912) the following concerning the enforcement of the Magyar tongue:

The forcible Magyarization in the schools is one of the chief causes of the pitiful cultural backwardness of the non-Magyar peoples. For, where the nationalities live in their close settlements far away from the Magyar culture, all school Magyarization is impossible because the school with its four hours of instruction is quite impotent against the twenty hours of real life. If, in every village of the great Rumanian settlement in Transylvania, every elementary school were to consist of children blessed with the linguistic talent of Count Albert Apponyi [in those times the chief exponent of this policy of artificial Magyarization] and if every elementary school were a model institution and not a single crowded room with one or two poorly paid and poorly qualified teachers, even then the Magyar language of instruction, forcibly imposed could have only the result that the children would learn some phrases in Magyar which life would soon erase from their memory, whereas they could not learn many useful things indispensable to daily life. . . . .[22]

The situation in the secondary schools was quite another as instruction was far more intense here and the schools were situated in larger towns where, even in the nationality regions, there was always a certain amount of Magyar social life. As a matter of fact the greater part of the intelligentsia of the non-Magyar peoples learned the Magyar language very well, nay some of them became excellent Magyar orators and writers. But from the point of view of Magyar assimilation there was no advantage in this process because the non-Magyar youth, recruited from these schools, became the most ardent supporters of the claims of their races, and the mechanical drill of Magyarization had as its result the embittered fight of these "Mag-

[21] S. Kunfi, *The Crimes of our Popular Education* (Budapest, 1908). In Hungarian.
[22] *The Evolution of the Nation States,* pp. 471–72.

yarized elements" against the school system of assimilation and sometimes against the Hungarian state itself which they identified with
the system of forcible Magyarization. Another part of the non-Magyar youth went abroad into the schools of their co-nationals beyond
the frontiers and this intercourse kindled even more the fire of irredentism. Prague to the Slovak youth, Bucharest to the Rumanian,
and Belgrade to the Serb appeared as a kind of national Eldorado
and there began a mass emigration of the souls which was even more
dangerous than the physical emigration in consequence of the pressure of the large estates.

Another important instrument of Magyarization seemed to be the
administrative machinery, especially the local administration of the
counties. Instead of rebuilding the former organs of the feudal self-
government of the counties into those of popular self-government (as
the founders of the Nationality Law had imagined) in which, without
hurting the unity of the state, the cultural and administrative needs
of the nationalities could have been easily satisfied, they became more
and more monopolistic positions of the landed nobility and of the elements attached to it, a kind of a nursery of the gentry in which those
members of this class who were unfit for economic or other professions,
found elegant and secure jobs. This tendency of the ruling classes to
secure for themselves all the more influential offices in the state and in
the local administration became a chief factor in the growing intensity
of the nationality struggles because this effort, as it has been already
emphasized in another connection, was accompanied by the ideology
that the middle class of the nationalities is traitor to the country, is
infiltrated with Pan-Slavistic and Daco-Rumanian ideas and, therefore, must be kept away from the more important offices and should be
employed only in the lowest grades of administration. As a matter of
fact this doctrine was applied with the utmost lack of consideration,
and there was not the slightest possibility of a social and moral penetration between the Magyar ruling class and the middle class of the
nationalities. Only some few renegades of the nationalities were accepted by fashionable society which fomented even more the exasperation of their self-conscious elements. The Jew in the Middle Ages
could not have lived more in isolation in their ghettos than the middle
class of the nationalities in the capitals of the counties. Louis Mocsáry regarded this situation with despair because he foresaw its outcome quite accurately. At the end of the eighties of the last century
he made a calculation according to which out of 9,541 officials employed in the more important branches only 199 were Rumanians, a
fact upon which he made the following comment: "Of the officials just
quoted only 2 per cent are Rumanian whereas the Rumanians constitute 20 per cent of the total population and even these 2 per cent are

employed in the lowest grades. . . . ."[23] This ratio was even more disadvantageous from the point of view of the weaker nationalities with
the exception of the Saxons of Transylvania who were utilized by the
government as suitable allies against the Rumanian masses. The
cause of this fact must be sought in the economic and cultural significance of the Transylvanian Saxons which surpassed not only the
Rumanian average but in some respects also that of the Magyars.

This administrative monopoly of the Magyar ruling class made
the state seemingly unilingual, but behind this uniformity of language
was lurking the backward cultural state of the masses and the exacerbation of the middle class of the nationalities. This latter class, in
order to get its livelihood, sought employment in the establishment of
a network of financial institutions, introducing a fanatically chauvinistic spirit into a kind of economic activity which anywhere else fo-
ments rather international feeling. The situation was further envenomed by the spirit of this "national administration" the exponents of
which, as has already been shown, regarded themselves not as public
servants, but rather as the masters of the people by the right of conquest. The whole population of the country, not only the nationalities
but the Magyar peasants and workers also were surrendered to the
arbitrary will and corruption of this administration. But whereas
these administrative abuses were represented by the Magyar people as
social evils, the nationalities regarded them as proofs of Magyar oppression. Nothing could be more detrimental from the point of view
of a rightly understood Hungarian state ideal than this exclusive
Magyar rule.

But even more pernicious than the brutality and corruption of the
system was its total misunderstanding of the popular currents and
aspirations. The oligarchic ruling class had not the least interest in
coming into closer contact with the real or imaginary needs of the
people. Only under such an administration could have occurred, for
example, the terrible massacre of Csernova in 1906 when it tried to
force the meek population of this small Slovak village to abandon its
cherished priest (the popular Slovak leader, Hlinka) and to compel
its new church to be dedicated by two unknown clergymen. The people
resisted, whereupon the gendarmerie, held in anticipation, began to
shoot, causing the death of fifteen and the more or less serious wound-
ing of sixty.

As a matter of fact this cultural and administrative policy could
be carried on only with the help of that antiquated and corrupt electoral system which we have already described in a previous chapter.
The chief evil of this system was not so much the small number of the

[23] In his pamphlet, *Some Words on the Nationality Problem* (Budapest, 1886).
In Hungarian. This just and brave man adduced many other important facts in order to convince his compatriots and his party of the extreme danger of the situation.

voters, not even the excessive gerrymandering to the detriment of the nationalities and of the Magyar small peasantry who favored the traditions of Kossuth. (The so-called "Democratic Circles" of the Magyar peasantry continuing the traditions of Louis Kossuth and urging the distribution of the big landed estates were ferociously suppressed immediately after the establishment of the Compromise.) That which made this electoral system according to the judgment of Rudolf Kjellén "the most reactionary system of Europe," and Hungarian electoral corruption according to the statement of Joseph Redlich "unique in Europe,"[24] was the fact that even this restricted and artificial arrangement was not carried out in a fair way but was falsified by pressure and violence for which the ignominious institution of "public voting" gave ample occasion. Very often public voting was not even employed, but the electorate was simply kept away from the polls by *vis major* artificially created. Cases occurred when bridges were destroyed or declared impassable in order to compel the voters of the opposition parties to make a long detour on foot; when all the horses in remote villages were put under veterinarian control by false pretext in order to check the transportation of the electorate; when the main roads of the district were reserved exclusively for the use of the governmental party, whereas the opposition was driven to use side roads in very poor condition because of bad weather; when the electors of the opposition were exposed for the whole day of election to rain or snow in order to persuade them to abandon their attempts to vote or to vote for the candidate of the government.

These administrative chicaneries were supplemented by an intricate system of corruption, by regaling the electorate with eating and drinking, by intoxicating them with alcohol, by buying their votes in open market, by promising them governmental jobs or by menacing them with their withdrawal, by a sudden execution of the arrears in taxes, and by giving abrupt notice of withdrawal of their bank loans. But generally even these procedures did not suffice to break the will of the electorate. In such cases the joint army of the monarchy was utilized, without scruple, to curb the renitent masses. For instance on the occasion of the last general elections before the collapse (1910), we witnessed such a concentration of the army that it gave foreign observers the impression of a general mobilization. In spite of the fact that there were in those times 120 battalions of infantry and 72 squadrons of cavalry in Hungary (not counting the national *Honvéd*-formations) large masses of troops were imported from lower Austria, Styria, and Moravia. The opposition accused the government of having employed troops in 380 out of the 413 constituencies of Hungary.

[24] It is questionable, however, whether after the terrible experiences of the postwar period these distinguished authors would uphold their statements without further qualifications.

As an answer to this criticism, an official statement was issued declaring that the calculation of the opposition press was an erroneous one and "only" 194 battalions of infantry and 114 squadrons of artillery were used "to maintain public order." Even the more far-sighted leaders of the army were, as has already been emphasized, deeply alarmed by this procedure because they foresaw that it would augment the centrifugal tendencies in the monarchy. It became a favorite topic of foreign newspapers to describe the Hungarian electoral atrocities. These foreign observers, however, did not see that the method of intimidation of the electorate was not only applied against the nationalities but that the same practices were in use with equal ruthlessness and unscrupulousness also against the Magyar masses who opposed the Dualistic System or tried to break the monopolies of the large estates. This will explain the widely spread Magyar proverb: "Politics is the roguish trick of the gentlemen."

This system restricted more and more the participation of the nationalities in the legislation of the country. For instance in 1887 in consequence of the electoral atrocities the two and a half millions of the Hungarian-Rumanians were only represented by one single deputy, by a former general of the joint army, Trajan Doda, but even he resigned with a declaration that he was incapable of defending the interests of his nation alone against more than 400 deputies. And as he expressed himself in passionate language in his resignation, he was brought before a tribunal which condemned him to two years in prison. Also the Slovak deputies were continually persecuted because of their "seditious behavior." In 1894 the Rumanian National Party, the only political organization of the Rumanian people, was dissolved as "unconstitutional" by an administrative act of the government.

These few facts and instances will sufficiently characterize the whole electoral system and explain how it was possible that there was not a single representative of the working-classes and of the landless peasantry (the great majority of the country) in the pre-war Hungarian parliament and that there were only 8 Rumanians and Slovaks out of a total membership of 413 in a country in which only 54 per cent of the inhabitants spoke Magyar as their mother-tongue. (We can omit in this respect the Saxon deputies of Transylvania because they belonged always to the inventory stock of the government.) But even these few representatives of the nationalities did not have a fair opportunity to express the aspirations of their peoples. It was a custom in the Hungarian parliament to shout down these men whenever they dared to denounce their national offenses. They were simply treated as traitors to the country. In this manner there was no opportunity for the nationalities to express their grievances; not even in the press, because the crime called "instigation to national hatred" gave sufficient opportunity to the juries, recruited exclusively from

the Magyar speaking population, to send to prison the writers of the
nationalities who attacked the policy of Magyarization. Concerning
these persecutions the statistical figures, shown in Table XV, were
gathered by the nationalities relative to the period 1886–1908.

TABLE XV

CONDEMNATIONS

	Cases	Years	Months	Days	Fine (in Crowns)
Slovaks, 1896–1908.........	560	91	7	26	42,000
Rumanians, 1886–1908......	353	131	10	26	93,000
Germans, 1898–1903.......	14	2	10	10	7,000
Ruthenians, 1904..... ...	7	5	....	....	2,000
Serbs, 1898–1906..........	4	1	1	....	2,000

See for detail: Scotus Viator (R. W. Seton-Watson), *Racial Problems in Hungary* (London, 1908),
pp. 441–66.

At this juncture it must be emphasized very strongly that the doctrine according to which the nationalities must be excluded from parliament and the doctrine that the Magyar State was incompatible
with a truly democratic system of representation were not only the
outbursts of demagogic passion fomented by the jingo press and by
politicians eager to become members of parliament, but were the central dogma of all the responsible Magyar statesmen of the last generation before the collapse. In this connection Michael Károlyi who
knew the leading men more intimately perhaps than any other contemporary (it was often stated that Hungarian political life was almost
exclusively directed by three or four leading counts and their family
clique; by the Tiszas, Andrássys, Apponyis, and Károlyis) and who
until the War shared their nationality bias, narrates the following interesting observations in his memoirs which characterize the situation
better than any abstract considerations:

In 1910, when I was still under the influence of Tisza's impassioned
reasoning, ... he once expounded to me his contention that first of all
the non-Magyar half of the twenty million Hungarian citizens had to be
Magyarized, and that only when that had been accomplished would it be
possible to consider democracy for Hungary. . . . . Julius Andrássy and
Albert Apponyi held precisely the same views as Tisza on the question of
the nationalities. But Tisza was more consistent than they. He scouted the
idea of democracy. Andrássy and Apponyi flirted with it. . . . . Apponyi
imagined that the country could be cut into two parts like a cake: into
Magyar and non-Magyar districts. He would have accorded to the Magyars, in theory at any rate, the very rights which he flatly refused the non-
Magyars. On this point, for all his sensitive and delicate tact, he had lost
the sense of what might be reasonably advocated in public and what could
not; in his speeches he made no attempt to conceal his intention to rob half
the population of the country of their national rights. . . . .[25]

[25] *Op. cit.*, pp. 67–69.

There were also other methods which were applied in order to build up a unitary Magyar state. Such were: the Magyarization of village names even in regions where there was practically no Magyar-speaking population; the Magyarization of family names which was in many cases the expression of a sincere loyalty but later it was extended by governmental pressure in order to manifest the Magyar character of the state before foreign public opinion; Magyar agricultural colonization in the midst of compact nationality settlements which had naturally no other result than the assimilation of these Magyar islets in the sea of the nationalities; the distribution of Magyar nobility which had a great prestige value, especially among those who tried to be accepted by the gentry. But a greater and more dangerous effect than these petty means had the so-called "Magyar Cultural Associations." Such associations were sorely needed in the country, indeed, because the Magyar people were terribly diminished by tuberculosis and emigration, the infant mortality was very high, and the illiteracy of many regions made a healthy cultural life impossible. The promoters of these associations, however, did not care for the cultural elevation of the Magyar masses but their aim was the quick Magyarization of the Rumanians, Slovaks, Germans, and Serbs. And they tried to obtain this purpose not so much by cultural means, by the establishment of libraries, museums, hospitals, dispensaries, better means of communication, industrialization of the country, or by the distribution of scholarships; but they were rather satisfied by the arranging of noisy banquets, denouncing on every occasion the treasons of the nationalities, and by instigating the government and the counties to apply more efficient and energetic means of Magyarization. Of course the only result of this "cultural activity" was the establishment of certain sinecures for the members of the privileged classes and the heightening of the exasperation of the nationalities which established their own cultural associations, tried to develop the national consciousness of their peasant masses, and opened their hearts and ears to hidden irredentist propaganda.

If we take into account all these methods and instruments of Magyarization, we can understand that even a scholar so friendly to the Magyars and so sincere an admirer of the greatness of Francis Deák and Joseph Eötvös, as Joseph Redlich, wrote the following destructive judgment concerning this policy:

In the whole history of the nineteenth century—omitting the oppressions of the Poles by the Russians—there was scarcely a second example of such a comprehensive and premeditated denial and annihilation of all legal enactments and procedures concerning the majority of the total population of the country, disregarding the political rights and privileges accorded by law by the Magyars to the nationalities, than that carried on by the Magyar upper classes and rulers of the country since 1867, against all their citizens of a foreign tongue and culture.[26]

This statement of the eminent scholar, however, needs certain qualifications. Before all there was a certain equality in the system. In the social and administrative field the same feudal methods were applied, as already mentioned, against the Magyar landless peasantry and the whole Magyar proletariat. And without justifying at all the Magyar manners against the nationalities I would say in fairness that they never reached the brutality of the English against the Irish or that of the Prussians against the Poles. Besides, the formal injustice was considerably alleviated by the indolence and inertia of Magyar administration. And what is still more important, the pressure of the whole system was felt far more by the small strata of the intelligentsia of the nationalities than by the bulk of the population which in its backward cultural state did not fully realize the importance of the issues. Finally, it must be emphasized that in many districts the Magyar nobility and their assimilated elements spoke to a certain extent the language of the people and therefore the Magyar administration pressed less heavily on the daily life of the peasant masses.

F. MAGYAR CURRENTS AGAINST MAGYARIZATION

In this connection a fact of great importance, already alluded to, must be emphasized which had a considerable rôle not only in the Magyar problem but in all cases where a fanatical nationalism tried to assimilate the racial minorities. The process delineated above did not manifest itself at all in the consciousness of Magyar public opinion as a forceful oppression. On the contrary, the majority of those who applied this system and the bourgeois and intellectual circles were deeply convinced that in Hungary there was no nationality persecution, but that the Magyar nation had accorded so many liberties and privileges to those "inferior" peoples with which it lived that its liberalism was unparalleled in history. At the same time it was regarded as an unheard of ingratitude that these second-rank peoples rewarded this generosity by accusations and calumnies inciting foreign public opinion against the Magyar nation. This public opinion was to a large extent a *bona fide* conviction, as a result of the Magyar civic education and press propaganda not counterbalanced by any other influences. The more cultured and more highly politically trained circles of the Magyars, as already mentioned, were in no contact with the intelligentsia of the nationalities. They had not the slightest idea of their points of view and aspirations, even when they lived in the

[26] *Das Österreichische Staats- und Reichsproblem,* II, 290.

same town with them. They never observed the realities of daily life but knew only the commentaries announced by the chauvinistic politicians, publicists, and teachers concerning them. Now according to these commentaries the nationalities had an excellent situation in Hungary, and if they were still complaining, it could be only the result of some foreign plots or irridentistic agitation. Anyone was called Pan-Slav or Daco-Rumanian who dared to criticize the Hungarian conditions, especially the electoral and the administrative systems. Even less was sufficient to involve anyone in the suspicion of high treason. I remember that in the fashionable Magyar society of a Slovak county I heard on one occasion the following remark: "It is unbearable with what openness and impertinence these Pan-Slavs have begun to behave themselves. Today, for instance, I was compelled to travel in a first-class compartment with five Pan-Slavs who did not even hide what they were." Inquiring about the circumstances of this terrifying experience, I was informed that those gentlemen conversed with each other in the Slovak tongue and from this fact the Magyar observer drew the conclusion that they were Pan-Slavs because no gentleman would speak Slovak. Similarly a Slovak or Rumanian song or the bearing of the popular colors by the people could arouse grave suspicions of international complications in some regions excited by national struggles.

If such was the attitude of the intelligentsia and the bourgeoisie, we can imagine how this problem was visualized by the so-called "historical classes" during the decades of this policy of assimilation. Among these and the masses of nationality, there was such a feeling of historical and social distance that even the idea of the oppression of the nationalities was absurd. John Stuart Mill once made the keen observation that true morality is possible only between equals. This statement is even more true concerning political morality because men feel far less those injustices which are the results of political means. There are many people who would be incapable of stealing or of attacking someone on the street. But this same man will settle political monopolies detrimental to the public interest or let the gendarmerie shoot into masses exasperated by a policy of exploitation. The inherited feudal attitude, the right of conquest, the dogma of "we are here masters and we will remain masters" made an equitable discussion of the nationality problem in these circles impossible. National oppression could not even exist on the basis of historical right. Magyar domination was a command of Destiny. Only a traitor of the country could protest against it.[27]

[27] That was the real attitude of the system which often even foreign observers of first rank misunderstand. So, for instance, Louis Eisenmann, one of the most astute students of the problem of the dual monarchy expressed recently the opinion that the effort of the Magyarization was not sincere, but was only an endeavor to impede the cultural and moral evolution of the non-Magyar people. [See his re-

There were only very few who realized the impossibility of such a policy of assimilation and who perceived that the "Magyar national state" remained a pure fiction, a sheer façade which could be maintained only on the basis of the cultural backwardness of the masses and of an oligarchical absolutism. Perhaps nobody saw these truths more clearly than Louis Mocsáry, the last guardian of the Kossuth traditions in the Party of Independence, emphasizing the fact that the country would never be capable of securing its independence from Austria as long as the Habsburgs could continue the old recipe of 1849, mobilizing the nationalities against the Magyar efforts. In a parliamentary speech of 1887 he said the following:

The Magyarization of Hungary is a utopian idea and only demonstrates that the Magyar cannot acquiesce in the thought that there are citizens of another tongue in this country because he believes that a good patriot of the fatherland can be only a man who speaks Magyar. That is a fatal error. . . . . It seems to me that the government does not regard as its proper task the checking of chauvinism in its wrong and aimless rampages but it fosters it rather by its complacence. This attitude gives rise to the surmise that all is allowed for the propagation of Magyarization, that the aim sanctifies the means, that one can acquire by such deeds immortal merits. . . . . I do not think that such should be the task of the government but rather a pure objectivity on behalf of the nationalities. . . . . The government should never forget that it governs a country of many tongues, that it should be equally a government of the Magyars, of the Slavs, and of the Rumanians, that the country is not a "cultural association" but that there are living citizens of various nationalities with whom not only the burdens but also the right should be divided in equal ratio.

In many other utterances and writings he emphasized the same point of view, denouncing the nationality policy of the country as a system of "unfortunate hallucinations." And nothing demonstrates more clearly the terrible growth of Magyar chauvinism than the fact that this man of a brilliant capacity, noble character, and complete financial independence, and what counted more in Hungary, belonging to the oldest nobility in the country, remained entirely isolated in Hungarian public life and was expelled by his own party, usurping the name of Kossuth.[28] This result appears even more strange when one knows that Kossuth did not cease to maintain his policy of compromise toward the nationalities. He denounced the policy of Mag-

---

markable essay, *La Hongrie Contemporaine, 1867–1918* (Paris, 1921), p. 152]. This ultra-Machiavellian point of view seems to me erroneous. The truth is that the desire for Magyarization, the aspiration for a united nation state was backed by an enthusiastic and sincere public opinion and it was the *only* "moral force" of the whole system. That was the case, even in the mass of the party of Tisza, though naturally, its feudal elements were more interested in "domination" than "assimilation."

[28] On one occasion when he finished his speech in favor of the nationalities, a member of his own party shouted, wildly applauded by the majority, "And now let us open the windows!"

yarization as an impossibility and when Mocsáry paid a visit to him in his exile, the great statesman flushed with indignation when his guest mentioned the nationality policy in Hungary.[29]

After the political retirement of Mocsáry, Magyar nationalism rolled on without any serious check. At the beginning of the present century the spirit of an intolerant jingoism invaded even the most conservative circles of society which in other countries tried to mitigate social and political conflicts.[30] Only Julius Justh, a strong and noble man, a convinced follower of Kossuth and for a short period the speaker of the House, tried to soften and counterbalance the spirit of growing chauvinism whose danger for the cause of Independence he thoroughly realized. Beside him a very small group of the Hungarian Socialists and the Sociological Society of Budapest (the so-called "Magyar Fabians") acknowledged the fatal gravity of the nationality problem and tried to draw the attention of the country to its dangers lest it would not be solved in the spirit of justice and equity. This supreme aim was before the eyes of the writer of this book when, in the two decades of the present century, he published many treatises and a comprehensive book concerning the problem of nationality in Europe and particularly in Hungary. He tried to demonstrate that the experiences of the forcible assimilation in Hungary corroborated completely those made by Bernard Shaw concerning the English-Irish, by Hugo Ganz concerning the German-Polish, and by Johannes Tiedje concerning the German-Danish nationality struggles. All these experiences had convincingly demonstrated, both in Hungary and in the foreign countries the following sociological generalizations:

1. The policy of a forceful assimilation leads in the oppressed people to the strengthening of its own national feelings and aspirations. Whereas the patriotism of the ruling class becomes more and more a jingoism, void of any constructive content, in the persecuted nationalities, there arises a current of a sincere and self-sacrificing patriotism.

2. The policy of forceful assimilation demoralizes the ruling nation, while it elevates both intellectually and morally the better elements of the oppressed nationalities. It is an extremely dangerous moral attitude to shoot from well-guarded positions, protected by the whole state power, on unarmed, poorly equipped masses. It is inevi-

[29] *The Balance Sheet of the Dualistic System*, p. 216.

[30] In this regard, the following highly characteristic little episode is narrated by Joseph Kristóffy (former minister of the Interior and the man who tried to introduce universal suffrage into Hungary): On one occasion he was walking with Alexander Dessewffy, bishop of Csanád and member of the House of Lords, through the latter's garden discussing the problem of suffrage. Dessewffy asserted that "there does not exist a problem of nationality in Hungary," and, menacing with his cane he shouted that not a single nationality deputy would be allowed to enter into the Hungarian parliament. When such was the attitude of the *grands seigneurs* we can imagine how chauvinistic the stump oratory was!

table that a moral brutalization should befall those who continue this policy. A psychosis of the battue will soon follow. At the same time the policy of the forcible assimilation has the effect of a wedge on the moral standard of the oppressed: it debases even more the worthless elements but it heightens the morally healthy.

3. The policy of forcible assimilation results in the fact that the solidarity of the oppressed nationality will conquer all class divisions because it cannot realize other problems than those of its racial oppression. This retards economic and social progress.

4. The linguistic results of the policy of forcible assimilation, in every case where the work of the schools is not protected by the real atmosphere of economic and social life, are very poor and lower the general standard of culture.

5. The policy of forcible assimilation damages the general culture not only by the anti-pedagogic enforcement of the linguistic instruction in a foreign tongue but also by its method of making the schools a kind of a chauvinistic nursery. This nationalistic mechanical drill spoils the intellectual elasticity of the souls of the children.

6. The forcible assimilation impedes not only the economic and cultural progress of the oppressed nationality but, at the same time, that of the whole country.

7. The forcible assimilation makes a real assimilation in feelings and interests impossible. The natural assimilative forces of a higher culture become bankrupt in the face of those repulsive tendencies which the anti-economic means of violence arouse. All real assimilation in modern times can be based only on the spontaneous exchange of spiritual and economic values. This exchange is uprooted by the policy of forcible assimilation.

I endeavored to prove these propositions by facts from the history of the nationality struggles in Europe and finally submitted the following, almost mathematical calculation to the Magyar chauvinists. I so wrote in 1912:

. . . . Behold only the experiences of foreign countries, 52 million Germans were incapable in spite of their colossal military and economic supremacy of assimilating by force 3 million Poles, 210 thousand French, and 160 thousand Danes; 42 million English, in spite of their world domination, were incapable of overcoming 3 million Irish and they apply now toward them a method of complete liberalism; the Russian colossus with its 90 million Great Russians stands impotent against 7 million Poles, 3 million Germans, and as many Armenians, nay even against 5 million Jews. Looking upon these facts who could be so naïve or silly as to think that 9 million Magyars could assimilate by forceful means the other half of the country, 9 million Magyars saturated with half-assimilated elements, in constant conflict with the economic and political supremacy of a colonizing Austria? And they are faced not by small nationality diasporas but there live as many or more Germans, Slovaks, and Rumanians in Hungary as

Denmark, Alsace-Lorraine, Greece, Norway, and Serbia have inhabitants. Is it not money, etc. . . . . thrown away, every million which we devote to the Magyarization of the nationalities with the only result that we arouse hatred and distrust against us utilizable by Austria for the promotion of her antagonistic interests? And if the English world-capitalism could regard apathetically for a long time the misery of Ireland, the cultural backwardness of the Celtic fringe of Wales and Scotland, can poor Hungary suffer the impeded economic and cultural life, the terrible atrophy of production and consumption of half of the country? If the policy would be really the carrying out of the principle of Bentham, this whole problem could in half an hour be taken from the hands of crude and impotent assimilation by force.[31]

But I knew very well that the Benthamite principle had nothing to do with the Magyar nationality policy and such and analogous facts as these had the least effect on the ruling political classes. Progressive Hungary unfortunately never had a word in the directions of the affairs of the country. And when finally, in the days of the catastrophe, in November, 1918, I had the opportunity of announcing to the Rumanian leaders in Arad my old policy as the platform of the government of Count Károlyi and to offer them an honest scheme of national autonomy, it was too late: they preferred to join Rumania rather than to accept a belated compromise.[32] Only in the younger generation and in the ranks of the proletariat did there begin to dawn a better conception. At the same time Andrew Ady, the greatest poet of the period before the collapse and a real national prophet, admonished his people with the great power of his genius that they were on the wrong track which must lead to a new Mohács, a new catastrophe. In many writings and poems he preached accordance and harmony with the nationalities and his powerful muse impressed large strata of the intelligentsia with a new vision. Let me quote one of his mighty rhymes in a pale translation:

> Why out of a thousand stiffened desires
> Doesn't there arise a solid will?
> Yet Magyar, Wallach, and Slav sorrow
> Remains always the same sorrow. . . . .
>
> Yet our disgrace, our grief and pain
> Are since a thousand years akin
> Why do we not meet, roaring,
> On the barricades of the Spirit?

[31] *The Evolution of the Nation-States*, pp. 486–92.

[32] To which Colonel Glaise-Horstenau, a great admirer of Tisza and hater of Károlyi, remarks: "Had Tisza offered them the same thing two years before—full autonomy in the frame of an Eastern Switzerland—the thought would probably have fallen on propitious ground. Now it was too late. . . . ." I think the Colonel errs. The personality of Tisza was so unpopular with the Rumanian people and the rigidity of his feudal attitude was so well known, that nobody would have believed in the sincerity of his promises.

Similar messages were sounded by some impartial and acute foreign observers. So among others Otto Bauer, the Austrian Socialist leader already quoted, answering a questionnaire which I submitted in 1908 to several leading intellectuals of Europe when Count Julius Andrássy introduced his new electoral bill trying to paralyze the Magyar agrarian proletariat and the non-Magyar voters by a system of plural votes and open ballot, thus expressed the opinion that the continuance of the exclusion of the non-Magyar nationalities from political participation

will push Hungary into a course which will lead inevitably toward political catastrophies. . . . . The rise of the working-classes and of the nationalities will be accomplished in any case; but if the road of a calm parliamentarian evolution will be closed, then it will come to the general strike of the industrial workers, to the revolts of the landed proletariat, and to irredentistic agitations. Such an evolution will become, for the Hungarian state more dangerous since the state constitutions of Eastern Europe are by no means so rigid as the nationally homogeneous states of the West. . . . . If an inevitable social and national process will be turned aside from a peaceful road into revolutionary tracks, then these movements will enter into a many-sided and reciprocal action with those upheavals which will happen on the stage of the surrounding countries. . . . . Then, in the coming political catastrophes which the infatuation of the ruling class conjures up in Hungary, nothing less will be at stake than the very existence of the Hungarian State.[33]

But the leading classes of the country followed the old way. Immediately before the World War, Count Stephen Bethlen, the present Hungarian Premier, wrote a pamphlet in which he advocated a policy against the Rumanians of Transylvania, analogous to that which was applied in Posen by the Prussians against the landed property of the Poles.[34] And when under the pressure of circumstances the crown urged the extension of the suffrage, the three drafts of a bill, prepared successively by Count Andrássy, Count Tisza, and Dr. Vázsonyi (the last already during the World War) all started from the axiom that Magyar supremacy must be maintained in the old artificial way and the nationalities must be further restricted by the old procedures.

The nation ran toward disaster and the ghost of the nationality problem, which already in 1848 defeated Hungary and led toward Világos, now in the World War raised its head again and drove the country toward Trianon.

[33] In *La Hongrie Contemporaine et le Suffrage Universel*, pp. 229–30.
[34] *Magyar Landed Property Policy in Transylvania* (Budapest, 1913). In Hungarian.

CHAPTER IV

THE FUNDAMENTAL ANTAGONISM BETWEEN THE AUSTRIAN AND THE HUNGARIAN SYSTEM

This very summary parallel between the chief tendencies of the Austrian and Hungarian nationality policy will suffice to make the reader understand the basic and unbridgeable antithesis of the two systems.

Though, as we saw, the old feudal structure survived in Austria too and manifested its influence conspicuously in the more backward parts of the country, nevertheless the general character of life became more and more bourgeois-like in the Austrian part of the monarchy and the control of the great popular parties had a growing influence. Even the most casual observer could realize very easily the great change in the inner and outer character of social life when he passed the Austrian frontier and entered Hungary. Putting in a single formula the whole difference, I would say that Austrian feudalism became more and more bureaucratized whereas Magyar bureaucracy became more and more feudalized. City life had a decisive influence on Austria, while in Hungary the village character of the country continued. And this village character was substantially colored by the masses of a wretched, uncultured, agricultural proletariat. Even the great urban agglomerations, especially in the Magyar plains, retained this distinctly peasant character. For instance, in 1912, in sixteen important provincial towns there was not a single public bath, a situation the more amazing as there were practically no private baths in the single apartments. The intellectual consumption was of a similarly low level. Charles Keleti, a noted Hungarian statistician, came to the conclusion that under normally healthy conditions—according to their financial possibilities—at least 100,000 men should buy and read books in Hungary whereas even popular works seldom reached a circulation of 2,000 to 3,000 copies, while a scientific book had 1,000. On the basis of such and similar facts a careful Hungarian observer, Dr. Robert Braun, who made a comparison between the Austrian and the Hungarian cultural structure, came to the conclusion that the relative cultural power of the Hungarian cities in the second decade of the present century was not greater than that of the Austrians about 1880.[1]

This contrast becomes even more striking if we compare the composition of the Austrian and the Magyar Parliament. The Austrian

[1] "A Parallel Between the Austrian and the Hungarian Inner Policy," in the review, the *Huszadik Század,* September-October, 1917. In Hungarian.

parliament, based on universal, equal, and secret ballot, was a tolerably true expression of the relative force of the various nations.

Among the chief parties of the Austrian parliament the seats were divided in 1911 as shown in Table XVI.

On the other hand in the Hungarian parliament in 1910 there were as already mentioned 405 deputies belonging to the Magyar parties and only 8 deputies (3 Slovaks and 5 Rumanians) belonging to the nationalities; whereas, if the nationalities had been represented according to their ratio in the population, 215 Magyar and 198 non-Magyar deputies would have been seated in the Hungarian parliament (Croatia-Slavonia excluded). But if we assume a cultural and economic advantage of 100 per cent in favor of the Magyars and if we further assume that the Magyars would have conquered in consequence of this supremacy 100 mandates more than corresponded to

TABLE XVI

Parties								Mandates
German	.	.	.	.	.	.	.	185
Czech	.	.	.	.	.	.	.	82
Polish	.	.	.	.	.	.	.	71
Jugo-Slavs	.	.	.	.	.	.	.	37
Ruthenians		.	.	.	.	.	.	30
Italians	.	.	.	.	.	.	.	16
Rumanians		.	.	.	.	.	.	5
Socialists	.	.	.	.	.	.	.	81
Other smaller groups		.	.	.	.	.	9
Total	.	.	.	.	.	.	.	516

their numerical strength (manifestly a very improbable assumption), even in this case beside the 315 Magyar deputies there should have been 98 non-Magyar deputies in the Hungarian Parliament!

This difference in the social and political structure makes us understand that, whereas the nationalities of Austria progressed year by year on the road of their national culture, the nationalities of Hungary showed rather an opposite tendency and the strongest Hungarian nationality was in its political and public life weaker than the weakest of the Austrian nationalities. So for instance 3 million Hungarian-Rumanians sent to the Hungarian parliament as many deputies as less than 300 thousand Austro-Rumanians sent into the Austrian but with the difference, however, that whereas the Rumanians were almost outcasts in the former, it became a custom in the latter to retain one of the vice-presidencies for the Rumanian club.

In the cultural fields we find this same glaring contrast. The Hungarian writer just mentioned compared the cultural situation of the strongest of the Hungarian nationalities, of the Rumanians (2,948,-000) with that of one of the weakest Austrian nationalities, the Slovenians (1,250,000), on the basis of the latest statistical figures before the war. His chief results were as follows: the number of university students were 414 Rumanians, and 375 Slovenians; the number of polytechnical students were 54 Rumanian, and 141 Slovenian; the number of middle schools were 1 Slovenian, and 7 Slovenian-German, giving a total of 8; 5 Rumanian (2 of them with lower classes), and 2 Rumanian-Magyar, totaling 7; the number of the students in middle schools were 4,164 Rumanian, and 3,827 Slovenian; the number of elementary schools were 2,257 Rumanian with 227,234 students, and 995 Slovenian with 167,915 students; the number of newspapers were 39 Rumanian, and 101 Slovenian; the number of dailies were 2 Rumanian, and 5 Slovenian; the number of literates were 830,809 (28 per cent) Rumanian, and 952,234 (76 per cent) Slovenian.

And whereas the Slovenians had a very intensive political and cultural life and the organs of local administration were mostly Slovenians, the political and cultural life of the Rumanians of Hungary was severely controlled and persecuted by the police, and the number of Rumanian officials compared with the Magyar employees was the following: in the state administration there were 105 Rumanians, and 8,124 Magyars; in the county administration there were 137 Rumanians, and 4,130 Magyars; in the city administration, 91 Rumanians, and 4,680 Magyars. This disproportionate participation becomes even more conspicuous when we know that the Rumanian officials occupied generally the lowest grades in administration.

If we compare the elementary education of the two countries (which is the most important from the point of view of the masses), we can generally say that it was an acknowledged principle in Austria that the peoples should be instructed in their maternal tongue from which there were only rare exceptions, as survivals of older conditions, whereas in Hungary there was a constant tendency, which became very much accentuated after the eighties of the last century, to enforce Magyar public instruction to the detriment of the languages of the nationalities. The results of this policy have been already explained.

Parallel with these cultural and political facts, the ideology of the public life was diametrically different in the two countries. The equality of all the nations was a political axiom in Austria, at least theoretically accepted, while the idea of the united Magyar national state and of the Magyar supremacy was the common dogma of all the Magyar parties, the questioning of which was equivalent to high treason. There was no official state language in Austria, the German had a certain hegemony only as far as the inner language of the central administration made a certain unification necessary. (*Innere Amtssprache.*) In Hungary the Magyar state language was enforced even in the smallest spheres of local administration. This antagonism found an almost symbolical expression in the common notes of the Austro-

Hungarian bank. Whereas on the Austrian side of these notes the inscriptions were made in the languages of all the peoples of Austria as coequals in the state, on the Hungarian side only Magyar inscriptions could be read. (And what is still more characteristic of the mental attitude of the two countries is that after the World War, when in consequence of the Peace Treaties, Austria became an almost exclusively German state and Hungary almost exclusively Magyar, the Austrian bank notes of today have only German inscriptions whereas the Magyar notes are printed not only in Magyar but also in the languages of all those nations which previously belonged to Hungary in order to emphasize the inalienable right of the Crown of St. Stephen to the "conquered territories.")

This fundamental contrast between the Austrian and Hungarian system made, as a matter of fact, a more intimate moral penetration between the two countries impossible. On the contrary, the more the nations of Austria progressed along the road of national self-determination, the greater was the contempt of the Magyar upper classes concerning this so-called "confused conglomerate of peoples." And what was still more dangerous for the future of the monarchy was that the more the nations of Austria grew in political and cultural power and the more they demanded the remolding of the dualistic, oligarchical Constitution into a new one satisfying the claims for national independence of the Czechs and the Jugo-Slavs, the more vehement and exacerbated became the reaction of the Magyar ruling classes against these endeavors which menaced not only their political and administrative monopolies in the empire but, at the same time, their national supremacy in Hungary proper. Therefore, any serious effort for the reform of the Constitution broke down on the irresistible wall of the Magyar oligarchy. Even so late as 1917 when the menacing dissolution of the monarchy became manifest, Dr. Wekerle, the Hungarian premier, declared emphatically that the Hungarian parliament would not tolerate any plan for the federalization of the monarchy and the old frontiers of the crownlands must be maintained.

The German-Magyar hegemony, however, offended more and more the feeling of *Ebenbürtigkeit* ("of equal dignity") of the other nations, exactly to the extent to which their equality in actual life was established. For instance the Czechs could employ against the Magyar monopoly in constitutional life the following arguments: "On the basis of what right did the Magyars arrogate to themselves a monopolistic situation in the Constitution of the monarchy, when our industry surpasses conspicuously the Magyar; when we have practically no illiterates in contrast to the 31 per cent illiterate in Hungary; when in our Czech elementary schools we have as many pupils as they have in their Magyar schools; when we have in the Czech university of Prague 4,200 Czech students, that is, only 1,800 less than are Magyars at Budapest University but at the same time we have 3,000 Czech students at our polytechnical schools at Prague and Brünn, that is, almost 800 more than the Magyars have at their polytechnical institution at Budapest; when the 1,500 Hungarian newspapers are confronted by 1,300 Czech; when the co-operative organization of the Czech peasants is far more democratic and efficient than that of the Magyars? Or do you oppose our equality on the basis of historical right? But your greatest men, Széchenyi and Kossuth themselves acknowledged that we have the same right of national independence as you have. . . . ."

Such and similar facts began to attack the Dualistic Constitution, which lost more and more its basis in the economic and cultural conditions. Austria, however, menaced in its existence, could not rejuvenate itself because the Magyar upper classes in the possession of their "united national parliament" shouted a *noli tangere* against all plans of reform of the Constitution which would diminish their relative influence in the monarchy. Hungary was sufficiently powerful to force Austria to remain in the Procrustean bed of the Dualistic Constitution.

Therefore an impossible situation arose which could only have been transitorily maintained provided the two hegemonic nations, the German and Magyar, had stood in a close alliance with each other and the Magyars had established a tolerable compromise with the Croats. But just the opposite happened, there broke out a violent constitutional crisis between the two hegemonic nations and the Magyars came into a violent conflict with the Croats. The German-Magyar conflict manifested itself at the same time as one between the Magyar upper classes and the Crown because the Dualistic System was a compromise between these two factors of the Constitution. In this manner not only the unsolved national problems of a dozen peoples but also two grave constitutional conflicts pressed heavily upon the Habsburg monarchy. We must now turn to the analysis of these conflicts.

CHAPTER V

HUNGARY VERSUS AUSTRIA

As we have seen, the chief cause of the Dualistic System was the débâcle at Königgrätz and the longing of Habsburgs for revenge against triumphant Prussia. That is the reason why the new era inaugurated by Beust tried to appease Hungary at any price. Without a loyal and satisfied Hungary nothing could be undertaken for the restoration of Austrian hegemony. In order to achieve this aim the Emperor guaranteed the independence of Hungary in the spirit of the laws of 1848, restored the rule of the Magyar noble classes in the internal administration of their country, and delivered his former allies, the nationalities of Hungary, without any check or counterbalance to the will of the Magyar ruling classes. On the other hand the Dualistic Constitution, with the help of an artificial electoral system, secured the supremacy of the Germans in Austria who received at the same time, as a second gift of the Compromise of 1867, the "Constitution of December" on the basis of a parliamentarian government. As compensation for these concessions the German liberals accepted, though unwillingly, the Compromise which the Emperor concluded almost without their consultation with the Magyar ruling classes.

There can be no doubt that Austrian public opinion (not only the Slav but the German too) regarded the Dualistic Compromise with great dissatisfaction, and from the beginning serious voices arose which denounced the *Reichsteilungspakt* ("the Empire-Division Pact" as it was bitterly called) as shaking the very foundations of the monarchy. Later events demonstrated that this point of view was justified because the Compromise concealed in itself the germs of unavoidable crisis. The chief cause of this uncertain equilibrium was the fact that the new "constitutionalism" which the Compromise created, delivered the great majority of the peoples of the monarchy to the German bourgeoisie and bureaucracy on the one hand and to the Magyar feudalism on the other. In both countries the system from the beginning was only workable on the basis of a very restricted and artificial electoral law which was combined in Austria with the application of the ill-famed "paragraph 14" of the Constitution (giving to the crown practically an absolute power in all issues which could not be settled by parliament) and in Hungary with administrative corruption and use of armed force in the face of electoral difficulties. But what made the situation even more unbearable was the fact that both the Germans and the Magyars became more and more resentful against the Compromise which was the very basis of their hegemony in spite of its beneficent economic results for the ruling classes of both countries, and in spite of the opulent monopolies which these classes enjoyed in the administration of their countries and in the leadership of the monarchy. As a matter of fact antipathy grew from year to year against the Compromise and its maintenance faced graver and graver difficulties.

The cause of this strange phenomenon was in the first place a historical one. The Compromise was born out of the spirit of mutual distrust. It was the result of an embarrassing situation. The Emperor needed the Magyars for the realization of his anti-Prussian policy whereas Hungary tortured, dismembered, and weakened by the absolutistic régime needed a breathing period for the regeneration of its economic and political forces before the old struggle for independence could be resumed. The two contracting parties, therefore, were animated by just opposite desires. The Emperor tried to maintain as far as possible the unity of his empire in his army, in the direction of the foreign policy, and in the main economic issues, whereas Francis Deák tried to develop, as far as possible, the entire independence of the Magyar state. The point of view of Deák was the traditional Magyar principle which beyond the community of the crown, established by the Pragmatic Sanction, was not willing to accept any kind of a common empire, or a common state life, or a common government. The very words of "emperor," "empire," "joint government," or "common parliament" sounded almost like an insult to Hungarian public opinion. On the other hand the Emperor, too, had a vivid recollection of the "rebellions" of the Magyar nobility, of its "disloyalties," of its conspiracies with foreign powers and, therefore, his primary effort was to maintain his royal privileges intact in the matter of his army and the foreign policy of the country and to safeguard the unity of the empire in the most important issues.

Out of this mutual distrust and of this half conscious, half unconscious mental reservation, there was born a very vague, very uncertain, very loosely defined law in which both parties sought for formulations which would sustain their hidden point of view. The Hungarian Law of 1867, XII, put an end to the unity of the former absolutistic monarchy (which as we saw was never completely achieved) and established two distinct states. One, the historical Hungary (the dismembered parts of which were again reunited), the other, Austria proper, called by some Austrian patriots with bitter irony, the "anonymous Austria" which did not even have a distinct name but was generally mentioned as "the other countries of His Majesty" or "the kingdoms and countries represented in the Central Parliament (Reichsrat)." These two distinct states had a completely separate parliament, administration, and judiciary system. Even the common sovereign (in Austria called Emperor and in Hungary King) had often a different title according to the different historical past of the two states. (For instance Emperor Charles VI in Austria was King Charles III in Hungary; Emperor Charles I in Austria was King Charles IV in Hungary, etc.) But in spite of this the two states assumed a certain unity from the point of view of international relations because the community of the army and of the diplomatic representation was acknowledged as a corollary of the unity determined by the Pragmatic Sanction. On the basis of this conception there were established three governments: two open and one hidden; one Austrian, one Hungarian, and one common, consisting of the three joint state departments, War, Foreign Affairs, and Finance (as far as the budget of the common administration was concerned). There was also, properly speaking, a need for three parliaments. Again two open and one concealed; one Austrian, one Hungarian, and the so-called "Delegations" which were committees sent out by the Austrian and the Hungarian parliament on the basis of parity for the discussion of the joint affairs. The situation was made even more complicated by the fact that though the community of the international, commercial, and custom relations as well as that of the state bank were not acknowledged as joint affairs emanating from the Pragmatic Sanction, nevertheless they were regarded as affairs which should be settled by a common accord and, therefore, periodically (generally every ten years) new compromises were made between the two governments in order to establish the common principles of their handling.

This constitutional construction, very complicated in itself, became confused by the loose stipulation of the law, already mentioned, in such a manner that even Hungarian jurists were debating for generations concerning the jural nature of the Austro-Hungarian Compromise, whether it should be regarded as a "personal" or a "real" union between the two countries. As a matter of fact the Austrian and the Hungarian points of view diverged even more radically because important differences arose in the text of the Austrian and the Magyar law regulating the Compromise. It is not surprising, therefore, that the Austrian interpretation of the law saw the establishment of a common state power in the Compromise whereas the Magyar emphasized the absolute distinctness of the Hungarian state and the entirely transitory character of the joint affairs for the period in which the Pragmatic Sanction was in force. This uncertainty was still more aggravated by the traditional spirit of the Magyar ruling classes which, continuing the feudal spirit of the politics of *gravamina* and disregarding the economic, social, and international conditions of the Compromise, studied always with the ardor of an attorney the loose and contradictory expressions of the legal text from which they could extract and demonstrate all the theses which were in favor with their momentary standpoint. And whereas the founders of the Compromise,

Francis Deák and Count Julius Andrássy, remained loyal to the spirit
of the Compromise and repudiated the idea of a purely "personal
union" between the two countries and emphasized the necessity of a
military and economic co-operation with the nations of Austria beyond the community of the person of the Monarch, the legal interpretation of the next generation made the discovery that the Compromise
acknowledged the possibility of an independent Magyar army and
that the Compromise was exclusively an act of the Hungarian nation
and of the Crown and, therefore, could be changed in disregard of
the will of the nations of Austria which should not be considered as
contracting parties in the Dualistic Constitution.

The confusion of the situation was still more accentuated by the
institution of the Delegations, already mentioned. It is quite evident
that for the control and direction of the military and foreign policy
of a great empire the necessity arose that all the nations could have
discussed among themselves the most important problems of their political co-operation. But for this same kind of a central parliament
would have been essential. As a matter of fact the Austrians at the
beginning contemplated the institution of the Delegation from this
point of view. This conception, however, broke down in consequence
of the constitutional intransigence of the Magyars who would not even
hear of a common state organ because they maintained the fiction that
there was no common empire or super-state in the monarchy. To what
hair-splitting argument this point of view was leading is almost comi-
cally shown by the following announcement of Count Goluchowski, a
foreign minister of the monarchy, manifestly made under Magyar
pressure in 1907:

I don't know a common state because such a common state does not
exist. . . . . But what I know is the Austro-Hungarian monarchy, which
on the basis of the Pragmatic Sanction, stands as an organic whole in relation to foreign countries, quite apart from the institutions which regulate
the co-operation of the two states of the monarchy.

That this non-existing common state could exact at any moment millions of the treasure of their nations and could drive hundreds of
thousands to the slaughtering bench in case of war, such considerations did not interest the high priests of this constitutional dogmatism. For them it was a matter of no importance that the military
and foreign policy of the country should be directed by the real interests of all the nations concerned; but it was a very grave problem
that the fiction of the absolute independence of the Hungarian state
should be maintained. That was the reason why the two Delegations
of the two parliaments were not allowed to discuss their common problems in a joint meeting, but were compelled to exchange only written
messages; and if they could not agree, they met only for a common
vote under the obligation of abstaining from any debate. It, there-

fore, entirely justified the ironical criticism pronounced by a German liberal deputy during the discussion of the Compromise bill in the Austrian parliament, when he said:

. . . . I cannot imagine a stranger spectacle from a parliamentarian point of view than that which these Delegations offer. This project is capable of only one further improvement, namely, to propose an amendment that the Assembly should meet in the dark and then everything would go on easily and smoothly. . . . . For an Assembly which meets in silence and votes in silence is nothing more than a voting machine. . . . . As a matter of fact, this new political construction reminds me of a child's game, familiar to our youth, in which one makes his presence known by a low piping. . . . .

Indeed, in this Assembly there could not be a serious control of the common affairs of the monarchy. Convoked only occasionally, the 60-60 delegates of the two parliaments constituted an artificial, aristocratic atmosphere easily controlled by the governments and the court. In the great majority of cases the Delegations constituted only a parliamentary show-window beyond which the will of the Crown and of his confidant, the foreign minister (who was at the same time the minister of the Imperial House) had practically no check at all. As a matter of fact public opinion was generally entirely apathetic concerning the debates on international relations, the same public opinion which was seized by a fit of paroxysm at news of an electoral scandal or the report of a scuffle in a university hall between students of various nationalities. There was scarcely a man besides the foreign minister and some of his intimate counselors who would have been interested in international relations. Nay, the politicians regarded these problems with a kind of holy terror because it was well known that the Emperor took these matters very seriously and anyone would lose his chances of becoming a state minister if he should dare to intrude into the private reservation of the Crown. On the other hand neither did the press have a serious foreign service but its reporters only trimmed up the official communications and information received from the *Ballhausplatz* (Foreign Office). A distinguished Austrian writer on foreign policy (one of those white ravens who studied seriously international relations) narrated to me that he was always the target of irony and was regarded as an incorrigible snob because he dared to have independent opinions on foreign problems. . . . . Besides, the nations were so absorbed by the nationality struggles and the Socialists by the affairs of their own class that the political parties lived under a false perspective: they overestimated the significance of the domestic policy and underestimated in a quite disproportionate way that of the foreign policy. At the same time the attention of the Hungarian public opinion was entirely absorbed by the fight for the Magyar army and state bank.

Only in such a political atmosphere could it have happened that the World War was determined by the decision of five gentlemen without the least participation of the nations of the monarchy; that the very organ of foreign policy was convoked only in the fourth year of the war and, therefore, the war was conducted without any efficacious parliamentary control; that the Austro-Hungarian monarchy was perhaps the only warring power in which even the most outstanding state ministers had no idea concerning the most important facts of the foreign policy. What kind of a constitutional control could have existed in a monarchy in which members of the cabinet themselves did not even surmise that Count Czernin announced as early as 1917 the position of the Central Powers as a hopeless one in a report addressed to the Emperor? The minister of finance of Austria during the war, Dr. Spitzmüller, wrote concerning it the following confession:

What should one say to the fact that we, state ministers of important departments, did not have the least idea of such a report? I learn only now in December, 1918, that in April, 1917, one of the Central Powers explained to another that things could not go on any longer and that an end must be made. This was not communicated at all to the minister of finance, to the minister of public alimentation, to the minister of commerce, to the minister of agriculture. . . . . That is horrifying.[1]

The conception that the Austro-Hungarian monarchy did not form any real unity and, therefore, could not have any real common organs led sometimes to absurd conclusions. For instance the officials of the joint ministries were joint officials of the two countries but they could not be regarded either as officials of Austria or officials of Hungary nor those of Austria-Hungary because the Magyar doctrine repudiated even the allusion to a super-state. This doctrine was the source of practical complications too. When Bosnia-Herzegovina was annexed, this unhappy province hung in the air from a constitutional point of view because it did not belong in reality either to Austria or to Hungary, but was only administered as by a legal fiction through the joint state department of finance. The historical right of the Hungarian Holy Crown to this province was theoretically acknowledged but it was regarded, as that of Dalmatia, as actually dormant. This constitutional subtlety, in the eyes of the Magyar nationalists a case of tremendous importance, was the more remarkable, almost mysterious, as the Magyar ruling classes did only lip-service to it because the very idea of a unification of these provinces with Croatia-Slavonia seemed to them an extreme danger, menacing by a Jugo-Slav integration the very foundations of the Dualistic Constitution.

Similar susceptibilities made the solution of the problem of the escutcheon of the monarchy impossible almost to the end of the Com-

[1] A destructive criticism of the situation may be found in Dr. Spitzmüller's, *Der Politische Zusammenbruch und die Anschlussfrage* (Wien, 1919).

promise. In the joint army the old Austrian eagle was applied but that emblem shocked the historical sensitiveness of the Magyars and led repeatedly to scandals and conflicts. On the other hand a new escutcheon could not be found because the Magyar point of view repudiated all state community. Only during the convulsions of the World War was a shrewd statesmanship able to settle the intricacies of the problem, and its solution is almost a symbolical expression of the fragile relations of the two countries.[2]

But what undermined and discredited the Dualistic Constitution finally was not so much the ambiguity of its jural construction as its economic arrangements, according to which the participation in the expenses of the joint budget (the percentage of the mutual contribution for the maintenance of the army and of the foreign administration), the so-called *Quota*, was discussed and determined periodically every ten years by the Delegations. Similarly the most important economic affairs which were regarded as matters of common interest to both states (custom regulation, international commercial treaties, and the Austro-Hungarian bank) were submitted to periodical regulations by the parliaments of the two states. If in the question of the Quota the Delegations could not agree, the controversy was decided by the Emperor-King.

This constitutional mechanism led to absurd results from the point of view of the monarchy. It was always uncertain how long Hungary would be inclined to maintain the common economic relations which were not acknowledged as obligations following from the Pragmatic Sanction but as purely matters of a provisional contract. There could be no doubt that from year to year Magyar public opinion was less disposed to continue these economic connections. In this manner every ten years the economic foundation of the monarchy was called into question, and with this the very existence of the empire. For in case of the dissolution of the customs union, the commercial policy, and the currency, the community of the army and of the diplomatic relations themselves would have lost their sense and possibility in consequence of the growing antagonism of economic interests. But not only the feeling of nervous incertitude aggravated the political atmosphere but whenever the Quota or other economic negotiations were

---

[2] The new escutcheon was a triple one. The Austrian and the Hungarian escutcheons stood beside each other but separate. Between these two, connecting their peripheries, stood a small escutcheon, that of the Imperial House. Under the escutcheons winds a ribbon on which the motto, borrowed from the Pragmatic Sanction: *Indivisibiliter ac inseperabiliter*. This ingenious construction tries to demonstrate that the two states were somehow connected but there was still no common state because the Crown on the Imperial escutcheon (in consequence of its smallness) was situated lower than the Crowns on the escutcheons of the respective states. In this manner the able author of this constitutional mystery saved the community of the Monarchy, the inviolability of the hereditary right of the Monarch, and the complete independence of Hungary.

renewed between the two countries, the two contracting parties stood always as unscrupulous brokers, each against the other. Both, in order to acquire more advantages in those economic controversies, agitated its whole press and all their economic organizations with a view to portraying its economic situation in the most gloomy and sinister colors imaginable and to make the other partner appear as a cruel Shylock. Instead of determining the ratio of the mutual contributions on the basis of constant objective criteria (for example the population, the results of taxation, and of the savings accounts, etc.) with the help of a pre-established measure, all such transactions were carried on by both partners in the spirit of a demagogic propaganda and left behind them a great amount of bitterness and distrust. Indeed this system of a *Monarchie auf Kündigung* (a "monarchy at short notice") as it was ironically called was perhaps more detrimental to the Dualistic Constitution than all its other weaknesses. The Austrian governments under the difficulties of the Compromise negotiations tried, by concessions given to the various nations, to save the stranded ship of the dualistic system whereas the Magyar Parliament in the feeling of its national unity could generally secure more advantages in the dualistic bargains. The Emperor, who had an instinctive horror of democracy and did not dare to shake the foundation of the system, tried to satisfy as far as possible the will of Budapest against Vienna, enfeebled by nationalistic struggles. Of course, from a Magyar point of view, his concessions were never adequate while from the Austrian point of view they were exaggerated and, therefore, his prestige and popularity was damaged from both sides. And when he decided the controversies concerning the Quota (according to the Compromise it was his duty to determine the Quota when the Delegations failed to agree) he appeared partial to one of the parties. It became a fashion in Austria talk of "the absolutism of the Magyar king against the Emperor of Austria."

Under such circumstances the schism between the two countries became deeper and deeper. Karl Renner, one of the keenest observers of the situation, announced the bankruptcy of the Compromise because it became a constitutional absurdity, being an *Organgemeinschaft ohne Willensgemeinschaft* ("a community of organs without a community of will"). Not only the Slavs hated the dualistic system but also the leaders of the German liberalism regarded it with growing distrust. Ten years after the conclusion of the Compromise, Heinrich Friedjung, the influential Austrian historian, wrote the following statement:

In all public localities and in every social circle the decay of the state is openly discussed and provinces are divided among the neighboring states. . . . . This evil is due to the fact that we simply do not know to which

state we belong and to what principles we owe loyalty. . . . . Are we at
all Austrian citizens? The official terminology knows an Austria-Hungary
but no Austria. . . . .

On the other hand some Christian Socialists also began to attack
bitterly the Compromise and denounced it in their popular demagogy
as an alliance of Magyar feudalism with Jewish capitalism. And if the
Germans, the chief usufructuaries of the dualistic system besides the
Magyars, became so inimical to it, it is easy to imagine what the feelings of the Slavs were toward it, those Slavs who regarded the Compromise from the beginning as an attempt against their constitutional liberties and who remained the ardent followers of Palacký, who
coined the very phrase "Dualism means Pan-Slavism."

Not only the Germans and the Slavs, but the Magyars too, who
were regarded as the first beneficiaries of the Compromise, turned
more and more from the achievements of Deák and Andrássy, nay
they became the most accentuated of the centrifugal forces of the
monarchy. The truth is that the Compromise never had a majority in Hungary. That the nationalities had no use for it, is quite
evident as the dualistic system meant an exclusive Magyar domination
in the country. But the Magyar masses too, the small peasantry and
the bulk of the artisans combined with a large strata of the intelligentsia, opposed the new system from the beginning, largely on a historical and sentimental basis because they expected nothing good from
Habsburg militarism and absolutism even though it now assumed a
semi-constitutional form. Only the more wealthy elements of society,
the big landed proprietors, the rich capitalists, the higher bureaucracy, and the leading staff of the intelligentsia acknowledged the
Compromise as a historical necessity for the country. Professor
Szekfü himself, the historian of the present Hungarian counter-revolution, a supporter of the Habsburgs, a naïve admirer of the German-Magyar supremacy and of the Compromise has demonstrated
that the dualistic system was from the first moment of its foundation
bitterly opposed by the masses and it could be maintained only by a
systematic corruption of public life and with the help of a restricted
and brutally controlled electorate.[3]

From the beginning of the eighties of the last century, there became more and more manifest those forces which tended to loosen and
finally to burst asunder the connection between Austria and Hungary.
These endeavors started as a matter of fact from the camp of the
traditional ideology of independence represented by men who regarded themselves as followers of the policy of Louis Kossuth. But this
party, in consequence of the restricted suffrage and the corrupted
electoral machine, was such a small minority in the political arena

[3] *Three Generations*, pp. 327–39.

that it did not signify a real danger to the Dualistic Constitution, protected by the big landed and financial interests. The real danger from the point of view of the Compromise arose only at that time when the ideology of independence and the hatred of Austria began to permeate even those parties and circles which stood on the basis of the Compromise as very influential elements in the higher nobility, bureaucracy, and local administration. Of course these exponents of the new ideology of independence (represented especially by Count Albert Apponyi and his followers) did not take this idea very seriously and they never dreamed of a separation from Austria or from the Habsburgs (for the big landed interests in Hungary were entirely solidary with the Habsburgs because the ruling class clearly understood that a real struggle for independence would have meant such a tension of democratic forces as would have inevitably led to a distribution of the landed estates and a local self-government for the nationalities), but they flirted more and more with the idea of the "expansion and development of the Compromise" in order to secure new privileges in the army and in the diplomatic representation of the state.

In this manner many factors contributed to the reviving of the idea of independence and of the traditional *Kurucz* feeling of the country. A demagogic propaganda was carried on which denounced the joint army and the common institutions of the monarchy as an emanation of the bad spirit of "cursed Vienna." Certain social and economic changes forced public opinion in the same direction: the proletarianization of large strata of small artisans who succumbed because of the competition of Austrian capitalism; the dominant position of the big Austrian finance in Hungary which retained a great part of the Hungarian industry as their vassals; the development of a large intellectual middle class in Hungary which could not find employment in the public offices, and the weakened position of one part of the Hungarian nobility which collapsed under the system of economic liberalism and was extremely desirous of getting new administrative, diplomatic, and military sinecures by the restriction of the joint institutions and by the development of the Magyar state ideal.

This tendency toward independence was further strengthened by the general current of civic education in Hungary under the sway of which two generations grew up which regarded the whole co-operation among the various nations of the monarchy with a kind of megalomania: they underestimated the rôle of Austria and especially that of the Slavs, whereas they overestimated the importance of the Magyars and disregarded entirely the Hungarian nationalities as a negligible quantity.

But there was also another factor which perhaps more than those already mentioned made the movement for independence more acute.

That was the antiquated electoral system of Hungary which was becoming less and less representative of the real interests of the country. Properly speaking, only those classes and strata were represented in parliament who stood for the Compromise or who opposed it bitterly on a historical and sentimental basis. On the other hand those classes and masses, the fundamental interests of which were not concentrated around the Dualistic Constitution but for which the agrarian policy or the social policy or the nationality policy had a paramount importance, the Magyar "dwarfish" peasantry, the agrarian proletariat, the industrial working-class, and the nationality masses were hermetically excluded from the Hungarian Parliament either by law or by the corrupt electoral practices.

This situation had a further danger from the point of view of the wholesome development of the monarchy. The ideology of independence became—more or less consciously—a kind of a *Verdrängungsideologie* ("an ideology of repression") against all efforts which endangered the interests of the ruling classes. Every historical society exercises a half-conscious, half-unconscious selection concerning those problems the discussion of which it considers advantageous or agreeable from the point of view of the dominant interests. This almost sociological law resulted in Hungary in the disproportionate predominance of the so-called "national problems" and of the *fine fleur* of these problems, of the constitutional and army problems to the detriment of the more serious economic and social considerations. Anyone who was anxious for a career or desirous of laurels turned toward those more dignified problems. On the contrary the agrarian problem, the *morbus latifundii*, the social problems of the working-classes, a new point of view in the nationality problem aroused the distrust and antipathy of the most respectable citizens. Under such circumstances it is only natural that as the demands of the agricultural laborers became louder, as the big landowners were molested by agricultural strikes, as the urban proletariat became a misunderstood and terrifying factor in Hungarian society (Socialism was treated for decades as exclusively a matter of police administration), and as the underground rumor of the nationalities became more audible, the "national problems" proved to be an excellent instrument for canalizing the economic and social unrest of the masses against Austria and for presenting the bill of the lower classes to Vienna and to the Habsburgs instead of to the feudal nobility. That was one of the reasons why important elements in the aristocracy embraced more and more the program of independence, and even the government of His Majesty accepted doctrines which stood in flagrant opposition to the fundamental ideas of the Dualistic Constitution.

The new nationalistic current began with an exuberance of the old constitutional slogans and with a demagogic propaganda against the "cursed common institutions" which they portrayed as treason against the independence of the country. It was for decades the chief occupation of the leading politicians to explore the remotest corners of the Compromise in order to demonstrate that the old independence of the nation was surrendered or that important national privileges were forgotten or disregarded. As a consequence of this attitude there were endless and exasperating debates in parliament concerning the colors of the *porte-épée* and of the flags, the displaying of the emblems and escutcheons, the use of the army language, the singing of the imperial hymn, and the tactless behavior of some of the army leaders. Hypnotized by these and similar attacks, Magyar public opinion demanded more and more passionately the introduction of the Magyar language into the Hungarian regiments and later the establishment of an independent Hungarian army. At the same time the movement for independence was carried on also in the economic field and the Party of Independence spread continuous propaganda in favor of the economic separation of the country from Austria by the erection of customs barriers and by the establishment of an independent national bank. Every new draft of a bill concerning the necessary development of the joint army became a source of vehement scandals in parliament, lasting sometimes for several years. It became customary for the opposition to demand so-called "national attainments," from the government as a kind of compensation for the passing of the army budget and the granting of the new contingent of the recruits. But these so-called national attainments concerning the independence of the country and the Magyarization of the army were confronted by the prerogatives of the Crown, jealously safeguarded by the Emperor in all matters regarding the internal organization and direction of the army and, therefore, the relation became more and more envenomed between the King and the Hungarian parliament. Even the modest concessions made by the King to the chauvinistic opposition could not relieve the situation. On the contrary they were only as oil on the burning flame of national enthusiasm. For instance a long and embittered fight was carried on to change the title of the joint army from Imperial-Royal Army to Imperial *and* Royal Army. When finally in 1889 this magic word for the placation of the national feeling was granted, it proved to be inefficient. In the absence of any other economic, cultural, or social-political food, public opinion threw itself with a more and more rabid exasperation into the national and constitutional problems and exciting scandals arose between the Habsburg army, the Austrian *soldatesca* and the *Kurucz* gentry, the small bourgeoisie and intelligentsia. Such and similar affairs always connected with the imperial hymn, the *Gott erhalte*, or the Austrian flag abounded and envenomed the whole moral and political atmosphere of the country. (Affairs Janszky, Nessi, Ugron, etc.)

Under the pressure of this public opinion the opposition began a more and more turbulent fight against the government, and a series of obstructions were launched in parliament whenever new army bills were introduced. As a result of these obstructions the parliament, this famous united, efficient Hungarian parliament, was paralyzed and the country was plunged into a state of so-called *Ex Lex:* the government had no legal authority for exacting taxes and for enrolling recruits. This situation became, in 1904, so acute that the then Premier, Count Stephen Tisza, by a sudden coup openly violated the rules of parliament in order to secure the acceptance of the army bill. But the forceful measure of the Premier did not help. The opposition, both the Party of Independence and those on the basis of the Compromise, demolished all the furniture on the floor of the House and attacked with the broken pieces the Parliamentarian Guard established by Tisza. The Premier, in order to restore normal conditions, appealed to the "nation" because he was convinced that the usual electoral machine would function without difficulty. But the nationalistic public opinion of the country was so exasperated that the calculations of Tisza failed. The elections in 1905 led to the fall of his party and the so-called "national coalition" of the opposition gained a majority, and inside of this majority the Party of Independence, under the leadership of Louis Kossuth's son, Francis, became the most powerful party of the new parliament. Thereafter the antagonism between the Crown and the constitutional opposition became even more embittered. In this critical situation the "most constitutional Monarch" made an extra-parliamentarian experiment and the Minister of Interior of this "illegal" Cabinet, Joseph Kristóffy, menaced the rebellious ruling classes with the promise, made to a deputation of the Social-Democratic Party, of a universal, secret ballot. Kristóffy maintained that the real cause of the conflict between the King and the nation should be sought in the fact that the parliament did not represent the real will of the country because its laboring elements were excluded from the Constitution. There was only antagonism between the Crown and the privileged classes whereas the working-people of the country and the King would understand each other without difficulty.[4]

This new doctrine, the renewal of the spirit of Josephinism, shook the very foundations of Hungarian public life. The national coalition, the county administration, and the whole oligarchical structure of the country announced a struggle of life and death against the illegal government and those who participated in its administration.

[4] Compare pp. 111–12, 182–83.

The situation became almost revolutionary and "the most constitutional King" appointed a plenipotentiary royal commissary and dissolved parliament by armed force (February, 1906). And now the country witnessed a spectacle which astonished European public opinion. The people of the entire country saw and suffered without protest the destruction of their time-honored Constitution. It became manifest that behind this Hungarian parliament, glorified as strong, united, and strictly national as compared with the despised Austrian, there were practically no public forces. Not even a single mass-meeting, a single placard, or a single popular proclamation protested against the new era of the "Viennese absolutism." On the contrary the working-masses and nationalities regarded with malicious joy the impotent struggle of the national oligarchy.

There are many, both in Austria and in Hungary, who regard this date of 1906 as of decisive importance in the whole history of the monarchy and are of the opinion that, if the Emperor had then introduced universal suffrage by a royal decree and had opened the door (as he did later in Austria) for the free political expression of the working-classes and the nationalities of Hungary, the monarchy could have evolved along the line of Federalism, which would have substantially mitigated the international tension and would have even checked the outbreak of the World War. Those however who take into consideration that the irridentist propaganda against the monarchy was at this time already very advanced and who realize that the masses, excluded from the Constitution for centuries and lacking even the most elementary civic education, could not be made in a few years self-conscious factors in a complicated and gigantic political transformation (as this of the remolding of the Dualistic Constitution into a Federalistic one), those will be entitled to doubt whether the last decade would have been a sufficient period for the salvation of the monarchy. Be that as it may, there can be no doubt that the Monarch committed grave faults in the handling of this most critical situation. It became manifest that he utilized the promise of universal suffrage as a sheer bugbear against the Magyar upper classes and as soon as the Magyar coalition abandoned its claims against his army prerogatives, he called it into the government and accepted the falsification of universal suffrage (giving his previous sanction[5] to the electoral bill of Count Julius Andrássy, based on the principle of an oligarchical plurality and of open voting) in order to obtain, as a kind of compensation for his royal favor, the assistance of the Magyar ruling classes in the annexation of Bosnia-Herzegovina (1908). This behavior of the Crown contributed very much to the final moral

[5] This "previous sanction" was a Hungarian curiosity according to which no bill could be introduced by the cabinet before the legislature without the "previous sanction" of the king. This institution functioned like an "absolutistic check" because no premier would have dared a conflict with the monarch.

disintegration of the monarchy because it exacerbated not only the
working-classes but also it showed clearly to the nationalities that
they could not hope for any improvement of their situation from internal reforms.

As a matter of fact this cynical pact of the ruling classes and the
Crown did not lead to a real consolidation and the struggle for "national concessions" in the army became recrudescent. The opposition
again tried to restrict the royal prerogatives, the government again
made some concessions (the so-called "Resolution Crisis" in 1912)
but the Emperor repudiated brutally the new "rebellion" and the end
of the powerless struggle of the opposition was once more that Vienna
needed "the strong hand" of Count Tisza who, as in 1904, and now in
1912, rushed through the army bill by the violation of the rules of
parliament, casting out by armed force the renitent deputies.

These tumultuous incidents (one of the deputies shot at Count
Tisza with his revolver in parliament) made it obvious to all clear-
headed observers that Hungarian parliamentarism had become merely an instrument of Habsburg absolutism because the principle of majority, in the name of which Count Tisza broke down with armed force
the obstruction of the opposition, was manifestly only a pretext under a constitution which excluded the overwhelming majority of the
nation from the suffrage and which terrorized the minority possessing
the suffrage by the system of open ballot, corruption, and the mobilization of the army. Perceiving the danger of this situation, about
fifty Hungarian publicists and politicians addressed a memorandum
to foreign public opinion drawing the attention of European progressive thought to the international peril of the renewed absolutism.[6] At
the same time the more far-sighted elements of Vienna emphasized repeatedly the entire bankruptcy of the Magyar parliamentarian system. But the Crown and the official circles regarded things apathetically since Tisza secured for them with his "strong hand" 300,000
more recruits and 400 million Crowns more for military expenses.
Though new promises were made for parliamentarian reform, it was
continually frustrated by the ruling class and in May, 1912, Count
Tisza choked in blood the manifestation of the working-class at Budapest. Even during the tempest of the World War and in spite of the
unheard of sacrifices of the Hungarian peasantry and working-classes,
the cause of electoral reform could not make any real progress. Count
Tisza, in the blindness of his class standpoint, made the following declaration before the correspondent of the *Frankfurter Zeitung:*

Not the people demands, with us, the suffrage but the politicians. The
Hungarian soldier in the trenches does not care about the suffrage; he is
only longing for a leave of two weeks in order to till his lot; he doesn't
think of the suffrage but only of his folks and the Fatherland. . . . . We
have become unworthy of these brave soldiers. . . . .

[6] *Die Krise der Ungarischen Verfassung* (Budapest, 1912).

How this mightiest statesman of the monarchy, under the sway of his traditional point of view, was incapable of understanding the general world-situation was characteristically demonstrated by a declaration of his made to the editor of his official German paper *(Pester Lloyd)*, who admonished him of the extreme importance of the electoral problem. Count Tisza emphasized the fact that such a problem did not exist in Hungary and that he himself, who knew thoroughly the moral attitude of the period, "dared to prophesy" that after the war a new *Biedermeier* epoch (so the extremely peaceful, narrow-minded, philistine attitude was called before the Revolution of 1848) would be born all around the world and the soldiers would be happy if, after their terrible sufferings, they could return to their work and their families.

Not only in the field of the constitutional and military problems did Magyar nationalism grow more and more acute, but also in the economic sphere. Louder and louder became its claims for a customs union independent of Austria, for a national bank, and for a Magyar foreign economic representation. From year to year it became more difficult to maintain the former economic unity. In 1902 the Sugar Convention at Brussels was already separately signed by Austria and Hungary as by distinct parties. The economic Compromise of 1907 faced such difficulties that well-informed public opinion both in Austria and in Hungary regarded this Compromise as the last one between the two countries and was convinced that Hungary would soon assume complete economic independence. The causes and psychology of this growing tendency for economic independence, we have already analyzed in another connection. At this juncture I wish only to allude to the fact that the ideology of independence was also considerably strengthened by certain foreign events, such as, for instance, the separation of Norway from Sweden, which had a great repercussion upon Magyar nationalism, while the erection of a Washington Memorial in Budapest by the American Magyars was enthusiastically appreciated as a symbol of independence.

The facts which demonstrated the growing force of the separatistic movements in all fields of social and political life gradually became more numerous. In 1900 at the occasion of the morganatic marriage of Archduke Francis Ferdinand, the Hungarian parliament made a declaration according to which "the Pragmatic Sanction did not establish a common order of heredity to the throne with Austria"; in 1903 Count Tisza called the Austrian premier in the Hungarian parliament a "distinguished foreigner," whose dilettante declarations had no political significance; in 1909 Count Albert Apponyi, then minister of public education, issued a decree which in all textbooks, maps, and globes supplanted the expression of the Austro-Hungarian monarchy by that of "Hungary and Austria"; somewhat later under the auspices of the same minister a historical textbook was written in which the Habsburg dynasty was portrayed as a foreign conqueror, a Germanizing power sucking the fat of the country. . . . .

This antagonism grew during the war into a real frenzy. Magyar public opinion accused Austria of utilizing the Magyar soldiers as cannon fodder instead of its own treacherous nationalities. Austria on the other hand accused Hungary of promoting famine in the monarchy by its selfish policy of alimentation. As a matter of fact the Hungarian government introduced so many limitations of circulation inside the customs union during the war that the economic unity of the two countries became *de facto* illusionary. This, however, did not impede the Austrians from smuggling out of Hungary in torpedo boats great quantities of corn which led to parliamentarian scandals. And the more desperate the war situation became the more grew the hatred and animosity between the two countries. It was a usual topic in the Austrian newspapers that the dualistic system had become for them a nuisance, the maintenance of which would not be worth while after the war. On the other hand the Magyar newspapers kindled by an extreme demagogy the flame of the traditional hatred of Vienna. For instance, *Az Est*, the most widely circulating and influential Magyar daily wrote in August, 1918, in such terms: "We do not care in the least how Austria helps herself nor with what wire she fastens her body. . . . ." Or, on another occasion: "For the present moment it is entirely irrelevant for us what advice the preservation instinct dictates to this country in order to lengthen its life. . . . . And if Austria is compelled to undergo an operation, it is entirely her own affair. . . . ." It is characteristic that this newspaper wrote no less than twelve leaders in such a tenor during this month, which is the more significant because it always followed servilely the fluctuations of public opinion.

From all these it becomes patent that the whole edifice of the Compromise, both in its spirit and its practice, began to crack and crash and that the antagonism between the two hegemonic nations, nay between the Hungarian King and the Austrian Emperor, was even greater than the conflict between the hegemonic nations and the second rank nations. The centrifugal forces broke out more and more ruthlessly in the whole field. And to make the dissolution even more chaotic, to the constitutional conflict between Austria and Hungary was added a second one which, by the foreign complications aroused by it, gave later the final death-thrust to the old monarchy, paralyzed by the hydra of internal struggles. This conflict was the Hungarian-Croatian conflict.

CHAPTER VI

CROATIA VERSUS HUNGARY

It has often been said, and with full justification, that the relation of Croatia-Slavonia to Hungary showed in its essence, though in smaller proportions, still with even greater consequences, the same dangers and difficulties as the relation between the two leading states of the Monarchy. The Hungarian-Croatian relation, however, in contrast to the Austro-Hungarian, was for centuries quiet and undisturbed. Since the beginning of the twelfth century and since the death of the last independent Croatian King, Croatia entered into a union with the Crown of St. Stephen, the jural nature of which is not very well known to us. It is probable that it was one of those loose feudal connections which the nobilities of two countries established for the more efficient defense of their mutual interests. Geographical proximity, the fear of the smaller state of international complications, the identity of the economic and social structure, and expanding commercial relations made this connection advantageous from the point of view of both parties. Generally speaking, it was maintained without serious difficulties, according to our historical reminiscences, until the first decades of the nineteenth century. The Croatian nobility became simply a part of the Hungarian *una eademque nobilitas* and the exclusive use of the Latin language between them eliminated all national antagonism. State activities in the proper sense were, before the arrival of the modern period, very restricted whereas the local administration of the counties gave the nobility of the respective regions almost the independence possessed by a small state. Both nobilities kept their bondsmen aloof from all rights and the fear of riots became as much of a factor in political cohesion between them as did later the growing threat of the Turks and the fight against them. The Turkish advance changed the Croatian settlements substantially, pushing them back toward the north, securing a hegemonic position to the Hungarian state and to its administrative organization throughout the whole kingdom. In the period of the enlightened absolutism the unifying policy of the Habsburgs brought the Croat nobility more and more into a union with the Magyars, and with them they made common cause against the reforms of Joseph II and later against the ideas of the French Revolution which terrified and exasperated the Croatian estates not less than those of the Magyars. It became a fashion that the Croat nobles, in order to demonstrate their solidarity with the Magyars, wore Magyar apparel and also in other respects the relation between the two noble classes seemed to be very cordial.

In spite of this we should not think of a common modern state idea in this connection. If their interests were at stake, the Croat nobility would adopt an almost independent state policy. Thus, for instance, after the collapse at Mohács the Croatian estates elected Ferdinand as their king in 1527, quite independently of the Magyars, and acknowledged at the same time the hereditary succession of the Habsburgs, that is, 160 years earlier than the Magyars. They also hastened to accept the Pragmatic Sanction (manifestly in order to attain special royal favors) ten years earlier than the Magyars (1712). From these facts, however, one should not conclude that the Croat state was entirely independent but only that the special state consciousness of the Croatian nobility remained unaltered and that they expressed it now and then, when their interests demanded it, in isolated political acts without disturbing the practical union and co-operation with the Hungarian Kingdom. It seems also a well-established fact that apart from the Hungarian central parliament the Croatian *Sabor* (the local parliament at Zagreb) had a broad autonomy and that the laws passed by the Magyar parliament were ratified in some cases by the Sabor.

This loose feudal state and its method of political co-operation resulted in nothing serious except when the Magyar nobility was aroused to national consciousness, and when after the thirties of the last century, they tried to introduce the Magyar state language into Croat territories. After that the Magyar state idea came into a more and more violent conflict with the Croat state idea.[1] The memories of the common historical past and the often loose and contradictory stipulations of the Hungarian and the Croat laws were utilized by both parties for the strengthening of their antagonistic standpoints by the semblance of historical right. The Croats tried to demonstrate that they had never as a state lost their independence, that Croatia-Slavonia had always been regarded as a *regnum socium*, that their parliament had always been entitled to pass independent laws. In opposition to this thesis, the Hungarians maintained that, since the union there had never been an independent Croatian state, their local parliament had only the significance of a provincial assembly and it was therefore subordinated in all important issues to the Hungarian parliament and consequently Croatia and the territories belonging to it were only *partes annexae* of the Hungarian kingdom.

This growing constitutional and sentimental antagonism broke out in full force at the Diet of 1843–44 when the Magyars passed a law providing that the Magyar state language should be employed— as mentioned before—throughout the whole territory of Croatia as the common state language of the two countries. This measure exasperated Croatian society because the Croat national idea based on the

[1] Compare p. 305 of the present book.

historical conception of Illyrism had already permeated the masses of
the Croatian people and the mighty personality of Ljudevit Gaj succeeded in arousing the distinct historical consciousness of the country. Public opinion advocated now not only the political independence
of Croatia-Slavonia, but at the same time the re-establishment of the
old Croatian Kingdom on the basis of the re-annexation of certain
territories (which had belonged, in earlier times, to the Croatian
state,) of Dalmatia, of the important harbor, Fiume, and the Croatian
military confine.[2] The Croatian Sabor had in 1848 already echoed
these ideas and declared the Croatian language a state language in
the whole territory of Croatia. At the same time it issued a manifesto to all the Slav tribes living in the Habsburg monarchy which formulated with striking lucidity the ideology which became later the
Austro–Jugo-Slav program:

The time of the nationalities has come, the nations will group according
to their language and protect each other against foreign aggression. . . . .
Following out this principle we accepted the fraternal alliance of the re-
awakened Serb Voivodina [the Serb territory of Hungary] with our triune
Kingdom and expect the accession of all the Jugo-Slav-Austrian brothers in
order to maintain the Austrian Empire on the basis of a confederation in
which our nationally homogeneous organism will peacefully cooperate with
the other peoples of Austria organized on the same principle. . . . .

When, therefore, the Hungarian Revolution of 1848 did not acknowledge these claims but, on the contrary, tried to establish the
authority of the Hungarian state and the use of the Magyar language
throughout the whole Kingdom, including Croatia, public opinion in
the Serbo-Croat territories became so exasperated that the Viennese
Court had no difficulty in utilizing and mobilizing it against the Magyar revolutionary nobility and peasantry. As a matter of fact, as it
has already been described, the Croatian *banus* (the governor of the
country), Jelačić, and the Jugo-Slav military forces organized by
him played an important rôle in defeating the Magyar struggle for
independence.

After the collapse of the Hungarian revolution, Croatia became
an independent crownland but the Croats were very dissatisfied with
their new conditions and complained about the ingratitude of Vienna
because the unification of Dalmatia with Croatia was refused and the
pressure of centralizing absolutism was not lighter on the loyal Croats
than on the rebellious Magyars. The later constitutional experiments
even increased the exasperation of the Croats because the "October

---

[2] The Croatian Military Confine, a part of the greater Military Confine, was a
large territory at the southern frontier of Croatia and Hungary militarily organized
as a defensive bulwark against the Turks throughout two centuries. One of the advantages which the Compromise gave to Hungary was the reincorporation of this
territory into the country and the reintroduction of the state administration instead
of the military rule.

Diploma" of 1860, in order to appease the Magyars, reunited Fiume
and the so-called Mur-territory with Hungary. The Compromise of
1867 and the subsequent Magyar policy envenomed the situation even
more. Though no objective observer will deny that in the so-called
Hungarian-Croatian Compromise which followed the Austro-Hungarian Compromise (the Law of 1868, XXX) Deák and the other leading Magyar statesmen were animated by a spirit of benevolence and
equity, the second-rank rôle which this Compromise offered to the
Croats in the Habsburg monarchy seemed to them inacceptable after
the events of the revolution and the memories of absolutism. As a matter of fact the Compromise, following the traditional Hungarian point
of view, did not acknowledge Croatia-Slavonia as an independent state
but gave to it only a provincial autonomy inside the Hungarian state.
In their internal administration, in the judiciary, and in the educational department the Croats obtained a perfectly free hand, but in all the
other walks of public life they belonged to the competency of the Hungarian parliament to which the Croat Sabor sent a delegation. The
Croats felt this self-government only as a shadow of self-government
the more as the *banus,* the head of the Croatian government, was nominated by the King, not on the proposal of the Sabor but on that of
the Hungarian government, that is to say, his position was not a parliamentary one toward his own country but it had the character of
a Hungarian royal commissary. There can be no doubt that the great
majority of the Croatian people were from the beginning inimical to
the Compromise which was only accepted by a packed Sabor created
by an agent of the Hungarian government, Levin Rauch, with the help
of some nobles and bureaucrats, loyal to the Magyars and called ironically by public opinion the "Magyarons." But not even this obedient
Sabor could be induced to accept paragraph 66 of the Compromise
which declared the town, harbor, and district of Fiume to be a special
body connected with the Hungarian crown. Originally the Croat text
was at variance with the Hungarian, stating that concerning this
question no agreement could be reached. And nothing could be more
characteristic of the spirit of the time than the fact that the harmony
between the two antagonistic versions was reached by a purely mechanical procedure, namely, that a thin strip of paper containing the
translation of the Magyar text was pasted over the respective portion
of the Croat text when the two versions were submitted for the King's
signature. That means that the Compromise was based not only on
electoral and administrative corruption, but also on the falsification
of an important state document!

    In spite of this it is conceivable that Croat public opinion might
have become accustomed to the large local autonomy offered to it and
might have acknowledged, in the long run, its several real advantages
if it had been managed by the central government with complaisance

and justice, and particularly if the promise of the Compromise concerning the uniting of Dalmatia with Croatia on the basis of the historical right of the Hungarian crown had been fulfilled. But just the opposite happened. The unification did not take place and Croat public opinion was continually irritated by Magyar inscriptions, Magyar emblems, and Magyar officials not knowing the language of the people. At the same time in the majority of cases men were put at the head of Croatian administration in the office of the banus who had no root in Croatian national life and who appeared before it as obedient instruments of the Budapest administration. As a matter of fact one can say that Croatia from the beginning of the Compromise until the collapse, with the exception of short intervals, was governed in an absolutistic way, which absolutism was more open and brutal than that on which the dualistic system was based, because, in such a unilingual and uniracial country as Croatia, this policy could only be based on the small and continually diminishing group of the "Magyarons."

Under such conditions the new system could only be maintained by a corrupt electoral and administrative practice which reached its culmination in the era of Count Khuen Héderváry, who governed the country for twenty years (1883–1903) with the help of his ill-famed method of the "horsewhip and oats." This crudely Machiavellian system may be regarded as the second spoiled and Balkanized edition of the system of Metternich. For, while the system of Metternich was mitigated by the extraordinary and highly cultured personality of the chancellor, the policy of Count Khuen introduced the most shrewd and ruthless methods of the Balkan politicians. Men of independent and honest conviction were persecuted, ousted from their offices and imprisoned, and were replaced by unscrupulous instruments of the absolutistic régime.[3] Thus the country was demoralized for generations. This policy was not only violent and corrupt, but even flagrant infringements of law were often applied. But the most fatal feature of this system of a Magyar *pashalic*[4] (as Otto Bauer characterized it) created by Khuen was the new *divide et impera* by which he played off the Serb minority against the renitent Croat majority, utilizing the religious and cultural difference between the two closely related tribes. The blind politician of violence did not perceive that this policy encouraged, properly speaking, the Serb irredenta directed against the monarchy. The Serbs were allowed to use their tricolors, the flag of

[3] The memoirs of Stephan Radić published by Charles H. Beard in *Current History* (October, 1928) casts a flood of light on these conditions. They demonstrate that even so malleable a personality as Radić, always inclined to compromise (he was capable of defending the imperialistic annexation policy of Aehrenthal in Russia!), migrated, so to say, from prison to prison under what he called the "slavery to Hungary and Austria."

[4] Turkish province where the Christian population was ruthlessly exploited by the ruling Turkish authority.

the Serbian kingdom, their schools were disproportionately favored, the Serbs newspaper subventioned from Belgrade remained undisturbed, whereas the Croatian papers were confiscated from day to day. In this manner the relative importance of the Serbs was artificially augmented to the detriment of the Croats in order to foment dissension and hatred between the two groups. This policy systematically undermined the foundations of the Magyar state. But Count Khuen saw only the petty struggles and tricks of his daily politics. His so-called Magyar patriotism was exhausted in carrying out all the measures ordered by Budapest, though he was not a Magyar chauvinist at all but rather an agent of the imperial policy of Vienna. The Magyar opposition called him a "Graničar," alluding to the blind loyalty to Vienna of the soldiers of the former military confines.

This system of absolutism, corruption, and artificial fostering of national struggles exasperated more and more Croatian public opinion. At the same time the separation of Croatia from Dalmatia and the other Jugo-Slav territories was increasingly felt as a burden in so far as national consciousness and the unity of the Jugo-Slav race was more clearly realized. The general dissatisfaction was further accentuated by the total apathy of Vienna concerning the complaints of the Croats. The people of Jelačić considered it a galling ingratitude that the Emperor, for whom they fought so strenuously in the drama of '48, now surrendered them completely to the absolutism of Khuen, to the rule of a man whose honor was publicly attacked without his obtaining satisfaction from the tribunal. The exasperation of the Croats spread throughout the territory of the Jugo-Slav monarchy. In 1903 the deputies of Dalmatia and Istria, members of the Austrian parliament, asked an audience of the Emperor in order to draw his attention to the sufferings of their co-nationals in Croatia. But the influence of the Hungarian government was sufficiently strong to obstruct the reception of the delegation. Habsburg repudiated ostentatiously his former allies who saved his throne. This affront had far-reaching consequences. The Croats, the most loyal nation of the monarchy, definitely lost confidence in the curing of their grievances with the help of the dualistic system. At the beginning of the twentieth century a new generation became active which had studied in foreign universities and which—enlightened especially by the teachings of Professor Masaryk—had acquired a clear conception of the solidarity of the whole Jugo-Slav race. The struggle of the Serbian kingdom for liberty and independence aroused the enthusiasm of many of the Croatian people. There was a growing conviction that the interests of the Serbs and Croats were common and that the *divide et impera* policy of Count Khuen meant only the oppression of both nations. The difference in religion and in the written language (the Croats use the Latin, the Serbs the Cyrillic alphabet) was of less and less significance in the face of the growing consciousness of the community of their national interests. Since 1903 the symptoms of a revolutionary movement became manifest in the entire Jugo-Slav world. The Macedonian uprising, the collapse of the Obrenović dynasty in Serbia, and the defeat of the Khuen system in Croatia were signs of the same changing spirit. The Hungarian constitutional crisis, the struggle of the Magyar national opposition against the crown contributed very much to the establishment of the Serbo-Croat unity. The politicians of Croatia and Dalmatia gave credit to the assertions of the Magyar coalition that they were fighting for a true democracy, not only for the rights of Hungary but also for the constitutional liberties of Croatia and that they were willing to fight for the union of Dalmatia with Croatia on the basis of the right of the Crown of St. Stephen. In this spirit the so-called "Resolution of Fiume" in 1905 made a declaration according to which "Croats and Serbs are the same nation, both by blood and language," and that they have the right "to decide freely and independently concerning their existence and future." Animated by this feeling the Croats and Serbs offered their alliance to the Magyar parties fighting for the independence of Hungary against the "Viennese camarilla." This turn caused great alarm in Vienna because it meant no less than that the successors of Jelačić, the sons of the "black-yellow[5] bodyguard of the Emperor" (as the Jugo-Slav officers were often called), would make an alliance with the son of Louis Kossuth, then leader of the Magyar coalition. Consequences of the greatest importance could have arisen from this new situation if the Magyar opposition, which soon came into power, had respected these principles and aided the Jugo-Slavs in the attainment of their unity and liberty inside the Hungarian crown. The greatest obstacle to a reasonable federalization of the monarchy would have been eliminated. But just the opposite happened. The Magyar opposition, in which naturally the great landed interests dominated, after having gained power betrayed not only universal suffrage promised to their own people, but also the principles embodied in the Resolution of Fiume. This episode, however, was advantageous to the Croats, since the elections in 1906 were relatively free and there was assembled a Sabor which expressed the real will of the country. The old methods of a half-hidden absolutism could not be continued. And when, a year later, the former leader of the Magyar coalition, then minister of commerce, Francis Kossuth, the unworthy son of the great exile, reassumed the policy of Magyarization on the Croatian lines of the state railways, the Sabor resisted energetically and the whole Croat-Serb public opinion attacked the government so violently that the banus, Baron Paul Rauch, the son of that Levin Rauch who forty years earlier carried through the Compromise by

---

[5] Black-yellow were the Imperial colors.

illegal means, was compelled to employ open absolutism. He tried also to continue the *divide et impera* politics of Khuen but in another direction, playing the Croats against the Serbs. But this reprise in Machiavellian politics was unsuccessful this time: the Croat-Serb unity proved to be unshakeable. Unfortunately, Hungarian public opinion did not understand at all, not even now, the extreme gravity of the situation. The chauvinistic press made a wild race and one of the most popular and influential organs wrote thus in March, 1908:

If we cannot convince the Croats, we must subdue them. We must prophesy that Hungary will still have bloody conflicts with the Croats and Hungary will be obliged to reconquer Croatia. It is not absolutely necessary that there should be a Diet in Zagreb. Laws must only be kept in the face of a nation which respects them. If Croatia cannot be governed in a constitutional way, it will simply be governed in an unconstitutional way. The positive work of Magyarization must finally begin in Croatia. . . . . If the Croats do not understand that they do not form an independent state beside Hungary, they must be convinced by arms.

And the most sorrowful aspect of the situation was that these and similar utterances were not only the shoutings of a jingo journalism but the emanations of a generally accepted doctrine according to which Croatia had no right to an independent constitutional life.

And the more the inner conflict became acute, the greater the Balkan chaos grew on the frontiers of the monarchy, the more the exasperation of the Christian Balkan peoples reached the boiling-point against Turkish rule: the more the dualistic *status quo* became difficult to maintain, the rulers were compelled to employ desperate methods. In order to discredit the Croat national movement and at the same time to justify, before international opinion, the action of foreign minister Aehrenthal, in the final annexation of Bosnia-Herzegovina, in the summer of 1908, a *razzia* was made against the Croat-Serb coalition, fifty-three members of which were arrested under the pretext that they had treacherous connections with Serbia. The monster process which was launched against them in March, 1909, made it manifest to any impartial observer that the documents of accusation were forgeries of police agents, and the moral depravity of the chief witness was proved without any doubt. In spite of this a packed tribunal, which refused the hearing of the witnesses of the defense, condemned most of the accused.

No wonder that such political machinations directed by the banus himself had a terrible effect on Jugo-Slav public opinion throughout the monarchy. This effect was even strengthened when Dr. Friedjung, the noted Austro-German historian, in connection with the scandals in Zagreb, produced documents against several Jugo-Slav politicians in order to demonstrate their conspiracies with Serbia. The men whose honor was attacked and life imperiled brought suit for defama-

tion against the historian which was carried on before a Viennese
tribunal, not under Balkan forms as the Zagreb process, but by distinguished judges and lawyers. Besides, domestic and foreign public
opinion was greatly aroused as it was widely known that Dr. Friedjung was a kind of an attorney of the foreign minister and his documents were given to him by the state department. The proceedings
entirely cleared the situation. The attacked politicians were able to
prove that Friedjung's documents were forgeries made with the special intention of compromising the Croat-Serb coalition and of justifying the policy of annexation of the monarchy. But even more than
this became public. In a session of the Austrian Delegation (February, 1910), Professor Masaryk, the present president of the Czecho-
Slovak republic, demonstrated that those documents upon which the
whole high treason comedy was based, had been forged in Belgrade in
the Austro-Hungarian embassy with the assistance of Count Forgách,
the Austro-Hungarian minister. Masaryk called Forgách a second
Azev (that was the name of an ill-famed Russian *agent provocateur*)
and the foreign minister was unable to defend the Serbian representative of the monarchy. In spite of this, Count Forgách remained in
foreign service, nay, he was rewarded by promotion.

These two processes undermined the entire moral prestige of the
monarchy not only in Croatia but in the whole Jugo-Slav world. After
the years of absolutism and oppressive politics no one could believe
that a state in which such things could occur, would be capable of a
just solution of the complicated problem of the Jugo-Slav state aspirations. All clear-sighted men of the monarchy realized the extreme
gravity of the situation. Archduke Francis Ferdinand himself saw
with despair the growing dissatisfaction of the Croats, and on one occasion he sent the following message to the Croat people by one of
his Croat friends: "Please tell your Croats that they may once more
safeguard their traditional loyalty. As soon as I succeed to the
throne, I shall correct all the injustices which have been done to them."

But the situation became more and more desolate. The events
both of the internal and external policy were alienating the hearts of
the Jugo-Slavs of the monarchy. Even the last formalities of constitutionalism ceased to exist in Croatia under the royal commissariat
of Cuvaj. At the same time Count Tisza again subdued the Hungarian parliament by force and suppressed in blood the demonstrations of the proletariat of Budapest for universal suffrage. There
was not the slightest beam for the future in the whole monarchy. On
the other hand, the peasant democracy of the Serb kingdom advanced
more year by year in the building up of their nation state after a
brutal military revolution had shaken off the hated yoke of Obrenović. The whole Jugo-Slav world of the monarchy began to regard
Belgrade as a central point of the unity of their race. And when Ser-

bia in alliance with the Bulgarians and the Greeks began, in 1912, its victorious campaign against the Turks for the liberation of Old Serbia and Macedonia, almost all the Jugo-Slav population of the monarchy trembled with the solidarity of national consciousness. Even the Slovenians who both geographically and in their historical evolution stood the farthest from the community of the Jugo-Slav world, greeted with enthusiasm the liberators of their kindred folk: "There at Tshataldsha," said a Slovenian Catholic priest, Janez Krek, the great reformer and social politician of his people, in the Austrian parliament, "they fight for the last Slovenian peasant of the threatened Carinthian village. . . . ." The Jugo-Slav policy outside the frontiers of the monarchy began to interest the masses more deeply than that inside. Because inside of the frontiers only the system of absolutism continued, spiced with renewed attempts against the person of the hated banus.

The ghost of the irredenta gradually strangled the monarchy and the dynasty which was incapable of maintaining the final loyalty not only of the "rebellious" Magyars but also of the Croats who, three generations earlier, saved the throne of the Habsburgs.

PART VI
THE DANGER OF IRREDENTA

CHAPTER I

GENERAL CHARACTER OF THE PROBLEM

Rudolf Kjellén, looking back on the dissolution of the Habsburg monarchy, wrote the following conclusion:

A Great Power can endure without difficulty one Ireland, as England did, even three, as imperial Germany did (Poland, Alsace, Schleswig). Different is the case when a Great Power is composed of nothing else but Irelands, as was almost the history of Austro-Hungary. . . . .

This remark points without doubt to the immediate cause of the collapse of the empire, but we should not regard this process as an unavoidable historical necessity. As a matter of fact the monarchy has been surrounded with countries, the peoples of which were closely related in blood and language with the nations of the monarchy. Therefore all these peoples exercised an inevitable attraction on each other.[1] It is evident that the attraction of Germany for the Germans of Austria, that of Russia for the northern Slavs of the monarchy, that of the Serb kingdom for the Jugo-Slavs, that of Rumania for the Rumanians of Transylvania, that of Italy for the Italian settlements of the monarchy, aggravated the internal political situation, but from this fact we are not at all entitled to draw the conclusion that all these so-called irredentistic movements had the same significance or that the dissolution of the monarchy was unavoidable under the pressure of these forces.

If we analyze the irredentistic problems of the Dual Monarchy more carefully, we shall see that among them there was only one which could be regarded as insolvable in its essence: the Italian; whereas the solution of all the others was not at all a sociological or historical impossibility. On the contrary the key to the situation was in the hands of the monarchy and if it had seized the possibilities at the right time and if it had followed consequently a prudent policy for the satisfaction of the national interests of its peoples, the fate of the Austro-Hungarian monarchy would have taken an entirely different turn. Of course, I know that the adherents of a rigid mechanical determinism regard all discussions concerning a historical *fait accompli* as sterile and ridicule the question of whether a given, already accomplished, historical process could have taken a different turn, whether better and more fertile

---

[1] Perhaps in no country in the world was the connection between the inner and the foreign policy of the state so intimate and full of dangers as in the former Habsburg monarchy. On the theoretical foundation of this connection excellent remarks may be found in the book of Rudolf Goldscheid, *Das Verhältnis der Äussern Politik zur Innern* (Wien, 1914).

results could have been achieved by a more prudent and fair policy. Opposed to this materialistic point of view, I accept the theory of Renouvier, of the reversibility of the historical process, and regard the chief utility of all historical and sociological investigations to be to admonish us of the alternative possibilities of history.

Regarding the Habsburg drama from this point of view, we may note two opposite policies in dealing with the problems of the monarchy. One policy was represented by Eugene of Savoy, the great war lord and statesman, the benignant French genius of the monarchy, who clearly visualized as its chief task the expansion of Western culture and civilization toward the Balkans and the East, in territories in a backward state because of Turkish occupation. In order to attain this aim he urged at the peace negotiations of Passarović in 1718 the annexation of the liberated territories, especially parts of Bosnia and Serbia, Wallachia and Moldavia, to the monarchy. At a time when the national consciousness of these territories was almost entirely dormant and when the most elementary conditions of culture were still lacking, such an enlargement of the Habsburg empire, combined with an efficient economic and cultural policy, could have put an end to all those external complications which envenomed the history of the whole nineteenth century and could have facilitated immensely the peaceful national integration of these territories. This road was not closed to the monarchy even later. The Habsburg empire in the first half of the nineteenth century was in economics and culture at least a hundred years in advance of the Balkans and Eastern Europe. If this advantage had been utilized in a prudent way, if a system of national autonomy had been established for all the nations of the monarchy, and if the empire had been gradually transformed into a system of a free confederation of peoples, the monarchy could then have developed an irresistible attraction for the related nations living outside its territory. It was not written in the book of Destiny with a fatal inevitability that the Jugo-Slavs of the monarchy must gravitate in any case toward Belgrade, nor that the Rumanians of Transylvania must tend of necessity toward the center of Bucharest; under appropriate conditions just the opposite tendency could have been operative and the Serbs in the Serb kingdom could have gravitated toward Zagreb in order to attain Jugo-Slav unity or the Rumanians of the Rumanian kingdom could have tended toward Transylvania as the Piedmont of the united Rumanian national state. Not only the powerful German and the comparatively highly developed Magyar and Czech cultures could have exercised the influence of a magnet, but there began also to develop a very propitious Croatian, Serb, and Rumanian culture in territories of the Hungarian crown which under adequate constitutional conditions would have attracted their semi-barbarous co-nationals beyond the frontiers into the orbit of the monarchy. The Hungarian Serb town, Novi Sad was called for a long time the "Serb Athens" and it was said that the "brain of Transylvania migrated to Bucharest and Jaşi." At the same time Zagreb was a real cultural center in a period when Belgrade was scarcely more than an oriental village.

As a matter of fact the road indicated by Eugene of Savoy never disappeared completely from the consciousness of the peoples and of the abler statesmen. That was the spirit which inspired the constitution of Kremsier, the reforms of Hohenwart-Schäffle, the plans of the Czech Austro-Slavism, the revival of Illyrism in the form of Trialism, which animated the political conception of Fischhof and Eötvös and even the anti-Habsburg confederation vision of Louis Kossuth. The kernel of all these plans and visions was the idea that the complicated national problems of the monarchy and of the Balkans could only be solved on the basis of a reasonable federalism which would have secured the peaceful expansion of the Western culture toward the backward countries but at the same time also the individual development of each nation and an appropriate unification of its ethnographic settlements. On the basis of this conception the monarchy should have assumed the rôle of a protector of the Christian Balkan peoples then languishing under the Turkish yoke, the rôle of an elder brother, endeavoring to promote with action and advice the future of its weaker and oppressed brothers.

Opposed to this policy never seriously tried in the monarchy was another idea, the conception of Metternich, the policy of the *status quo* and of the stabilization which regarded the national problems exclusively from the point of view of the legitimist dynasties. From the point of view of this policy the struggles of the Balkan Christian nations for emancipation against the Turks were revolutionary upheavals against the *status quo* of the legitimist powers and they tried, therefore, to conserve the Turkish rule which became entirely corrupt and obsolete. Metternich used to say:

The Porte is like a person who became incurably sick with a chronic disease. Her maintenance is an important thing for her friends and even for strangers because her death would be harmful for their interests. . . . . The great powers, especially Austria, face as advisory physicians the task of prolonging as far as possible the life of the patient, her salvation being impossible. . . . .

But in reality this policy was not so innocent as portrayed by the Chancellor and Freiherr von Stein, the great Prussian statesman, was perfectly right when he said of Metternich that "he oppresses the Greek in order to hinder the Russian movement and sharpens and directs the murderous knife of the Turks."[2] This policy in its later de-

---

[2] Cf. Heinrich Ritter von Srbik, *op. cit.*, II, 470, 625, 684.

velopment, in the hands of the weaker successors of the chancellor, became chiefly an instrument for the frustration of the growing efforts for Jugo-Slav unity. The system became more and more a playing off of the various Balkan nations against each other in order to avoid the unification of a Jugo-Slav state which would have menaced the fundamental thought of the Dualistic Constitution: the German-Magyar hegemony.

With the consequences of this policy we will deal later as the most fatal force which undermined the monarchy. At this juncture I would like only to emphasize that the extreme danger of this policy of the *status quo* and the cogent necessity of rebuilding the monarchy by utilizing the federative aspirations of its peoples became more and more a *communis opinio* not only in the eyes of the more objective foreign observers but also in the opinion of the more thoughtful politicians of Austria. At the beginning of the twentieth century an extensive literature arose which (however different may have been the individuality of its writers and their political tendencies) was based on the common thought that the system of the German-Magyar hegemony had become untenable, that the monarchy should be transformed in the spirit of a confederation in order to make it possible that the natural attraction between the Slavs and the Rumanians of the monarchy toward their brethren beyond the frontiers should lose its destructive character. In this manner the Habsburg monarchy, instead of becoming the Eastern and Southern bridge of the German imperialism, should have been transformed into a state organization of conciliation and separation between the Pan-German and Pan-Slav imperialistic tendencies.

Amid the tempests of the annexation crisis, when the final incorporation of Bosnia and Herzegovina put Europe on the verge of a world war, a Serb statesman, Stojan Protić, said with great clearness in the Parliament of Belgrade:

Between Austria-Hungary and the Balkan states peace and good neighborhood can only be established when the Danube monarchy decides to assume the rôle of an Eastern Switzerland. As long as it continues to play the rôle of a Great Power, it will be under the necessity of making new conquests in the Balkan peninsula. . . . .

This opinion was corroborated from a retrospective point of view by one of the ablest diplomats of the former monarchy. Baron J. Szilassy in a courageous book has demonstrated that the annexation policy of Aehrenthal was the most fatal blow to the monarchy and that the system of dualism made the peaceful solution of its problems impossible. In this connection he made the following profound remark:

It should not be forgotten that if instead of the Dual System there had existed a large Danube Federation, several of the national Irredentas could have been appeased inside of its frontiers. I am thinking chiefly of the

Jugo-Slavs. Some of their distinguished statesmen have preconized this solution. . . . . A well balanced federation would have created harmony, as history has shown in many examples. . . . . This Danube Federation . . . . would not have been forced to make a common cause with the German Empire, not yet satiated. . . . . Rather it would have every reason to seek a close connection with the Western Powers, interested chiefly in the maintenance of their possessions. . . . . Western Europe would have every interest in protecting this liberal federation against eventual desires for expansion of Russia or Germany. . . . .[3]

But none of the active German or Hungarian statesmen of the monarchy visualized the gravity of the existing situation, with the only exception of Count Michael Károlyi, then leader of the Independent Party, who made a last effort to regalvanize the policy of Kossuth for a Danube Federation. For this scope he advocated universal suffrage and dismemberment of the *latifundia* in the internal policy and a rapprochement toward France and the Slavs in the external policy by terminating the Dualistic Constitution. Guided by these principles he went to Paris in 1913 and discussed the possibilities of such a new orientation with Messrs. Poincaré and Clemenceau. This latter remarked that the idea was excellent, but it came too late because Austro-Hungary was already too much engaged in the opposite direction.[4]

[3] *Der Untergang der Donau-Monarchie* (Bern, 1921), pp. 40–42.
[4] *Fighting the World*, pp. 78–80.

CHAPTER II

THE PSEUDO-IRREDENTAS

A. THE GERMAN SEPARATISM

If we regard more carefully the so-called irredentistic problems of the monarchy, we find that among them the German, the Czech, the Polish, and the Ruthenian were not real irredentas nor could they ever develop into such if a prudent and constructive policy had been followed.

As to German separatism, we have seen already in another connection that there never was a serious German irredentistic movement in Austria, that it signified rather a sentimental attachment to Germany or at best a sulky protestation against the growing influence of the Slavs which menaced German hegemony. But the force of the dynasty, of the army, and of the Church was so strong in Austria that a real German separtistic movement could not develop. We saw that the *Los von Rom* movement with outspoken anti-Habsburg tendencies ended in a complete fiasco and the Pan-German idea never had behind it a truly revolutionary movement. It is true that some of its leaders, for instance K. H. Wolf, spoke publicly of a *Germania Irredenta* and that enthusiastic young men began to sing seditious rhymes:

> Wir schielen nicht, wir schauen
> Wir schauen unverwandt,
> Wir schauen voll Vertrauen
> Ins deutsche Vaterland. . . .[1]

But the entire movement remained always a rather sentimental or tactical protestation, the more as the leading circles of Berlin never sympathized with this tendency. The German official policy followed to the end the conception of Bismarck, who with his keen sense of reality understood very well that the union of the Austrian Germans with Germany would lead not only to a renewed armed conflict between the Habsburgs and the Hohenzollerns but that it would possibly also kindle a world war because the Slav peoples of Austria would develop the most exacerbated resistance to such a policy. This price would have been too high from the point of view of the German empire, the more so, since the Austrian Germans could render more precious services to the whole German nation outside of the German empire than inside without the Slavs or struggling with a disparate Slav minority. "The German Austrian," said Bismarck, "is justified to aspire for political

---

[1] We leer not, we look, we look steadily, we look trustingly to the German fatherland.

leadership and should safeguard the interests of Germandom in the Orient, serving as the tie of contact between Germans and Slavs by hindering their collision."[2] As a matter of fact Austria played more and more the rôle of a bridge between Germany and the Danube basin, and the Balkans. This German economic and cultural expansion was quite natural in consequence of the geographical position of Germany and of her technical and scientific superiority, and this tendency would have been even more prominent if the saber-rattling German imperialism and the anti-Slav dualistic system of the monarchy had not aroused more and more the antipathy and distrust of the Slav and if the wise maxim of Bismarck had been followed, according to which "he was not willing to sacrifice even the bones of a single Pomeranian grenadier" for the Balkan policy of Austria.

One can say that until the World War and until the conception of a *Mitteleuropa* which followed the first victories of the Central Powers, the official standpoint of the German empire remained the unaltered retention of the Habsburg monarchy. To the report of Prince Lichnowsky, already quoted (in which he gave an account of the symptoms of dissolution of the Austrian monarchy) the foreign secretary, Bernhard von Bülow, gave the following answer, better say, categoric instruction to the Prince (June, 1898) :

. . . . Our political interest, to which all platonic sympathies should be subordinated . . . . lies in the maintenance of Austro-Hungary in its present independence as a Great Power. This interest demands that we be on our guard to discourage disintegrating tendencies in Austria whether they come from the Czech, Polish, or German side. The German-Austrians should not remain in doubt that as long as their struggle for the German cause is animated by an effort to safeguard Germandom as a cement for the inner cohesion and further maintenance of the Austrian state in its present form, we follow their aspirations with the most complete sympathy. But at the same time they should know that as soon as this struggle has as its final aim the separation of the German provinces from Austria and with this a return to the *status quo* of before 1866, the German nationalists cannot count on the promotion of their plans from our side. . . . .

B. THE CZECH SEPARATISM

In the same sense one could not speak of a Czech irredenta in the proper meaning of the term, because the essence of the Czech separatistic tendencies was the same as that of the Magyars: an effort for constitutional independence, the unification of the countries of the Czech crown under national government. There was no foreign point of attraction, the union with which could have been a really serious aim of the Czech policy. Not even the thought of a union with their kindred folk, the Slovaks of Hungary, was in their minds, until the

[2] Quoted by Richard Charmatz, *Österreichs innere Geschichte* (Leipzig u. Berlin, 1918), II, 95.

World War, a realizable program. The state independence of the Czech historical territories in Austria and a moderate autonomy for the Slovaks inside the Hungarian crown would have satisfied both the Czechs and the Slovaks completely if such a constitutional reform would have been carried on at the right time.[3] The Czech separatism, therefore, signified just the same thing as the Magyar: the guaranty of the independence of the state in the spirit of the historical right. This was clearly felt by the leader of Hungarian independence, by Louis Kossuth himself, who, in his devastating criticism against the Dualistic Compromise, wrote among others the following statement:

Bohemia, from the point of view of historical justice, has the same right to regard itself as a distinct autonomous state as Hungary; even, if possible, it would have more right because it is a fact that Bohemia had already been a flourishing state for centuries, when we Hungarians were not yet in Europe.[4]

One might even say that Czech separatism was far less dangerous from the point of view of the monarchy than the Magyar. For the Czechs, from the first awakening of the democratic national spirit until the dissolution of the monarchy, were not disinclined to accept the plan that the future independent Bohemia would become a part of a federal state and they would have willingly participated in a central parliament including all the nations of the monarchy as equal members. Just the opposite was the Magyar point of view, even that of the loyal dualistic circles, namely, that Hungary could not accept any state community or super-national central organ with the other nations of the monarchy.

And if, in spite of this, the danger of Pan-Slavism had always irritated the German and the Magyar leading elements and if it became a fashion to denounce Czech national aspirations as a result of Russian propaganda, that was the result of this unfortunate policy which by the German-Magyar hegemony, by the Magyar policy of assimilation, and the brutal handling of the Jugo-Slav problem always offended the Slav nations of the monarchy, especially the very developed

[3] At the beginning of a conscious national movement in the nineteenth century a serious literary and cultural movement was started among the Slovaks of Hungary under the leadership of Stur, Hurban, and Hodža for the elaboration of the Slovak language and culture distinct from the Czech. If instead of the policy of a forcible Magyarization this movement would not have been hindered, but protected by the Hungarian government, it is very probable that the gap between the Slovaks and the Czechs would have assumed proportions hostile to any efforts for unification. National culture and autonomy of the Slovak territory could have become a powerful bulwark against the Czech influence the more as the historical atmosphere, the national temperament, and the social customs of the Slovaks were nearer to the Magyars than to the Czechs whose nationalism, hussitism, and business efficiency is still a factor for misunderstanding, even hatred among the two kindred peoples. (A good analysis for this situation was given by R. W. Seton-Watson in his book, *The New Slovakia*, Praha, 1924.)

[4] *Writings of Louis Kossuth*, VII, 367–68. In Hungarian.

constitutional and cultural conscience of the Czechs. We have seen already that the claims for national autonomy of the Czechs were never satisfied, nay, that the most solemn pledges of the Emperor were broken in order to maintain unaltered the German-Magyar hegemony. Under such circumstances it was quite natural that the Czechs fixed their eyes more and more on the big Russian brother when they saw that they could not guarantee their national independence in a peaceful, constitutional way and that only a new catastrophe, a new Königgrätz could solve their problem. But this feeling of solidarity never was a serious irredenta, because it could not be such. A union with Russia was an impossibility from a geographic, an ethnographic, and a cultural point of view. The Czechs were separated form their remote Russian brothers by the national settlements of the Poles and the Ruthenians, peoples with which the Czechs had no real cultural connection. Besides the Czech culture was entirely a Western one, penetrated by the ideals of Humanism, the Reformation, and democracy. There was, therefore, no serious possibility for a union with Tsarist Russia and that romantic Pan-Slavistic plan which talked of a union of the smaller Slav nations under Russian hegemony from the future center of Constantinople was not only then a Utopia but it will probably remain such for centuries.

Under such circumstances the flirting of the Czech intelligentsia with Pan-Slavism, their pilgrimages to Russia, their enthusiastic cultural connections with Russian intellectual life, and the growing emphasis of Slav solidarity did not signify a possible or serious irredentistic movement but rather a tactical and also a sentimental position. It signified the magic charm of the Slav world-empire to the youthful spirits; it signified the canalization of the national exasperation into the sea of Pan-Slavism; it signified the attraction of national affinity, the possibility of imposing threats for Czech politicians against the Viennese court and government; it signified the moral and material protection of Czech intelligentsia by the Russian pan-Slavistic literary and scientific associations; and, finally, it signified the propaganda of the Russian emissaries who promised the guaranty of a brilliant Czech future when the day of last judgment, the *dies irae, dies illa,* between Pan-Slavism and Pan-Germanism comes.

Of course, the more things became envenomed in Austria, in Hungary, and in the Balkans, the less was the prospect probable that the aspirations of the northern and southern Slavs for their independent states would be realized within the frontiers of the monarchy. And the more all Europe was segragated into two military camps which by a system of alliances and counter-alliances prepared feverishly for the final fray, the more important became the card of sentimental and cultural Pan-Slavism in the hands of the leading Russian circles for utilizing the hatred of the Slavs of the monarchy against the countries which refused to accept them as equal partners in their constitutional life.

We have seen that this propagandistic effort of Russian imperialism was to a large extent successful during the war and became one of the chief causes of the dissolution of the monarchy. This process however was not a fatal, unavoidable one. On the contrary, we have shown already in our historical analysis that the most serious and influential elements of the Czechs, beginning with their great leader, Palacký, embraced quite sincerely the point of view that Austria should be maintained on the basis of the equality of their peoples. This conception was enlarged by several northern and southern Slav political writers to a doctrine called *Austro-Slavism* which opposed the sentimental romanticism of Pan-Slavism with the distinct national individuality of the Slav peoples and advocated the maintenance of a democratized and federalized Austria as a natural bulwark for the free development of the smaller Slav peoples. The most consequent exponent of this tendency was the brilliant political thinker of the Czechs, Karel Havlíček (1821–56). He put the consciousness of his nation above the Slav solidarity. The Slav peoples are distinct national individualities as, for instance, the French and Spanish. The Austrian monarchy could become the supreme protector of the Czech and the Illyrian nationality. He emphasized the fact that the Slavs have four fatherlands and the idea of a general Slav patriotism was as vague as the idea of cosmopolitanism. "I am not a Slav, I am a Czech," he used to say and urged the Austrian government to defend also the Ruthenians against the oppressive tendencies of the Poles. After the revolutionary collapse in 1850, he admonished the ruling circles that an Austria protecting the Slavs would be capable of drawing also the Jugo-Slavs into its sphere of influence and of acquiring, by the way of a spontaneous gravitation, the largest part of the Turkish inheritance which would be an excellent change for the Italian territories, maintainable only by armed force.

This spirit of Austro-Slavism was sometimes called a hypocrisy or a purely tactical chess game, but it represented without doubt a sincere and natural tendency. The Czechs had no serious interest in fostering a policy of irredentism if they could have an opportunity of developing their own national state inside the monarchy. As a matter of fact, until the dissolution of the empire there were never lacking influential and authoritative voices which emphasized the necessity of such a solution. Not only the small group of Professor Masaryk, called the Czech Realists, sought peace and compromise with the other nations of the monarchy but even the leader of the younger Czech nationalists, Karel Kramař, though he was a leading man of the Russian solidarity, emphasized the possibility of a Czech compromise if they could build up their own national state as the Magyars did.

Nay, even after the World War, after the creation of an independent Czecho-Slovak state, in 1926, the same Kramař upheld retrospectively the correctness of this point of view which was desirous of solving the Slav problems without arousing catastrophes, a point of view advocated even during the World War by several Austro-Slav politicians. In regard to such plans Kramař wrote:

Was not a prudent and honest Austrian policy possible, such a one as our men since Palacký and Havliček have advocated, because they wished sincerely the continuation of Austria, a policy which would have made also the Serbs friends of Austria by becoming so just toward them that they would not aspire for a state beyond the frontiers and would estimate as superfluous the arousing of a catastrophe which might have ultimately also a sinister outcome for the Serbs and the Slavs . . . .?

The Czech statesmen gave an affirmative answer to this question. Naturally, for obtaining this aim quite a different policy, a different public morality and above all a different civic education would have been necessary.

C. THE POLISH SEPARATISM

That the problem of irredentism is not directed by a special mystical affinity and that it is not inevitable that a people in the minority must ogle beyond the frontiers or foment irredentistic plots but that the tendency of the national minorities is determined by the "law of the least social and national resistance," was clearly proved by the history of the Polish national minority of the monarchy. The Poles were for a long period the most restless and unreliable elements of the monarchy. Metternich regarded them with complete distrust. "The 'Polonism,'" he said, "is only a formula, a slogan, beyond which the revolution is hidden in its crudest form, it is the revolution itself." Indeed, as a matter of fact both in 1846 and 1863 the revolutionary dissatisfaction of the Poles flared up violently. But the situation changed when the Viennese government assumed a conciliatory attitude and when, abandoning the policy of German centralization, a complete national autonomy was granted to the Poles in Galicia. Especially the Compromise of 1867 made the influence of the Poles in the monarchy very conspicuous since, for the maintenance of the dualistic system the Austrian governments needed the votes of the Polish Club in the Viennese parliament. In consequence of the new equilibrium the Poles became the pampered children of the leading circles, the *Zunge an der Wage*, and they were allowed to build up an almost national state in Galicia which was often victorious over the Central administration. The Poles were not hindered in establishing their administrative, cultural, and economic organizations, nay, the Viennese government tacitly tolerated the continuous effort of the Polish nobility to curb under their yoke the Ruthenian peasant masses, almost half of the population of Galicia. Whereas the Poles of Prussia sighed under the heavy burden of the Germanizing policy and of the system of forcible expropriation and whereas the autocratic brutality of Russian Tsarism strangled the Polish minority, Austria became the envied province of Polish liberty and independence. The Austrian Poles, or to speak more correctly, the Polish nobility (because there was an enormous gulf between the Polish landlords and the wretched peasantry) began to feel themselves comfortable and became the most loyal subjects of His Majesty and the most important offices and diplomatic positions of the monarchy were intrusted to them. Since they had their own national autonomy and the possibilities of a free cultural development, not the slightest revolutionary ripple or irredentistic agitation was to be observed among them. On the contrary, their co-nationals under Prussian and Russian oppression began to extol the Galician conditions as a model state where, especially in the city of Cracow, a powerful center of Polish literature, science and art arose. Of course, the Austrian Poles continued to cherish the dream of the re-establishment of the former historical unity of the Polish state but this seeming Utopia had not the least sentiment against Austria and, therefore, the Polish nobility could develop unchecked their national aspirations. They were not only undisturbed in this but their attitude was rather sympathetic from the point of view of the ruling elements who understood that in the case of unification Austria would have a powerful attraction for all the Poles. Futhermore the Poles were so satisfied with their constitutional situation in Austria that when on the Austro-German side plans were made according to which Galicia should receive a complete autonomy analogous to that which Croatia had toward Hungary (in order that by the absence of the Poles, a German majority could be secured in the Austrian parliament) such plans aroused not the least sympathy among the Poles who enjoyed and utilized their power in the monarchy.

During the World War, too, strong sympathies were manifested for the monarchy which could have exercised a considerable force in favor of the Central Powers if the reminiscences of the Prussian policy in Posen had not pressed on a part of the Poles and if the monarchy and Germany had not been so short-sighted and hesitating in their Polish policy, but had accepted openly and determinedly the program of a united Poland as an independent state of the Habsburg empire. But the dualistic system in Austria and the Prussian policy in Germany made such a policy unworkable. Later the adventure in the Ukraine, as we have already seen, made the Poles enemies of the monarchy. Leon Bilinski, the Polish statesman who was several times Austrian and joint minister of finance and who became for a period minister of the newly created Polish state, wrote his memoirs before his death still in a loyal spirit to the Habsburgs and came to the conclusion that the dissolution of the monarchy was due to three facts:

to the incapacity of the Habsburg to conclude the Austro-Polish solution, to the megalomania of the German government on the occasion
of the peace negotiations in 1917, and to the fatal nationality policy
of Hungary.[5]

D. THE RUTHENIAN IRREDENTISM

The Ruthenian separatism shows the same tendencies as the Polish,
though in another direction. The Ruthenian population of Austria
was for a long time famous for its loyal dynastical attitude. They
were called the "Tyrolians of the East" or the "Galician Piedmont"
because the Ruthenian settlements of Austria began to exercise a certain attraction on their Ukrainian brothers of the same racial stock
who were languishing under the yoke of the Russian autocracy and
forceful assimilation. This Ruthenian minority was regarded for
some time as a good balance against the revolutionary Polish nobility.
At the same time the development of a special Ruthenian culture was
favored and protected in Vienna as a bulwark against undermining
endeavors of Russian imperialism.

This attitude, however, of this loyal people was changed radically
after Galicia was surrendered to the Polish nobility which interfered
with the national and political rights of the Ruthenian minority. This
Polish-Ruthenian antagonism, made even more acute by the economic
and social pressure of the big Polish estates, proved to be an efficient
instrument in the hands of Russian Pan-Slavism for fostering irredentistic tendencies in Galicia and Bukowina. Indeed, Pan-Slavism
was successful in arousing a pro-Russian feeling in some regions of
the Ruthenian peasantry. The Ruthenian people in its cultural backwardness (in Bukowina 54 per cent and in Galicia 41 per cent of the
population over ten years were illiterate) and in its social misery did
not know that their Ukraine brothers in Russia were even more oppressed than they and that the rôle of the Polish nobility was played
there by the Russians. Russian Pan-Slavism made its propaganda not
only by the "rolling of rubles" and manipulating the feelings of the
people, exasperated by social and political abuses, but also by utilizing the deep religious mysticism of the people which instinctively resented the papal union of its clergy and on which the old orthodox religion had a great sentimental appeal. Therefore, in certain regions
the political propaganda was administered under a semi-religious disguise and the Tsar became a kind of divine protector for the persecuted Ruthenians of Austria.

This Pan-Slav propaganda was carried on almost openly without
being counterbalanced by any effort for a reasonable civic education.
On the contrary, the Poles, knowing the low cultural standard and the
unorganized state of the Ruthenian peasantry, did not take this move-

[5] *Reminiscences and Documents* (Warsaw, 1924–25). In Polish.

ment seriously but even fostered it because it counterbalanced the political influence of the Ruthenians loyal to Austria, their really serious
opponents, and at the same time they could extol themselves as guard-
ians of the Austrian state idea against the "treacherous Ruthenians."
This political play was so ruthless and hypocritical that in the younger Ruthenian generation a revolutionary spirit arose, which led to
the killing of the governor of Galicia, Count Potocki, by a Ruthenian
student in 1898. Though a part of the Viennese circles knew very well
the nature of the problem and the ambiguous rôle of the Polish nobility, the government did not dare to interfere with it, according to its
policy of *Fortwursteln* ("bungling along in the old groove"). For in
order to extirpate the Ruthenian irredenta certain fundamental reforms were needed, among them the elimination of Polish supremacy, a
courageous agrarian reform, complete religious equality, all things
with which Vienna could not experiment the less so because these necessary reforms would have again created a Polish separatism, would
have irritated the Roman Catholic church, the pillar of the empire,
and what was the most important, they would have endangered the
Dualistic Constitution itself which rested partly on the shoulders of
the Poles. Under these conditions it was quite natural that the dynasty and its government chose rather the seemingly harmless, rather sentimental irredentism of the peaceful, weak, and unorganized Ruthenian subjects and abdicated from the "Eastern Tyrolians" to the
benefit of the Polish *Szlachta*.

The irredentistic movement of the Ruthenians of Hungary was
even more naïve and sentimental. The social and cultural background
was even darker than in Austria. Illiteracy, slow starvation, the pressure of the big estates and of the feudal administration, ruthless usury, the alliance of the Greek Catholic church with the corrupt county
potentates were a propitious field for Pan-Slavistic propaganda,
which, under the disguise of orthodox Greek oriental religion, was administered as a species of social narcotics. As a matter of fact this
wretched people had no idea of the political motives of the Pan-Slav
propaganda but embraced enthusiastically the traditional religion of
Russia, exciting its religious imagination and at the same time offering to the poor peasants sacred books in their own language in a surrounding where the Magyarization policy of the schools and of the administration left the intellectual longings of the people unsatisfied.

Immediately before the World War a sensational process was en-
acted against the so-called schismatic Ruthenians who tried to secede
from the Greek Catholic church and to join the Greek Oriental church
of Hungary. Though this aspiration was perfectly legitimate from a
jural point of view, the Greek Catholic church denounced it as a plot
of high treason fomented by the Pan-Slav agitation. This process
carried on at Mármarossziget, a town of Northeastern Hungary,

aroused an international excitement because some leading figures of the Russian Pan-Slav movement were also involved in it. The better part of the Hungarian intelligentsia saw with despair the dark, medieval atmosphere of the whole process fomented by a greedy clergy who feared that the religious secession of the Ruthenian peasantry would diminish their ecclesiastical incomes. It became manifest that though the Russian propaganda played without doubt a certain part in this tragic religious hysteria of the Ruthenian people, it was mainly a result of their cultural isolation, economic misery and of the abuses of the local administration. A Hungarian attorney for the defense of the accused peasants wrote:

The chief lesson for us of the Ruthenian schismatic movement is that the religious persecution arranged by the Greek Catholic clergy, allied with the local administration [the people of the villages were surrounded by gendarmerie, then heavily fined because they performed secretly during the night those religious exercises forbidden by the authorities], created the possibilities of a Russian religious propaganda. That this religious propaganda found, curiously enough through America where the emigrated Hungarian Ruthenians narrated their sufferings to their co-nationals, the Ruthenian schismatics, this is in its final result only a painful episode of the Hungarian democracy.

It is quite natural that in this atmosphere the Russian religious propaganda should begin to assume a national color too and that the Ruthenian peasant, persecuted in his religious life,[6] should regard more and more the mystic personality of the Tsar as his liberator from the ecclesiastical and administrative yoke which he felt in his naïve consciousness simply as a Magyar yoke. . . . .

[6] The superstitious, but at the same time extremely popular character of the Greek Orthodox religion which makes its priests in the culturally backward provinces almost magicians or primitive "medicine-men" had a great influence in the "nationalistic propaganda" (A. Bonkáló, *The Slavs* [Budapest, 1915], pp. 22–27. In Hungarian).

CHAPTER III
THE TRUE IRREDENTAS

As for real irredentas, in the proper sense, meaning the effort of a national minority to secede from the community of the state and to unite with another, to that of their co-nationals, there were only three in the monarchy: the Italian, the Rumanian, and the Jugo-Slav. Of these, only the first was a problem insoluble in its essence.

A. THE ITALIAN IRREDENTA

Since the formation of the Italian unity, it was inevitable that the Italian kingdom should exercise a great and irresistible influence on the Italian minority of Austria. (A population of about seven and a half hundred thousands before the World War.) This minority lived partly scattered, partly as compact settlements in southern Tyrol, in the southwestern parts of Görz and in the western regions of Istria. The attraction of the Italian territories toward Italy was quite natural, though it did not perhaps permeate the deepest strata of the population. The spell of an old historical culture, the community of the historic traditions, the desire for an economic and cultural unity would have manifested itself to a certain degree even in case Austria had signified a higher culture and a greater freedom. However, it did not signify this, but foreign rule, the obstacle to a richer cultural development, and the absence of a free local autonomy. And combined with these were the terrible memories of the Austrian *soldatesca* in their mother-country. Add to all this the continuous propaganda of Italian imperialism and of nationalistic romanticism for the Tyrolese and Triestene irredenta and for the *mare nostro*. One should not forget that Garibaldi had already conquered southern Tyrol in 1866, and though he was unable to hold the provinces, this memory was kindling enthusiasm in Italian public opinion.

Under such circumstances the Italian territories meant a debit item for Austria, a source of internal strife and external complications which heightened the dangers of the other irredentas. A really enlightened Austrian policy therefore would have been a final conciliation with Italy by the cessation of its closed national settlements. As a recompense for this policy Austria could have easily obtained the agreement to declare the harbors of Trieste and Fiume free cities, *porto franco*, international centers for the trade. This solution would have been the most advantageous both from the Austrian and Italian point of view because the hinterland of these harbors was mostly Slav and Magyar. This policy would have been without doubt a perfectly workable one if carried on tactfully with a prudent appreciation of the difficulties of the Italian policy. Before the catastrophe of König-grätz the Italian government made a formal proposition to Austria for the purchase of the province of Venezia and at the same time for Italian Tyrol it offered recompensation for the Habsburgs in another direction. The proposition was refused without any consideration.[1] Even during the World War there were serious endeavors to maintain the neutrality of Italy by pursuing this road.

The present-day imperialistic state, however, in consequence of its very nature and of the dogma of "the prestige of a Great Power and of national honor" could not follow such a policy of "abdication" even if such would be highly beneficial for the immense majority of the population of both countries. Instead of this, both parties prepared for a policy of catastrophe through which the people of Austria-Hungary finally lost their harbors and the German Tyrolese territory. The crime of this policy was the greater because the leading circles of Austria were perfectly aware of the fatal gravity of the Italian irredenta. One for instance who reads the book of Alois Ritter von Haymerle, a colonel of the general staff, written in 1879 under the title, *Italicae Res*, will see that the Austrian officer has unveiled all the details of the Italian intrigues. Haymerle has shown that this current was not restricted to a few romantic dreamers but embraced broad circles of society and enjoyed the secret protection of the government. At national festivals it was a custom to carry the flags of Trieste and Trentino covered with a mourning veil; the whole country was permeated with the organizations of the "Italia Irredenta"; on the maps used in the public schools, the political frontier facing Austria was drawn through the Brenner and southern Tyrol was designated as *Provincia del Trentino;* the patriotic irredentistic festivals were often frequented by high officials of the state, and by the members of Parliament and of the army leadership. Witnessing such and similar currents, the Austrian staff officers did not even mention a plan of compromise but his final conclusion was simply an appeal to the right of arms.

As a matter of fact this rigid conception of the right of conquest determined Austrian policy until the end. This policy was the more light-minded and short-sighted because at the same time no serious step was taken to satisfy the just claims of the Italian minority which could have appeased somewhat the tension between the two countries. The demand of an autonomy for southern Tyrol was frustrated by the German bureaucracy and chauvinism. Similarly without result remained the desire of the Italian minority for the creation of a university in the Italian tongue, a privilege enjoyed for a long time by other

[1] V. Bibl, *op. cit.*, II, 288.

nations of the monarchy which were less conspicuous in culture and national traditions. But the Austrian government was frightened by this plan because it feared (and not without reason) that under the envenomed conditions such a university would strengthen the irredentistic current. For this reason the cause of the Italian university was postponed and finally a half-measure was adopted to establish an Italian faculty connected with the German university of Innsbruck (the southern bulwark of the Germans) instead of the Italian scheme to create a university in Trieste, the real center of Italian life in Austria. The result of this tactlessness was a real battle between Italian and German students in the *Aula* of the university of Innsbruck which had a bloody continuation in the streets (1909). After this calamity the Italian faculty was transferred to Vienna but there the German-Italian fight broke out even more violently. The cause of an Italian university died and the result was only this, that it poured new oil on the fire of Italian irredenta: "instead of a university the Italian students received cudgels and revolver. . ."

The inflammatory acuteness of the Austrian-Italian relations was further accentuated at the occasion of the Triestine festivals in 1882 when Austria held an exposition to the memory of the fact that Trieste belonged for five hundred years to the Habsburg monarchy. During these festivals, the police detected three attempts with bombs against the members of the dynasty and the Emperor himself. The organizer of one of these plots, Oberdank, was sentenced to death by a tribunal and became, thereafter, an Italian national martyr, a real symbol of the Italian irredentistic movement.

The relation, envenomed more and more between the two countries, was not improved but rather aggravated by the conclusion of the so-called Triple Alliance (1882) which was the true expression of the immoral policy of imperialism in not considering the real feeling of the people. Italy, under the patronage of Bismarck, entered into the Alliance of Germany and Austro-Hungary in order to manifest its dissatisfaction against the Tunis policy of France. This treaty, the text of which was not then published, signified the worst continuation of a Machivellian policy between the new allied powers, Italy and Austria, which were rightly called the "strangest allies of the world" because they made incessant war preparations against each other, they erected fortifications on their respective frontiers, and the hatred of the Italians and the Austrians was systematically kindled. This spirit of animosity exploded already during the Annexation Crisis when the whole Italian political world assumed a passionately hostile attitude against the Austrian "ally" for its "robbery" in the Balkans and asked for compensations on the irredentist territories. The exacerbation of Italian public opinion was so great that Prime Minister Giolitti could scarcely pacify it and was himself compelled to play, almost unhidden, irredentistic tunes, speaking in Parliament of "premature impatience."

The Italian irredentism became more and more ruthless. For instance, General Asinari, commander of the Corps of Milano at the occasion of the inauguration festivity of the flag of a new cavalry regiment at Brescia, renewed in a speech the memory of the Austrian terror which reigned in this city half a century earlier and expressed the hope that Destiny would allow him some day to lead his soldiers against the traditional enemy. . . . . At Udine a doll representing the features of Francis Joseph was fabricated and was burned by the mob. . . . . At the same time the irredentistic literature became more and more violent. Under the title *La Preparazione*, a military-political periodical was started with the program of preparation for the future irredentistic war. And while the governments talked always officially of the "best," of the most cordial relations between the Allies, the propaganda of Gabriele d'Annunzio gained thousands and thousands for the irredentistic ideal and his book *La Nave* engraved the desire of the reconquest of the "Italian Sea" in the heart of the masses.

Meanwhile the turning of Italy toward the Entente became manifest and even an Italian-Slav rapprochement was skilfully arranged under French protection which had an open tendency against the Austro-Hungarian monarchy. It is quite natural that in this tense atmosphere the Austrian war party, too, made desperate efforts. In the first place, Conrad von Hötzendorf, who became chief of the staff in 1906, was quite aware that the Austrian-Italian relation was near to explosion and urged a preventive war against the Italians because he came to the right conclusion that things were rapidly tending toward an Italian-Jugo-Slav-Russian coalition against the Habsburg monarchy. That is the reason why Conrad advised, in 1911, when Italy had serious difficulties in Tripoli, an attack on the "ally," that is to say, to administer this "stab in the back" which, according to the Austrian terminology, Italy performed against her ally during the World War.

B. THE RUMANIAN IRREDENTA

The nature of the Rumanian irredenta differed substantially from the Italian. Speaking in round numbers, three and a quarter million Rumanians lived in the territory of the Habsburg monarchy (the bulk of whom, about three millions, were in Hungary) and six millions in the Rumanian kingdom. Therefore the Rumanian irredenta was not a small minority, as was the Italian, compared with the whole nation, but it was a very conspicuous settlement, the population of which liked to regard themselves as the successors of the Roman inhabitants of Dacia. The tradition of this Dacian affinity heightened very much the national consciousness of the Rumanians of Transylvania and the doctrine of the Daco-Rumanian origin became the chief ideology of the irredentistic thought and of the endeavor to unite all the Rumanian territories. Though the historical foundations of this doctrine are hotly debated, it is probable that a part of the Rumanians of Transylvania belonged to the oldest elements of the country and the history of Transylvania was always a Magyar-Rumanian history. The Transylvanian and the Hungarian Rumanians had, therefore, all reason to regard Hungary as their native land.[2] (The Rumanians of Bukowina, numbering about 250,000, we can omit in the consideration of the irredentistic situation, because they lived in an almost complete separation from the Rumanian settlements of Hungary, as there was no direct railway connection between Bukowina and Transylvania. The interest of the Rumanians of Bukowina was absorbed in the Rumanian-Ruthenian antagonism and, therefore, their rôle in the irredentistic current was an insignificant one.)

There were also other reasons which would have made it possible that a Rumanian irredenta should not develop or that it should take quite another direction, that it should gravitate not toward the Rumanian kingdom but toward Transylvania. Namely, the Habsburg monarchy compared with the Rumanian kingdom, which not until the beginning of the sixties of the last century adopted the forms of Western civilization, could have exercised a mighty economic and cultural attraction upon all the Rumanians if it could have secured the unimpeded national development of the Rumanians inside its own frontiers. Besides, the real kernel of the Rumanian culture was first developed in Transylvania where some far-sighted Hungarian princes promoted intentionally the linguistic and ecclesiastic culture of the Rumanian race. Under such circumstances it would have been a comparatively easy task to maintain the cultural and economic hegemony of the Rumanians of Transylvania over those in the kingdom. At the same time the Rumanians of Transylvania surpassed in discipline, administration, Western culture, and moral restraint the bulk of the Rumanian population in the kingdom, which was corrupted by the Phanariot rule, by those Greeks who under Turkish patronage governed the country in an Asiatic spirit. Another cause which could have turned the line of irredentistic tendency was the traditional loyalty of the Transylvania Rumanians to the Habsburg dynasty, the better exponents of which often protected them from the abuses of Magyar feudalism.

For all these reasons, if the monarchy had been capable of satisfying at the right time the national needs of its peoples in the spirit of a reasonable federalism, Transylvania would have become a Pied-

---

[2] Compare pp. 306–7 of this book.

mont of the Rumanians which, with its more advanced culture and liberty, could have exercised a powerful attraction upon her connationals beyond the frontiers. As a matter of fact such a Rumanian irredenta, *tending toward the monarchy* manifested itself for centuries. Already, Michael the Courageous, a Rumanian prince (1593–1601), made an effort to unite their territories with the empire of Rudolf II and similar endeavors were renewed during the seventeenth century, desiring to unite all the Rumanians under Habsburg rule.[3] The fear of the isolated Rumanian race before the growing Pan-Slav tendencies was also operative in the same direction. In 1848, some Rumanian leaders made the proposition to the German national assembly in Frankfurt that all the Rumanian settlements should be united in an autonomous country intimately connected with Austria. In the revolutionary period the Rumanians were ardent supporters of the Habsburg and almost until the collapse of the monarchy they stood in close connection with Vienna and their loyalty toward the dynasty was uncontested. One of their ablest political thinkers, Aurel C. Popovici, a leader of the Rumanian national party of Hungary who fled to Austria in order to avoid imprisonment in consequence of a pamphlet which he wrote against the policy of Magyarization, published as late as 1906 a sensational book under the title *Die Vereinigten Staaten von Grossösterreich* ("the United States of Greater Austria") in which he advocated the federalization of the monarchy in an entirely loyal spirit toward the Habsburg. He tried to demonstrate that only a constitution based on the equality of the nations of the empire could save it and at the same time make it the center of attraction for the East and South.

All these facts, which could be easily supplemented by others, demonstrate sufficiently that the irredentistic movement tending toward Bucharest, which since the end of the nineteenth century alarmed more and more Austrian and Hungarian public opinion, was not at all an inevitable one but the result of an erroneous internal policy. A fatal irredenta directed against the Habsburg state was the less unavoidable because, since 1866, there were Hohenzollerns on the Rumanian throne who, in accordance with their education and traditions, were in harmony with the idea of a German–Hungarian–Rumanian alliance which was regarded by them as a bulwark against the growing waves of the Moscovite Pan-Slavism. As a matter of fact both King Charles and King Ferdinand were sincere supporters of this policy and did their best to check the Rumanian irredenta in Transylvania and to find a *modus vivendi* with the Habsburg monarchy.

That this policy of conciliation proved to be impossible, nay, that the irredentistic current grew rapidly in Transylvania was a conse-

[3] F. Kleinwaechter, *op. cit.,* p. 168.

quence of the unhappy nationality policy of Hungary which by the Magyarization of the schools, by the vexatious control of the Rumanian church, and by the ousting of the Rumanian intelligentsia from the state life and local administration fostered the centrifugal tendencies of the Rumanian citizens. This irredenta was in the beginning rather sentimental and literary, but it assumed more and more political forms. A considerable part of the Rumanian intelligentsia of Hungary which could not find an appropriate livelihood at home or which came into collision with the Magyar juries, began to migrate to the Rumanian kingdom and became there a nucleus of an irredentistic campaign.

Immediately before the outbreak of the World War, the symptoms which indicated the growing acuteness of the Rumanian irredenta became more numerous. A Rumanian deputy in the Hungarian parliament, Vajda-Voevod, one of the most influential leaders of the Rumanians in Transylvania, wrote in 1913 in the October issue of the *Österreichische Rundschau* (the magazine of the leading Viennese circles) a passionate accusation against the Magyar chauvinistic policy, summoning Archduke Francis Ferdinand to carry on "the pacification of the Mongolia of Europe." In his vehement article the Rumanian leader denounced in detail the whole policy of artificial Magyarization.

These and similar complaints, a great part of which could not be refuted, heightened the exasperation of the Rumanian irredenta the more since a new wave of political persecution arose. At the same time the movement began to infiltrate also into the popular masses. The riot of Kismajtény and the criminal trial of Szatmár which followed it (1914) aroused a new current of ill-feeling. But something still more alarming happened in the same year. The Vicar-General of the bishopric of Hajdudorog, which was created for the Magyarization of the Rumanian uniates, became the victim of an infernal machine sent by unknown criminals by post. The detonation of this machine wounded seriously several priests of the diocese.

Such events made the antagonism between the two nations more and more acute and the *Liga Culturale* of Bucharest held a series of protest meetings in several cities of Rumania against the oppression of their brothers in Hungary. This current had such a violent repercussion that it began to alarm seriously even the so-called Great Policy of the monarchy. Immediately before the outbreak of the World War, Conrad von Hötzendorf, chief of the staff, declared in 1913 that Rumania must be regarded as lost to the Triple Alliance in consequence of the exasperation which the Magyar chauvinistic policy aroused among the Rumanians. Count Czernin, then minister at Bucharest and later foreign minister, admonished Vienna repeatedly that the nationality policy of Hungary must be changed because oth-

erwise Rumania would secede to the Entente. As a matter of fact the
secret treaty between Rumania and the Triple Alliance was never published because the Rumanian government knew very well that it would
have been swept away by the indignation of Rumanian public opinion.
In one of his reports Count Czernin quoted a declaration of King
Charles accórding to which "as things stand at the moment, Rumania
in a war could not go with the monarchy. . . . ."

The danger of the Rumanian problem in Transylvania began also
to frighten the Berlin circles. When Emperor Wilhelm visited Archduke Ferdinand at Konopischt, this problem was one of the chief
points of their conversation. The heir apparent attacked passionately the policy of Count Tisza in Transylvania and complained that
the Hungarian Premier did not keep his previous promises made to
him at Schönbrunn concerning the pacification of the Rumanians.
The Archduke urged the Emperor to convince Count Tisza of the
necessity of the revision of the Hungarian nationality policy (June,
1914). As a matter of fact the German ambassador at Vienna, von
Tschirschky, was charged to admonish Count Tisza on every possible
occasion of the urgency of a change in his policy toward the Rumanians. The Emperor told the Archduke that Count Tisza should
always be addressed with the words : *Herr, gedenke der Rumänen* ("Sir
remember the Rumanians!"). Under these difficulties Count Tisza
had previously begun negotiations with the leaders of the Rumanians
of Hungary, but the political atmosphere was already so envenomed
and the point of view of the Hungarian Premier was so biased by his
feudal attitude that he was incapable of settling any compromise. He
was always under the sway of the rigidity of his general political conception in which the people did not exist as a conscious factor of public life. In this manner he saw in the Rumanian problem only some dissatisfied bishops and bank-directors and was convinced that this grave
question could be solved by giving certain privileges to the gentlemen-
like elements of the Rumanians, disregarding the social and economic
grievances of the masses. He used to call the Rumanian problem
"treading on the corns" of the Rumanian intelligentsia and admonished Magyar public opinion to discontinue the impolite practices,
hurting in social life the sensitiveness of the Rumanians. In this way
the most serious problem of the country, an almost cancerous disease
of the social and political body appeared before the almighty leader
as an "aching corn."

Both Vienna and Berlin followed with excited interest this new
policy of Count Tisza. On one occasion the German Emperor tried
personally to soften the Hungarian leader and to calm him with the
assertion that "the Kingdom of Rumania did not demand a 'great action' on the part of the Hungarian government, but only concessions
in smaller issues concerning the schools and local administration."

At the same time the Emperor tried to play on another string by which he hoped to overcome the resistance of Count Tisza. According to a report of von Treutler:

His Majesty drew the attention of the Hungarian statesman also to the point that Hungary had every reason to stand firmly with the Germans against the Slav wave and pointed out that the best guaranty in the face of this danger would be a German Austria and a Magyar Hungary standing as firm pillars of the dual monarchy. . . . . Count Tisza answered with enthusiastic agreement. . . . .[4]

That means that in March, 1914, the German Emperor and the most influential statesman of the Habsburg monarchy were in complete accord as to the maintenance of the Dualistic Constitution and of that anti-Slav policy which made the gravest irredentistic problem of the Austro-Hungarian monarchy, the problem of Jugo-Slav unity insoluble and which caused ultimately the catastrophe of Sarajevo.

[4] *Die Grosse Politik der Europäischen Kabinette.* Vol. XXXIX, Nos. 15,715, 15,716, 15,735, 15,736, 15,737.

THE JUGO-SLAV IRREDENTA AND THE ROAD TOWARD THE WAR

Even that most dangerous irredenta which finally gave rise to the World War and destroyed the monarchy, the Jugo-Slav irredenta itself, cannot be regarded as an insolvable problem in its very nature, a problem which must have inevitably led to the dissolution of the Habsburg monarchy. On the contrary, the chief factors of the Jugo-Slav situation would have made it possible to have the unavoidable tendency of the Jugo-Slav peoples toward national unity take a course propitious to the monarchy since national integration could have been achieved not from Belgrade but from Zagreb or Sarajevo.

As a matter of fact the Jugo-Slav irredenta, in one way or another, was really an unavoidable sociological necessity but the conditions and the process of its achievement depended to a large extent on the policy followed in this question. The whole history of the nineteenth century is a demonstration of a sociological law, according to which among masses of the same nationality, living under different sovereignties, there develops, with the rise of economic and cultural life, an irresistible current tending toward the unification of the whole national body into one single economic and political organization. The whole process of Jugo-Slav unity was in its essence the same as that of Italian or German unity. At the end of the nineteenth century, every careful observer could see that the tendency toward Jugo-Slav unity had become an inevitable mass-psychological necessity. The intrigues and rivalries of the great powers could retard or accelerate this process but they were not its real causes. Anyone with the slightest historical or sociological sense will repudiate *a limine* this naïve propagandistic point of view which holds that Jugo-Slav unity was the result of the undermining influence of Russian Pan-Slavism and of the diplomatic intrigues of the Entente, though both factors without doubt, have intensively ripened and accelerated the historical process.

A. THE DISPERSION OF THE JUGO-SLAV FORCES

The majority of the Jugo-Slav peoples of Europe, at the beginning of the nineteenth century, lived under foreign domination. The Austrian Slovenians under German, the Serb immigrants of Hungary under Magyar,[1] the Dalmatian Slavs under Italian, the Slavs of the

---

[1] Under the Turkish rule there was a slow, but continuous infiltration of Serb elements into the southern parts of Hungary. The largest wave of this immigration came in 1690 when about 40,000 Serb families under the leadership of the patriarch of Ipek were colonized by the imperial authorities in the counties of Pozsega, Szerém, and in Bácska. Emperor Leopold I bestowed upon them wide privileges which made their settlements almost a small state in the state.

Balkans under Turkish rule as subject peoples, without the leadership of a national historical class, without a state life or local self-government. Only the Croats were successful in safeguarding their state life and historical continuity to a certain extent.

The wars of the Habsburg monarchy against the Turks naturally aroused also the Balkan Slavs, languishing under Turkish exploitation, and threw into these peoples the sparks which kindled the Slav consciousness, leading after half a century of struggling for independence, in the peace of San Stefano (1878), to the acknowledgment of an independent Serb state. At the same time the independence of the small principality of Montenegro was also recognized by which Serb national life and culture acquired two new centers in the Balkans. From this moment, as a matter of fact, the Serbian state became the natural leader and continuer of the movement which tended toward the elimination of Turkish feudalism from Old Serbia and Macedonia, a movement which in the Balkan Wars of 1912, obtained in the main its aim parallel with the exuberant development of Serb national consciousness. During the decades of the national struggles there developed a vigorous Serb middle class and intelligentsia which absorbed eagerly the revolutionary ideas of the West and which, with a southern impetuosity and a ruthless cruelty acquired in the guerilla warfare with the Turks, embraced the program of entire Jugo-Slav unity. By this the Southern Slav world achieved two powerful centers of attraction: one in Zagreb, in the capital of the Croatian kingdom belonging to the Crown of St. Stephen; the other in Belgrade, in the capital of the independent Serbian kingdom.

These two centers necessarily exercised a great influence on the totality of the Southern Slav peoples, who were divided among six distinct state territories and inside these among a number of distinct provinces. These artificially divided parts of a common national body led for a long time a different economic and cultural life and the feeling of the local particularisms remained for an extended period stronger than the feeling of national unity. But all that which promoted in these national fragments the economic and cultural development augmented from year to year the natural cohesion among them, the consciousness of the ethnographic solidarity and the hatred of the foreign rule.

The comprehension of the nature of the whole process will be facilitated by the following table which shows the Jugo-Slav population of the various countries, distinguishing the Catholic Slavs (Croats, Slovenians) from the Orthodox Serbs. Though the statistical figures from the Balkan territories before the war were not entirely reliable, we can accept the calculations of R. W. Seton-Watson as an approximately correct estimate of the Jugo-Slav forces before the establishment of Jugo-Slav unity.[2]

[2] Analyzed in detail in his book, *The Southern Slav Question* (London, 1911).

Tables XVII and XVIII show that more than twice as many
Jugo-Slavs lived in the monarchy than outside of it, around the newly
developed Serb centers, and, therefore, by the sheer force of numbers,
according to the law of mass attraction, an irredentist movement toward the monarchy would have had a greater probability than a tendency toward secession from the monarchy. But beside the numerical
conditions there have been even more powerful forces at work which
could have changed the line of irredentism in favor of the monarchy.
Thus, above all, the majority of the Jugo-Slav peoples living under
Habsburg rule had a tremendous advantage over the Jugo-Slavs of the

TABLE XVII

Jugo-Slavs inside the Habsburg Monarchy (in Round Numbers)

I. In Austria (Carniola, Carinthia, Styria, Istria, Dalmatia)

a)	Slovenes	1,400,000
b)	Croats	700,000
c)	Serbs	100,000

II. In Hungary

a)	Croats	300,000
b)	Serbs	500,000

III. In Croatia-Slavonia

a)	Croats	1,750,000
b)	Serbs	650,000

IV. In Bosnia-Herzegovina

a)	Croats	400,000
b)	Serbs	850,000
c)	Mohammedan Serbo-Croats	650,000
	Total	7,300,000

TABLE XVIII

Jugo-Slavs outside the Habsburg Monarchy

I.	In Serbia	2,600,000
II.	In Montenegro	300,000
III.	In Turkey	400,000
	Total	3,300,000

Balkans in economic organization, in general culture, and in administrative efficiency. Let us suppose that the monarchy, by the help of a
Federal Constitution, had bestowed complete cultural autonomy and
national independence upon its seven million Jugo-Slav citizens, that
they could develop without any hindrance in national force, culture,
and economic life. Would it have been a utopian dream to suppose
that this Society of Nations around the Danube, counting fifty-one
million population and in which, besides Vienna, Budapest, and Prague,
Zagreb would have been the most important economic center of the
Federation, would have exercised an irresistible attraction for those
three million Balkan–Jugo-Slavs who were in dire need of a cultural,
economic, and scientific leadership?

Moreover, the Habsburg monarchy would not have been under the
necessity of hastening the work of integration, but could prepare it
at leisure, slowly and cautiously, acquiring step by step new sympa-

thies and affinities. For, as a matter of fact, as has been mentioned, the consciousness of national solidarity grew comparatively slowly among the Jugo-Slav tribes. At the beginning they faced each other like foreigners with a distrustful attitude. The Croats and Slovenians of the monarchy in their Roman Catholic creed, brought up in the spirit of Western Roman culture, utilizing the Latin alphabet, belonging to the natural blood circulation of Vienna and Budapest, regarded themselves for a long period as distinct from and superior to their Serb kindred folk who formed the southwestern projection of the Byzantine culture, following the orthodoxy of the Greek Oriental religion, utilizing the Cyrillic alphabet and on whom the incessant Komitadji fights and the bloody struggles against the Turks during centuries impressed a somewhat barbarous, Asiatic color. On the other hand, the Serb minority felt distrustful toward the Croat-Slovenian majority which it considered as vassals of Vienna and Budapest. Under such conditions it was quite natural that the Western majority did not care very much in the beginning for their poor Balkan relatives but it cherished the political ideal of the so-called Illyrism, the conception of which was the restoration of the unity of the three countries of the former Croatian crown. This Illyrism had no hatred at all against the Habsburgs, nay, it was the most decided affirmation of their empire which proved to be, through the powerful propaganda of Ljudovit Gaj, the most efficient ideological force by which Vienna gained the armed support of the Jugo-Slavs against the Magyar fight for independence. . . . .[3] But even later, through almost three generations, the Croats played the rôle of the most loyal citizens of the Habsburgs, their regiments fought strenuously for the monarchy even during the World War, and the majority of the Catholic Jugo-Slavs followed the tradition of their great national leader, the Banus Jelačić, who wished to unite his race under the rule of the Habsburgs. Even as late as May 30, 1917, a resolution of the Jugo-Slav club vindicated without ambiguity the unification of all the Jugo-Slavs of the monarchy inside its frontiers.

But not only among the Catholic Southern Slavs of the empire but even in the Serb kingdom there were not lacking currents and aspirations which were in favor of a movement of unification tending toward the Habsburg monarchy. At the very beginning of the nineteenth century Kara Georg, the leader of the Serb national struggle against the Turks, asked repeatedly for the protection of Emperor Francis and declared himself willing to accept the Austrian suzerainty.[4] Similar endeavors continued in recent times also. A Serb Premier himself, Dr. Vladán Georgievič, narrated in the columns of a Viennese

[3] See pp. 96, 261–62, 310, 368 of the present book.
[4] For details see Alfred Fischel, *op. cit.*, p. 212.

newspaper, his proposition made to Aehrenthal, then Foreign Minister of the monarchy, in which he offered the willingness of Serbia to enter into the Austro-Hungarian monarchy, claiming in return only such a degree of independence as was possessed by Bavaria inside the German empire. But the Austrian statesman was not willing to give any consideration to this plan.[5] Immediately before the World War, in 1912, Nicolas Pašić, the Serb Premier, was also very anxious to build up a far-reaching economic approachement and asked Professor Masaryk, the present President of the Czecho-Slovak Republic, then a leading member of the Czech opposition, to present his plan to Count Berchtold, the Foreign Minister of the monarchy. But this unfortunate statesman was not inclined to discuss the matter with the Czech scholar because in a typically Austrian spirit, he believed that "Masaryk wanted to create a commission and we are not here to help people to commissions. . . . ." A similar intervention of Joseph Redlich and of Dr. I. M. Baernreither, a member of the Upper House, was equally unsuccessful.

B. THE ORIGINS OF THE JUGO-SLAV IRREDENTA

Confronting such and similar facts, it is not only not natural but it asks urgently for explanation of the cause of that vehement Jugo-Slav irredenta which getting a hold not only over the Serbs but over large masses of the Croatian and Dalmatian younger generations,[6] led directly to the dissolution of the monarchy. Whoever is desirous of obtaining an accurate answer to this question must read the detailed history of the movement for Jugo-Slav unity as it was described by R. W. Seton-Watson, P. Südland, and above all by Hermann Wendel.[7] Here I must restrict myself to the emphasis of some of the most salient facts which had the greatest influence in the formation of an irredentistic movement directed against the monarchy.

In this connection, before all, the oppressed conditions of the Jugo-Slav territories of the monarchy must be pointed out. The greatest political fault was the scandalous direction of the all-important Croat problem, the most outstanding events of which have been already described in another chapter.[8] Out of a country which could have become the natural Piedmont of the Jugo-Slavs the ruling classes of the monarchy made a dissatisfied province and later, in the immoral

[5] F. Kleinwaechter, op. cit., p. 157.

[6] In July, 1917, the organ of the loyal Habsburgist Party in Croatia (the so-called Frank Party) emphasized the fact that 90 per cent of the Croatian intellectuals were following the "chimera of Jugoslavia."

[7] The books of R. W. Seton-Watson and of Hermann Wendel have been already quoted. The Austrian standpoint was elucidated by Südland, Die Südslavische Frage und der Weltkrieg (Wien, 1918).

[8] See pp. 366–75 of this book.

hands of Count Khuen Héderváry, a kind of a Balkan colony which could only be ruled by armed force and absolutism, accompanied by riots, student upheavals and, after Khuen, by attempts against the lives of the exponents of the system. Already in 1871 it had become manifest that the new era was on a bad track. In the so-called "Plot of Ogulin," a widely spread conspiracy was detected which could only be suppressed by considerable military force. At the same time the Slovenian minority was consequently hampered in its cultural prog-- ress, whereas Dalmatia, this brilliant center of old Slav culture, played the rôle of the Cinderella of the monarchy, where for a long period a dwarfish Italian minority ruled over a population 98 per cent of which was Jugo-Slav. Besides, Dalmatia was neglected both economi- cally and culturally. About three hundred villages had no schools and in some regions the number of illiterates surpassed 90 per cent. The whole situation could be best characterized by the unique fact already mentioned that the capital of Dalmatia had no direct railway commu- nication with Austria to which it belonged and Zara could only be reached by sea or by carriage.

These and similar evils could only be cured by an independent and self-determining state but the unification of the Jugo-Slav territories broke down before the barrier of the Dualistic Constitution of the German-Magyar hegemony. On the one hand, Hungary claimed a his- torical right over Dalmatia and later also over the occupied Bosnia- Herzegovina, but at the same time it was rigidly opposed to any effort tending toward the unification of the Jugo-Slav territories of the mon- archy because this aspiration would have meant the end of the dual- istic system, the breakdown of the German-Magyar hegemony. The Hungarian anti-Slav attitude found a staunch ally in the higher Ger- man bourgeoisie, especially in the leading financial circles, for which the dualistic system signified unassailable monopolies in all parts of the monarchy. This alliance became adamantine by the protection of the German imperialism, for which a federalized Habsburg monarchy, led by a Slav majority, would have become valueless.

This attitude of the Magyar upper classes against Jugo-Slav uni- ty remained unaltered even during the World War and gives a key to the understanding of Count Stephen Tisza's position which was often misrepresented by official propaganda and superficial foreign observ- ers. When Count Tisza, the most steadfast and class-conscious de- fender of the big landed interests of the monarchy, tried to avoid the war with Serbia,[9] his policy was not the outcome of a desire for peace

---

[9] It must also be noted that his resistance against the catastrophe-policy of Vi- enna was very platonic and lukewarm. The truth is, rightly emphasized by Count Theodore Batthyány, a state minister and one of the best informed men of the war period, in his recent memoirs (published in Hungarian in 1927), that Tisza could have impeded the outbreak of the World War if he would have refused to accept the constitutional responsibility for the ultimatum sent to Serbia. Why? Because the

or of moderation. Tisza did not have any "pacifistic bias" at all. He was as convinced as all the other leading statesmen of the monarchy that a war with Russia was inevitable. Already in 1889 in a public speech he declared that the European war was imminent and urged the country to prepare for it.[10] As already mentioned, he twice broke violently the rules of the Hungarian Parliament in order to make the

old Emperor—at least at the beginning—seems to have received unwillingly the plan of the war party. The hatred of the majority of the peoples of Austria against the war adventure was manifest. Therefore, an energetic resistance on the part of the "solid" Hungary through her most powerful statesman, the Magyar "superman" would have been sufficient to counterbalance the influence of the Viennese war party. But Tisza alleviated his conscience by purely verbal arguments. Later he became the most ardent supporter of the war party, helped to make the ultimatum unacceptable for Serbia, moved for the refusal of Sir Grey's conciliation plan (July 31, 1914), and already two weeks earlier went to the German ambassador emphasizing the necessity of the war. (The revocation of his former standpoint earned for him the enthusiastic marginal remark of the German Emperor: *Na, doch mal ein Mann!* "Now, there's a man for you!"). This conversion of Count Tisza, of the "strong man" of the monarchy, "the ablest and most striking political figure" of the period, became a riddle for many foreign students and must remain such for all those who try to explain the decisions of the leading statesmen exclusively on the basis of individual psychology instead of analyzing the general mass-psychological situation. The key for the solution of this "problem" lies in the fact that Tisza, like all other Hungarian premiers, could never dare to oppose the will of the Emperor or that of the dominant court-groups at Vienna. The dangers of such a resistance would have been too great, due to the fact that there was never a real majority public opinion behind the Magyar premier who represented not the country, but only the ruling oligarchy maintaining the Dualistic System. (See the analysis of this system on pp. 357 ff. of the present book.) In the case of conflict (as the case of 1906–7 clearly showed) Vienna could always mobilize against the ruling classes the overwhelming majority of the country, the Magyar proletariat and the nationalities, promising them universal suffrage. And universal suffrage with secret ballot would have meant immediately the end of the latifundist system and the Magyar supremacy in the monarchy, two things which represented the deepest aspirations of the Magyar feudal classes whose uncontested leader Count Tisza was. Therefore the position of a Hungarian premier was not like that of the premier of England, backed by majority public opinion and practically independent of the Crown, but of a royal commissary, an exponent of the feudal interests, entirely dependent on the will of the king. That was the situation when Count Tisza saw in those critical weeks that his memoranda were repudiated in a rather harsh way by the monarch and when he saw the growing war passion of the ruling militaristic and diplomatic circles. His resistance broke completely, *laudabiliter se subjecit.* The tragedy of Hungary was sealed.

But this was only his derivative sin, the consequence of his whole system, which by the rigidity of its feudal economic structure, by the disrespect of the Nationality Law, by the maintenance of the corrupt electoral law made the racial problems of the monarchy insolvable and led directly to the explosion of the Jugoslav irredenta. Therefore, one of his greatest admirers, but a man of independence and a broader conception, Mr. Glaise-Horstenau, is right in calling him "the grave digger of his beloved thousand-year-old fatherland" (*op. cit.,* p. 112).

Exactly the same thing happened with the occupation of Bosnia-Herzegovina which was the beginning of the apocalyptical ride of the monarchy. Again a Magyar statesman, Count Julius Andrássy, was chiefly responsible for it. Now we know from the reminiscences of his son (Count Julius Andrássy, *The Antecedents of the World War,* I, 20–21, in Hungarian) that the founder of the Dualistic System opposed very energetically this scheme. Later, he became its leading protagonist. Again the Hungarian premier was an instrument of Habsburg expansion and was unable to maintain his original standpoint.

[10] Joseph Redlich, *Kaiser Franz Joseph,* p. 406.

Army Bill accepted which the military circles demanded from him as a necessity for the future war. His attitude toward international relations was a strictly Machiavellian one. He wrote to the Emperor in his first memorandum for the maintenance of peace (July 1, 1914) the characteristic words: "In face of the present Balkan situation it would be my smallest concern to find an apt *casus belli*. When the time comes for the striking of the first blow, it is easy to construct from the various questions a case for war. But before this we must create a diplomatic constellation which will make the relations between the powers less unfavorable for us."[11] His famous *politique de longue main* was not a peace policy, but the preparation of a new military alliance for the future war.[12] His "moderation" was determined by two chief considerations: In case of a defeat, the whole monarchy would be lost; in case of a victory, the annexation of the Jugo-Slav territories of the Balkans would be demanded by all those military and diplomatic circles which were aware of the fact that without the unification of the Jugo-Slav tribes, the irredentistic danger would continue and envenom as before the whole atmosphere of the monarchy. But annexation and unification would have signified Trialism or Federalism, the end of the German and Magyar hegemony. And exactly this was the most dreaded thing for the beneficiaries of the big landed interests. Count Tisza upheld this leading point of view until the last. When Serbia and Montenegro were occupied by the victorious Central Powers and some leading Viennese circles, influenced by Conrad, were for a final annexation of them in order to solve the Jugo-Slav problem by a radical operation, Count Tisza bitterly opposed this policy. And doing this he was motivated again not by a feeling of moderation of justice toward the Serbian state, or by cautiousness to avoid further international complication, but by the perfectly clear vision that the unification of the Jugo-Slavs would lead immediately to the federalization of the monarchy. He favored, therefore, the mutilation of Serbia by a strategic correction of its frontiers, by giving parts of it to its rival neighbors, he favored a policy of complete economic domination over the defeated state. Generally speaking, his point of view was the continuation and petrifaction of the *status quo*, the maintenance of Serbia in its position of a state embryo, incapable of any serious independent economic and political life. When, after the defeat, he insulted, as it was shown, the Serb leaders at Sarajevo, he was animated by the same fears and hates toward the Jugo-Slav world. Therefore, the whole attitude of the powerful Hungarian statesman during the World War was completely in harmony with his fundamental dogma of the Dualistic Constitution, but his plan, if successful, would have perpetu-

[11] *Diplomatische Aktenstücke zur Vorgeschichte des Krieges 1914* (Wien, 1919), I, 17.

[12] S. B. Fay, *The Origins of the World War,* II, 191–92.

ated the tension in the Balkans and the irredentas in the monarchy. The war would have meant only a breathing space for new and more vehement convulsions. The other bulwark of the Dualistic Constitution, the old Emperor himself, shared completely this point of view of Magyar feudalism and regarded it as an axiom that Jugo-Slav unification must be crushed. In an autographed letter written to William II immediately after the catastrophe of Sarajevo, he advocated the plan of a Balkan League which "will only be possible if Serbia . . . . is eliminated as a political factor in the Balkans."[13]

Under the pre-war conditions just analyzed, the Jugo-Slav problem of the monarchy became more and more inflamed because it is in the nature of irredentism that such a tendency grows in a direct ratio with the economic and cultural development of the respective territories. This situation was further aggravated by the fatal foreign policy of the monarchy which, seeing a mortal danger in the Jugo-Slav aspiration for unification, was by necessity animated by the purpose of checking the Serbian kingdom in its independent economic and political development and of retaining it in its rôle of an abortive state embryo. This unfortunate attitude, which later threw the Serbs and large masses of the other Jugo-Slavs into the arms of the Russian propaganda, found already a symbolical expression in 1876 when, during the fight of the Serbs and Montenegrenians for independence against the Turkish rule, Magyar public opinion broke out in clamorous manifestations for the Turks. A sword of honor was sent from Budapest to the Turkish generalissimus and Svetozar Miletić, the popular leader of the Serbs of Hungary and member of the Hungarian parliament, was imprisoned for several years because he tried to organize a Serbian volunteer troop in Hungary in order to help their Balkan brothers in their struggle against Turkish absolutism. Svetozar Miletić became insane in prison and his tragic figure constituted one of those sentimental barriers which separated the Serbs from the ruling dualistic system.

C. THE DANGER-SPOT, BOSNIA-HERZEGOVINA

But the most important issue which fomented irredentistic feelings among the Jugo-Slavs was the occupation of Bosnia-Herzegovina in 1878. Extensive and controversial literature has been written concerning this expansion of the monarchy but its sense and meaning is quite clear. The fatal decision had two chief motives. One was the old desire for conquest of the Habsburg imperialism which, after so many humiliations, became again victorious and could recompense itself with an important province for its losses in Italy. If anyone should deny this motive, I would simply allude to an interesting docu-

[13] *Diplomatische Aktenstücke zur Vorgeschichte des Krieges 1914*, I, Teil, p. 3.

ment which sheds sufficient light on the real purposes of the leading circles. Even at the end of 1913, that is, half a year before the catastrophe, this Habsburg empire, pressed by so many unsolved problems and preparing for new wars under the dreadful burdens of its irredentas, continued feverish diplomatic negotiations for acquiring colonies in the territories of the then vacillating Turkish sovereignty, in Cilicia, a province in Asia Minor. Obviously, they did not yet have sufficient irredentas and they were anxious to supplement them with an Asiatic one, and to excite the Turkish world, too, against their empire. Count Berchtold had no such scruples when he declared before the German ambassador that "especially in the circles of Hungarian parliamentarians there is a keen desire to get an economic footing in Asia Minor."[14] The booty of Bosnia was not enough to satisfy the appetite of dualistic imperialism.

The other cause for the war of occupation against Bosnia-Herzegovina was the growing desire to check the natural extension of the Serb state and of Jugo-Slav unity. The Serbs have interpreted the occupation of Bosnia-Herzegovina in this manner from the beginning and the wrath of national paroxysm shook the whole Jugo-Slav world in the Balkans, a paroxysm skilfully utilized by Russian propaganda in fomenting the conviction that against the mortal enemy, Austria, Serbia can trust only a Pan-Slav protectorate. The Jugo-Slav world considered the new provinces conquered by Austria as the oldest center of its national culture and, therefore, the Habsburg occupation was regarded as the projected arm of the German imperialism for the frustration of Jugo-Slav unity. From this moment the Serbs became implacable enemies of the monarchy and the occupation of the new provinces, imagined by Count Julius Andrássy, then foreign minister and author of the project, as a simple *Parademarsch* (a march in dress parade), became a very bloody adventure involving great and serious losses in life and property. After it an extremely envenomed press campaign was started against the monarchy both in Serbia and in foreign countries, exciting also public opinion inside the monarchy. This anti-Austrian feeling broke out in 1882 in a stubborn and widely spread riot in certain regions of southern Dalmatia and of the occupied provinces (the so-called "upheaval of Crivoscie"), the suppression of which cost a real warfare of nine months during which the Delegations were repeatedly convoked and an extra appropriation of thirty million florins were granted for the pacification of the "riotous provinces." The dual monarchy was compelled to mobilize an armed force of nearly a hundred thousand men against the Jugo-Slavs and its victory was filled with bad forebodings because regular military enrolments could not be carried on for long years and the immediate

[14] *Die Grosse Politik der Europäischen Kabinete,* Vol. XXXVII, Part II, Nos. 15,045, 15,048, 15,052, 15,054, 15,057, 15,069, 15,070, 15,072, 15,079, 15,100.

effect of the military expedition was that nearly 10,000 men emigrated from the monarchy to the territory of Montenegro.

This incident aggravated very much the acuteness of the Jugo-Slav problem, during which the Joint Minister of Finance, Szlávy, acknowledged publicly in the Delegations that the very idea of the occupation of the provinces was to drive a wedge into Pan-Slavism. This policy could have been defended as an act of prospective self-defense from the point of view of a higher cultural mission if, at the same time, it had made the way free toward the national and economic development of Bosnia-Herzegovina by the unification and self-government of the Jugo-Slav territories of the monarchy. But just the opposite happened. The monarchy took under its control, without any far-reaching conception, the new provinces, simply as a capitalistic colony. In consequence of the Austro-Hungarian rivalry, already analyzed, not even the constitutional position of the occupied territories could be determined. Bosnia-Herzegovina was put under a military commander, under the protection of whom an intense economic activity was started but not from the point of view of the interests of the inhabitants but from that of the capitalistic colonial enterprises. The province was administered by German, Magyar, and Polish-Jewish officials who did not have the least idea of the real needs of the population. Bosnia-Herzegovina remained the classic country of illiteracy (90 per cent!) and the government based its power, primarily, on the Mohammedan feudalism which continued its rule over the Christian Slav bondsmen. The old Habsburg practices were renewed and the Joint Finance Minister, Kállay, the head of the civil government, was anxious to promote artificially a specific "Bosnian nationalism" against the Jugo-Slav tendencies toward unification. Besides, the system of spies was far more virulent than in the other parts of the monarchy and the pressure of the government on the public schools was so exacerbating that student strikes were not infrequent and the high school of Mostar was closed for a whole year (1913).

This system aroused the most vehement form of Jugo-Slav irredentism in the new province. The Balkanic atmosphere; the Southern romanticism, not reckoning with real facts; the confused revolutionary propaganda of half-educated young men, systematically exploited by the Pan-Slavistic agents; the brutal terror of the military absolutism piled high the popular passions which exploded at Sarajevo. But even previously, in 1910, a Serb student fired at General Varešanin, the military commander of the province. The attempt was unsuccessful and the student committed suicide. According to a widely spread rumor the general kicked the corpse of the unfortunate youth. Perhaps this story was only invented but it became one of those legends which created the type of the Jugo-Slav revolutionaries from which also the murderer of Archduke Ferdinand was recruited. (We must not forget that the catastrophe of Sarajevo was the seventh attempt in four years directed against the representatives of the monarchy by exalted young men!) This revolutionary type united within itself, in a strange and awful way, the national idealism of a Mazzini with the violence of a Bakunin and a nebulous ideology of Communism. Many members of this revolutionary generation studied in the West and some were in direct connection with Trotsky and the Russian *emigrés*.

One of the most terrifying products of this feverish and envenomed public atmosphere was the widely diffused conviction which I heard personally from serious Jugo-Slav intellectuals concerning the brothels of Sarajevo. These ill-famed places were generally known in the military circles of the monarchy, both by their number and their quality. The Austrian authorities showed probably a cynical indulgence toward them but scarcely a greater one than in the other great military garrisons of the monarchy. Jugo-Slav public opinion, however, shared by many from the middle class, was that the brothels were an intentional creation of the Austrian policy in order to envenom the blood and the morals of the native population by the lust of the colonizing foreigners. A more dreadful accusation was perhaps never formulated against foreign invaders!

These morbid conditions, growing worse year by year, were not bettered by the final annexation of Bosnia and Herzegovina which was forced through by Aehrenthal in 1908 among many diplomatic blunders. This unfortunate and thoroughly unmotivated diplomatic coup (for the annexation did not make any *de facto* change in the situation of the provinces, whereas *de jure* it made the Habsburg imperialism more odious) resulted in drawing the circle of the Entente more tightly around the monarchy and in inciting speeches in the Serb *Skupština* against it.

D. THE ATTITUDE OF THE DANUBE MONARCHY TOWARD SERBIA AND THE PIG WAR

Besides Croatia and Bosnia-Herzegovina, the third and most important current of the Jugo-Slav irredenta was born in the Serbian kingdom. This robust peasant people, full of life, scarcely liberated from the Turkish yoke of many centuries, raised in a medieval warlike atmosphere, proud of its democratic constitution, unaccustomed to feudal pressure, a classic type of an independent, self-conscious small peasantry, naturally felt most clearly its national aims and the obstacles to the unification of its race. At the same time the terrible situation of the Christian population in Macedonia, the eternal fights against the Turks, and among the various armed bands hired by foreign imperialism or Balkan interests was a powerful incentive toward unity and elimination of foreign rule. Year by year, 2,000 political murders were committed on the average in Macedonia, a country with less than three million inhabitants. And in these statistics the rapines, ravishments, and arsons were not included. In this bloody chaos the Serbs felt themselves the most interested.[15] The young nation was exasperated by the situation of its kindred folks within the frontiers of the Habsburg monarchy, and felt continually on its own body the lashes of Viennese policy. Instead of playing the rôle of a protector and educator toward its young neighbor, Austria regarded it from the beginning as an undesirable competitor, the material and political growth of which must be checked at any cost. Foreign Minister Count Kálnoky (1881–1895) informed his Minister in Belgrade that "he did not count on Serbia adhering to us for love; she will have to do so from fear and material interests and these I consider as far more reliable motives than the changing feelings of such half-wild peoples. . . . ."[16]

This unhappy principle remained to the end the ruling idea of official policy in spite of some diplomatic enunciations in a milder tone. King Milan, the tyrannous Obrenović, became a real vassal of the Viennese court who under the protection of Austrian arms continued his fatal policy against his own people (1882–1889). King Milan saw more and more clearly that his position was becoming precarious against the growing national consciousness of his people. On one occasion he ran to Vienna in order to convince the leading circles of the uncertainty of his crown. Concerning this episode, Crown Prince Rudolf wrote the following reminiscence and his words throw much light on the Balkan policies of the Habsburg monarchy. The Crown Prince narrates that in the Foreign Ministry the Serb King was told that:

He should not see everything so black but should continue calmly his previous course without provoking a public scandal. This is easy to say, thought the poor king to himself, and openly declared both before the Emperor and Count Kálnoky that only two roads were open for him: either to turn and to throw himself into the arms of the Russian Pan-Slavistic policy or to remain a good Austrian and take up a struggle against his own people. For such a course, however, it would be necessary that on the frontiers Austrian troops should be concentrated.

Meanwhile the situation became so acute in Serbia that King Milan made concrete propositions in Vienna concerning the annexation of Serbia by the Habsburg monarchy (1885).[17] It is a startling fact that a sovereign asked for the incorporation of his country,

[15] The moral and political impossibility of the *status quo* was stated by Réné Pinon in, *L'Europe et l'Empire Ottoman. Les Aspects Actuels de la Question d'Orient* (Paris, 1908), pp. 152–54.

[16] Quoted after Corti by R. W. Seton-Watson, *Sarajevo: A Study into the Origins of the Great War* (London, 1925), p. 23.

[17] Bibl, *op. cit.,* II, 424.

against the will of his people, by a foreign and hated empire and it demonstrated the extreme envenomed state of the Jugo-Slav problem. As a matter of fact, the system of Milan could only rule Serbia by means of an Asiatic absolutism, delivering the little state completely both economically and politically to Austria. This policy poured fresh oil on the fire of Pan-Slavism and Jugo-Slav irredentism. In the seething atmosphere of political imprisonments and murders a new generation was rising, intoxicated by the most radical socialistic and anarchistic ideas of the West and regarding the history of Italian unity as a symbol: Italy too had sighed in former times under the yoke of the Habsburgs. . . . . The conception of a new Serbia, of a Piedmont of the Jugo-Slav world conquered the souls of the youth. . . . . At the same time these young men who began to attend frequently foreign universities rejected more and more the antiquated conception of a Serb, Croat, and Slavonian patriotism and under the influence of the Western ideas, especially under the sway of the mighty personality of Professor Masaryk at the University of Prague, the consciousness of Jugo-Slav unity was further developed.

In 1903, three events of great importance indicated that this new public spirit stirred already the very masses of the Jugo-Slav world. The Macedonian uprising against the Turkish rule, the murder of King Alexander, the son of Milan, and of his wife by the military revolution at Belgrade (which broke out in consequence of the enforcing of an absolutistic constitution) and the fall of the corrupt and hated system of Count Khuen in Croatia were manifestations that the Jugo-Slav revolution all around was progressing. . . . . Under its new, very democratic constitution and influenced more and more by the Pan-Slavistic agitation, Serbia came into increased conflict with the monarchy. The most statesmanlike moderation and the introduction of deep organic reforms would have been necessary in the dual monarchy in order to avoid the eruption of the Jugo-Slav crisis. But just the opposite course was followed. Under the pressure of the overwhelming feudal interests, the Austro-Hungarian government started a light-minded and pernicious customs war, the so-called Pig War, with Serbia (1906).[18]

There is not the least doubt that this frivolous and brutal economic policy, detrimental not only to Serbia, but also to the great majority of the Austro-Hungarian population, was "the chief cause"

[18] The most important literature on the customs war crisis is in the following:
Von einem aufrichtigen Freunde der Österreichischen Landwirtschaft: *Der Serbische Handelsvertrag, ein Sieg der Agrarier* (Wien, 1908).
Alfred Simitsch, Reichsritter von Hohenblum, *Materialien zur Vorbereitung des Österreich-Ungarischen Handelsvertrages mit Serbien* (Wien, 1903).
Otto von Zwiedineck, *Die handelspolitischen Beziehungen Serbiens zu Österreich-Ungarn,* Harms, Weltwirtschaftliches Archiv, Band 6.
Karl Renner, *Die Aera Hohenblum. Der Ruin unserer Staats- und Volkswirtschaft* (Wien, 1913).

which made Serbia the irreconcilable enemy of the Habsburg monarchy. The responsibility for the World War lies to a great extent on those circles which provoked this customs war, a real class war, against the interests of the Serb producers and Austro-Hungarian consumers. Since 1882 the monarchy had had a fairly liberal commercial treaty with Serbia which made a comparatively close economic relation possible between the two countries. Before 1905, 60 per cent of the grain and 95 per cent of the cattle imported by the monarchy came from Serbia, whereas 87 per cent of the Serbian imports were furnished by the monarchy.

As early as 1903 this highly beneficial commercial treaty was attacked in an impetuous way by the big landed interests both in Hungary and in Austria. Count Stephen Tisza and Ritter von Hohenblum were the chief champions who favored the exclusion of Serbian agricultural imports, especially cattle, from the monarchy. This agitation, backed by the all-powerful political influence of the big estates, made it impossible to renew the commercial treaty with Serbia in 1906. The Austro-Hungarian government presented almost impossible conditions to Serbia: they were not to bring in live cattle and at the same time were obliged to buy all materials for railway construction and all war munitions from the monarchy. This cruel and narrow-minded policy was motivated not only by the traditional anti-Slav feeling of the monarchy and the rapacious agrarian interests, but it had also two other motives. The one was to put Serbia under pressure to recede from the Serb-Bulgarian customs-union treaty, already unanimously accepted by the parliament of Sofia at the end of 1905. The other, to induce the Serb government to give an order for twenty-six million francs to be expended in cannon manufacture to the Austrian Skoda plant. And though Serbia withdrew from the customs union and gave other signs of its conciliatory spirit, the pressure of the agrarian interests both in the Austrian and the Hungarian parliaments was so ruthless that the Foreign Minister was compelled to abandon the successful negotiations with Serbia. And when, in 1908, a new provisional solution was inaugurated, though the international atmosphere was already full of dangers, the agrarian circles of the monarchy, led by Ritter von Hohenblum, Count Tisza, Count Berchtold, and Count Stürgkh, started an envenomed propaganda against the liquidation of the customs war; and in Austria the government was menaced with the threat of concentrating peasant masses around the Viennese parliament. This infamous policy made the prices of meat at Vienna so excessive that public opinion of the cities demanded the importation of meat from Argentina. At the same time it aroused a degree of hatred and exasperation in Serbia, the like of which was only surpassed in the crisis of annexation.

Following this episode the Serb people regarded the Habsburg

empire not only as a national enemy but as the promoter of a plan of
trying to starve the whole country, which at the beginning of the customs war had no commercial possibilities except in the Austrian markets. At the same time this was the period when the pressure of Hungarian absolutism on Croatia was the most vexatious. It is no wonder
that the Serbian and the Croatian disaffection met each other and
that the consciousness of Jugo-Slav national unity was further developed as a symbol of national independence and economic progress. It is
quite natural that this hypertense situation was ruthlessly and demagogically exploited by the growing Pan-Slavistic propaganda against
the dual monarchy. The governments in Belgrade and Cetinje became
more and more obedient instruments of the Russian diplomacy. At
the same time the various Serb literary and cultural societies assumed
increasingly a political color for the unification of the Jugo-Slavs.
Whereas, the earlier association of this kind, as the *Zora* ("Aurora,"
founded at Vienna in 1863) or the *Omladina* ("Youth," founded in
1866 in Novisad) maintained more or less their legal and peaceful
character, the *Narodna Obrana* ("Society of National Defense"), established in 1909 after the Bosnia Crisis, employed more and more
provocative hues. Finally, a secret society was started in 1911, the
so-called "Black Hand" or "Union or Death," which under the leadership of the demoniac personality, Dragutin Dimitrijević (in 1913 he
became head of the Intelligence Bureau of the Serb General Staff),
frankly accepted the methods of murder and terrorism as the unique
means for unification and liberation. The Serbian government made
unsuccessful (probably not quite seriously meant) efforts to check or
suppress its activities which made the revolutionary fever more and
more acute and led directly to the murder-plot of Sarajevo.

This growing danger did not escape the attention of the more
thoughtful statesmen and observers. Conrad von Hötzendorf saw
quite clearly that conditions were becoming unbearable. Under the
sway of these pessimistic prospects, after 1906, when he became the
Chief of the Staff, he urged constantly and passionately a preventive
war against Serbia,[19] but also a radical solution of the Jugo-Slav
problem through the unification of all Slav territories, giving them a
complete autonomy. It became manifest that without the solution of
this problem, the Jugo-Slav irredenta would explode and lead to world
complications, a world war, the chances for the success of which would
become worse from year to year in consequence of the advance of the
French and English policy in creating the Entente against imperi-

[19] "Not counting the period 1906–1912 . . . . it may be noted that in the seventeen months from January 1, 1913, to July 1, 1914, the chief of staff had, according
to his own statements, urged war against Serbia no less than twenty-five times" (S.
B. Fay, *The Origins of the World War*, II, 224). And the reader should not forget
that Conrad was not an isolated maniac but the exponent of the all-powerful military and diplomatic leading circles!

alistic Germany. And when, in 1912, the Balkan War inflamed the national consciousness of the Serbs still more and the armed interference of the monarchy seemed to be inevitable, Conrad von Hötzendorf, who became for the second time Chief of Staff, urged passionately the military solution of the Jugo-Slav problem. He declared in one of his memorandums that "the union of the southern Slavs is one of those nation-moving phenomena which cannot be denied or artificially prevented," the only question to consider was whether this union should be created under the protection of the monarchy or against it. This statement of the Chief of Staff was almost a verbal repetition of a diagnosis made a year earlier by an English observer, by R. W. Seton-Watson, who, in his book on the Jugo-Slav problem, said:

The movement in favor of Croato-Serb unity has many obstacles to surmount. . . . . But as surely as Germany and Italy have won their liberty and unity, so surely will it be won by the Croato-Serb race. The real problem is the manner of its achievement: and here we are at once faced by two alternatives. Unity can be obtained either inside or outside the Habsburg monarchy, either by the latter's aid and under its auspices, or in defiance of its opposition. . . . . Upon Austria's choice of alternatives depends the future of the Habsburg monarchy. . . . .

And though the number of those who recognized the fatal importance of the Jugo-Slav problem grew continually and though, as we have seen, the later victim of this problem, Archduke Francis Ferdinand, urged desperately its solution, not only nothing happened in this direction but the national consciousness of the Slavs of the monarchy was constantly irritated, whereas against Serbia the traditional hostile policy was continued. In the same year in which the victorious arms of the Balkan Slavs swept out the corrupt Turkish rule, heightening almost disproportionately the national consciousness of the Southern Slavs, in Croatia the system of open absolutism envenomed public opinion and led to repeated political attempts against the life of the hated exponents of this rule. And when the bullet of a young fanatic directed against the detested banus, "the Royal Commissary" of the Budapest government, failed to hit its target but killed instead a high employee accompanying the banus (June, 1912), an enthusiastic Austrian patriot, Theodore von Sosnosky wrote the following diagnosis of the situation:

As long as the present system continues, as long as the Croatian Banus is not the representative of the Croatian people but the exponent of the Hungarian government . . . . the system of political murders cannot be eliminated. . . . . Therefore, it is unspeakably silly to describe this attempt as the individual deed of a single man as the official press tried to cause it to be believed. . . . . On the contrary it was a typical symptom, an early flash of lightning from heavy thunder clouds which are gathering menacingly in the southeastern part of the monarchy. . . . .[20]

[20] *Die Politik im Habsburger Reiche* (Berlin, 1913), II, 366–67.

Golden words, which were equally true of the later attempts and especially of the catastrophe of Sarajevo.

The official circles of the monarchy, however, did not learn anything. No one dared to attack the holy dogma of the Dualistic Constitution but the whole statesmanship of the empire was exhausted in
a diplomacy which tried to impede Serbia in its natural development.
During the Balkan War the monarchy mobilized and the military circles would have liked to interfere in order to break down the victorious
Serb Piedmont. . . . . For this purpose a disgusting legend was officially propagated concerning the terrible mutilation of the Austrian
consul in Prizren, Mr. Prochaska. Not a single word of this rumor was
true as it was simply intended as a means of propaganda for the contemplated war. And when, under the pressure of the Great Powers,
the armed interference of the monarchy was prevented, Bulgaria was
encouraged by the Austro-Hungarian diplomacy to the second Balkan War against Serbia. After the failure of this experiment, the dual
monarchy was successful in carrying out, under the disguise of the
Albanian national independence, a feeling quite rudimentary at that
time, the establishment of an impotent Albanian buffer state serving
as a barrier between Serbia and the sea (in order that the economic
dependence of Serbia should be maintained) and as a naval base for
Austrian and Italian imperialism. The cup of despair was filled for
Serbia. She could use no other solution than a war against the hated
dual monarchy under the protection of her big Russian brother.
And Count Polzer-Hoditz, the chief of the Cabinet of the late Emperor Carl, the last Habsburg, after demonstrating long and copious-
ly the innocence of the monarchy in the World War comes, as a kind
of Freudian outburst after a long "Verdrängung," to the following
confession:

Nobody thought of revising our Balkan policy for this would have
involved a complete change also in the inner policy. The understanding
that the hatred of Serbia and Rumania . . . . was caused by ourselves, by
our custom policy, that the Southern Slavs did not want anything else than
to unite themselves and to get an outlet to the sea, that by our unfortunate
Albanian policy we have closed the last valve and therefore an explosion
became inevitable: this understanding was never attained by the ruling
elements. . . . .[21]

E. THE GROWING DANGER OF THE WAR

In this manner a mass-psychological situation was created inside
the monarchy and on its frontiers which forced the dualistic system,
step by step, toward explosion, making the struggle between Habsburg imperialism and Russian Pan-Slavism more imminent from year
to year. It became almost a political dogma that this life and death

[21] Arthur Graf Polzer-Hoditz, *Kaiser Karl* (Wien, 1928), p. 246.

struggle was totally inevitable and in the last decades the leading military circles in both camps prepared feverishly for the final clash. And it was really inevitable in the sense that nothing serious was undertaken for the solution of a vital problem, the colossal gravity of which was clearly felt by all intelligent observers, both national and foreign, as the immediate cause of the approaching historical catastrophe. This conviction was expressed with an almost cruel lucidity by the German ambassador at Vienna, von Tschirschky, in a report addressed to the chancellor of the empire, Bethmann-Hollweg, November 18, 1912. The ambassador made an analysis of public opinion of the non-Slav political and military circles at Vienna and summarized his observations as follows: "We are tumbling into the war" (to which the German Emperor made the marginal note: "Drifting!"). The ambassador emphasized that this war would be very popular in this camp if it should be utilized for the solution of the Jugo-Slav problem in accordance with the German point of view. The general staff and the feudal circles were extremely depressed and ashamed that the monarchy did not dare to draw the conclusions of the situation.

They see with astonishment and anguish the sudden [It was "sudden" only for the official circles!] swelling of the Slav wave and on all lips is fluttering the anxious question, what will happen to Austria? The Germans are disheartened. One of their leaders told me recently in the House of Lords: "That is the end of the Germans in Austria." [Marginal remark of Emperor William II: *Kopf hoch!*]. They will lose all influence in the monarchy and I ask myself if they will not be compelled to secede. . . . .

Later the ambassador called attention to the fact that it was becoming more and more difficult to retain the seven million Jugo-Slavs inside the boundaries of the monarchy. "A new Lombardo-Venezia has been born in the southeastern part of the empire, an irredenta which must unavoidably fall beyond the frontiers to the new great, independent Serb state. . . . ." The ambassador asserted that the ruling circles scarcely believed that the Slav regiments could be utilized against Serbia in the case of war and the pessimism of many is so great that they think that "after the dissolution of Turkey, Austro-Hungary will be next." (Marginal remark of the Emperor: "*So was!*") The ambassador stated with despair that after the Balkan victories the religious difference among the Jugo-Slavs will no longer be a serious obstacle for their national unity. Von Tschirschky summarized his conclusions in the following weighty and characteristic words:

The idea of a united Empire, the feeling of solidarity disappears more and more. . . . . The picture which the internal structure of the Austro-Hungarian monarchy shows at the present time is not a cheerful one, also not cheerful from the point of view of the German ally. It would require great wisdom and energy of the central government [Marginal remark of William II: *Mit Blut und Eisen sind die Kerle noch zu kurieren* ("By blood and iron the fellows can still be cured.")] to maintain the centrifugal forces of the strongly developing Slav peoples serviceable for the purpose of the state and to carry on further a policy of a great power beside the German ally. . . . .[22]

But from where could this wisdom and energy have emanated in the period of the dissolution and approaching catastrophe, when these qualities were totally lacking for half a century under circumstances far more propitious for the monarchy? It may well be doubted whether, after the victorious Balkan War of the Southern Slavs, any amount of wisdom and energy would have been useful so completely had the monarchy lost the confidence and esteem of the Jugo-Slavs and its other nationalities. Under such circumstances and under the growing pressure of the Pan-Slavistic current only the road to war remained open.

Regarding things from this perspective, only the roughest outline of which have I been able to give, the problem of responsibility for the World War gains another sense and significance. This immense literature which has been developed around this question is, according to my opinion, in its largest part worthless because in a naïve and childish way it seeks only individual responsibilities in such events which were not the work of individual men but the results of old institutions, of heavy national and social sins. These naïve historians (who are to a large extent the so-called "war criminals" themselves) investigate only the calendar date of the outburst of the world crisis and they forget that if the catastrophe had not broken out in 1914, it could have exploded (always under the hypothesis of *rebus hic stantibus*, under the existing national and social complications) some years later, as it was already near to explosion in 1887 and 1912.[23]   No diplomatic *finesses*, no Kellogg Pact, or treaties of amity could have avoided this explosion whose real roots were in the social, economic, and national structure both of Russia and of the Dual Monarchy. The point where the feudal, pseudo-constitutional political structure of the former monarchy, clinging desperately to its dualistic monopolies, impeding the development of the overwhelming majority of its population and partly also, that of the neighboring states, came into conflict with the Pan-Slavistic, militaristic currents of the Czarist autocracy longing for Constantinople and the half sentimental, half imperialistic "lib-

---

[22] *Die Grosse Politik der Europäischen Kabinette,* XXXIII, No. 12,402.

[23] How the peace of Europe in the two decades before the World War was repeatedly saved by the firmness of the German diplomacy against the sturdy war passion of Austria, was aptly shown by Alfred Frankenfeld in his *Österreichs Spiel mit dem Kriege* (Dresden, 1928).

eration" of the Slav brothers . . . . here was the real danger spot of Europe for three generations. All the other factors, the English-German capitalistic rivalries, the lust for revenge in France, the Italian irredentism, the sabre-rattling dementia of the Kaiser, his pathological *Alarmblasenkatarrh* were only of second importance in the undermining of Europe. No artificial diplomatic arrangements (Europe was full of them for three generations) could have avoided the world catastrophe, but only a radical cure of social and political reforms: the elimination of the feudal system in Austria-Hungary, its federalization, a free trade policy toward the neighboring nations. And at the same time the breakdown of the Czarist absolutism, a democratic and liberal Duma, and the agrarian reform of Stolypin, carried on at least two decades earlier than they were initiated. . . . . But even with an autocratic Russia another European equilibrium would have been possible. Imagine that the negotiations of Lord Haldane (in 1912) had been successful in establishing a solid compromise between Great Britain and Germany and imagine an Austro-Hungarian monarchy which would have become, on the basis of a democratic confederation, a real fatherland for all its peoples and one can hardly see how the unscrupulous propaganda of Russian Tsarism could have thrown Europe into the wholesale slaughter of its most cultured nations.

But the growing irredentistic movements of the monarchy not only made the internal tension among the peoples unbearable but they strengthened at the same time, as a result of interference, the Russian Pan-Slavistic parties which covered their imperialistic aims by the partly true, partly false ideology of the liberation of the Slav brothers. One should not forget that the natural reactionary alliance among the three emperors, among the German, the Austrian, and the Russian autocrats was not dissolved by their personal rivalry but under the pressure of a widely spread national public opinion which demanded from the Tsar a more energetic defense of the oppressed conationals. We must remember that as late as 1905 a personal treaty was made between the German Kaiser and the Tsar but the Russian autocrat could not get the treaty accepted by the ruling circles who were under the sway of nationalistic public opinion.

F. THE SOCIOLOGICAL RESPONSIBILITY FOR THE WAR

From this point of view the responsibility for the war falls, in the first place, upon the Dual Monarchy which by its antiquated dualistic constitution and by the narrow-minded economic and nationality policy disseminated during generations the germs of the world conflagration. A personal responsibility can only be established in the sense of placing the blame upon those statesmen who hastened the date of its outbreak. In this respect it can easily be demonstrated that the leading generals and diplomats of the monarchy tried at any price to utilize the catastrophe of Sarajevo for a war with Serbia and possibly with Russia. They did this not because they were a bit more warlike or imperialistic than their colleagues in the camp of the Entente but because they considered the war as inevitable and, seeing the feverish war preparations of their antagonists, they came to the conclusion (perfectly legitimate under the condition of the national and social *rebus hic stantibus*) that every additional year could only increase, to their detriment, the chances of a future war. That was why Conrad von Hötzendorf urged, since 1906, a preventive war against Italy and Serbia; why he told at the outbreak of the World War that "in 1909 the war would have been a game with open cards, in 1913 it would still have been a game with chances, in 1914 it had become a game of *va banque*, but there was no other alternative"; why Premier Count Stürgkh said in that fatal Crown council which determined, July 7, 1914, the destiny of the monarchy: "It must come to decisive action; a purely diplomatic history will not suffice us. . . . . If, from international points of view, the course of a previous diplomatic action must be entered upon, it must be carried on with the firm intention that this action can only finish with a war."[24] That is the reason why the ultimatum to Serbia was purposely so conceived that Serbia would not be able to accept it; why a previous jural opinion from Professor Hold was demanded as to what legal pretext could be found if Serbia should submit; why the offer of the Tsar to present the conflict to the tribunal at the Hague was rejected; why they watched carefully that all foreign interference for the maintenance of peace should be eluded under diplomatic evasions; why the consent of the hesitating old Emperor, Francis Joseph, was forced by the false announcement of the battle at Temes-Kubin which really never occurred; why this petrified monarch himself calmed the war party at the time of the Annexation Crisis with the memorable words: "This war will come by itself, unaided. . . . ."; and why in the final crisis he said with resignation: "If the Monarchy must perish it should at least perish with decency. . . . ." And that is also why the whole official and semi-official press, both feudal and capitalistic, agitated unscrupulously for war;[25] why in Budapest officially paid and arranged demonstrations were made in order to arouse enthusiasm for the Serbian War;[26] why even so cultured a gentleman as Count Albert Apponyi

[24] *Diplomatische Aktenstücke,* Part I, p. 31.
[25] See for details Heinrich Kanner's *Kaiserliche Katastrophenpolitik* (Wien, 1922), pp. 59, 122, 325.
[26] One of the best-informed and most reliable journalists of the pre-war period writes me: "I could observe it for many days how the scum of the population, for a daily payment, shouted on the streets of Budapest for war against Serbia. Realizing my responsibility, I can assert that in Budapest masses organized and paid by the police demanded the war."

greeted the Serbian war in the Hungarian parliament with an enthusiastic "At last!"; and finally why Count Moltke, the Chief of the German Staff shared the point of view of Conrad, that "all retardation would mean the lessening of our chances," and as late as July 31, 1914, reminded Conrad of the seriousness of the warlike will of the Central Powers.

These and similar facts, which might easily be extended, demonstrate that the Austro-Hungarian monarchy did not wish to postpone the war. And this wish was motivated by no frenzied imperialism but by the conviction that its internal situation had become unbearable because it could not solve its own problems; because it came into conflict more and more with the will of its people; because in the atmosphere of the continual attempts against the lives of the exponents of the state, the leading circles of the monarchy lost their heads (how characteristic, for instance, that William II was urged not to come to Vienna to attend the funeral of Francis Ferdinand for, according to reliable information, his life would not be secure in the imperial city on account of Jugo-Slav plotters!) ; because its military and diplomatic experts were convinced that, if a few more years should be granted to Russia for the repairing of its loss in blood and treasure caused by the Japanese defeat, the chances of war would have become desperate for the dual monarchy.

This series of facts and not sheer diplomatic machinations leads us toward a better understanding of the problem as to the "immediate" cause of the war (which, I repeat, is a problem different from that of "war guilt" and must be sought in the sins of omission and commission of the national and social policy followed for a century). From this point of view, Dr. Heinrich Kanner, based on the memoirs of Conrad von Hötzendorf, has shown with clear and strong argument the preponderant importance in the outbreak of the war of the "secret military convention," convened by the chiefs of the German and Austrian Staffs under the auspices of the two Monarchs and the other responsible factors in 1909, in which the former strictly defensive alliance contracted by Bismarck was extended into an offensive alliance between the two states in case Austria should find it necessary to start a preventive war against Serbia.[27] It may be doubted whether this agreement can be called a "military convention" in the strict sense, as Mr. Kanner has done, but there can be no reasonable doubt that the existence of such a "binding agreement" influenced profoundly the attitude of the Austrian war party. One should not forget that Bismarck, as long as he was in office, always resisted strenuously the Austrian efforts (in 1882 and 1887) to extend the *casus foederis* to the case of an offensive war also, because, according to his own words, he feared the "desire for war" *(Kriegslust)* and the "light-minded-

[27] *Der Schlüssel zur Kriegsschuldfrage* (München, 1926).

ness" of the Austrians and was not willing "to pay them a premium for a pretext of their quarrels with Russia" (eine Prämie auf das Händelsuchen mit Russland). When, however, Bismarck was no longer in power, and when in Austria the foreign policy was directed by Aehrenthal, a chief exponent of the so-called "active" policy, and when Conrad von Hötzendorf, the apostle of the preventive war, was put at the head of the Staff, there was no longer any obstacle to the remolding of the defensive alliance into an offensive one. Beginning with 1909 the Habsburg monarchy could count on the assistance of its powerful ally even in case it found it necessary to start a war itself. It may be doubtful whether Germany really acted under the stipulations of this agreement but it cannot be doubtful that the World War was born under the shadow of it and the daring advance of the Austrian war party would be unimaginable without this psychological motive. (The military agreement was later supplemented almost yearly by written or oral negotiations.)

This fatal military convention or "binding agreement" was the expression of the conviction of the leading circles that the situation of the dual monarchy had become untenable and could only be saved by the daring operation of a preventive war. In this saving of the monarchy the German empire was naturally deeply interested not only on behalf of the Nibelungentreue but also in consequence of the fact that its policy in Asia Minor and in Africa aroused against it the jealous antagonism of the other imperialisms. After having repeatedly refused the English offers for a solid compromise, after the unhappy policy "of the loud mouth" and of the pose of a continuous "sabre rattling," Germany stood perfectly isolated in Europe, bound to Austria for life and death. What the genius of Bismarck could avoid, the policy of his successors precipitated: Germany was compelled to follow its fatal ally into its leap to death. It did this not from the motive of a frenzied imperialism but under the stress of the system of the balance of power. Its situation was clearly analyzed by an objective German historian, Wolfgang Windelband in the following weighty statement: "If Germany had not wished to acquiesce in the destruction of its power—and a spontaneous yielding would have been the symptom of the most dangerous internal rottenness—it was obliged to maintain its alliance with Austro-Hungary because the possibility of a more advantageous one was lacking in consequence of its own sin. Very sharply did the change in the situation become manifest: Germany was dependent on Austro-Hungary and was therefore compelled to accept its interests. . . . ."[28] This was the real motive of the German participation, the motive of the balance of power, and not the alleged indignation against the Serbian criminal maneuvers. How hypo-

[28] Die Auswärtige Politik der Grossmächte in der Neuzeit. Zweite, durchgesehene Auflage. (Stuttgart und Berlin, 1925), p. 411.

critical this argument was, has been vigorously stated by Prince Lichnowsky, the last German imperial ambassador to London, in the following note made in January, 1915:

Has not the Italian unity arisen by perfectly similar means and does not the same thing which happened between 1848 and 1866 in Italy repeat itself with the Jugo-Slavs? There in the Lombardo-Venetian provinces the Austrians tried to crush the national movement by violence, sword, and gallows . . . . the Italians, too, utilized bombs and daggers for political aims and laid violent hands on the Divine Right and even on the Holy Father! Did we, therefore, refuse to make an alliance with Italy or did we declare war against Italy because Orsini threw a bomb at Napoleon? Is not the foundation of Italy exactly as "revolutionary" as the tendencies of the Great Serbian movement directed against Austria? . . . . Why must the German people rush into a World War in order to crush the Jugo-Slav movement for unity?[29]

G. THE "PERSONAL WAR GUILT"

In the honest and serious literature on the so-called "war guilt" problem one of the most outstanding is, without any doubt, the recent book of Professor Fay, already referred to, who made a compr. hensive and admirable effort to disentangle all the various currents leading to the World War. He was successful in demolishing the propagandistic legend of the exclusive war-guilt of the Central Powers. The great importance of this work imposes the duty on the author of the present book to make his standpoint clear concerning certain points in which he disagrees with the presentation of Professor Fay. In his noble ardor for justice he follows too much the present swing of the pendulum of public opinion when he does not see, that the Central Powers, *though they alone did not cause the World War, they determined the date of its outbreak.* His attitude is decidedly pro-German and sometimes biased by some inaccurate private information.[30]

---

[29] Published in the *Berliner Tageblatt,* November 8, 1927, from the memoirs of Prince Lichnowsky: *Auf dem Wege zum Abgrund.* The Italian situation in 1859 and the Serbian in 1914 have so general and striking resemblances that one has the impression that we here face a sociologically determined typology of the crisis for national unification.

[30] For instance, Herr Leopold Mandl, for two decades the semi-official mouthpiece of the Ballplatz and the organizer of a press campaign against Serbia, is called by him the "Austrian historian." Mr. Wendel is qualified as a "pro-Serb German writer" which he really is. But at the same time none of the fanatic anti-Serb pamphletists whom he quotes abundantly is qualified by him as an anti-Serb German writer. Dr. Kanner, one of the most acute students of war-responsibility, is called the editor of the former *Viennese Socialist Daily.* Probably Dr. Kanner was characterized before him in this way by the German nationalists in order to portray him as a rabid Communist. The truth is that Dr. Kanner has published a solid liberal bourgeois daily *(Die Zeit).* Whereas he quotes the worthless German anti-Freemason pamphletists and the Viennese propagandistic journal of the Soviets to the discredit of the existing Balkan governments, he does not even mention the great historical work of the leading authority, Professor Bibl, who though a staunch supporter of the German cause, shows that Austria could not postpone the war at the time given.

It seems to me that the great number of facts given by Professor Fay alone show abundantly and conclusively that the leading Viennese circles by all kinds of Machiavellian means precipitated the war because, according to Conrad, the position of Austria would have become more untenable from year to year in the case of a warlike complication. They knew that with the completion of those military reforms which were going on in Russia and France, and with the growth of the anti-Austrian irredentistic propaganda the odds for Austria in a later war would have become practically null. The only power which could have crushed, as it did several times in the past, the war will of Austria, was Germany. But the Germans—to quote Professor Fay— "made the grave mistake of putting the situation outside of their control into the hands of a man as reckless and unscrupulous as Berchtold. They committed themselves to a leap in the dark. They soon found themselves involved in actions which they did not approve . . . . but they could not seriously object and protest . . . . because they had pledged their support to Austria in advance, and any hesitation on their part would only weaken the Triple Alliance at a critical moment when it most needed to be strong. . . ." (II, 223), So a *carte blanche* was given to Germany (*ibid.*, p. 255) which was practically equivalent to a declaration of war. It is true that Germany got the ultimatum of Austria less than twenty-four hours before the Austrian Minister was to present it at Belgrade, but (according to Professor Fay) "even if Bethmann and Jagow had been informed of the text earlier, it is not to be assumed that they would have modified or stopped it" (*ibid.*, p. 267). That is absolutely sure, because previously the *carte blanche* was given to Austria.

But it is not sufficiently clear why the German military circles who several times in the past stopped the light-mindedness of Austria became at once so meek and indulgent. The only explanation is that they saw that Austria was headed for catastrophe and that they agreed with Conrad that this was the last possibility for Austria, their only ally, to risk a war to save its existence which was more endangered from year to year. Only those social and political factors which we analyzed in this book can really explain the motives of both Austria and Germany.

Therefore it is quite evident that *Austria fixed the date of the conflict and Germany did not stop her ally.* Here lies the primordial responsibility of Austria, motivated not by personal crimes of her statesmen, but by the social and national sins of the whole system. And here lies the responsibility of Germany which was rather an omission than a commission. From this point of view the vexed problem of the war-guilt assumes almost a mathematical simplicity. Is it true or not that after the catastrophe of Sarajevo none of the Entente Powers had any motive to start a war in 1914? The whole world opinion was so terrified by the crime that to attack the ramshackle empire *at this time* was a mass-psychological impossibility. But it was a good opportunity for Austria to utilize the general indignation of the world to crush the stormy center of Serbia. (That was the leading point of view not only of Vienna, but of Berlin too!) Then I ask further is it true or not that Austria without a German backing was not in the position to begin a war? A small logical experiment will suffice to decide this question. Let us suppose that in the last critical week a single telegram would have been sent from Berlin to Vienna with the following short text: "Germany cannot promise any participation in a war as long as all the diplomatic means are not exhausted to settle a fair compromise." I do not say that this course was open for Austria without the complete collapse of her prestige on the Balkan. But I do say that under such a step of Berlin no ultimatum could have been sent from Vienna. The War would have been stopped for a few years!

This is the simple truth both from a logical and a historical point of view. And besides all the facts which I enumerated there is also the direct testimony of the late General Max Hoffmann, one of the ablest German military leaders who in his memoirs, recently published, made the following sincere and outspoken statement:

"To be sure, we could have ducked our heads again in the summer of 1914; then the Entente would not have struck until 1917, since they were prepared only for this period. In this sense we began the war, that is true. . . . ." ("Natürlich hätten wir uns auch im Sommer 1914 wieder ducken können, dann hätte die Entente erst 1917 losgeschlagen, denn zu diesem Termine waren sie erst fertig. Insofern haben wir den Krieg angefangen, das stimmt. . . . .")[31]

In these few words the whole war-philosophy of the Central Powers at the outburst of the war is vigorously stated. And this philosophy was perfectly sane under the clausula of *rebus hic stantibus*. Only deep organic reforms could have avoided the war and for these reforms there was no more time.

---

[31] *Die Aufzeichnungen des Generalmajors Hoffmann* (Berlin, 1929), I, 155.

PART VII
CONSCIOUS EFFORTS IN CIVIC EDUCATION

CHAPTER I

OBSTACLES TO CIVIC EDUCATION

It is manifest that in the framework of those historical forces, constitutional life and public mentality which we have become acquainted with in this volume, there was no real opportunity for a conscious effort in civic education. The whole monarchy has never been considered as a problem of the people who constituted it but only as a problem of the dynasty and of the ruling classes. The real outstanding and fundamental question of the monarchy, how to satisfy the different national and cultural claims of the various nationalities in such a way as to give them ample possibilities to develop their historical individuality and consciousness but at the same time to build up a supernational consciousness of a state solidarity among them, this question, as we have seen, with very few exceptions, was not even perceived or formulated. Really the whole moral and constitutional atmosphere of the monarchy made such a conscious effort in civic education impossible. To solve this problem would have meant, in the ultimate resort, the federalization of the monarchy. The problem could have been solved only "between equals," or at least potential equals. But the whole system of the monarchy was the formal denial of such an equality. The German-Magyar hegemony was the real bulwark of the Constitution, the unshakeable rock upon which the whole system was built. And inside of this framework a *divide et impera* policy in Austria, and the strict repudiation of any idea of national equality or super-national federalization in Hungary. And though a relatively great progress was achieved in Austria toward the cultural self-expression of the various nations as a result of continuous struggles and compromises, the problem as a whole, in a systematic, conscious, constructive manner was never touched. Mr. Strakosch-Grassmann in his valuable book on the history of the Austrian public instruction has acutely shown that a bettering of the general conditions in the recent decades was a direct result of the growing decentralization in popular education and of the growing elimination of the paralyzing influences of the centralized administration, but this manifest progress could not bear the desired fruit because the process was checked by the antiquated framework of the Dualistic Constitution.

The lack of a solid will, which has characterized the Austrian state administration since 1879 in an ever increasing measure, was also manifest in the field of public education. . . . . The want of any political plan and the absence of any ethical consideration are characteristic of the whole state administration.

434 DISSOLUTION OF THE HABSBURG MONARCHY

And his final conclusion was that the "national organization of public instruction in Austria would presuppose the organization of all the nations into political and administrative units." Each nation should have the incontestable right to establish its own schools at its own expense. The educational items should disappear from the budget of the state and should belong exclusively to the competence of the single nations.

The federal state, following the example of the United States, of Switzerland, and of the German empire, is the only solution of the problem as to how the Austrian state can continue. But the antiquated crownlands should be replaced by the political organizations of the Nations. . . . . The old Austria, in which officials of the central Viennese administration have governed the whole empire, no longer survives. . . . . The individual nations of a state composed of so many heterogeneous peoples exist not to be kneaded into a unitary state, but the state should be transformed in such a way that each individual nation could have the greatest possible amount of self-determination. . . . .[1]

As a matter of fact the internal evolution of Austria, as has been demonstrated, was dominated though in an unconscious and chaotic way by this principle. An organic solution, however, of the whole problem was impossible on the basis of the Dualistic Constitution. The growing floods of national energy could not find a sufficient natural outlet. This situation was further aggravated by the fact that civic education in Austria and in Hungary followed not only different, but totally antagonistic principles.

[1] *Geschichte des Österreichischen Unterrichtswesens* (Wien, 1905), pp. 349–53.

CHAPTER II

THE AUSTRIAN SYSTEM OF CIVIC EDUCATION

Generally speaking, the whole public instruction in Austria was permeated by the old dynastic and patrimonial conception of the state. Austrian history was described, almost exclusively in all the textbooks as a history of the dynasty and its war lords. After the perusal of the accepted textbooks in civics and history, one has the impression that all the events were personal acts of the Emperors. The whole history as it was taught was a glorification of the dynastic force, a kind of a vast *dynastic epopoeia*. All the chapters of the widely spread texts, all their pictures emphasized and extolled the same point of view. One has the feeling that the peoples were only mute personages in the anational drama of the Habsburgs, purposeless instruments in the hands of the Emperors, their war lords, and ministers. The school festivals were celebrations of the birthday of the Emperor and of other important family events. All patriotic songs were the glorification of the Sovereign or of the exploits of his successful generals. It is quite characteristic that the only Austrian song which could be called patriotic in a popular sense, the song glorifying the memory of Andreas Hofer, is not an expression of an Austrian solidarity but of the loyalty toward "the good Emperor Francis" and of the love "of the holy country, Tyrol."

This tendency to describe Austrian history as the personal work of the Habsburgs; to extol all their military exploits, even the smallest; to eliminate as far as possible the memory of their defeats, errors, or faults; to qualify all movements opposed to the Imperial Majesty as pure crimes or rebellions was a constant feature of all the popular textbooks. They are permeated with the spirit of a nauseating Byzantinism. Some few examples will elucidate the extreme morbidness of the whole atmosphere. For instance, Dr. Emanuel Hannak, former director of the Teacher's Seminar in Vienna gave the following instruction to his pupils under the heading "Formation of Character and Will":

The rapturous feeling of love and esteem clings primarily to the leader of the state, whose picture is already known to the child from his earliest infancy by the money in circulation and by its presence in a dignified place both in the home and the school. He learns to venerate him as the father of the fatherland and extends this reverence to all the members of his majestic family. . . . .[1]

[1] *Methodik des Unterrichtes in der Geschichte* (2d ed., Wien, 1907), pp. 14–15.

When the minds of the children were filled with a great amount of useless details and servile adulations, the most important economic, cultural, and national connections of Austrian history were entirely neglected. For instance, concerning the Viennese revolution of 1848 an extensively used textbook narrates that "for such troubles the too benign Emperor felt himself not a match, he left Vienna and went to Olmütz, to his residence. . . . ." On the other hand all the results and achievements of a period are exclusively portrayed as the personal work of the sovereign. A popular little textbook, for example, though containing only seventy-nine small pages, enumerates under the title "What Emperor Francis Joseph Did for His Peoples" in a long series of items all the creations of this great emperor, beginning with the granting of a constitution and finishing with the water-supply of the capital.[2] Naturally all the new universities or hospitals were a personal present of the magnanimous sovereign to his beloved nations.

But in spite of the exuberance of this dynastic patriotism, the real results of the system were very small. Especially in the non-German regions the dynastic enthusiasm spread by the schools was only "a cold lip-service of the teachers," whereas in an unofficial manner they extolled and cherished the national aspirations of their respective peoples. This growing chasm between dynastic and national patriotism could not be bridged by the anxious efforts of the official administration. So for instance it became a system, especially in the non-German regions, to have the students write so-called "Patriotic Tests," an endeavor to bring into harmony the regional patriotism with the Habsburg patriotism. The better teachers, however, felt always the futility of such an attempt. What could the poor school do against the impetuous flood of national dissatisfaction, against the acrimonious criticism of the popular leading articles of the daily press and against the continuous national scandals in the Diets and in Parliament? The more serious teacher, therefore, avoided as far as possible these patriotic experiments because they were perfectly aware of the fact that such and similar artificial worship of the dynastic state was useless and could only debase the moral character of the pupils. At this juncture I remember a characteristic episode. A new governor of Dalmatia, dissatisfied with the growing Slav spirit of a high school, asked somewhat bitterly the director of this institution why its moral atmosphere could not be as good and patriotic as that of a *Kadettenschule* (colleges for the education of future officers). To which this acquaintance of mine replied: "Sir, if you were capable of putting all

[2] Al. Swetina, *Das Wichtigste aus der Österreichischen Geschichte* (5th ed., Sternberg, 1908), pp. 56–57.

the children of this province under the same conditions as your cadets, separated from their family, in the dynastical hothouse of a secluded college, we could obtain exactly the same results. . . . ."

This courageous answer gives really the true key to the problem of civic education in Austria. The only institution of the monarchy, as has been already emphasized in another connection, which was really successful in creating for a long period a type of man in whom the idea of a dynastic patriotism and of the interests of the super-state was stronger than the national aspirations of his race, was the imperial army. Why? Because it constituted a real state within the state, a dynastic island in the sea of the growing national and social struggles. Upon this island there was quite an artificial cultural vegetation. And the chief textbook of the *K. K. Armee* (Imperial-Royal Army), the famous *Dienstreglement* (Rule of Service), was a real Bible of Habsburg patriotism. It is highly characteristic that the traditional oath taken by the soldier was purely and simply an oath of vassalage toward the Emperor and his official officer staff, without a single word of any duty of the soldier toward his fatherland, people, or constitution. On the other hand, a very scrupulous and tactful care was maintained that the members of the imperial army should feel themselves as equals not disturbed by national rivalries or chauvinistic particularisms. Thus, for instance, paragraph 5 of the *Dienstreglement* emphasized in a solemn and resolute manner that

the destiny of the army, uniting many thousands in a lofty purpose, demands a common spirit and unity both in the singular organized bodies and in the totality of the armed force. This common spirit is rooted in the feeling of solidarity and in the realization of the necessity of subordinating private interest to the well-being of the whole. It creates the professional feeling (*Standesbewustsein*), fosters a severe self-denying accomplishment of duty, and develops the highest military virtues. . . . .

But this very definition of the dynastic patriotism shows its fragility for the modern times. It created not a state consciousness but a professional consciousness for the imperial service. Therefore, any progress in national and cultural development of the various peoples lessened this professional solidarity and strengthened the national, strictly opposed to the imperialistic super-state. The leading circles were perfectly aware of this situation and it became a kind of governmental maxim to keep the "loyal army" as far as possible aloof from the general population infected with the bacilli of a more liberal and national public opinion.

In this dilemma only a new type of civic education could have found a way out: a civic education convincing the various peoples of the monarchy of the necessity and advantages of a mutual, economic and cultural co-operation under the patronage of a free federal state.

But nothing was done in this direction. The ten nations of the monarchy and its various nationalities were total strangers to each other, and the whole system of public education was entirely incapable of closing this gap. Discussing this problem retrospectively with some outstanding educators of former Austria, their opinions converged on the point that the whole system of public education never faced this problem in its real importance and seriousness.

The chief interest of Austrian history—so a former educational leader wrote—was not concentrated upon Austria as a state of various nations but it was always directed upon the Habsburg state under the hypothesis of the political and cultural preponderance of the Germans. . . . . Though this spirit was far less chauvinistic than that of the Western nation states, it was also devoid of any genuine enthusiasm, and the idea of a general reconciliation of the nations was never considered. . . . . There was scarcely the opportunity and still less the desire to learn the languages of the non-German peoples and a mutual intellectual penetration, therefore, was out of the question. Especially the distance between Austria and Hungary became more and more unbridgeable; the general Austrian student left school with the impression that beyond the Leitha an entirely foreign country began. . . . . Though a certain amount of political geography concerning the various nations was taught, this teaching was entirely a dead letter, giving no impetus toward a better mutual understanding and co-operation. The strangeness of the people to each other was the cause of the downfall of the old Austria and our school system did nothing to prevent it.

Another eminent expert emphasized to me that the purely dynastic accent of Austrian history was detrimental to a state idea and even in the nationally mixed territories the German students rarely learned the non-German languages. Besides, the most important chapters of modern Austro-Hungarian history were treated in a very summary way, giving to the students very slight opportunity to understand the essence of those changes which led to the dualistic remolding of the constitution. All the actions and movements against the Habsburg dynasty were naturally portrayed as riotous upheavals without any real justification.

Speaking generally, however, one might say that public education in Austria committed sins of omission rather than commission. In the cool dynastic and bureaucratic atmosphere of this system everything was omitted which could have led to mutual hatred among the students and to the artificial fostering of national and racial antipathy. Unfortunately the other great factors in civic education, political life, and local administration, the daily press and the social organizations of the citizens worked in quite another direction. In all these fields of public life the spirit of an intolerant nationalism grew stronger and stronger. In so far as national consciousness permeated more and more all the various ethnical elements of the monarchy, the emphasis and fostering, the lip-service and adulation of this feeling became a springboard for all business politicians and demagogues. National feeling in its vagueness, elasticity, and traditional sentimentalism gave an excellent opportunity for building up a united national front against the "common enemy," for canalizing all economic and social dissatisfaction of the masses, and for hiding class antagonism and cultural differences for the benefit of a loud, confused national demagogy. The dynamics of this process have already been described elsewhere.[3] At this juncture I would like only to emphasize that neither the state nor society tried to counterbalance, on the basis of a constructive policy, these dissolving tendencies. The immense majority of the Austrian newspapers, especially the most powerful German capitalistic press, found it excellent business to promote the wave of national paroxysm. The same was done by the so-called national and cultural associations, an extended network of which covered all the countries of the monarchy. Each nation had its own national-cultural associations motivated by the necessity of safeguarding its national rights against the aggressive tendency of another nationality by fostering national consciousness; by organizing the still apathetic strata; by founding schools, choirs, libraries, and other cultural organizations in order to strengthen the nation as a whole. No one can deny that these associations were an important factor in the development of national consciousness, especially among the more backward nations of the empire. But from the point of view of a state-solidarity their effect was strictly detrimental because they soon were transformed from an instrument of self-defense and consolidation into a demagogic apparatus, a chauvinistic machine for the benefit of the political bosses and of sinecure officials, shouting the most envenomed slogans of national hatred. The political parties and the local administration, and later, as we have seen, the state administration itself, came more and more under the sway of the hypertrophy of the nationalistic feeling created by these pseudo-cultural associations.

[3] Compare pp. 284–87 of this book.

CHAPTER III

THE HUNGARIAN SYSTEM OF CIVIC EDUCATION

Just the opposite was the situation in Hungary where, after the Compromise of 1867, all Habsburg administration was completely eliminated and the time-honored Hungarian state reassumed its complete internal sovereignty. The ruling Magyar classes, triumphant against the centralizing Viennese administration, regarded as their only historical mission the building up of a unitary Magyar state. The acknowledgment of the other nations as not only agglomerations of individuals but as distinct political units of the country was repudiated as an offense against the very idea of the Hungarian nation. Though a cold lip-service was paid to the dynasty by the official circles, by the high clergy and aristocracy, as long as the sovereign did not interfere with the claims and interests of the ruling class, this dynastic loyalty did not permeate the vast strata of the population of the Magyars who combatted through centuries Habsburg absolutism and Germanization. Therefore, this dynastic religion which determined to a large extent civic education in Austria was almost entirely lacking in the Magyar nation and animated only certain circles of the nationalities which, owing to the traditions of the past, continued to regard the Habsburgs as a kind of potential bulwark against the growing tide of Magyar nationalism.

The main features of this nationalism, its tendencies toward an artificial, if necessary, even forcible Magyarization of the non-Magyar nationalities, were described elsewhere.[1] In this connection I would like only to emphasize that in opposition to Austria the Hungarian state had a very systematic, even highly dogmatic conception of a civic education devoted exclusively to the conception of a Magyar national state. The leading circles of Hungary regarded the Hungarian state, in spite of the small Magyar majority of the country, as a united national state, entitled to this dignity by the same historical reasons by which the English, the French, the German, and the Italian nations have a right to build up a completely homogeneous national state, disregarding any other ethnic elements as constituting parts of state sovereignty. All the moral and spiritual energies of the state were devoted to this unique aim of national assimilation, centralization, and consolidation. The entire educational system of the state served, almost with a religious fervor, this supreme dogma of national unity. In the absence of a bourgeois class in a Western sense and in the absence of an organized peasantry and an efficient labor movement, this

[1] Compare pp. 327 ff. of this book.

ideology of national unity and solidarity was carried on almost exclusively according to the traditions and social values of the feudal classes. If I called the public training in history in Austria a dynastic epopoeia, I must characterize the Hungarian system of civic training as a *feudal epopoeia*. The whole public education, press, and cultural activity of social associations described and portrayed the history of the Magyar state as a unique effort for national independence and solidarity under the exclusive leadership of the Magyar nobility. All the uprisings and rebellions of the feudal classes against the Habsburgs were glorified as national struggles for emancipation in a modern national sense. All the selfish opposition of the feudal classes against the reforms of the enlightened absolutism was explained exclusively by high national motives. The whole history of the country was set forth as a classless history of national enthusiasm against the devilish plans of Habsburg centralization and the even more devilish plots of the Rumanians and the Slavs, who in spite of the unheard of magnanimity of the Magyars, made common cause with the Austrian aggressors. The imperialistic episodes of Hungarian history, the Greater Hungary of a Louis the Great and King Matthias were enthusiastically commented upon not only as things of past glory but also as future possibilities provided the nation should reconquer its ancient unity and warlike virtues.

I had the opportunity of getting some interesting replies on a questionnaire which I sent to some educational authorities of the former Hungary inquiring about her pre-war experiences in this field. One of them, the former head of a very important instructional district, characterizes the knowledge of the Magyar students concerning the culture and aspirations of the non-Magyars as follows:

The non-Magyar peoples of the country were only mentioned in the political geography and in a very cursory manner. The only thing which the students knew about them was in what parts of the country they lived and what was their numerical strength. Their achievements in history were narrated as perfectly hostile actions against the Hungarian nation under the devilish excitation of the Habsburgs. (For instance, the riot of Hora-Kloska, the upheavals of the nationalities in 1848–49.) Never a word was said concerning their ethnic particularities, culture, literature, or popular art. Generally speaking, when occasionally the non-Magyar peoples were mentioned they were always portrayed as of an inferior culture and as enemies of the Magyars who made common cause with the Habsburgs from sheer malevolence, envy, and hatred of the Magyars. The psychological cause of this attitude was never explained to the students, at best the fact was alluded to that, as they were formerly conquered by the Magyars when the state was created, later they tried to avenge themselves against their rightful masters. That pre-eminently economic and social causes contributed to this antagonism, especially the pressure of the latifundist system, the repulsion against the feudal administration, and the defense of their national language was concealed by silence by all our books and teachers. The Compromise of 1867 was glorified as the work of the "sage of the nation" and described as giving total independence to the country and guaranteeing the supremacy of the Magyars over the nationalities. But never was reasonably elucidated what was the part of the Magyars in the Constitution, what were their duties and obligations toward the other nations of the monarchy. On the contrary the illusion was fostered that Hungary was an entirely independent, free, and self-sufficient country which could do what it liked. The other nations of the monarchy, the Germans themselves, were disregarded as mute and insignificant partners in the Magyar epic. A kind of romantic symbolism permeated all instruction. The Magyar nation became the innocent poor fellow of the popular tales who was attacked on every side by malignant enemies, but he, by his incredible courage, was always victorious over the treacherous assailants. Similarly, until the Compromise the Habsburgs were described as monsters who attacked the loyal Magyar nation without any serious motive, exclusively led by hatred and antipathy. That this struggle was largely due to the economic and social privileges of the feudal classes, which checked all efforts of the King in building up a modern state, was never mentioned or analyzed.

In this atmosphere the Magyar student never learned the languages of the other nations, even in nationally mixed territories where there was a possibility for doing so. It was the very intention of the administration that in the high schools and similar institutions the non-Magyar languages should play a minor rôle. Therefore, there was no intellectual or cultural co-operation between the Magyars and non-Magyars. Generally speaking, the whole elementary and secondary education was characterized by the fact that the child's face was turned backward, he could look only upon the past. He could never see himself in his relation to the present. And this past was an artificially constructed picture in the center of which stood the heroic Magyar nation, surrounded by few friends and many enemies. No wonder, therefore, that the student, graduated from high school, did not know anything concerning the real cultural and economic forces of his country and the opposite historical traditions of the various other nations. . . . .

All the other experts whom I questioned narrated very similar experiences. The non-Magyar nations were regarded as peoples without history, having no special mission, the Magyarization of which could be the only possible issue in the long run. All the festivals, literary and social associations fostered the same spirit. The chivalrous Magyar nation was terribly abused by its pernicious enemies, both by the dynasty and the nationalities, but the time is near when it will reconquer its former glory, its entire independence and unity. All the moral and financial forces of civic education were concentrated toward this ideal, which represented the most sincere and serious conviction of the Magyar society and of the leading educational staff. For three generations Magyar public opinion, almost without any counterbalance, regarded the history of the country and of the whole world through this distorted perspective.

Following the relative consolidation and material prosperity of the period after the Compromise, the spirit of this exclusive nationalism became more and more intolerant. Even the catastrophe of 1849, when the Russian intervention made the struggle against Austria impossible and when the heroic leader of the Magyar forces was obliged to lay down his arms, even this tragic episode became as oil on the fire of national conceit because public opinion embraced the legend eagerly that General Görgey, the Hungarian generalissimo, was a traitor and without this devilish personality the Magyar would have been triumphant over both the Austrians and the Russians.

In spite of the inherent fallacies of this system of civic education, it seemed for a long period to be efficient and victorious, especially in the big cities and in all those circles where Magyar economic, cultural, and political life was sufficiently intensive. Magyar public opinion was under the mirage of this optical illusion, disregarding the fact that in the rural districts and in the small towns many millions of non-Magyar nationalities were untouched by this trend of exuberant patriotism. It was dazzled by the results of the brilliant Hungarian capital and certain other important commercial centers where the German and the Jewish middle class and even many members of the other nationalities became ardent supporters of the Magyar state idea. The meaning and significance of this process has been previously analyzed. In this connection I would like to emphasize again that it was to a large extent a spontaneous assimilation due to the ardor and passionate driving-force of this civic education. In a recent historical novel Louis Hatvany reconstructed with ability the psychology of this process. He narrates how the teacher Mihályi (formerly a Slovak with the family name of Mihalek) shouted to the boys of his class "like a student reciting his lesson that on the Eastern rampart of Europe the handful of Magyars defended European civilization against the Turks and fought its solitary fight, poor abandoned race, for the liberty of the world. . . . ." Also the enthusiasm of the Jewish assimilated elements is excellently portrayed by the same author. An old Jew ridicules the ardent Magyar feeling of his son:

"Who speaks Magyar? Nobody understands the Magyar tongue beyond Pressburg." Now the voice of the son was choked. But only for a moment, then he replied courageously: . . . . "And if we, like our King Matthias, will reconquer Vienna, then even there everybody will speak Magyar." . . . .[2]

The feeling out of which such and similar attitudes arose was in most cases perfectly genuine, nourished by national festivals through

[2] *Lords and Men* (Budapest, 1926), I, 263. In Hungarian.

which patriotism, especially the memory of March 15, 1848, the beginning of the Hungarian revolution (interpreted almost exclusively as a
national upheaval against Austria and not as a proclamation of human
rights, which it was at the same time) and the tragic remembrance of
the thirteen Hungarian generals murdered at Arad by the imperial
justice in 1849 was extolled with an ardent enthusiasm. The growing
fervor of these memorial days alarmed certain circles and a loyal premier, Baron Desider Bánffy, tried to counterbalance them by establishing a new national holiday tending to bring into harmony the Magyar feeling with loyalty toward the King. Therefore, a law was passed
in 1898 which declared April 11, as the national holiday, as the fiftieth
anniversary of the day when, in 1848, the laws of independence proposed by the Hungarian parliament were sanctioned by the Monarch.
As a matter of fact the new national holiday received only a very cool
lip-service because public opinion did not forget that the same laws
were ignominiously violated by the Habsburgs within a few months.
The only result of this charmed loyalty was, therefore, to re-enforce the
enthusiasm of the real national festivals.

Another successful instrument in the promotion of Magyar solidarity was the Magyarization of the family names. The origin of this
fashion may be found in the imperial administration when Joseph II
ordered that the Jews should adopt German family names. Especially
the liberal enthusiasm of 1848 and 1867 induced many people to accept Magyar names as a symbol of their loyalty to the victorious nation which was willing to share its privileges with the other nationalities. Later the tax on applications for the new names was reduced to
a nominal sum which made this patriotic custom quite usual and widely spread. By it a great number of sincere Magyar patriots were created but at the same time it opened the door for adventurers who tried
to find admittance into feudal society by their new names. The government greatly favored these measures in the state offices, it even applied certain compulsory procedures. As the participation of the
Jews and Germans was disproportionately high in the Hungarian economic and intellectual life, the Magyarization of names was an excellent instrument for showing to foreigners the non-existent racial unity
of the country. The true motive of the leading circles was unmasked
after the war when Hungary was dismembered and the non-Magyar
territories detached. The ruling element did not need any longer the
assistance of the Jews in its fight against the nationalities and consequently its public opinion changed radically. The Magyarization of
names is no longer favored. On the contrary the state makes grave
hindrances against the Jewish applications.

As in Austria, in Hungary too, the press and the so-called cultural associations played a great part in the creation of national consciousness and solidarity. There was, however, a great difference be-

tween the two systems in the fact that whereas the Austrian state kept itself farther and farther from the national struggles and avoided intentionally the impression of a German state, in Hungary both press and the system of cultural associations served as a powerful means in the hands of the state authorities against the nationalities and for the propagation of national unity. An extended network of Magyar cultural associations was artificially fostered and those of the Ruthenians, Slovaks, and Serbs demolished. Only the Rumanians and the Germans had sufficient strength to maintain to some extent their cultural associations. But the slightest cultural movement of the nationalities was severely controlled and its "irredentistic" aims vehemently denounced, even in many cases where they were really purely cultural, whereas the similar Magyar associations enjoyed not only complete freedom but were allowed to employ a licentious language. In a study relative to the activity of these associations, a Hungarian observer made the statement that they had the tendency to become instruments of the political machine and jingo organizations against the nationalities :

They confide to the government that the Slovaks will establish a reading-room and, therefore, the country is in danger; that the state inspectors are not sufficiently severe with the Slovak teachers; that the Rumanian teachers intend to hold a meeting for the bettering of their financial status; that the Hungarian Vend pupils frequent the schools of the Austrian Slovenians and that the authorities give too much freedom to the movements of the nationalities. The cultural associations squandered great energies and their leaders are unable to understand that their activity is not only futile but positively detrimental. . . . .[3]

Still more dangerous, from the point of view of a true state solidarity, was the activity of the Magyar press. While the press of the nationalities was often molested and persecuted, accused of anti-state tendencies, the language of the most influential Magyar organs became more and more vehement and offensive against all political and cultural movements of the nationalities. Only a few Magyar statesmen and publicists realized the extreme danger of this attitude by which the very sources of state consciousness were envenomed. Louis Mocsáry denounced repeatedly this system by which the nationalities were constantly irritated and Magyar public opinion misled. The utterances of the nationality press were very often not only misquoted but intentionally falsified and, as the Magyar circles were unable to read the press of the non-Magyars, the fear complex of the nationality danger grew parallel with the national consciousness of the various peoples. The non-Magyar nations were not only accused of disloyalty but were often insulted by the vituperation of their most

[3] Victor Aradi, "The Cultural Work of Our Cultural Associations," *Huszadik Szdzad,* January, 1914.

cherished national traditions. Let me quote only a single example. In 1901 when Svetozar Miletić, the once popular leader of the Hungarian Serbs, who was imprisoned because of his attitude at the time of the Serbian war against the Turks when he offered to raise a corps of Serb volunteers in the cause of Christian Slavdom, died, a Magyar daily, which claimed to be the organ of the radical Magyar intellectuals, wrote the following obituary:

A traitor died, the country which he betrayed was the Hungarian fatherland, this endeared fatherland. . . . . Against this glorious fatherland was he a traitor, this base man, whose corpse now lies in state. . . . . There was nothing in his heart but an inextinguishable hatred against the land where his cradle rocked and which he knew would receive his putrefying cadaver. . . . . The venomous spider gave out his death gasp in his own web. . . . . The pen in our hand shudders from contempt when we put on paper the name of Svetozar Miletić. . . . . We would like to restrain it but we cannot check our feelings, not even before the bier. . . . . As long as it was warm, this exposed body, excited, propagated, and organized riot; as long as this death-pale lip could speak, it taught hatred against the fatherland. . . . .

To this terrible outburst of a base demagogy, Louis Mocsáry wrote the following remark:

Is it permitted to write in such manner? Must we copy the habits of the hyenas, digging out the dead for the presentation of Magyar feeling and patriotism? It may be a case of hyperpatriotism but this habit is not a Magyar one. One thing is certain, that by such utterances one can infiltrate inextinguishable hatred into exasperated breasts which at a given occasion will burst out in atrocities. . . . .[4]

It is manifest that the behavior of the Serb leader was not patriotic from a Hungarian point of view and would have aroused anger in any other country too. On the other hand this episode demonstrated with many other symptoms that in a country where the hero of a national minority could be attacked in such a way without any interference on the part of the state against the perpetrator, when at the same time all the manifestations of the nationality press were continually persecuted, there was no idea of a true system of civic education trying to coalesce the various national traditions into a state consciousness. What really happened was a licentious exaggeration of Magyar feeling and a hidden exuberance of the nationality consciousness among the intellectuals of the non-Magyar peoples.

[4] *The Balance Sheet of the Dualistic System,* p. 238.

CHAPTER IV

DYNASTIC PATRIOTISM VERSUS NATIONAL PATRIOTISM

Looking over the general tendencies of the two systems, we must say that the Austrian system was entirely incapable of establishing any kind of a popular state consciousness, whereas the Hungarian civic education was overdoing Magyar national consciousness to the detriment of a spontaneous state consciousness of the non-Magyar nationalities. And the danger of the situation was even greater: the Magyar state consciousness in its robust exclusiveness denied not only the existence of the non-Magyar nationalities as corporate entities of the state, but at the same time denied more and more the very existence of a super-state regulating the joint affairs of Austria and Hungary. Under such conditions the loyalty toward the common sovereign, the dynastic patriotism of the patrimonial state became the only uniting tie between the two countries and the various nations. But this feeling became, as a matter of fact, weaker and weaker, an artificial flower in a time when the idea of the self-determination of the nations was growing. The artificial escutcheon of the dualistic state, on which a small dynastic weapon held together the larger weapons of the "anonymous Austria" and of the seemingly united Magyar national state, is almost a symbolical expression of the extreme weakness of the whole structure. The middle weapon, the dynastical patriotism of the Habsburgs, became more and more pale, losing its real driving-force. But not only this curious escutcheon, monument of a desperate statesmanship, the various national hymns too, this real emanation of the popular souls symbolized even more strikingly that Habsburg patriotism was incapable of checking the national patriotism. Let us compare some characteristic utterances of the imperial hymn with those of the national songs of the peoples. The famous Austrian Popular Hymn almost gives the impression of an occasional poem of a high-school teacher by its banal and rigid loyalty in spite of the wonderful music of Haydn

> God save, God guard
> Our Emperor, our country!
> Powerful with the Faith's protection
> Shall he lead us with wise hand!
> The Crown of his Fathers
> Shall defend us from all enemies:
> Closely with the Throne of Habsburgs
> Austria's fate remains united.

How differently ring the national songs of the various nations!
For instance the beginning of the Magyar anthem was this:

> Unshaken to thy Fatherland
> Be loyal, O Magyar!
> It is thy cradle, it is thy grave
> Which nourishes thee and covers. . . . .

Or of the Rumanians:

> Awaken, Rumanian, from thy deadly sleep
> Into which thou wert forced by barbarous tyrants!
> Now or never: create another fate for thyself
> To which even thy cruel enemies should bow!

Or of the Slovaks:

> Up, ye Slovaks, still is living our true Slovak language,
> While our loyal hearts are beating truly for our nation.
> Living, living, yea and deathless is the Slovak spirit:
> Hell and lightning, Hell and lightning rage in vain against us.

Or of the Czechs:

> Where is my Fatherland?
> The waters rumble in the fields
> The pinewoods roar on the rocks
> In the gardens bloom spring flowers
> 'Tis a Paradise on earth
> And this is the beautiful country,
> The country of the Czechs, my Fatherland. . . . .

And of the Croats:

> Flow Sava, flow Drava,
> Neither thou Danube lose thy strength!
> Whenever thou roarest, tell to the World
> That the Croat loves his nation
> Until his soil is not lit up by the sun,
> Until his oak forests are struck by the lightning,
> Until his body is covered by the grave,
> Until his heart no longer beats.

It is highly characteristic that the only nation of the monarchy which did not produce a national hymn in the proper sense was the first leading nation of the monarchy, the German. Why? Because the center of gravity of the German national consciousness, even for the Germans of the monarchy, was not the anational Austria but the German empire as a nation state. At the same time the German leading nation in Austria was so intimately connected with the Habsburg dynasty that the glory of the monarchy as a whole held back the expressions of a special German patriotism within the empire.

No wonder that the intensity of all these national feelings was stronger than the artificial suggestions of a receding dynastic patriotism. And this growing trend of national feeling and conscious-ness was neither checked nor co-ordinated by any other moral syn-thesis. The Habsburg empire became more and more a conglomerate of various nationalistic feelings among peoples which did not know each other but which hated each other bitterly. The dynastic patriot-ism, the faith of some ten thousand officers, aristocrats, priests, bu-reaucrats, and industrial magnates was powerless against the popular enthusiasm of the exuberant national individualities. The state of the Habsburgs collapsed, in the final analysis, because it was unable to offer a real solidarity to its various nations by the help of a system of serious civic education. The more enlightened Habsburgs knew very well the fatal importance of this problem but they could not solve it. The means which were employed were far too mechanical and incoherent. Outside the army we have not a single example of a real type of civic education. Only Crown Prince Rudolf made an attempt in this direction by editing under his patronage a monumental work of many volumes under the title: "The Austro-Hungarian Monarchy in Writing and Pictures." But this enterprise had a very small influ-ence in an atmosphere already envenomed by constitutional and na-tional struggles.

Perhaps no one understood more keenly the situation of the mon-archy from the point of view of public education than Karl Möring, a great soldier, military engineer, statesman, and a careful student of the United States. In his famous anonymous book *Sibyllinische Bü-cher aus Österreich*, dedicated to Archduchess Sofia, mother of Em-peror Francis Joseph, he wrote in 1848 the following prophetical lines:

Must oligarchy and bureaucracy push the monarchy from year to year nearer to the abyss until, standing on the verge and shaken by the slightest thrust, it loses its equilibrium and tumbles down? Such a curse would be terrible and would exclude any hope or possibility of reform. There ex-ists one means still, but only one. It must be applied because it is a mat-ter of life and death. And this only means is public opinion, this appeas-ing, equalizing, and harmonizing intermediary between people and Throne which translates freely the adversities of the state into the language of the truth and not into the jargon of the bureaucracy. It puts clear spectacles before the eyes of the Monarch and not those colored by the oligarchy or ground according to its needs. . . . . Yea, public opinion, this tested Palladium of England, this trumpet of the wholesome voice of the people, it alone can be the Savior of Austria. . . . .[1]

The diagnosis of Karl Möring remained true until the collapse. There never was in the monarchy a public opinion in the Western sense, only an agglomeration of group opinions, led by oligarchical interests.

[1] Hamburg, 1848, I, 153–54.

That the crucial problem of the existence of the monarchy was that of civic education was finally realized by the last Emperor himself when, in the desperate hours of the beginning dissolution, he made among others the following statement to the great pacifist and humanitarian, Professor F. W. Foerster, who, almost as a political physician, was called in July, 1917, to the deathbed of the agonizing empire:

My proclamation of amnesty has aroused much uneasiness and contradiction in some circles. . . . . But it was my firm conviction for a long time that the hopelessly entangled situation of the Austrian people cried for a radical change, the tradition of narrow-mindedness and short-sightedness is so deeply rooted that we can be saved only by an entirely new disposition of mind. . . . . I know that many thousands among my people have long been anxious for such a new beginning, but abroad they do not understand this, nay they do not surmise for what purpose we were united by Providence in this South-eastern corner of Europe: Austria is, as a matter of fact, neither a German nor a Slav state. Though the Germans were the founders of the Danube Monarchy, they are at the present time a minority surrounded and interspersed with many ascending peoples. . . . . Under such circumstances they can remain the leaders of the younger cultures only if they are able to give the example of the highest culture . . . . and to meet the newly evolving nations with love, esteem, and generosity. . . . . Sins were committed on all sides; all the faults must now be corrected . . . . therefore we must turn over a new leaf! . . . . The unity of the state cannot be imposed by force—less than anywhere else—upon the nations of Austria . . . . it must arise from the moral union of these peoples. . . . . Already the youth should be influenced by this spirit: instead of the text-books on both sides which incite to racial hatred, rather such books should be created in which the great qualities and virtues of the Slavic race should be brought home to the German youth . . . . and in the same way it should be honestly told to the Slavic youth what Germandom has contributed to the general culture and particularly to the young nations of the Slavic South-eastern world. . . . .[2]

According to Foerster, the monarch spoke these words in great emotion and with strong emphasis. But this imperial lecture on civic education came too late—not to mention that there was no recipe for the Hungarian problem, the cornerstone of the whole system, in the program of the last Habsburg. He did not even dare to mention this other side of the situation. . . . . The reasons for it are obvious.

[2] Quoted by Polzer-Hoditz, *op. cit.,* pp. 462–63.

RETROSPECT AND PROSPECT

Some general remarks may be added to the chief conclusions of this work concerning both the past and the future.

As to the historical meaning of the process of dissolution, the reader will perhaps share the impression which I experienced the more my investigations proceeded, namely, that the collapse of the Habsburg empire was not anything surprising but rather the long continuance of this amalgamation of peoples without a common state idea, based on the mutual hatred and distrust of the various nations. Manifestly their inner revolutionary forces were not sufficient, in time of peace, to get rid of the Habsburg yoke. Regarding the process as a whole, the most outstanding groups of causes which undermined the cohesion of the old patrimonial state were threefold:

1. The growing national consciousness of the various nations which could not find place for a true consolidation and adequate self-expression in the rigidity of the absolutistic structure, later not changed but only modified by the semi-absolutism of the Dualistic System under which neither a confederated constitution nor even a sound local national autonomy could be achieved.

2. The economic and social pressure of the feudal class rule, allied with a usurious kind of capitalism, which did not allow the productive forces of the various nations to be developed. Vienna was not only a natural economic leader but at the same time an economic exploiter of the weaker nations through her financial and administrative monopolies. The national exasperation of the peoples was strengthened by the feeling of being a kind of a colony for German capitalism. At the same time the hunger-belt of the latifundist system paralyzed to a large extent the beneficent influences of a united customs territory. A true division of labor among the various territories remained rudimentary whereas a new national middle class arose everywhere which felt its economic interests incompatible with the supremacy of big Viennese finance.

3. The lack of any serious kind of civic education. All the nations lived as moral and intellectual strangers to one another. Both the dynastic epic in Austria and the feudal in Hungary were incapable of creating a sufficiently strong and cohesive state idea. Finally these two fallacies pushed the two hegemonic nations into a fatal conflict, even more pernicious than that in which they were engaged with their lesser nationalities.

This growing dissolution and final collapse of the Habsburg empire was mainly the work of three factors:

1. The continuous growth of the various nations which realized more and more clearly that their hope for the rebuilding of the Habsburg empire and for their reasonable national independence was a fallacious one. The ideas of separation or secession became stronger.

2. The irridentistic propaganda of those surrounding countries which harbored a claim for their co-nationals living under Habsburg "oppression," partly from sentimental reasons, partly animated by the imperialistic conceptions of the respective war parties.

3. The disintegrating influence of the World War which made the latent hatred of the nations burst into flame and gave opportunity to the dissatisfied intelligentsias to form fighting diplomatic and military organizations against the empire. This internal dissension and antagonism gradually paralyzed the moral and economic forces of the monarchy.

At this juncture the emphasis of a theoretical consideration seems to me important from the point of view of a clearer understanding of the nature of warlike conflicts. Present-day pacifism, both of a bourgeois and a proletarian type, with very few exceptions, is inclined to think that all wars are exclusively undertakings of the ruling diplomatic and military gangs, allied with certain financial interests and having no connection with deeper popular currents. This war theory, though true in many cases, cannot be regarded as a serious analysis of the social transformations affected by warlike conflicts. It describes, using the terminology of Hegel, only the *List der Idee* and not the *Idee* itself. War is sometimes a kind of revolution and does the same thing as a victorious civil war: it ousts and eliminates antiquated and petrified social and constitutional structures, however unintentioned this effect may be from the point of view of those circles which launched the war. In the case of the last war, it destroyed four petrified political structures, that of the Habsburgs, of the Romanoffs, of the Hohenzollerns, and of the Sultans. In consequence a great number of state embryos in Central Europe, in the Balkans, and in the Baltic grew into an independent life and for many millions of people the road was opened toward national and social emancipation. All these oppressive dynastic structures could have lived indefinitely without the World War, because no successful internal revolution is imaginable in the period of great standing armies as long as their military force remained unshaken. This conception is naturally no justification of the war methods. It is only the assertion that on the basis of the *status quo* real peace cannot be maintained. It is with wars as with revolutions: they can only be eliminated by the elimination of their causes, of those national or social dissatisfactions which envenom the internal or external relations of the countries. No kind of jural or contractual agreement can create real peace as long as the injustices of a given situation continue. The collapse of the Habsburg monarchy is a very decisive corroboration of this thesis.

Unfortunately, war is a very crude and poor substitute for reason and morality. Like revolution, it can solve problems only in an incomplete and summary way, arousing new difficulties, new injustices. The Habsburg monarchy was destroyed without its problems having been solved in a complete, fair, and systematic way. Though many of the old irridentas were eliminated, some new ones were created which will endanger the European situation unless better methods are employed by the new states than those utilized by the Habsburgs. As a matter of fact the newly created states are, from an ethnographic point of view, more firmly built than was the former monarchy. However, they are not national states at all in the Western sense, but are permeated with important national minorities. Thus, for instance, only 81 per cent of the Jugo-Slav state, 71 per cent of Rumania, 64 per cent of Czecho-Slovakia, and 62 per cent of Poland belong to the ruling nation and in the majority of these countries not even the ruling nation is homogeneous but is divided into important antagonistic regional groups. Also the new Russian state faces all the problems of a nationality state, complicated by many serious issues in local autonomies. Therefore, the spectre of the past Austro-Hungarian monarchy could admonish these states not to forget the disastrous lessons of this unsuccessful experiment. Their situation is even more difficult from a certain point of view because the new irridentas formed by the peace treaties are not the backward nations of the former monarchy but, in several cases, equals or superiors in cultural strength and national consciousness to the so-called state-building nations. And if it be replied that in spite of these difficulties the new situation is far more stabilized because the international friction is diminished and there are no powers which could stir the fires of irredentism in these countries, I would answer that this is hardly even true of the present situation and in the near future serious steps could be taken in this direction. Already at the present time the propaganda of the Soviets in the Balkans is far more nationalistic than Communistic, and Fascist Italy utilizes the national dissensions of the newly created states. Magyar irridentism is almost a religious dogma of new Hungary and an influential public opinion in Germany regards the Eastern frontiers as entirely transitory. The *Anschluss* movement in Austria makes rapid progress among the masses, and Albania has taken over the former rôle of Serbia as a storm center of Europe.

The dangers which most of the newly created states face are exactly the dangers of the former Habsburg monarchy: overcentralization and a system of artificial assimilation. Local, ethnic, cultural, and often religious differences have no opportunity to find adequate constitutional channels, whereas the new ruling nations continue here and there the same political and cultural methods by which before the war Germans, Magyars, and Poles tried to maintain their hegemony to the detriment of the subject races. It is outside the task of the present book to enter upon these new experiments in the field of the old policy of artificial assimilation. Suffice it to say that some of the victorious nations did not learn from the tragic fate of the Habsburg empire and many of the old proceedings are continued both in the educational field and in public administration. Here and there the worst excesses of the nationalistic fever envenom the public atmosphere.

In a recent publication[1] a group of Hungarian professors gave us a critical survey of the public instruction of the Magyar population detached from Hungary and annexed to the new states. I am not in a position to judge how far their information is accurate. In any case a certain caution is needed because some of the authors were in prewar times ardent adherents of the Magyar policy of artificial assimilation. Nevertheless, there can be no doubt that in several cases public spirit was not changed but only inverted. Many passages of the book sound almost as servile repetitions of the same procedures which I have portrayed in the present book, describing the methods and spirit of national intolerance and megalomania. I know that several political leaders and statesmen of the new states deplore this attitude but in many cases the governments are not willing or not able to check the chauvinistic tendencies strengthened by a sudden victory, the reminiscences of the past, and the difficulties of the present situation. The dangers of the new illusions of nationalism and the new irridentas are very great.

Unfortunately Western public opinion does not understand sufficiently the new constellation. Many think that the methods of a purely jural pacifism and of a peaceful humanitarian propaganda will be sufficient to appease the haughtiness of the victors and the revenge of the vanquished. Anyone, however, who is in more intimate touch with the psychology of Central and Eastern Europe knows very well that these methods alone cannot suffice without serious organic reform. A very interesting document in this connection is the preface of the previously mentioned book written by Professor Julius Kornis of Budapest University and President of the Hungarian Pedagogical Society. The author ridicules the endeavors of the International Commission for Intellectual Co-operation of the World Federation of Educational Associations to promote peace by the method of a pacifistic education and mutual understanding and advocates openly the necessity of maintenance of the warlike spirit. Let me quote one or two of his most characteristic passages because they throw a beam of light on the real situation of this new unstable equilibrium:

[1] *The Public Instruction of the Detached Magyar Population* (Budapest, 1927). In Hungarian.

. . . . Should we vanquished people, begin to eradicate the natural antipathy against the neighbors who robbed our property for a thousand years when our detached brothers are tortured by these neighbors with the most unbounded cruelty? . . . . The peace of today . . . . is only a silent continuance of the state of war, it is even worse than the bloody wars. Open war is destruction, suffering, death, but the present peace is the silently choking terror of brute force in which the shrieking from pain is smothered by the new international law and the courteous phraseology of the international pedagogy. . . . . In the name of universal humanism, refuted daily by the armament of the imperialistic Great and Little Entente, and by the oppression of national minorities, they will forbid the new Magyar generation the understanding and realization of the warlike exploits and glory of our ancestors, ... the learning of the power of the force which maintained this country through a millennium and which alone can reconquer it in the future. . . . . The sorrowful content of this book will convince the peace enthusiasts that the brilliant epoch of true peace and international good will is on the Eastern European fields not only a Utopia but a Uchronia. Here the words of Kant are particularly true: "Eternal peace? A good inscription for the door of a cemetery!" . . . .[2]

If political reality reflects itself so terribly in the brain of the leader of Hungarian education and if a professor of philosophy misunderstands so completely the great pacifistic message of Kant, the reader can realize the wild and brutal atmosphere of hatred and revenge which is still the dominating current of Eastern Europe. And that is not an isolated symptom but many thousands of the German so-called intellectuals echo the same feelings and convictions whenever they speak in perfect sincerity. Under such conditions only deep organic reforms could cure this envenomed mass-current which will inevitably lead to future wars. What these organic reforms should be, the lesson of the great historical drama which we have investigated in this book shows us with perfect clearness. The roads toward real peace and consolidation can be only the following: First, revision of the frontiers in all cases where homogeneous national minorities can. be attached without difficulty to their connationals. Second, organization of all the national minorities in public bodies entitled to carry on their own cultural and educational system, limited only by their loyalty to the state. Third, decentralization of the overcentralized and bureaucratic states in the spirit of free local government. Fourth, elimination of trade hindrances and augmentation of the possibilities for economic and cultural co-operation. Fifth, eradication of that type of intellectualism and civic education which is represented in the above-quoted utterances.

If the League of Nations should not be capable of carrying on these fundamental reforms, all its jural and educational work will be futile. The disastrous rôle of the former Austro-Hungarian monarchy will be undertaken by other nations.

[2] *The Public Instruction of the Detached Magyar Population, op. cit.*, pp. 10–12.

BIBLIOGRAPHY

I. GENERAL

ABBOTT, J. S. C. *The Empire of Austria.* New York, 1902.

ANONYMOUS (ANDRIAN-WERBURG, VON). *Österreich und seine Zukunft.* Hamburg, 1841.

ANONYMOUS. *Der Zerfall Österreichs. Von einem Deutschösterreicher.* Leipzig, 1867.

AUERBACH, B. *L'Autriche et la Hongrie pendant la Guerre.* Paris, 1925.

————. *Les races et les nationalités en Autriche-Hongrie.* Paris, 1898.

BAHR, H. *Wien.* Wien-Stuttgart, 1907.

BAUER, O. *Die Nationalitätenfrage und die Sozialdemokratie.* Wien, 1907.

————. *Die Österreichische Revolution.* Wien, 1923.

BIBL, V. *Der Zerfall Österreichs* (2 vols.). Wien, 1922.

BIDERMANN, H. J. *Geschichte der österreichischen Gesamtstaatsidee (1526–1804)* (2 vols). Innsbruck, 1867, 1889.

BRUCK, L. FREIHERR VON. *Die Aufgaben Österreichs.* Leipzig, 1860.

CHAMBERLAIN, H. S. *Foundations of the Nineteenth Century* (2 vols.). London, 1911.

CHARMATZ, R. *Geschichte der auswärtigen Politik Österreichs im 19. Jahrhundert.* Leipzig, 1912.

————. *Österreichs äussere und innere Politik von 1895 bis 1917.* Leipzig und Berlin, 1918.

————. *Österreichs innere Geschichte von 1848–95* (3d ed.). Leipzig und Berlin, 1918.

COLQUHOUN, A. R. *The Whirlpool of Europe.* London and New York, 1907.

DINER-DÉNES, J. *La Hongrie, Oligarchie, Nation, Peuple.* Paris, 1927.

EISENMANN, L. *Le Compromis Austro-Hongrois de 1867.* Paris, 1904.

EÖTVÖS, J. FREIHERR VON. *Der Einfluss der herrschenden Ideen des 19. Jahrhunderts auf den Staat* (2 vols.). Leipzig, 1854.

————. *Die Garantien der Macht und Einheit Österreichs.* Leipzig, 1859.

————. *Die Nationalitätenfrage.* Pest, 1865.

————. *Über die Gleichberechtung der Nationalitäten in Österreich.* Pest, 1871.

FISCHEL, A. *Das österreichische Sprachenrecht.* Brünn, 1901.

————. *Materialien zur Sprachenfrage in Österreich.* Brünn, 1902.

————. *Studien zur österreichischen Reichsgeschichte.* Wien, 1906.

FISCHHOF, A. *Ein Blick auf Österreichs Lage.* Wien, 1866.

————. *Österreich und die Bürgschaften seines Bestandes.* Wien, 1869.

FRIEDJUNG, H. *Der Ausgleich mit Ungarn. Politische Studie über das Verhältnis Österreichs zu Ungarn und Deutschland* (2d ed.). Leipzig, 1877.

GENNEP, A. VAN. *Les élements extérieurs de la nationalité, 1922.*

GLAISE-HORSTENAU, E. VON. *Die Katastrophe.* Wien, 1929.

GOLDSCHEID, R. *Das Verhältnis der Äussern Politik zur Innern.* Wien, 1914.

GOOCH, G. P. *Nationalism.* New York, 1920.

GUMPLOWICZ, L. *Das Recht der Nationalitäten und Sprachen in Österreich-Ungarn.* Innsbruck, 1879.

―――. *Österreichische Reichsgeschichte.* Berlin, 1896.

HERRNRITT, R. H. VON. *Nationalität und Recht.* Dargestellt nach der österreichischen und ausländischen Gesetzgebung. Wien, 1899.

HEVESY, A. DE. *L'Agonie d'un Empire: L'Autriche-Hongrie.* 1923.

JÁSZI, O. (ed.). *La Hongrie Contemporaine et le Suffrage Universel.* Paris, 1909.

JÁSZI, O. *The Evolution of the Nation States and the Nationality Problem* (in Hungarian). Budapest, 1912.

―――. *Der Zusammenbruch des Dualismus und die Zukunft der Donaustaaten.* Wien, 1918.

KAHLER, E. VON. *Das Geschlecht Habsburg.* München, 1919.

KJELLÉN, R. *Die Grossmächte und die Weltkrise.* Leipzig und Berlin, 1921.

KLEINWAECHTER, F. *Der Untergang der österreichisch-ungarischen Monarchie.* Leipzig, 1920.

LANG, O. *Das österreichische Staatsproblem und seine Lösung.* 1905.

LASKI, H. J. *A Grammar of Politics.* London, 1925.

LAVELEYE, E. DE. *The Balkan Peninsula.* London, 1886.

LAVISSE, E. *Vue générale de l'histoire politique de l'Europe.* Paris, 1904.

LEGER, L. *La Save, le Danube, et le Balkan.* Paris, 1884.

LOISEAU, C. *Les Balkan-Slaves et la Crise autrichienne.* Paris, 1898.

―――. *L'equilibre Adriatique.* Paris, 1901.

LUSCHIN, A. VON. *Grundriss der österreichischen Reichsgeschichte.* Bamberg, 1914.

MASARYK, T. G. *The Making of a State.* New York, 1927.

MITSCHERLICH, W. *Der Nationalismus West-Europas.* 1920.

MOCSÁRY, L. *The Balance Sheet of the Dualistic System* (in Hungarian). Budapest, 1902.

MUIR, R. *Nationality and Internationalism.* London, 1917.

OPPENHEIMER, F. *Grossgrundeigentum und soziale Frage.* Jena, 1922.

―――. *Der Staat.* Jena, 1926.

Österreichs Staatswörterbuch. Herausgegeben von Professor Dr. Mischler und Prof. Dr. Ulbrich. Wien. (4 vols.)

PALACKÝ, F. *Österreichs Staatsidee.* Prag, 1866.

Popovici, A. C. *Die Vereinigten Staaten von Gross-Österreich.* Leipzig, 1906.

Přibram, A. F. *Austrian Foreign Policy (1908–1918).* London, 1923.

Redlich, J. *Kaiser Franz Joseph von Österreich.* Berlin, 1928.

———. *Das österreichische Staats- und Rechtsproblem* (2 vols.). Leipzig, 1920, 1926.

———. *Österreichs Regierung und Verwaltung im Weltkriege.* Wien, 1925.

René, H. *Question d'Autriche, Hongrie et question d'Orient.* Paris, 1904.

Rose, J. Holland. *Nationality in Modern History.* New York, 1916.

Samassa, P. *Der Völkerstreit im Habsburgerstaat.* Leipzig, 1910.

Schücking, W. *Das Nationalitätenproblem.* Eine politische Studie über die Polenfrage und die Zukunft Österreich-Ungarns. Dresden, 1908.

Schüssler, W. *Das Verfassungsproblem im Habsburgerreich.* Stuttgart und Wien, 1918.

Schuselka, F. *Das provisorische Österreich.* Leipzig, 1850.

Sealsfield, C. *Österreich wie es ist.* Wien, 1919.

Seignobos, C. *Histoire Politique de L'Europe Contemporaine* (2 vols.). Paris, 1924.

Seton-Watson, R. W. *Racial Problems in Hungary.* London, 1908.

———. *The Rise of Nationality in the Balkans.* London, 1917.

———. *Sarajevo. A Study in the Origins of the Great War.* London, 1925.

———. *The Future of Austria-Hungary and the Attitude of the Great Powers.* 1907.

———. *The Southern Slav Question and the Habsburg Monarchy.* London, 1911.

Sieger, Dr. R. *Die geographischen Grundlagen der österreich-ungarischen Monarchie und ihrer Aussenpolitik.* Leipzig und Berlin, 1915.

Sosnosky, T. von. *Die Balkanpolitik Österreich-Ungarns seit 1866.* Wien, 1913.

———. *Die Politik im Habsburgerreiche* (2d ed.). Berlin, 1912.

Spitzmüller, Dr. *Der politische Zusammenbruch und die Anschlussfrage.* Wien, 1919.

Springer, A. H. *Österreich nach der Revolution.* Prague, 1850.

Springer R. (Karl Renner). *Grundlagen und Entwicklungsziele der österreichisch-ungarischen Monarchie.* Wien, 1906.

———. *Der Kampf der österreichischen Nationen um den Staat.* Wien, 1902.

———. *Staat und Parlament. Kritische Studie über die österreichische Parlamentskrise und das System der Interessenvertretung.* Wien, 1901.

Steed, H. W. *The Hapsburg Monarchy.* London, 1913.

Südland, P. *Die südslavische Frage und der Weltkrieg.* Wien, 1918.

SYNOPTIKUS (KARL RENNER). *Staat und Nation.* Wien, 1899.

SZILASSY, BARON J. *Der Untergang der Donaumonarchie.* Bern, 1921.

TEZNER, F. *Das staatsrechtliche und politische Problem der österreichisch-ungarischen Monarchie.* "Archiv des öffentlichen Rechts." 1913.

————. *Die Wandlungen der österr.-ungarischen Reichsidee.* Wien, 1905.

ULBRICH, T. *Die rechtliche Natur des österreichisch-ungarischen Monarchie.* Prag, 1879.

VAUSSARD, M. *Enquête sur nationalisme.* Paris, 1924.

VERBÖCZY, S. *Corpus juris hungarici.* Budae, 1822.

WALLAS, G. *Human Nature in Politics.* New York, 1921.

WENDEL, H. *Aus dem südslavischen Risorgimento.* Gotha, 1921.

WIESER, F. VON. *Die Vergangenheit und Zukunft der österreichischen Verfassung.* Wien, 1906.

————. *Österreichs Ende.* Berlin, 1919.

ZANGWILL, I. *The Principle of Nationalities.* New York, 1917.

ZIMMERN, A. *Nationality and Government.* London, 1918.

II. HISTORICAL

ACSÁDY, I. *History of the Hungarian Empire.* (2 vols.; in Hungarian). Budapest, 1903.

ANONYMOUS (HORMAYR, J. VON). *Anemonen aus dem Tagebuche eines alten Pilgersmannes* (4 vols.). Jena, 1845–47.

APPONYI, COUNT A. *A Brief Sketch of the Hungarian Constitution and of the Relations between Austria and Hungary.* Budapest, 1908.

ARNETH, A. RITTER VON. *Geschichte Maria Theresias* (10 vols.). Wien, 1863–79.

————. *Prinz Eugen* (3 vols.). Wien, 1864.

BACH, M. *Geschichte der Wiener Revolution, 1848.* Wien, 1898.

BACHMANN, A. *Geschichte Böhmens* (2 vols.). Gotha, 1899, 1905.

BAGGER, E. *Franz Joseph, Emperor of Austria, King of Hungary.* New York, 1927.

BEIDTEL, I. *Geschichte der österreichischen Staatsverwaltung (1740–1848)* (2 vols.). Innsbruck, 1896, 1897.

BERZEVICZY, A. *The Period of Absolutism in Hungary, 1849–65* (in Hungarian). Budapest, 1922.

BIBL, V. *Die niederösterreichischen Stände im Vormärz.* Wien, 1911.

BRIGHT, J. F. *Joseph II.* London, 1897.

BROGLIE, A. DUC DE. *Marie Thérèse impératrice. 1744–1746.* Paris, 1892.

COXE, W. *History of the House of Austria, 1218–1792.* London, 1847.

CZOERNIG, K. FREIHERR VON. *Österreichs Neugestaltung. 1848 bis 1858.* Stuttgart, 1858.

DENIS, E. *La Bohême depuis la Montagne Blanche* (2 vols.). Paris, 1903.

FESSLER, I. A. *Geschichte von Ungarn.* Leipzig, 1877.

FISCHEL, A. *Der Panslavismus bis zum Weltkrieg.* Stuttgart und Berlin, 1919.

FOURNIER, A. *Historische Studien und Skizzen.* Prag, 1885.

———. *Wie wir zu Bosnien kamen.* Eine historische Studie. Wien, 1909.

FRAKNÓI, W. *Ungarn vor der Schlacht bei Mohács.* Budapest, 1886.

FRANKENFELD, A. *Österreichs Spiel mit dem Kriege.* Dresden, 1928.

FREEMAN, E. A. *The Ottoman Power in Europe.* London, 1877.

FRIEDJUNG, H. *Der Kampf um die Vorherrschaft in Deutschland* (2 vols.). Stuttgart, 1897.

———. *Der Krimkrieg und die österreichische Politik.* Stuttgart, 1907.

———. *Österreich von 1848 bis 1860.* Stuttgart und Berlin, 1908.

GEORGEVITCH, W. *Das Ende der Obrenovitch.* Leipzig, 1905.

GINDELY, A. *Böhmen und Mähren im Zeitalter der Reformation* (2 vols.). Prag, 1857, 1858.

———. *Geschichte des dreissigjährigen Krieges* (4 vols.). Prag, 1869–80.

———. *Rudolf II. und seine Zeit (1600–1612)* (2 vols.). Prag, 1862, 1868.

GRAHAM, W. *New Governments of Central Europe.* New York, 1926.

GRÜNWALD, B. *The Old Hungary* (in Hungarian). Budapest, 1910.

HAYES, C. J. H. *A Political and Social History of Modern Europe* (2 vols.) New York, 1924.

HELFERT, J. A. FREIHERR VON. *Geschichte der österreichischen Revolution im Zusammenhange mit der mitteleuropäischen Bewegung.* Freiburg, 1907.

———. *Kaiser Franz und die österreichischen Befreiungskriege gegen Napoleon.* Wien, 1867.

HORMAYR, J. VON. *Das Land Tirol und der Tiroler Krieg von 1809.* Leipzig, 1845.

HORN, G. *Le Compromis de 1868 entre la Hongrie et la Croatie et celui de 1867 entre l'Autriche et la Hongrie.* Paris, 1907.

HORVÁTH, J. *Modern Hungary, 1660–1920.* Budapest, 1922.

HORVÁTH, M. *Geschichte des Unabhängigkeitskrieges in Ungarn. 1848 und 1849* (3 vols.; 2d ed.). Pest, 1872.

———. *Kurzgefasste Geschichte Ungarns* (2 vols.). Pest, 1863.

———. *25 Jahre aus der Geschichte Ungarns. 1823–48* (2 vols.). Leipzig, 1867.

HUBER, A. *Geschichte der österreichischen Verwaltungsorganization bis zum XVIII. Jahrhundert.* Innsbruck, 1884.

———. *The Hungarian Rebellion.* London, 1872.

IRÁNYI AND CHASSIN. *Histoire politique de la Révolution de Hongrie 1848–49.* Paris, 1859–60.

JORGA, N. *Geschichte des rumänischen Volkes* (2 vols.). Gotha, 1905.

KÁLLAY, B. VON. *Geschichte der Serben.* Budapest, 1878.

KLAPKA, G. *Der Nationalkrieg in Ungarn und Siebenbürgen in den Jahren 1848 bis 49.* Leipzig, 1851.

KNATCHBULL-HUGESSEN, C. M. *The Political Evolution of the Hungarian Nation.* London, 1908.

KRAUS, V. VON. *Zur Geschichte Österreichs unter Ferdinand I. 1519–1522.* Ein Bild ständischer Parteikämpfe. Wien, 1873.

KRONES, F. *Handbuch der Geschichte Österreichs* (5 vols.). Berlin, 1876–79.

⸻. *Ungarn unter Maria Theresia und Joseph II.* Graz, 1871.

KUPELWIESER, L. *Die Kämpfe Ungarns mit den Osmanen.* Wien, 1895.

LEFAIVRE, A. *Les Magyars pendant la domination Ottomane en Hongrie (1526–1722).* Paris, 1902.

LEGER, L. *Histoire de l'Autriche-Hongrie depuis les origines jusqu'à l'année 1894.* Paris, 1895.

⸻. *A History of Austro-Hungary.* London, 1889.

LÜTZOW, COUNT. *The Hussite Wars.* London, 1904.

MAILÁTH, GRAF J. *Geschichte der Magyaren.* Regensburg, 1917.

MARCZALI, H. *Hungary in the Eighteenth Century.* Cambridge, 1910.

⸻. *Ungarische Verfassungsgeschichte.* Tübingen, 1910.

⸻. *Ungarns Geschichtsquellen.* Berlin, 1882.

MÁRKUS, D. *Ungarisches Verfassungsrecht.* Tübingen, 1912.

MARX, K. *Revolution und Kontrerevolution in Deutschland.* Stuttgart, 1896.

MAURICE, C. E. *The Revolutionary Movement of 1848–89 in Italy, Austria-Hungary and Germany.* London, 1887.

MEYNERT, H. *Geschichte der k. k. Armee* (2 vols.). Wien, 1852–54.

NOWAK, K. F. *Chaos.* München, 1923.

⸻. *Der Sturz der Mittelmächte.* München, 1921.

OTTENFELD, R. VON, UND O. TEUBER. *Die österreichische Armee 1700–1867.* Wien, 1895.

PALACKÝ, F. *Geschichte von Böhmen* (5 vols.). Prag, 1836–67.

PINON, R. *L'Europe et l'Empire Ottoman. Les Aspects actuel de la question d'Orient.* Paris, 1908.

REICH, E. *The Magyar County: A Study in the Comparative History of Municipal Institutions.* London, 1893.

ROGGE, W. *Österreich von Világos bis zur Gegenwart.* Leipzig und Wien, 1872–83.

RÜSTOW, W. *Geschichte des ungarischen Insurrektionskrieges 1848–1849.* Zürich, 1860–61.

SALAMON, F. *Ungarn im Zeitalter der Türkenherrschaft.* Leipzig, 1887.

SAYOUS, É. *Histoire générale des Hongrois.* Paris, 1876.

⸻. *Histoire des Hongrois et de leur littérature politique de 1790 à 1815.* Paris, 1872.

SCHAPIRO, J. S. *Modern and Contemporary European History.* Boston, 1922.

SCHEVILL, F. *History of the Balkan Peninsula.* New York, 1922.

SCHULER, F. VON. *Siebenbürgische Rechtsgeschichte* (3 vols.; 2d ed.). Hermannstadt, 1867–68.

SCHWICKER, J. H. *Politische Geschichte der Serben in Ungarn.* Budapest, 1880.

SKENE, A. VON. *Entstehen und Entwicklung der slavisch-nationalen Bewegung in Böhmen und Mähren im 19. Jahrhundert.* Wien, 1893.

SOREL, A. *L'Europe et la Révolution française.* Paris, 1904.

SPRINGER, A. *Geschichte des Revolutionszeitalters.* Prag, 1849.

———. *Österreich nach der Revolution.* Prag, 1850.

———. *Protokolle des Verfassungsausschusses im österreichischen Reichstag 1848–49.* Leipzig, 1885.

———. *Geschichte Österreichs seit dem Wiener Frieden. (1809–1849)* (2 vols.). Leipzig, 1863, 1865.

STRAKOSCH-GRASSMANN, G. *Geschichte der Deutschen in Österreich-Ungarn.* Wien, 1895.

SZALAY, L. VON. *Geschichte Ungarns* (3 vols.). Pest, 1866–75.

SZEKFÜ, J. *Der Staat Ungarn.* Stuttgart, 1918.

SZILÁGYI AND COLLABORATORS. *The History of the Hungarian Nation* (in Hungarian) (10 vols.). Budapest, 1895–98.

TELEKI, COMTE L. *De l'intervention Russe I, II.* Paris, 1849.

TELEKI, GRAF L. *Die Ereignisse in Ungarn seit dem März 1848.* Leipzig, 1849.

TEMPERLEY, H. *History of Serbia.* London, 1917.

TEUTSCH, G. D. *Geschichte der Siebenbürger Sachsen.* Kronstadt, 1899.

TIMON, A. VON. *Ungarische Verfassungs- und Rechtsgeschichte* (2d ed.). Berlin, 1909.

TSCHUPPIK. *Die tschechische Revolution.* Wien, 1920.

VÁMBÉRY, A. *The Story of Hungary.* London, 1922.

WACHSMUTH, W. *Geschichte des Illyrismus.* Leipzig, 1849.

WARD, A. D. "The Revolution and the Reaction in Austria (1848–49)," in *Cambridge Modern History,* Vol. XI.

WENDEL, H. *Der Kampf der Südslaven um Freiheit und Einheit.* Frankfurt am Main, 1925.

WERTHEIMER, E. *Geschichte Österreichs und Ungarns im ersten Jahrzehnt des 19 Jahrhunderts* (2 vols.). Leipzig, 1884, 1890.

WINDELBAND, W. *Die Auswärtige Politik der Grossmächte in der Neuzeit.* Zweite durchgesehene Auflage. Stuttgart und Berlin, 1925.

WREDE, A. VON. *Geschichte der k. und k. Wehrmacht.* Wien, 1898.

XÉNOPOL, A. D. *Histoire des Roumains* (2 vols.). Paris, 1894.

ZENKER, E. V. *Die Wiener Revolution 1848 in ihren sozialen Voraussetzungen und Beziehungen.* Wien, 1897.

III. ECONOMIC

ADLER, E. *Die Lage des Handwerks in Österreich.* Wien, 1898.

ADLER, M. "Anfänge der merkantilen Gewerbepolitik in Österreich," *Wiener Staatswissenschaftliche Studien,* Vol. IV. Wien.

ANONYMOUS (Von einem aufrichtigen Freunde der Österreichischen Landwirtschaft). *Der Serbische Handels Vertrag, ein Sieg der Agrarier.* Wien, 1908.

BEER, A. *Die Finanzen Österreichs im 19. Jahrhundert.* Prague, 1877.

————. *Die österreichische Handelspolitik unter Maria Theresia und Joseph II.* Wien, 1898.

————. *Die österreichische Handelspolitik im 19. Jahrhundert.* Wien, 1891.

————. *Studien zur Geschichte der österreichischen Volkswirtschaft unter Maria Theresia.* Wien, 1894.

BETHLEN, COUNT S. *Magyar Landed-Property Policy in Transylvania* (in Hungarian). Budapest, 1913.

BONER, C. *Transylvania: Its Products and Its People.* London, 1865.

BUDAY, L. *Dismembered Hungary.* Budapest, 1922.

————. *The Economic Unity of Hungary.* Budapest, 1919.

BUNZEL. *Studien zur Sozial- und Wirtschaftspolitik Ungarns.* Leipzig, 1902.

DARÁNYI, I. *The State and Agriculture in Hungary.* London, 1905.

DEUTSCH, J. *Geschichte der österreichischen Gewerkschaftsbewegung.* Wien, 1908.

EXNER, W. F. *Beiträge zur Geschichte der Gewerbe und Erfindungen in Österreich.* Wien, 1873.

FÉNYES, A. *Statistik des Königreichs Ungarn.* Pest, 1843.

Geschichte der österreichischen Land- und Forstwirtschaft und ihrer Industrien 1848–98 (4 vols.). Wien, 1899–1901.

GONNARD, R. *La Hongrie au XX siècle. Étude Économique et Sociale.* Paris, 1908.

GRATZ AND SCHÜLLER. *Die äussere Wirtschaftspolitik Österreich-Ungarns. Die mitteleuropäischen Pläne.* Wien, 1925.

Grossindustrie Österreichs. Jubiläumswerk (3 vols.). Wien, 1908.

GRÜNBERG, K. *Die Agrarverfassung und das Grundentlastungsproblem in Bosnien und der Herzegovina.* Wien, 1911.

————. *Die Bauernbefreiung und die Auflösung des gutsherrlich-bäuerlichen Verhältnisses in Böhmen, Mähren und Schlesien* (2 vols.). Leipzig, 1894.

————. *Die handelspolitischen Beziehungen Österreich-Ungarns zu den Ländern an der unteren Donau.* Leipzig, 1902.

————. *Studien zur österreichischen Agrargeschichte.* Leipzig, 1901.

GRUNZEL, J. *Handelspolitik und Ausgleich in Österreich-Ungarn.* Wien, 1912.

HAINISCH, M. *Einige neue Zahlen zur Statistik der Deutschösterreicher.* Wien, 1909.

————. *Die Zukunft der Deutschösterreicher.* Eine statistisch volkswirtschaftliche Studie. Wien, 1892.

HERTZ, F. *Die österreichisch-ungarische Bank und der Ausgleich.* Wien, 1903.

————. *Die Schwierigkeiten der industriellen Produktion in Österreich.* Wien, 1910.

HERTZKA, T. *Österreichisch-ungarische Streitfragen.* Wien, 1912.

————. *Die österreichische Währungsfrage.* Wien, 1875.

HÜBSCH, F. L. *Versuch einer Geschichte des böhmischen Handels.* Prag, 1849.

JÁRAY, G. L. *La question sociale et le socialisme en Hongrie.* Paris, 1909.

JEKELFALUSSY, J. (editor). *The Millenium of Hungary and Its People.* Budapest, 1897.

————. *Der tausendjährige ungarische Staat und sein Volk.* Im Auftrage des ungarischen Handelsministeriums herausgegeben. Budapest, 1896.

KOVÁCS, A. *The Development of the Population of Hungary since the Cessation of Turkish Rule.* Budapest, 1920.

KUN, E. *Sozialhistorische Beiträge zur Landarbeiterfrage in Ungarn.* Jena, 1903.

LANDAU, H. *Entwicklung des Warenhandels in Österreich.* Wien, 1906.

LÁNG, L. *Hundert Jahre Zollpolitik 1805–1905.* Wien, 1906.

LUSCHIN, A. VON. *Die Handelspolitik der österreichischen Herrscher im Mittelalter.* Almanach der kaiserl. Akademie der Wissenschaften. Wien, 1893.

MAJLÁTH, COMTE J. *La Hongrie rurale, sociale, et économique.* (Paris, 1919.

MAJLÁTH, GRAF J. *Studien über die Landarbeiterfrage in Ungarn.* 1905.

MATLEKOVITS, A. VON. *Das Königreich Ungarn volkswirtschaftlich und statistisch dargestellt* (2 vols.). Leipzig, 1900.

————. *Die Zollpolitik der österreichisch-ungarischen Monarchie und des deutschen Reiches seit 1868 und der nächsten Zukunft.* Leipzig, 1891.

MATLEKOVITS, A., AND GELLÉRI, M. *Die Entwicklung der ungarischen Industrie.* Wien, 1902.

MICHELIS, E. *Die Zolltrennung Österreich-Ungarns in handelspolitischer und volkswirtschaftlicher Beleuchtung.* Wien, 1908.

MISES, L. VON. "Die Entwicklung des gutsherrlich-bäuerlichen Verhältnisses in Galizien 1772–1848," Aus: *Wiener Staatswissenschaftliche Studien,* Vol. IV. Wien.

NÁVAY, A. *La Hongrie, son rôle économique.* Paris, 1911.

OFFERGELD, W. *Grundlagen und Ursachen der industriellen Entwicklung in Ungarn.* Jena, 1914.

PANTZ, F. REICHSRITTER VON. *Die Hochschutzzollpolitik Hohenblums und der österreichische Bauernstand.* Wien, 1910.

PŘIBRAM, K. *Geschichte der österreichischen Gewerbepolitik von 1740 bis 1860.* Leipzig, 1907.

RAUCHBERG, H. *Der nationale Besitzstand in Böhmen* (3 vols.). Leipzig, 1905.

RÉCLUS, E. *The Earth and Its Inhabitants.* London, 1880.

RENNER, K. *Die Aera Hohenblum: Der Ruin unserer Staats- und Volkswirtschaft.* Wien, 1913.

SCHWICKER, J. H. *Statistik des Königreichs Ungarn.* Stuttgart, 1877.

SCHWIEDLAND, E. *Kleingewerbe und Hausindustrie in Österreich.* Leipzig, 1894.

SIEGHART, R. *Zolltrennung und Zolleinheit. Geschichte des österr.-ungarischen Zwischenhandels.* Wien, 1915.

SIMITSCH, A., REICHSRITTER VON HOHENBLUM. *Materialen zur Vorbereitung des Öst.-Ung. Handelsvertrages mit Serbien.* Wien, 1903.

SKENE, A. *Ein Beitrag zur Beurteilung der österreichischen Agrarfrage* (2d ed.). Wien, 1885.

STIASSNY, P. *Der österreichische Staatsbankrott vom Jahre 1811.* Wien, 1911.

STIEVE, F. *Der oberösterreichische Bauernaufstand des Jahres 1626* (? vols.). München, 1891.

SZÉCHENYI, GRAF S. *Über den Kredit.* Pest, 1830.

SZENDE, P. "Der Staatshaushalt und das Finanzsystem Österreichs und Ungarns" in *Handbuch der Finanzwissenschaft.* Tübingen, 1928.

TEIFEN, T. W. *Die Besitzenden und die Besitzlosen in Österreich.* Wien, 1906.

SZÉCHENYI, GRAF S. *Über den Kredit.* Pest, 1830.

VÁGÓ, J. *Memorandum concerning the Renewal of the Austrian-Hungarian Customs and Commercial Treaty* (in Hungarian). Budapest, 1916.

ZWIEDINECK, O. VON. "Die handelspolitischen Beziehungen Serbiens zu Österreich-Ungarn" in Harms, *Weltwirtschaftliches Archiv,* Band 6.

IV. NATIONALITIES AND THEIR STRUGGLES

ANONYMOUS. *Die Magyarisierung in Ungarn.* Nach den Debatten des ungarischen Reichstages über den Unterricht der magyarischen Sprache an den Volksschulen. München, 1879.

ANONYMOUS. *Masaryk the Liberator* (in Czech). Praha, 1922.

BEARD, C. A., AND RADIN, G. *The Balkan Pivot: Yugoslavia.* New York, 1929.

BEKSICS, G. *La question roumaine et la lutte des races en Orient.* Paris, 1895.

BERNHARD. *Die Polenfrage.* Leipzig, 1910.

BERTHA, A. DE. *Magyars et Roumains devant l'Histoire.* Paris, 1899.

Beschwerden und Klagen der Slaven in Ungarn, vorgetragen von einem ungarischen Slaven. Leipzig, 1843.

BIDERMANN, H. I. *Die Italiener im Tiroler Provinzialverbande.* Innsbruck, 1874.

———. *Russische Umtriebe in Ungarn.* Innsbruck, 1867.

———. *Die ungarischen Ruthenen, ihr Wohngebiet, ihr Erwerb und ihre Geschichte* (2 vols.). Innsbruck, 1862, 1867.

BLAGOYÉVITCH, V. *Le principe des nationalités et son application dans les traités de paix de Versailles et de Saint Germain.* Paris, 1922.

BÖLDÉNYI, M. J. *Le magyarisme ou la guerre des nationalités en Hongrie.* Paris, 1850.

BONKÁLÓ, A. *The Slavs* (in Hungarian). Budapest, 1915.

BOURLIER, J. *Les tschèques et la Bohême contemporaine.* Paris, 1897.

BOWEN, F. *Hungary. The Rebellion of the Slavonic, Wallachian and German Hungarians against the Magyars.* Cambridge, Massachusetts, 1851.

BROTE. *Die rumänische Frage in Siebenbürgen und Ungarn.* Berlin, 1895.

ČAPEK, T. *The Slovaks of Hungary.* New York, 1906.

ČERVINKA. *On the Roads of Our Revolution* (in Czech). Praha, 1920.

CHEKREZI, C. A. *Albania, Past and Present.* New York, 1919.

CLOPOTEL, J. *The Revolution of 1918* (in Rumanian). Cluj, 1920.

ČOROVIĆ, DR. V. *Black Book* (in Serbian). Beograd-Sarajevo, 1920.

CZÖRNIG, C. FREIHERR VON. *Ethnographie der österr.-ungar. Monarchie.* Wien, 1857.

DASZYŃSKI. *Four Years' War* (in Polish). Kraków, 1918.

DJORDJEVIĆ. *Serbia and the Jugo-Slavs* (in Serbian). Beograd, 1922.

FÉNYES, A. *Ungarn im Vormärz, nach Grundkräften, Verfassung und Kultur.* Leipzig, 1851.

FICKER. *Die Volkstämme der österreichisch-ungarischen Monarchie.* Wien, 1869.

HAYMERLE, A. RITTER VON. *Italicae Res.* Wien, 1879.

HELFERT, J. A. FREIHERR VON. *Geschichte der süd-ungarischen Bewegung und Kämpfe gegen die Zumuthungen des Pan-Magyarismus.* Wien, 1908.

———. *Österreich und die Nationalitäten.* Ein offenes Wort an Franz Palacký. Wien, 1850.

HERMANT, J. *La Révolution hongroise de 1848: Les nationalités, leurs luttes et leurs revendications.* Paris, 1901.

HODŽA, M. M. *Der Slowak: Beiträge zur Beleuchtung der slawischen Frage in Ungarn.* Prag, 1848.

HUNFALVY, P. *Ethnographie von Ungarn.* Budapest, 1877.

———. *Die Rumänen und ihre Ansprüche.* Wien, 1883.

JANCSÓ, B. *Historical and Present State of the Rumanian National Aspirations* (in Hungarian). Budapest, 1899.

JANCSÓ, B. *Our Struggle for Independence and the Daco-Rumanian Aspirations* (in Hungarian). Budapest, 1885.

KRASINSKI, COUNT V. *Panslavism and Germanism.* London, 1848.

————. *Montenegro and the Slavonians of Turkey.* London, 1853.

KRATOCHVIL. *The Road of Revolution* (in Czech). Praha, 1922.

KUPZANKO, G. *Das Schicksal der Ruthenen.* Leipzig, 1887.

LAURIAN, M. A. *Le Principe des Nationalités et l'Unité nationale roumaine.* 1923.

LÖHER, F. VON. *Die Magyaren und andere Ungarn.* Leipzig, 1874.

LOISEAU. "Les Yougoslaves d'Autriche-Hongrie pendant la guerre" in *La vie des Peuples,* Tome II. Paris, 1924.

MASARYK, T. G. *Der Agramer Hochverratsprozess und die Annexion von Bosnien und der Herzegowina.* Wien, 1910.

MELTZL, O. *The Position of the Transylvanian Saxons in Hungary* (in Hungarian). Nagy-Szeben, 1878.

MERCATOR. *Die Nationalitätenfrage und die ungarische Reichsidee.* Budapest, 1908.

MORACZEWSKI. *A Sketch of the Polish Cause in the Present War* (in Polish). Lausanne, 1915.

NIEDERLE, L. *Le race Slave.* Paris, 1911.

PAPÁNEK. *La Tchécoslovaquie.* Prague, 1923.

PHILIPPS, W. A. *Poland.* London, 1915.

PICOT. *Les Serbes de Hongrie.* Prague, 1873.

PODWOJSKI. *The Truth about Czecho-Slovakia* (in Russian). Moscow, 1918.

POTOČNJAK. *From the Emigration* (in Croatian). Zagreb, 1919.

PULSZKY, F. *Die Stellung der Slovaken in Ungarn.* Prag, 1843.

RADL, E. *Der Kampf zwischen Tschechen und Deutschen.* Reichenberg, 1928.

RAŠIN. *The Upheaval of October 28th* (in Czech). Praha, 1919.

ROMANCZUK, J. *Die Ruthenen und ihre Gegner in Galizien.* Wien, 1902.

ROSNER. *In Critical Time* (in Polish). Wien, 1916.

ROTH, S. L. *Der Sprachenkampf in Siebenbürgen.* 1842.

ŠAZINEK, F. *Die Slovaken.* Prag, 1875.

SCHIERBRAND, W. VON. *Austria-Hungary: the Polyglot Empire.* New York, 1917.

SCHULTHEISS, F. G. *Deutschtum und Magyarisierung in Ungarn.* München, 1898.

SCHWICKER, J. H. *Die nationalpolitischen Ansprüche der Rumänen in Ungarn.* Leipzig, 1894.

SEMBRATOWYCZ, R. *Polonia irredenta.* Frankfurt am Main, 1907.

SETON-WATSON, R. W. *Absolutism in Croatia.* London, 1912.

————. *Corruption and Reform in Hungary.* A study of electoral practice. London, 1911.

————. *German, Slav, and Magyar.* London, 1916.

————. *Political Persecution in Hungary.* London, 1908.

————. *Roumania and the Great War.* London, 1915.

SMOLKA, S. *Die Ruthenen und ihre Gönner in Berlin.* 1902.

Sollen wir Magyaren werden? 5 Briefe geschrieben aus Pest an einen Freund an der Theiss, von D. H. Karlstadt, 1843.

SOUKUP AND RAŠIN. *The National Committee on October 28th. The National Assembly in the First Year of the Republic* (in Czech). Praha, 1919.

SPALAJKOVIC, M. *La Bosnie et l'Herzegowine; étude d'histoire et diplomatique et des droits internationales.* Paris, 1899.

STEIDLER. *The Czecho-Slovak Movement in Russia* (in Czech). Praha, 1921.

STÚR, L. *Das XIX. Jahrhundert und der Magyarismus.* Leipzig, 1843.

SUCIU, A. *De la Nationalité en Roumanie.* 1906.

SYDACOFF, B. VON. *Die panslawistische Agitation und die südslawische Bewegung in Österreich-Ungarn* (2d ed.). Berlin, 1900.

SZÁSZ, Z. *The Minorities in Rumanian Transylvania.* London, 1927.

THUN, GRAF L. *Die Stellung der Slowaken in Ungarn.* Pest, 1843.

TOBOLKA. *Czech Policy in the World War* (in Czech). Praha, 1922.

TOMIĆ. *Jugo-Slavia in the Emigration* (in Serbian). Belgrad, 1921.

Die Völker Österreich-Ungarns. Ethnographische und kultur-historische Schilderungen. Wien, 1881. 1, Schober, *Die Deutschen in Niederösterreich, Oberösterreich, Salzburg, Steiermark, Kärnten und Krain.* 2, Bendel, *Die Deutschen in Böhmen, Mähren.* 3, Schwicker, *Die Deutschen in Ungarn.* 4, Egger, *Tirol.* 5, Hunfalvy, *Ungarn* (Magyaren). 6, Slavici, *Rumänen.* 7, Wolf, *Juden.* 8, Vlach, *Tschechoslaven.* 9, Szujski, *Polen und Ruthenen.* 10a, Suman, *Slovenen.* 10b, Stare, *Kroaten.* 11, Stefanovic, *Serben.* 12, Schwicker, *Zigeuner.*

WESSELÉNYI, BARON N. *Eine Stimme über die ungarische und slavische Nationalität.* Leipzig, 1844.

V. POLITICAL

AJTAY, J. *The Hungarian Question.* London, 1908.

ANDRÁSSY, J. GRAF. *Ungarns Ausgleich mit Österreich seit 1867.* Leipzig, 1897.

ANONYMOUS (KRONPRINZ RUDOLF). *Der österreichische Adel und sein konstitutioneller Beruf.* München, 1878.

ANONYMOUS (LANG, O.). *Grundzüge für die endgültige Lösung der Nationalitätenfrage in Österreich.* Wien, 1897.

ANONYMOUS (SCHUSELKA, F.). *Deutsche Worte eines Österreichers.* Hamburg, 1843.

————. *Ist Österreich deutsch?* Leipzig, 1843.

BAERNREITHER, T. M. *Zur böhmischen Frage.* Eine politische Studie. Wien, 1910.

BERTHA, A. DE. *La Constitution Hongroise.* Paris, 1898.

BROCKHAUSEN, K. *Österreichische Verwaltungsreformen.* Sechs Vorträge. Wien, 1911.

CHARMATZ, R. *Der demokratisch-nationale Bundesstaat Österreich.* 1904.

———. *Deutsch-österreichische Politik.* Studien über den Liberalismus und über die auswärtige Politik Österreichs. Leipzig, 1907.

CHÉRADAME, A. *L'Allemagne, la France et la question d'Autriche* (3d ed.). Paris, 1905.

———. *L'Europe et la question d'Autriche* (4th ed.). Paris, 1906.

CHLUMECKY, L. FREIHERR VON. *Österreich-Ungarn und Italien. Das west-balkanische Problem.* Leipzig, 1907.

CRENEVILLE, GRAF L. *Grossösterreich?* Betrachtungen über unsere staat-liche Zukunft und die Möglichkeit nationaler Versöhnung. 1908.

DEÁK, F *Denkschrift über das Verhältniss zwischen Ungarn und Kroa-tien.* Wien, 1861.

———. *Ein Beitrag zum ungarischen Staatsrecht.* Bemerkungen über Lustkandls ungarisch-österreichisches Staatsrecht. Pest, 1865.

EÖTVÖS, JOSEPH FREIHERR VON. *Die Reform in Ungarn.* Leipzig, 1846

———. *Die Sonderstellung Ungarns vom Standpunkte der Einheit Deutschlands.* Pest, 1861.

FELDMANN. *Geschichte der politischen Ideen in Polen.* München, 1917.

FERDINÁNDY, G. *Staats- und Verwaltungsrecht des Königreichs Ungarn und seiner Nebenländer.* Hannover, 1909.

FISCHEL, A. *Die nationalen Kurien.* Wien, 1898.

FISCHHOF, A. *Der österreichische Sprachenstreit.* Wien, 1888.

HELFERT, J. A. FREIHERR VON. *Revision des ungarischen Ausgleichs.* Wien, 1876.

JELLINEK, P., AND PLIVERIK, J. *Das rechtliche Verhältniss Kroatiens zu Ungarn.* Agram, 1885.

KRAMÁŘ, K. *Anmerkungen zur böhmischen Politik.* Wien, 1906.

———. *Das böhmische Staatsrecht.* Wien, 1896.

LECHER, O. *Der Kampf gegen die Sprachenverordnungen.* Znaim, 1897.

LUSTKANDL, W. *Föderation oder Realunion?* (2d ed.). Wien, 1870.

———. *Die josephinischen Ideen und ihr Erfolg.* Wien, 1881.

MENGER, M. *Der böhmische Ausgleich.* Stuttgart, 1891.

NASTIČ, G. *Finale* (2d ed.). Sarajevo, 1908.

NAUMANN, F. *Deutschland und Österreich.* Berlin, 1900.

OFFERMANN, A. FREIHERR VON. *Die Bedingungen des konstitutionellen Österreichs.* 1900.

PEABODY, E. P. *Crimes of the House of Austria against Mankind.* New York, 1852.

PETROVIĆ, A. *Die madjarischen Sonderbestrebungen im Reiche der Habsburger*. Berlin, 1904.

Protokoll der Verhandlungen des Parteitages der deutschen sozialdemokratischen Arbeiterpartei in Österreich. Wien, 1917.

RADIĆ, S. *Die slavische Politik in der Habsburgermonarchie*. 1902.

REDLICH, J. *Verfassung und Verwaltungsorganization der Städte*, Band 6: *Österreich*. Leipzig, 1907.

———. *Zustand und Reform der österreichischen Verwaltung*. Wien, 1911.

RENNER, K. *Der deutsche Arbeiter und der Nationalismus*. Wien, 1910.

———. *Österreichs Erneuerung*. Wien, 1916.

SCALA, R. VON. *Was uns not tut*. 1903.

SCHUSELKA, F. *Deutsch oder russisch? Eine Lebensfrage Österreichs*. Wien, 1849.

———. *Deutsche Volkspolitik*. Hamburg, 1846.

SETON-WATSON, R. W. *Europe in the Melting Pot*. London, 1919.

SKENE, A. FREIHERR VON. *Der nationale Ausgleich in Mähren, 1905*. Wien, 1910.

SPRINGER, R. (KARL RENNER). *Die Krise des Dualismus und das Ende der deákistischen Episode*. Wien, 1904.

STRAKOSCH-GRASSMANN, G. *Das allgemeine Wahlrecht in Österreich seit 1848*. Wien, 1906.

STREET, C. J. *Hungary and Democracy*. London, 1923.

SZALAY, L. VON. *Zur ungarisch-kroatischen Frage*. Pest and Leipzig, 1863.

TEZNER, F. *Ausgleichsrecht und Ausgleichspolitik*. Wien, 1907.

VI. MEMOIRS, BIOGRAPHIES, AND PERSONAL REMINISCENCES

Friedrich Adler vor dem Ausnahmegericht. Berlin, 1920.

ANDRÁSSY, GRAF J. *Diplomatie und Weltkrieg*. Berlin, 1920.

ANONYMOUS (MÖRING, K.). *Sibyllinische Bücher aus Österreich* (2 vols.). Hamburg, 1848.

ANONYMOUS (SZÉCHENYI, GRAF). *Blick auf den Rückblick*. London, 1860.

ANSTED, PROFESSOR D. T. *A Short Trip in Hungary and Transylvania*. London, 1862.

APPONYI, GRAF A. *Lebenserinnerungen eines Staatsmannes*. Wien, 1912.

ARNDT, E. M. *Erinnerungen aus dem äusseren Leben*. Leipzig, 1840.

BAERNREITHER, J. M. *Bosnische Eindrücke*. Wien, 1908.

BETHLEN, COMTE M. *Memoires historiques du Comte*. Amsterdam, 1736.

BILINSKI, L. *Reminiscences and Documents* (in Polish). Warsaw, 1924–25.

BISMARCK, FÜRST O. *Gedanken und Erinnerungen* (2 vols.). Stuttgart, 1898.

BLIND, K. *The Life and Labors of Francis Deák*. London, 1876.

BORN, BARON I. *Travels through the Bannat of Temesvar*. London, 1770.

472 DISSOLUTION OF THE HABSBURG MONARCHY

CHARMATZ, R. *Adolf Fischhof. Das Lebensbild eines österreichischen Politikers.* Stuttgart, 1910.

CHISHULL, E. *Travels in Turkey and Back to England.* London, 1747.

CONRAD, FRANZ FREIHERR VON HÖTZENDORF. *Aus meiner Dienstzeit 1906–1918* (5 vols.). Wien, 1922–25.

CSENGERY, A. *Franz Deák.* Leipzig, 1877.

————. *Ungarns Redner und Staatsmänner.* Leipzig, 1852.

CZERNIN, GRAF O. *Im Weltkriege.* Berlin, 1919.

ELLIOTT, C. B. *Travels in the Three Great Empires of Austria, Russia and Turkey.* London, 1838.

FADEJEW, GENERAL R. *Neueste Schriften.* Leipzig and Wien, 1871.

FORST, O. *Ahnentafel Seiner Kaiserlichen und Königlichen Hoheit des durchlauchtigsten Herrn Erzherzogs Franz Ferdinand.* Wien und Leipzig, 1910.

FRANKFURTER, S. *Graf Leo Thun.* Altenburg, 1894.

FRIEDJUNG, H. *Benedeks nachgelassene Papiere.* Leipzig, 1901.

GAJDA. *My Reminiscences* (in Czech). Vinohrady, 1920.

GÖRGEI, A. *Mein Leben und Wirken in Ungarn in den Jahren 1848 und 1849* (2 vols.). Leipzig, 1852.

GRÄFFER, F. *Franziszeische Kuriosa; ganz besondere Denkwürdigkeiten.* Wien, 1849.

GRANT DUFF, SIR M. E. *Notes from a Diary, 1851–72.* London, 1897.

GUGLIA, E. *Friedrich von Gentz.* Wien, 1900.

HATVANY, L. *Das verwundete Land.* Leipzig, 1921.

HOFFMANNSEGG, GRAF. *Reisen über Ungarn.* Görlitz, 1800.

HORMAYR, J. FREIHERR VON. *Österreichischer Plutarch oder Leben und Lebensbildnisse aller Regenten und der berühmtesten Feldherren, Staatsmänner, Gelehrten und Künstler des österreichischen Kaiserstaates.* Wien, 1807–20.

HORN, E. *François Rákóczi II, prince de Transylvanie 1676–1735.* Paris, 1906.

JÁSZI, O. *Revolution and Counter-Revolution in Hungary.* London, 1924.

KANNER, DR. H. *Kaiserliche Katastrophenpolitik.* Wien, 1922.

————. *Der Schlüssel zur Kriegsschuldfrage.* München, 1926.

KÁROLYI, COUNT MICHAEL. *Fighting the World.* New York, 1925.

KECSKEMÉTHY, A. VON. *Graf Stephan Széchenyis staatsmännische Laufbahn, seine letzten Lebensjahre in der Döblinger Irrenanstalt und sein Tod.* Pest, 1866.

KEITH, SIR R. M. *Memoirs and Correspondence.* London, 1849.

KEYSLER, J. G. *Travels through Germany, Bohemia, Hungary.* London, 1757.

KLAPKA, G. *Memoirs of the War of Independence in Hungary.* London, 1850.

————. *Aus meinen Erinnerungen.* Zürich und Wien, 1887.

Kossuth, L. *L'Europe, l'Austriche et la Hongrie* (translated by J. Ludvigh). Bruxelles, 1859.

———. *Meine Schriften aus der Emigration* (3 vols.). Pressburg, 1880–82.

———. *Ungarns Wünsche.* Leipzig, 1843.

Krausz, A. *Die Ursachen unserer Niederlagen.* München, 1922.

Lányi, B. von. *Die Regierung Fejérváry, Juni 1905 bis April 1906, in regierungspolitischer und verfassungsrechtlicher Beziehung.* Berlin, 1909.

Levy, A. *La Filosofia Politicq di Guiseppe Mazzini.* Bologna, 1917.

Margutti, General Baron von. *Kaiser Franz Joseph, Persönliche Erinnerungen.* Wien-Leipzig, 1924.

Maria Theresia und Joseph II. Ihre Korrespondenz samt Briefen Josephs an seinen Bruder Leopold. Herausgegeben von A. Ritter von Arneth. (3 vols.). Wien, 1867, 1868.

Mendelssohn-Bartholdy, K. *Friedrich von Gentz.* Leipzig, 1867.

Mitis, O. von. *Kronprinz Rudolf, Neue Österreichische Biographie,* Vol. II. Wien, 1925.

———. *Das Leben des Kronprinzen Rudolf.* Leipzig, 1928.

Mitrofanov, P. von. *Joseph II. Seine politische und kulturelle Tätigkeit.* (Aus dem Russischen übersetzt.) Wien, 1910.

Molden, B. *Alois Graf Aehrenthal.* Stuttgart, 1917.

Nikitsch-Boulles, P. *Vor dem Sturm, Erinnerungen an Erzherzog Thronfolger Franz Ferdinand.* Berlin, 1925.

Palacký's politisches Vermächtnis (German translation; 2d ed.). Prag, 1872.

Plener, E. Freiherr von. *Erinnerungen.* Stuttgart, 1911.

Polzer-Hoditz, Graf Arthur. *Kaiser Karl.* Wien, 1928.

Przibram, L. Ritter von. *Erinnerungen eines alten Österreichers* (2 vols.). Stuttgart, 1910, 1912.

Pulszky, F. von. *Franz Deák. Eine Charakerstudie.* Leipzig, 1876.

———. *Meine Zeit, mein Leben* (4 vols.). Pressburg, 1880–83.

Rákóczi, Francis. *Secret Memoirs relating to the Present War between the Confederates and the French King.* London, 1707.

———. *The Demands of the Malcontents.* London, 1706.

———. *A General Collection of Treaties, Manifestoes, Etc.* London, 1705.

Redlich, J. "Heinrich Lammasch als Ministerpräsident" in *Heinrich Lammasch. Seine Aufzeichnungen, sein Wirken und seine Politik.* Wien, 1922.

Rudolf, Kronprinz. *Briefe an einen Freund, 1882–1889.* Wien, 1922.

Schäffle, A. E. F. *Aus meinem Leben* (2 vols.). Berlin, 1904.

Springer, A. *Aus meinem Leben.* Berlin, 1892.

Srbik, H. von. *Metternich, der Staatsmann und der Mensch* (2 vols.). München, 1925.

SzÉCHENYI, GRAF S. *Ein Blick auf den anonymen Rückblick.* London, 1859.

———. *Licht oder aufhellende Bruchstücke und Berichtigung einiger Irrtümer und Vorurteile.* Pest, 1832.

TELEKI, COUNT L. *The Case of Hungary Stated.* London, 1849.

———. *La Hongrie aux peuples civilisés.* Paris, 1849.

TISZA, GRAF S. *Briefe (1914–1918).* Berlin, 1928.

VEHSE, E. *Geschichte des österreichischen Hofes und Adels und der österreichischen Diplomatie.* Hamburg, 1851.

WERTHEIMER, E. VON. *Graf Julius Andrássy. Sein Leben und seine Zeit.* Stuttgart, 1910.

WIDMANN, K. *Franz Smolka.* Wien, 1886.

VII. CULTURAL AND RELIGIOUS

ALEXICE, G. *Geschichte der rumänischen Literatur.* (Aus der Sammlung "Die Literaturen des Ostens.") Leipzig, 1906.

BERTHA, A. DE. *La Hongrie Moderne.* Paris, 1897.

BEZOLD, F. VON. *Zur Geschichte des Hussitismus.* München, 1874.

BIBL, V. *Einführung der katholischen Gegenreformation in Niederösterreich durch Kaiser Rudolf II.* Innsbruck, 1900.

BRÜCKNER, A. *Geschichte der polnischen Literatur.* (Aus der Sammlung "Die Literaturen des Ostens.") Leipzig.

CHASSIN, C. L. *La Hongrie, son génie et sa mission.* Paris, 1856.

DOUMERGUE, E. *La Hongrie Calviniste.* Toulouse, 1912.

DUBOSCQ, A. *Budapest et les Hongrois.* Paris, 1913.

EÖTVÖS, BARON J. *The Village Notary.* London, 1850.

FELBERMANN, L. *Hungary and Its People.* London, 1892.

FRIESS, G. E. *Der Aufstand der Bauern in Niederösterreich am Schlusse des 16. Jahrhunderts.* Wien, 1897.

GASTEIGER, G. VON. *Die Zillertaler Protestanten und ihre Ausweisung aus Tirol.* Meran, 1892.

GÉRANDO, A. DE. *La Transylvanie et ses habitants.* Paris, 1845.

GINDELY, A. *Geschichte der Gegenreformation in Böhmen.* Leipzig, 1894.

HANNAK, DR. E. *Methodik des Unterrichtes in der Geschichte* (2d ed.). Wien, 1907.

HELFERT, J. A. FREIHERR VON. *Bosnisches.* Wien, 1897.

———. *Die Österreichische Volksschule* (3 vols.). Prag, 1860.

HEVESI, L. *Österreichische Kunst, 1800–1900.* (Aus der Sammlung "Geschichte der modernen Kunst") (2 vols.). Leipzig.

HORN, E. *Le Christianisme en Hongrie.* 1905.

HUCH, R. *Das Risorgimento.* Leipzig, 1909.

HUNFALVY, P. *Die Ungarn oder Magyaren.* Wien, 1881.

JAKUBEC, J. *Geschichte der tschechischen Literatur.* (Aus der Sammlung "Die Literaturen des Ostens.") Leipzig, 1907.

KLEIN, A. *Geschichte des Christentums in Österreich und Steiermark seit der ersten Einführung desselben in diesen Ländern bis auf die gegenwärtige Zeit* (7 vols.). Wien, 1840–42.

KOLLAR, J. *Über die literarische Wechselseitigkeit zwischen den verschiedenen Stämmen und Mundarten der slawischen Nation* (2d ed.). Leipzig, 1844.

KONT, J. *Geschichte der ungarischen Literatur.* (Aus der Sammlung "Die Literaturen des Ostens.") Leipzig, 1906.

KORNIS AND COLLABORATORS. *The Public Instruction of the Detached Magyar Population* (in Hungarian). Budapest, 1927.

KRALIK, R., *und* SCHLITTER, H. *Wien, Geschichte der Kaiserstadt und ihrer Kultur.* Wien, 1911.

LEWIS, L. *Die Geschichte der Freimaurerei in Österreich im allgemeinen und die Wiener Loge zu St. Joseph insbesondere.* Wien, 1861.

LIPPERT, J. *Sozialgeschichte Böhmens in vorhussitischer Zeit* (2 vols.). Wien, 1896, 1898.

LOESCHE, G. *Geschichte des Protestantismus in Österreich.* Tübingen, 1902.

——. *Von der Toleranz zur Parität in Österreich, 1781–1861.* Leipzig, 1911.

MAJLÁTH, GRAF J. *Die Religionswirren in Ungarn* (3 vols.). Regensburg, 1845, 1846.

MATTHEWS, S. *Patriotism and Religion.* New York, 1918.

Die österreichisch-ungarische Monarchie in Wort und Bild. Unter dem Protektorate des Kronprinzen und der Kronprinzessin herausgegeben. Wien, 1886–92.

PESCHEK, C. A. *Geschichte der Gegenreformation in Böhmen* (2 vols.). Dresden, 1844.

PETROVICH, C. *Serbia, Her People, History and Aspirations.* New York, 1915.

PULSZKY, F. *The Jacobins in Hungary.* London, 1851.

PYPIN, A. N., UND SPASOVIC, V. D. *Geschichte der slavischen Literatur.* Leipzig, 1884.

RECOULY, R. *Le pays magyar.* Paris, 1903.

REISNER, E. H. *Nationalism and Education since 1789.* New York, 1922.

RIEGER, F. L. *Les Slaves d'Autriche.* Paris, 1860.

RUDNITZKY, S. *The Ukraine and the Ukrainians.* Jersey City, 1915.

SCHERER, J. E. *Die Rechtsverhältnisse der Juden in den deutsch-österreichischen Ländern.* (Aus "Beiträge zur Geschichte des Judenrechts im Mittelalter.") Leipzig, 1901.

SCHWICKER, J. H. *Die Katholiken-Autonomie in Ungarn.* Pest, 1870.

SLAVICI, J. *Die Rumänen in Ungarn, Siebenbürgen und der Bukowina.* Wien, 1881.

SMITH, A. T. *Education in Foreign Countries, 1912–13.* Washington, 1914.

————. "Education in Hungary," *Encyclopedia of Education* (edited by Monroe). New York, 1912.

SRBIK, H. VON. *Die Beziehungen von Staat und Kirche in Österreich während des Mittelalters.* Innsbruck, 1903.

STEAD, A. *Servia and the Servians.* London, 1909.

STRAKOSCH-GRASSMANN, G. *Geschichte des österreichischen Unterrichtswesens.* Wien, 1905.

SUNDERLAND, J. T. *Three Centuries and a Half of Unitarianism in Hungary.* Boston, 1900.

SWETINA, A. *Das Wichtigste aus der österreichischen Geschichte* (5th ed.). Sternberg, 1908.

SZLAVIK, M. *Die Reformation in Ungarn.* Halle, 1884.

TEUTSCH, F. *Die Siebenbürger Sachsen in Vergangenheit und Gegenwart.* Leipzig, 1916.

TROLLOPE, F. *Vienna and the Austrians.* London, 1838.

UJFALVY, C. E. *La Hongrie, son histoire, sa langue, et sa littérature.* Paris, 1872.

VERESS, S. *Einfluss der kalvinischen Grundsätze auf das Kirchen- und Staatswesen in Ungarn.* Tübingen, 1910.

WEISS, A. *Geschichte der österreichischen Volksschulen* (2 vols.). Wien, 1904.

WIESNER, A. *Denkwürdigkeiten der österreichischen Zensur vom Zeitalter der Reformation bis zur Gegenwart.* Stuttgart, 1847.

WOLF, A. *Die Aufhebung der Klöster in Innerösterreich, 1782–1790.* Wien, 1871.

WOLF, G. *Geschichte der Juden in Wien.* Wien, 1876.

YOLLAND, A. B. *Hungary.* London, 1917.

ZENKER, E. V. *Geschichte der Wiener Journalistik.* Wien, 1892.

INDEX

Görgey, General, 97
Goethe, 299
Goga, O., 18
Goldscheid, R., 378
Goluchowski, Count, 104, 352
Gott erhalte, 360
Grand imperial title, 34
Graničar, 57
Greek Catholics, population, 160
Greek Orthodox religion, 393
Green Cadres, 20
Grillparzer, F., 11, 44, 78, 84, 89, 106
Grünberg, K., 226
Grünwald, B., 70, 71, 329
Gumplowicz, L., 253

Habsburg, Rudolph, 33
Habsburgs: absolutism, 17, 20, 26, 38, 48,
  49, 59, 74, 104; and Estates, 45 f., 68, 81,
  149 f.; causes for failure, 31, 130, 449,
  453 ff.; centralizing policy of, 49; clerical-
  ism, 48, 66, 160; dethronisation of, 96;
  foreign policy of, 411; foundation of em-
  pire, 40; *Hausmacht*, 92; imperialism, 34,
  35; legend, 6; marriages, 33, 150; ma-
  terialism, 25; militarism, 18, 141 ff.;
  monarchy, causes of dissolution, 98;
  state idea, 45, 66 f.
Havlíček, K., 388
Haymerle, A. von, 395
Haynau, General, 97
Héderváry, Count Khuen, 370 ff., 408
Hentzi affair, 119
Herder, influence of, 250 f.
Hertz, F., 187, 193, 201, 203
Hilferding, R., 204
Hofer, A., 80
Hoffmann, General M., 429
Hohenwart, Count, 112
Holy Alliance, 74
Holy Roman Empire, 35 ff.
Hora-Kloska revolt, 68
Hormayr, 51 f., 78
Hörnigk, P. W. von, 36
Horthy, Admiral, 142
Horváth, M., 311
Hötzendorf, C. von, 116, 145 f., 397, 400,
  418 f., 424
Hungary: Catholic church, 161; Diet, 59;
  feudalism, 67, 216; literature, 260 ff.;
  literary renaissance, 83; system of civic
  education in, 441
Huss, J., 47

Hussarek, 20
Hussitism, 136, 157

Illyrism, 261 ff.
Industries, 201 ff.
Innere Amtssprache, 346
Irányi, D., 316
Irredentism, 379 ff.
Italian irredenta, 394 ff.
Ius Placenti, 69

Jacobins, 77, 83
Jancsó, B., 54, 218
Jelačić, General, 96
Jesuits, 47, 79; colleges of, 156; education
  of aristocracy, 153
Jews: in capitalism, 172 ff.; Magyarization
  of, 325; population, 160. *See also* Anti-
  Semitism
Joseph II, Emperor, 63, 66, 70, 74, 79, 164,
  222, 252, 301
"Josephinist system," 67, 75
Jouanovič, J. N., 124
"Judaeo-Magyars," 174
Jugo-Slavs: irrendenta, 402 ff., 413 ff.;
  population, 404 f.; problem, 419; tribes,
  distrust of, 406; unity of, 403, 408
"Junction of Annaberg," 191
Justh, J., 340

Kanner, H., 425, 427
Karácsonyi, 306
Karadžić, V., 264
Karlovicz, Peace of, 54
Karlsbad, decisions of, 79
Károlyi, Count J., 200
Károlyi, Count M., 114, 233 f., 335, 342, 383
Kazár, 234
Kazinczy, F., 72
Kemény, Baron S., 215 f.
Kestranek affair, 284
Kjellen, R., 177, 239, 333, 379
Kleinwaechter, F. F. G., 139, 143, 151, 164,
  168, 288, 407
Kmets, 225
Königgrätz, 314
Körber, E. von, 12, 167
Kollár, J., 264
Kollonics, Archbishop, 55
Konkurrenznationalität, 253
Kornis, J., 456
Korošec, 217